IN THE ARENA

IN THE ARENA

A Memoir of the 20th Century

Caspar W. Weinberger

with GRETCHEN ROBERTS

Since 1947
REGNERY PUBLISHING, INC.
An Eagle Publishing Company • Washington, DC

Weinberger, Caspar W.
   In the arena : a memoir of the twentieth century / Caspar W. Weinberger, with Gretchen Roberts.
      p. cm.
   Includes bibliographical references and index.
   ISBN 0-89526-166-9
     1. Weinberger, Caspar W. 2. Cabinet officers—United States—Biography. 3. United States. Dept. of Defense—Officials and employees—Biography. 4. United States—Politics and government—1945–1989. 5. United States—Foreign relations—1945–1989. 6. United States—Military relations. 7. Weinberger, Caspar W.—Friends and associates—Anecdotes. I. Roberts, Gretchen. II. Title.

   E840.8.W44 A3 2001
   973.927'092—dc21
   [B]

                                             2001048334

Published in the United States by
Regnery Publishing, Inc.
An Eagle Publishing Company
One Massachusetts Avenue, NW
Washington, DC 20001
www.regnery.com

Distributed to the trade by
National Book Network
4720-A Boston Way
Lanham, MD 20706

Printed on acid-free paper
Manufactured in the United States of America

10 9 8 7 6 5 4 3 2 1

Book design by Sun Young Park
Set in Berkeley

Books are available in quantity for promotional or premium use. Write to Director of Special Sales, Regnery Publishing, Inc., One Massachusetts Avenue, NW, Washington, DC 20001 for information on discounts and terms or call (202) 216-0600.

DEDICATION

Eleven years ago I dedicated my first book, *Fighting for Peace: Seven Critical Years in the Pentagon,* to my wife in these words:

"And then there is Jane, my wife, who was there at the beginning when we were both in the army, and who was at the next beginning running my first campaign for the California legislature, and who is always a constant source of the support and inspiration we all need, and a constant example of the courage we all should have—and it is to her I dedicate this book."

The past decade has only reinforced the feelings and opinions I expressed then.

Jane has continued all her activities: her writing and publishing many books, her gardening, the organization and management of our homes, her splendid entertaining, and the good she does for so many people in all walks of life. She is still very much the constant source of support and inspiration we all need, and still a constant example of the courage we all should have.

It is to her I repeat these words, and to her I dedicate my autobiography.

CONTENTS

PREFACE

M y God, you're going to live forever!" Katharine Hepburn's mother exclaimed when she read my palm at her home in 1936, after being exposed to the conservative views of a very young Harvard student—views quite repugnant to her liberal soul.

I have indeed lived a very long time since that summer day, though not quite forever, and I have known numerous joys and challenges and many extraordinary people.

Since I always prefer reading first-person accounts of events to second- or thirdhand versions, I decided to set down on paper my own recollections while my memory still serves me reasonably well. Experiences always seem to me much more vivid when told by someone who was actually there, and I am fortunate to have been a participant in a number of exciting activities, particularly within government. I hope that in this memoir, I have succeeded in conveying a real sense of what it was like to tramp through the jungles of New Guinea in wartime; to feel for the first time the electricity that Ronald

Reagan brought to any gathering he attended; to struggle with congressional committees over funds; to help plan military actions; and to struggle with other members of the administration over policies such as Strategic Defense and support of the British in the Falklands, as well as the daily combination of minutiae and great issues that are the staple of holding an office.

It is my hope that this book will be more practical and compelling than academic in tone. Policy issues are certainly examined, but in the context of my own experience rather than from a theoretical standpoint.

Undoubtedly, there will be people who remember things differently than I do, or who disagree with some of what I have written in these pages, but my purpose here is only to record some of the history I saw, as I remember it.

Unlike my first book, *Fighting for Peace*, which focused primarily on my years at the Pentagon, this book covers a much longer time span—more than three-quarters of a century—from my childhood in San Francisco to the present. This volume is organized, for the most part, chronologically.

A common thread throughout the story of my life is my abiding interest in politics and the workings of government. Since I was very young, I have been fascinated both by the ideals upon which our country was founded and by how our democracy generally works. As early as 1924, I followed the national party conventions closely, and, at the age of fifteen, I asked a congressman to send me the *Congressional Record*, which I read avidly and daily. By the time I was in high school, I rewrote my school's student constitution, modeling it after the U.S. Constitution, and many of my school papers reflected my strong opinions, even then, about the virtues of a market economy and the inherent evils of repression and big government.

I became more outspoken with my conservative views by the time I was in college at Harvard, and expressed them, no doubt at tiresome length, both in classes and in editorials for the daily *Harvard Crimson*. My first direct (though quite limited) participation in national politics came during this time, when I served as an usher at the 1936 Republican convention. In 1938, my last year in college, and the next three years of law school, my interest in domestic politics was completely superseded by deep interest in, anxiety about, and incessant discussion of the war.

It came as no surprise to anyone who had to listen to me then that I enlisted in the infantry almost as soon as I had finished law school in 1941. Indeed it was only my father's strong and logical persuasion that kept me in law school. My desire to serve my country and her allies in World War II was very strong indeed, and was fueled by Winston Churchill's eloquent and inspirational rallying cries against appeasing Germany. I considered my participation in the war effort not merely a duty, but a privilege—an opportunity to further a noble cause in which I believed passionately.

I felt that same exhilaration of being a part of something larger than myself, being a part of history, throughout my civilian career in government. A few years after the war was over, I embarked on my political career—first as an assemblyman in the California legislature, then in the ranks of the California Republican Party, and later, as a cabinet member in the administrations of Governor Reagan, President Nixon, President Ford, and President Reagan. My service in these various capacities was periodically interrupted by my return to work in the private sector (which, admittedly, had its financial advantages), but I always found public service far more rewarding and satisfying. Each post brought exciting new challenges and a sense of honor that I felt could not be matched outside of government. And yet, paradoxically perhaps, I always wanted government to be small and nonintrusive.

In the process of writing this book, I have drawn on the extensive collection of personal papers in the Library of Congress (it seems I

saved nearly everything!), and on the recollections of a great many
people who have been subjected to me or whose lives intersected
mine over the years, to help spark my memory. As I tried to call up my
own reminiscences, I often found myself thinking of John Buchan's
autobiography and particularly its title, *Memory, Hold the Door*.

As anyone who read the introduction of my first book knows,
Theodore Roosevelt is a great hero of mine, and his words best
summed up my wish to be in the arena, and not in the stands with
the timid souls:

> Service is rendered...by the man who...is actually in the
> arena, whose face is marred by dust and sweat and blood; who
> strives valiantly; who errs, and comes short again and again,
> because there is no effort without error and shortcomings; but who
> does actually strive to do the deeds; who knows the great enthusi-
> asms, the great devotions; who spends himself in a worthy cause;
> who at the best knows in the end the triumph of high achievement
> and who, at the worst, if he fails, at least fails while daring greatly,
> so that his place shall never be with those cold and timid souls who
> know neither victory nor defeat.

I originally thought that the title *In the Arena* best expressed my
belief that one should be down on the playing field, taking an active
part in great events.

However, shortly after my publisher accepted the title and began
the long task of entering it into all the various systems in the book-
selling network, I found that Charlton Heston had already used that
title, as indeed had Richard Nixon some years before.

I told my publisher I wanted to change it and call the book *And
Not to Yield*, from *Ulysses*, a favorite Tennyson poem:

One equal temper of heroic hearts,
Made weak by time and fate, but strong in will
To strive, to seek, to find, and not to yield.

But apparently, mechanically, it is virtually impossible to change a title once it is selected and initially advertised.

So with my apologies to my friend Charlton Heston, whom I have greatly admired for many years, we will have to continue our joint use of the same title.

When I give speeches, I always try to include a question period, because that way I am reasonably sure that at least one person in the audience is interested in what I am saying. Unfortunately, there is no such opportunity when writing a book, so I can only hope that what is of interest to me is also interesting to the reader. So without more, let us begin.

IN THE ARENA

PROLOGUE

$\mathcal{T}$he air in Washington was crisp and cold on January 20, 1981, and a gray blanket of clouds stretched to the horizon. For the first time, a presidential inauguration ceremony was taking place on the West Front of the Capitol, at the request of President-elect Ronald Reagan. West, after all, is the direction of California, indeed, of America. Thousands of people covered the lawn that sloped down from the inaugural platform built out over the west steps of the Capitol. Stands were also banked steeply up behind the platform, where sat, shoulder to shoulder, members of the outgoing Carter administration and the incoming Reagan appointees. President Carter looked gaunt and weary—a defeated man in more ways than one.

But when President-elect Reagan took the inaugural oath, his voice infused the air with his characteristic confidence and sparkling vigor, lifting the pall and almost literally parting the clouds. As I had witnessed many times before, Reagan effortlessly summoned brightness; a golden stream of sunlight broke through the dark sky, first shining only on him, then showering everyone present. It was as if he carried the sun in his breast pocket everywhere he went, warming everyone around him with the hope and faith and optimism that were as much a part of him as his modest smile.

After concluding the oath of office by adding, "So help me God," the new president began his inaugural address. As he spoke, I began to reflect on how I came to be there, sitting behind a new president as his secretary-designate of defense.

> The orderly transfer of authority as called for in the Constitution routinely takes place, as it has for almost two centuries, and few of us stop to think how unique we really are. In the eyes of the world, this every-four-year ceremony we accept as normal is nothing less than a miracle.

My mind drifted back to nights in San Francisco, over fifty years earlier, when my father would sit between my brother's and my beds and weave for us the exciting story of the Constitution. He made it come alive for us, telling us how the document was drafted, the points of debate, how agreement finally was reached, and how close we had come to the whole convention's dissolving in disagreement—an outcome that would have left us simply a group of separate, small, impotent states. And now, here I was, watching, and indeed part of, this quadrennial miracle. It was the latter that I found most difficult to realize. For to a far greater degree than in previous inaugurations, I felt the sudden transfer from spectator to being part of the ceremony itself. I suppose I felt the sudden onrush of responsibility.

The president had turned to the problem of inflation—the cruelest tax—which had been gripping the country for at least half a decade. When he said, "Ending inflation means freeing all Americans from the terror of runaway living costs," I thought back to my days at the Office of Management and Budget (OMB), under President Richard

Nixon. We believed that a large part of the inflation problem was caused by runaway government expenditures. I recalled many days, and nights, when we struggled to roll back spending—paring departmental budget requests and eliminating ineffective, redundant, or unnecessary programs—only to be overruled by Congress (and sometimes by the president). Particularly, I had a brief recollection of the time when, as director of OMB, I had pointed out to President Nixon that a proposal to increase Social Security benefits was not justified because we had recently increased them beyond what even inflation required. "But, Cap, it is an election year." The tone of that message precluded any idea of an appeal I might have had in mind.

I also remembered President Reagan's unprecedented feat when he had been governor and I was director of finance: the state's constitutional requirement for a balanced budget had forced him to ask for a tax increase, but, thereafter, we were so successful in cutting state spending that he was able to return the substantial resulting surplus to the taxpayers of California. "If government is running a surplus, taxes are too high," he said then. "Government is not in the business of earning income." He had been willing to defy the conventional wisdom and make cuts where needed despite the presumed popularity of many programs. He understood that government had its place, but that place was primarily protecting and not burdening the American people.

I again focused on his inaugural speech as he was saying, "It's not my intention to do away with government. It is rather to make it work—work with us, not over us; to stand by our side, not ride on our back." I knew that if anyone could tame inflation and slow the cost and growth of government, Reagan could.

President Reagan did indeed make us feel good about ourselves, and he knew that when Americans regained pride and self-confidence, there was no limit to what we could do. His words and this deep belief could bring out the best in people.

> With all the creative energy at our command, let us begin an era
> of national renewal. Let us renew our determination, our courage,
> and our strength. And let us renew our faith and our hope.

Then he spoke of everyday American heroes who exemplify these very qualities and who, together, make up our national character. I thought about some of my own heroes—Theodore Roosevelt and Winston Churchill—leaders who inspired by their example and who rallied nations to their highest callings. But those were not the kind of heroes President Reagan was speaking of that day. He was speaking of people like my mother and father, who quietly enabled their sons to be educated at Harvard. And not only was I able to attend Harvard for four years of undergraduate study and three years of law school, but my parents also made it possible for me to make those long train trips across the country four times a year so that I could spend Christmases and summers at home. All of this during the Great Depression.

Then, I heard the president repeat what he had many times discussed with me: how vital it was that we rebuild our military strength and credibility as an ally. As he spoke, a scene from my training in the army during World War II flashed across my mind. We had been so unprepared for war, and so lacking in basic war materiel, that we had to train with World War I–era rifles, or even wooden replicas of them, and blocks of wood labeled "hand grenade" in white paint.

> We will again be the exemplar of freedom and a beacon of hope
> for those who do not now have freedom. . . . As for the enemies of
> freedom, those who are potential adversaries, they will be
> reminded that peace is the highest aspiration of the American peo-
> ple. We will negotiate for it, sacrifice for it; we will not surrender
> for it, now or ever.

Our forbearance should never be misunderstood. Our reluctance for conflict should not be misjudged as a failure of will. When action is required to preserve our national security, we will act. We will maintain sufficient strength to prevail if need be, knowing that if we do so we have the best chance of never having to use that strength.

Above all, we must realize that no arsenal or no weapon in the arsenals of the world is so formidable as the will and moral courage of free men and women.

The cadences in that matchless voice rolled on, and I could almost feel the eagerness of the crowd's response. What he was saying was what Americans had been waiting to hear. The president was pointing the way for what we desperately needed to do at the Pentagon—the effort that he intended me to lead as his secretary of defense. The vast responsibility with which I was entrusted swept over me again. I still was not sure why the president had chosen me, but I felt a renewed determination to do what he and I knew the country—indeed the world—most needed.

At that moment, President Reagan read from the diary of Martin Treptow, a World War I infantryman:

My Pledge:
America must win this war. Therefore I will work, I will save, I will sacrifice, I will endure, I will fight cheerfully and do my utmost, as if the issue of the whole struggle depended on me alone.

I knew again that kinship I always felt for the infantry and the pride that I had served in it so long ago.

But as daunting as our task may have been in 1981, President Reagan's imperishable optimism and confidence made it all seem possible if we only worked at it hard enough. He had always had the ability to imbue his audience with the same spirit he had, an ability that was evident from the first time I saw his smile light up the room at a political rally in California years earlier. As he concluded his inaugural address, he lifted us all to that higher plane:

> The crisis we are facing today...requires...our best effort and our willingness to believe in ourselves and to believe in our capacity to perform great deeds, to believe that together with God's help we can and will resolve the problems which now confront us.

Filled with this exhilarating hope (tempered by vague reservations about my ability to do all of this), I took one more look out over our beautiful capital city, with its gleaming monuments to the great people who ensured the beginning and the continuity of our republic, and I recalled the last line of Arthur Hugh Clough's poem that Winston Churchill quoted when World War II looked its darkest: "But westward, look, the land is bright."

For me, the West represented much of my own personal history and the forces in my life that had brought me to this day. My abiding interest in government had been formed in my San Francisco childhood, and grew continuously, there and during my years in the East at Harvard, and through my army service in the South Pacific, and up and down California as a legislator and state finance director. I always knew I wanted to serve in government, and had already served in the army and at the federal level under Presidents Nixon and Ford. But I never imagined I would serve as the secretary of defense, at such a critical time in our history.

From the inaugural platform, we moved back into the Capitol, where the Congressional Inaugural Committee gave the traditional luncheon in honor of the new president and vice president in one of the large caucus rooms. It was there that President Reagan received word, and was able to announce, that the fifty-two American hostages who had been held for over a year in Iran were on their way home.[*] I believe this came about largely because the captors knew full well that President Reagan would not stand idly by while American citizens were held by kidnappers. To others, it was evident that Iran had great contempt for former president Carter.[†]

Whatever the reason, the hostages' release was an auspicious beginning for the Reagan administration and was particularly welcome after the president's uplifting inaugural speech. But later, as I rode down Capitol Hill and along Pennsylvania Avenue to the inaugural reviewing stand in front of the White House, and during the long afternoon parade that followed, my thoughts were not about the pageantry but about the tasks ahead—and where it all began.

[*] One of the most moving events I experienced as secretary of defense was on January 27, 1981, when I had the great privilege of helping to welcome the hostages home. I flew by helicopter with Vice President Bush, Al Haig, Howard Baker, and Tip O'Neill to Andrews Air Force Base in Maryland and formed part of a receiving line on the tarmac to greet them. As stirring as it was for us, their emotion far exceeded anything we could have been feeling, and it was expressed differently in each person. Some shouted for joy. Some kissed the ground. Some wept openly. Some still wore the mask of weary stoicism.

They had undoubtedly changed because of their ordeal, but they were coming home to a changed country as well. There was new hope, new confidence, new patriotism, ushered in by Ronald Reagan and I think they could feel it from the moment they stepped off the plane.

The compassion of the American people was also apparent as we all rode in a bus motorcade to the White House for an official welcoming ceremony with the president. Lining the route were thousands of countrymen waving flags and holding signs, an overwhelming outpouring for the freed hostages.

On the South Lawn of the White House, along with families, friends, government officials, a military honor guard, and surviving members of the attempted rescue mission, they met their new president face-to-face—the man whose resolve and strength of character, I believe, were the catalysts for the hostages' release.

[†] Peter Goldman illustrated this well in the February 2, 1981, Newsweek: "Teheran, having helped in [Carter's] ruin, piled on a final insult by holding the freedom flight on the ground until just after the rite of succession and so depriving Carter of a bow and a bit of refracted glory."

CHAPTER 1

A CALIFORNIA CHILDHOOD

*T*his memoir begins during the First World War. Nineteen-seventeen was the year the United States reluctantly joined the three-year-old "war to end all wars" in Europe. German submarine attacks on British and American merchant and passenger ships finally convinced President Wilson that we could no longer ignore events an ocean away. He was well aware of the strong isolationist sentiment in this country, and for that reason, and also because of the vague hope (which he called "idealism") that events in Europe would make it unnecessary to decide, he had hesitated and displayed the indecisiveness and weakness that so enraged Theodore Roosevelt. Particularly galling to TR and those who thought Germany was wholly to blame was Wilson's insistence on America's fighting as an "associated power," not a full ally of Great Britain and France.

That same year also saw the birth of the world's first Communist state—the USSR.

San Francisco in 1917 was settling into maturity after the bawdy opiate of the Gold Rush and the devastating 1906 earthquake and fire that had shattered all the illusions of invincibility with which San Franciscans cloaked their idea of their city.

But the Panama-Pacific Exposition in 1915, with all of its fantastic buildings and ethereal lights, was San Francisco's declaration to the world that it not only had survived but had triumphed over even such devastation as the earthquake and fire had wrought.

Indeed, Californians have always possessed indomitable optimism and a pioneer spirit—as did my father, who moved to San Francisco in the early teens of the century, because he felt that Colorado was getting too crowded!

So, when I was born in my parents' San Francisco home in 1917, I, by right of birth, was naturally endowed with this generally sunny, optimistic nature.

I was named Caspar, after a great friend of my mother's from Denver, Mrs. Stanley Caspar, who became my godmother.

It was my father who first called me Cap. There was a novel about San Francisco shipping life at that time called *Cappy Rix*. The Cappy Rix character in the book was a skipper of one of the ships, and for some reason, my father started calling me Cappy, and then Cap. Later, in grammar school, I was often teased about my unusual name. I told my tormentors they were just jealous because they did not have a unique name, but that did not seem to deter them. Finally a small fight settled the matter. Maybe this was the beginning of a feeling that occasionally confrontation is better than compromise.

My father's father, Nathan Weinberger, emigrated from what was then Bohemia in the late 1800s and opened a general store—a small forerunner of the department store—in the small mining town of Idaho Springs, Colorado, a few miles from Denver. My father, Herman, was born there. He supported himself while he was in high school by working nights as an operator at the town's telephone exchange. He was always fascinated by, and good at—then and later—working with all things electrical. In the town telephone office he rigged up a system that would ring a bell and wake him up whenever a call came in. That way, he got at least *some* sleep on a bunk that he had also constructed. The telephone and electricity were the high technology of that time. Today my father would have been a skilled and fascinated user of computers, the Internet, and cyberspace. In retrospect, I have wondered why my father chose the law rather than some scientific or technological pursuit as his lifework.

In 1904 my father went to the University of Colorado in Boulder. To help put himself through college, he ran a successful boardinghouse for students, ordering the food and hiring the cooks. He also edited the *Coloradoan*, the class album, and ran the school newspaper, the *Silver and Gold*. In addition, he was involved and successful in debate contests. My father, in a quiet but determined way, was always striving. He completed the university's A.B. and LL.B. programs in six years instead of seven by taking his last year of college and his first year of law school in the same year.

During one summer in law school, he served as a clerk to the Judicial Committee of the Colorado legislature. After graduation, he practiced law with a partner for a couple of years in Boulder, and at the same time he was appointed general manager of student activities at the university. It was during that time that he met my mother, Cerise Carpenter Hampson, who was a young, talented violin artist and teacher from Denver.

Shortly thereafter, my father went to California to practice law. He soon found a job as a very junior attorney and manager of the office boys at the San Francisco law firm of Chickering & Gregory. He lived in a boardinghouse and walked downtown (more than twenty blocks) every day to the firm's offices in the Merchants Exchange Building at California and Montgomery Streets, in the heart of San Francisco's financial district.

Some of his friends and classmates told him and me later that he would have undoubtedly become governor of Colorado had he stayed and followed the well-recognized paths to political success there. Indeed, many years later, when a not-too-brilliant classmate *was* elected governor, my father expressed this thought himself—but not with much regret.

In January 1913 he returned briefly to Denver to marry my mother and bring her to San Francisco, where they rented a small house on Tenth Avenue in the Sunset, an older, moderately priced area of San Francisco. My father continued as an associate at Chickering & Gregory, but left in 1918 to open his own law office (in the same building), where he practiced for the rest of his life.

My father felt responsible for all his family members, no matter how distant. I, on the other hand, did not. It seemed to me that some relative of his was always showing up, and it was my father's instinct and practice to entertain them, with dinners at home or long drives around the city. My father was very proud of San Francisco and always showed it off to visitors with a slightly proprietary air. I cared little for those visits by relatives, frequently pointing out that they were relatives only by an "accident of birth." I particularly disliked it when they smoked long, evil-smelling cigars in our car. I fear I was just not nice about family.

But perhaps a couple of them deserve mention. Of my father's two brothers and three sisters, two stand out in my mind. Bella was deaf, and quite a remarkable lady—she learned to read lips and taught school in New York City. I visited her there a few times when I was attending Harvard and was always amazed at her ability to read lips and at her courage. Another sister, Luella, married a man named Harry McNeil. They lived in Sheboygan, Wisconsin, and had a son, Don, who later hosted a famous radio program, which some mid-westerners might remember: *Don McNeil's Breakfast Club.*

My mother was an only child, the daughter of Charles Marshall Hampson and the former Lillian Louise Carpenter of Denver. Charles, whom I always called Charlie, was a successful mining engineer who patented a few of his inventions, including a railroad turntable. His wife, my grandmother, always called "Mumsie," was an active newspaper reporter and writer for Denver's *Rocky Mountain News*. She was a spirited, modern lady for her time and drove to her various assignments in Denver's first electric auto.

My mother's inclinations were more musical, and when she was very young she learned to play the violin. In fact, at the tender age of fourteen, at her own request, she went to Leipzig, Germany, to study violin. Mumsie accompanied her to Baltimore, and from there she set out alone on a transatlantic ship. not knowing German or the family with whom she was to stay. But she spent a very fulfilling year or two there, studying under a pupil of the renowned violinist Leopold Auer.

After returning to the States, she gave some concerts and taught violin, both in Denver and at the Grand Island College Conservatory of Music in Grand Island, Nebraska, before she married my father and moved to California. After that she gave up her career, played the violin less and less, and concentrated entirely on homemaking and raising her children.

Mother was close to her parents, and shortly after I was born, they moved to San Francisco as well. They were frequently at our home, and some of my earliest memories are of sitting on my grandfather Charlie's lap at our house. He had a wonderful Charles Evans Hughes–type beard and moustache, and altogether was a most impressive figure. At that late stage of his life, after retirement from all his engineering activities, he started selling life insurance door-to-door and office-to-office—something at which he excelled and which he apparently genuinely enjoyed. He studied the whole insurance business thoroughly, leaving several old texts on the subject in our library. He was a patient, devoted grandfather, and I have only the happiest memories of him.

My older brother, Peter, was born on Halloween Day in 1914. He was more outgoing and venturesome by far than I, as well as much more handsome and athletic. We didn't do very many of the same things, especially as we got older. By the time he was in high school, he had largely broken away from home—always going out with his friends (and, I'm sure, even with *girls*—creatures who terrified me at the time). I still did not see Peter much when later we roomed together at Harvard. He did his own thing, and I was still very shy and quite overwhelmed with the volume and difficulty of my studies and, later, with my virtually full-time preoccupation with the *Harvard Crimson*. But although he and I were quite different, he was a wonderful brother. I recall how vigorously he worked for me when I ran for office years later, walking the San Francisco precincts and putting in many hours campaigning in my behalf.

On religious matters, many people assumed that I was brought up in the Jewish faith, but I was not, and neither was my father. Two or three generations back, in Bohemia, there had apparently been some kind of quarrel in his family over various factions in the Jewish synagogues, which left my father—and his father as well—with a feeling of indifference toward virtually any church. I do not think my father knew any of the details of the argument (at least he never talked of it), but he was completely inactive in religion throughout his life, although supportive of my mother's attachment to the Episcopal Church.

My mother's family had been Quakers. She, however, became an active Episcopalian, playing violin in many church services before she was married. Mother taught us the Lord's Prayer, the Ten Commandments, and various other basic tenets, and we occasionally went to a nonsectarian Sunday school, and that was about the extent of our involvement in religious matters. The secular aspects of all holidays—

Christmas, Easter, etc.—were special occasions and cause for major celebration.

During college and World War II, I gradually became more active in religion, occasionally attending the college chapel services in the morning and on Sundays going to Christ Church, the Episcopal church across the street from Harvard Yard. Occasionally I went to informal church meetings in the evening at the home of the Reverend Kinsolving, our Episcopal minister. He urged me to go into the ministry after graduation, but I never considered it, although my faith and belief were and are unshaken and my trust in God has been an enormous influence and comfort all my life.

I did attend services as regularly as I could while I was overseas during the war. (I suppose I felt I needed all the help I could get.) Then, when I returned to San Francisco in 1945, I became actively affiliated with St. Luke's Episcopal Church of the diocese of California, and remained so for many years. I was elected to the vestry of St. Luke's and later became chancellor and then treasurer of the diocese, and was a delegate to various church conventions.

It was in 1918, when I was not even a year old, that my father moved our family into a larger, shingled house he bought in the new Forest Hill area of San Francisco, only a couple of blocks from the Twin Peaks Tunnel streetcar station. Forest Hill was a wooded and up-to-then undeveloped part of the city, with a great deal of open space around it. From the outskirts of our little enclave, rolling sand dunes ran west toward the ocean—literally to the edge of the continent. Then northward, along the beach, one came to Golden Gate Park, where I remember with fondness several happy boyhood afternoons with my family, picnicking and riding the beautiful old carousel. Farther north was, by the 1920s, Playland, an oceanfront amusement park correctly called the "Coney Island of the West."

Ours was the end house of the first four new homes on Merced Avenue, and my father also bought the lot on either side of the house—one for a garden and the other for baseball, football, and occasionally tennis. It was a modest house, but it seemed like a castle to me, with six or seven rooms, a half basement, and a storage attic. It was one of the only homes in the area with a freestanding garage. There was also a porte cochere (which I, for years, thought was spelled "porker sheer") and a flight of stairs from the driveway up to the front door.

Soon after we moved in, my parents enclosed the big back porch, which became the bedroom my brother and I shared when I got a little older. I remember the conversion fascinated me, and I was frequently out on the old porch—undoubtedly very much in the way—as it was being made over. About this time, there was a worldwide influenza epidemic that struck our family as the construction was going on. It must have been a terrible time for my parents, but I remember no complaints.

We never moved from our comfortable home. The house stayed in the family until around 1970.

I was often at home because I had frequent mastoid infections. Whenever I got the flu (which was a regular occurrence), it would always settle in the ear. Doctors made house calls then, and Dr. Gelston made many visits to our home. Without anesthetics or antibiotics, the doctor would lance my eardrums with a needle and tell me to stay still for several hours while it drained. Many days in bed followed, because you had to have a 98.6 temperature for three days before you were allowed up.

The only diversions I had were reading and conducting mock battles with my toy tin soldiers, placing them strategically in the trenches and hilltops of the sheets. The battlefield was large, as my parents often let me appropriate their bed for these long periods of recuperation. (Where *they* slept all that time, I don't know, but I do not recall being very concerned about that at the time.) In any case, of course, I had no inkling then that later in my life I would be responsible for the deployment and safety of *real* troops.

At the age of six, I spent an interminably long month in the children's hospital with a staph infection that required a mastoid operation. My mother spent hours reading to me and providing solace. She must have gone home occasionally and helped with Peter, but my memory is that she was always at the hospital. One night when the operation started bleeding, my father was hastily summoned to the hospital to donate blood for a transfusion. Even after the mastoid operation and the long hospital stay, ear trouble persisted throughout my childhood.

Earlier that same year, 1923, my mother had become ill. Both of her parents had recently died, and not long after that, Mother suffered a nervous breakdown, or what I suppose today would be called depression. She stayed in bed in a darkened room for a number of weeks, which was probably the worst thing for her to do. (I have never liked dark rooms since then.) My father hired an in-home nurse and a couple of ladies to help with the housework, the cooking, and looking after Peter and me.

Mother made a full recovery but tended to stay at home. She was shy and retiring, never really interested in outside activities, and preferred taking care of my brother and me to anything else. Only reluctantly did she agree to go with my father on a business trip to Los Angeles not long after her recovery (Dad felt that she needed a change of scene). I still have a letter she wrote to me during that trip, and it was clear that she could hardly stand to be away: "I miss my little boys every second—more than words can tell, and I would start right back tonight if Daddy would not mind, but he would be so disappointed."

My immediate family was close-knit, and our home was always warm and secure. I was very fond of both my mother and father, and they clearly felt the same way toward me and Peter (and were careful not to favor one of us over the other). It seems to be rather fashion-able now to dwell on unhappy childhoods or insensitive parents. I can claim neither. I had a happy home and loving parents.

My brother and I did not get an allowance; instead, my father devised a "point" system by which we would earn points for doing certain tasks around the house—cutting the lawn, helping with the dishes, and so forth. Conversely, we would lose points for "conduct unbecoming." Once we reached a certain number of points, we would get a baseball mitt, or some other thing we really wanted. The system worked well.

I do not remember getting into any trouble as a child; my brother and I probably received occasional paddlings, but certainly nothing particularly traumatizing. In fact, I suspect that I escaped such pun-ishment more often than Peter, simply because I was so ill and weak so much of the time. (There were a *few* advantages to being sick.)

One incident I do recall, however, occurred one day when I was about five. I don't remember exactly what prompted it—I was prob-ably being a particularly obnoxious little brother—but Peter picked me up and threw me over a hedge, breaking my arm in the process. It certainly would not have done me any good to get into a physical fight with him (he was obviously much stronger than I), but I'm sure he suffered dire consequences. Incidentally, my arm recovered completely.

Most of the time, though, Peter and I got along well, and we shared a few activities. We both started piano lessons at a very young age and continued until we went to college. As was the case with many chil-dren, we were basically forced into it, but now that I am older, I am glad we were. It gave me a lasting appreciation of music.

In piano, as in athletics, Peter was much better than I; he had bet-ter technique (and could play "The Minute Waltz" in fifty seconds or so), though I was said to have a nice touch. Our teacher, Melba Brookshier, was an "older" lady (she was probably all of twenty-five), and she sometimes played duets with us and occasionally with my mother, who had begun to play the violin again. I enjoyed the lessons, but not practicing, and recitals were occasions of terror. However, my first experience with public speaking occurred at these recitals, where I read short biographical sketches I had written about some of the composers.

Both Peter and I much preferred baseball. We played "indoor" baseball—that is, with a larger, slightly softer ball than the regulation "hardball"—but the game was of course played outdoors, usually on the lawn right next to our house. Peter and I, and a very good friend of ours, George Kristovich (who later became a schoolteacher and coach), formed a neighborhood league. Our team was known as the Merchants, and the rival team was the Robins. I was usually the pitcher and also the manager. (I guess the idea was that if I couldn't play very well, at least I could do that!) We meticulously kept track of our scores, batting averages, and every other imaginable detail of our games—it was all very serious business, and along with many other childhood items, I kept these records for years.

We also spent quite some time working on our electric trains, which my father had helped us set up in the basement of the house. We had an extensive array of train-related paraphernalia: not only a variety of cars, which usually came as Christmas gifts, but also all of the accessories—tunnels villages, signals, and so forth. We even wrote up a charter for "The Weinberger Railroad Lines" and elected my father president; I was vice president and general manager, and Peter was consulting engineer.

Dad was deeply involved in this hobby—he knew all about things mechanical and electrical, and I know he had as much fun as we did. I remember one Christmas day, very early on, when a terrible storm blew a tree over, which consequently knocked down the main power line near our house. My father wanted so much to get the new trains hooked up and operational that he went outside in the pouring rain and tried to piece together the power line himself. He was not successful (and, fortunately, not injured either). Finally, late that night, the power company came out and fixed it, but not in time for us to try out our gifts on Christmas. Fixing the power line was vital for another reason. We had one of the few electric ranges in the city and there could be no Christmas dinner until the electricity was restored.

Another favorite activity that filled a good bit of my childhood was reading. I suppose this came partially because I spent a lot of time ill in bed, but it was also because my parents read a great deal to me and to Peter when we were quite young. My father even made up a long bedtime story, told over many nights, about the Constitutional Convention. This would not normally hold the attention of youngsters, but he told it so dramatically that it came alive for us and was, I believe, one of the foundation stones on which my lifelong interest in government was built.

My mother introduced me to Hugh Lofting's Doctor Dolittle books, which I enjoyed greatly and read to my own children many years later. I was also very fond of *My Book House*, a six-volume anthology of children's stories, which included "Hans Brinker (or, The Silver Skates)" and "The Nuremberg Stove." They were very handsome books, beautifully bound, and I remember that my parents bought the set from a door-to-door salesman, something practically unheard of today.

Peter also read to me early on—tales of King Arthur and histories of England and our Revolution—and even helped teach me to read. This led to my lifelong interest in English history and, indeed, all things English.

When I got a little older, I spent quite a lot of time at the Mechanics' Institute Library in downtown San Francisco. The Mechanics' Institute was founded in 1855, originally to provide "schooling for indigent mechanics." The library was, at first, only a small part of it, but after the University of California and the state school system were founded, the Mechanics' Institute concentrated less on giving classes and more on building up its library. By the time I started using it, the institute had become, and still is, entirely a private library, and a very good one. I liked it because it had open stacks and allowed you to browse, as in a bookstore, whereas at the public library you had to fill out a form and wait forever for someone to bring a book out.

I was a rapid reader, so I was able to absorb a great many books; I usually checked out three or four books at a time. I had a catholic, eclectic taste. I read many mysteries by Edgar Wallace, Sax Rohmer, and others, as well as history, particularly English history, biography, archaeology. And books about dogs, thanks to Albert Payson Terhune's Sunnybank Lad books. It was because of Terhune's stories that we eventually got a collie. (Before our collie, we had a cocker spaniel named Buster, and even before he, or I, came along, my father had a fox terrier named Judge. Judge was so jealous when my brother was born that my father had to give the dog away.)

My greatest interest, however, was politics, an early passion largely engendered by my father. I had one of my first brushes with a political figure in 1923, when my family was vacationing at Brookdale Lodge near Santa Cruz. We were having dinner one evening in a beautifully rustic dining room, through which a small creek ran, when I spotted one of California's U.S. senators, Samuel Shortridge. Being a reasonably good campaigner, Shortridge noticed the enormous interest with which I was watching him, and he came over to our table and introduced himself. My father was very pleased, and I was quite astonished, at the age of six, to have shaken the hand of a United States senator!

I followed the 1924 national party conventions as closely as I could from the newspaper, and I listened intently to the 1928 and 1932 conventions on our Atwater Kent radio. I was enthralled— particularly by the 1924 Democratic convention, because it took 103 ballots to determine the nominee.

In the election of 1930, the mayor of San Francisco, James Rolph Jr., was running for governor of California. Being from northern California, he wasn't given much chance of winning, but my father knew him and thought he was a good man, so we (Dad let me pull the lever in the voting booth) gave him a "courtesy" vote—and he won.

When Herbert Hoover was running for president in 1928, Dad took me to a campaign rally. I remember that as Hoover shook hands with people, he would sort of pull them through, to discourage them from standing and talking. He was not a very cheerful-looking man, and with his high, stiff collar and rather frozen expression, he seemed interested in getting the reception line over with rather than in meeting the people. Still, I was a strong Hoover supporter and was awed to see him in person.

On Election Day 1932, President Hoover came home to vote, and I went with my classmates to see him in front of City Hall. He knew that he had probably been defeated. He looked more tired, discouraged, and depressed than I had seen anyone look.

That same year I wrote to our congressman and was placed on his list to receive the *Congressional Record*. It always came about a week late, but I read each issue cover to cover. Through it, I gained a reasonably good knowledge of congressional procedure, though the *Record* was, and is, a highly sanitized document: congressmen and senators still take out everything they don't want in and add anything they wish they'd said had they thought of it at the time—all of this under the rubric of "revising and extending their remarks." So it was not an entirely faithful record, but it interested me nonetheless. I also used to save any letters that a congressman wrote back, because of the letterhead of the U.S. Congress on them; I was intrigued by all such governmental trappings.

The whole mechanism of democratic elections—conventions, campaigning, returns, counting of the votes—fascinated me. I put together scrapbooks of newspaper clippings about conventions, elections, and political events. I considered assembling these scrapbooks an absolute priority. I worked very diligently on them, meticulously pasting in articles, and even sent away for postelection copies of newspapers around the country, because our own had very little news about elections in other states.

I found that my burgeoning political views and preferences were increasingly those of the Republican Party. When my political consciousness was first beginning to take shape, Calvin Coolidge was president, having succeeded to that post after President Harding's death,* and then winning it in his own right in 1924. Coolidge's laissez-faire, probusiness policies and his cuts in taxes and federal expenditures seemed reasonable and proper to me (and my father) as instinctively the right course to follow, even before I had formally learned about economics. I knew that business was good for my father and for his clients, and that the country was enjoying unprecedented prosperity. All of that convinced me that the Republicans were doing something right.

President Franklin Roosevelt's tremendous expansion of the federal government in the Depression-wracked 1930s only solidified my views that the best government was the least government. Many credit FDR and his alphabet soup of programs with bringing the

---

* I have particularly vivid memories of President Harding's death in August of 1923. He had fallen ill on his way back from an official trip to Alaska and so stopped over in San Francisco. The balcony outside his rooms at the Palace Hotel on Market Street was hung with U.S. flags and bunting.

Then there were headlines that his condition had worsened, and one afternoon when I picked up our phone to call my father, the operator, instead of the usual "Number, please," said, "The president is dead." That was my first encounter with the mystical aura that surrounds the presidency. Later, the newspapers devoted their full front page to pictures of the president with, in huge type, the words "President Is Dead" superimposed over the picture. The flags on the balcony at the Palace Hotel were changed to heavy black draperies. All of this filled an impressionable six-year-old with awe and excitement.

country out of the Depression; I believe that that, if anything, made things worse. New Deal spending was almost entirely financed by taxation—which left people with even less to spend—which meant less consumer demand—which meant less supply was needed—which meant companies were not hiring—which meant there was widespread unemployment—which left people with less money to spend—and so went the vicious circle.

I felt quite strongly in 1932 (and have ever since) that expanding the power of the federal government was not the answer. Nor was strangling individuals and businesses with the noose of regulation. I was particularly troubled by the Soviets' "master plans" and successive "five-year plans," which I felt was the kind of system that completely foreclosed all opportunity for the individual to flourish. I feared that the more the New Deal developed, the more we would become like the Soviets—the more power the government had, the less power there would be for each individual to chart his own course and rise as far and as fast as his abilities could take him.

As it was, I believe it was only our entrance into, and massive mobilization for, the Second World War that brought some improvement in our economy. But long before Pearl Harbor, millions of Americans were suffering; virtually no one was untouched by the Depression.

During the building of the Golden Gate Bridge in San Francisco, I remember lines of desperate, out-of-work, able-bodied men who would wait, day after day, for one of the construction workers to fall or injure himself so they could take his place.

Those years were very difficult times for my father as well. In such economic straits, it was generally felt that, while food and utilities had to be paid for, doctors and lawyers didn't, so Dad lost quite a bit of regular income. It was especially hard for him since he had a one-man law practice, but even in the worst times, he never let on or even discussed finances. We always lived comfortably, though not lavishly by any means, and Dad never gave any indication that we did not have enough money for whatever we needed. The subject simply never came up. I learned only later what a great strain it had been for him to pay the bills.

I followed big news stories avidly. One that I particularly remember was a major effort to get flu anti-toxins to Alaska during an epidemic. I tracked their progress by air and then dogsled. I can still see the big headline: "Anti-toxin Reaches Nome."

Air travel was in its nascent stages, and its development was thrilling to witness. Each new achievement was a cause for national celebration. I remember, when I was very young, my parents went out to see Colonel Maugham land on the old Crissy Field in the San Francisco Presidio, after the first dawn-to-dusk flight across the United States. He had left from New York in the early morning, in a biplane, and arrived in San Francisco shortly after sunset. Of course he made many stops along the way, but it was still considered a tremendous feat.

Then, in 1927, Charles Lindbergh made his historic solo, nonstop flight across the Atlantic. As in many cities around the country, a huge parade was held in his honor in San Francisco. There were no stands along the parade route, which made it difficult to see anything unless you were in the front row. So my father rented a small room at the old Federal Hotel on Market Street, and my family crowded in there to watch the parade. My father had one of the first Bell & Howell home movie cameras. He later edited his home movies and showed them for years. Lindbergh was an authentic American hero and could do no wrong—until his isolationist views before World War II meant he was in opposition to the Allies.

In 1932 the Lindbergh baby's kidnapping made constant head-lines. Americans became familiar with H. Norman Schwarzkopf, head of the New Jersey Police Department, who gave innumerable press conferences regarding the investigation. Little did I know that many years later, I would interview his son and then approve his appointment to head the U.S. Central Command, in which capacity he led our forces in the Gulf War.

Prohibition, which was in effect for most of my childhood, didn't bother my father. He had seen the effects of drunkenness in Idaho Springs—the miners, who worked six days a week, would get paid on Saturdays and then go out and destroy themselves with liquor. They had to be dragged back to work on Monday mornings. So my father was essentially a teetotaler, but he wasn't fanatical about it. In fact, in 1932, when the repeal of Prohibition was in the works, my brother was very anxious to try a can of 3.2 percent beer (the first thing legalized). Dad went down to Marshall's Pharmacy to get one for him. I had a taste of it, but I did not like it—it was sour and bitter, and didn't taste anything like chocolate! I much preferred wine, which I tried many years later. It was not a question of principle or prejudice, but simply that I never liked the taste of most alcohol.

My first experience with school was dreadful. Starting in the early 1920s, my family often spent the summers at a garden apartment, the Kingscote, on the Stanford campus, about thirty miles south of San Francisco, and one summer my parents thought it would be a good idea to send Peter and me to the Palo Alto Military Academy.

I do not remember the classes, but I most vividly recall the marching. We had to wear terribly hot, scratchy, World War I–era uniforms and march in formation out on a dusty field in the blazing sun. I also remember that everyone was required to eat at the same time, and to eat the same thing, which was something absolutely ghastly and always included rice pudding. In short, there was little room for individuality or individual development at the military academy. After only about a month, my parents decided the whole experience was counterproductive and mercifully took us out of the school. It was fortunate, as it later turned out, that this brief experience did not adversely affect my view of the military in general.

After we returned to San Francisco at the end of that summer (1925), Peter began attending Commodore Sloat, a public grammar school, and a home tutor, Miss Dorothy Rector, was engaged to provide my instruction. Since I had been ill so much, it was thought that I needed to gain my strength back before entering school, and by that time, I would need to be prepared to enter the fourth or fifth grade. Miss Rector came to the house for four or five hours a day. I remember her as a nice young lady and a good teacher, and I enjoyed preparing for schoolwork.

In 1926 my parents sent me to the Frederic Burk School. It was a progressive school that allowed each student to advance at his own pace in various subjects. This was the so-called Dewey system, then a very advanced idea. This school was chosen mostly so that I would not fall behind when I was absent with frequent illness, as I would have in a traditional school. It was a good system, and classes were small, so every child received individual attention and encouragement.

The school was part of the laboratory of the San Francisco State Teachers' College, and all of my instructors were in training for their teaching careers. My favorite teacher was Miss Violette Kindt, and we kept in touch by letter for quite a while after I started high school.

One other faculty member that I recall was Miss Spozio, the principal. She was a formidable and imposing woman. If you were sent to Miss Spozio, you were in deep trouble, and I was exceedingly relieved that I never had to make a trip to her office. Years later, I met a lady commissar in Tashkent, in the Soviet Union, who reminded me strongly of Miss Spozio.

I basically enjoyed grammar school. I made decent grades and was class treasurer and editor of the school newspaper.

It would have been most logical for me to go on to Lowell High School, which was considered the "academic" high school; most pupils who were planning to go on to college went to Lowell. But my brother was already attending Polytechnic High School, and he had impressed on me, and I fully agreed, that "real men" went to Poly. So in 1930 I started high school there.

Polytechnic was oriented more toward manual and mechanical training, at neither of which I was very good, but they did have all of the normal courses. I especially enjoyed English and all kinds of history, and of course I was particularly interested in anything that had to do with government and politics. Many of my school papers reflected my strong opinions, even then, about the virtues of democracy and the inherent evils of Communist repression and New Deal economics. In a number of my essays, I warned against "the Soviet Menace," economic planning, and the views espoused by Professor Rexford Tugwell, a radical, early "Brain Trust" adviser of President Franklin Roosevelt. Indeed, my writing then, and now, shows a certain consistency (or perhaps more properly, a lack of growth).

I was extremely shy as a child, a trait I no doubt developed from my mother, and which, I am sure, was exacerbated by the fact that I started school so late. But at Poly, I took part in a number of extracurricular activities, which brought me out of my shell somewhat.

When it came to girls, however, I was still incredibly timid. It's not that I wasn't interested; I certainly was, but I never felt I could advance the cause myself. I was always afraid I'd be bothering the girl. (I didn't realize until much later that many of them actually *like* to be bothered.) If a girl showed interest in me and took the initiative, then that was fine, but not many of them did, so I would mostly just admire them from afar and pine for better days.

I was much more comfortable with other endeavors. I joined the Drama Club and worked mostly behind the scenes—if you lacked talent, you were put in charge of the lights. But I did have a small part in a mystery play called *The Thirteenth Chair*. My big line was, "It's no use—he's dead." (Why I so clearly remember that particular bit of trivia, while I've forgotten so many other things, I don't know.)

In my senior year, I was elected president of the student body. I had run on a platform promising to establish a new constitution. With the help of my father and my faculty adviser, Miss Polly Hatch, I drafted a constitution that provided for a legislative body similar to the U.S. Congress, a student court, and other institutions borrowed from federal government models. I felt that this would be a good way to learn about the American government, but primarily I wanted to carry out my campaign promise to establish such a constitution. It took me several months and at least ten drafts to get it completed, but it was eventually voted on and ratified.

By my senior year, I knew that I wanted to be involved in government in some way. My graduation speech was on "The Honorable Profession of Politics." I know that many thought it a rather strange title, but the idea came to me after reading results of a poll that showed about 70 percent of parents did not want their children to have anything to do with politics. I told the audience I firmly believed that while politics can indeed be a dirty profession—just as dirty as we let it become—politics can also be an honorable profession—just as clean and honorable as we want it to be. We can make and keep it honorable by our own participation. The choice is ours.

After I graduated from Polytechnic in December 1933, I took a few more courses there during the spring semester, including economics, Pacific relations, and California history to nourish my insatiable interest in government affairs (and to fill up the time until the college years began). I also made extensive use of Stanford's library during our summers on the Stanford campus, a trip we made almost every year of my childhood. One summer there, I drifted into the back of some classes on American politics and political parties. Professor Barclay was the instructor, and these classes further fueled my interest in all of these matters.

My father had a client from England who had encouraged both Peter and me to think about a Rhodes Scholarship and applying to Oxford. Being a confirmed Anglophile even then, I found that a very attractive idea, but I soon learned that I had to attend an American college first. It seemed to me, from what I had heard and read, that Harvard was the best college in the United States, and I have always wanted to go to the top. Inquiries about Harvard led me to the Harvard Club of San Francisco, which annually awarded the William Thomas Scholarship. This was the only scholarship at that time named for a living person, and Mr. Thomas, an elderly San Francisco attorney, personally selected the winner. After an enjoyable interview with him, he announced that I was his choice to be that year's recipient.

Needless to say, I was delighted, and I set about meeting Harvard's entrance requirements. Fortunately, I was able to do that without much difficulty because Harvard exempted from all college entrance examinations those applicants who were in the highest seventh of their high school if their school was in an area not served by the College Entrance Board Examination. San Francisco and I both fit these exemptions.

So now my course was set. I had not the slightest doubt then—or since—that Harvard was indeed the finest university in the land.

CHAPTER 2

THE FINEST UNIVERSITY

My whole family—Mother, Dad, Peter, and I— loaded our newly acquired one-year-old Cadillac (with twelve cylinders—at that time Cadillac made the only twelve- and sixteen-cylinder engines) on a late summer day in 1934 and set out for Cambridge, Massachusetts. (After attending Stanford for a year, and the University of California at Berkeley for one semester, Peter transferred to Harvard when I received my scholarship.) It was a long trip, and the longest time my father had ever been away from his law practice.

For me, the highlight of the trip was our stop in Washington, D.C. Being such an avid student of government, it was wonderful actually to see and set foot in our capital city—the place I had read so much about. Indeed, in our spare time on the drive across country I had read my *Washington Standard Guide* and paid fifty cents for the paperback 1932 edition of *The Challenge to Liberty* by Herbert Hoover— his first attack on the New Deal of his successor.

We stayed at a hotel near Union Station in full view of the Capitol, which, lighted at night, seemed to me to be the most beautiful sight I had ever seen. Although Congress was not in session, we visited the empty House and Senate chambers. My imagination supplied the vision of the members whose words (or an approximation thereof) I had been reading in the *Congressional Record*. A passage of fevered prose that I had scribbled down from what I think was a Washington guidebook perhaps summed up my impressions best:

> Here transpire daily events that will leave their impress on the future, and one cannot look upon the scenes where the future destiny of the nation is being formed without feeling that he has touched the very pulse of the government and felt its living throb.

After nearly a month on the road, we came to Boston, with all of its history, crossed the gleaming Charles River, and journeyed into Harvard. The grand, redbrick buildings, standing like stately, wise old men, deeply impressed me. I saw the Harvard Yard bustling with eager, young, confident students and was assailed by doubts. How could I ever acquire such assurance, such a sense of belonging as most of those students seemed to exude? They seemed a world apart, until I found many as uncertain, but few as shy, as I was. Many of all types became my good friends, but early on, I felt out of place and unsure of everything except my political opinions. I expressed these quite didactically, and I am sure quite irritatingly.

My mother took an apartment on Prescott Street, one block over from the Harvard Union. She was a worrier, unhappy at our separation, and decided she would stay until Christmas to "get us started" while my father hurried home to his law practice. He would return to spend Christmas with us at Harvard, and then my parents would return together to San Francisco.

Peter and I shared a room in the Union, a building just behind the Yard, in which were located the dining hall and a few meeting rooms for freshmen. There were only five or six large residence rooms on the top floor, a library and language rooms on the second floor, and the dining hall on the first floor. I remember being impressed, even then, with the way the West Point cadets, who came for the Harvard-Army football games, would file into the dining hall. With impeccably straight posture, they were quite a contrast to their slumped and sloppy Harvard hosts who followed.

My brother continued to be much more outgoing than I, so although we roomed together, we really did not see much of each other. While he often went out with friends, I was quite overwhelmed with work and often in Stillman Infirmary because of chicken pox, measles, and recurring ear infections. I really had led quite a sheltered life up until then, so admittedly, it was helpful that Mother was nearby. My father came back to Cambridge as planned for that first Christmas. We celebrated the holidays in Mother's small apartment, with a tree and wreaths—everything as much like Christmas at 60 Merced as possible.

After my parents left, I set aside time nearly every other day, usually around 5 P.M., to write letters home. (Fortunately, I was a fairly proficient typist, so I spared them the eyestrain of trying to decipher my awful handwriting.) My parents wrote to me almost as often. Whenever I returned to Cambridge from a summer or Christmas vacation, my first stop would be the Western Union office in Harvard Square to wire them that I had arrived safely.

The cross-country trips were a financial strain for my father, as indeed were my college years, coming at the depth of the Depression. But somehow my parents always made it possible for me to come home for summers and Christmas The four-day, three-night train trip seemed interminable, but I was always grateful to be able to do it. It helped considerably that I had won the scholarship that covered my first year's tuition—the princely sum of four hundred dollars. That was a major turning point in my being able to attend Harvard, though my father called it a "loss leader," meaning, "they got you into the store with what looked like a bargain, but then all the other prices went up." I did not hear the expression again until I was at the Federal Trade Commission and discovered it was an unfair trade practice.

Once I was at Harvard, I watched my expenses closely and sent my father a regular accounting. As in the earlier years of the Depression, however, my parents always made it work with a minimum of strain on Peter and me, and I remember more than one instance when, boarding the train to return to Harvard at the end of a summer or Christmas at home, I discovered that Mother had deposited a dollar bill or two in my jacket pocket. I tried to tell her in subsequent letters that that had been entirely unnecessary—if much appreciated. A dollar in those days could buy a subway ticket into Boston and back, a haircut, a couple of football programs, or a few greeting cards, with change left over.

I also tried to earn a little income of my own. For a couple of summers when I was home from Harvard, I wrote editorials for the *Argonaut*, a fairly conservative, business-oriented, and now long-defunct weekly San Francisco magazine. I covered local issues and events, such as the deportation case of longshoremen labor union leader Harry Bridges, and other industrial disputes, but occasionally I would cut loose against the big government agenda of President Roosevelt or the appeasement policy of Neville Chamberlain.

At Harvard, I wrote a regular column for the *Argonaut*, entitled "Along the Atlantic Seaboard," providing Californians with a window on "how the other coast lived." I reported on local politics, weather, sports, the arts, and other goings-on throughout New England and the East. My experience with the *Argonaut* perhaps kept alive my latent interest in journalism, already fueled by work on the *Harvard Crimson* (of which more later). And I have to admit, an added attraction was the reasonably regular income (ten dollars a column as I recall it).

When I first started college, I had no specific plans for the future. I suppose there was an unspoken assumption that I would go to law school, though, frankly, I wasn't all that enthusiastic about it. As was the case with many college students, I rather drifted from one idea to another. The thought of being a doctor appealed to me, since I had been ill so much as a child, but the science courses were not congenial. A few highly cynical newspapermen with whom I interviewed shortly before graduation talked me out of a journalism career. "This is the worst profession in the world," the editor of the old *New York Sun* told me (he was a college friend of my father).

I majored ("concentrated" in Harvard's usage) in American government but found my courses lifeless and taught with a liberal bias. Indeed, I was often the lone conservative in class. I did, however, greatly enjoy English history and literature courses, and by my third year, I wished I had started out on that track instead. Of course, at that point it was entirely too late to start over, and Harvard did not offer "minors."

The class workload was extremely heavy. I was quite ill-prepared for it, coming from a relatively easy, carefree existence at San Francisco's Poly High. Another problem was Harvard's language requirement. To graduate, students had to have a reading knowledge of an ancient and a modern language. I did well enough with Latin, since I had studied the basics of it in high school. For a modern language, I chose a double course in German, largely because my mother had studied violin in that country. After prodigious efforts, I passed with the only two C's of my college career, but I was happier to have those two C's than any of the higher grades I received later, because they met the required reading knowledge of a foreign language and relieved me of the need for further language courses. But I now regret that I never mastered a foreign language, and I think it is a great mistake that our public schools do not require foreign language instruction starting in elementary school. When I was in the California legislature, I secured passage of a bill requiring teaching of a foreign language by or before the sixth grade. Sadly, the teachers' union forced its repeal only a few years later because "there were not enough qualified teachers." I suggested we use educational television, but it turned out that that was precisely what the teachers' unions most feared.

Harvard also had an athletic requirement for graduation, which included swimming fifty yards. Because of my chronic ear infections, I had never learned how to swim. After two years of trying, followed by several successive ear infections, I was granted a waiver. I still cannot swim, which was later a great worry to my wife and the Secret Service detail whenever I would take my motorboat out alone in Maine. It was also inconvenient to me as an army lieutenant leading troops across various shallow (I hoped) jungle streams in New Guinea.

With all of Harvard's other requirements, however, I did reasonably well. My professors were of course well known and respected in their areas of expertise, and many were the world's authorities. The great majority of them were considerably more liberally inclined than I; some were genuine New Dealers, and most favored expansion of federal government power.

As war clouds gathered over Europe, many were, if not isolationists, at least far more interested in domestic matters. This bias was apparent even in the thesis topic I was given. The last of my tutors,[*] Professor E. Pendleton Herring, pressed me to write my senior thesis on the Farm Credit Administration (FCA), then recently created as

---

[*] Every student had a "tutor," usually a tenured professor, to guide him in his class selection, supervise his class work, and help with his thesis. For many, the work with a tutor was more important than classroom work.

part of Roosevelt's New Deal. (Theses were required if one wanted to graduate with honors.) I, of course, would have preferred to write on political parties or conventions or other aspects of politics, but I let myself be persuaded to write about the FCA. I am sure that from an educational viewpoint it was a suitable subject, for I knew absolutely nothing about farms or credit policy—but I did not know a great deal more even after writing the thesis.

As a freshman, I joined the Union Debating Society; I had heard many of my father's stories of his work on debating teams at the University of Colorado. I also felt that debating might help me overcome some of my shyness, which it did. It may have even fostered my interest in law. I stayed busy in politics, too. At election time, I worked with newly formed college committees for local Republican candidates. I was elected treasurer of the student council, which was fun but not terribly challenging, since student government at Harvard was neither very strong nor considered very important. My work there consisted mostly of evaluating scholarship applications, recommending courses to new students, and keeping track of the council's limited finances. The best part was working with my classmate Francis Keppel, who was the president of the council. He was a brilliant, thoroughly charming New Yorker who had an exuberance and enthusiasm comparatively rare among my classmates. He had wide-ranging interests, studied sculpture in Rome after graduation, and later was appointed dean of the Graduate School of Education—one of the youngest deans in Harvard's history. I was a guest in his parents' homes in New York City and in Peekskill, and it was always a delight to be with him and see his quick and brilliant intellect in action.

The most fun of all, next to the *Crimson*, was the Signet Society, a literary club to which I was elected in my junior year. The society often held readings and concerts, and it housed a wonderful library in the Dunster Street clubhouse (into which, I recall, entry was gained by pressing on a loose board alongside the front door). The Signet also served excellent food; I often went there for lunch and enjoyed the food as much as I did the conversation.

Initiation into the Signet involved hazing which, by today's standards, would seem quite mild. Great quantities of alcohol would be consumed (though not by me), while the candidates were required to read aloud amusing poems or stories they had written themselves, and then be questioned by a boisterous audience. I wrote a short poem, the topic of which I have now forgotten, but which was well received—primarily, I believe, because of the inebriation of the audience.

Initiation also included the tradition of giving each new member a rose, which the member was then to send back to the Signet upon publication of his first book, at the time of his first concert, or on the occasion of his first literary, artistic, or musical achievement, whatever it might be. The rose would then be framed and kept at the Signet Society house. The roses of several accomplished members, including T. S. Eliot, are on display. Regrettably, I lost track of my rose and so was not able to carry out this tradition when, in 1990, my first book, *Fighting for Peace*, was published.

My fondest memories of my years at Harvard are of the many long hours I spent at the *Harvard Crimson*—"Cambridge's Biggest [and only] Breakfast Table Daily."

In April of my freshman year, I, quite audaciously for me, tried out for the news board of the *Crimson*. There were four boards: editorial, photographic, news, and business. Forty or fifty people competed for a spot on one of these boards; ultimately only two or three new candidates were elected to each board from the two or three competitions held every year.

As a news candidate, I was given various assignments, which included everything from doing menial tasks to covering football games to getting interviews. We were also encouraged to develop and write stories of our own and not just carry out assignments.

Interview subjects were not specified, but I was able to talk with and write about quite a motley, if small, cast of characters, including the eldest son of one of my great heroes, Theodore Roosevelt.* TR Jr., in Boston for one of his speaking tours, was extremely friendly, eager to put me at ease, and most helpful. He gave me good quotes and never seemed to worry about what I might write about him.

My big triumph (at least in *my* mind), however, was to "get" Tallulah Bankhead. It happened that she was in Boston, starring in *The Little Foxes*, and simply by calling the theater I was able to get an appointment with her in her dressing room after a performance. I had not been able to get a ticket for the play, and the *Crimson* did not provide one, but after she expressed some initial disappointment that I had not seen the play, Miss Bankhead was very helpful and answered all my questions. (It was not until December 6, 1941, that I actually saw her in the play in San Francisco, the night before Pearl Harbor, of which more later.) I was quite flattered that she called me "darling," in her broad Alabama accent—until I later learned that she called *everybody* "darling." In any case, I considered the interview quite a triumph.

But I think it was another coup that got me on the board. British Labour Party economist Harold Laski (not one of my heroes) was

---

* Theodore Roosevelt had been a hero of mine since boyhood. I believe it was my father's strong admiration for TR that started me on this track. My father had seen and heard Roosevelt when he came to Denver, probably in 1910 or 1911, and was most surprised that he had quite a high voice that without any public address system could be heard two or three blocks away. I admired greatly the fact that Roosevelt had willed himself to change from a sickly boy into a man of enormous physical vitality and strength. I also was greatly attracted by TR's writing and other abilities, his early entry into active politics, his war record in the Spanish-American War, and his extraordinarily rapid rise to state and national fame. All of these early impressions were recalled and heightened when, much later, I reviewed the excellent eight-volume collection of TR's letters, and still later when I read Edmund Morris's biography, of which alas only the first volume has been completed. I greatly regret that Morris's biography of Ronald Reagan fell far short of his work on TR.

giving lectures in Boston, but he absolutely refused to be interviewed—and was very unpleasant about refusing. So I went to one of
his lectures, and during the question period I managed to ask him
three questions before he realized he was being interviewed. I wrote
it up as if it were an actual interview, and I have a feeling that helped
greatly in earning me a slot on the news board.

Once on the staff, from the beginning of my sophomore year, I spent
almost all of my spare time at the *Crimson*. I usually had classes, sometimes three in a row, in the mornings on Mondays, Wednesdays, and
Fridays, and then my day at the *Crimson* would begin around two in
the afternoon. The printing deadline was 2 A.M., so despite the late
start, it was indeed a full-time job. There were always numerous varied
tasks to be done: developing and writing stories, editing issues, making
up dummy pages, helping to run the next competitions, and proof-
reading. I learned to read type from the galley proofs upside-down
(inverted so that it would print correctly from the Linotype machine),
and I also became quite good at helping repair the ancient printing
press, which broke down periodically—inevitably around 1:30 A.M.

On one occasion, members of the *Lampoon* staff raided our office
and shut down the press. It took quite a long time to counterattack
and oust them, so it was not until 5 A.M. that the paper rolled off the
press and was folded. We then had to deliver it ourselves, completing
the task about 8 A.M. Although that *Lampoon* raid did not succeed, it
was considered essential to retaliate and harass the *Lampoon*. We used
to stage frequent raids back and forth, and once the *Crimson* even
managed to steal the metal ibis from the top of the *Lampoon's* quaint
building. (I understand that the bird has been bolted down since.)
Then there were the hoax issues of the *Crimson* put out by the
Lampoon, and vice versa. (The *Advocate*, Harvard's other publication,
considered itself to be intellectually above such pranks.)

In those days, the *Crimson* could not afford to subscribe directly to
the wire services, so every night, usually around 11 P.M., one of my

duties was to take the subway into Boston to pick up the United Press International dispatches from a kind *Boston Herald*. These nightly outings gave me quick familiarity with snow and extreme cold, weather I had not encountered before moving to New England.

The "Red Ink Sheets," the first proofs of the paper, were a source of great anxiety and occasional embarrassment. These resembled freshman themes returned with the professor's comments; the major difference was that the "Red Inks" were required reading for all and replete with the managing editor's comments and criticisms written in red ink, rarely tactfully expressed. The most intolerable error involved infinitives: they were *not* to be split. Factual errors were corrected with scorn; I am sure this improved our writing and accuracy, although usually only after the error had appeared.

Many of the *Crimson*'s editorials in those years were very biased (for which I would like to claim some credit). We tried to keep the news pages free of political prejudice, but in one example I remember, we ran a picture of Alf Landon after he was defeated by Franklin Roosevelt in the 1936 presidential election, along with the cutline "Landon Beats Lemke!" William Lemke, a former North Dakota senator, was a third-party candidate. We did not mention FDR's victory until later in the story.

We also did a rather provocative editorial entitled "Are You Mice or Men?" complaining with tongue in cheek that the present crop of students was too weak and meek to have any riots, as they had in the old days. This, of course, caused the deans great anguish and, predictably, produced a riot by students the next night.

I worked my way up to the positions of assistant managing editor and managing editor and was elected president at the end of my junior year. Up until that time, there had always been two managing editors and two presidents from each class per school year. But I felt that that system did not really allow sufficient time to learn how to do the jobs right, so when I was president, we secured the members' consent to have only one president and managing editor a year. However, this did not apply until the next year, so only halfway through my senior year, my term was over and I relinquished the chair to my classmate Morris Earle. Although I did not recognize it at the time, this may have been one of the first examples (besides my constitutional work at Poly High) of my penchant for reorganizing existing systems, which I was called upon to do, and did, a number of times later in life. As for the *Crimson*, I believe my one-president-a-year policy continues to this day.

I made a few other, more minor changes during my term as president. We improved the sports coverage, added more photos, and, in a move that perhaps stemmed from my own sedentary inclinations, installed a copy chute to the basement so editors would not have to walk downstairs every time something was ready to be printed.

As president, I took an active interest in editorial policy. Although I wrote only a few editorials myself, I did try to "improve" some of them with my own biases, particularly those on national and international issues. It was on my watch that, for the first time in a long time, the paper made a small profit, which we distributed among the staff in the form of a dividend.

In addition to the daily paper, the *Crimson* revived publication of *The Confidential Guide to Harvard Courses*, which had been discontinued some years earlier. The guide, largely compiled through student opinion surveys, assessed the courses offered at Harvard and particularly the quality of teaching. It was really the only criticism and evaluation available and was designed to help students choose what courses to take. We did try to be fair, but, not surprisingly, it was viewed with some disdain by the faculty, except those favorably mentioned. It was, however, very popular with students. Its publication was another example of the complete freedom we enjoyed as students.

All of these activities, in addition to heavy class work, left little time for a social life. Most of my time was spent studying at Widener

Library or in my room at Dunster House, or working at the *Crimson*. As a result, most of my friends were from the *Crimson*: J. Sinclair Armstrong, a close friend who became my daughter's godfather; his roommate, Morris Earle, now my son's godfather; Shippen Goodhue; and Cleveland ("Clip") Amory, who became a professional writer with several well-received books to his credit.

Ellsworth Grant and Tom Calhoun were also good friends from the *Crimson*, and right after our spring exams in 1936 we drove up to Fenwick, Connecticut, to see the boat races and visit Ellsworth's fiancée, Marion, a younger sister of Katharine Hepburn. Many years later, Tom wrote an entertaining article about me on that trip for the *Hartford Courant*, but I'm afraid that the way I remember it is not quite as glamorous or prescient as his version.

We stayed at the Hepburns' rambling old house on the water. Katharine was there for part of the time (with her former husband, which I thought a rather strange arrangement). Her mother, Mrs. Hepburn, was a vigorous, earthy woman who had all kinds of views and ideas that for the time were very liberal and advanced. She was particularly vocal on birth control and women's rights and the more liberal parts of the New Deal. At dinner one night, she listened to me defend, in a rather halting and shy way, some of my conservative beliefs, and finally she grabbed my hand and said, "Let me see your palm! Where *do* you get all this?!" She studied it for quite a while, and then, with great irritation, pronounced, "My God, you're going to live forever!" This made me even more ill-at-ease, but I do not recall that she made any other predictions, as Tom Calhoun reports it, about any great power or military responsibilities I might have in the future. I probably would not have believed her anyway!

Three other men in my class who went on to gain prominence, but whom I did not know well during college, were the Pulitzer Prize–winning biographer Arthur Schlesinger Jr., the prolific corre-spondent, historian, and China expert Theodore H. White, and Wiley

Mayne, a skilled and talented attorney and a congressman from Iowa during the same time that I served in the Nixon administration.

I never knew him well, but John F. Kennedy, class of 1940, was on the *Crimson* business board. I saw him only a few times but remember him as a thin, gangly youth. His older brother, Joe Kennedy Jr., later killed tragically in the war, I knew much better. Joe was a vigorous, enthusiastic man, as quick to defend the New Deal and the Democrats as I was to attack them during several meals we had together in Dunster House. He was an easy man to argue with, and likeable and friendly. I am sure he would have made at least as popular a president as his brother. In fact, all the rumors were that his father was even then grooming him for that office. Joe had a strange (to me) accent. It was a combination of Boston street twang and pure eastern preparatory school. I never could imitate it. I often wondered how *I* sounded to him!

In my junior year, I got to know Clip Amory's younger sister, Leonore, or "Leo," as we called her. She was still in prep school at the Milton Academy Girls School, and I saw her frequently at her parents' home. I most enjoyed the casual weekends we spent at her family's home in Milton, Massachusetts, not far from Cambridge. I generally felt awkward around girls, but I was more comfortable with Leo, perhaps partially because she was relaxed and very bright and knew how to play baseball. (In fact, one of the main reasons I returned to Harvard for law school was to be close to her.)

Her family was always extremely nice to me and seemed to welcome me at their home, but I am sure they never considered a serious relationship between their daughter and me. Indeed, the first, almost automatic Boston response to any matters of that type was, "Who are his people?" In any event, nothing came of it.

Boston and its surroundings had a completely different feel from San Francisco. Of course, it is much older, staid, and smugly proud—a perfectly pressed dinner jacket to San Francisco's well-worn favorite sweater. More attention was paid to social strata and who one's "people" were—an environment I had not directly experienced before. After a few years in Boston, I began to understand and be much amused by the fact that "Lowells speak only to Cabots, and Cabots speak only to God." I amused at least myself by wondering aloud whom Godfrey Lowell Cabot, a most illustrious Brahmin, could possibly talk to.

After freshman year in the Union, students were assigned to one of the houses, massive brick residence halls along the Charles River. I was assigned to Dunster House, and during my sophomore year I again shared a room with Peter. Later I had fine, large quarters to myself for my junior and senior years. This last suite overlooked the courtyard and, beyond its gate, I had a view of the Charles. Dunster House sits in a residential neighborhood, surrounded mostly by private old homes, and is a good ten-minute walk from the Yard and Harvard Square.

The university tried to get a cross section of students in each house, but Dunster, at that time, seemed to have a preponderance of students studying government or economics and while this encouraged study groups, I preferred to study alone until I entered law school.

The houses were like full-service apartments. Each house had its own library; Dunster's was long and narrow, with rich, dark paneling and plenty of deep, comfortable chairs and couches to sink into. The rooms were homey, and some suites had fireplaces. There were maids (or "biddies" as they were disparagingly called in those politically incorrect days) who cleaned the rooms and were generally nice old Irish ladies. They told me I was one of the neatest residents, a distinction I was proud of but kept to myself. Meals were served in the beautiful paneled dining hall on the first floor by waitresses and student help. The dining hall, consciously modeled after the Oxford and Cambridge colleges, had many paintings of old Harvard and New England figures, including, of course, Henry Dunster, the first president of Harvard. I generally ate breakfast and dinner there (and lunch at the Signet Society),* and I considered the food at Dunster mediocre at best. When I was later in the army, I was ashamed that I had criticized Harvard's food. Army meals made such an impression on me that when I became secretary of defense more than forty years later, I made improving the food, particularly the MREs (Meals Ready to Eat), a priority.

In the summer of 1936 I had my first real, though very limited, taste of participatory politics. I was an usher (along with my good friend, Bruce Griswold, with whose family we stayed) at that year's Republican National Convention in Cleveland. The convention was sparsely attended and I had little to do, being assigned to a section of seats at the very top of the arena. I was also included, though, in a small dinner given by Nelson Rockefeller. Nelson's brother David was on the *Crimson's* business board, and he has been a much admired friend and Maine neighbor for years.

At the convention, former president Herbert Hoover's appearance brought the crowd to its feet, and his address was far more politically appealing than the rather scholarly talks he had made in his losing campaign four years earlier. The delegates rallied in support of Alf Landon, the venerable governor of Kansas and one of the few GOP victors in 1934. He easily won the nomination. I was convinced that all that enthusiasm was going to translate itself into votes. So confident was I that when I rode back to Harvard afterward with classmate Ben Welles, I bet him (too much) that Landon would defeat Roosevelt. Unfortunately—for my pocketbook, as well as for the nation, in my opinion—I lost the bet. I have never bet on anything since.

---

* In major contrast to most any place today—*especially* colleges—in those days, one could not even get into the dining hall without having a tie on. Indeed, the standard attire of the day for college men included a tie and sports jacket.

My undergraduate years at Harvard were crucial ones for my personal development. It was during that time that I seemed to come out of my shell and gain confidence in myself. I also had a real opportunity to expand my knowledge in many fields. As daunted and out of place as I had felt when I first came to Harvard in 1934, in four years' time I found that I could measure up to the high intellectual standards of the Ivy League and, more important, get closer to my own aspirations, which were even higher.

At the end of my undergraduate career, I ranked third out of 127 men in the government department, and sixth out of 355 in the whole division of history, government, and economics.

On a glorious, bright, early summer day in 1938, I graduated magna cum laude at ceremonies in Harvard Yard. My emotions that afternoon were mixed. Obviously, pride was the predominant feeling, but it was mingled with disappointment that my parents had not been able to afford the trip east to share it.

After the ceremony, I walked back to Dunster House, leaving the Yard through Dexter Gate at the head of Plympton Street. I paused for a moment to read again the inscription above it, which had fixed itself in my memory the first time I saw it back in 1934. It has been an inspiration to me ever since. On the street side it reads, "Enter to Grow in Wisdom," and on the Yard side is engraved, "Depart to Serve Better Thy Country and Thy Kind." It seemed to me then, and now, a good beacon to have before one.

My graduation also brought a degree of uncertainty. I had been awarded the Lionel de Jersey Harvard Studentship, which would have given me a year of relaxed study in Cambridge, England, with residence in John Harvard's old rooms at Emmanuel College, Cambridge. Instead, I entered law school, both mindful of my father's hopes and for other reasons. This was 1938. I have made many mistakes since, but turning down that chance to go to England before the war was one of the stupidest things I have ever done.

If I thought the undergraduate coursework was strenuous, law school was about threefold as difficult, as anyone who has done both well knows. There seemed to be barely enough hours in a day to do all the studying necessary to keep up with the classes.

I never decided what area of law I wanted to practice, but I quite enjoyed classes that strongly emphasized English history, such as real property law and the history of the common law.

The faculty was distinguished, but the *manner* of teaching had a great impact on how much was actually learned. I particularly remember George K. Gardner, professor of contract law, who delighted in being an absolute sphinx and carrying the Socratic method well beyond suitable limits. He only asked questions and would never give the answers, even at the end of the hour, an approach I found maddening. Others, such as Professor Warren Seavey, were far more effective for young students. They would use Socratic questions until about ten minutes before the hour and then clarify and explain the answers to which the questions had been leading.

Professor Edward Warren, known as "Bull" Warren for the vigor and animation with which he taught, was one of the best known and most respected law professors at Harvard. Unfortunately, my own experience with him was cut short when he became ill and retired during my freshman year. Luckily, the professor who replaced him, James Casner, was an extraordinary teacher.

Probably the most useful and helpful component of my law school education was the moot court work, done outside of class. This work, done under the title of the annual Ames Competition, was not compulsory, but everybody took part, as it provided the only real opportunity to go beyond theory into practice. You were elected to a law club—mine was the "Pow Wow"—which then worked as a team, writing briefs and preparing and giving oral arguments for the moot appellate court presentations, which were the heart of the competition. This was a lot of extra work but well worth it. The whole experience was quite realistic, especially once you reached the finals. At that stage, the judges who heard the cases were actual justices from the Massachusetts Supreme Judicial Court or the U.S. Court of Appeals or occasionally even the U.S. Supreme Court. They rendered decisions in our cases immediately after our presentations. The judges also wrote critiques and opinions, which inevitably helped us to improve our preparation and performance the next time around.

In the summer of 1940, I had an additional opportunity for real-world experience, working in the New York law firm of Simpson, Thatcher, Bartlett, a position arranged for me by my father. My useful but unexciting duties focused on researching state laws regulating the issuance of stock by corporations.

More enjoyable was acting as a proctor for undergraduate freshmen in Matthews Hall in the Yard, particularly because I recalled how helpful some of my own proctors had been in my freshman year. I found that I greatly enjoyed counseling individual students who were making their way in a new environment. Occasionally, some who found their new total freedom at Harvard exhilarating, after the strict rules at most schools, also required other help, such as being carried upstairs to their rooms after late-night parties in town. Being a proctor had its advantages. I had my own spacious, ground-floor suite, and I even drew a salary of two hundred dollars a year.

My third and final year of law school proved to be the most difficult. Not only was it the busiest and most crucial period of my law school career, I was also hit with another serious ear infection. I had to spend three or four weeks in the infirmary and lost almost two months of class and study time. I was treated with one of the new antibiotic drugs, despite some misgivings by my fine conservative Boston physician, Dr. Gooddale. He said later that the new sulfanilamide had probably cured me.

During most of my stay in the infirmary, I was required to lie flat, which made it nearly impossible for me to write. So some of my friends, primarily Sinc Armstrong, helped by writing letters to my anxious parents from my dictation. Sinc was enormously helpful during this time, and his kindness and generosity continued after I was released: he and his new bride let me stay with them at their home while I made a full recovery, which took another three or four weeks. I managed to catch up with my coursework and graduate on time, but it was a struggle.

Although I started and ended my Harvard career with extended illnesses, I consider the seven years at Harvard some of the best of my life. In fact, I enjoyed Harvard so much that it took a world war to get me out of there.

CHAPTER 3

OVER HERE

*E*arly in my first year of law school at Harvard, it seemed evident to me that Europe and England were rapidly sinking into disaster. Winston Churchill seemed virtually alone in recognizing the folly of appeasement. In late 1938 a Gallup poll indicated that 65 percent of my fellow Americans approved of the Munich agreement. However, I firmly believed that America's interests required us to be active participants in what later came to be called the "Good War." It seemed to me clear then, as it does now, that we could not exist in a world in which our European friends were overrun by the Nazis (or later by the Communists). I agreed with Churchill that appeasement is the vain and foolish hope that if you keep on feeding the crocodile, he will eat you last. But my fervor was shared by few of my fellow students, and my parents were completely opposed to my desire to fight in Europe.

In the summer of 1940, when the Battle of Britain was at its height, the Royal Air Force (RAF), in affiliation with the Royal Canadian Air

Force, was doing some confidential—and, I suppose, illegal[*]—recruiting at a San Francisco hotel. Filled with the crusading spirit, I volunteered but was rejected because I had "no depth perception." I asked if that really made a difference, and the examining doctor said, "Not really—you'll simply try to land the plane fifty feet above the ground and walk away from it!" For the rest of the summer, I did eye exercises, but it was to no avail; the RAF would not take me. It was only later that I realized what a major investment it was to train a pilot.

My parents were relieved, to say the least; my father had tried to dissuade me from leaving law school early, and I reluctantly promised that as long as the United States was not directly involved, I would not try to enlist.

As additional incentive to keep me out of the war, my father arranged a postgraduation position for me on the legal staff of the Securities and Exchange Commission, a new regulatory agency created under FDR. I, however, was determined to join the military after law school, at the latest, and rejected the position.

My father, hoping to keep my participation stateside, then arranged for me to talk with an army intelligence unit at the Presidio in San Francisco. I did meet with recruiters for the unit but concluded that the work there would be extremely limited. I was also put off by the Shell Oil Company maps on the walls; this did not seem like the highly classified information I thought we should be working with.

As it turned out, the United States was not brought into the war before I finished my three years of law school. I graduated with an LL.B. degree in June 1941, and after passing the New York bar exam, I came home and enlisted in the army in September 1941, asking for assignment to the infantry.

* Because of our officially neutral stance.

The infantry was, in my mind, the most honorable way to serve, a sentiment which I suppose came partially from my mother's New England heritage and the ethic that only the most difficult, disagreeable path was morally right and that anything enjoyable must be wrong. But my fascination with the infantry was also strongly influenced by the novels of Siegfried Sassoon, particularly *Memoirs of an Infantry Officer*, which I had read in high school or early in college. The book by no means glamorized the infantryman's existence—quite the opposite—but Sassoon's eloquent account stirred my patriotic passions and brought out the idea of noble service and total dedication to a cause; even though Sherston, Sassoon's protagonist, was against World War I, he fought in it bravely. Martyrdom is perhaps too strong a term, but I seemed always to have this compelling inclination to do what I thought was the right thing, even if it was difficult, unpopular, or actually disagreeable. I thought it essential that this war be fought, and I could not imagine not being involved myself.

I was sworn into the army at the San Francisco Armory. Most of the other men had been drafted and had little interest in saving the world. I should mention here that my brother, Peter, was married and had one child at this time, so he was not eligible for military war service, though he did have a civilian job with the navy, first in Hawaii (before Pearl Harbor) and then in Fresno He served in the army later, in Korea. In any case, he did not particularly share my crusading fervor. While he was supportive and understanding of my desire to fight, he was also very concerned when I eventually went overseas; I believe he could think of no one less able to take care of himself abroad than I.

But I was more than eager to jump into the fight. My first army assignment was to the Presidio of Monterey, which was basically just a holding site for new recruits while it was determined where we would go next. No real military training was conducted there except for some routine close-order drills; to keep us occupied, we were sent to a huge warehouse to receive canned goods for distribution to other military units in California. We would stack tons and tons of Del Monte canned tomatoes and apricots on one side one day and then move them all to the other side of the warehouse the next. For me, this was varied with latrine duty.

After three weeks in Monterey, when I was starting to believe my father may have been right, I was sent to Camp Roberts in central California. This was the Infantry Replacement Training Center.

When I arrived in October 1941, much of Camp Roberts was still under construction, so a good deal of our time was spent building its infrastructure. The first major task was digging sewers under the main parade ground. All men with college and graduate degrees had been assigned to one company—and this was our assignment.

Aside from digging the sewer, most of our time was devoted to marching and more warehouse stocking. What little training there was was far from realistic. We had no real weapons to practice with: we carried wooden "rifles" and used blocks of wood labeled "hand grenade." We had to pass a couple of World War I–era rifles around among us during instruction in what our regular army instructor called "the normanclature of the rifle." "Normanclature," we were told, "is a Latin word meaning 'parts.'" The complete lack of equipment and preparedness was a lesson that I carried with me to the Pentagon many years later.

It was also as an enlisted man at Camp Roberts that I got a good idea of what is important to enlisted men and their morale, which proved invaluable when I served as secretary of defense.

At Roberts, training meant long marches with heavy packs, slithering under old rusted barbed-wire fences, and on a few rare occasions "dry firing"—that is, *not* firing—at the rifle range. There was training in how to use the rifle sling and in the proper prone, kneeling, and standing positions from which to shoot. In later weeks, we had a strong incentive to keep down, as live firing exercises were conducted over the fences under which we were crawling.

Toward the end of my three-month stint at Camp Roberts, I was moved to a clerkship under a tough first sergeant. He was aptly named Tartar, and his favorite expression was "Soldier boy, you've been in the army long enough to know..." followed by a long and detailed list of various infractions and errors. One recruit asked our drill sergeant why we wore *two* dog tags. The answer, delivered in the army's best singsong monotone: 'One is cut off and sent to the next of kin; the other stays on the body."

On the weekend of December 6, 1941, I happened to be home on one of my few leaves. Saturday evening, December 6, was innocuous enough; my father and I went to see *The Little Foxes*, starring my one-time interview subject, Tallulah Bankhead.

The following morning, we heard on the radio that the Japanese had attacked Pearl Harbor. At first I thought it was just another Japanese threat. But the reality was soon confirmed. Fear rippled through San Francisco as people realized that if Hawaii could be surprised by an attack, we might be next.

The army immediately canceled all leaves—all military personnel were to return to their bases. So my father took me to the train station late that afternoon. I'll never forget that ride through the city: the Japanese areas, and even Chinatown, were in a complete state of siege. The National Guard and police were out in force—partly to protect Japanese-Americans who lived there, but also to guard against sabotage from possible Japanese collaborators.

I took a troop train to Camp Roberts, arriving around 2 A.M. on December 8. Now there were armed sentries at each barracks. I was stopped by a guard of apparent Japanese descent, and my first thought was, "My God—they've already taken over!" But, of course, he was Japanese-American, and as loyal to the United States and the army as the rest of us. In fact, he hesitated to let me in because I could not come up with the correct password, which had been issued after the bombing.

On December 8, after the United States declared war on Japan, our training took on a new relevance—now no one was merely going through the motions; we were preparing to fight a specific enemy.

President Roosevelt's address to Congress and the nation that day, which I and my fellow soldiers gathered around the radio to hear, made it all too real, especially for those of us on the West Coast: "The attack yesterday on the Hawaiian Islands has caused severe damage to American naval and military forces. I regret to tell you that very many American lives have been lost. In addition, American ships have been reported torpedoed on the high seas between San Francisco and Honolulu. . . . I ask that the Congress declare that since the unprovoked and dastardly attack by Japan on Sunday, December 7, 1941, a state of war has existed between the United States and the Japanese Empire."

Soon thereafter, I heard about Officers' Training School and immediately applied. A lot of the men I was training with did not *want* to be officers, which I could not understand. I thought if anyone was in an organization, he would, of course, seek to rise to the top.

I nearly missed my chance, however, because the first order that came in was for me to be assigned, as part of a big bloc of infantry trainees, to a battalion in Alaska. But within a week, my application for officer training was approved and I was ordered to Fort Benning, Georgia, to attend the Infantry Officer Candidate School.

I joined Officer Candidate Class 14, along with about one hundred other soldiers, for thirteen weeks of far more rigorous training than at Camp Roberts. In addition to the standard requirements of physical exercises, negotiating obstacle courses, marching, and map reading, there was target practice with live ammunition and real guns. We learned how to conduct night maneuvers through swamps, how to dismantle and reassemble weapons under difficult circumstances, and what to do in various other demanding situations. Physical skill had never been my strong suit, and that deficiency was exacerbated by the fact that I had not had much real basic training at Camp Roberts.

There was one nerve-wracking exercise that made quite an impression on me—almost literally. Our whole officer candidate class gathered around a young lieutenant who was to give us our instructions. Before he began, he came over to me and asked if I remembered him.

"Actually, no sir, I really don't," I replied. This was before I ran for office and learned to be much more reluctant to admit I could not remember someone.

"Well, you should," he said, "because I met you when I was in competition for the *Harvard Crimson*."

"Ah, yes," I said, smiling cheerfully. "Did you enjoy the *Crimson*?"

He responded in an even tone of voice, "Not after you cut me from the competition."

This took me rather aback, and I was trying to think how best to respond to it, when he turned back to the group and began explaining the day's exercise.

This exercise was a result of French troops' not knowing how to deal with mass tank attacks. The tanks engendered a great deal of fear and panic, and the troops frequently surrendered or ran away. There was to be none of that in the American army, the lieutenant said, and we were going to practice some tactics that our strategic planners had come up with. This seemed reasonable enough.

Basically, what the exercise entailed was digging a small foxhole (easier said than done in the hard, red clay of Georgia), which had to be narrow enough that it would support the heavy weight of the tank without caving in, but also deep enough that you could get your entire body into it, crouching so that the top of your helmet was below ground level. This still seemed reasonable enough.

In addition, a new, small, plastic grenade had been developed, and we were to push one into the tread of the tank as it passed over the foxhole. Anticipating some of our worries, he explained that the timing of the fuse had been worked out so that it would not go off until about fifteen or twenty seconds after the tank had rolled on past. It was beginning to sound a little less reasonable, but still rather a neat idea—for someone else.

However, the lieutenant then announced that we did not have time for the whole class to practice this, and so only a handful of us would do it. I suppose I shouldn't have been surprised that he pointed a stubby finger at me first and yelled, "You!" Four other names were rattled off quickly, and we were given entrenching tools (the formal army name for the shovels we carried under our packs) and mock grenades made out of something like Play-Doh because we did not have any of the real plastic grenades.

A bugle sounded, meaning we had sixteen minutes before the tanks arrived. We started scrabbling away frantically at the Georgia clay, probably the most impermeable substance that had yet been discovered by man. Soon there was, in the distance, a rumbling sound, which we assumed were the tanks, although none of us had ever actually heard or seen a tank in action before. The rumble increased, as did our efforts, and finally I got to the point where it was possible, by assuming practically a fetal position, to wedge myself into the foxhole.

Shortly, the sunlight was blotted out, and I saw, too close for comfort, the tank tread above me. Somehow I was able to get one arm up and push the Play-Doh as hard as I could into the tread. I was never so glad to see the blistering Georgia sun as when the tank finally rumbled off. I counted fifteen seconds, but my Play-Doh did not explode, so the realism was over.

I extricated myself from the hole to see that my four colleagues had apparently long since emerged from theirs. Relieved laughter swept the group, and we stood around sort of anticipating the congratulations of our leader. But he had moved on to the next exercise—with what I thought was a fairly disappointed look.

In other training, I was surprised that I excelled at rifle practice, perhaps because I'd had no previous experience (except a BB gun at home and the dry runs at Camp Roberts). I simply did exactly what the instructors told me to do. Many of my fellow candidates had trouble, I suspect, because they had hunted extensively and had already learned other methods of shooting.

For the relatively short amount of time we spent in the barracks, a couple of vivid memories stick in my mind. Both involved the radio. A large, burly fellow infantry officer candidate named "Tex" Charlton had somehow hooked up his radio and phonograph so that when the lights came on every morning at 5 A.M. and the bugles blew reveille, his phonograph would blare out "Deep in the Heart of Texas." This was not then one of my favorite songs, nor did the passing mornings endear it to me.

The other thing I most remember was Prime Minister Churchill's radio addresses. The first of these talks that I heard was a rebroadcast of his address to the Joint Session of Congress not long after Pearl Harbor. I had been in the mud all that winter day, and all the equipment needed thorough cleaning before another execrable dinner. But Mr. Churchill's great prose delivered in those matchless tones (even on the small, tinny barracks radio) revived any flagging spirits, just as he inspired the people of England and of occupied Europe.

In May 1942 I was commissioned as a second lieutenant. My new officer's cap and gold bars made me feel important and proud of myself. I was sent home for a five- to seven-day leave before being deployed overseas. The week turned into two weeks, and ultimately into about five weeks, because there was no transport available.

Almost the last day I was at Fort Benning, we had been asked to fill out a questionnaire stating where we wished to be assigned. I put down England as my first choice and Northern Ireland as my second, since the United States was starting to build air bases there. But I doubt if anyone even read those questionnaires (a point I mentioned to the army many years later). Within six weeks I was on a ship to Australia.

CHAPTER 4

⌒

OVER THERE

*S*hortly before I shipped out, I had an inkling that I probably was not going to England. My orders said I was to
go to "SUMAC." I assumed this was some obscure
secret location, but I soon learned that SUMAC stood for "summer
arctic," which meant that I would be in a climate that required both
summer and arctic uniforms. Actually, on further reflection, I realized
that could have meant England, but I guessed that it would most
likely be the South Pacific.

My journey got off to a rather inauspicious start in July of 1942
when my mother and father were seeing me off at the dock in San
Francisco. My mother had packed a box of her cookies and brownies for my trip. I set it down momentarily with my luggage while I
went to the entrance of the pier to say good-bye to my parents, as
they were not allowed beyond that point. When I returned, the cookies and brownies were gone. A rather traumatic departure, I thought.

The ship, the USS *Mt. Vernon*, was actually a converted ocean
cruise liner, but needless to say, it was no longer a luxury ship.

Sandwiched into the five-high, sea-tossed canvas bunks were hundreds of other naive young men like me—in the same boat, literally and figuratively. Some were—or at least acted—swaggeringly confident and almost fanatical in their zeal to convince "the Japs" that *nobody* pushes the United States around. But in the creaking and pitching dark of the vast ocean, I am sure that most soldiers aboard felt at least some slight panic and nauseating aloneness. Those were the times, I suspect, when many of us clung to the images of such simple things as the curtains on our bedroom windows at home, our aproned mothers making our favorite meal, summer football games with our brothers and childhood friends. Those days seemed so innocent and so young and so far from where we were now, and as we sailed off to an uncertain future, it began to occur to us, perhaps for the first time, that maybe we were not all that invincible.

The cabin to which I was assigned was unbelievably hot because it was right over the laundry. Occasionally I slept out on deck, which was fine until the nightly General Quarters alert was called and everyone scrambled to their posts, usually trampling me in the process.

The eighteen-day journey to the Pacific theater did have its good points. Soon after we were under way, I noticed a young, red-haired nurse playing checkers with an "elderly" ship's officer. He must have been all of fifty years old. Later, I learned that this was the father of one of her friends. She was an army nurse, one of only four on board, being sent as a replacement to a station hospital in Brisbane.

I had found a sheltered spot on deck and taken refuge there with my books. After a while, I was interrupted by one of the nurses bent on rescuing a lonely soldier. She kept up a lively though one-sided conversation, asking if I played various games, to all of which I had to answer no. Finally she inquired what, if not cards, dice, or shuffleboard, did I play. In the hope of being left in peace, I admitted to chess—whereupon she insisted that I come down to their cabin to meet the nurse who played chess. I did, and to my surprise—or maybe to my hope—it was the one I had noticed earlier—Lieutenant Rebecca Jane Dalton from the state of Maine, as she informed me. She, too, was a second lieutenant, but outranked me, as she had been commissioned a few months earlier than I. She also outplayed me at chess, and having won that first match, she never played again, saying she had sense enough to quit when ahead. Luckily, I now have a delightful red-headed grandson who plays a great game.

Anyway, on that long-ago transport, chess no longer mattered, for as I started to leave that evening, thinking I had taken too much of her time, I said I thought I would take a walk around the deck. "Not without me, you won't," she replied, and that was the first of many star-filled evening walks. From then on, we spent every free moment together talking, walking, reading, sometimes just watching the sea, and mostly ignoring the rest of the world.

We could not share meals together since all the women—four nurses and eighteen Red Cross ladies—were required to eat with the higher-ranking army officers in the navy officers' dining room. But she took pleasure in smuggling me cakes and cookies, even a sandwich now and then, which were a great improvement over the meals served on the lower decks.

To our dismay when we disembarked in Sydney, we were separated: I went to a makeshift barracks at Randwick Racetrack outside the city, and Jane, to a hotel called 52 Maclay Street.

With a bit of rearranging, however, we were soon together again, and against all regulations, we were quietly married in Sydney. We had two days there before she left by train for Stuartholm, a convent that had been converted to an army hospital in Brisbane. I had been at the racetrack barracks when I returned to find that all the nurses were leaving with a train full of soldiers. Told that it would take a day or two for them to get to Brisbane and that there would be no food available except what you could purchase at stops, I quickly got a box lunch of sandwiches and cheese and a bottle of sherry. The train was about to pull out when I got there, but I was able to deliver the lunch to Jane and say a quick good-bye.

I informed my mother and father of our marriage by letter after the wedding. They were, of course, surprised because I was so shy, and my mother had all the normal reservations that all mothers have about any daughter-in-law.

Several days after Jane left, I took off by the same train for Rockhampton. Having been told how long each stop lasted, I was able to get off the front of the train in Brisbane, spend an hour with Jane at the hospital, and get back on board at the rear before it cleared the station. While she was in Brisbane, I was also able to visit now and then on supply trucks going back and forth between there and Rockhampton.

Then she was sent to Southport, a delightful little seaside town, to join a hospital group being made ready to relieve a unit at a camp in the Beanley Mountains. It was on the first of several visits to Southport that I had my first airplane ride. It was in a Royal Australian Air Force DC-3, whose pilot was quite willing to add me to his cargo of spare aircraft engines.

I was not there when the nurses left Southport by truck, sitting sideways on planks, for the long ride up the mountains. How they survived the trip is hard to imagine.

Jane and I did not meet again until she came back to Brisbane as a patient with dengue fever. Routine exams indicated that she was pregnant, and our marriage became public. Spouses were not allowed to stay in a war zone together. As a result, with other evacuees, she was ticketed for the next available transport home. I wrote my parents to expect her. When news of our marriage reached Jane's family, her somewhat catty sister-in-law said that "she always knew Jane would go and marry some soldier." One of Jane's favorite stories is to quote that and add, "Well, she was right. I did, and after fifty years, he is still *some* soldier."

Jane and I knew that we would miss each other dreadfully, but she would be safer at home and I would soon be moving up to New Guinea.

After a seemingly endless trip back to the States on a Danish freighter that kept breaking down, she arrived in San Francisco. She visited with my parents briefly before returning to Maine.

On the 27th of April, 1943, our child was born, weighing barely five pounds, but vigorous and healthy. A few days later I received a telegram: "Daughter born—all is well." Through some error, I received the same message three times in the next few days, so I wondered if we had had triplets. It turned out to be just one—Arlin Cerise Weinberger, named for Jane's adoptive mother, Stella Arlin Newcomb, and my mother, Cerise Hampson Weinberger—and my wife and daughter moved to San Francisco, waiting for the end of the war and my return. They stayed with my mother and father, an arrangement that underwent the normal strains of wartime living in close quarters. Jane and my father had an immediate fondness for each other, and my father was fascinated with Arlin. My mother, on the other hand, had some reservations about my new bride, as I suspect she would have had no matter whom I had married. Later, Mother came to like and depend on Jane.

I never met Jane's family. Her mother died before I made it to Maine, and Jane's father, a retired banker, had died earlier.

My mother and father and I continued to correspond frequently; my father wrote once a week, my mother more often, and Jane nearly every day. The mail arrived in batches, so I'd get four or five letters at once, sometimes two to three weeks apart. Finally, they started numbering their letters, so I would read them in the correct order. As every soldier knows, mail call is the highlight of the week (or whenever it arrived), and I was fortunate to have such a close-knit family and a devoted wife. Years later, remembering the trauma of waiting for the mail, I was determined as secretary of defense to improve the speed of mail delivery to the troops.

My own letters were written as frequently as possible. When we were in a rear area with some spare time I would write rather illegible scrawls. Occasionally I used "V-Mail," a form of photostatted mail that was designed to save space and weight but was very public. Years later someone saw a V-Mail letter from me to my family in a Seattle bookstore and bought it for me.

When I went overseas for duty, I was classified as a "Casual Unassigned." It was not until after I arrived in Australia that I was assigned to the Forty-first Infantry Division. The core of the Forty-first, a National Guard division mostly from Oregon and Washington, was already there but was understrength. We, the newly arrived crop of soldiers, were to "bring them up to strength," which seemed to me a gross misuse of the language, because we knew less than they did. Besides being very green we were also, I sensed, seen as interlopers. Indeed, as a National Guard outfit, most of the soldiers in my unit were from the same small town, Baker, Oregon, and had trained together for years. War does not allow much freedom of choice, so we inevitably grew to depend on each other, to have confidence in and trust each other, which is essential for a military unit.

After a few days in Sydney, I was sent north to Rockhampton for some field training. Shortly after we arrived, one of the men in my platoon was killed in an awful accident. We were practicing advances through jungle territory, putting out flank guards on each side of the line of advance and a point man in front. If the point man encounters opposition, you cover him, and he motions the rest where to go to avoid fire. We were using live ammunition, and when the maneuver called for shooting, someone behind me fired excitedly and hit the point man from behind. I actually heard the bullet on its way past my ear. That was my first experience with a casualty by so-called friendly fire. We had had a few live-fire exercises at Fort Benning, but no accidents. When I saw him go down, it seemed to me to be far too realistic a fall. I halted the exercise, ran forward, and tried to do what little I could for my fellow infantryman, a Hispanic corporal. I called for a stretcher and tried to comfort him and stop the flow of blood oozing from his back. We finally got him to a hospital in Rockhampton. He lived for two or three days, and I visited him in the hospital; when he died, I attended the funeral Mass in a small Rockhampton church. I wrote to his mother and father, telling about his burial after a high Catholic Mass. Ever since, the term "killed by friendly fire" has had a special and terrible meaning for me.

After more training, including night maneuvers, our regiment in early 1943 was sent up to New Guinea, landing at Port Moresby. Then we were flown to the Buna/Dobodura area on the north side of the island, over the Owen Stanley Mountains, one of the most rugged areas in the world. It probably would have taken two to three weeks to march over, and we all would have been in terrible shape by the time we got there. So the army pulled together air transport—a whole group of disparate planes—and that took quite a while. We had to wait twenty-four to thirty-six hours at the Port Moresby airstrip, during which time we had no food. (We were supposed to be fed when we reached Dobodura on the other side of the mountains.) Finally, they did issue us United States Army Field Ration D, which was a chocolate bar. Being a confirmed "chocoholic" and very hungry, I immediately devoured the whole thing. What I did not understand was that this was not an ordinary chocolate bar. It had, packed into it, a large number of highly concentrated and enhanced vitamins and, in fact, was the equivalent of a one-day, three-meal pack; you certainly weren't supposed to eat it all at once. Needless to say, I was terribly, terribly ill during the very turbulent flight over the Owen Stanleys. Once we landed, I, being the platoon leader, was supposed to organize the platoon and begin the march from the rudimentary airstrip to the sea, which I managed to do. I was almost hoping that the Japanese would attack immediately so that at least I could lie down. They did not, however, so we marched over a very rough log and mud road for

God knows how many hours and eventually got to our bivouac area in a coconut grove just inland from the beach.

While on the northern coast of New Guinea, we sustained a few Japanese air raids, generally just three or four planes at a time—nothing remotely resembling what Europe was enduring. When they came, you were supposed to get into a foxhole; the first time I did, I found a coiled snake as my companion. I decided that I would rather get hit by a bomb. From then on, I stayed around the tents (and later, shacks) during air raids, which was more stupidity than bravery.

Once in the Buna area, we mostly conducted patrols through the thick jungle. The Japanese were defending the Buna airstrip, and they had a nasty habit of tying snipers into trees. Once they even hauled a naval gun up a tree, and it and its crew stayed there for two or three days until we were able to locate and dispose of it. None of the infantry manuals prepared us for dealing with that. But we rarely encountered the enemy; eventually the Japanese abandoned the airfield, and we occupied it.

After several months in the Dobodura area, we were sent to Milne Bay on the eastern tip of New Guinea for more patrolling. We also patrolled further west for some months, and that was interspersed with building perimeter defenses and slightly more sophisticated living quarters. Every day we patrolled the jungle, manned the perimeters of our camp at night (the Japanese were always expected to attack at dawn), and cleaned and recleaned rifles and artillery pieces.

When our situation permitted it, I used to talk to the men in my platoon in an informal way, usually gathered in a rough circle, sitting on logs. They had all kinds of questions, ranging from trying to understand why particular orders had been given to asking why the mail took so long and who would get to go home. The most frequently asked question was, Why are we in New Guinea?

I tried to point out that we could not have stayed out of the war, that, that even the United States could be attacked, and in any event, we could not live in the world were both Europe and Asia overrun by the enemy. I told them I would much rather defend California or Oregon from New Guinea than from California itself.

Many seemed to enjoy these sessions. I found it a good way to try to keep up morale, for with periods of inaction and uncertainty about what we were to do, questions and doubts and the desire to go home multiplied.

There was a rough outdoor area used to show the very occasional film sent over by the USO to entertain the troops. There was also an area for religious services on Sunday mornings when the situation permitted. A rough entrance portal had been constructed and a handmade sign erected on which was a quotation from Emerson's *Sacrifice*—"'Tis man's perdition to be safe, when for the truth he ought to die."

My law school education was put to use in a couple of court-martial cases that underlined why a new Code of Military Justice was enacted after the war. One was a desertion case, and when the jury showed signs of not believing the evidence, the regimental commander ordered the trial adjourned and summoned all to his tent. He said he did not want to hear any nonsense about an acquittal: "When I charge a man, he is guilty." He also mentioned that he made out the efficiency reports for all the officers. The implication was clear.

I was also assigned as a regimental gas officer and sent back to Australia for two weeks' training in dealing with poisonous gases. The school was just outside of Brisbane. There are two things I particularly remember about it. One was that the food was infinitely better than anything we'd had in months and months in the field; the second was that we lived in a big old house that was not by present standards luxurious but that at the time seemed like a four-star hotel.

Here we had very realistic training that included putting a drop of mustard gas on your arm so that you could see its actual effects. I still have the scar.

Shortly after I returned to my regiment, I became very ill with malaria and spent two or three weeks in the hospital. In New Guinea, 70 percent of my regiment had become ineffective because of malaria. Had we been subjected to a major attack at that time, we would probably not have been able to hold any of our positions.

In the field, we had introduced preventative water sanitation measures in an effort to destroy the mosquitoes that transmitted the disease. This consisted largely of turning over anything in the bivouac area that could gather water (usually old coconut shells) and spreading oil over any puddles to eliminate standing water where mosquitoes could breed. We created a fifty-yard perimeter with no standing water around our positions because fifty yards was supposed to be the flight range of the average mosquito. Our methods worked and the percentage of men well enough to fight increased.

For those not familiar with malaria, there are two kinds. There is vivax, or benign tertian, malaria, which is relatively mild, though it recurs for many years. When it does, it lasts for three days. Plasmodium falciparum, on the other hand, is a malignant, virulent, lethal strain. It has one advantage: if you get over it, it does not recur.

I had a fever of about 105, but the doctors could not identify which kind of malaria I had. They got me up one day and made me run up and down a hill behind the hospital tent. Then they were able to get a positive smear and found it was indeed falciparum. Since the treatment for both types (quinine, Atabrine, and bed rest) seemed to be the same, I did not understand why it was so important to determine which type I had. I was not in the best condition after my high-fever run, but at least it was an effective rapid-weight-loss treatment—had I needed to lose any weight then. I did eventually make a full recovery.

One other memory I have of that station hospital was a visit by Eleanor Roosevelt. We were supposed to have everything spruced up for her and then stand by our beds when she came in. After I used up some remaining energy cleaning the place, I took refuge in the gentlemen's lounge so that I would not have to see her. I took my politics rather too seriously then.

The only other health problem I encountered during the war was a slight hearing loss, due mostly to too much exposure to the 37mm antitank gun, which sounded like a loud, angry Pekingese. Ear protection during test firing was not introduced until much later.

Later in 1943, I was promoted to the rank of captain and transferred to General Douglas MacArthur's headquarters to serve in the Combined Operational Intelligence Center, a move to which I objected seriously. Being young and foolish and still filled with the crusading spirit, I wanted to stay in the field with my platoon and company and do some good, or so I thought. But the army wanted someone with legal and/or newspaper experience to join General MacArthur's staff in Brisbane, Australia.

When I arrived at my new post, I sought an interview with General Chamberlin, of General MacArthur's staff, to request reassignment to the division. It was a short interview. He looked me up and down and said, "Young man, in the army you go where you are sent. The army knows what is best for you."

I actually found my new duties interesting. I was on duty two days and two nights, then off a day, and back on for two days. My task was primarily to analyze intelligence reports coming in and then write situation briefs for the general. I would also draft communiqués that he would send to other theater commanders. In the jungle, platoon officers were lucky if they knew what was happening fifty yards on either side of them; from my new vantage point, I could see the whole Pacific campaign as it developed day by day.

General MacArthur was a tremendously imposing man. I worked on the same floor where he had his office—in the Australian Mutual Provident Society, or AMP Building. I could always tell when the general was on duty because he kept his hat on top of a file cabinet that I could see from across the courtyard.

One evening, after he had left—or at least his hat was gone—I walked out into the corridor, toward the elevator, and suddenly I saw him and his whole entourage heading for the same elevator. He saw me pull back and said, in those deliberate, sonorous, organ-like tones, "Come, ride along with me, Captain." I felt it was a royal command. We got in the elevator, and I stood at rigid attention—which was hard to do for eight or ten floors—the general in full uniform, with more rows of ribbons than I could imagine and a presence that inspired awe.

There was one other occasion on which we met at close range. The United States had a small amphibious invasion force at sea, preparing to land at dawn on a small Pacific island (I've forgotten which one). An intelligence signal came across my desk around midnight. Japanese naval units were sighted in the vicinity. I decided the situation was important enough to inform General MacArthur—and I was the only person on duty, so I had to be the messenger. I ran the four blocks from headquarters to Lennon's Hotel, where he lived, and eventually got through all the security to find the general in his bathrobe, but looking as if he were in full uniform, with impeccable posture and dignified formality. He read the intelligence report carefully. "Well, what do *you* think, Captain? What would you do?"

"Well, sir," I said nervously, "I think the Japanese are there by chance. I don't think they've discovered our plan. I don't think they'll interfere with the invasion."

"That's what I think, too. Good night." I raced back to my desk and spent the rest of the night fearing that I had been wrong. Much to my relief, our assessments turned out to be correct. Our landing succeeded unopposed.

My position gave me a minor part in discussing a possible landing on Japan, dubbed Operation Olympic. If we had not dropped the atomic bomb on Japan, we almost certainly would have lost more than two divisions in any ground assault on the home islands of

Honshu and Kyushu. Indeed, the first two divisions, one of them the Forty-first, were written off as assumed total losses. There would have been many more deaths in lost ships; a massive and prolonged engagement would have meant even more casualties on both sides; and there was no certainty that even a successful invasion would lead to a Japanese surrender. That is why I have always felt the decision to drop the bomb was correct.

After having been with MacArthur as his Intelligence Headquarters moved from Australia to New Guinea and then to the Philippines as the war progressed, I was offered the chance to go with him to Japan as part of the occupation force. But I was also offered, at about the same time—late summer of 1945—the chance to go home for good, because I had a very high number of points. (One received points for the number of months served overseas. the total length of time in the service, number of dependents, and so forth, so I was one of the first people selected to go home.)

I quickly decided to do that. My father had died the previous September when I was home on a brief leave, and I had had to go back to the war almost immediately, leaving the rest of my family to deal with the grief and not really dealing with it myself. I had carried a vague. dolorous feeling in the pit of my stomach since that time, but only now were the details starting to come back to me.

After returning from a business trip to Los Angeles, on the Southern Pacific train called the "Lark," and after a normal day at the office, my father had gone to bed. But my mother woke me close to midnight, concerned that he was feeling ill and short of breath. I ran up the street to get Dr. Shwartz, a friend of the family. When he arrived at our house, he immediately diagnosed heart trouble and called for an ambulance. The doctor at the hospital would not let my mother and me in to see my father for a couple of hours, and when we did go in, we were taken aback to see him in an oxygen tent; neither of us had seen such a thing before.

My father died about a week after the original attack, which doctors diagnosed as a massive coronary occlusion. I think he probably would have survived with current treatment and medications, but at that time, they could not do anything to unblock the clogged arteries. I'm afraid that his death was hastened by his constant worrying about my military service; he was only fifty-seven years old.

In any event, with the war essentially over, I wanted to return home to stay and get started on my law practice. By the end of September 1945, three years after I had gone to war, I was home.

My service in World War II was invaluable training for when I became secretary of defense in 1981. In particular, I was struck by the terrible lack of foresight that had left America so unprepared—materially, psychologically, and in trained manpower—for war.

In 1941 very, very few people were ready to teach new recruits. There was a total lack of preparation for many of the things we ultimately had to do and the conditions in which we had to fight. Those of us who were assigned to units in the Pacific had read about the jungles but had no training in jungle fighting or living in a jungle environment. In fact, we had no specialized training at all. For the most part, our knowledge of the South Pacific was limited to films that starred Dorothy Lamour.

The United States was totally unready for a war then. If anybody had been willing to look and listen, we could have seen it coming—at least a few months before it was upon us. Few did and most would not have believed any warnings. In fact, we made a large sale of scrap metal to Japan on December 3, 1941. Right up to that point there seemed to be no belief that we could ever be at war. We were not psychologically prepared as a nation. I learned many lessons from that and felt keenly the necessity of adequate training of men and procurement of materiel.

In 1981 I saw that, again, we had basically the same shortages of equipment and qualified personnel that we had had before World

War II and were facing—at the height of the Cold War—an aggressive global threat. I intended to rebuild our military strength very
quickly, greatly improve our transport capability, and pre-position
weapons in Europe so that we could mobilize rapidly. In World War
II, we had had the blessing of time. But we could no longer take
shelter behind our two great oceans when ballistic missiles could
cross those oceans in eighteen minutes.

In 1981 General Jack Vessey and I were among only a handful of
people left in the Pentagon who had seen active duty—as both
enlisted men and officers—in World War II. Of the secretaries who
immediately preceded me—Brown, Laird, Schlesinger—none had
had any wartime military experience. I felt I was very lucky and was
proud to have served in the infantry, and even given the vastly different situation of the 1980s, I knew the infantry was and is still the
infantry. Without it and its ability to take and hold enemy ground, we
would never be able to win wars.

CHAPTER 5

SETTLING DOWN

By late summer of 1945 I was quite ready to come home. The war had been won and I had been in the army for a little over four years. I was glad I had served, and still think that everyone should serve his country in some way.

But I never considered a career in the military. I was anxious to begin my law practice. I arrived at Fort Mason in San Francisco after a long, slow trip on a very crowded troop ship, the ship still zigzagging because the Japanese surrender had not yet been signed. From there I was sent to Camp Beale at Marysville, near Sacramento, to be officially discharged. It was there that I was reunited with Jane. She had taken a bus from San Francisco after receiving my one permitted call to say that we had actually docked. I suddenly realized I had never seen her in civilian clothes—but that made little difference.

The town was packed far beyond its capacity with returning soldiers and their families. We finally secured a room with a beautiful view of the freight yards—which also brought an all-night cacophony of clanging trains. Still, Marysville was a neat, clean little town—quite a pleasant contrast from the gritty army life. As Jane and I strolled through its manicured park the next morning, we decided to stop in a nearby church, which we later learned was Baptist. We could not help noticing that the church reverberated with jubilant singing, clapping, and shouts of "Hallelujah!" I had never before seen people so thoroughly enjoying themselves at church; I had known only Episcopal and Anglican church services—solemn, quiet events. At first, I felt almost like a child reluctantly taking part in a prank at which I was certain we would get caught. But the enthusiasm was contagious, and I soon found myself enjoying the atmosphere.

After that, Jane and I continued our walk and pondered our future. Jane wondered what we would do next. Quite spontaneously, I burst out that I wanted to be famous. A Harvard classmate and fellow *Crimson* editor, Hans Zinsser Jr., had hoped, before the war, that I wouldn't be "just a lawyer." He had it exactly right—I wanted to practice law, but not be "just a lawyer."

I think that, somewhere in my mind, I aspired—if only in general terms—to the example of one of my great heroes, Theodore Roosevelt. Ill and weak for much of his childhood, as I was in mine, he compensated later by engaging in a mentally and physically vigorous life. I had no desire to hunt buffalo in the Badlands or scale Europe's peaks, but I felt I had to prove that I had overcome earlier weaknesses and make something of myself. But at the same time, I felt the same uncertainty that Roosevelt once expressed: "I wonder if I won't find everything in life too big for my abilities." To overcome this, I subconsciously made extra efforts. Jane has often reminded me of our talk that day.

After my separation from the army, we took a bus back to San Francisco to the house where I had grown up and where Jane, Arlin, and my mother were living. To my daughter I was a stranger, but she seemed to me a beautiful child with a strong will and decided opin-

ions of her own. My mother looked much the same as when I had last
seen her in 1944 and kept herself busy by doing radio surveys—
something like the Nielsen ratings for television—by phone from
home. A few months later she took a position at a children's clothing
and toy store near our house. It bothered my brother terribly; he
thought it was awful that she was working, particularly because she
did not need to, but she seemed to enjoy it.

As for myself, I had an offer with a small New York firm and had
passed the New York bar examination in 1941, but I wanted to stay
in San Francisco and looked for leads at the San Francisco Harvard
Club. The club directed me to a local attorney, Roger Kimball, who
was interested in helping anyone who had been to Harvard and
served in the war. He arranged a number of interviews for me,
including a law clerkship with a judge newly appointed to the U.S.
Court of Appeals for the Ninth Circuit. This was William Orr, former
chief justice of Nevada. I met him in his chambers in the Post Office
Building at Seventh and Mission. I had occasionally gone to that
court with my father when he argued cases there, but I had never
seen the judges' chambers. They were very grand—large, airy rooms
with beautiful redwood paneling. The law clerk's office also seemed
palatial as far as I was concerned, but then, I was coming practically
straight out of a tent.

The entire building was a lavish federal building by any standard.
It had been rebuilt after the devastating San Francisco earthquake of
1906. Something like $7 million had been appropriated for the
reconstruction, but surprisingly, the final cost was way under that—
somewhere around $5½ million. There was, at that time, a peculiar
federal budgetary provision: by law, the surplus could not be returned
to the Treasury. So they went back through the building and added
embellishments. They paneled the offices with redwood and added a
great deal of marble, among other things, so it turned out to be an
extremely opulent building in an old-fashioned sense.

Judge Orr was cordial, pleasant, dignified, respectful, and a man of obvious talent. And he was a very western judge. From time to time, he wore a white cattleman's hat. He also had a dry, laconic, western sense of humor and knew numerous frontier jokes. He was a patriot as well, and admired anyone who had served in the war. The only clothing I had at the time that came remotely close to fitting (I had lost about fifty pounds) was my uniform. I wore it at our interview, and I think that was 95 percent of his reason for hiring me.

I was totally unprepared and ill-equipped to help a judge, or really to do anything except be an infantryman, and we had a great surplus of those then. I had been away for four years and had not even passed the California bar examination. Luckily, the judge had one other employee—an experienced, gray-haired lady named Grace Arnold, who had served with other judges and knew everything there was to know about federal courts. Shortly after she told me she had been a Red Cross nurse in World War I, she rather abruptly asked, "How old do you think I am?" Being stupidly more interested in accuracy than feelings, I did a rapid calculation and came up with precisely the right answer mathematically. "However did you know that?" she replied testily. It took several days to restore a cordial relationship, but she became a close friend of both my wife and me.

As soon as I was ensconced in my beautiful office and had begun my new job with the judge (less than a month after I had returned from overseas), I enrolled in a bar examination preparation course. It was an evening course given by Bernard Witkin, who had written a few textbooks and was famous in California law circles, both for his legal treatises and for his preparation course. The course accomplished its purpose, but it was the antithesis of Harvard Law School. There, they generally used the Socratic method in which professors would bring out the law by questioning you and having you give the answers. In the bar preparation course, in effect, Mr. Witkin bored a

hole in your head and simply poured in, night after night, the things
he knew you would need to pass the bar.

Meanwhile, my wife was busy house-hunting. Ultimately, she
found a house in Sausalito for around $5,000. It was financed not by
a bank but by the very effective California State Veterans' Program. If
the state was satisfied with the price, the state would buy the house
outright, and you would then pay the state back in very small
monthly payments. As I recall, our monthly payment was about $40,
which fit nicely with my court salary of $200 a month.

We moved in shortly after Christmas 1945. It was a very good first
home. Perched on the side of a hill and nestled in a virtual tent of
trees, the tiny house had three floors, but with basically one room on
each floor. It was cozy, with a porch and a fireplace, and the living
room had a cathedral ceiling. The trees framed a huge picture window that afforded an absolutely glorious, 180-degree view of the bay
and of San Francisco. Leaf-blanketed log steps crawled from our
street clear down to the center of Sausalito, at least one hundred
steps that I counted every time I climbed them with groceries. I was
in pretty good shape then, as walking was, and had been during the
war, my primary mode of transportation.

Our lot was not only steep but narrow, so we were quite close
to the neighbors' homes. We could hear their dog barking, and they
could, on occasion, hear Arlin crying. A nice older couple who lived
on one side of us often spoke of how terrible the war must have been,
and whenever they heard Arlin crying, they sympathized with Jane.
They were quite sure that I was suffering from war trauma and
probably beating the child. Actually, the only "war trauma" I experienced, which no doubt was the same for many soldiers, was a recurring nightmare: for years I dreamed I was holding a hand grenade
about to go off, and I would wake up perspiring profusely and grinding my teeth.

In January 1946 I took the California bar examination, and around May I was informed that I had passed and now had a chance to practice what I had been trained for. I enjoyed my work with Judge Orr, but there was no ladder to move up. Still, I knew it would be a wrench to leave Judge Orr, with whom I had formed a lasting friendship. He was not only a great judge but a first-class teacher and role model as well. He was the first to teach me, not by purposeful intention, but by example and by his kindness and great help, that not all Democratic appointees were necessarily bad! I fear the degree of my partisanship then was virtually limitless.

Judge Orr was a man of simple tastes who abhorred all pretense or affectation. He was completely a man of the people but not a populist, and he never forgot the dignity, without pomposity, he felt was required of a judge. He would frequently take me to a simple lunch at a cafeteria (I believe it was called, ironically, the Clinton Cafeteria) on Market Street, a few blocks from the courthouse.

In any event, I resisted the temptation to stay on, and I started looking for another job. Within a couple of months, I took a position as a very junior associate in the old San Francisco law firm of Heller, Ehrman, White & McAuliffe. At first, my new position seemed almost like a step down. My initial salary was barely more than before, and instead of having my own spacious, paneled office I now shared a tiny office with another associate, Robert Harris, and all of the firm's many years of files. I was the newest, youngest, and lowest in the firm, and the legal profession now seemed to me not quite the noble vision of it that I had carried in my mind since the day I graduated from law school. On that day, along with our diplomas, we were given Harvard's traditional dictum: "You are awarded the degree of Bachelor of Law, and admitted to the study and practice of those wise restraints that make men free."

The firm, located in the old Wells Fargo Bank Building (the bank was our principal client), had about eighteen people at that time:

twelve partners and six associates, an unusual ratio. Today, Heller, Ehrman has well over four hundred attorneys and offices in several cities. I have frequently pointed out to my former colleagues that the firm achieved its huge growth and prosperity shortly after I left them.

The job consisted almost completely of legal research in the firm's law library. Occasionally, abstruse points required a trip to the city law library, but generally you were "confined to quarters," to use the old army term. Very rarely did you get to court. When you did, it was to carry books and serve as a lowly assistant to the real counsel. But it was the best way to learn how to be a lawyer—something that neither law school nor the bar examination really taught.

One example of the large degree of naiveté I possessed at that time came in connection with our client Hiram Walker, the big Canadian distiller. The problem involved various state regulations concerning alcoholic beverages, and I was asked to get the regulations dealing with fermented wines. I promptly produced the regulations that governed the sale of distilled spirits. Not knowing there was a difference, I was quite surprised when this was pointed out to me rather forcefully. My "research" was immediately rejected.

Later, I also wrote briefs for cases on appeal and occasionally argued preliminary motions before trial courts, usually in probate matters involving wills and trusts. While these were minor problems, I prepared as carefully as if it were a law school mock trial. But some briefs were handed to me as I started on the streetcar trip to City Hall, and my preparation had to be limited to the ten minutes or so that those trips required.

One of my more interesting assignments was a criminal antitrust case brought against several California rice milling companies. This trial showed me how powerful, and absurd, the government can be.

The rice companies had been asked by the U.S. Department of Agriculture to get together as rapidly as possible and send a huge shipment of rice to war-devastated Japan.

They did so, and the U.S. Department of Justice then charged them with criminal violations of the antitrust law for working together to fill the order.

We worked on the case for nearly a year; it took about a month to try, and the jury took only about thirty minutes to acquit all the companies. But there was no reimbursement to the companies for their heavy legal expenses.

For me, the case offered a great opportunity to work with a number of San Francisco's best trial lawyers, representing the several defendant companies, and to observe a not-always-courteous judge in action. The principal lesson I learned from my colleagues was that there was no substitute for the most thorough and detailed preparation of every phase of a trial combined with enormous patience for snappish, irritable federal judges who had lifetime tenure.

Because the law firm was my principal source of income, I felt I *had* to like it, but I felt then, and know now, that spending my whole career as an attorney would have been stultifying for me.

A couple of years after I started at Heller, Ehrman, I began doing some extracurricular work, which my wife came to call my "nonprofit activities." Some of them did bring in a little extra money, but I was motivated more by the need to do something other than practice law.

At that time, my brother was teaching a business course at Golden Gate College, a downtown night school affiliated with the YMCA, and he knew that the dean of its law school was looking for additional faculty to teach the big influx of law students coming in on the G.I. Bill. The school was kind enough to take me on at my brother's suggestion and let me teach a class one night a week. At about the same time, I was also offered and accepted a teaching position at Hastings College of Law, which was part of the University of California.

Hastings was noted for its "65 Club." This was an interesting plan under which Hastings employed professors from other law schools all over the country who had been compulsorily retired at age sixty-five. This compulsory rule was nearly universal, but a great mistake because many of these professors were the most famous in the country. They clearly had seven, eight, nine years or more of good teaching left in them. So Hastings had an amazingly distinguished faculty in these professors, including many former law school deans. But even with the "65 Club," Hastings was still short of teaching staff, so it recruited some young practicing attorneys.

At Golden Gate I taught "Practice and Procedure," which was a good course for me because I needed to learn a lot about it. It covered the mechanical fundamentals of how to practice law—things that were not taught at Harvard Law School. I had to work hard to keep ahead of the class.

At Hastings, I was assigned to teach "Bills and Notes" and "Negotiable Instruments"—essentially the same thing—which was not my first choice, as it was a rather narrow area of law. Later, I was asked to teach the law of corporations, a somewhat more interesting topic. This teaching experience was very valuable for me. It helped me get over some of my natural shyness, and I learned how to answer unexpected questions. This stood me in good stead for later political and legislative debates. The second year of teaching was much easier because by then about 90 percent of the questions the students would ask were not unexpected. Aside from some brief experience training enlisted soldiers when I was an officer in the army, this was really the first public speaking I had done. I found that, both in the army and in the law schools, I greatly enjoyed teaching and taking questions, and I gradually became more comfortable speaking informally and without notes, appearing before groups, and answering questions. I have always tried to avoid reading speeches.

As if my schedule were not already full enough, I took up book reviewing. It was something I had always wanted to do, and my friend Bill Coblentz, another San Francisco attorney, had done a couple of reviews for the *San Francisco Chronicle*. The *Chronicle* was one of the few papers then that had not only a Sunday book review section but also a daily book review, and as a result, they received a great many more books than the permanent staff could handle. So, with Bill's encouragement, I called the paper and they agreed to let me try a couple. They seemed to like them, so I wrote reviews for them regularly for many years. Reviewers were not paid; the reward was the book. In addition, I could keep other new books I liked that the regular critic had decided not to review. So I would go up, usually on Fridays, and take at least five or six books (as many as I could conveniently carry) and review one or two of them. Occasionally books would be assigned, but generally I was able to choose which ones I wanted to review, which is why my library is so heavily overloaded with English history and biography. Art and music books and travel studies also caught my eye.

By the summer of 1948, we had saved enough money—roughly $2,000—to get a car, but money was not all you needed to buy an automobile then. There was almost as great a demand for automobiles as there was for housing in those postwar years. Factories were still making the transition from production of war materiel back to domestic production. Each auto company had huge backlogs of orders for new cars.

Again my brother helped. He knew a local dealer, and he somehow arranged that I could buy a car if I could pick it up in Detroit. By that time, I had two weeks of vacation due from Heller, Ehrman, so I took the train to Harvard for my tenth college class reunion.

Then, once I found the factory in Detroit on my way back, I had the great thrill of getting into the first car I ever owned. The gleaming, "Horizon Blue," two-door DeSoto sedan had literally just come off the assembly line, so when the odometer said zero, it *meant* zero.

As I slid in behind the huge steering wheel and first pressed the accelerator, I almost felt I was driving into a new phase of life, much as the country was at that time. After the clouds of war had finally drifted away, everyone breathed a collective sigh of relief, as when relatives who have overstayed their welcome finally leave. We were weary, but eager not to waste a minute of our new freedom.

Later that year, we began looking for a house in San Francisco proper. For one thing, in January 1947, we had welcomed a splendid new addition to the family, Caspar Jr., and we were rapidly outgrowing our little hillside home in Sausalito.

Cap Jr. had a big, welcoming smile almost from the first day. He was a healthy, happy baby, and as I recall, from the perspective of some fifty years, he slept all night—a very big plus.

We found a roomy, three-story, wood-shingled house on the narrow end of Pacific Avenue, overlooking the Presidio Wall* and the Julius Kahn playground, a key feature for a growing, young family. Even more important, the neighborhood boasted some excellent schools.

Pacific Heights was home to the old-money mansions of many of the city's leaders and business names, such as Spreckels, Sutro, Huntington, and Flood.

Fortunately for us, the house we liked was unusually low-priced, especially for that area. The owners had divorced, and part of the divorce settlement was that the wife would sell the house and the husband would get half the proceeds. She apparently disliked him intensely, so she deliberately sold it for a very small sum, about $27,000—unthinkable for a big house in that prize location. Our Sausalito house sold quickly, and we moved into our new home about the end of 1948.

I was always very fond of that house, with its fine view of the bay and the Golden Gate Bridge. A view has always been important to

---

* The southern boundary of the Presidio military base, headquarters of the Sixth Army.

me. Having a home in the city was also important because I was becoming more involved in local Republican politics.

The event that propelled me into an active role in politics was Governor Thomas Dewey's stunning loss to President Harry Truman in 1948. California did miserably for Dewey and Republicans, particularly in San Francisco. I decided I could no longer just sit on the sidelines and assume the right people would win.

Earlier that year I had campaigned a bit, working with a fellow attorney I had met in the bar examination course, Joe Martin Jr., a warm and witty man who had been taken prisoner by the Japanese early in the war and confined for the duration. He and I worked for William Farnham White, the Republican candidate for Congress from San Francisco. White lost ingloriously, as he deserved to, and joined the ranks of so many other fallen Republicans in that election.[*] It was during the course of this campaign that we discovered that there was no effective Republican organization in San Francisco.

The members of the County Central Committee, led by longtime chairman Herbert Hanley, had been entrenched in their positions throughout the 1940s and were mired in lethargy and incompetence. Their goal seemed to be to attend Republican events. They made no apparent effort to recruit more members into the party or to give more than token support to Republican candidates; they did not even recognize the Young Republican organization or work with other party groups.

We, on the other hand, wanted to win elections, and we knew that required aggressive leadership, active scouting for quality candidates, and expanding the base of the party, numerically and ideologically.

---

[*] Our support for him, based almost entirely on the fact that he was the Republican candidate, melted swiftly after he told a home meeting we had arranged that he preferred women who stayed home instead of "being political."

So Joe Martin and I, along with Robert Harris (the same with whom I shared an office at Heller, Ehrman), determined to oust the Hanley regime. In the 1950 primary we and a small group of like-minded Republicans—"Grand New Party" Republicans, as we called ourselves—put forward a reform slate of candidates to run for seats on the County Central Committee. With the help of newspaper publicity and an active and vigorous campaign—highly unusual for a county committee election, where incumbents almost automatically win—our slate took twenty-one of the forty seats, while the incumbents held on to eighteen. (An independent won the remaining seat.) Hanley's group contested the results immediately and went to court to try to prevent our nominees from being certified. I was one of the attorneys representing the new group, and ultimately we won. So, after a long and major effort, we became the majority party on the county committee and were able to throw out all of the previous officers who had done such a poor job.

In 1952 I myself ran for an open state assembly seat. Arthur Connally, a popular Republican attorney who had been one of San Francisco's assemblymen for several years, decided to retire and move down the peninsula. After encouraging calls and talks with several of our new Republican group (I must confess I did not require much encouragement), I decided to run for Connally's seat. Other potential and actual GOP candidates appeared, and for a time I thought I would not continue because I did not want to split the party. But finally I decided to stay in the race. My wife was very instrumental in this decision and, indeed, throughout my campaign. She knew that I was not deriving much satisfaction from the law practice, and she was well aware of my great interest in politics and saw this as a logical step. In fact, I think it is fair to say that if Jane had not vigorously encouraged me to run for office and stay in the race, I probably would not have felt I could do it after it turned into a contested primary.

When I first mentioned the idea of running for the assembly to the partners at Heller, Ehrman, they objected. Their immediate reaction was, "We employed you to be a lawyer, not a candidate." But when I kept raising the question, Lloyd Dinkelspiel, who was then the head of the firm, finally relented, saying, "You know, we spend a lot of time urging people to participate in government, and here we have the chance and we have turned you down. Well, we're changing our mind. The partners have agreed. You should run." Florenz McAuliffe, another senior partner and a major behind-the-scenes power in San Francisco politics, became interested in my race. He was the epitome of the old-style city politician—and an excellent lawyer. Many years of smoking long, strong cigars (probably Cuban since no one had heard of Castro then) gave him a throaty growl when he spoke, which could be intimidating. He was short with a bull neck and penetrating eyes, hidden behind thick glasses. He tolerated no shoddy work, and he was not troubled by self-doubts.

As I later learned, no one in the office felt I had a chance to win the race. Mr. McAuliffe decided he would try to make me a winner. His support and that of several of my fellow young Republicans— particularly Bob Harris, Joe Martin Jr., and Roger Lapham Jr., whose father had been mayor—were a huge boost.

My wife was an extremely active campaigner. She set up and manned the headquarters office (which was in our home) and put together a number of supporting women's church and neighborhood groups. They came to be known collectively as "Your Neighbors for Good Government," an organization that loyally resurrected itself for my subsequent campaigns. My children, aged ten and five at the time, also were recruited to help out at headquarters and to pass out campaign literature. They seemed very willing foot soldiers and particularly enjoyed putting up small signs called "quarter cards," which extolled my virtues and carried a retouched earlier picture.

For me, the campaign was another exercise in confidence building. I was constantly struggling to overcome my shyness at pushing my own candidacy. When I went door-to-door, I rather hoped no one would be home. But my confidence gradually grew as I found that the vast majority of people were nice and seemed both surprised and pleased that I was calling on them personally; it was unusual at that time for candidates for state office to do that. When I handed out my election card, many asked, "Are you him?" or they would call out to other family members, "It is Weinberger."

The Twenty-first District encompassed a large and reasonably upscale area of the city, including the Marina, Chinatown, the Presidio, part of the Richmond area, and part of Pacific Heights.

My principal opponent in the Republican primary, Milton Marks, was a young lawyer whose father had been active in San Francisco politics—so much so that when I tried to get supporters, many people said that they had to back Marks because they had roomed with his father in college. I began to think his father must have lived in the biggest dormitory in the University of California.

Marks ran a fairly traditional campaign, concentrating on getting endorsements from various organizations. I, on the other hand, tried to emphasize issues, particularly reducing the state budget and cutting state taxes. In addition, there was one local issue in which I was personally quite interested and which I brought up in the campaign: the restoration of the Palace of Fine Arts. This was a much-loved but crumbling relic of the 1915 Panama-Pacific International Exposition. The exposition site was located in the Marina, a major part of the Twenty-first District. It was highly unusual to have a local issue in the state legislative races, and the people seemed to like my pledge to try to restore the palace.

I did something else that was rather unconventional at the time. In San Francisco, it was considered bad form and bad politics to emphasize your party affiliation, especially as a Republican in a heavily Democratic city, but I did not hesitate to do just that. In fact, my campaign slogan (coined by my wife) was, "In a Republican year, elect a real Republican." This was in 1952, which indeed turned out to be a Republican year, with war hero General Dwight Eisenhower winning the presidency and the GOP gaining a majority in both houses of Congress. A lot of this was due to dissatisfaction with Truman.

Something I did must have been effective, because I won the Republican nomination in the primary by about eight hundred votes, and with cross-filing, then allowed in California, I even came in fourth (out of eight candidates) on the Democratic ballot. Marks actually had more total votes than any of us, but he finished second on both tickets. Under the law then, a candidate had to win the nomination of his own party to get on the ballot for the general election. So my emphasis on my Republican roots seemed to have helped.

For the November finals, I continued on in much the same way, but this time with substantially more support from many sources. The Democratic nominee I was running against in the general election was a large and deceptively old-looking San Franciscan named William Blake. He was a cheerful, friendly opponent who ran a ship-repair business on the San Francisco waterfront and had many friends among old-line San Francisco politicians. My friends turned it largely into a campaign for a new, young face in the legislature, and we managed to win by a substantial margin this time—about sixteen thousand votes. Blake remained friendly and supportive throughout the campaign. I think he was the nicest man I ever ran against. At one of our joint appearances, he even said to my wife after my speech, "You know, if I weren't running against him, I'd vote for him!"

CHAPTER 6

LEGISLATIVE LIQUIDITY

D wight Eisenhower helped sweep many Republicans into office in 1952. Not only was he elected president, but the party also won control of both houses of Congress and increased its ranks in many state legislatures. Voters believed that Eisenhower and his fellow Republicans would clean up what was generally regarded as corruption and cronyism in the Truman administration and would reduce government intrusion into people's private lives. They also hoped that the military deadlock in Korea could be broken. General Eisenhower's pledge to go to Korea appealed to many voters who thought that his very presence there could accomplish wonders. I was, of course, but a tiny cog in the Republican wheel, but I could not help feeling a real exhilaration at being a part of this great new crusade under Eisenhower.

After two days of discouraging house-hunting, we found the perfect new, affordable apartment near the beautiful Capitol grounds. Our new landlord agreed that we could bring a "small dog." I felt our collie qualified, so we moved to Sacramento at the beginning of 1953. The regular legislative session ran from January through June in odd-numbered years, which corresponded nicely with spring semester in the schools.* The children were at an age where they were more excited about moving than unhappy about leaving their friends (they knew we would be back home on many weekends), and once in Sacramento, they seemed to enjoy it thoroughly. Arlin learned to ride her bike on the grounds of the Capitol, and both Arlin and Cap Jr. enthusiastically worked as pages on the floor of the assembly during the Easter school recess. I was much amused by the fact that as "employees of the state" for five days, both children had to take the then-required loyalty oath,† swearing that they were not then, nor had they been, members of a Communist organization at any time in the past five years. Caspar Jr. was about five at the time, so he was not forbidden by his conscience from signing.

My mother remained in San Francisco, which was only about an hour away from Sacramento, but I called her nearly every day and wrote her occasional letters.

I drove home whenever I could. I had the bad habit of driving much too fast as I was thinking about other things. And once I start toward a target, I like to get there as soon as possible. On one such occasion, I was stopped by a highway patrolman. When he came

---

* In the even-numbered years, the legislature usually met for only one month, and for those years my family remained in San Francisco.

† As relations chilled after World War II between the United States and our wartime ally the Soviet Union, a "Red Scare" swept across the country, permeating every level of government. This was similar to the atmosphere immediately after World War I. The House Un-American Activities Committee led the way in 1947, with hearings of a sensational and highly charged nature. The California legislature followed, requiring a loyalty oath for all state employees. It was not until 1967 that the state supreme court ruled that the oath, as formulated by the legislature, was unconstitutional.

up to my car, he said, "I'm very sorry, sir—you were going so fast, I didn't see your legislative license plate."[*] He had clocked me doing eighty-five miles an hour, and I acknowledge that that *was* entirely too fast regardless of my plates, but I must confess a bit of pleasure at discovering what kind of perks my new position afforded. I was not used to being the object of such deference.

When the legislature was not in session and there was no committee work, I spent substantial stretches of time in San Francisco. During these "off" times, I continued to work at the law firm, though it was understood that I could not be made a partner until after I left the legislature. An assemblyman's salary then was only three hundred dollars a month, plus a small per diem living allowance which generally was exhausted shortly after breakfast. But money, or the lack of it, was never much of a factor for me. State government held my interest because I could debate and work on issues of major importance, whereas my law practice often seemed to deal at endless length with rather petty matters. A friend of mine put it another way: "The trouble with Weinberger is, he can't stand making money."

I won reelection to the assembly in 1954 and again in 1956, running unopposed each time. I was glad because I preferred legislating to campaigning. When I learned that I was unopposed, I returned all individual contributions to the donors—which was unheard of. I was fortunate to have achieved some early accomplishments as a legislator and gotten quite favorable press coverage. The press corps even voted me "Most Able Member of the Legislature" in 1955.

---

[*] Legislators were issued special license plates: a green "A" designated an assemblyman, followed by the number of the district one represented, "21" in my case. A red "S" was for senators. I was quite proud of these, but after this encounter with a particularly kind patrolman, I realized that while rank had its privileges, rank was also supposed to behave well.

In the California legislature in those days, there was a friendly, collegial atmosphere that cut across party lines.* Most of us seemed to be there for something bigger than ourselves. Added to this was the fact that many of us were in our thirties or early forties, with young families, and we generally became good friends as well as colleagues.

Most of us shared offices (in the new Capitol Annex) with other assemblymen—in my case, a fellow Republican from San Jose, Bruce Allen. Bruce Allen was a taciturn, laconic, and skilled lawyer and legislator who was loyal, friendly, and much admired for his rugged, almost frontier-like honesty. He left the legislature when he was appointed a judge of the Superior Court and served in that post until his very untimely death. Our office arrangement felt almost like a college dormitory: we each had our own room, but we shared a common reception area where both of our secretaries worked.

If the Capitol offices were the dormitories, then the old Senator Hotel, just across Twelfth Street from the Capitol, was the student union. Most of the lobbyists lived there and lavishly (for the time) entertained legislators in their suites. Some lively cocktail party or meal or informal gathering was always under way.

Don Cleary was an amusing and popular old-style lobbyist for the city of San Francisco who often served grand gourmet meals at the Senator. Since they were for the cause of discussing legislation affecting San Francisco, I felt little compunction about going to those functions. Cleary always said, "With some of the legislators, you can get 'em with money; with some, you can get 'em with women. But with Weinberger, you need lamb chops." He was nearly right.

Fellow legislators also gave parties to showcase products from their districts, one of the best-known being Eureka assemblyman Frank Belotti's famous annual crab feed.

---

* The only major partisan issue seemed to be the reapportionment of legislative districts that took place after each census.

Legislators' wives added to the atmosphere of camaraderie as well, hosting luncheons and other activities. Jane was a popular hostess, entertaining with great style and graciousness. Her cooking and buffets became quite famous in legislative circles, primarily because she did it all herself.

Of course, none of these events was purely social; there was always a political undercurrent. Even so, I had little time for them. I was working far harder and far longer than I had at the law firm. I often began the day with a breakfast meeting around seven, followed by committee meetings around nine or ten. Then the assembly itself usually went into session at ten or eleven, and I tried to attend all of the actual sessions on the floor.* More committee meetings generally filled up the remainder of the afternoon and evening, and I often took reams of paper home to prepare for the next day's activities. That was a good eighteen-hour day—and I relished it.

Republicans had control of both houses of the legislature, but given the spirit of bipartisanship, divisions were more apparent *within* the party.

I was considered a somewhat liberal Republican, in part because I was one of the few who supported the Fair Employment Practice Act, which was basically a forerunner of later state and federal civil rights acts. Sponsored by Byron Rumford, a black Democrat assemblyman and a close personal friend from Berkeley, the act essentially tried to eliminate hiring discrimination against minorities. I had thought in the

---

* The assembly chamber was a large, well-proportioned room. Green was the predominant color—a throwback to the House of Commons in England. Red was the predominant senate color (as it was in the House of Lords). The members' desks—two abreast—were arranged to form a broad semicircle. The voting banks were at the front of the chamber, facing the desks, and to either side of the Speaker's rostrum. The votes were frequent and electronically recorded, and as each member turned the key on his desk, a green (yea) or red (no) light was illuminated after his name. Vote changes were permitted until the vote was closed. Frequently, on major issues, some would hold back until it was clear which side would win.

past that there had not really been any discrimination. But when I had tried to help some black and Hispanic friends get jobs in San Francisco, I found that there really were elements of discrimination. Many employers, particularly larger businesses like department stores, were reluctant to hire blacks because they were afraid it would hurt their stores' sales. So we did a survey of people coming out of a San Francisco department store, asking them if they had been waited on by a black clerk or a white clerk. Most of them had no idea, which confirmed my belief that the color of employees had no effect on business.

In general, I opposed government interference in the private sector, but in this case, it became increasingly clear to me that blacks would not be given a fair chance for employment (in many cases because of ignorance or unjustified fears) unless state law prohibited discrimination. The Fair Employment Practice Act did not become law until 1959, after I had left the legislature, but I had been an early and vocal proponent of the measure. This convinced some old-time legislators and lobbyists that I was not "fundamentally sound."

I think it is fair to add that another reason for my stand was my strong admiration for Byron Rumford. He was a large, capable, and friendly pharmacist who had been in the legislature for many years. Everyone who knew him liked him, particularly children—he always had a bit of candy or other gift for them handy. Our children were very fond of him and our families became great friends.

Byron was also particularly helpful on alcoholic beverage reform. He served on my committee loyally and skillfully, even though there were many pressures on him from old-time lobbyists to oppose everything we were trying to do. Much later, when I was chairman of the Federal Trade Commission, I had the great pleasure of appointing Byron to a key regional post in California where he again served with distinction.

Another action that placed me in the more "liberal" wing of the Republican Party was that I voted for the more moderate Republican candidate, James Silliman, for Speaker in the 1953 session. He was from the Fresno area and represented what he called the "Clean Government," antilobbyist approach as opposed to the more traditional "old boy network" way of operating. A number of young Republicans—including Laughlin Waters, a Republican leader who later became a federal judge; Charles Conrad, an actor-legislator from North Hollywood; Luther "Abe" Lincoln from Oakland; and I—were part of the reform group that elected Silliman by a narrow margin.

It was fortunate that I, as a new assemblyman, had decided to support Silliman, because at that time the committee assignments were all made by the Speaker. As a freshman, I was assigned to my first-choice committees: Ways and Means, which heard the budget; Government Organization; Elections and Reapportionment; and Judiciary.

As it turned out, I spent most of my time and energy on issues before the Committee on Government Organization. My first major challenge came when I was made chairman of that committee's Joint Subcommittee on Alcoholic Beverage Control. It was considered sort of an in-house joke that this new, young, eager assemblyman was put in charge of this subcommittee. The truth was that nobody else would take it; everyone else was smart enough not to get anywhere near it. I don't think anyone really expected that anything significant would be done. The liquor industry lobbyists were considered the strongest in Sacramento. The Board of Equalization's administration of liquor licensing and other parts of the liquor law was scandal-ridden, but previous attempts at reform had gone nowhere because the Senate Governmental Efficiency Committee always killed everything that would have changed the status quo. That committee was considered the graveyard for liquor legislation.

I knew absolutely nothing about alcoholic beverage control when I was elected, but I worked hard to learn. The seeds of the problem seemed to lie in the Board of Equalization, a curious anachronism originally designed to equalize the distribution of tax revenues to schools. There were many counties, particularly in the northern part of the state, that had vast areas owned by the federal government—national parks or national forests—which were exempt from local taxation. Consequently, these counties had a very low tax base. The Board of Equalization was created in 1879 to provide these areas with the same kinds of educational opportunities as the more populated, tax-rich areas of the state. Oddly enough, it was an elective board, with one member from each of four districts whose boundaries—despite massive population shifts—had been left virtually unchanged since 1879. The board was completely independent of the governor. (California was the only state where this was the case.) It was also independent of the legislature, could not be impeached, and in practice usually left each member to make his own decision in his own district. Few voters cared about it, generally automatically reelecting incumbents, which left the board virtually autonomous.

These problems were compounded when the board fell under the sway of the strong liquor lobbies. After Prohibition was repealed, these lobbies succeeded in transferring to this strange board the responsibility for collecting liquor taxes and the liquor licensing function. The lobbyists were able to control the board because they were the only major contributors to board members' elections. By the time my subcommittee was assigned to study the board's operations in 1953, corruption was pervasive. Liquor licenses were limited and could be sold, and were sold, for ever increasing prices. Issued to special friends of the board for $525, they were frequently resold for $10,000 to $20,000. The new purchasers frequently did not meet even the very lax standards set by the board for licensees.

Also, the basis on which licenses were granted by the board in the first place was not apparent. Some district administrators who testified were evasive about how they decided who were to be the favored few. But we soon learned that liquor licenses were being issued without anything resembling an adequate investigation of either the premises or the individual applicants. Licenses for the sale of liquor were issued to vacant lots; to applicants who submitted blueprints of premises they promised to construct, but the dimensions of which could not possibly fit the premises; and even to cemetery lots and, occasionally, to people who were deceased. The decision of whether to approve or disapprove an application apparently depended solely upon the applicant's relationship with the district liquor administrator or the board member for that area.

I scheduled five hearings around the state for late 1953 and early 1954. It seemed to be general practice, at that time, for committee *staff* to determine the agenda and direction of hearings and then actually to run them, with the legislators asking only occasional questions. But I felt this was an important enough issue that legislators, and particularly I, should be more involved since this was more along the lines of a criminal investigation. The other members of the bipartisan subcommittee—Assemblymen Byron Rumford and Glenn Coolidge (a Republican) and Senators Hugh Donnelly (a Democrat) and Ed Johnson (a Republican)—were also quite interested and active and extremely helpful in the proceedings. The legislative auditor's office—primarily Arthur Buck, the staff member assigned to our subcommittee—was a major research asset. I did much of the preparatory work and questioning myself, including lining up many of the witnesses. The subcommittee heard testimony from everyone from Board of Equalization members to licensees to law enforcement officers to concerned citizens.

Our investigation uncovered numerous improprieties, weak or no law enforcement, outright fraud, and, indeed, a complete abandonment of the rule of law in favor of the rule of a few men—exactly the kind of concentration of power our government was supposed to forbid.

Many of these abuses were perpetrated and perpetuated by close cooperation between Artie Samish, the self-proclaimed "Secret Boss of California," who headed one of the big liquor lobbies, and William

Bonelli, the Board of Equalization member from the southern California district—the largest district, by far, in terms of population.

Bonelli felt he was absolutely invulnerable at the polls and simply denied any responsibility for the abuses we found.* Samish, on the other hand, flaunted his power and was almost clownish about it. He was quoted as saying, "I'm the governor of the legislature," and he claimed that he had "the damnedest Gestapo you ever saw." In his autobiography, he bragged about how he selected, elected, and kept in power those he believed would best serve the liquor industry's interests. He also was not shy about removing people from office if they did not play his game. As one example, he wrote, "I considered Senator Ralph Swing the best mind in the legislature. . . . But one year when he was chairman of the Government Efficiency Committee, he got in my way. All of a sudden he wasn't chairman of the Government Efficiency Committee any more." He made many of these boasts to writers in the old *Collier's* magazine, which then had a wide circulation in California.

After months of testimony at public hearings and long meetings to go over the evidence, we put our findings in our Subcommittee Report to the Legislature, and at our urging, Governor Goodwin Knight called a special session in early 1954, primarily to address the alcoholic beverage control issue and the recommendations we had made. Our efforts at reform were distinguished from previous attempts by the evidence we had gathered; by a dozen specific remedial bills and a recommended constitutional amendment attached to our report; and by the fact that our report was submitted to the legislature with the

---

* He publicly denied any responsibility for administering or enforcing liquor laws, saying that all he did was "rubber stamp" the recommendations of the district liquor administrator. (The liquor administrator disagreed.) I asked Bonelli in one of our hearings, "You really pay very little attention to the actual liquor control function?" To which he responded, "I don't have the time nor the inclination nor the responsibility."

unanimous support of the bipartisan subcommittee. I must take credit for the idea of making specific recommendations in the form of already drafted bills. I wanted action on these bills and the constitutional amendment, not just another report that would gather dust, so I worked continuously from the beginning of the hearings to try to get unanimous support. We also gained support from Paul Leake, the member from the Third District (encompassing much of northern California). Leake was an honest, straightforward Democrat and publisher of a Woodland newspaper. He had been appointed to the Board of Equalization to fill a vacancy in late 1952, and when he saw the tremendous corruption, he attacked it publicly and fearlessly, before the legislature did and before most people even knew of it. When my subcommittee began its investigation, Leake started out (as did many people) feeling that this was going to be just another whitewash. But when we named him as our first witness and set our first hearing in Woodland, he realized it was going to be a real investigation. We worked closely together and became good friends for the rest of his life. He was also particularly effective in persuading many of his press corps colleagues that we were determined to clean up this mess. In particular, Art White of the *Los Angeles Mirror* and Carl Greenberg of the *Los Angeles Times*, both of whom had covered San Diego and Los Angeles, where the worst of the liquor licensing scandals had taken place, were extremely helpful in working closely with the committee, as was another state senator, Arthur Breed of Oakland.

And as we began uncovering more and more evidence of corruption, the attorney general's office also became interested and started its own investigation, though I think that was essentially because Pat Brown, the attorney general, was planning to run for governor and did not want to be left behind.

Eventually, most everyone got on the bandwagon, for our evidence could not be refuted. A consensus agreed that something had to be done. And something was done.

The main recommendation we put forth was to create a Department of Alcoholic Beverage Control with a director appointed by, and serving at the pleasure of, the governor. The department would administer liquor licensing and would be assigned all liquor law enforcement responsibilities. The Board of Equalization would be stripped of all its power over alcoholic beverages. We considered it crucial that the director of the new department be appointed by the governor, be subject to confirmation by the senate, and be removable by either the governor or the legislature. As an extra safeguard against an all-powerful director of the new department, a provision was added later by the conference committee to create an Alcoholic Beverage Control Appeals Board to hear appeals from some of the director's decisions.

The constitutional amendment containing all of this was the centerpiece of our reform plan, and it was introduced by our committee as Senate Constitutional Amendment #4 (of which I wrote quite a lot of the final wording). It was adopted by a combined vote of both houses of the legislature, by a vote of 105 to 3. As with all proposed constitutional amendments, it was then placed on the ballot, where it appeared as Proposition 3 on the November 1954 ballot. It became law when voters supported it two to one.

The legislature also adopted several additional recommendations of the joint subcommittee. These laws were meant to crack down on the many illegal activities that seemed to be connected to liquor licenses—from narcotics dealings to prostitution. We also created a new Alcoholic Beverage Rehabilitation Commission, a particular interest of Assemblyman Glenn Coolidge, to study problems of alcoholism and its treatment. The commission would be financed by a license-fee increase we enacted. We felt there was a particular need for research into the causes and possible cures of alcoholism, because we had seen various figures on the amount of crime that was traced to alcoholism, much like drugs and crime today. Unfortunately, other committee recommendations, such as prohibiting the sale of licenses, were rejected by the senate after having been passed by the assembly.

As for the former liquor czars, many were indicted and convicted and served jail time. A 1955 indictment against Bill Bonelli accused him of conspiring to violate the election code and to obstruct justice. He fled to Mexico, where he apparently stayed for the rest of his life. Later there was a big question as to whether he could get his pension as a state officer. As I recall, the ultimate court decision was, incredibly, that he could. I have always wondered where they sent the check—some post office box in Mexico, I assume. He later wrote a bitter book about me and the subcommittee. Samish was convicted of tax evasion.

But the main victory, in my mind, was cleaning up the way the state's liquor laws were administered and enforced. The whole endeavor had taken a tremendous amount of work and time, as my young daughter pointed out when a teacher asked if her father could come and speak to her class. Arlin replied by repeating the joking response she had heard me make to similar requests: "Oh, no. Daddy's so immersed in alcohol these days, he doesn't have time for anything else." The teacher was a bit nonplussed.

In the 1955 regular session, I had another big assignment. This one involved the single most important issue in the state: water. There was no *shortage* of water, but 70 percent of it originates north of Sacramento, while almost 80 percent of the people live south of the capital. Just before World War II, the state's population was about 6.9 million, and by 1955, it had nearly doubled—with that population explosion concentrated in the south. As demand went up, water resources became more scarce, somewhat like the 2001 power crisis in California and other western states. The Owens River Project had been built many years earlier to get water from north and east of Los Angeles to the city, but the river was drying up; water from other sources, such as the Colorado River and Hoover Dam, was already overallocated; and attempts to convert seawater to potable water were prohibitively expensive. The need to move more water from the north to the south was an inescapable fact.

But the north had its problems as well. Flooding was far too regular an occurrence, and it reached unprecedented levels of devastation in December 1955 and January 1956. This dramatically emphasized the desperate urgency of securing flood control and regulating the runoff of the great rivers of the north, from which billions of gallons of water washed out to sea every year.

The obvious solution to help control floods in the north and deliver some of its surplus to the south was recognized in the early 1950s and evolved into what came to be known as the California Water Plan. This essentially entailed constructing a whole new river over one thousand miles long (most of California's major rivers flowed east to west). While this would be a huge and complex undertaking, it was felt, like most problems in California, to be entirely solvable. (We were all optimists then.) The new river would require a huge dam at Oroville, a whole series of aqueducts, pumps, reservoirs, and power plants to divert the new river around the mid-California delta (which was subject to heavy salt-water intrusion), and huge generators to create the power to lift the water over the Tehachapi Mountains just north of Los Angeles—higher than water had ever been lifted—before it would tumble down into southern California.

To me, the water problem was a fascinating subject that involved engineering, law, economics, and politics, and I flung myself into every detail—how to trap and transport the water; how much power was required to lift it over the mountains; how it would be distributed once it reached the south—to say nothing of the violent north-south fights on the political side.[*] It really was a full education for me; I did

---

[*] As Mark Twain once observed, "Whiskey is for drinking, water is for fighting over."

not have a rural, agricultural background. In fact, I knew nothing about water except that when you turned on the tap, the water came out. So to understand and convey the urgency of southern California's water needs through my many speeches and presentations on the subject, I asked audiences to picture what it would be like if they turned on the tap and nothing came out. And, to emphasize the need for a quick solution, I hammered away on the point of how long it would take to build the California Water Project and how few years we had before we would actually face real shortages.

Naturally, the plan for diversion of water to the south encountered major political resistance, primarily from many of the northern senators, who were absolutely determined that none of their water was going to go south. Many felt that their sparsely populated counties would someday be as large as Los Angeles if they could keep all their water.

Some of their objections were reduced when it was suggested that they could conceivably get "replacement" water from the Columbia River in Oregon, or even ultimately from the huge runoff of the rivers in Washington. We also acknowledged the need to help northern California with flood-control measures.

Another problem was the haphazard way in which the state government was organized to handle water issues. This was the area where I, as chairman of the Assembly Government Organization Committee, became most involved. As we studied our assignment (to recommend the best organizational structure to develop, use, and regulate California's water), we found that there were well over fifty California agencies that dealt with water in one way or another, very little coordination among them, and no one overall agency. Nor was much direction or control provided by the state. Much like the Board of Equalization before we reformed it, these state water boards and agencies were virtually independent of the governor and the legislature and had little communication with local boards and local governments. At the same time, none of these many agencies had the authority—or the expertise or the funding, for that matter—to build or manage a big water project. Before, they had been concerned mainly with water quality, water rights, and piecemeal flood control, not transporting or distributing water on a large scale.

My remedy for all of this, and the recommendation of our committee, was to consolidate the myriad boards and agencies into one streamlined department (under a director appointed by the governor) that could build and then efficiently administer the water project and effectively deal with any future water issues.

Our proposal, which came to be called the Weinberger Bill, was based on certain principles I believe should underlie any governmental organization: it should be integrated, unified, and capable of effective action—in short, it must have the power to carry out policies—and it must be responsible to the people by having its director appointed by, and reporting to, the governor.

Not surprisingly, there was strong opposition to the idea from the many employees of the various ineffective regional boards. And throughout the process, there was still the basic north-south rift. The south, of course, had a majority in the assembly, apportioned on the basis of population. The senate was still apportioned by counties, but the population-heavy south was about to change that.

The governor, at my urgent request, called a special session to consider our committee's recommendations and to try to solve our water problems. On the very last day of that 1956 special session, after extensive debate, the final conference report incorporating the unanimous recommendations of our bipartisan committee was adopted. I was greatly aided in the effort by the fine support of Senator James Cobey, a Democrat of Merced County. He was a particularly effective supporter coming from a nonsouthern county.

The bill created the Department of Water Resources. Responsibility for water quality and water resource development was transferred to this new department, thus eliminating the need for most of the separate water boards and agencies. Heading the department would be a director appointed by and removable by the governor. The only water-related function that was kept separate from the Department of Water Resources was the determination of water rights, for which our legislation created a State Water Rights Board. Water rights were as important as land titles in California, and indeed, a whole history of the state could be written based on fights over water rights. Unfortunately, the senate could not be persuaded that a constitutional amendment recognizing the need to protect the interests of both north and south was the fairest solution. But we did have a new, properly organized state department to finally fulfill the water needs of the whole state.

With the new administrative organization in place, a $1.75 billion bond issue (the largest ever considered by any state up to that time) to finance the California statewide water project was passed in 1960 by popular vote. The project's main beneficiaries, the water users, repaid most of the huge bond issue and paid most of the annual operating costs. Some state tidelands oil and gas revenues were also used, but little federal money (only about 1 percent of total project costs) was required, and that was mainly for some of the flood-control aspects of the project.

Actual work on the water project began shortly after the bond issue was passed, with the construction of the Oroville Dam on the Feather River, the first phase of the plan. By 1973 the bulk of the facilities had been completed, with water reaching the Los Angeles metropolitan area. I took great pleasure and, I must admit, some pride in coming out from Washington to attend the dedication ceremonies.[*] But the final phases to reach regions even farther south have yet to be finished.

---

[*] Governor Reagan turned on the activators to start the power generators. In a rather comic development (although not seen as such at the time), the first time he turned the switches, nothing happened! It finally worked the second or third time around.

The Department of Water Resources is still in existence today, with essentially the same responsibilities it was given at its creation—administering the use of the state's water resources and ensuring that there is and will be enough water for all.

But, unfortunately, water administration in California has again become fragmented and confusing, with a new proliferation of water agencies, many of which have overlapping responsibilities. A cursory perusal of the *California Water Resources Directory* reveals the extraordinary number of federal, state, and local agencies and departments that currently have some interest in the state's water. The fight to keep government streamlined, and bureaucracies from multiplying, is never-ending. I hope some young California assemblyman will take up the cudgels again.

The California Water Project moved from the drawing board to reality in the 1960s because we established the management and administrative foundation and framework that such a huge project required. We will have to keep and strengthen that unified administrative structure if we hope to ever realize the benefits of a completed system.

Though these major, statewide issues of alcohol and water were extremely interesting to me, as indeed was virtually everything connected with state government, one local subject was especially close to my heart. Relatively speaking, it was fairly unimportant, but I was sentimental about San Francisco's beautiful Palace of Fine Arts.

The Palace of Fine Arts was one of the many temporary exhibition buildings built for the Panama-Pacific Exposition of 1915 in the Marina District of San Francisco. The rose and blond structure, with its eclectic details and neoclassical rotunda and columns, was said to have been the re-creation of a dream its architect, Bernard Maybeck, had once had. My father was fond of the palace and spent a lot of time at the exposition, taking many photographs of it. It had captured the imagination and affection of many San Franciscans, and it was the only structure of the exposition that was not razed when the fair was over. My family often visited it when I was a child. Over the years, it had been used for art displays, tennis courts, and even army storage during World War II, and it had always escaped occasional calls for its demolition.

By the early 1950s, the elegant, much-loved, temporary building had fallen into disrepair. The city of San Francisco had not done anything to preserve or even maintain it, even though the palace was part of the city park system.

So I made it a campaign issue when I first ran for the assembly; it was the one local issue I took to the state level. In fact, it was the only issue of local concern in the campaign. All the other candidates talked about their own virtues and, in general terms, about education, welfare, and so on. I was the only one who talked about a real local issue and a specific plan. I think the voters liked that. I felt I could do something about it in the legislature.

Even before I took office, I had drafted a bill to present to the 1953 session that would make the palace and its grounds a state park. As such, it would be maintained and restored by the state. (One friend in the legislature, Assemblyman Thomas Caldecott, who ultimately supported the bill, joked that I was proposing to build the largest all-marble birdbath in the world.) After my bill was introduced, the State Parks Department people strenuously objected. They did not want comparatively scarce state funds used for a park they had not chosen. They wanted all the money they could get for their standard mix of campgrounds and beaches.

I tried to make the proposal more palatable by offering an amendment allowing the state to lease the Palace of Fine Arts back to the city of San Francisco, with the city responsible for maintenance and operation and the state responsible for only the original repair cost. The bill passed in both houses, after some strenuous lobbying on my part, but Governor Earl Warren vetoed it following the advice of the

Parks Department. Governor Warren prided himself on the distance he kept from partisan matters and from legislators in general. It would have been virtually unthinkable for him to sign a bill opposed by one of his department heads.

By the 1955 session, Goodwin Knight was governor,* having taken over when Earl Warren was appointed to the Supreme Court. Along with Warren, many of the state officials who had opposed the Palace of Fine Arts restoration had also left state government, so when I reintroduced my bill I was quite hopeful. But sadly, Governor Knight proved just as amenable to the State Parks bureaucracy as had Governor Warren, even though the bill had once again passed both houses of the legislature.

Despite these discouraging setbacks, I was absolutely determined to save the palace. In fact, on one occasion, although I had contracted

---

* Governor Goodwin Knight was an interesting example of a successful California politician. He had been appointed a judge in Los Angeles, but unlike many judges, he had his eye on higher political office. He was once asked by one of his early supporters, "Judge, would you like a little publicity?" Knight replied instantly, "No—what do I do to get a lot?" He was a Republican and spent a large part of his time strengthening his party ties and building his own political organization. He and his friends frequently presented him as a conservative alternative to Governor Warren, who took increasingly liberal or nonpartisan positions.

Ultimately, Knight was elected lieutenant governor. a position with few duties but with increased opportunities to demonstrate his opposition to Governor Warren's above-it-all aloofness from the internal machinations of California politics.

It was widely expected that he would run for governor himself at the first opportunity. That came unexpectedly in 1954 when President Eisenhower appointed Governor Warren to be chief justice of the United States.

Goodwin Knight was then governor and could run in that year's election as an incumbent, a powerful advantage. Feeling that he had most of the conservative Republican sentiment strongly in his pocket, he quickly began to court leaders of organized labor and supported many prolabor programs that he had previously criticized. He also supported my alcoholic beverage bills and, later, the water bill. He and I got along well, and I always admired and was amused by his buoyancy, general good humor, and easy ability to gain support from widely differing areas of the political spectrum. In any event he was retained as governor in the 1954 election and then set his sights, as he always did, on the next election.

mumps from my children, I insisted on presenting the bill to the committee session. Committee chairman Caldecott entertained a motion to move the bill out of committee as quickly as possible—along with the author.

When the bill passed a third time, in the 1957 regular session, Governor Knight signed it over the continued objections of the State Parks Department. By that time I had succeeded in getting the liquor and water reforms through, and I guess I was listened to a little bit more. So the palace became a state park and would be run (after restoration) by the city of San Francisco.

A provision that I had added to the bill somewhere along the line was that the state's financial contribution to the restoration of the palace—then estimated to be about $2 million—would have to be matched by the city of San Francisco. The most feasible way to do this, I felt, was through a city bond issue, which was put on the city ballot as Proposition B in November of 1958. Sixty percent of voters supported it, but that fell short of the two-thirds majority vote required for passage of a bond issue. Many civic groups backed the bond issue, but I suppose our defeat can be attributed to the fact that, outside my legislative district where it received a big majority, city voters did not turn out in sufficient numbers to give us the two-thirds majority.

It was shortly after this defeat, when it seemed that our years of effort had been in vain, that a financial angel, in the person of Walter S. Johnson, came forward. He had made his comfortable fortune heading an early adding machine company, the Marchant Company, and had been active in the campaign to pass the bond issue. He loved the palace and appreciated its beauty, artistic quality, uniqueness, and its sentimental importance to the city.

At a meeting to discuss resubmitting the bond issue, Mr. Johnson turned to me and asked, "Wouldn't it be simpler if I just gave the money?" Completely astounded, I said, "Yes, I guess it would." He did, and, finally, the palace was saved.

The next problem, though a relatively simple one, was *how* to restore the palace. Since it had been built as only a temporary building, it was made of lath and plaster, inferior materials that were not designed to last more than a few years. It had deteriorated significantly and was literally crumbling and falling apart. Much of it had to be taken down and completely rebuilt. Some structural steelwork was done and concrete was poured, and also a new, fairly malleable kind of fiberglass was used to cover the whole structure. That made it easier for the sculptors to work on.

Once begun, the whole process took only about three years, from 1964 to 1967. It had been fifteen years since I started my campaign to save the building, and the number of defeats we had suffered along the way far exceeded the victories.

But in the meantime, there was the question of what to do with the space—not in the rotunda itself, which needed to be kept open, but in the semicircular exhibit hall behind it. A group of benevolent San Franciscans had formed the Palace of Fine Arts League in December of 1957 in order to determine just that (as well as to promote the 1958 bond issue). Many proposals were offered, everything from a concert hall to a museum. There was even a very small but vocal group that wanted nothing but tennis courts in the whole huge building. Eventually a theater was put in one end, and then, in 1969, the rest of the building was occupied by a science museum called the Exploratorium, which is still in operation today. It was one of the first of the "hands-on" museums, in which visitors could operate many of the exhibits. I am proud to have been a part of saving the graceful Palace of Fine Arts that my father had so loved.

All of my six years in the California legislature were most rewarding. It was gratifying to see the results and feel that I was accomplishing something of some lasting benefit. I particularly felt that that was the case with liquor control reform and California's water plan.

I was sorry when I thought it was time to leave the legislature, just as sorry as I had been to leave the law clerkship under Judge Orr many years before. Probably it was the more or less subconscious fear of changing the known for the unknown. Of course, while I was in the legislature I had not actually left the law firm, so I knew what was awaiting me there. I also knew that I owed it to my family to earn a more substantial living in the law practice, uninteresting as that sounded in comparison to the previous few years. But before I returned to practice law, there would be one more political campaign. I could scarcely have chosen a worse year!

CHAPTER 7

THE BIG SWITCH

*B*y 1958, I had been in the legislature for five years, so I felt it was time to do something else. However, I had enjoyed state government work much more than I had earning a living at the law firm. Some people, on the basis of my legislative achievements in the liquor and water areas, talked of my running for governor of California, but I thought that would be premature.

After the Alcoholic Beverage Control investigation and passage of the constitutional amendments in 1954, many people had urged me to run for attorney general. I did not want to do that then, fearing that people would think I was trying to turn the liquor investigation into a personal political campaign. Now, almost four years later, the idea of the attorney-generalship—representing all the people in the state and working on all of the highly varied legal activities and other major responsibilities that went with that post—seemed very attractive. It would also mean continuing to work on state governmental issues. And so I decided to run for that office in the 1958 election, although after five years on a legislator's salary, I should have returned to more gainful employment.

After considerable encouragement from my family, I announced my candidacy in September 1957. Soon thereafter, Governor Knight made one of his jokes: "Why would anyone want a good, honest man for attorney general?"

My campaign apparatus was a little rusty, but my wife soon resurrected "Your Neighbors for Good Government." Several of my fellow attorneys joined our team, as did former law school students and many other well-wishers. Especially helpful, of course, were the enthusiastic efforts of my children, my brother, and my wife. Jane spent nearly every day at our headquarters, writing letters, making phone calls, organizing volunteers.*

It was largely an all-volunteer operation. We did not have professional campaign "managers" or big fund-raisers, and that, of course, was part of the problem in statewide races.

Most of all, statewide campaigns needed money, and we had little. So initially our campaign activities were minimal—mostly just billboards and basic headquarters expenses. Fortunately, I had no Republican opponent for the primary, and I was hoping for major GOP financial support in the general campaign. Rapidly shifting politics changed that. The problem was "the Big Switch." Senator William Knowland (who had presidential ambitions) decided early in 1958 that, instead of running for reelection to the U.S. Senate, he would run against incumbent Goodwin Knight for governor of California in order to support a proposed "right to work" law that union membership could not be made a requirement for getting a

---

* A letter she wrote to potential supporters exemplified her characteristic deft blending of purpose, charm, and humor: "In giving me his permission to write these letters Cap said I simply couldn't ask for campaign contributions. I won't but...Robert Harris...is the Treasurer and I understand is joyfully accepting all offerings, great and small."

job. This was a very divisive issue and guaranteed fierce labor union opposition to Senator Knowland in the fall. But Governor Knight was vulnerable to a Republican challenge because he had become increasingly close to the unions. He was eventually persuaded that he would lose in the gubernatorial primary. So he decided to run for Knowland's Senate seat, rather than seek reelection as governor.

Vice President, and Californian, Richard Nixon tried to orchestrate Knight's switch, in order to avert a Republican primary fight and to keep a united California Republican Party two years later when Nixon would run for president. I do not know whether or to what extent Nixon was involved, but Knight was not a willing pawn. Initially, he had felt his chances against Knowland in the primary were good, especially with labor support, but when told that major Republican contributors would back Knowland for governor, Knight realized, as he put it, that "Standing on the burning deck in mid-ocean, I had no choice."

"The Big Switch" divided the party anyway, and not until Ronald Reagan ran in 1966 were the various rifts healed so the GOP could triumph again.

As part of the fallout from "the Big Switch," a southern California congressman, Patrick Hillings, who had intended to run for the Senate seat, decided not to challenge Knight in the GOP Senate primary. Instead, he entered the attorney general race, having previously assured me that he would not.

I never liked contested primaries, because they usually meant a divided party and wasted resources—things that Republicans could not afford. The demographics of the state were changing, and Democrats now had a strong majority of registered voters. If I had known that the primary for attorney general was going to be contested and the party so disastrously split, I might not have entered.

I think everyone assumed I would drop out, but I had already made what I felt were irrevocable commitments to my supporters. So now we had a hotly contested primary race that turned pretty much into a north-against-south fight, with many independent voters disgusted by Republican infighting.

Filled with practiced and carefully cultivated bonhomie, the ruddy-faced former Democrat Patrick Hillings had succeeded Richard Nixon as congressman from the Twenty-fifth District in southern California when Nixon moved up to the Senate in 1950. In the attorney general race, Nixon did not *publicly* endorse either of us, but Hillings was widely known as Nixon's protégé (oddly enough, because Hillings had been an active FDR supporter in college), and he opened practically every speech by saying, "I've just come from a meeting with Dick Nixon." Hillings was close to then-chairman of the Los Angeles County Republican Committee Robert Finch, who supported him with a million-person mailing to L.A. Republicans urging his election in the primary. And Hillings, not surprisingly, won the endorsement of the *Los Angeles Times*, though the *Los Angeles Mirror-News*, a smaller paper which was owned by the *Times*, endorsed me. And, during the campaign, I believe Hillings encouraged the sudden entry of several other GOP candidates for attorney general—to divide the northern California vote.

Indeed, almost all the party support that could be had in southern California had been nailed down by Hillings in support of his Senate candidacy. When he switched to the attorney general race, much of that support stayed with him.

Thinking that I would have no challenger for the primary, I had not yet concentrated a very large effort in the south. After Hillings came onto the scene, Jane and I established a southern California headquarters at the old Alexandria Hotel in Los Angeles, but by then it was too late to be very effective.

There was also a smear campaign against me by Fulton Lewis, a right-wing extremist radio commentator. He seized on an old article in a California Communist newspaper, *People's World*, which warned its readership to watch me carefully because I had been effective in the California legislature. Lewis alleged on his radio program that the Communists were praising me and suggested I was actually a Communist. This was ludicrous—but damaging, nevertheless, and played into Pat Hillings's strategy of painting me as a dangerous liberal.

Some in my campaign wanted me to sue Lewis and the radio station for libel, and I rather liked that idea because I thought it was a way to set the record straight. But we soon realized that nothing could be decided by the courts until years after the election. We did, however, demand an apology, which Lewis gave half-heartedly. But a lot of damage was done, and it takes a long time to eradicate the negative effects of even absurd attacks.

My campaign emphasized that I was a practicing attorney— Hillings had never done any actual law practice—and was far better suited by experience to run the largest law office in the state. It was, in fact, the largest law office in the country outside the U.S. Department of Justice.

I spent the last month before the primary campaigning exclusively in southern California, before returning to San Francisco. The early returns—which were largely from the Bay Area—showed me running well ahead, but I knew that my lead would quickly be diminished when votes in Los Angeles were counted. When a reporter asked me early in the evening for a victory statement, I replied that if I weren't running so far ahead, I'd concede right then! It turned out that I did win in most counties, except for Los Angeles and Orange Counties, but that still was not enough to win the race.

My defeat, I am sure, was partially the result of some of the political factors I have already mentioned, but I think the main problem was simply that we did not raise enough money. We had many dedicated campaign supporters and volunteers, and I borrowed from the bank a substantial amount, for me, which took about five years to pay off. These sources combined gave us roughly $50,000, but in those days you needed at least a couple hundred thousand to mount an effective statewide campaign. The race taught me at least one lesson: that if I ran for elective office again, I would never put my own money into it.

The California GOP also learned the cost of division. We had forgotten the cardinal rule for California Republican victory: our candidates needed to be able to win about 80 percent of the GOP vote and attract about 20 percent of the registered Democrats. I am sure Senator Knowland and Governor Knight could have done this and easily won reelection if they had stayed in their respective posts. As it was, nearly all of our candidates lost. Stanley Mosk, a strong Democrat with a lot of labor union support, beat Pat Hillings for attorney general in the general election—a race I think I could have won. Stan Mosk served well as attorney general and later became a most able member of the California Supreme Court and a good friend.

After this disaster for California Republicans, many felt it would take years to restore the party. In 1958 California elected Democrat Edmund G. "Pat" Brown as governor and gave him Democratic legislative majorities in both houses. This was part of a national trend. The Democrats in 1958 made their biggest gains in Congress since the New Deal and won a net of five governorships, probably because we had had six years of Republican victories and many people wanted a change.

You never know, but I still think the California GOP could have survived this 1958 tide had we stayed united. After all, just two years later Richard Nixon carried the state against John F. Kennedy in the race for president.

CHAPTER 8

GRAND OLD POLITICS

*B*y 1960, Richard Nixon had already led a distinguished life in government—four years as a congressman, two years in the Senate, and eight years as President Eisenhower's vice president.

I had known him—I suppose as well as anyone could really know Richard Nixon—since 1950, when, as a California congressman, he ran for and won a seat in the U.S. Senate. It was during that campaign that I first saw him at a small gathering of San Francisco GOP supporters in a mezzanine room at the St. Francis Hotel. His main theme was that he wanted to "help clean up the mess in Washington"— mostly some real transgressions by some dubious Truman appointees (although I have to add, quite minor transgressions compared to today's). Nixon had a garden shovel that he displayed rather sheepishly as an instrument he would use in this cleanup endeavor. I sympathized with him; I would not have wanted to wave a shovel around either.

He was a good candidate and a good political speaker, expressing solid conservative views, and he was popular within the Republican party. He was a favorite son of the California Republican Party, but there were always liberals who hated Richard Nixon from the moment he defeated the radical Democrat Helen Gahagan Douglas in the 1950 Senate campaign. Mrs. Douglas was a media favorite and professional Nixon-haters always spoke of his "dirty tactics" in that race. But it was really the same atmosphere that surrounded any other hotly contested California seat.

In his memoir, *RN*, Nixon wrote:

> Throughout the campaign I kept her pinned to her extremist record. I pointed out that she had voted against Truman on military aid to Greece and Turkey, the key plank of the Truman Doctrine, which I had supported. She had also voted against bills requiring loyalty checks for federal employees and was one of only fourteen members of Congress who had voted against the security bill that allowed the heads of key national defense agencies, such as the Atomic Energy Commission, to discharge government workers found to be security risks. . . .
>
> Mrs. Douglas had often appeared at meetings and addressed organizations that had been cited by the Attorney General's office during Truman's administration as "Communist and subversive."

Some in the Nixon campaign, if not Nixon himself, took to calling her the "Pink Lady." In return, Douglas dubbed Nixon "Tricky Dick." I think one of Mr. Nixon's main campaign problems was that he allowed some less scrupulous or less careful campaign advisers to take over. In the early days of Nixon's political career, a Los Angeles attorney named Murray Chotiner was a good example. He was a likeable enough rogue whose enthusiasm for doing in his opponents sometimes exceeded his judgment. Of Mr. Chotiner it was frequently said that "Wherever you find Murray Chotiner, there is a trail of blood behind." One of his favorite ploys was to telephone someone from a booth in a corridor of the Senate Office Building and to open the conversation with. "I am calling you from the vice president's office."

In 1960 I felt that, as the Republican nominee for president, Nixon deserved the support of the party—all our party. I was adamant that my other political supporters not hold a grudge because of the Pat Hillings race against me for attorney general. It is a fundamental law of successful GOP campaigns that they are a process of *inclusion*, not of continuing old enmities.

So when Mr. Nixon asked me, I became a campaign cochairman in northern California. Basically that meant I was to arrange speaking engagements for him in the area, help coordinate his campaign appearances, plan rallies, and try in the usual ways to drum up party and independent support for him.

I also attended the national convention in Chicago that year, as an at-large delegate selected by Nixon. The three major party leaders in California—Nixon, Senator Knowland, and former governor Knight—each nominated one-third of the delegates for the 1960 convention, a sign of how the division in our party still hadn't healed. This selection process was a way of avoiding a major fight as to who was the "leader of the California party." But at least it ensured unity behind Nixon.

The convention itself was fairly uneventful, although all the paraphernalia, noise, and standard demonstrations (such as stunts with live elephants) were there in full measure. There was no organized opposition to Nixon—only a brief and minor challenge by supporters of Governor Nelson Rockefeller of New York, far too late because the delegates were already pledged to Nixon. This was considered by Nixon managers to be the "last gasp" of the "Eastern Establishment" that had run the party.

The basic theme of Nixon's 1960 campaign was "Peace, Prosperity, Progress," which was a continuation of the Eisenhower years that had delivered these three P's in the sure hands of the experienced Richard Nixon against the young Democratic nominee, John F. Kennedy.

There were no major ideological divisions in the country. The Cold War was at its coldest, and both men promoted their qualifications for dealing with that. Senator Kennedy frightened people with talk of a "missile gap" between the United States and the Soviet Union (a gap that he later admitted did not exist). Nixon, of course, was the quintessential anti-Communist, and much of his campaign literature emphasized this. As vice president, he had stood up to Soviet premier Nikita Khrushchev in the "kitchen debate," extolling the virtues of capitalism as they toured a Moscow exhibit of a model American home with all of the latest technology. Also, as a congressman in 1948, Nixon had successfully uncovered the spying activities of former State Department official Alger Hiss.

In the final analysis, however, the personalities and personal appeal of the two men were the deciding factors to many voters. That, unfortunately, did not work to Nixon's advantage. As many recall, the presidential debates (the first to be televised) were significant. Kennedy appeared young, vigorous, and handsome, as indeed he was. Nixon, on the other hand, came across poorly in the first of the four debates. He had the flu, he had recently hurt his knee, and a nonstop travel schedule had not allowed him any preparation time. Moreover, his "five o'clock shadow" made him look rather sinister and, compared to Kennedy, quite old. He came across better in the subsequent debates, but the first, being new, had the most impact.

It is interesting to note the influence television was already having in elevating style above substance. People who watched the debates on television felt that Kennedy was the winner, but those who listened on the radio decisively picked Nixon as the victor. Sadly, even this did not help Nixon, since the television audience was about five times larger than the radio audience.

Still, the election turned out to be a very narrow defeat for Nixon—with considerable evidence of vote fraud, particularly in a few precincts in Illinois and Texas, without which the election may have gone in his favor. Local bosses in both states had, through illegal counting and manipulation, provided ammunition for a major challenge. Nixon, to his credit, immediately decided to accept the election results. He admired Kennedy as a former Senate colleague and did not want to embarrass the country and the new, apparent president with a vigorously pursued recount.

As 1962 approached, a number of people encouraged Nixon to run for governor of California, as a natural platform for another presidential campaign. I was then the state party vice chairman and I was one of those urging him to run for governor, because I thought he could be elected. After all, he had barely lost the presidential election in 1960 and had carried California against the popular young Kennedy.

When Nixon decided to run for governor, he asked me to be the full-time manager of his campaign. This was tempting, but I declined. I did not feel safe in giving up my principal means of income, my law practice. There were also many nonprofit activities I was engaged in (of which more later), and I knew that running a gubernatorial campaign was more than a full-time job in itself. I did, however, serve as an informal adviser, occasionally meeting with Mr. Nixon on strategy or issues, and I made a few speeches, but I did not hold any formal or paid position.

Nixon was a reluctant candidate in this race, because his greatest interest was foreign policy and he did not know state issues well, which is one reason I think he wanted me to run his campaign. Someone had asked him about a local problem in Los Angeles, and he said, "See, Cap, I don't know how to answer things like this. I don't know anything about the sewage disposal problems in Los Angeles." (He did not call it "sewage.") When I told him that governors do not deal with such issues, he replied, "Well, you see, I don't even know that!"

Another factor that substantially weakened Nixon in this race was the party split caused by a far right-wing Republican challenger, Joe Shell. Shell had been a colleague of mine in the assembly and was quite popular in southern California. He was a former football player at USC, which in southern California was practically a passport to political advancement. An ultraconservative, Shell supported the dubious John Birch Society,* a small but very vocal extremist faction of the party that Nixon had condemned in an act of political courage for the time.

Nixon won the primary, but he did so without generating much GOP enthusiasm, which was deadly given that he was running against an incumbent Democratic governor, Edmund G. "Pat" Brown, who had not done anything particularly iniquitous. In California, incumbents of either party are hard to unseat. So Nixon lost the election, and the next morning, feeling understandably depressed and regarding himself as a political failure, unable ever to achieve the presidency—the only thing he really cared about—he held his disastrous "You won't have Nixon to kick around anymore" farewell press conference, lashing out, rather incoherently, at the press.

---

* The John Birch Society was a relatively new organization, established in 1958. Anti-Communism was its main thrust, a prevalent sentiment in the country at that time, but its members' rigid intolerance of anyone whose degree of fervor was less than theirs struck me as somewhat hypocritical.

I remember one particularly raucous meeting of the Republican State Central Committee in early 1963 that exemplified this. During a roll-call vote on a resolution to restore cross-filing (which had been eliminated in 1959), Birchers loudly disrupted the meeting in an effort to keep supporters of the resolution from hearing their names being called. For maximum effect, they even positioned themselves in a diamond formation around the room, just, as vote-recorder Emily Pike pointed out, "like the Communist handbook recommends it." Their opposition to the measure, however, was based on their basic belief that any Republican who would run for office on both the Republican and Democratic ballots was obviously not sufficiently conservative.

Shortly after that defeat, Nixon gave up California as a residence and political base and moved to New York. He also did a great deal of traveling and speaking abroad. where he was still very popular; practiced law," and kept in close touch with his most loyal party supporters. One loyalist and admirer, Bob Haldeman, believed that Nixon's 1962 gubernatorial race was crucial to his eventual election as president, because it kept him in the public's mind as an active politician rather than as merely a former vice president.

I never knew if Nixon himself actually felt that his political career was completely finished after his gubernatorial defeat. He certainly seemed to think so the morning after that election, but he proved to be a most remarkable political phoenix. I am sure this was because of both his meticulous planning and his dogged perseverance in the face of overwhelming odds.

I regretted having urged Nixon to run for governor, because it was bad for him to have entered a race in which he had comparatively little interest. Admittedly, I had been thinking almost entirely of the welfare and success of the state Republican Party rather than that of Richard Nixon personally.

In spite of my own loss in the 1958 GOP primary for attorney general, I kept a hand in politics as well. That year, I had been asked by Senator Knowland and agreed to become secretary of the Republican State Central Committee (RSCC)—the official GOP organization.[†] Its main purpose was to raise funds for state candidates, persuade good potential candidates to run, keep county party organizations

---

* Leonard Garment, one of his law partners in New York, has written in his autobiography, *Crazy Rhythm* (New York: Times Books. 1997), the best history of this part of Nixon's post-California career.

† The RSCC then consisted of all Republican members of the legislature and all other elected state GOP officials. Each of these had the right to appoint three other people to the organization.

going, and draft state party platforms in election years. The chairman
was spokesman for the party.

But in the early 1960s the California Republican Party was fac-
tious. The party was used to winning, but when it split over degrees
of conservatism it almost guaranteed defeat.

This was very much in evidence when I agreed to the urging of
many friends that I run for the vice chairmanship of the RSCC in
1960. Some of the legislative leaders I had known when I was in the
assembly came to me at the state convention and said they knew
I did not have enough votes and I would be humiliated, and they
urged me to drop out of the race. But my strong impression was that
if they had the votes to defeat me, they would not bother to suggest
I drop out. That conclusion turned out to be correct: I won on a roll-
call vote. My opposition was largely based on the impression that I
was relatively more "liberal" than my opponent, Vernon Cristina, and
hence less "reliable" in the coming fight for the 1964 presidential
nomination. Cristina, who ran a trucking company south of San Jose,
was a pleasant man whom I liked, so there was little personal rancor
between us.

The vice chairmanship was very important because the vice chairman almost always became the chairman two years later. So the more
"conservative" faction, including Joe Shell, kept trying to oust me at
each subsequent meeting.

I called several additional meetings in an effort to keep everybody
active and interested in the party. Those meetings were usually contentious. Far too many Republicans would rather pass a resolution,
even if ridiculous or unhelpful in persuading voters, than win an
election. I soon learned that it was quite unsafe to call very many
meetings because I spent half my time trying to survive the attempts
to replace me with a "Goldwater man."

Still, in 1961, I developed for the RSCC a strategy that came to be
called the Weinberger Victory Program. One element of this program

was to register voters and bring more of them into the party. This was fairly successful.

Another part of the program was to make a concerted effort, particularly in marginal legislative districts, to win control of the legislature, which had already become considerably more partisan than when I had served in the assembly. The legislature was scheduled to reapportion the state after the next census, and we strongly preferred that the reapportionment be done by a Republican majority. We concentrated our resources on the most promising districts, developing precinct organizations, setting up phone banks, and sending out mass mailings.

Of even more importance was recruiting promising candidates, endorsing them strongly, and providing them with plenty of public opportunities to present their views.

The key to all of this, I felt, was to start two to four years before an election, because if you followed the standard practice of waiting until only a few weeks before, it was too late, and you would probably be stuck with a candidate who was not electable. Having *continuous* party activity, even many months or years away from an election, was a new idea. Of course, all of this planning was made more difficult by the efforts of the Goldwater people, who were uninterested in promoting candidates they felt were not conservative enough.

At the state convention in 1962, I faced a challenge from Gardiner Johnson for chairmanship of the party. He was a fellow San Francisco attorney and a friend. Senator Knowland nominated him in a speech that lost some of its intended dramatic effect because the senator forgot to mention Johnson's name. Johnson's nomination was part of an additional effort by the Goldwater people to gain control of every state party in preparation for the 1964 election, so I never felt it involved any opposition to me personally, although of course it might have. I did manage to win the chairmanship, again by a close roll-call vote.

The Goldwater faction was persuasive, had money, made a lot of noise, and worked hard throughout the year, but it also kept us riven with internecine squabbles and hurt our efforts to attract independents and wavering Democrats.

When Barry Goldwater became the Republican presidential nominee in 1964, his people expected all the rest of us in the California Republican Party to fold up and resign our positions. That did not happen—moderates retained leadership—but I supported Goldwater because he was the nominee of the convention, and I urged others to do the same, even though I would have preferred Nelson Rockefeller. I thought he had been an excellent governor of New York and was more electable, but I was careful not to make any public statements to that effect before or during the convention. One fellow state committeeman, however, was not so reluctant. Joe Martin, a "Grand New Party" colleague from 1950 and the California member of the national committee, resigned from the state committee to support Rockefeller.

The 1964 Republican National Convention, held at San Francisco's Cow Palace,* was raucous and divisive. When Rockefeller spoke, he was booed and hissed. The hatred toward this Republican governor was palpable, and it was shocking to many television viewers.

Even though I backed Goldwater after the convention, his people still did not regard me as "reliable." They did not, for a long time after the convention, accept my offer to help. Finally, Goldwater himself did, and at his request I made a couple of speeches on his behalf in October.

---

* San Francisco had hosted the Republican convention only eight years earlier but was chosen again because it had a good convention hall as well as good and plentiful hotel space—and, of course, it is a very attractive city that everyone likes to visit. I had made a couple of presentations in Washington, urging the selection of San Francisco to the national committee, which selects the convention site. The Cow Palace was so named because it was the home of county fairs with agricultural and cattle exhibits.

Goldwater won only six states (he lost California). He had been labeled as an extremist, and many worried that he would expand the Vietnam War and cut Social Security. President Johnson won reelection easily—and went on to expand the Vietnam War. One cartoonist summed it up rather neatly by showing a caricature of President Johnson telephoning Senator Goldwater after one disastrous Vietnam debacle and asking, "Barry, what was it you were going to do next in Vietnam?"

Though considered extreme, Goldwater was simply a conservative and proud of it. He had none of the bitterness that extremists feel toward the less ideologically pure. In fact, later, in the Senate, he sometimes voted for measures considered quite liberal.

It was Ronald Reagan who made the most notable speech on Goldwater's behalf in 1964, and it was Reagan who would soon express the kind of conservatism that could win elections.

CHAPTER 9

TELEVISION IN CALIFORNIA

nvolvement in politics kept me busy enough in the late 1950s and early 1960s to satisfy my addiction, but with a recent defeat in elective politics and a large (for that time) campaign debt to pay, I reluctantly concluded that I should concentrate on more profitable pursuits, namely, my law practice. Some people talked of my running for city attorney or mayor of San Francisco, but I really had no interest in those positions. I wanted to be where I felt I could make a real contribution in public service, not just run for an office for the office's sake. Besides, I'm sorry to say, municipal politics has never really interested me, even though I know it is a vital part of citizen participation in government.

Actually, even if I had wanted to pursue a position in San Francisco city government, I could not have because by 1959 I was no longer a resident. The previous year, after our vigorous campaign for attorney general, our family's summer camping vacations were replaced with a much-needed rest for a month in the hot, dry climate of California's wine country. The summer home we rented had a swimming pool.

This, in turn, led to family queries as to why this sort of thing could not go on all the time. So we moved down the peninsula to Hillsborough, where swimming is possible, if not all year, at least for a large part of it.

My professional life remained in San Francisco, though, and I soon understood all the jokes about commuting. I returned to Heller, Ehrman, and I became a partner in 1959. While I worked hard at the law practice and liked some of it, I never enjoyed it as much as what my wife called my "nonprofit" activities. I do not think I made a conscious effort to find other, more interesting things to do than the law, but I certainly did not resist too strongly when various offers presented themselves.

The first of those came around January 1959, just as my final term in the legislature was coming to an end. Jon Rice, general manager and one of the founders of KQED, San Francisco's local, and fairly new, educational television station, called and asked if I would be interested in being the moderator for one of their public affairs programs. I had always been interested in educational stations, and as an assemblyman I had secured passage of a bill amending the Education Code to permit public schools to spend money for educational television programs. This had provided KQED and other early educational TV stations with urgently needed public funding that helped them to survive.

Profile: Bay Area, the program I was asked to host, was essentially a weekly public affairs discussion program covering all sides of a wide range of topics of local, state, and national interest. *Profile's* first moderator, Roger Boas, had served as host of the show for its first year or so but then wanted to move on to a career in local politics. KQED liked the program and knew that a lot of people watched it (half a million, by some estimates). I had been on a few similar programs involving state legislative matters and enjoyed them. So Jon's offer fell on surprised but willing ears, and I accepted.

Our crew on *Profile* consisted of myself, a permanent studio cameraman, and the producer/director—a bright, brilliant, energetic lady named Virginia Duncan. She was largely responsible for the considerable success the program enjoyed.

Virginia and I worked closely together on all aspects of the program: deciding the topics to be covered, lining up the guests and interviewing them ahead of time to ensure that all points of view were presented on controversial subjects, writing the scripts and preparing questions, and so forth. All of this was time-consuming but quite helpful—indeed essential if we wanted to present an intelligent, fair, and balanced program.

Still, things did not always go smoothly. Sometimes pressing work at the law practice, or the lack of firm commitments from guests until a day or so before the program, made it impossible for me to interview or meet with the guests ahead of time. I always regretted this because I felt the preprogram interviews with the guests were a vital part of the program, particularly because frequently my knowledge of some topics was extremely limited, such as with modern art. For that program, we interviewed Richard Diebenkorn, the famous modern artist from Berkeley about whom sadly I previously knew nothing at all.

We generally wrote out an introduction and background for me to read, but I did not stick rigidly to the various questions we drafted. This allowed for more spontaneity and give-and-take among the guests.

The only special visual effects or graphics were pictures I was allowed to pick up from the *San Francisco Chronicle*'s morgue to illustrate the show's opening. I usually walked there from the law office around 6 or 7 P.M., selected the pictures, and then took them to the small KQED studio on Fourth Street, which was "South of Market"— a rather seedy part of town at that time, and quite a long walk. The *Chronicle* was very cooperative about letting me wander through its files and picture collection, even when its rival, the *Examiner*, was sponsoring *Profile*.

We did the program live at 9 P.M. every Thursday, which I much preferred to taping. Originally, the show was only a half hour long, but viewer requests for more thorough discussions allowed us to extend to forty-five minutes and eventually to an hour.

We always tried to have at least four guests, two on each side of an issue. I would start talking with the guests in the studio several minutes before airtime so that when the camera actually started rolling, they would be warmed up and ready to continue, rather than start, the discussion. I acted as moderator and did not impose my own opinions. We had many highly vigorous debates. In one program, on public education, an actual fistfight developed afterward between two academics.

Occasionally we received letters from viewers who said the program was slanted because I was a fairly prominent Republican. We always wrote back and asked these people to point out one specific incident where my personal opinion had intruded, and they were invariably unable to do so.

We covered a wide variety of topics, including riots at City Hall, political campaigns, narcotics, loyalty oaths, state water problems, the San Francisco Symphony, professional boxing, rapid transit, disarmament, baseball, and Vietnam. As Jon Rice said, "There's no subject the program won't tackle. It was the first in the nation to deal with the relationship between cigarette smoking and cancer." I remember that program quite vividly because one of the guests, a doctor who opposed theories linking smoking to cancer, defiantly and ostentatiously smoked cigarettes, blowing smoke over the other guests throughout the program. A few years later he died—of cancer.

Profile occasionally even directly influenced policy. One example was when we discussed capital punishment the night before one of the many scheduled executions of rapist Caryl Chessman. Chessman's attorney, as part of his *Profile* presentation, made a dramatic—and successful, as it turned out—plea addressed to the governor, turning to talk to him as if he were actually in the studio. The governor was indeed watching, and later that night he granted another stay.

Once, following the death of a boxer who had absorbed a terrible beating in the ring, our subject was whether professional boxing should be allowed. We had a retired boxer who was contemptuous of efforts to ban professional boxing and a brain surgeon who had told me that this barbarous sport should be banned. My first question went to the surgeon: "Why do you think professional boxing should be abolished?" "Oh, I don't. I've changed my mind," he replied. That left me with about fifty-eight minutes to fill with two guests who agreed with each other.

Our guests were as disparate as the subjects we presented. Among them were state and local political candidates; farm labor spokesman Cesar Chavez; the inventor of the hydrogen bomb, Edward Teller; and an extremely eloquent and persuasive Malcolm X shortly before his assassination.

The program I remember most vividly was one in October of 1966 that illustrated, with considerable force, the problems underlying riots at Hunters Point, a low-income, predominantly black area of San Francisco. The root cause of the riots seemed to be primarily the difficulty for residents there to get satisfactory jobs, so Virginia and I decided to devote a special two-hour show to the issue, to try to find out what obstacles they were facing and to discuss some possible solutions. Our panel included city, state, and federal employment officials, labor leaders, an NAACP representative, and several representatives of youth groups and residents of Hunters Point.

I felt that we had assembled a pretty balanced group of participants, but about an hour into the show, a handful of disgruntled, agitated young men from Hunters Point cut into the discussion from one side of the stage. They said that since they were the ones who were closest to the situation, their position should be heard. I agreed and asked for their point of view, but they simply kept repeating who they were and that we should listen to them. I quickly realized that this exercise was not productive, so I returned my attention to the invited panel.

Soon, however, the interlopers surrounded the table, pressing themselves and their indignation further and further onto center stage. I would have been pleased to hear their opinions and some of their suggestions, but it was difficult to have any kind of calm discussion about it because they all spoke at once and seemed determined to disrupt the program.

I was becoming rather irritated as well because our invited guests, who were kind enough to take time to be a part of our panel, were hardly getting a chance to speak. When I tersely suggested to the intruders that part of the problem might be that they were not willing to listen to anyone else, their anger—and volume—only rose, with fists pounding the table and fingers pointing.

Partly because I was trying to maintain order and partly, I think, because I represented to them every white man who had discriminated against them, I became a convenient target for their ire. The exchange that perhaps revealed their complete frustration and disillusionment best was when I said it was difficult for anyone to be heard when they kept interrupting, and one man got right in my face and replied, "You've been interrupting me since the day I was born."

That program won a couple of prizes for best educational television program, and much was written about it in the newspapers. It was lauded mostly for the "realism" and spontaneity provided by our unexpected participants.

The invasion brought home to many of our viewers, in a way that little else could, the desperate frustration of a group of people to whom most of us could not relate. Program panelist and city supervisor Terry Francois described it well: Though he "could not excuse the intemperate, rude behavior" of the angry young men who had invaded the studio, "the intense hostility, the feeling of alienation, and the total rejection of middle-class standards which were exhibited came as no surprise. We have told them that they didn't belong for so long and treated them as though they had no stake in society, that it is not surprising that they have come to see themselves as a group apart and not bound by any of the rules of the group."

Much later, we learned that a week before that show, this same group had poured into the reception area of the station and demanded to be heard on another program. A rather frightened manager offered them each five dollars to go away. So I think most of them came back not so much to disrupt *Profile* as to get their five dollars.

The program, and indeed the station, was run on a shoestring budget, supported largely by individual contributions, occasional corporate sponsors, and some school funds. The *San Francisco Examiner* sponsored *Profile* for a time, and we tried to get foundation grants, but most of the time only our permanent cameraman was paid; the producer/director and I received nothing at all. Over the roughly nine years I moderated the program, I doubt if I received much more than five hundred dollars in all. But we enjoyed it thoroughly and were dedicated to producing a fair and accurate discussion program.*

Aside from my continued but rather minor involvement in the Republican Party during these years, two other opportunities turned up that allowed me to combine my passion for government and my interest in journalism.

Around 1959 I made a speech to the California Newspaper Publishers' Association, the gist of which was that while there was plenty of coverage of local matters and a lot of coverage of national

---

* I remember how astonished I was when I appeared on NBC's *Meet the Press* in Washington for the first time, in 1970, after I was appointed chairman of the Federal Trade Commission. There were about thirty people in the studio—everything from cameramen to scriptwriters to assistant producers and directors to make-up people to lighting experts and graphic artists—all working on a single discussion program.

and international events, the state government was rather badly neglected in most newspapers outside of Sacramento. With such minimal coverage, I argued, there was very little understanding of it, certainly not as much as I thought people ought to have in view of the numerous ways the state affected the lives of so many people. One or two of the publishers came up to me afterward and said, "You're complaining about this; what are you going to do about it? Why don't you write us some stories, or even a column?"

That idea greatly appealed to me, so I started writing a regular column (a couple of times a week) about state government issues. I tried to explain each issue as objectively as I could and then give readers an idea of the pros and cons as well as the interests behind each side. My own opinion usually came out toward the end of the column. Occasionally, however, I would unabashedly push my view from the start, as I did, for example, when I advocated allowing taxpayers to file as their state income tax return a simple carbon copy of their federal return. I also gave my opinion frequently when writing about measures that would affect the areas I had worked on as an assemblyman, particularly alcoholic beverage control and the state's water needs.

Ultimately the column ran in twenty to thirty papers around the state. Each one paid a small amount (ten to twenty-five dollars as I recall) for each column. I did this for about nine years. It certainly did not bring in a large income, but, like my other extracurricular activities, I enjoyed it much more than my work at the law firm. My personal secretary at the law firm, Marguerite Klapka, did too, in fact. She was always enthusiastic and helpful with this, as well as with all of my other outside activities. I have been so fortunate over the years, for the secretaries and executive assistants with whom I have worked have all been very helpful, enormously able, and loyal, and have usually become good friends.

I also did a daily radio commentary for the local NBC station. The program initially was sponsored by a group called the Republican Alliance, which wanted to get Republican views on the air, but before long the only ones paying for the airtime (we had no "production costs") were old friends and Hillsborough neighbors, John Renshaw and his wife, Hope. They were longtime, hardworking Republicans. The station was reluctant to sell the time at first because it was afraid it would lose its audience and would have to offer equal time to a Democratic spokesman. Neither scenario materialized.

It was only a fifteen-minute, live program (daily, and later, weekly), sandwiched between the evening news and prime time. I would walk up to the station around 5 P.M., reading over notes I had made about some events that had happened during the week and that seemed to me to demonstrate the need for Republicans to be elected. I did not like to use a prepared script, as the studio urged me to do. I would go on the air and talk informally about these six or eight topics. Unlike on *Profile*, here I did express my personal views. The station was quite pleased with the program because it got far more favorable than negative reactions. We did it for about two years, until our efforts turned more directly to the 1966 governor's race.

CHAPTER 10

THE GOVERNOR WHO TURNED THE STATE AROUND

The main Republican contenders for governor of California in 1966 were George Christopher, former mayor of San Francisco, and a personable, handsome actor named Ronald Reagan. It may surprise some that I supported Christopher in the primary, but I had pledged my support to him before Mr. Reagan decided to run. Christopher was a fellow San Franciscan, a political supporter in my own bids for office who had made the very first contribution to my 1952 campaign. I was very busy with my law practice, so my support was limited to a few speeches in which I was always careful to extol Christopher rather than attack Reagan. I had no problem after the primary in joining the Reagan gubernatorial campaign because I admired him and appreciated all he had done for our party.

Ronald Reagan had a star quality and a popular message of personal and economic freedom that helped him win that primary and, ultimately, every major race he entered. He eloquently presented a picture of reduced state government expenditures and reduced government involvement in people's daily affairs, both of which meant increased power and freedom for individuals. It was exactly the message and the picture most people wanted to hear and to achieve.

Moreover, he was fully committed to rebuilding the party *within* the state and was enormously effective in doing so. His celebrity status helped, but even beyond that, he had an electric quality about him and a way of making each person in the audience, no matter how large or small the gathering, feel as if he were speaking directly to him or her. He could articulate their hopes and ideals—or persuade them to share his.

Also, as I had seen when I was chairman of the State Central Committee, Reagan was willing to go anywhere, however small or remote, even though he did not like to fly, to preach the Republican message—a message that no one could express more personably or with more inspiring vision.

I went with him to some campaign rallies, did a few radio programs on his behalf, helped draft some speeches, and gave a few of my own. I also met occasionally with his personal campaign staff. But in the 1966 general election, it was his own tireless efforts and the appeal of his philosophy that translated into his overwhelming victory over incumbent Governor Pat Brown.*

Reagan immediately set about translating his beliefs into action. In fact, he was so anxious to get started that he even asked to be sworn in, in the rotunda of the State Capitol, immediately after midnight on Inauguration Day, January 3, 1967, instead of waiting until the more traditional noon ceremonies.

---

* Governor Brown did his part too, though. A master of malapropism, he often hurt himself more than anyone else could. A good example was when he flew over a flood-damaged area and proclaimed, "This is the worst disaster since I was elected governor."

His goals in office were essentially his core philosophy that he had talked about in the campaign—that is, smaller government and more individual freedom and responsibility. He wanted to reform welfare by removing some of the incentives to stay on the welfare rolls and by adding a work requirement. He wanted to improve schools by raising standards, not necessarily by raising budgets. And he wanted to reduce taxes. But first, he had to get rid of the budget deficit that Governor Brown had left. The state constitution required a balanced budget.

During the transition, Governor-elect Reagan asked me to head a small ad hoc task force to recommend ways to make the state's executive branch more efficient, less cumbersome, less expensive, and more responsive to the governor's direction.

It was through this endeavor that I first met Bill Clark, a rancher and attorney who was, at that time, one of Reagan's senior campaign advisers. For Bill, the son of California ranchers, his greatest love, after his lovely wife, is indeed his ranch and ranch life. I believe that one of the reasons he had been attracted to Reagan's candidacy was the fact that Reagan personified the best of the frontier virtues that Bill admired. We each subsequently served in Reagan's gubernatorial and presidential administrations, and it was evident to me from our first meeting that Bill Clark was a thoroughly decent, completely honest man, totally devoted and loyal to the cause of Mr. Reagan's success. Bill always served Mr. Reagan extraordinarily well, because he innately understood the way Reagan thought and operated. He also understood better than most that extremist versions of Reagan's beliefs, which some of the governor-elect's friends were recommending, would hurt him at the polls and beyond.

As cabinet secretary, and later, as the governor's executive secretary, Bill did an excellent job of organizing the governor's office and staff; he worked well with all of the various interests competing for the governor's time and was well liked by the press. Bill brought order to the generally chaotic early days of any new administration. I have always thought that Reagan's enormous success as governor, particularly in his first term—the term that propelled him onto the national stage—was in large part due to Bill Clark. Bill has always been completely selfless, and although he was rewarded by high judicial offices, those appointments were the governor's initiatives, not Bill's. Of course, I was prejudiced in his favor. Bill has been unfailingly thoughtful and generous to me; indeed, Jane and I consider him and his wife, Joan, our closest friends. All in all, he is one of the most able people with whom I have ever worked.

We worked closely on the governor's reorganization task force in late 1966. This group, which included management consultants and business executives I had appointed, held a series of meetings in my San Francisco law office (and a few in Los Angeles) and prepared a thorough reorganization plan. Essentially, this called for clustering groups of state agencies together according to the types of things they did—agriculture and services, business and transportation, human relations, and natural resources. Each of these four broad areas would be headed by executive vice presidents or secretaries, who would then report to the governor. As it was, there were well over one hundred agencies reporting directly and separately to the governor, so our plan significantly streamlined communications.

To get legislative approval for this plan would probably have been very difficult and taken many months because the legislature was heavily Democratic and suspicious of any reorganization plan. So, at Bill Clark's suggestion, we put the essence of the plan into effect immediately by executive order, on the theory that the governor would use this new plan simply as a means of communicating with his appointees. This did not require any statutory authority. Governor Reagan used this organization for most of his two terms, and I believe that his successors have used some versions of it as well. Some aspects were subsequently enacted formally through legislation.

Several years later, President Nixon implemented a similar plan, essentially consolidating federal departments and agencies performing generally similar activities under four or five "counselors to the president." Mr. Nixon appointed me counselor to the president for human resources. Not surprisingly, individual cabinet members, and some of the White House staff, did not like the arrangement because it subordinated their role to these counselors. And members of Congress, as was the case with the state legislature, were wary of the reorganization because they felt it changed their relationship with the executive departments and agencies. Taking a page from Governor Reagan's books, President Nixon put the plan into effect without formal congressional approval. Actually, it lasted only about six months, and then Watergate overtook everything and nothing more was done about it—or indeed much else until President Nixon's forced resignation.

We tried to put in the same kind of plan later, when Reagan was president, but there was too much opposition from some members of the White House staff, who were afraid it would reduce their influence with the president, and from potential cabinet appointees who wanted to report directly to the president.

As Governor-elect Reagan's administration was taking shape, Bill Clark urged Reagan to name me director of finance. Bill liked my work on the reorganization task force and knew of my earlier work in the legislature, and he apparently felt, correctly, that I would be completely loyal to the governor. There was, however, strong opposition from southern California ultra-conservatives who still considered me a liberal Republican. In any event, interested as I was in helping the governor, I was preparing for a major antitrust case, so a full-time state job was out of the question.

There was, however, another way both the governor and Bill felt I could help. They asked me if I would serve as Reagan's first appointee to, and chairman of, the Commission on California State Government

Organization and Economy. This "Little Hoover Commission," as it was also known, had been in existence since 1961, and it had investigated a variety of individual questions, largely based, it seemed to me, on the personal interests of its members, some of whom were appointed by the leaders of the assembly and state senate, and some by previous governors. The commission had never looked at overall reorganization of the executive branch; it was our task force that really did the work on that.

It was difficult to reach a consensus on anything because the governor's appointees and those within the Little Hoover Commission appointed by the legislative leaders, mostly Democrats, were usually at odds. The majority of the commission also insisted on keeping a singularly inept and partisan staff, added to which were a couple of particularly unpleasant holdovers from the Brown administration.

Nevertheless, I have always found it difficult to say no to governors and presidents, and since the commission met only once or twice a month, I accepted the position. We managed to complete some reasonably useful investigations and projects, but I cannot say I enjoyed the experience.

As 1967 went on, more and more people inside the administration recognized the ineffectiveness of Governor Reagan's first director of finance, Gordon Paul Smith. Smith had come from a management firm and was not experienced at dealing with the legislature. He was generally not very knowledgeable about state government, and little had been done to deal with the state's deficit. So, toward the end of that year, Bill Clark, who was by then the governor's executive secretary, renewed his efforts to have me appointed director of finance. When Governor Reagan called me about the job, I was waiting for the jury's decision after a ten-week trial in the antitrust case. The case involved predatory pricing in the dried sandblast sand industry, and I had learned far more about sandblast sand than I wanted to know. So when Mr. Reagan asked again, my reply was, "No—when do I start?"

I planned to serve as finance director for only a year, and the law firm reluctantly agreed to my taking a leave of absence. I think by then the firm realized that practicing law was not my top priority.

The salary of the director of finance was about $30,000, which was a significant cut in pay from the law firm, and there was no living expense allowance. My wife noted that I had cut my own income and doubled my expenses—which made me seem a very dubious budget director.

In any event, I accepted the position, and we rented another apartment in Sacramento across the park from the Senator Hotel and fairly close to the one we had rented when I was in the legislature. Our new apartment was later Governor Jerry Brown's "pad," as he called it (which he chose over living in the newly built governor's mansion). Apparently, he moved all the furniture out and slept on the floor in accordance with his widely publicized monastic views, and he was pleased to describe it as spartan. But we found it very comfortable with the furniture in, and it had a splendid view of the beautiful park and Capitol grounds.

It was only a short, pleasant walk from there to my office, which was on the ground floor of the Capitol and faced the same beautiful park. The governor had flowers from the gardens in the park grounds brought to his office daily, and I quickly got my office on the list too. The gardeners were delighted to have somebody else who liked flowers. However, I was not fond of potted palms, which were the standard decor—I did not want any reminder of the jungle—so I immediately had the regular-issue plants removed from my office in favor of fresh, multicolored flowers.

I was sworn in on March 1, 1968, in the governor's office, with Jane and my brother, Peter, and most of the other cabinet members in attendance. As I recall, there was a San Francisco newspaper strike on at that time, so my hometown saw very little coverage of the event. In fact, the news apparently barely made it around Sacramento, as I learned shortly after I took office. I was to attend a press conference by the governor, to which only the governor's staff and cabinet and properly credentialed members of the press were admitted. I was held back at the door by a policeman who did not know I was the new director of finance. One of the governor's secretaries ultimately got me in. I found the whole thing very funny. Incidentally, that incident *did* make the papers.

What was not so amusing, however, was the shape of the state's finances. In fact, in a postscript on his letter of appointment to me, Governor Reagan wrote, "By now, you must think you've been appointed receiver in a bankruptcy case." The state was still operating in fiscal year 1967–68, the budget for which had been prepared by the previous administration. Governor Brown had left a deficit of nearly $1 billion, but by using some dubious accounting methods, he had been able to show the budget closer to balance than it actually was and thus avoid raising taxes in an election year. This accrual method allowed him to reflect, on the books, revenue to be received as if it had already been received, making it appear that there was enough revenue to cover expenditures.

The California State Constitution required a balanced budget, and Governor Reagan most reluctantly concluded that he could close the huge deficit only by raising taxes even though that went against everything he stood for. He succeeded in pushing a large tax increase through during his first year in office, and it did not meet with *too* much public resistance, probably largely because the governor was able to explain effectively to the people the nature and scope of the financial mess in which the state found itself. And the Democrats really could not criticize the tax increase because they knew the dire fiscal situation was largely their doing.

The combination of the governor's first-year tax increase and some budget cuts resulted in a surplus of about $100 million. Reagan wanted to give the surplus revenue back to the people. I said that sounded great, but of course it had never been done before. To which he replied, 'Well, we've never had an actor for governor before either." Governor Reagan went directly to the people, immediately appearing on television to announce the surplus and the intended refund—a tactic which thwarted potential opposition in the legislature. Most of the refund was in the form of a 10 percent rebate on 1970 income taxes, and it was enormously popular.

But the governor believed that, in addition, there needed to be fundamental reform of the tax system. Californians were paying too much,* and the state was spending too much. The best way to impose fiscal discipline, Governor Reagan felt, was to limit the amount of taxes that could be collected by fixing an objective standard, such as the previous year's expenditures plus inflation. This novel idea was bitterly opposed by the lobbyists, particularly the education lobby. We actually qualified a revenue-limitation measure for the state ballot (by obtaining the required number of signatures), but sadly, it was defeated, largely because of the argument that it would force local taxes higher. This would have been true only if local governments refused to cut their own expenditures, but the scare tactic used by the governor's opponents succeeded in inflicting a rare loss on him. Even so, the people recognized that he had been the one trying to hold their taxes down.

Another component of the governor's 1969 tax reform plan was to reduce the regressive residential real estate tax and to shift more than half of it to three other imposts that are directly related to ability to pay: sales tax, income tax, and nonresidential real estate taxes. That new state revenue would then be used to finance a large part of the

---

* In the second decade of the century, it took the average citizen only a couple of weeks to earn enough to pay his whole year's taxes. By 1970, it took over three months, with thirty-seven cents of every dollar going to the government. Of course, it's even worse today.

cost of public schools. Unfortunately, several senators in the Democrat-controlled legislature blocked the proposal. It was not until much later that California's real estate taxes were finally reduced by the famous Proposition 13 in 1978.

In addition to the governor's tax reduction efforts, I recommended ways to improve the administration of taxes as well. I thought it would be much better to put all of the responsibilities for administering and collecting taxes into a single new department headed by an official appointed by the governor. The existing laws split the tax responsibilities between the Franchise Tax Board (consisting of independently elected state officers, serving ex officio) and the independently elected Board of Equalization. A new Department of Revenue, I estimated, could save up to $7 million a year, which was a fair-sized saving then.

Another of my suggestions was that the state adopt a carbon copy of the federal tax return—that is, when you filed your federal return, you would simply make a carbon copy for the state and pay California at a rate designed to bring in the same revenue as the state's income tax. This caused a great outcry, primarily among the Franchise Tax Board employees, who correctly saw that they would be out of a job. They raised the specious argument that the carbon copy tax return would infringe on "California's sovereignty," but the voters, in 1966, had only narrowly rejected a constitutional amendment authorizing the change. I had advocated both of these ideas back when I was in the legislature, but there, too, without success.

I made one additional suggestion to Governor Reagan, based on my legislative proposals. This was to get rid of duplicate taxation and burdensome and redundant filing requirements. I urged that we eliminate California's gift and estate taxes, as these areas were already taxed heavily at the federal level. In return, the state would get something back on the federal collection of income taxes. Unfortunately, this proposal was never put into effect either.

Along with tax reform, Governor Reagan and I believed that it was imperative to reduce expenditures significantly as well. Indeed, one of the first things the governor had wanted to do as soon as he took office was to implement a 10 percent across-the-board spending cut. But he found that was not possible because close to two-thirds of the budget was made up of dedicated funds—special funds automatically allocated by law for specific purposes—which had to be paid on a regular basis regardless of revenue or other factors. To change any of these automatic allocations, the legislature would have to agree, a most unlikely event, particularly since Democrats controlled the legislature for six of Governor Reagan's eight years in office.

So there was very little room for discretionary cuts, and those could be made only from the remaining one-third of the budget. That one-third of the budget comprised the General Fund, which funded things like some education programs, welfare, health, construction, bond interest, and conservation programs. So if there were to be any real overall reductions, we had to hit some of these politically sensitive areas very hard. For example, in the 1969–70 budget, in order to achieve a tax reduction and a balanced budget, and also to fund sufficiently the governor's priorities, such as school aid and care for the mentally ill, we had to reduce other General Fund expenditures by more than $500 million. Still, each year's budget was higher than the previous one, due largely to the untouchable dedicated funds. Initially, we were able, at least, to hold down the *rate* of increase.

As I had in the legislature, I tried, again unsuccessfully, to get some of the dedicated funds released. For example, I wanted to make some of the highway gas tax monies available for rapid-transit construction. But, as with all of the dedicated funds, the gas tax highway fund was backed by strong, entrenched special-interest groups. My suggestion was opposed by the highway construction lobby, gas companies, automobile clubs, and a number of labor unions, none of whom wanted any of "their" gas tax money diverted for other uses. There always seemed to be a large number of opponents to everything I wanted to do!

One way I *was* able to address the governor's desire for budget cuts was to switch from the standard, long-used budget procedure to the so-called program budget. Under the existing method, each agency's budget was basically determined by taking the amount it had had the previous year and adding cost-of-living and salary increases—in other words, automatically funding the same things each year, only at a higher price.

What I did, in effect, was to go back and start from zero (so-called zero-basing) and then try to determine what each department really needed for the programs we wanted to continue. The program budget incorporating these concepts (which we fully adopted for the first time in the fiscal year 1969–70 budget) thus enabled us to see more than just how much it cost a particular department for all of its employees, typewriters, automobiles, and so on. The program budget allowed us to determine the cost of a particular program, such as firefighting, educating undergraduates, or improving safety on the highways. It also gave us the opportunity, by measuring the amount of effort and dollars that we put into a program and, even more important, by measuring the results we got from that program, to determine whether the results justified the cost.

Oddly enough, one of the greatest difficulties we encountered in switching from the traditional to the program budget was the reluctance—and, in some cases, the inability—of various departments to put into simple, understandable narratives precisely what it was their department was doing, why they were doing it, and what results they hoped to achieve.

Hand in hand with the new program budgeting, I also tried to get away from the general practice of having the departments independently determine their budgets and then submit their requests to the Department of Finance. Those requests, for the most part, had been included in the state budget, so each year's budget was bound to be larger than its predecessor. Instead, we began giving the departments and agencies guidelines so that their budgets would fit into our overall estimates of revenue. This was important because of the state constitutional requirement of a balanced budget. This is also what I did later in Washington at the Office of Management and Budget.

It was bound to be an inaccurate science, because all revenue estimates were based on guesses of future economic activity—inflation, employment, sales tax revenues, and so forth. And these estimates (which had to be done eighteen to twenty months ahead) had one distinguishing feature: they were always wrong. But we always tried to make them as accurate as possible because, as I frequently pointed out to the governor, the state was not a business—we were not aiming for a surplus; we needed to have only enough revenue to pay for necessary and effective programs. The governor agreed and frequently used the phrase "If a government has a surplus, it is because taxes are too high."

It was also while I was director of finance that we began the practice of trying to make five-year estimates. With those, I wanted to show the long-term implications of passing a new program. We might be able to fund a new program this year, but what is it going to cost in subsequent years? By doing that, the governor, and particularly the legislature, could see what effect adopting a new program (or expanding an old one) might have down the road.

As director of finance, I tried to be involved in all aspects of the budget process. I held hearings and personally met with the department and agency heads to go through their budgets and to instill in everybody the Reagan administration's policy to *reduce* spending overall and not just to finance all program desires, particularly when doing that would require a tax increase.

I also, of course, represented the administration on fiscal matters in the legislature, as our first objective was to secure passage of the governor's budget. The first year I was there, the budget negotiations went into the night of June 30, the last day of the fiscal year and the date when the existing appropriations ran out. Around 3 A.M., the lights all went out in the Capitol. I joked that the Sacramento Municipal Utilities District had assumed that they were obviously not going to be paid, so they shut the lights off. Actually, somebody had accidentally cut a cable, but the timing could not have been more appropriate.

The following year, the legislature was again a few days late in passing the budget act—which has happened many times since, but that was one of the first times. When the press asked me what was going to happen, I facetiously said that the first thing we'd have to do if the legislature failed to pass any budget was to dismiss the guards at all the jails and mental institutions. This was quoted in newspapers across the state and might have helped put additional pressure on the legislature to pass our budget.

All of our efforts to keep spending down and to keep taxes and government intrusion from becoming onerous and stifling were important factors in maintaining the state's strong economy and impressive prosperity. By 1970, if California had been a country, its gross national product would have been sixth in the world, and Governor Reagan was determined not to let anything interfere with that.

My duties as director of finance, happily for me, went far beyond budgetary matters. I was a member of the governor's small cabinet, which met at least once a week in the large conference room just off the governor's office. The room evoked the Old West, with a huge Mission-style table and heavy, high-backed Spanish chairs. In many ways, the atmosphere reflected qualities of the governor himself: solid, uncomplicated, and surefooted.

As a cabinet officer and fiscal adviser, I recommended to Governor Reagan whether to sign or veto any bill that had a fiscal impact (and that was most bills).

During cabinet meetings, Governor Reagan would ask a few questions, but mostly he just listened as we made presentations to him and discussed the issues at hand. He normally did not make a decision right then, particularly on more contentious questions; he would take in everything that was said, and after his questions had been answered, he would move on to the next agenda item. Typically there were many items. Bill Clark, as the executive secretary to the governor, was instrumental in formulating an inclusive agenda and keeping all of us on track. In many ways, our cabinet meetings were more substantive and helpful than many of the federal cabinet sessions in which I later participated.

Governor Reagan has sometimes been characterized as being absentminded or uninterested because he was not more active in the discussions. On the contrary, he clearly weighed each issue carefully and thoughtfully, and it was important to him to hear all sides. It was clear from his questions that he knew exactly what were the issues and the implications of his decisions. He did not want us to present a united front just for the sake of consensus; he preferred to hear the pros and cons discussed in front of him, so that he could make an informed decision himself. And he was anxious that our comments not be filtered. Further evidence of this was that he established a direct phone line to his desk for each cabinet member, always assuring full access. I could see him virtually at will. When you walked in, he always seemed delighted to see you.

Of course, I tried not to take advantage of this wide-open access very often, but it was particularly important to have during the all-consuming task of preparing the budget.

In addition to my duties as a member of the cabinet, along with three or four others, I informally assisted the governor in preparing for press conferences, which he held at least once a week. We would brief him on a variety of issues that were likely to come up. With his extraordinarily retentive memory, he did extremely well in press conferences. Questions out of the blue did not faze him, but if he felt that someone else could answer a particular question better than he could, he would ask one of us, who always stood in the back, to supply an answer. Though he rarely needed to call on us, it was rather like modern-day presidential press conferences—anxious staff members were always there standing along the wall.

At the start, the press was somewhat hostile toward Governor Reagan because they felt it was a serious aberration in the state's history that this untutored movie actor was governor. Moreover, so many of his views violated the conventional wisdom that many in the press automatically opposed him. But that feeling was soon erased; it was impossible to dislike Ronald Reagan or to doubt that he was serious about improving state government. The press in Sacramento were much more objective than the press in Washington. Reporters in Washington were essentially advocates of liberal causes and very adversarial.

Occasionally I would also help Governor Reagan prepare some of his speeches, though he wrote quite a few of his own. I always felt his own were the best. But often he did not need a written speech or even very much lead time before an event. The governor had the impressive ability to absorb a cursory briefing—about his audience and its main concerns—in the car on the way to the speaking engagement, and then he would deliver a most eloquent, thoughtful talk that delighted his audience.

Humor, in both content and delivery, was one of the governor's strongest points. He liked people to be happy, and to leave people laughing, and so he would always try to open and close a meeting or a speech with a joke of some kind, most of which were very funny and set the stage for a receptive audience, no matter their initial feelings toward him.

Even hostile reporters couldn't hide Reagan's easy, genuine, and natural wit. It helped establish warm, personal relationships between himself and other leaders. This, in turn, often surmounted policy differences they might have had. I remember one meeting, when he was president, with Canadian prime minister Brian Mulroney. They each had thick briefing books covering serious issues like acid rain and trade. Reagan began by telling an Irish joke. Mulroney responded in kind, and they traded jokes for almost half an hour before they even touched the briefing books. It was frequently said of Reagan that he could quickly make a warm admirer out of almost anyone, but for the people who really hated him and his views, it sometimes took as long as ten minutes.

This great friendliness did not translate into going soft on his principles and beliefs. When he was governor, I heard some political advisers warn him that his proposed budget cuts in education spending were seen by many as dooming his chances for reelection. He responded, characteristically, "But I didn't come up here to get reelected." He also asked how, if teachers were not doing a good job (as was frequently pointed out), paying them more was going to help. No one could answer that.

This is not to imply that Governor Reagan was antieducation; he simply felt that no one should be exempt from fiscal belt-tightening, which was not stringent in any event. He proposed, for example, not *cutting* the budgets of the University of California and the state colleges but simply holding down the rate of increase and securing some revenue by small tuition charges.* As veteran political reporter Lou Cannon put it, "The university, which for years had demanded and received the cream of the state budget, was now being served skim milk"†—but it *was* being served.

---

* Charging tuition was a revolutionary idea for California at that time—and one only reluctantly agreed to by the UC Board of Regents. Governor Reagan felt strongly about this issue, often saying that "higher education in our state colleges and universities is not a right, it is a privilege."

† Lou Cannon, *Ronnie and Jesse: A Political Odyssey* (New York: Doubleday, 1969), 231.

Governor Reagan was heatedly opposed by narrow special-interest groups, but he enjoyed wide popularity and support. He was saying and doing things many people believed in but that had not been said before by government officials. By 1968, a group of Reagan loyalists was pushing the governor hard to run for president. I was not in favor because I thought he should finish his gubernatorial term. I'm not sure that the governor himself ever really authorized a campaign. It was only at the Republican convention that year that he reluctantly allowed his name to be presented as a candidate. But he was a realist, and though he received quite a few votes, he quickly told backers to support Richard Nixon, which they did—though the Nixon people continued to harbor a distrust of the Reagan people.*

Still, I campaigned for Nixon and thought he was far superior to the Democratic candidate, Vice President Hubert Humphrey, on the big issues of the day. I was, of course, so busy as director of finance of California that my participation was limited just to making a few speeches.

In fact, I was so completely absorbed with California's fiscal affairs and state matters that I did not pay as much attention as I should have to national and international issues. And there was indeed a great deal going on in the country and the world during those years—1968 and 1969. Of course, the biggest of all issues was the Vietnam War.

I thought America's involvement in the conflict was fair enough, but I was disturbed that we were trying only to "contain" Commu-

---

* Although I was basically opposed to a Reagan candidacy for president at that particular time, I did, as a member of his cabinet, attend the convention, as did my son. Cap Jr. had studied film at Harvard and had become quite fascinated with it. So, for the convention, he created and produced a triple slide show on Governor Reagan's record in California called "The Governor Who Turned the State Around." This was one of the early uses of three screens to show a series of slides simultaneously, creating the effect almost of a moving picture.

nism rather than win the war. I thought it was very wrong to ask our soldiers to risk their lives for a war we did not consider important enough to win. I also thought it impossible, as time went on, to fight a war abroad at the same time we were fighting the American people's opposition to the war at home. These vivid impressions influenced me many years later, when I was secretary of defense.

The Vietnam War affected my own family only peripherally. My daughter, Arlin, was married in 1965, and shortly thereafter she and her husband moved to Canada because both opposed the war and he was anxious not to be drafted to serve in it. Of course this was very distressing for me and our family. My wife and I were particularly unhappy that Arlin was not able to come back into the United States freely as long as she was married to someone who was evading American law. After a few years, she apparently reached the same conclusion. She divorced and returned alone to live in San Francisco, and my wife and I were delighted to have her back.

Our son, Caspar Jr., was not eligible for the military because he has no hearing in one ear. He graduated from Harvard in 1968, which coordinated nicely with my own thirtieth class reunion. My mother, my wife, and I attended Cap Jr.'s commencement, as well as some of my reunion activities. The atmosphere in Cambridge still had a comforting familiarity to it. There were a few visible signs of the tumultuous unrest sweeping college campuses across the rest of the country. (Later, of course, and to my considerable surprise, this unrest engulfed Harvard too, with University Hall being occupied by rioters.) Even the graduation ceremony was much the same as in 1938. There were a few changes: Cap Jr. received his diploma at Dunster House rather than in the Yard. And this occasion was particularly special for my mother because she and my father had not been able to attend my commencement.

After Cap Jr.'s graduation, he became a producer for KRON, a San Francisco television station owned by the Chronicle Publishing

Company. He enjoyed it and even won a prize for a documentary he produced and directed about the strains and stresses of being an air traffic controller.

In September of 1969, my wife and I went to Europe—our first vacation in several years. But after only a few days there, my son called from San Francisco and said he had some bad news. I assumed that meant my mother had fallen ill or died; she was then eighty-three. I could not believe it when he said my brother, Peter, had died. He was fifty-five—only three years older than I. He had had a sudden heart attack while in San Francisco.

It was a great shock, and naturally I began revisiting in my mind all the good times we had had together and the support he had given me, particularly in my political endeavors. He had come to my swearing-in ceremony and was very proud when I became director of finance.

About a year before that, he himself had been appointed to Governor Reagan's administration as director of employment, and in early 1969 he became head of the Department of Industrial Relations. People may have assumed that since he was my brother I would give his department special treatment or exemption from budget cuts, but that was not the case. He came in and made his presentation, and I asked the usual questions (bound to be found unpleasant by department heads), and ultimately we did knock his budget back a bit. I had not seen him much lately, however, as we were both busy with our respective jobs. As a result, my grief was compounded by my anguished thoughts of what I should have done differently and by wishes that I had spent more time with him during his short life.

I returned to San Francisco for his services and to try to be of some help to my mother and Peter's widow and their four sons. I was particularly concerned about my mother and how she would handle Peter's death. She simply refused to accept or acknowledge it—a reaction her doctor called "automatic rejection," or denial. From that time on, she was confused about who various people were. Her altered state of mind was very difficult to witness, but I think it was really the only way she was able to go on.

It became clear that she should no longer live by herself, so it was decided that she would move into our home in Hillsborough.

Peter's death was a shock, but I think Peter had been afraid of a heart attack ever since our father had died so unexpectedly of a massive and sudden coronary occlusion. He was similar in build—thick and strong through the chest and arms—and, also like Dad, Peter had always enjoyed good health, even prided himself on it. Neither had ever had any previous signs of heart trouble.

I have never paid much attention to my own health, and, aside from my childhood mastoid problems, I have been free of most health problems until very recently.

Of course, there were the usual stresses and long hours that go along with such a demanding job as finance director, and I undoubtedly added a lot to that by insisting on actually reading the entire budget. I also wanted personally to see as much of the correspondence, both incoming and outgoing, as I could, so I usually spent at least twelve hours at the office each day, and then I would take two or three briefcases of work home in the evenings.

But I did not mind any of that because the post was a marvelous platform from which to see the whole government in action. My longtime interest in state government never flagged the whole time I served in it. I enjoyed it all thoroughly—participating in the cabinet and staff meetings, advising the governor on a wide range of issues, hearing the department heads present their budgets, and trying to make all the pieces fit into an overall budget plan. I learned and gained experience in a number of areas that helped me later in the federal government: I was running a large organization and working with a large variety of problems that had an important bearing on the way the government works. I was also dealing with both the legislative and executive branches, as well as the press. For someone as fascinated as I was in all things governmental, being director of finance was really an ideal position. I always said it was no way to earn a living, but it was a lot of fun.

My wife, however, was not nearly as enthusiastic about it. She did not like the demands of the job, the long hours, the being "onstage" constantly, and she was anxious to get back to a quieter, more private way of life. She had always urged people to contribute something to their community, and she believed, as I did, that you cannot have a democracy unless everyone participates, but by this time, she had come to feel that I had overdone it. So she was not very pleased when, in the late summer of 1969, I got a call from Washington.

CHAPTER 11

JUMPING RIGHT OFF
THE DOCK

On August 5, 1969, White House aide Peter Flanigan called me in Sacramento and told me that President Nixon was interested in having me come to Washington to head either the Federal Trade Commission (FTC) or the Federal Communications Commission (FCC).

This took me completely by surprise. I was flattered and wanted to learn more about what they had in mind, but I did not feel that I could take the time out from my budget work just then to go to Washington. From midsummer to December was the heart of the budget timetable in California. Peter Flanigan then offered to have his deputy, Jon Rose, meet me halfway in Chicago so that I could return to Sacramento the same day. I agreed because I wanted to know far more about both the FTC and the FCC before I made a decision.

I flew to Chicago a few days later, but when I landed at O'Hare, there was no Jon Rose to be seen. Just as I was about to leave, a red-faced young man rushed up to me, out of breath and apologetic. He announced himself as Jon Rose, and he had apparently run the length of the concourse. Stout and short and a bit flustered, he quickly proved himself to be extraordinarily friendly and helpful—and clearly anxious to succeed in his mission, which apparently was to persuade me to take the post at the FTC.

We settled into a relatively quiet airport conference room, and he gave me a frank assessment of the sorry state of the FTC[*] and the heavy criticisms that had been levied at it from diverse sources. When I asked whether there would be any other Republican appointees named to the FTC, he said no, that I would fill the only GOP vacancy and that the president would name me as chairman. It could not be described as an especially appealing offer, but the challenge of trying to do something that obviously needed doing was a point in its favor as far as I was concerned.

In the following weeks, I met with Peter Flanigan and, later, with President Nixon himself at San Clemente to discuss it. This was the first time I had visited San Clemente, the president's home in California. The compound was on a bluff, with trails leading to the beach. The residence itself was in the Spanish Mission style and sat well in from the ocean. There were various other buildings, standard utilitarian temporary structures, where most meetings were held.

Physically, Nixon seemed much the same as he had been in the 1950s. But there was also an intangible aura about him, as well as numerous appurtenances that come with being president: Secret Service everywhere, numerous staffers hurrying about (staff people rarely moved slowly), and an occasional glimpse of a magisterial Henry Kissinger.

I told the president that I was actually more interested in the Federal Communications Commission because I was more familiar with, and had had some personal experience in, television and radio,

---

[*] I inquired about the FCC, which had sounded more interesting because of my interest in television, but Jon said he thought that was no longer on offer.

but the president felt that there was a greater need for management and guidance at the FTC. The Federal Trade Commission was, as Jon Rose had said, in terrible shape, and it had been the subject of several critical reports, including ones by the American Bar Association and Ralph Nader's group, all of which by that time I had read, along with reports of various congressional hearings. The president wanted me to come back and "clean it up." When I pointed out that I had no experience in consumer protection, an area that was rapidly becoming an important facet of the FTC's responsibility, he said he felt that my unfamiliarity was one of my strongest assets. We needed an "open mind," he said. I tried to tell him there was a difference between an open mind and an empty mind, but he was not interested in arguments. He was convinced that I was the man for the job.

While we were on the subject of the right man for the right job, I took the opportunity of this one-on-one meeting to tell Mr. Nixon that I was delighted to see him as president for several reasons, but particularly because I had always felt somewhat guilty about having urged him to run for governor of California in 1962. He said, "If I hadn't lost that one, I'd never have won this one."

Before we concluded our meeting, he said he wanted to assure me that I would have a full seven-year FTC term, which struck me not as an inducement but as a rather ghastly prospect. I certainly did not want to spend seven years cleaning up the FTC—in fact, I could not imagine doing *any* one thing for seven years. I said that if I came, I would come for only a year to implement the kinds of urgent reforms the commission obviously needed, but then I would return to California. The president smiled and said, "I doubt if you can do the job in just a year, and anyway, I doubt if you will need to go back after only one year."

I think the task appealed to me because it was a major challenge, especially in light of the heavy criticism the agency was receiving. And, too, the fact that this provided an interesting alternative to going back to the routines of law practice after two years as finance director was no small factor.

When I discussed the matter a bit later with Dick Guggenhime, the managing partner at the law firm, he very kindly said he would hold my position for me during my year at the FTC, but my feeling was that if I went to Washington, I might get into a possible conflict-of-interest position without even knowing about it. So I decided I would have to resign entirely from the firm and relinquish my relatively new partnership.

My primary concern, of course, was my responsibility as California's director of finance and my commitment to Governor Reagan. I told the governor and Mrs. Reagan of the FTC offer at their large, ranch-style home in the Los Angeles hills in mid-August. I assured the governor that if I took the Washington post, I would not leave Sacramento before the end of the year, so that I could get the 1970–71 state budget finished. He said he wanted me to stay on in Sacramento but would not object if I went to Washington. As usual, he was able to see the situation in a positive light. It would help the Nixon administration to have more Californians at a federal level, he said. And it might give me some national exposure, which could help if I ever decided to run for the Senate, a thought that he always seemed to have in the back of his mind. Nancy Reagan (who provided the governor with a healthy-looking salad lunch) was more firm in her opposition to my leaving the governor's administration.

I finally concluded that I had done as much as I could do as director of finance in the nearly two years I had been there, and I kept thinking that I should not turn down a request from a president. I suppose I accepted mostly out of a sense of duty and a desire to help the Nixon administration, which I had strongly supported.

On August 29, I called the White House and accepted the FTC chairmanship. Then I told the governor I had decided. He was very complimentary about my service as finance director, and he said he hoped I'd be a frequent visitor in Sacramento.

My wife was not enthusiastic about moving to Washington, or, perhaps more precisely, moving away from our home and family, and I admit I too was not all that eager to pull up my California roots and sell our lovely home in Hillsborough. On the other hand, we both knew that I would find little satisfaction if I returned to the law practice and that this new opportunity might be something I would really enjoy doing. As she has so gallantly and selflessly done so many times, before and since, Jane rallied to support the decision.

I was fortunate to have my own personal "advance man," so to speak: my good friend Bill Clark, who had left Governor Reagan's administration to become a California judge.[*] He knew that I was busy with the budget until the end of the year, so he took a leave of absence from the bench and, with his family, went back to Washington for a couple of months in late 1969 and, in effect, laid all the groundwork for me. He made it a smooth transition indeed. He set up my office; he met a lot of the permanent civil service staff and advised me as to which ones he thought were the most reliable; and he interviewed a number of people for appointive positions and recommended good candidates to me. He was extraordinarily helpful and truly a great friend to spend his time, including his Christmas, smoothing the way for me so that when I arrived in Washington, everything was ready. This enabled me to concentrate on finishing my work on the budget and to prepare for my confirmation hearings and our move.

---

[*] Bill later was appointed to be a justice on the California Supreme Court and, still later, came to Washington as President Reagan's deputy secretary of state, national security adviser, and secretary of the interior.

On October 1, I held a press conference (embargoed until the next day, at Washington's request) in Sacramento to announce my appointment. It was important to me to make clear that I was not leaving Governor Reagan's administration because of any dissatisfaction with him or with my job there, and I tried to convey that in my announcement. It was also at this press conference, I believe, that I was asked what was the prime requirement for a director of finance. I replied, "Survival," almost without pausing to think.

On October 2, I flew to Washington for the official announcement at the White House, followed by a press conference with the White House press corps. This was my first encounter with the Washington media, and they seemed notably different from their California counterparts. Reporters' questions in Sacramento showed genuine interest in government and in establishing facts about a policy. In Washington, however, the questions were designed to elicit controversy. They seemed particularly interested in my views on smoking and tobacco policy. Some appeared quite gleeful when I said I did not smoke.

I later learned that the Senate disapproved of press conferences held prior to confirmation, because senators wanted the first chance to question an appointee. I never held a preconfirmation press conference again.

My arrival in Washington also meant my first visit to the White House. The building inspired a feeling of awe and wonder—accompanied by some degree of astonishment at my being there at all. No matter how often I was there after that time, those feelings were just as strong, and the sense of history was palpable.

In mid-October, I made another quick trip to Washington, making the required courtesy calls on several senators and congressmen. I called not only on the senators on the Commerce Committee, the committee that would vote on my confirmation, but also on senators and congressmen with whose committees I would deal after taking office (assuming I was confirmed), such as the Appropriations and

Judiciary Committees. Generally, they were courteous and interested in my views and experience (which was virtually nil at the time), and some went out of their way to make me feel at home.

When I returned to Sacramento, I spent as much time as I could trying to prepare for my confirmation hearing. which was very much like an oral examination for a degree. I felt it especially important to try to be familiar with everything the commission might have done or might be doing in the future. I tried to anticipate the questions as much as I could; I succeeded to some extent, but I was pretty much on my own as far as learning about the FTC ahead of time.

I talked with members of the commission, most of whom were Democrats. One, however, was particularly helpful—retiring commission member James Nicholson.* Nicholson was a Democrat, but he was interested in reforming the FTC and thought I could bring positive change. He even came to Sacramento to help me in my preparation and provided me with valuable thumbnail sketches of my new colleagues-to-be. He was most helpful, and I immediately felt I could trust him completely.

My confirmation hearing took place in mid-November 1969 in a Senate committee room, the physical arrangement of which was most imposing. The committee members were seated a long way from the witnesses—and several steps above them and the audience. Authority was clearly delineated by the massive, curved wooden bench from behind which they peered down. The arrangement was similar to the grand dais with which I had become familiar in appellate courtrooms, but this was on an even more intimidating scale. I was surprised and impressed also with the large number of staff,

---

* It was his resignation that created the vacancy I filled. I replaced him as a commissioner, but he had not been chairman. Rand Dixon had been chairman for many years, and when President Nixon named me as chairman, he had to step down but remained on as a member of the commission.

press, and others who were present. I suppose this was probably in part because I was a new appointee and also because of the vast number of special-interest groups that were concerned with the FTC.

Some of the committee members' questions were designed to discern my attitude and the positions I would take on various matters, such as consumer affairs, warnings on tobacco products, and advertising. But the senators were mainly concerned with my thoughts on the FTC's relationship with Congress and with the president. I told them frankly that since I would be head of an independent regulatory agency, appointed by the president, the Congress would not be my primary allegiance. Many in Congress believed they owned these independent agencies. My incautious remarks angered several senators and congressmen, particularly Senator Warren Magnuson, chairman of the Commerce Committee, who rather pointedly asserted that the Federal Trade Commission was an arm of Congress and that the only connection the president had with the agency was the power to appoint commissioners. Chairman Magnuson then and later was generally pleasant to me personally but remained prickly on several issues.

On November 19, the day after my hearing, the full Senate confirmed my nomination.

On that same trip to Washington, Jane and I looked at homes in the Georgetown, Kalorama, and Capitol Hill areas. We finally settled on a narrow, yellow, three-story row house on Capitol Hill, mostly because it had a small pool, which Jane would enjoy. It was not all that far from the Federal Trade Commission building at Sixth and Pennsylvania Avenue, and local legend had it that Abraham Lincoln had lived nearby during his one term in Congress. On pleasant days, I walked down the hill to the FTC building, even though I had a driver assigned to me. Our real estate agent tried to talk us out of living in the Capitol Hill neighborhood because of its higher crime rate, but it seemed all right to me, and besides, I did not expect that we would be there more than a year. I often walked our beautiful collie, "Mr. Buffington," on the grounds of the Supreme Court and around the construction site for the new Library of Congress Madison Building, and never had any problem with crime, although the papers reported various holdups and shootings in the area.

There was one other interesting thing about the neighborhood, which I learned after we were actually living there: for a time, whole blocks were classified by the always strange District government as eligible for welfare benefits, so at one point we qualified simply by virtue of where we lived, and an "outreach office" suggested that we should apply.

After my confirmation I returned to California and the governor held a splendid farewell dinner for me at the executive residence.* Governor Reagan appointed the able and affable Verne Orr to succeed me as director of finance. Orr had been a deputy in the Finance Department and was later appointed, at my request, to be secretary of the air force when I was secretary of defense under President Reagan.

In late December 1969, with the California budget completed and ready for submission to the legislature, and after a final Christmas in our wonderful, large Hillsborough living room (which looked as if it had been designed for Christmas), my collie and I flew to Washington to start moving into our new home in Washington. Bill Clark assisted even with that, helping me and the movers carry pieces into the house. On December 31, Jane and my mother followed. Arlin came down from Toronto to help, too, and that is how I met the press.

---

* The partners and staff of my law firm also gave a fine farewell dinner for me at a private San Francisco luncheon club, the Villa Taverna. I have always been fond of the Villa Taverna, which was named after the U.S. ambassador's residence in Rome and offers a most pleasant atmosphere in a simple, Italian tavern–like setting.

Jane had arranged for someone to come help for a few days. So when the bell rang (our first visitor), Arlin went to the door to see a pleasant, brisk, tall young lady—obviously the new helper. Arlin was unpacking and making up beds and invited her to help. The lady said she would like to meet me and promptly began asking pertinent questions about the FTC. When I arrived and began to question her, she turned out to be Nina Totenberg, a TV and radio reporter at PBS, hot on the trail to get the first interview with the new chairman of the FTC.

In addition to the huge task of moving out of Hillsborough and getting the Washington house settled, Jane spent a great deal of time taking care of my mother—and did all this admirably and without complaint. On January 1, we had our first Washington dinner at a small nearby Italian restaurant which had the great advantage of being open New Year's night. We went out because none of our china or utensils had yet been unpacked, there was no food, and the refrigerator did not appear to be working.*

Almost as soon as we arrived, we experienced firsthand, and more glaringly than anywhere else, poor customer service, outright fraud, and other consumer frustrations—the very issues that would occupy much of my time as FTC chairman. Washington is an interesting and most beautiful city, but living there does take patience; I was certain that neither my wife nor I would suffer Potomac Fever.

In the first week we were there, our pipes froze. When the plumber finally came, he said he couldn't do anything about it and that he would be back "in the spring." We were, of course, billed for his "service." (Jane solved the problem by holding a lighted candle up to the pipes until they thawed—a risky procedure, but it worked.)

---

* My wife's description of our move is far better. See *As Ever* by Jane Weinberger (Mount Desert, ME: Windswept House Publishers, 1991).

Prices of furniture went up between the time we looked at it and the time we called to order it only a few hours later. It took weeks to get lamps delivered. I had assumed we could pick them up at the store that afternoon, but a horrified salesman told me they had to come from a warehouse that was at least nine miles away. After living a short while in Washington, I never doubted the need for stronger consumer protection.

There had been complaints that the FTC coddled big business and neglected consumer complaints. President Nixon clearly wanted to change that. When I was sworn in, the president said, "Business had better look out now! On the basis of what Cap Weinberger did in California, he'll make life difficult for them."

My swearing-in, on the afternoon of January 13, 1970, was held at the White House in the Roosevelt Room,* giving my appointment more ceremony than usual. Even President Nixon attended. So did my mother, and when the president came in, she loudly asked, "Why is *he* here?" I explained as quietly as possible that he was the president and he *lived* here. At which point she announced, "I've never liked Nixon." This was quite out of character for my normally quiet and reserved mother, but at least the press seemed not to have heard her.

When asked to raise my right hand to take the oath, photographers and several reporters noted, I for some unfathomable reason raised my left hand. Then, assuming the Bible was mine to keep as a memento, I took the Bible home. Within an hour, H. R. Haldeman's office was on the phone asking to have it returned, presumably so it could be used for the next event.

The chairman's office at the FTC was still occupied by the previous chairman, Rand Dixon, a hearty southern, courthouse-type politician

---

* When a Republican is president, Theodore Roosevelt's portrait hangs above the mantel; FDR's portrait graces the spot in Democratic administrations.

and Democrat. He was even friendlier when I told him he could keep his big office and that I would take another. This was as practical as it was generous. I did not see any way he could possibly move out—it was the most cluttered place I had ever seen. It looked like about six antique shops merged into one big room.

The office I took was big enough for me, and comfortable. My secretary thought it needed a fireplace, but when she gave me the General Services estimate of the cost, I decided I'd much prefer not to read about the expense in the press.

Occasionally, the other commissioners and I held formal hearings up in the commission room, which looked much like an appellate courtroom. We had only three or four formal hearings during the time I was there. Most of the real work was done in closed, once- or twice-weekly informal meetings, which were held in the conference room adjacent to my office. These were more relaxed, and many staff would attend, in addition to the five commissioners.

The commissioners, most of whom had served for several years and had fairly firm agendas of their own, presented quite a set of contrasts. Everette MacIntyre, a Democrat from North Carolina and a longtime commissioner, had formal and courtly manners. I think he did not care for my informal meetings. I generally did not call on people to speak unless two or three were clamoring to do so all at once. If somebody wanted to say something, he or she would just say it, and this went against MacIntyre's style. He was rather like an old English solicitor, slow-spoken and precise, and he always called ahead if he wanted to come in to my office and talk (which was good, because if you were going to have a discussion with Everette MacIntyre, you had to set aside a couple of hours). But he was kindly, extremely polite, and plainly rather puzzled by this California attorney.

Phil Elman was another Democratic commissioner; indeed, he was an almost doctrinaire Democrat. Normally he and I would have been on opposite sides, but we were agreed that the FTC urgently needed reform. We worked well together on procedural matters and had a good personal relationship.

There was only one other Republican commissioner besides myself: Mary Gardiner Jones, an ambitious lawyer who was quite put out when I was appointed chairman. She was a tough lady, more aggressive than I had been used to dealing with. Once, she came into my office and startled me by snarling, "I want to get right down to the facts of this case," as she swung her feet onto my desk. She also smoked cigars.

It was not only among the commissioners that Republicans were in the minority. Almost all of the top staff were Democratic appointees. I felt rather like the British holding India with one battalion; of the roughly 1,200 people at the FTC, I found only one Republican. This was Basil Mezines, who had been a permanent staff member for years and who knew exactly way the commission needed dramatic reform. Bill Clark had told me Mezines could be trusted completely, and Basil soon became my closest adviser.

I brought in some new blood as well. I recruited San Francisco Republican Joe Martin to be general counsel; unfortunately, his arrival was delayed—almost to the time I left the FTC—because the White House staff discovered rumors that Joe's wife was a Communist, which was entirely mad. Joe eventually came on board and did a fine job of furthering my reforms. I also brought in Byron Rumford, my Democratic friend from the California legislature, who was a pharmacist and did a lot of work for us on fair drug pricing. The White House initially opposed his appointment as well, for partisan reasons.

In addition, I decided we should recruit the very best law students to strengthen our legal staff. All large law firms did this, and indeed I had done much of the interviewing at Heller, Ehrman. It seemed, however, an entirely new idea at the FTC—and one that was not looked upon kindly. Two or three of the permanent staff people told me, "This is exactly what we *don't* want. We don't want people who are that good because they're going to leave shortly. We want people who have tried and basically failed elsewhere, and will stay with us for the rest of their career." To me, that attitude explained a great deal about the FTC's problems.

In any event, we recruited several bright young attorneys, starting with the three law clerks authorized for the chairman. The first of these was Will Taft, who, as it turned out, stayed with me all the way to the Defense Department and did a superb job in every post.* In 1970 he was fresh out of Harvard Law School (I was willing to overlook the fact that he had gone to Yale for his undergraduate degree). He had been involved in Ralph Nader's group and its critical report on the FTC. Nader recommended him highly. I interviewed Taft myself and was impressed with how knowledgeable and pleasant he was. I instinctively liked him, and I brought him on board as my chief law clerk and legal adviser. He proved to be an extremely hard worker, and indeed indispensable, especially when it came to doing in-depth research, interpreting staff papers, and things of that kind. Besides his professional contributions, he was simply great fun to work with. He laughed at the same things I did, and he was familiar with the literary allusions I would make from time to time. It made for an easy camaraderie that I have enjoyed ever since.

My other two clerks were Robin Freer and another fine lawyer who was shy and reserved but knowledgeable about the commission. Freer was an ambitious and able young lawyer, eager to work, and energetic. Both were exceptionally good and helpful and had fine subsequent careers.

---

* After his great service at Defense, Will was appointed to be our ambassador to NATO.

Even before I learned firsthand about the FTC's problems, I did not have a very favorable impression of the commission. My only previous association with it had been when my wife and I took our children on a tour of Washington many years before. When we passed by those dreadful, early Soviet powerhouse-style statues of strange-looking men trying to control mighty horses, placed at the sides of the building, my son asked, "What are those?" The guide, an unwitting wit, said, "Oh, they represent the government restraining trade." I fear that was about what I thought, although I had had virtually no experience with the commission in my own practice.

But some had just the opposite opinion. As an *Advertising Age* article put it in 1970, the Federal Trade Commission had been called "the little old lady of Pennsylvania Avenue for half a century, because its timid performance never managed to make any significant impact on the marketing practices it was supposed to police."

In any event, as I started wading into the, for me, unknown depths of the FTC, I began to fear I may well have jumped right off the dock this time. The fact that the American Bar Association (in a study requested by President Nixon) and Ralph Nader's consumer group, which normally would have widely differing viewpoints, had reached similar conclusions after their separate studies should perhaps have given me a hint of what I was getting into.

Among the criticisms of the agency were that its activities were mired in a maze of antiquated procedures and incredibly slow execution. The entrenched, largely incompetent staff would spend two to three years and no one knows how much of the available resources on relatively small or unimportant cases. For example, an inordinate amount of time seemed to be devoted to whether the Robinson Patman Act was being sufficiently enforced. This aroused enormously strong emotions in grown men—including a couple of the commissioners. Rand Dixon had a fixation about upholding and strengthening the act, a measure designed to eliminate any purchasing advantages big business might have had over buyers of small to medium quantities. The problem with that was that it generally meant higher prices for consumers. So it was essentially an expensive subsidy for small business. I thought it was an important enough statute but not one that warranted the whole trade commission devoting so much attention to it.

I also found a curious situation in which the Federal Trade Commission and the Antitrust Division of the Department of Justice had overlapping responsibilities, with no clear line separating the authority between the two. On top of that, the liaison officers between Justice and the FTC were not speaking to each other. One of the original mandates of the FTC was to maintain fair competition in business, but by the beginning of the 1970s the consumer movement had become a groundswell, and I felt that taking on the responsibility for protecting consumers directly was more important than fighting with the Department of Justice over who was going to break up which monopoly. Of course, attacking monopolies was also a broad form of consumer protection, although regarded by consumer activists as too slow and cumbersome.

One of my top priorities at the FTC was to dismiss bureaucrats who did little but attend to the narrow special interests of certain congressmen. One congressman in particular—Joe Evins, a Democrat from Tennessee—was apparently under the misapprehension that he owned the FTC, and probably all of the other independent agencies, for that matter. He had, for a long time, been able to get the commission to do what he wanted because, as chairman of the House Appropriations Subcommittee for Independent Offices, he controlled their budgets. When I let some of his henchmen in the FTC go, Evins immediately retaliated by reducing our appropriations. But this did not have the usual desired effect—I fully agreed that our budget was much too big and should be cut. This confused him and caused quite a stir. Congress had never had anyone ask for a budget reduction.

We replaced marginal staff with bright and vigorous attorneys and professors who had no congressional ties and were eager to work. Then we cleared the dockets of old, relatively trivial cases. One of the more absurd examples that I recall was that the FTC had spent about seven years trying to determine whether Listerine really freshened your breath and whether its advertising was truthful. We also accelerated timetables to resolve cases and reduced the numerous cumbersome tests that were used to decide if a citizen's complaint warranted an investigation.

We reestablished communications with the Department of Justice and also divided our antitrust responsibilities with its Antitrust Division—actions that reduced wasteful bickering over turf. We encouraged businesses to set up policies themselves so that we didn't have to intervene.

Another priority of our reform program was decentralization. I personally visited some of the field offices, including those in Boston, New York, San Francisco, and Chicago, which, I discovered, were not allowed to do much on their own initiative. In late January 1970 I called the heads of each field office to Washington to get their ideas for improved performance. As a result of this and other meetings, we expanded the functions of the regional offices so that they could lead investigations, issue subpoenas, and take cases of deceptive trade practices and restraint-of-trade to trial. We also encouraged them to take an active part in protecting and educating consumers. To this end, I established consumer advisory boards, made up of businessmen and consumers as well as representatives from each level of government, for each of the eleven field offices. These boards basically determined if consumer complaints could be dealt with best at a local, state, or federal level, and by private or governmental organizations. Thus the attorneys-in-charge of the field offices were enthused and the officers reminded that their primary responsibility was to help consumers. This shift from essentially protecting small business—and bureaucratic institutions—to protecting consumers was literally an innovation, the first time the 1938 expansion of the FTC's responsibilities had actually been put into force.

A prevalent consumer complaint was mislabeling. Sometimes labels were just plain false, such as claiming an item was fireproof when actually it was only fire retardant, if that. Other labels were confusing. My favorite was a clothing label that said "Do Not Wash" on one side and "Do Not Dry Clean" on the reverse. In addition to dealing with these problems, I also thought that the public should be given much more product information on the labels so that they could make more informed decisions. We were able to make substantial strides in this area by vigorously enforcing the Truth in Labeling Act, which had been passed by Congress in 1966, and by working with various trade and professional organizations. Of course, advertising was another area where we cracked down on deceptive practices. I always preached that it was not only right but also very good business for all manufacturers and sellers to protect the public.

One company that I frequently cited as an example of how good business practices were indeed good for business was the Chrysler Corporation, which was giving its customers relatively lengthy and nearly unconditional warranties on its new cars—a program that boosted Chrysler sales. Warranties were not federally regulated until the Magnuson-Moss Act was passed in 1975, but many companies had proved the merits and profitability of offering customers such guarantees.

The cigarette industry was another big issue for us. When the surgeon general issued a report in 1964 confirming the link between cigarette smoking and various illnesses, including lung cancer, bronchitis, and even heart disease, FTC Chairman Rand Dixon announced that all cigarette packages and all tobacco advertisements would be required to print a health warning. Tobacco lobbyists argued, successfully, that the FTC's ruling was an usurpation of Congress's power.

The result was the Cigarette Labeling and Advertising Bill of 1965, which was essentially a victory for tobacco. The law made package warnings mandatory but prohibited the Federal Trade Commission, for four years, from requiring any warnings or statements in cigarette advertising.

In 1968 the FTC had strongly recommended banning radio and television cigarette advertisements. This cause was supported in Congress by Senator Warren Magnuson of Washington, chairman of the Senate Commerce Committee, and his Consumer Subcommittee chairman, Frank Moss, a Democrat from Utah. The two senators pushed the Public Health Cigarette Smoking Act through both houses of Congress in March 1970, and President Nixon signed it on April 1 of that year. This act accomplished three things. It prohibited cigarette commercials on television and radio, beginning January 1, 1971; it lifted the ban on FTC action regarding warning requirements for other forms of cigarette advertising; and it strengthened the health warnings already required on package labels. Instead of "Caution: Cigarette smoking may be hazardous to your health," the labels now had to read, "Warning: The Surgeon General has determined that cigarette smoking is dangerous to your health."

Now I notice this has been changed on some ads to the very innocuous "The Surgeon General has determined that smoking contains carbon monoxide."

Predictably, these measures prompted an outcry from the tobacco industry and the television and radio networks. But the cigarette companies, the advertising agencies, and the networks all survived. I hope many American people survived too, thanks to the dangers of smoking being made clear to them.

I personally was convinced of the need to protect the public from the perils of smoking, but my opinion had been formed long before and was based on much less erudite reasoning. When I was four years old, I had found a half-smoked, still-burning cigar on the street near our home in San Francisco, and naturally I tried to smoke it as I had seen others do. I still remember how ill it made me, and I never touched tobacco again. More important, I felt the dangers of smoking were an important consumer issue. Among my advisers on this and other consumer matters were Virginia Knauer, the president's special assistant for consumer affairs, and Elizabeth Hanford (better known now as Elizabeth Dole), who was then her deputy. We even, along with a number of others, held an unplanned "meeting" when we got stuck in an elevator after a White House Correspondents Dinner at the old Sheraton Park Hotel. After about an hour and a half, someone finally rescued us through the trap door in the ceiling of the elevator.

There were a great many dinners and events like that to attend in Washington, which was a comparatively new experience for me. Simply by virtue of being an officeholder, I was automatically invited to many of them—particularly the annual dinners of various trade associations—and I felt that I should appear at a fair number of them to show the government's interest in their activities. But adding this to what were very long days was a novelty that soon wore off and I grew weary of being "onstage" so much of the time.

Indeed there was a great deal to do during the days. As I had in my state government posts, I probably brought a lot of it on myself. The "in-basket" was overflowing at all times, and I tried to look at as much of it myself as I could. A large amount of it was simply informational—various studies, articles, and so forth—and there was a good deal of mail. As always, I particularly wanted to see the mail, congressional and other, and I personally dictated many of the responses. There were also numerous commission staff reports, recommendations for action, and meeting memoranda.

Aside from the paperwork there were regular meetings with the other commissioners, fairly frequent appearances before various congressional committees and subcommittees, phone calls to be made and returned, occasional travel, and many speeches to give. I wrote many of the speeches myself, often in consultation with Basil Mezines and Will Taft.

One of the first talks I gave in Washington was to the antitrust section of the American Bar Association (ABA). and I admit to feeling quite a bit of trepidation. There is always an element of considerable risk in talking to a group of experts about their own specialty. When I was in the California legislature, I found it far easier to talk to people who were not specialists in legislative affairs. My favorite group in that category was the Northern California African Violet Society, which asked me back several times.

Somehow I made it through my rather long-winded speech to the ABA, talking mostly about its report criticizing the FTC and the ways in which I had already addressed, and planned to continue tackling, the problems it raised. The whole evening was made more difficult because the dinner was long delayed but the cocktail hour was not. The lawyers were getting more raucous as time went on. I was pleasantly surprised when Supreme Court Justice William O. Douglas, whom I regarded as an irremediable liberal and who was at the head table, leaned over and said, "Very good, young man," after I finished. I think I liked the "young man" part of the compliment best.

Overall, I feel that we accomplished a great many things during the short time I was at the FTC. We also seemed generally to receive favorable press reports. The press seemed to think that what we were doing was right and necessary, and a number of positive editorials were written. Even Ralph Nader reluctantly gave us some credit.

I enjoyed working on these important issues at a national level, though it certainly was not easy. The biggest challenge was trying to persuade people of many different viewpoints—commissioners, permanent staff, business, consumers, and, of course, members of the

Senate and House—to get together and support the reforms that I felt were necessary. But it was gratifying when that did happen, and we were able to achieve, or at least set in motion, many of those reforms.

I was looking forward to continuing my work through the end of 1970, at which point I planned to return home to San Francisco and, presumably, to the law practice. But in May of that year, I learned that President Nixon had other plans in mind for me.

CHAPTER 12

DR. NO, ALIAS
"CAP THE KNIFE"

y wife and I returned from a meeting in Paris of the Organization for Economic Cooperation and Development (OECD) to a sultry June day in Washington. I had attended this OECD meeting as chairman of the Federal Trade Commission, and it was one of my first experiences at an international gathering representing the United States. When we landed at Dulles Airport, there was a message that the president wanted to see me, and I was to report to the White House immediately.

I was shown into the Oval Office, where President Nixon told me he intended to create a new Office of Management and Budget (OMB), as well as a Domestic Council—two things that had been recommended by the president's Advisory Council on Executive Organization. As the president explained it, "The Domestic Council will be primarily concerned with *what* we do; the Office of Management and Budget will be primarily concerned with *how* we do it, and *how well* we do it."

I was not sure exactly why he was telling me all of this, but I listened with interest. The Domestic Council was basically to parallel in domestic affairs what the National Security Council did with foreign affairs. The OMB was to replace the existing Bureau of the Budget and separate the management and budget-planning functions. To this end, there would be a deputy director for management and a deputy director for the budget. On the basis of my work in California as finance director, the president wanted me to be his first deputy director of OMB on the budget side.

"I want you to do for me what you did for Governor Reagan," he said.

George Shultz was to be shifted from secretary of labor to director of OMB, but the president assured me that I would have full authority and control over the budget; he wanted me to make the same deep budget cuts in the fat federal budget as I had in California's state budget.

The president quickly dismissed my concern that I had not finished my work at the FTC, where I had been less than six months, saying I had made a good start and somebody else could take it from there. Besides, he said, "That's not nearly as important as running the budget of the United States." I agreed to take the post—but one important matter needed to be settled first. Jane was not eager to stay in Washington and had grave reservations about Nixon and my working with him. But, as always, and to my gratitude, she supported my decision.*

On July 2, 1970, George Shultz; Arnold Weber, deputy director for management; James Hodgson, Shultz's replacement at Labor; and I

---

* I was concerned too about my FTC driver. I mentioned this to the White House chief of staff, Bob Haldeman, my friend from California days. I later learned from his book, *The Haldeman Diaries*, that he apparently felt that I wanted to keep my FTC driver simply as a "perk" that I expected in my position. The truth was that I wanted to be sure my driver's tenure would be protected if he came with me to OMB, as he wanted to do. And I was very fond of him. "Sarge" was quite a colorful character. As

were all sworn in at San Clemente, the "Western White House." Jane had come out with me from Washington, and our son and his wife came down from San Francisco. The OMB was now a reality.

Federal law says that a person "cannot hold two positions of honor and trust under the Federal government at the same time," so I drew only one salary, but for a couple of months I handled both my FTC and OMB jobs. I had recommended Bill Clark to succeed me at the FTC, but he declined to take it. He had returned to his judicial duties in California some months before and did not want to change again. Eventually, Miles Kirkpatrick, an excellent lawyer who had written the ABA report on the FTC, was chosen, and he did a fine job continuing the reforms I had begun.

Moving over to OMB meant moving into an office in the Old Executive Office Building. It has always been one of my favorite buildings, with its grand, sweeping staircases, mahogany railings, black and white tile floors, and high ornamental ceilings crowning great long corridors—a total waste of space that would never be permitted in government offices built these days.

My new office had previously been the secretary of war's office, a huge room with a balcony overlooking the Renwick Art Gallery across Pennsylvania Avenue. I have always been fond of light and open spaces, so I had one of the large windows made into a door so that I could go onto the large balcony. My friends joked that this would enable me to make speeches to the huge crowds gathered below. The massive, ornate desk had been Secretary Henry Stimson's

---

an enlisted man in our military, he had been in a Turkish prison for doing considerable damage to a non-U.S. soldier in a bar fight. I never did hear all the details, but it was enough to make it difficult for me to arrange the necessary security clearances for Sarge to follow me to a White House position. I always felt completely safe with him, and he was fiercely loyal to me. Happily, he was able to come to OMB as my driver and retain his same government benefits, so it worked out well for both of us.

and, earlier, General John Pershing's. The whole grand office, with its intricate moldings and a magnificent inlaid hardwood floor (which I discovered when I had an old and very ragged carpet removed), inspired awe and transported one to another era.

There were moments when I could hardly believe it was actually I in these rooms where so much history had happened. I had read volumes of history and had often believed the makers of that history to be larger than life. But now I, a schoolboy from California, was making decisions that might affect the course of history and, indeed, the course of many individual lives.

In the course of one's normal duties and the press of the nation's business, it was easy to forget to appreciate *where* one was. Sometimes, as I passed through the rooms of the West Wing, the White House itself, and the Old Executive Office Building, flashes of history came alive in my mind, from photographs I had seen or simply my own mental pictures that I had attached to the accounts I had read: Lincoln convincing at least some of his cabinet that the time had come to issue the Emancipation Proclamation; Franklin Roosevelt's somber moments in the Oval Office contemplating the speed of our regaining a war-fighting capability in World War II; even Teddy Roosevelt's brood frolicking through the state rooms.

I would generally have lunch in the White House mess, which was in the basement of the White House West Wing. The mess served excellent food, of which I particularly remember the splendid chocolate sundaes; indeed, they were the main reason I liked to go over there.

There were, in fact, *two* White House messes, this being a true Nixon operation. There was a "B" list and an "A" list. Nixon's people were always big on that sort of thing. This was simply due to overzealous, overprotective staff who wanted to insulate the president from any other influences, but it seemed to be a consistent characteristic of the people about him throughout his political career, or at least as long as I knew him.

There were, however, times when appointees were *expected* to be in touch with the president. He was always extremely interested in feedback (assuming it was favorable) on his public speeches, particularly his major Oval Office addresses. There was a standing request for us to listen to all of these speeches, no matter where we were, and to call in our opinions as soon as possible after he finished speaking.

It was from Don Rumsfeld, then head of the White House's "War on Poverty" office, that I learned a good bit of the art of supporting the president. Don and I and several other mid-level administration officials were taking a rare afternoon off in California to visit a new technology exhibit at Disneyland. On our way back to the hotel, we listened to the president on the car radio. No sooner had he finished than Don pulled into a service station, raced in to the telephone, and called in the required message of congratulations. I was impressed.*

I always felt somewhat of an outsider in the Nixon administration, and I doubt that I was the only one. Bob Haldeman and John Ehrlichman were the president's gatekeepers, and they granted minimal access to him.

I had known John Ehrlichman back in California, when he was one of Nixon's advance men and I was the state party chairman. At that

---

* I have been even more impressed with Don's later work, particularly the superb job he did in securing a unanimous report from a highly bipartisan commission of experts as to the nature and proximity of a nuclear threat to the United States. That report, completed in 1998, has done a great deal to convince many doubters that we should proceed with missile defense, and it was, I believe, one of the strong factors influencing President George W. Bush to name Don as defense secretary. This is the first time in our history that a person has been twice named to hold that position, and I know he will serve the president and the country with the same extraordinary skill and dedication as he always has.

time, he was open and friendly, but he had changed a good bit by the time he came to Washington. He rarely returned phone calls. When I walked over to his office to get answers I needed for my budget work, he was annoyed, distant, and buttoned up. George Shultz spoke highly of him, but I lamented the way Ehrlichman had changed.

Haldeman, on the other hand, had not changed at all. He had always been stern and brusque, but at least he would talk to you, and he was extremely efficient. I liked him, and we usually got along well. Haldeman was totally loyal to the president and venerated the office. A good part of his later trouble came from the fact that he seemed to believe that if the president wanted something done, not only did it have to be done but it also must be legal—just because the president wanted it.

The Nixon "inner circle" were difficult to work with, but I was later grateful that I was not close to them or privy to their activities.

I remember one morning when I came into my office and found white plaster powder on the floor near one of the telephone jacks. The White House "plumbers" had put a wiretap on my line (and, I assume, on others' as well) because Haldeman was trying to find out who was leaking to the press. I called him about it that day. He was furious that the workmen had been so careless—but that was all.

Most of the limited contact I had with Haldeman and Ehrlichman was at the daily White House staff meetings in the Roosevelt Room, attended by senior and deputy White House aides and various special advisers to the president. These were basically crisis avoidance meetings, at which participants would give progress reports on whatever issues they were handling and whether any problems were likely to arise. I would report on how the departments and agencies were meeting the budget goals set by the president. Generally, the OMB director presided at these sessions, but I also went because George Shultz did not go to many of our internal budget meetings and I had the most current budget information.

I gave Shultz progress reports almost every day, but he was hard to read and rarely expressed his own opinions until late in a conversation, if at all—all of which I found frustrating. He always seemed perfectly friendly, but I often felt I was representing OMB by myself because of all the meetings I attended. Even though I was only a deputy director, once I was told to be at a meeting of the Defense Policy Review Committee in the White House Situation Room— itself a rather intimidating setting. National Security Adviser Henry Kissinger rushed into the room late, announcing that he had just come from seeing the president. Then he looked around the room and, fixing his gaze on me, he growled, "I thought this meeting was for *senior* officials only." Feeling rather as if my credentials were being challenged, I could only smile and prepare to justify my presence. However, we quickly moved on to substantive matters. I greatly admired Henry then, and my admiration for him has only increased over the years.

After that rather humbling experience, I was surprised by the reaction some of my remarks generated soon after I came to OMB. In a television interview, I mentioned how vital I thought it was to balance the budget, and the next day the stock market plunged. Wall Street did not *want* the budget balanced because that would reduce government spending, and Wall Street *liked* government spending in those days.

I threw myself into this new job, working fourteen or fifteen hours a day. I did not begrudge the long hours for a moment; the OMB offered an unparalleled platform from which to see it all, and it was particularly good fun for someone as fascinated by government as I am.

I made it a point to be extremely well prepared for my congressional testimony on budget issues, especially when I was advocating unpopular budget cuts. I probably spent three times the length of each actual hearing in preparation for the hearing, including having staff people, playing hostile congressmen, bombard me with questions as difficult as they could devise. I was probably a bit too combative in some of my responses, using tactics from debates and cross-examinations in legal trials. I had seen many people testify who were obsequious and subservient, so I probably overdid it a bit in the other direction. I was also conscious of how the hearing would be reported in the press. I knew that if I made concessions for the sake of getting a favorable nod from a congressman, it would be reported that the administration was abandoning its program or wasn't sure of its position.

Hearings were physically wearing, sometimes running up to six hours at a time, during which time congressmen could come and go, but the witness could not. All the while, you had to pay the closest attention to every detail of what was said. My wife often says that I "tune out" sometimes in conversations, but you cannot do that in a hearing. One silly or ill-informed response would be the press focus of a six- or seven-hour hearing.

Dealing with Congress made my position one with inherent difficulties, because with more than three hundred congressional committees and subcommittees authorizing, as President Nixon put it, "spending for their favorite programs without direct regard for what the others are doing," fiscal irresponsibility was the norm, and convincing Congress of the need for fiscal discipline was not easy. There was also an increasing and unfortunate tendency to commit the federal government, through legislation, to outlays many years in advance. I preferred the California style, where the budgets of all departments were included in one bill, which was then considered as a whole by the legislature. In many other respects, the work at OMB was not that different from what I had done in California; you just had to add about nine zeroes to everything.*

---

* It was rather overwhelming at first, dealing in such huge numbers—hundreds of billions of dollars, as opposed to millions, which had been daunting enough. But I grew used to it and occasionally tried to lighten the weight a bit with humor. Shortly after I

The budget process within the OMB began nearly a year before the document was completed and submitted to Congress. In late spring each year, the OMB would hold its Spring Previews, which really entailed first a review of how, and how well, each department was using its previous year's funding. We looked not only at how much was needed in order to continue effective programs but also at what could be reduced or eliminated altogether. I felt that this could be most effectively accomplished by using zero-based budgeting, as I had in California—that is, starting from zero rather than the traditional method of simply increasing the previous year's amount enough to keep up with inflation. I believe I may have been the first to introduce zero-based budgeting on the federal level, and, needless to say, it was not accepted warmly by those who were used to receiving automatic increases without having to justify them.

By early summer, we would arrive at a tentative budget total and then adjust it as necessary according to estimates of revenue, the impact of inflation, any new high-priority programs of the president, new security problems, and so forth. Ultimately, of course, the total was set by the president, based on these factors as well as on OMB's recommendations.

Then we would give the departments the amounts each had to work with for the coming fiscal year and would ask how they would allocate it so that we could measure that against the performance data gathered during our Spring Previews. OMB did not just give a department a lump sum to do with as it pleased; we wanted to know specifically how it intended to use the money. Invariably, every department asked for more—requests I almost always turned down, although I admit I did have my own biases.

---

left OMB, I was asked at a dinner party how a certain agency could have an overrun of $127 million. I couldn't resist responding, "Don't nickel and dime me to death."

I was personally most interested in space exploration and cultural endeavors; many on our staff said I was "soft" on space and the arts. These areas were easy targets for budget cuts because neither had large constituencies. They needed advocacy, and I advocated for them. I was actually able to ensure useful and adequate budgets for them, despite regular calls by some members for reductions or eliminations.

I felt that the government spent a great deal on programs for the aged, the handicapped, and so forth, but very little on things other than redressing existing problems. Of course, funding was needed for many of these programs, but, in my opinion, not enough emphasis was placed on the future of the country—things like programs for gifted children, medical research and development (especially for *preventive* purposes), the arts and humanities, taming the space frontier, and, naturally, a strong defense.

Even then, more than a decade before I went to the Pentagon, I felt that a strong national defense was extremely important. I was and am convinced that if we do not have enough money allocated for defense, we will never know it until it is too late. Nothing can be accomplished if our borders are not safe—that is, unless we have both peace and freedom. So, to me, defense needs must always come first, and I was worried that the winding down of our involvement in Vietnam was leading to unjustifiable defense cuts. In fiscal year 1968, at the height of the Vietnam War, 45 percent of every dollar spent went to defense. The proportion going to human resources and similar programs was 32 percent. Those proportions were exactly reversed in 1973.

My responsibility as deputy director of OMB was to fit every department's budget into the overall budget total set by the president. This usually entailed denying many appeals for increases. My job, much like being director of finance in California, was clearly not conducive to popularity.

In the Fall Reviews, each department had the opportunity to present its problems and requests to the OMB. I met with the department secretaries and their representatives, usually in the same conference room where we held our daily OMB staff meetings, and we took up their requests one by one. They would all try to demonstrate what incredible damage we were doing to the Republic by imposing such a low spending ceiling.* These meetings would be followed by weeks of negotiating with the department heads, in person and by telephone, on the budget figures. They had their responsibilities and I had mine, but I always had in mind that increases in one year would inevitably mean even bigger increases in the following years. Occasionally, a cabinet officer would appeal directly to the president. Since I was in effect representing the president's overall desire for budget cuts, these appeals rarely met with success unless the White House saw some major political advantage in granting them.

Then would come the Director's Review, which took six or seven weeks, ordinarily in the late fall. Despite the name, I was often the one who ran this part of the process as well, even when I was deputy director. I determined all of the departments' final allocations, which were reached after considering and trying to reconcile myriad often-contradictory factors—the departments' own requests and appeals, the president's priorities and the initiatives he wanted to introduce (which would mean cutting back something else he wanted, in order to stay within the overall total), revenue estimates, economic conditions, and factors like that.

---

* No doubt, some of these ceilings may have seemed so low that department heads might have thought they were typographical errors. But in order to avoid raising taxes and fueling inflation, and to allow for administration initiatives, it was imperative that overall federal spending be reined in.

Finally, there was generally a list of ten to twenty decisions that the president would have to make. Getting a response from the president on these was easier said than done. For one thing, as I mentioned earlier, his aides rarely granted direct access. I probably met personally with President Nixon only half a dozen times during an entire budget season, which ran for nearly a year.

One of those times I particularly remember. The president was flying to Paris in November 1970 to attend French president Charles de Gaulle's funeral, and he wanted me to come along to discuss the budget on the flight, even though I was not originally scheduled to attend the funeral. This budget meeting was remarkable not just for the setting, on Air Force One, but also because President Nixon, on his own initiative, wanted to talk about the budget. He was much more interested in foreign affairs than domestic issues, and the budget was generally considered only a domestic matter, although the Defense and State and foreign aid budgets illustrated how thin the boundary between domestic and foreign policy had become. Many people said the president had MEGO—My Eyes Glaze Over—syndrome when they tried talking to him about domestic matters. But on this occasion, he did seem interested in the budget as a whole, and I was able to get some decisions from him.

I also particularly remember this meeting for another reason: Air Force One. It was, of course, very comfortable, as one would expect, but also grand in its simplicity. The most lavish thing about it was that meals (not your standard airline fare) were prepared by the White House chefs and served on White House china. There were several roomy cabins, a couple of conference rooms, and private quarters for the president and his family. A few senior staff and the press were always aboard, assigned to the back of the plane. At one point—I am not sure if it was on this trip—a blue jacket with the Air Force One logo on it was given to each passenger as a souvenir. Unfortunately, mine was later stolen.

Once the president signed off on the budget, it was then sent to be printed. Then the OMB staff and I, along with some White House aides, would spend many hours preparing the President's Budget Message, which accompanies the budget when it is sent to Congress. The budget has to be submitted on a fixed date when Congress reconvenes in January. This is roughly six months before that budget's appropriations are to take effect on July 1. In 1974 Congress moved the start date of the fiscal year to October 1 to give itself more time to consider the budget, but it still managed somehow to delay passage of several of the appropriations bills until after even that new deadline.

The OMB director would hold a major press briefing on the president's budget on the weekend before it went up to the Hill. This was to give the press time to write their stories, which were on an embargoed basis until the budget was released. I was always on hand for this briefing to follow George Shultz's overview with specifics and to answer most of the questions.

Once the administration's budget is in the hands of Congress, it wends its way through all of the various committees and subcommittees, where it is debated, challenged, and invariably criticized as containing not enough of this or too much of that. My primary role during this process was to represent the president and defend his authorization and appropriation budget before all of those committees and subcommittees.

Whether we were dealing with Congress or the executive departments, we in OMB were confronted with near-constant disagreement with the president's budget, so it was important to have a clear objective and remain firm. It was also vital to be ready to explain and defend an enormous amount of detail completely accurately. Even a few slight errors would be seized upon as an excuse for negative votes.

President Nixon's main budgetary concerns were to reduce both the high inflation and unemployment rates. Each was only around 5 percent in 1970, which seems moderate and acceptable now but was considered alarming at the time. I felt, and President Nixon agreed, that the spiraling inflation rate was due largely to the Johnson administration's government-spending policies. President Johnson had tried to conduct the Vietnam War without asking the American people to make any sacrifices at home. He was afraid that making cuts in domestic programs or raising taxes would weaken support for the war, so he charged ahead with full-tilt spending on both the war *and* domestic programs. The deficit as a percentage of gross domestic product soared above 10 percent in the early 1970s.

To combat inflation and bring down unemployment, President Nixon announced on television his New Economic Policy (NEP)[*] on August 15, 1971 (a Sunday evening, purposely chosen before the markets opened Monday morning). One component was a tax package that included personal income tax reductions and a job development tax credit. The NEP also suspended the convertibility of the dollar into gold, an action popularly known then as "closing the gold window," to stop the outward flow of our gold reserves.

But the cornerstone of the president's New Economic Policy was a ninety-day wage and price freeze, instituted by executive order. I personally opposed wage and price controls, because they simply do not work. They create a completely artificial factor in the economy and interfere with the operation of a free market. They really only postpone the real problem, because as soon as the controls end, everybody raises prices to make up for perceived "losses" during the period of the freeze. Thus, the overall inflationary effect is usually higher. As Herb Stein, a member of the Council of Economic Advisers, explained in a memo to the president, "Tightening the price-wage control system creates the danger of keeping the con-

---

[*] Only after it started using the term "NEP" did the administration learn that Lenin had used the same acronym for his own economic plan years before.

trolled rate of inflation too far below the free-market rate of inflation, so that the controls become impossible to terminate." George Shultz, whose concerns on this point also were ignored, compared it to Vietnam: "Once the troops are in, it's hard to get them out." The problem was also aptly described in one of the administration's own earlier issues papers: "Mandatory wage and price controls won't work. They deal with symptoms not causes. They are like clamping a lid on a boiling pot without turning down the heat—they can only produce a later explosion."

The thing that really brought home the absurdity of the whole idea, and that went against all of my core conservative beliefs, was an exercise conducted by the Cost of Living Council.* This was the group, mandated as part of the NEP, to oversee the new price controls. We met regularly and considered requests for exemptions from wage and price controls. One afternoon, council members spent about two hours trying to decide whether a shirtmaker could get a price increase if he put a pocket on *both* sides. The government has no business trying to restrain or control the free market, much less determining such things as how much a two-pocket shirt should cost.

Besides the economic effects of wage and price controls, as a practical matter, enforcement was a gigantic problem; with billions of transactions a year in our free market, it was nearly impossible to prosecute individual violations or even to know of them.

At first, President Nixon opposed wage and price controls, as did Director Shultz and I. Having expressed my opinion to Nixon and feeling confident in his concurrence, I had spoken to a Ditchley conference near Oxford and assured all in attendance that the president

---

* The Cost of Living Council was made up of five cabinet officers, representatives of the OMB and the Council of Economic Advisers, and several special assistants to the president.

would not institute wage and price controls. Within two months, he did just that. The planning for it had been done in great secrecy to avoid having businesses raise their prices before the controls took effect—such secrecy that I believe that John Connally, the newly arrived secretary of the treasury, was the only cabinet member who knew of the president's decision until very shortly before it was announced. President Nixon did tell a few of us on the night of August 14 at Camp David, but we were all sworn to secrecy until the full meeting the next day. As I recall, we were even told not to make telephone calls that night.

I think the president changed his mind on controls in large part because Secretary Connally, a lifelong Democrat, was a very persuasive advocate of wage and price controls. The president wanted to do something dramatic about inflation, and Secretary Connally convinced him that the shock effect of the controls would tame inflation. It did, but only for a short time;[*] soon after the controls were lifted, prices jumped even higher. Over the next three years, the president continued to use various forms of wage and price control, but none with lasting or good results.[†]

---

[*] The NEP, particularly the wage and price freeze, was initially very popular and temporarily calmed consumers' fears. Indeed, the day after it was announced, the stock market gained thirty two points—the largest one-day gain in history up to that point. The new confidence even carried the president to reelection victory, which was perhaps part of his intent. But the euphoria was short-lived, as the longer-term effects became more apparent. In fact, as late as the fall of 1973, 89 percent of Americans still considered "the high cost of living" the country's biggest problem, even though the Watergate scandal was taking over the headlines.

[†] Besides the fact that wage and price controls were counterproductive, some economists had said, before the controls were even implemented in mid-1971, that they were unnecessary because the economy was already showing small signs of improvement on its own. The main evidence they pointed to was that the inflation rate had stopped rising and, according to other economic indicators, seemed poised to begin subsiding.

Another means by which President Nixon addressed the problem of inflation was the use of the so-called Full Employment Budget. As the president's 1972 reelection campaign factbook explained, "By pursuing a policy of deficit spending at the level of full-employment revenues, sufficient expansion of the economy is assured to provide full employment, increased federal revenues, and thus automatically *remove the deficit* and excess economic stimulation before its effects lead to inflation [emphasis added]." In simpler terms, the Full Employment Budget was based on what the revenues and expenditures would be *if* the economy were at full employment. The theory was that if more people were working, they would pay more taxes, which would bring in more revenues, and at the same time government expenditures would be less because unemployment insurance and other federal relief payments would be low.

George Shultz was a big advocate of the Full Employment Budget. I most definitely was not. Operating *as if* the economy were at full employment was little more than a method of presenting things to look better than they really were, and a way of enabling political speakers to claim balance even though the actual budget was quite badly *out* of balance. It had no real effect on tax receipts or on the allocation of money to any departments or programs; Congress still looked at the *actual* numbers and I continued trying to balance the *actual* budget. I felt that anything we did to mask how large the deficit really was would weaken our attempt to cut spending.

As had been the case in California, only about 25 percent of the federal government's spending was discretionary—the rest was legally required, as written into the funding provisions of almost innumerable programs. These usually start as a pilot project, which turns into an essential program in about three years and becomes an urgent priority in three years more. The distance from an urgent priority to an untouchable sacred cow is usually no more than five fiscal years.

One of the first things I did when I became deputy director of OMB was to ask for a study on real ways the budget could be cut, and whether any so-called uncontrollables could in fact be changed. I also went through the budget myself, line by line. Everyone was horrified at some of the things I suggested as possible cuts, including such obvious impossibilities as postponing interest payments on the national debt. I felt it was essential to get everyone to realize how drastic was the need to cut and that we had to look at every possible option. My budget-cutting zeal earned me the nickname "Cap the Knife," coined by presidential speechwriter, and now distinguished columnist, Bill Safire. The biggest item that was relatively "controllable" was national defense, but both President Nixon and I were extremely reluctant to scale back the defense budget.

Contrary to his rhetoric,* the president was reluctant to make the deep cuts in popular programs that I thought were necessary. Spending reductions were especially unwelcome in a campaign year. In 1972 I strongly advised him against signing a debt ceiling bill because that bill also contained a 20 percent increase in Social Security. It was a well-known tactic of congressmen to include their favorite bills in the debt ceiling legislation because the latter eventually had to be signed. The president signed it, telling me bluntly he could not veto a Social Security increase in an election year. When Nixon asked why I was less successful cutting the federal budget than I was in cutting California's state budget, I told him, probably too bluntly, that it was because California had a chief executive who gave budget cuts the highest priority.

---

* In his second inaugural address, President Nixon put a conservative spin on the appeal President Kennedy had made to the American people exactly twelve years earlier, saying, "Let each of us ask—not just what government will do for me, but what can I do for myself?"

To his credit, President Nixon did, at least, slash the rate of increased government spending. His 1971 budget provided only a 1.5 percent increase over the previous year's spending, compared to an *annual* increase *averaging* 17 percent for fiscal years 1965–68.

The president also called for a $250 billion spending ceiling for fiscal year 1973, the budget I spent most of my time on during my tenure at OMB. I was able to keep the budget outlays under that— $246.3 billion—despite the protest of almost every executive department and agency. The bills incorporating the ceiling passed both houses of Congress, but in one of the Senate committees, various amendments were added that would have required the president to cut equally from all programs if he cut from any. This was administratively unworkable and required reductions in effective programs. So we opposed it.

Ultimately, Congress restored most of the funding we had cut from the $250 billion spending cap. Sadly, it is often the case that an administration's efforts at fiscal responsibility are thwarted by Congress's zeal to ensure that every pet project is fully funded. I frequently urged President Nixon to veto such inflated appropriation bills, but he rarely did.

One thing he did do, however, was to withhold some of the congressionally appropriated spending. This "impoundment," as it was called, dated back to 1803 when President Thomas Jefferson declined to use funds that Congress had appropriated for two gunboats, because the Indian wars for which the gunboats were appropriated had ended. Every president since had occasionally "impounded" funds, and it was a useful way to postpone a portion of spending until it was really required. The best way to visualize this is to think of all of the money that Congress appropriates at any one time as going into a large tank out of which several hundred little pipes lead. The valves on these pipes are opened and the money drops out into the proper slots and program allocations from time to time, as the given conditions are fulfilled—as contracts are prepared, designs are agreed upon, the site is selected for a building, and so on. I would think that every president would, at some time, use the impounding authority—because there's nobody to give the money to, or because it violates the debt ceiling, or because conditions have changed since the appropriation.

If President Nixon had had the line-item veto (a power that most state governors had), holding funds in reserve would not have been necessary. He did veto some appropriations bills in their entirety; on a few occasions, Congress then reduced the appropriations, but often the vetoes were simply overridden. When that occurred, the only option left to the president was to withhold funds.

Of course, this "impoundment" infuriated Congress. Congress held hearings on the subject and even considered impeachment of the president for executive intrusion on legislative authority. It was a fierce constitutional fight, and ultimately President Nixon was persuaded to sign away his authority (and that of all future presidents) to withhold funding, as part of the Budget and Impoundment Control Act of 1974—at a time when Nixon's political capital had been whittled away by the Watergate scandal.

A precursor to this act was a 1970 hospital construction authorization bill, in which Congress included language requiring that the entire annual appropriation be spent every year. President Nixon balked at this and vetoed the bill, but Congress overrode the veto and won another victory for mandatory spending.

President Nixon's policy of revenue sharing was more successful. I was and am a great advocate of revenue sharing because it makes for more efficient and effective spending. Essentially, it works like this: the federal government gives states a lump sum to pay for federally required programs, thus eliminating expensive federal bureaucracy and freeing the individual states and cities to determine their own funding priorities under broad federal guidelines. I have always felt

1920: Not even three years old, and already stubborn.

My mother, Cerise, was an accomplished violinist.

I'm on the left, with my father, Herman, and my brother, Peter.

At Polytechnic High School
in San Francisco, 1933.

A newly commissioned infantry
officer, 1942.

The nurse who became my wife,
Jane.

On duty in New Guinea, 1943.

On the campaign trail in 1952 for a seat in the California State Assembly.

In the California governor's office with Governor Ronald Reagan. I served as his director of finance.

Sworn in as President Nixon's secretary of health, education, and welfare at his western White House in San Clemente. Left to right are Governor Reagan; President Nixon; my wife, Jane; and Judge Thomas Caldecott.

At the White House with Nixon, discussing health care issues, 1974.

Showing my perfect shooting form, even in cufflinks, with a radar-tracking gun—one of the perquisites of being secretary of defense.

Sworn in as President Reagan's secretary of defense, January 21, 1981.

Showing Mrs. Lagorio of Italy and Mrs. Rinaldo Petrignari, wife of the Italian ambassador to the U.S., around the Air and Space Museum.

Discussing strategy with Secretary of State Al Haig and Deputy Secretary of State Bill Clark in the Roosevelt Room of the White House, 1981.

Meeting in the Cabinet Room with the Joint Chiefs of Staff and the National Security Council in 1982. Left to right are General Barrow (Commandant of the Marine Corps), Admiral Watkins (Chief of Naval Operations), General Vessey (Chairman of the Joint Chiefs of Staff), General Meyer (Chief of Staff of the Army), General Gabriel (Chief of Staff of the Air Force), Robert McFarlane, Bill Clark, Ed Meese, George Bush, Ronald Reagan, and James Baker. Missile defense was on the agenda.

With my stalwart friend Bill Clark in 1983.

Greeting Vice
President Bush at
the Pentagon, 1984.

Meeting Mrs. Weinberger.
Left to right are General
Secretary Gorbachev,
President Reagan, and
Chief of Protocol Selwa
"Lucky" Roosevelt; my
wife, Jane, is seated.

Saying good-bye to the president in the Oval Office. Left to right are my
daughter, Arlin; my grandson, James; President Reagan; my wife, Jane; my
granddaughter, Becky; my son, Caspar Jr.; and my daughter-in-law, Mavis.

Announcing my resignation and the appointment of Frank
Carlucci as my successor to head the Defense Department.
Behind me are President Reagan, Frank Carlucci, and a
young Colin Powell, November 1987.

With President Reagan at my retirement ceremony.

My last cabinet meeting as secretary of defense, November 19, 1987.

Outside of Buckingham Palace, displaying (at the request of the British press) the Knight Grand Cross just awarded by Queen Elizabeth II. Jane is with me.

With Colin Powell at my eightieth birthday party.

What I do now, touring the world for *Forbes*. Here I am with Kip Forbes, Steve Forbes, and Christian Frost on Wake Island.

that those closest to a problem are the ones best able to find and administer an appropriate solution.

The president had proposed revenue sharing in 1969, before I joined the administration, but I hope that my strong and active support for the idea had something to do with his making it the centerpiece of his recommendations for 1972.

In October of that year, President Nixon signed a $30.2 billion revenue sharing bill. But this came only after another protracted battle with Congress. Unsurprisingly, Congress opposed revenue sharing on the grounds that states would not spend the money or administer the programs as wisely or as well as the federal government did; the *real* reason was that congressmen liked doling out money to favored constituents.

By this time, June 1972, I had become the director of OMB. When John Connally resigned, George Shultz became the new treasury secretary and President Nixon asked me to direct OMB. Aside from taking over the management side of OMB, my duties grew but didn't change that much, though now I operated from a second-floor office in the West Wing of the White House.

Arnold Weber, who had done an excellent job as the deputy director for management, had recently resigned to return to university teaching. He was replaced by Frank Carlucci, who had done an admirable job running the Office of Economic Opportunity and serving as an associate director at OMB. He did a fine job on our management team as well.*

When I asked for staff suggestions on how to improve OMB, the responses focused on the need for more guidance and involvement from the director. This I was happy to do, as I had been involved

---

* Frank was a former career Foreign Service officer, and later he served with me at the Department of Health, Education, and Welfare and the Defense Department.

much more in the day-to-day activities of the budget than George Shultz had been.

I was constantly motivated by the size and scope of the job and by the idea that maybe what I was doing could make a difference. It was a continually challenging enterprise—and a vast improvement, in my mind, over the law practice, where one usually dealt with tiny, narrow disputes.

In early 1971 a number of my California Republican friends urged me to run for mayor of San Francisco against the incumbent, Joe Alioto. Some also wanted me to run for Congress.* But I thrived on the long days, heavy workload, and detailed policy of the budget, and did not let my mind think about much else, which, I am sure, made me a very dull fellow.

Fortunately, my wife, Jane, had become involved in a number of her own activities. When we first moved to Washington in 1970, she had immediately become active in the Folger Shakespeare Library, which was just down the street from our little row house on Capitol Hill. This more than fulfilled her long interest in Shakespeare and was a very good thing for the Folger. Later, she became chairman of the board.

She also continued some of the hospital volunteering she had done at St. Luke's in San Francisco. Being a nurse, she was drawn to this kind of work, and she enjoyed visiting patients in the wards of several area hospitals every week, as well as serving on the hospital boards.

In addition, she campaigned with some of the other cabinet wives for President Nixon when he ran for reelection in 1972. She was basi-

---

* My name bounced around quite a lot in this period. I later learned—to my great surprise—that Len Garment, a major adviser and the counsel to the president, suggested to the president that I would be a good appointee to the Supreme Court.

cally a rather reserved New England lady, but she became very effective at public speaking, television appearances, and fund-raising.*
None of this came naturally to her; she had taught herself the necessary skills, starting way back when she ran my first campaign for the California assembly in 1952.

Although I think she would have preferred to be home in California, I was pleased and proud of her successful activities and that she adapted so extraordinarily well to her role as a "Washington wife." Once again, she proved to be of tremendous support to me, and she found the bright side of the situation for herself as well.

We were both comfortably ensconced in our respective routines in 1972, but President Nixon's reelection that year brought an unexpected change.

---

* Jane even wrote and published her own how-to book on fund-raising called *Please Buy My Violets*, which was highly regarded and much in demand. It was one of the great successes of her publishing business, Windswept House Publishers, which she started in the early 1980s, operating out of the top floor of our home.

CHAPTER 13

A FIRST LESSON IN REALLY
BIG GOVERNMENT

*O*n Wednesday morning, November 8, 1972, the day after President Nixon's landslide triumph at the polls, the cabinet and the president's staff assembled in the Cabinet Room for what we expected would be the president's warm congratulations and hearty thanks for the work done on his behalf, and perhaps some indication as to what his immediate goals were for his second term. When he finally came in, he looked particularly angry and glowering, and only nodded when one or two people ventured to offer some congratulations. The first thing he said, as he picked up a stack of papers, was, "Can you imagine a million people voting for a fellow like that Schmitz?!" John C. Schmitz was a far-right California congressman who ran on the American Independent Party ticket. I thought it a rather odd comment from someone who had won 47 million votes.

After grumbling about that for a few minutes, the president said he had noticed in his study of history that second terms of administrations tended to lose a lot of energy and just coast along without accomplishing much of anything, and, by God, that was not going to happen in *his* second term. He was going to do some major reshuffling; he wanted everybody's resignation on his desk that day. With that, he got up and walked out. We did not hear the slightest sign of pleasure at being reelected. As we all sat there in rather stunned silence, Bob Haldeman cut in with what I thought was the most unnecessary comment of the year: "In case any of you didn't understand, the president wants your resignations." For anyone who was really obtuse, he added, "I have them here. You can all sign them now." So everybody resigned from office just as if we had lost the election.

As we all dispersed into the hall, there were some puzzled comments—and nobody had any idea what was going to happen next[*] or who was going to be in what position. I thought that, having recently started as budget director, I would probably continue there, if anywhere. In any case, it was quite apparent that there were to be many changes and that "energy" was to be infused into the second term.

Over the next couple of weeks, the cabinet members and other presidential appointees were taken by helicopter, in turn, up to Camp David to be told their fate. I rode up with Pete Peterson, secretary of commerce, who suggested a way we could tell, even before we reached Camp David, what the verdict was: "If there is a trap door in the floor of the helicopter, they're going to let us go halfway there. Then we can be reasonably sure we're not going to be retained." We both examined the floor fairly carefully but made it through the trip.

The Camp David proceedings were conducted with enormous secrecy—a phenomenon typical of Nixon's second term. Several of us had the same experience: as soon as we entered a room where the president, Haldeman, and Ehrlichman were, all talking immediately

---

[*] I think most assumed that the president would simply not accept the resignations until he was actually ready to move someone to another position or out of office entirely. Of course, having a formal resignation was a totally unnecessary step because we all served at the pleasure of the president and could be removed at any time.

stopped and everybody looked self-conscious. Clearly, he and his staff had been discussing things much too important to be heard by anyone else.

I cannot say that I would have been terribly disappointed if I had been let go, but apparently that was the farthest thing from the president's mind. When we met in his quarters at Camp David, he was cordial and complimentary, and said he had decided he wanted me to run the Department of Health, Education, and Welfare (HEW). The current secretary, Elliot Richardson. was moving over to Defense, an option the president said he had considered for me as well. But he felt that HEW was more in need of fiscal and managerial discipline; it was, at that time, the highest-spending department. The president said he thought it would be an interesting twist to send a budget cutter to HEW and a big spender to the Pentagon. Indeed, he felt I was better suited to HEW and shared many of his general goals for the department, such as reining in a runaway budget and devolving a good deal of power back to the states and the private sector.

I accepted, because I thought heading up HEW would be a great challenge and interesting work. My wife would have preferred to go home to California, but as always, she was supportive. In fact, she became very involved and did extraordinarily valuable work with many of the constituencies that HEW served, particularly in the health field and with organizations that represented some of the most needy groups in Washington.

My wife was not the only one who was less than thrilled with my appointment to head HEW. Outgoing secretary Elliot Richardson and much of the department staff were alarmed that a budget cutter was taking over, as were many senators and congressmen. Democrats like Senators Edward Kennedy and Harold Hughes of Iowa were particularly vocal in their opposition at my confirmation hearings, and liberal Republicans like Senator Jacob Javits had serious reservations about me. Javits's main reservation about voting to confirm me, he said, was that he was afraid I was not 100 percent in favor of all of HEW's programs. I told him that was absolutely correct—I felt that we needed to look closely at each one and have the courage to stop doing things that were not working so we could free some resources to try something else. This was not a satisfactory answer to him because he wanted the secretary to be a complete advocate for everything the department was doing.

I suspect that some congressional resistance stemmed also from irritation at President Nixon's thus-far-successful practice of impounding funds that Congress had appropriated. The vote on my confirmation was delayed for over a month, I'm sure in part to pressure the administration to release those funds. But the president did not yield, and finally, on February 8, 1973—long after most of the other cabinet members had been sworn in, and even after the inauguration—I was confirmed by a vote of 61 to 10, with the dissenting votes all cast by Democrats.

Frank Carlucci, my deputy at OMB, came over to HEW with me, at my urgent request, and was confirmed as undersecretary at around the same time. I was also fortunate enough to be able to bring Will Taft, who later became the department's general counsel and who served with all his usual skill and effectiveness. Also following me to HEW was my faithful driver, Sarge. Having familiar, competent people at one's side makes tackling major new challenges seem easier.

The delay in my confirmation meant that, officially, I was only secretary-designate of HEW during the inaugural festivities in January. The sign on my car in the parade said as much, as if to announce that I was not quite official. But that did not dampen my enjoyment of the grand quadrennial inauguration festivities.

The inauguration wrapped Washington in a jovial, celebratory atmosphere. As society writer Betty Beale described it, "This city has been a cross between Mardi Gras in New Orleans, peak hour at LaGuardia Airport, and the investiture of a new pope."

The occasion also provided a welcome opportunity to see some of our faraway friends. Governor and Mrs. Reagan, Ed Meese, and Mike Deaver came to Washington for the celebration, and Jane cooked a marvelous dinner for them the night before. Later that evening, we all attended a concert by the Philadelphia Symphony at the brand-new Kennedy Center.

The next day we invited our California guests back for breakfast. Jane had set the table the night before, only to find, when she came downstairs, that the party rental company had retrieved its table sometime during the night. Completely unfazed, Jane simply served breakfast buffet-style. She carried the whole thing off with her usual flair and good humor.

Later that morning, Jane and I assembled with the other cabinet officers and their families inside the Capitol, and then we were seated outside on the presidential inaugural platform built out over the east steps facing the Supreme Court building. There were people as far as the eye could see, from the driveway at the bottom of the stairs, back to First Street and beyond.

The seamless transition of power in a democracy is an event that many of us take for granted, but to witness it up close is a moving experience, even though some of that impact is lost when the president is sworn in for a second term. The oath, administered precisely at noon, when the previous term expires, never varies; it is prescribed by the Constitution. Also unvarying is the ceremony of a berobed chief justice swearing in the president, followed by the inaugural speech, delivered from the place where so many previous presidents-elect have stood. I wondered how some of these men, in the days before public address systems, could have been heard by more than a few rows of spectators. Indeed, many people probably could not even see their new president.

Immediately following the ceremony, we joined President and Mrs. Nixon, congressional leaders, and other cabinet members for lunch in the Senate Dining Room in the Capitol—a pleasantly spacious but rather featureless room near the Senate chamber.

Then my wife and son and I rode up Pennsylvania Avenue in the inaugural parade, in a top-down convertible sporting a large sign indicating my "half status" as secretary-designate of HEW. The rear seat was designed for only two people, and my son is not small, but the three of us squeezed in, which made for a warmer ride to the White House. As is typical in January, it was very cold, and I greatly admired the stamina of the Secret Service agents who trotted along beside the car for the whole length of the drive. The large crowds lining both sides of the avenue were generally friendly.

Upon arriving at the presidential reviewing stand on the north side of the White House, we took our assigned seats to watch the rest of the parade go by—which it did for hours. Fortunately, the reviewing stand was partially heated (and the seats for the president and vice president were, of course, protected by bulletproof glass).

The evening's activities included a dinner honoring Congressional Medal of Honor winners. As always, being in the presence of the bravest of the brave was a most moving experience.

Then there were numerous inaugural balls around town; we went to the one at the Smithsonian's beautiful Museum of Natural History, where the immense elephant greets everyone from his platform at the head of the main stairway. Inaugural balls are primarily huge crowds of people milling about a too-small dance floor. It is impossible to dance, and the crowd keeps growing as all await the arrival of the new president. He goes to all the balls and makes a few remarks at each, and perhaps enjoys a few brief dance steps with the first lady. Then they depart hastily for the next one.

The inaugural events provided a brief respite from the daily rigors of trying to rein in the federal budget at OMB, a pause that helped gird me for the challenges that lay ahead.

I was sworn into office on February 12, 1973, again at the Western White House, where President Nixon seemed to be spending much of his time. I was permitted to use our family Bible this time and made a conscious effort to raise my right hand instead of my left.

Between 1969 and my confirmation as secretary in February 1973, HEW's health budget had grown more than 100 percent, its education budget by more than 30 percent, and its welfare budget by roughly 75 percent, making it the largest of the executive departments and very unwieldy. When HEW was created in 1953, its budget was $7.6 billion. In 1973, only twenty years later, it had an $89.2 billion budget. Worse, only 6 percent of its budget was discretionary, the rest being mandated by law. Changing these automatic increases required the approval of Congress, which was not forthcoming. Congress, lobbyists, and departmental bureaucracies—the "Iron Triangle," as Theodore White called them—put up formidable opposition to any attempt to change the status quo. The special-interest groups who benefited directly, the civil service groups who did not want to lose their jobs, and the staffs of the congressional committees who didn't want to lose their control opposed our proposals to cut spending or even just to hold down the rate of increase of various programs. Indeed, in most cases, congressional committees appropriated more funds than the administration requested.

The more I thought about the difficulties of trying to control federal spending, the more I became convinced that we could never solve the problem solely by making cuts in various programs. The only way to achieve real budget reform was to limit the revenue government received—subject, of course, to various escape clauses for national emergencies and wars. By late 1974, close to 40 percent of the gross national product (GNP) went to support government. Many, myself included, felt that if that figure got much higher, it would be increasingly difficult to maintain our free-enterprise capitalist system. We needed to limit tax revenues to a fixed—and much lower—percentage of GNP. I outlined this idea to President Ford in November 1974, but he refused drastic policy changes until he could be elected president in his own right—but he wasn't, and my proposal went down to defeat with him.

It was also my feeling that a great many things HEW was doing could be performed as well or better by the states or by the private sector. I did not think that the federal government should try to operate general schools or public hospitals, for example. We ought to give the state and local governments grants they could use as they saw best, for what they determined to be their highest priorities. This was achieved, to a small degree, through revenue sharing, passed by the Congress in 1972, but this was not nearly as ambitious a program as the administration had wanted.

With regard to higher education, the Nixon administration was committed to ensuring that *all* qualified young people, be they rich or poor, black or white, male or female, could attend college. A key administration program passed by Congress in 1972 was the Basic Opportunity Grant program, under which federal assistance went directly to the *student*, who made his or her own decision as to which college he or she wanted to attend. This reversed the previous system of giving colleges the federal funds to disperse. But funding of the Basic Opportunity Grants was limited because Congress continued to prefer the traditional method of aiding schools rather than students.

All higher education institutions receiving federal contracts were subject to affirmative action requirements, both in their hiring and in student admissions. The colleges weren't happy about this, and I wasn't either. If a fair and broad search for qualified candidates—the proper goal—degenerated into fear that a college's federal funds would be endangered if it did not fill a specific number of vacancies with black or Asian or women appointees (or some other specific group), then we would achieve only quotas and reverse discrimination. That was certainly *not* my goal. Discrimination cannot be cured by practicing it.

In a celebrated case in 1973 and 1974, Allan Bakke, a white male, was denied admission to the University of California Medical School at Davis, even though his grades and test scores were higher than those of several minority students who were accepted. Bakke decided to sue the school, and the case went all the way to the Supreme Court, which, in 1978, ruled that racial quotas were not permissible and that, while an applicant's race could be considered, other factors such as aptitude and ability must be considered as well. This decision was a step in the right direction, but it provided rather nebulous guidelines.

Another education issue was school vouchers that would allow all parents to send their children to the school they prefer. I had supported this idea from the time I had been in the California legislature because I felt that poor children should have the same educational opportunities as any other children, but I was never able to persuade the administration. Organized public education lobbies, the National Educational Association, and various teachers' unions always violently opposed anything that enabled parents to choose private schools—because they feared the competition.

The main education issue on the table during my tenure was Title IX. Congress had passed Title IX as part of the Education Amendments of 1972 (to the Higher Education Act of 1965). Title IX was intended to prohibit sexual discrimination in educational programs that received federal money. HEW was assigned the task of developing the regulations—to set out in detail how Title IX would be administered.

It took three years from the time Title IX was passed to the time the president signed the final regulations. Many in HEW were reluctant to prepare the regulations, probably because the educational and college lobbies opposed the new law. If I had not kept pushing for it, I'm not sure the department would ever have finished the regulations. I felt that equal educational opportunity was very important and *needed* to be pushed instead of defeated by inaction.

Nondiscrimination in hiring at and admissions to federally funded educational institutions was at the heart of Title IX and encompassed the areas of financial aid and scholarships, but the most talked-about and controversial issue was athletics. As I studied the matter, I became convinced that women did not have nearly enough opportunities to participate in college sports. I was struck by the argument that women's athletics were supported by bake sales, while men's athletics were supported by football game revenues.

But remedies had to be tempered with common sense; as the final regulations explicitly stated, equal opportunity did not necessarily mean equal spending for men's and women's teams. For example, not as many women as men may *want* to participate in a sport. The intent of the law was that anyone who *wants* to participate in college and school athletics must have the opportunity to do so and must be provided with the necessary equipment, travel allowances, and so forth.

In June 1974, HEW published the proposed Title IX regulations, and I allowed ninety days for public comment on them. I took it one step further and held hearings around the country, in much the same way I had done around California when I was investigating the liquor laws in the 1950s. In general, it seemed that the NCAA and representatives of established, successful men's athletic programs objected to the idea that the revenue their sport produced would have to be shared to help support what they considered less important programs— women's sports. On the other side, the Association for Intercollegiate Athletics for Women felt that the regulations did not go far enough. As the Cedar Rapids *Gazette* put it at the time, "You know you have been fair if both sides are displeased."

Finally, in 1975, President Ford signed into law regulations designed to make access to all educational opportunities—academic as well as athletic—equally available to everyone.

Personally, I was especially interested in educational programs for gifted children. These children, in the same classes as everybody else, would finish their work sooner and quickly get bored—and bored children often get into trouble.

I believed we should cultivate gifted children—our future leadership—and provide them with the opportunities to advance at their own pace to more challenging activities. Not a little of my concern was derived from my own experience at the Frederic Burk grammar school I had attended in San Francisco, where each student was able to progress at his or her own rate and was given individual attention and encouragement.*

I was also a great proponent of the Head Start program, which gave early extra training to financially disadvantaged children, many of whom did not have helpful environments at home. This program produced dramatic results. I saw firsthand the difference it could make when I visited a poor area of Kentucky and saw how much more confident and eager to learn were the children enrolled in Head Start. Opponents said it worked *too* well—it gave these children a great boost that would only turn to disappointment when the standard public education system failed them. I argued that with Head Start at least some students would succeed against the odds.

Improving each individual's chances of success was also at the heart of my approach to welfare reform.

By the time I came to HEW, the welfare system, if it can be called a system, was a mess. It had exploded in the 1960s, partially, I think, due to pressure from special-interest groups that believed their influence would be increased if they had more people—clients, as they called them—participating in as many government programs as

---

* John Dewey, an educator at Columbia University and a leader in the "progressive movement," was a pioneer in this approach.

possible. So "outreach" to recruit more "clients" was their constant endeavor. This outreach idea was enthusiastically embraced by those who administered the programs. Instead of concentrating on helping people get off welfare, the whole system was geared to getting people *on* welfare. By the end of that decade, there were second-generation welfare families.

It was not until Governor Reagan's State Welfare Reform Act of 1971 that that trend was challenged. Robert Carleson, chief architect of the governor's welfare plan in California, explained it well: "Key elements were a work requirement, intensified scrutiny to determine initial and continuing eligibility, and stiff new laws under which welfare payments to a family that has been deserted by the father constitute a civil debt that the father owes to county welfare agencies. Savings realized from these reforms made possible a 27 percent increase in the size of cash grants to those genuinely in need."

Shame used to be associated with being "on the dole" in England, but that was not as prevalent in the United States (nor is it much in evidence in England now). To Americans welfare had become an entitlement. Many, of course, genuinely needed temporary assistance. Unfortunately, federal welfare programs in the early 1970s—such as Aid to Families with Dependent Children (AFDC), Food Stamps, Medicaid, and housing assistance—provided little or no incentive to get off the rolls and find work.

On the contrary, there were built-in inducements to stay on welfare: benefits increased the more children a family had; there was no real effort, by state or federal governments, to make absent fathers pay child support; and a recipient's benefits were slashed if he or she actually worked to earn income.

President Nixon wanted to find better ways of helping people. Sometimes he took a liberal direction. In early 1969 he expanded the Food Stamp program and increased individual benefits. Then, in August 1969, he proposed an interesting innovation—the Family

Assistance Plan (FAP). It offered a direct cash assistance grant to replace the many piecemeal welfare programs for poor families with children. I felt that it was a good idea to cut bureaucracy but that it did not go far enough. For one thing, it did not have a strong work requirement. And once Congress got hold of it, it would become yet another perpetual categorical grant. FAP twice passed in the House, the second time weighted down with congressional provisions and additions. Both times, FAP failed to reach the Senate floor for a vote. Critics killed it by saying that poor people would spend cash granted on liquor or lottery tickets; only bureaucrats could spend the money properly—a low opinion of poor people that I thought was thoroughly unjustified.

At about the same time, in the fall of 1972, another measure—the Supplemental Security Income (SSI) program—was cavalierly dumped into a Social Security bill near midnight and passed with no hearings. I strongly opposed this legislation, but, supported as it was by vigorous lobbies and members of both parties attached to traditional welfare, it became law anyway. The president could not be persuaded to veto a Social Security bill, particularly in an election year.

Basically, the SSI program required the conversion to a single *federal* system of the more than 1,150 then-existing state and county welfare programs of cash assistance to the aged, blind, and disabled. This task was assigned to HEW, and it had to be accomplished in only fourteen months. The SSI program was designed to ensure that people who cannot work have enough to eat, a place to live, and other essentials of living—certainly worthy goals, but this legislation, I felt, was poorly and hastily developed, with no hearings or opportunity for amendment, and its provisions were ill-defined. And of course, it required a great deal more money and a whole new layer of bureaucracy to administer it. These features ran counter to all of my core beliefs, as did shifting control of welfare away from states and counties—those closest to the problem—and giving it to the federal government. By extraordinary efforts on the part of many skilled people, we in the department did get SSI up and running in the required fourteen months.

On another front we had a presidential directive to find a way to reform welfare. I concluded—after more than a year of study—that a negative income tax, as proposed by Nobel Prize–winning economist Milton Friedman, was the best plan to limit government programs, slash bureaucracy, and give people more control over their lives.

The plan I proposed became known as the Income Supplement Program, or ISP. I preferred to call it "Welfare Replacement." Under this plan, the major categorical, means-tested programs—AFDC, the new SSI program, and Food Stamps—would be eliminated and superseded by a simple, universal cash transfer for families that fell below a certain level of income. The single cash payment would be reduced as a family's other income rose, until the combined total exceeded a predetermined break-even point. After that, even with a tax liability, a family earning more than the break-even amount would still have a higher net income than if it were receiving government assistance under the programs I wanted to abolish. The ISP would be integrated with the tax system and would provide work incentives because benefits would be reduced by only half of increased earnings. At the same time, those physically unable to work would be taken care of with a guaranteed minimum income.

I felt strongly that the ISP should be administered by the IRS rather than HEW or other departments experienced only in welfare. Coordinating the welfare and tax systems, as I wanted to do, was based on the fact that both have the same mechanical function—a cash transfer between the individual and the government—and the same rationale for computing the amount of the transfer: the ability to pay (or, negatively phrased, inability to pay) or need. And no new bureaucracy would be necessary.

Another major benefit in the ISP proposal was that it gave poor people what they needed most: money. Again, there was the argument, mostly from social workers, government bureaucrats, and other conventional-wisdom followers, that poor people do not know how to spend their money "properly"—an assumption I thought demeaning and wrong.

In general, liberals were concerned that ISP's benefits would be inadequate, conservatives were concerned about increasing the number of recipients, and the entrenched welfare bureaucracies were simply opposed to change.

Of course, we anticipated difficulties with Congress. First of all, jurisdiction over our proposal would cut across many committees, and this would threaten both Congress's own power and the categorical programs it loved so dearly. Second, I was sure it would have been sorely tempted to add benefits without eliminating any of the existing programs, such as Food Stamps.

Unfortunately, our Welfare Replacement plan never even reached Congress for consideration. President Nixon's highest priority became surviving the Watergate scandal, so our legislative agenda fell by the wayside, and President Ford, although favorably inclined, again deferred action until he could be elected president.

Another problem under my purview was health care costs, which were shooting upward in the early 1970s—not only for citizens trying to handle medical bills themselves but also for government programs such as Medicaid and Medicare. When President Johnson signed the Medicare program into law in 1965, he pledged that the doctors would be paid for whatever services they performed and that they would not have to get government approval ahead of time. Not surprisingly, costs skyrocketed. By late 1973, Medicare and Medicaid together were costing the government nearly $17 billion a year. The lifting of price controls, when President Nixon's Economic Stabilization Act expired on April 30, 1974, only exacerbated the problem.* Within two months, medical care costs exceeded other consumer costs by as much as 70 percent.

The administration tried to rein in these runaway health care costs in a number of ways. President Nixon advocated the concept of health maintenance organizations (HMOs), and in late 1973 he signed the Health Maintenance Organization Act, which authorized the federal government to test some HMO pilot projects around the country. The basic idea was to keep costs down by emphasizing *preventive* medicine. I felt that this was generally a good approach, but the structure of an HMO plan—requiring that only government-approved physicians be used—kept many people from choosing their own doctor, which remains one of the big problems with HMOs today, nearly thirty years later.

To avoid undue government interference in health care, I encouraged peer reviews—that is, other *doctors, not* Uncle Sam, would advise on proper treatments and various cost-saving proposals, such as how long to keep a woman in the hospital after childbirth. This was achieved by the formation of PSROs, or Professional Standards Review Organizations, and at first that did bring costs down. But technology, and its concomitant expense, was advancing rapidly and quickly overtook any gains realized from the PSROs.

President Nixon wanted a more comprehensive solution to skyrocketing health care and health insurance costs. In February 1971, he had introduced the National Health Insurance Partnership Act, which was seen as a good, middle-ground position between a complete federal takeover of the health insurance industry, as proposed by Senator Edward Kennedy, and minor changes in the insurance and delivery

---

* President Nixon and the Cost of Living Council voted to end price controls in all areas *except* health care because it was clear that medical costs were ready to explode. But Congress did not approve that exception, so all controls were allowed to expire.

systems, as proposed by others. The National Health Insurance Partnership Act required employers to provide health insurance for, and share the costs with, their employees, and it would augment or replace Medicaid assistance for poor families.

But during early debate on these issues, while I was at OMB, a number of deficiencies in the administration's bill became evident. It was widely criticized for its lack of universal coverage: low-income single people and childless couples were excluded. Democrats also objected that it did not provide for sufficient benefits, and Republicans and fiscal conservatives maintained that patients' cost-sharing requirements were not high enough, so the government's costs would go up.

This first administration attempt at health insurance reform was not enacted. When I came to HEW in early 1973, I began a thorough analysis of the entire problem, with all relevant staff involved. We worked diligently for most of that year, and by November we had developed a "new and improved" proposal designed to correct those deficiencies while maintaining the basic structure of the original plan.

As with the first plan, the crux of our new proposal was the requirement that all companies procure private insurance for their employees. The government's role was primarily to provide assurances that insurance companies were solvent, their policies comprehensive, their costs reasonable, and that all businesses had at least a minimum program to provide their employees with coverage. I felt it was important that the government only set standards and certainly not be so involved in the details of health care that it was virtually practicing medicine. An additional benefit of emphasizing private insurance was that premiums would go down as competition was fostered among insurance companies for the new big market for insurance.

This part of the proposal was called the Employer Plan, and employers would pay a percentage of the premiums. For employees who were not low-income, we proposed a higher deductible than was included in the previous bill. A fundamental principle that we followed was that higher cost-sharing with more comprehensive benefits was preferable to narrower coverage with lower cost-sharing. Also, we felt that a relatively high deductible would discourage overuse of services, which, in turn, would keep the cost of such services down. We did, however, include a maximum annual liability feature, which provided protection in case of lengthy illness and a guarantee to protect people from having to pay for catastrophic medical care costs.

The second major component of our new proposal was the Government Plan. Under this part, the federal government would arrange with the states, which would be expected to share roughly 25 percent of the costs, for the states to offer coverage by private insurance companies to all low-income people, as well as those with high-risk medical problems who were unable to obtain private coverage at affordable rates. The major group covered would be low-income people without steady employment. However, even people who were employed but had a total family income under $7,500 could choose to enter the Government Plan rather than the Employer Plan.

Both plans would cover a wide range of services, including hospital and physician services, outpatient and inpatient prescription drugs, preventive care, mental health services (very controversial then), and extended care.

A user-friendly feature that we included was a "Healthcard"—a credit card individuals could use to facilitate billing. So instead of going into the hospital and being required to write out a check when you are on a stretcher, you would simply present the card and be billed later. The card would also contain vital medical information about the holder.

Medicare would be retained but adapted to conform with the new plan, and Medicaid, for the most part, would be terminated. We estimated that the federal government's costs for the new proposal would be just under $6 billion a year—only about one-third what it was spending annually for Medicare and Medicaid.

I felt that our new health insurance plan would be particularly appealing, providing universal access to affordable insurance and using public financing only where private financing was not available.

Our Comprehensive Health Insurance Plan, or CHIP, as it was called, was introduced in Congress in February 1974, accompanied by the president's health message, in which he outlined the measures in the plan that were "designed to contain costs, improve the efficiency of the system, and assure quality health care."

Health insurance was a hot topic at that time, and Congress was awash with a great many competing bills on the subject during most of Nixon's presidency. In the Ninety-third Congress (1973 and 1974), over twenty-two separate bills were introduced to establish a national health insurance policy.

Late in 1973, Senators Long and Ribicoff put forward a bill that had fairly wide political appeal. One of its features called for substantial reform of Medicaid. There was no question it was a very inefficient and inequitable system, but I felt that simply tinkering with the existing structure or tacking further convoluted provisions onto it would not go far enough; it needed to be entirely replaced. The Long-Ribicoff bill also proposed measures designed to protect all citizens from the crippling costs of prolonged medical care (catastrophic illness), a goal that we shared. We differed mainly on how best to accomplish that.

Many liberals—led by Senator Edward Kennedy, who also introduced a bill in the Ninety-third Congress—favored the single-payer plan, the single payer of course being the government. Under this system, modeled on Canada's program, the government would pay everyone's health bills, which of course would mean that the government could tell doctors what they could and could not do, and there would be nothing to keep doctors from charging as much as they wanted. And patients had no incentive not to go to the doctor every time they had a hangnail. With no incentive to reduce costs or to stay well, medical costs would inevitably grow higher and higher. Social-ized medicine is a huge drain on any government, and citizens are not afforded the best care. Senator Kennedy's cradle-to-grave cover-age of every American citizen had strong backing from organized labor, but fortunately his bill did not even get out of committee.

The administration's bill made some promising progress, but it ultimately did not fare well either. By late summer of 1974, after substantial missionary work by many of us in the department, the insurance industry had come to support it, and even labor was start-ing to come around. We were able to get the powerful House Ways and Means Committee chairman, Wilbur Mills, on our side. He was determined to get a health insurance bill enacted that year, and he apparently felt that he could work with ours.

When President Ford took office in August, he strongly endorsed CHIP and authorized me to negotiate with Mills to try to reach an acceptable compromise, which we did later that month. Mills objected primarily to any deductibles or copayment provisions, but after many hours of our reasoning together, he eventually accepted them. So we were able to keep the main elements of our plan—health insurance provided by private companies and paid for by workers and employ-ers, and, in case of genuine need, the government.

The major change from CHIP in the compromise was to provide catastrophic coverage financed by a payroll tax. Mills believed this would be necessary in order to secure some liberal support. I had always opposed a payroll tax because of my dislike of more taxes and particularly those with revenues dedicated to a specific purpose. Also, I thought more payroll taxes would discourage more employ-ment. But we felt we could accept it since so much of our original plan would be retained.

Representative Mills told me he had almost convinced Senator Kennedy to go along with our compromise, despite labor union oppo-sition, when events conspired to prevent it. In October, Mills became otherwise occupied at the Tidal Basin, which quickly diminished his influence.* Fanne Fox did far more damage than she knew.

Then, even more damaging, in January 1975, in response to worsening economic conditions, President Ford announced a moratorium on new federal spending programs other than those related to national security or energy. Administration spokesmen expressed the hope of introducing a bill similar to CHIP once the economic climate improved, but the momentum was already lost. For many years thereafter, there were no comparable health insurance plans or indeed anything that even came close to securing the support that our compromise bill had won.

Throughout my tenure at HEW, most of my efforts in the health area centered around pushing for a viable health insurance program. In addition, there were a couple of other health issues in which I had a personal interest.

One of those developed after I came to HEW. As secretary, I visited a number of abused children at hospitals, and the scars they bore, physical and emotional, were horrifying to see. I had had no idea of the extent to which this went on and how little was apparently being done to address the problem. The lack of intervention exacerbated the situation: I was appalled to learn that most of these children I saw would simply be sent back to the same homes. There was apparently no legal way to separate them from the abusive parents. This only perpetuated the cycle—studies showed that those who were abused as children were more likely to abuse their own children. Almost as bad was abuse of women, and again we found that, after treatment, most abused wives returned to their husbands.

---

* When Washington police stopped Mills's car on one occasion, out jumped Fanne Fox, a stripper who somehow ended up in the Tidal Basin. This was quite a scandal at the time, and it proved to be somewhat of a pattern with Mills, who later admitted that an alcohol problem had contributed to his fall from grace.

As soon as I became aware of the severity of the problem, I initiated a child abuse prevention program, which funded studies on how to prevent, stop, and treat this tragic wrong to children. Child abuse has not been eradicated by any means, but I hope that increased penalties, more research, publicity, better treatments, and family counseling have significantly reduced its incidence and helped many children escape from abusive parents.

I was also interested in early child health screening, not only as a preventive, cost-saving tool but also based on my own early experiences. In classes at my grammar school in San Francisco, we were seated alphabetically, which meant that I was usually near the back of the room. Some children that far back could not see the board or hear as well as they should. These problems often went unnoticed and untreated, and it was generally assumed that the child was either unintelligent or just not trying hard enough. The Frederic Burk School I had attended was fairly progressive for its time, and the school nurse gave annual physicals of a sort for many pupils. As secretary of HEW, I realized that many children were not being properly tested for such basic things as vision and hearing or susceptibility to hereditary or other diseases. Therefore I pushed for early screening, so that deficiencies could be identified and treated as early as possible before they hindered a child's scholastic progress.

Another problem I learned about, unfortunately more from personal experience than from my work at the department, was the deplorable condition of some nursing homes and the incompetence of some in-home caregivers.

We had brought my mother with us to Washington, as her health was declining. Initially she lived with us in our small Capitol Hill home, and we tried to make her as comfortable as possible. We even rigged up a music system in her room, but for the first time in her life she expressed no interest in music.

We hired a series of nurses to help, but most proved uninterested in or incapable of giving her the attention she needed. One even failed to come at all when Jane and I were away on an official trip.

On a number of occasions we had to take her to the hospital. We concluded that it would be best if she had round-the-clock care in a nursing home. We tried several in the city, each one worse than the one before. Finally we found quite a good converted private home.

I visited her as often as I could, and I think she also enjoyed the outings we took her on—to see the Fourth of July fireworks from the Capitol, to view the cherry blossoms, or often just to walk in a nearby park. Once, while we were away at a conference, her doctor told us she was now quite ill. We hurried home and put her in the hospital.

On June 24, 1975, my wife called to tell me that Mother had died. The news was difficult but not a surprise. When I had seen her the night before, she had lapsed into a coma after a series of small strokes or cerebral hemorrhages. The doctor had said there was no way she could regain consciousness, and it was just a matter of hours until her body would shut down completely.

We had a private service for her—only my wife and I attended—and then, at her long-standing request, she was cremated and her ashes buried next to my father's grave in San Francisco.

The demands of my job did not afford me much time to grieve, but the appalling conditions I had seen in some of the nursing homes compelled me to work more actively to improve the standards of quality in such facilities, even without legislation.

The secretary of a major department, especially one as people-oriented as HEW, can do a lot to advocate causes by personally visiting institutions, programs, hospitals, and schools, and then stressing publicly the conditions that need improvement. This can focus attention on issues that are of personal interest to the secretary and can be especially helpful when funding is bogged down in

Congress. Such visits and speeches can also instill a fear of legislation which in itself can be helpful. I did a great deal of this, and I enjoyed having the opportunity to meet people all over the country and to learn firsthand what their concerns were and what was working and what was not.

Also at HEW, I took my first substantive overseas trip as an American cabinet official. I found I was becoming more interested in foreign and defense affairs, perhaps influenced by President Nixon's inclinations and activities in that direction. This interest was also stimulated by various security briefings I had received. I was always conscious of how global and interdependent the world was becoming. Of course, HEW was primarily concerned with domestic matters, so its international activities were comparatively small, but I felt that there would be some useful lessons in studying firsthand how other countries handled difficult issues such as welfare and health care. For some time, I was quite fascinated by England's cradle-to-grave health care program, which was completely government-run and tax-funded. I wasn't interested in doing it that way; I was interested in *not* doing it that way. Finding out what England's experience had been was most useful in my trying to discourage this "single-payer" system.

My first major trip as secretary was to Poland and the Soviet Union in the late summer of 1973, the period of détente, when the administration was trying to thaw Cold War relations and get to know our Communist adversaries. My visit was basically a gesture of goodwill, demonstrating cooperation on health issues and medical research; indeed, we set up with Moscow a sort of "health hotline"—a telex by which we could exchange research results on things like heart disease and vaccination effectiveness. This was all part of implementing a joint overall agreement with the Soviet Union, signed by President Nixon in Moscow the year before.

My wife and several of my staff accompanied me on the two-week trip. We went first to Poland, where, to my surprise, we were most enthusiastically received. The Poles openly expressed their unhappiness with Moscow's domination and their love for the counterexample of America. The Polish health minister and other officials told me they wanted to cooperate with the United States in exchanging research data and arranging reciprocal doctor visits but were blocked by the Soviets. (When I mentioned this to the Soviets later, they simply looked blank.) Polish foreign minister Stefan Olszowski even had on his wall, right beside the requisite photo of Leonid Brezhnev, a picture of President Nixon. When I commented favorably on seeing our president's photo, the minister said with an ironic smile, "Oh yes, we have friends all over, but he [gesturing to Brezhnev] is a much *closer* friend."

We traveled next to the Soviet Union, where we concentrated primarily on health issues. The Soviet minister of health, Boris Petrovsky, was a Santa Claus type—a short, rotund, ruddy-cheeked fellow—and a Red Army surgeon. He and his wife were very friendly, but in general, at least in Moscow, people were not as warm as in Poland. We were received correctly and politely, but with a strong undercurrent of suspicion. Direct contact with Americans was a relatively new thing, and we suspected the Soviet security forces taped all of our conversations.

Conviviality was, however, in evidence when it came time to eat and drink; indeed, drinking was a high priority. At our first dinner, the deputy minister of health explained the Russian custom of the first toast: the vodka (it was always vodka) had to be drunk completely and at once. To show that their glasses were empty, our hosts held them upside-down over their heads. If I had done that, I would have gotten some vodka shampoos. I generally did not drink except for a little wine, and I was concerned that our hosts would be offended. Fortunately, they did not mind if you only sipped subsequent toasts, of which there were many.

We were grandly entertained throughout our visit. We were treated to opening night of the Bolshoi Ballet, performing *Swan Lake* at a modern glass and aluminum Palace of the Congresses in the Kremlin;

a reception with the city council at a lovely dacha; a private tour of the Diamond Fund to see the czar's crown jewels; a tour of the Kremlin, including Lenin's apartment—spartan but with several English-language books behind an old-fashioned glass case; and a reciprocal dinner at our own embassy, Spaso House.

I was most interested in every aspect of our trip, taking photographs at every opportunity. I was also quite fascinated with what was one of my first experiences riding in a motorcade. The Chekka was a very square, uncompromising-looking car, sort of a cross between a London taxicab and a 1940 Dodge or Pontiac. It was a seven-passenger car, but it did not appear to be this long from the outside. It was very comfortable and there was an oriental rug in the backseat because, as it was explained to me, they try to make them as much like their homes as possible. In front of the motorcade, a yellow police car rode with a flashing blue light on top and a loudspeaker system, which constantly ordered drivers in the way to get to the right. The result was that we made astonishing time and quite frequently ran through the middle lane, or even off into the left-hand land, and gave only the slightest token concession to red lights.

Our days in Moscow were occupied mostly with visiting numerous health facilities: the Institute of Oncology, the Myasnikov Institute of Cardiology, the Soviet Academy of Medical Sciences, and Dr. Petrovsky's own First Moscow Medical Institute. Our stop at "Hospital Number 67" made a particular impression on me. We found a very large hospital, with approximately 1,200 beds, with a lady doctor as the director. This woman appeared extremely forbidding and disapproving at the beginning, and she was built along the general lines of a Russian tank, but she had extraordinarily fashionable platform shoes with very high heels that must have made the immense amount of walking she had to do up and down the corridors of that hospital extremely difficult. Despite the initial impression she made, she warmed up considerably as our tour continued, and she became downright friendly when we asked some questions indicating a real interest in the hospital. She also served a rather substantial spread, including some meat-filled rolls she had made herself, and had some very nice gifts for the party at the end.

I also vividly recall the brief trip we made to the then-Soviet republic of Uzbekistan aboard an Aeroflot plane that epitomized Communist backwardness. It was dirty, noisy, drafty, uncomfortable, and filled with people in various stages of disrepair. The plane took off in a long, shuddering roll. It seemed as if every bolt in the fuselage was coming out and rattling around on the floor. Eventually the plane took off, but the drafts were extreme (there was actually a hole in the plane's ceiling, which had been "repaired" by stuffing newspaper in it). The normal creature comforts were totally nonexistent. About three hours later we flew over Tashkent, then for some reason circled around the city for several hours before landing. For me, the major advantage of Tashkent—aside from its desert climate, a welcome relief from the cold rain of Moscow—was the equally welcome absence of vodka, a holdover from the Muslim roots of the area.

From Tashkent, we flew to Bukhara for a brief visit. As we were leaving, I noticed that a local band was playing, apparently for us. Soon a very large ring of people was there. Before I knew it, the deputy local mayor, a lady of about sixty who, it had been earlier reported to me, was feeling somewhat aggrieved because she had been photographed with me only about ninety-nine instead of a hundred times, appeared and motioned for me to dance. The dance was similar to high school dances of a few years earlier, with much gesturing of the hands and feet. I engaged as well as I could, telling them it was an ancient California dance. They seemed absolutely delighted, and I left with assurances that I could be elected to the council in Bukhara.

We returned to Moscow and then were taken to the airport for our return flight to the United States. In my travel book that I had kept during the trip, I recorded my general impressions:

September 9: The sense of relief even on getting onto a Swedish airline is unmistakable, although in a sense, this is unfair because our hosts could not have been more cordial, or more anxious to please us. Many of them are thoroughly delightful people, particularly Minister Petrovsky and his wife. The uniform impression you get from walking along the streets of Moscow is one of drabness. Women are extremely unfashionably dressed and most men are also. Public transportation is crowded, but very available and comes with great regularity and rapidity. They are a very proud people—almost totally unaware that anything is wrong, both as a matter of their pride and, I suspect, they're afraid of being reported as dissidents if they do complain or criticize. There's a noticeable contrast with the Poles. The Poles seem much more basically friendly and very anxious to be far more closely allied to us than Russia. They're deeply aware of the armored divisions on their border, and of what happened to Czechoslovakia and Hungary, and they know perfectly well that any revolt by them would not be supported by anyone else and would be crushed instantaneously.... But the Poles are extremely friendly and warm, and I thought it very significant that in my interview with [First Secretary] Gierek, he said to me, "You know, your people should not be so suspicious of us. We do truly want to be your friends and you should let us be."

The secretaryship of HEW brought with it not only several other opportunities for foreign travel but also a great increase in other public and official appearances. The department's public affairs office gave me an interesting summary of my activities in just the first nine months I was there: I had taken forty-six out-of-town trips; visited twenty-four states; visited all ten regional offices (for many, the first by any secretary); made sixty-four major addresses to local, state, and national organizations; held thirty-six news conferences; made twenty-nine major television appearances; and been interviewed on eleven radio programs. All of this was a marked change from any of the federal positions I had held previously, but I thought it was necessary to inform the public about the new direction we were taking in welfare, health, and education. All of this was demanding, but at the same time, I found it exhilarating.

Although I often brought work home in the evenings, Jane and I also tried to attend as many social events as we could, particularly embassy events, because failure to appear at some of these was considered an affront by some ambassadors. It seemed a glittering age of entertaining, with grand parties in the company of such Washington fixtures as the *Post's* Kay Graham, society writer Betty Beale, columnist Joe Alsop and Susan Mary Alsop, and philanthropist Brooke Astor, who frequently came down from New York. Social occasions also offered an opportunity to meet with congressmen and senators and help persuade them of the rightness of our agendas.

Unfortunately, when President Carter came in a few years later, he made a determined effort to be informal and what he called "folksy." The trouble was, he was so anxious not to be stuffy that he forgot to be dignified. He made quite a show, for example, of carrying his own bag (usually empty). President Reagan, thankfully, brought back much of the grace and style that had characterized the Nixon and Ford days—brightened by his own spirit of sunny conviviality.

I have to say, though, that being a cabinet officer often reminded me of the old anecdote about an aged senator at a party studying a small index card. His hostess asked if he was looking for his next appointment. "No, madam," he replied, "I am trying to find where I am now."

At HEW, there were numerous ex officio positions that went along with the secretaryship, so many that you could spend the whole time just on those. Every day I seemed to have enough meetings, briefings, hearings, and appointments to cover at least two days. As was my usual practice, I wanted to see and answer all the correspondence that I could,[*] so I requested that it be brought to my office. I dismissed staff warnings that I'd find it impossibly large. I received an object lesson when they brought in box after box after box; the secretary's office received something like six thousand letters a day. So I deferred to the staff, who drafted responses. But I still tried to read as many of the letters as I could, particularly congressional correspondence. I also felt it especially important to maintain direct communication with the media to prevent slanted reporting or stories that often seemed based on groundless speculation. Unfortunately, many of the things reported about some other members of the administration turned out to be true.

In the late summer of 1973, I heard rumors that Vice President Agnew would be indicted for bribery. Although I had not known Agnew before he took office, I simply could not believe that this was true. But then, when I was in the middle of a speech a couple of months later in Virginia, I was handed a note saying he had resigned. I tried not to break the flow of what I was talking about, but it was a great shock.

Two days later, on the evening of October 12, I, along with many other administration officials and press, gathered in the East Room of the White House for President Nixon's announcement of his choice to replace Agnew. As we waited for the president, longtime Soviet ambassador Anatoly Dobrynin came bounding in, beaming and shaking everyone's hands. One reporter said to another, "My God, you don't suppose...." That would be the ultimate in détente.

Of course, Nixon chose Gerald Ford—congressman from Michigan, House minority leader, supporter of our agenda, and vocal

---

* Ironically, I recently came across a letter I had written home from college in which I admonished my mother not to try to answer every Christmas card they received.

defender of the president. Ford's nomination was somewhat of a surprise because Nixon had come to regard Congress as his adversary.
At a cabinet meeting, he told us, "The Congress is going to continue
to be difficult, and if, at the end of some hearing, the committee
chairman tells you that 'you have been helpful,' you have failed."

Actually, the president seemed increasingly wary of everyone, and
he grew withdrawn and private, even with his closest advisers.
President Nixon appeared to regard cabinet meetings as a nuisance.
He used them mostly to announce policies and report on trips. He
did not regard the cabinet as a decision-making body.

Our cabinet meetings were not on a regular schedule; they were
usually called quite suddenly, which made it difficult for everybody.
I always felt that this practice probably stemmed from the eagerness
of the White House staff to keep a close hold on the reins of power
and not disperse any of it to the cabinet or anyone else.*

Bob Haldeman and John Ehrlichman resigned in the spring of
1973, which meant less White House interference with the departments. I also have notes from a cabinet meeting on May 1, 1973, that
their departure was meant as a warning:

> [The president] also said everyone should feel quite humble because
> there but for the grace of God might go anyone. He then said somewhat
> puzzlingly, "From time to time, I have defended all of the cabinet mem-
> bers who may have been under attack."

---

* The British have trouble understanding this random and rather informal nature of
American cabinet meetings. Even in President Reagan's administration, cabinet
meetings were not always on a regular schedule, and I remember one instance when
this caused Prime Minister Margaret Thatcher puzzlement and not a little alarm. I
was late to meet her at the Pentagon because of an impromptu cabinet meeting.
When I finally arrived, I found that they had held her motorcade so I could arrive
first and formally welcome her. When I apologized and explained that I had not
known about the cabinet meeting very far ahead of time, she assumed that there
must be some kind of crisis. That was not the case, but in her government, the cabinet was her chief decision-making body, and of course it met on a regular basis.

Perhaps this was an oblique call for us to stand by him come what may. I certainly urged my own department to concentrate on doing our work, concluding that if the Watergate "scandal" were permitted to cripple our constructive energies, that would be the greatest scandal of all. I thought Nixon was right to remove anyone from the administration who was even suspected of wrongdoing, and I continued to defend the president (as did my wife and several other cabinet wives), not so much because he might have expected it but simply because it was incomprehensible to me that he would have ordered the break-in at the Democratic headquarters; I attributed the incident to an overzealous staff and felt that the story was fueled and blown out of proportion by a hostile press corps. I even publicly called Watergate an "ephemeral" matter, which sent several reporters off to try to find out what ephemeral meant. But, of course, I was wrong. Watergate was far from ephemeral. It dominated everything and pushed other issues and policy to the shadows.

As the scandal continued to unfold and become more public, President Nixon became more defensive and angry, though he tried to maintain a business-as-usual facade. In one cabinet meeting fairly late in the game, then-chairman of the Republican National Committee George Bush, who sometimes attended cabinet meetings, ventured a question we had all been wrestling with. We have to be realistic, he told the president—we need to know how to respond when we're asked about Watergate. The president did not care much for that, and he replied curtly that it was not necessary for us to deal with it.

He was anxious to appear outwardly as if it were not necessary for him to deal with the growing scandal, but it was clear to those of us who had direct contact with the president that it was taking a heavy toll. I had a private meeting with him in the Oval Office, arranged entirely by the White House and designed to try to get the press to write about something else. The subject was federal scholarships for college students, and I was to confer with him about it and then come out and brief the press. But the president was totally uninterested in discussing the matter. He had spent the earlier part of the morning listening to tapes, and was probably going to spend the rest of the morning doing the same, so he was anxious to get our meeting over with as quickly as possible. As predicted, when I emerged, all the press wanted to know about was the president's mood and demeanor; they were not the least bit interested in student scholarships either.

I recall that at an August 1974 cabinet meeting when Mr. Nixon himself raised the question of resignation, the president said he had found no evidence of any impeachable offense. If there were, he said, he would not stay in office one more minute. He explained at greater length that the president is not in the position of an ordinary citizen. The Constitution says the president is to be impeached by the House and tried by the Senate. It was his view that he should not take a step, resignation, that changes the Constitution and sets a precedent that resignation should instead be the method. That would introduce a parliamentary system, and that precedent should not be set or even thought of. Any action of the president that may have been illegal should be handled, he said, as provided in the Constitution, not by resignation.

Only two days later—faced with collapsing congressional support and the Supreme Court decision that all of the White House tapes must be turned over to the special prosecutor—the president changed his mind. The day President Nixon announced his resignation, our Chilean housekeeper came to me trembling and frightened. "Oh, Mr. Weinberger, when will the National Guard come?" She was the widow of a Chilean army officer, and she assumed the military would assassinate everyone in the government and "take over."

My driver, Sarge, was also quite shaken and upset about the news of the president's resignation, so much so that he had a small accident driving me to a speaking engagement at the National Institutes of Health. (I ended up hitching a ride with a kind motorist.)

The next day—August 9, 1974—was a sad day for the country and wrenching for all of us in the Nixon administration. My wife and I and other cabinet members and White House staff filled the East Room, where we had been summoned to hear the president's farewell address. We were acutely aware that we were present at a historic event. As the president began, it felt as if we were collectively holding our breath— as though that would prevent the inevitable from happening. But through the apprehension, incredulity, and even grief that hung heavy in the air, a beaten president delivered a long, rambling talk in which he constantly mentioned his mother but never once made mention of his wife, who had stood by him and supported him throughout the whole ordeal, indeed through his entire career. This omission was noted by many, and I thought it was particularly unfortunate.

Shortly after Nixon departed from the White House by helicopter, Vice President Ford was sworn in as our thirty-eighth president. He then made a splendid short speech, beginning with, "My fellow Americans, our long national nightmare is over. Our Constitution works." He said exactly the right things, striking a perfect balance between compassion for Nixon and the importance that the country move on. The mood in the room improved palpably as he spoke. I tried to carry that feeling of hope to my own department, calling a meeting of all HEW employees, at which I encouraged them to seize this new beginning with President Ford. And it was a new beginning. Only two days later, I appeared on *Meet the Press* to discuss health insurance, and for the first time in months I actually was allowed to talk about policy rather than Watergate.

Even though President Ford knew public opinion was against it, he made the courageous decision to pardon President Nixon in order to put Watergate behind us. I believe it was the right thing to do because Nixon had already suffered far more intense personal anguish than any trial or jail sentence could have imposed; also, it was important that the country move forward.

Unlike President Nixon after his reelection, President Ford asked everyone to stay on. As I wrote of his first cabinet meeting, on August 10, 1974:

> The president said, "I don't want any resignations submitted to me." He said without reflecting on anyone or implying any criticism, "I thought the wholesale resignation called for after the 1972 election was just terrible."

Nevertheless, I offered to resign if President Ford had his own candidate for my job, but he kindly asked me to stay. President Ford told us in that first cabinet meeting:[*]

> "Everybody's style is different and mine will be different than President Nixon's. I like to see people. I am a better listener than I am a reader. I want you to come in. I also like to get business done and over with. I don't like a lot of chitchat, that isn't my style. Your time and mine is precious, and I want to observe that and protect it."
>
> I told him I thought this was a much better system than the one that had been in effect before, when not only was it impossible to get our memoranda through, but it was virtually impossible to get an appointment. He smiled sympathetically.

Unlike Nixon, President Ford sought advice from his cabinet members, including our recommendations for vice presidential candidates. The people I suggested were the same ones whose names I had submitted (unsolicited) to President Nixon when Agnew resigned: Nelson Rockefeller and Ronald Reagan. Both men, I felt, were superb governors, and either one would bring great strength to the ticket if President Ford decided to run for the presidency in 1976.

---

[*] The quote may not be exact; this is how I recorded it in my notes.

Governor Rockefeller was usually seen as a liberal, even though he often spoke of his admiration for Governor Reagan's conservative policies. Rockefeller himself did not worry about labels; he was an enthusiastic "idea man," vigorously supporting those he believed in, whether the ideas happened to be liberal or conservative.

When President Ford nominated Governor Rockefeller to be his vice president, he was confirmed, but only after long and disagreeable confirmation hearings marked by far more questions about the Rockefeller family wealth than anything substantive.

As I admired Nelson Rockefeller for his openness to ideas, I also admired President Ford because I found my meetings with him were far more substantive and productive than were my meetings with Nixon. As I wrote after one such meeting in May 1975:

> These working meetings in which the president actually makes decisions and follows closely domestic policy and has been well briefed in advance and is willing to have various others from the departments present . . . are a great improvement from his predecessor, and we all remarked on it following the meeting.

After two depressing years in Washington, I felt that the clouds had finally rolled away. Once again, I enjoyed government service.

But by April 1975, with my mother's health deteriorating, and with my wife suffering from arthritis and eager to return to California, I informed President Ford that I must reluctantly resign office as soon as he could find a successor. He said he was disappointed but understood my reasons.

I felt it was too bad to have to leave before I had completed everything I had set out to do, but I was proud of what we had been able to accomplish in my two years at HEW. We had put into effect some programs that had just been handed to me, such as the Title IX regulations and the whole SSI program. We had also succeeded in at least shifting the public debate from a concentration on huge federal government programs more toward individuals, even if we were not able to get all of our specific proposals through Congress. Unfortunately, though, Congress had often passed measures over administration protests, resulting in several increases in Social Security and Medicare payments which pushed HEW's budget up nearly 55 percent just in the time I was there. It was a huge, unwieldy department, but one that provided many exciting challenges and the opportunity to try to change things for the better.

In a meeting with the president to say good-bye, I suggested Frank Carlucci (then undersecretary of HEW), former treasury secretary John Connally, or Governor Reagan to succeed me, but he ultimately chose Dr. Forrest David Mathews. Mathews was a professional educator who had made some innovative changes at the University of Alabama, where he was then president.

The date set for Dr. Mathews to take over was August 8, nearly one year to the day since President Nixon had left office.

A number of people I had come to know during my five-and-a-half years in Washington gave some lovely farewell parties for us. One that was particularly special to me was a testimonial dinner given not only by my staff at HEW but also by those with whom I had worked at OMB and the Federal Trade Commission.

I also hosted a party (at Camp David, which President Ford was kind enough to let me use one weekend) for the HEW staff and their families to show my appreciation and gratitude for their great support of the work we had tried to do. I would venture that no other agency of government had such a diversity of professions and skills as those required to operate the roughly three hundred (at that time) programs of HEW efficiently. We had physicians, researchers, lawyers, educators, social workers, economists, actuaries, typists, the maintenance force—and all of them were dedicated to doing their jobs well and serving the many Americans who relied on them.

On the morning of August 8, my last day in office, I attended Dr. Mathews's swearing-in ceremony in the departmental auditorium. That afternoon, I went to a cabinet meeting and said good-bye to my colleagues and the president, who was very kind and generous in his comments.

I considered this the end of my government career. The main contribution I expected to make to the government from then on was to pay a large income tax. My wife and I loaded our dog into the car and literally drove off into the sunset.

CHAPTER 14

RETIREMENT FROM PUBLIC LIFE—OR SO I THOUGHT

The day after my resignation from HEW, I experienced a very peculiar sensation. It was the first time that I had been in Washington with nothing official to do. There were no meetings to get to, no press conferences, no congressional hearings, nothing to prepare for. At first, it left me feeling almost lost.

So we became sightseers. My wife and I spent a couple of days enjoying the beauty of Washington and then embarked on a cross-country journey. We drove northeast to Maine, where, two years later, we bought a house near Jane's childhood home, at the head of a meadow running down to Somes Sound, a long fjord flowing in from the sea on Mount Desert Island.

In that summer of 1975, we drove from Maine to Toronto to see Arlin, then back into the United States and down to California. We liked to get up early each day and start driving by six so that we would reach our overnight destination by early afternoon. That gave us some time to look around the towns or swim in the motel pools. I had not made such a trip since my college days, and then I was more interested in getting "there," wherever that happened to be, than in appreciating the scenery or resting anywhere.

Our new home was in Hillsborough, California, about twenty miles south of San Francisco. We decided on a lovely, old, white, Tudor-style house in the same neighborhood as our previous California home.

Everything about our new house was on a large and old-fashioned scale. It had spacious rooms, including a ballroom and a library. There were a couple of splendid redwood trees in an old garden (a garden much improved later by Jane) and room for a swimming pool, which we put in. All that new space worked out well when Cap Jr. and his wife and daughter lived there with us for a few years.

We had some remodeling done on the house, work that Bechtel, my new firm, kindly supervised before we arrived. They also put in gates and a fence for security.

Our first night in our new home was September 11, 1975. The next morning, I drove into San Francisco to begin work for Bechtel.

As early as June, Bechtel, a global construction firm based in San Francisco, had begun efforts to recruit me. My former colleague George Shultz was already there, and I had known some other Bechtel executives when I had practiced law at Heller, Ehrman, including Bill Slusser, Bechtel's general counsel. The company had a sterling reputation and track record. Warren Bechtel started the business in 1898 when he bought a team of mules and contracted to lay railroad tracks across what is now Oklahoma. By the 1970s, Bechtel was a huge firm involved in heavy construction of tunnels, pipelines, nuclear and other power plants, refineries, building complexes, transportation systems, and a number of civic projects of substantial size, which meant that our customers were often foreign governments. Bechtel would provide broad and varied work—not just legal work—and that and the overseas aspect particularly appealed to me.

The recruiting process had been flatteringly intense. Bill Slusser wanted to retire, and wanted very much for me to succeed him. Bill was a thoroughly charming, delightful, and persuasive man whom I had known for many years, through the Bohemian Club and elsewhere. Ultimately, I met with Steve Bechtel Jr., who had recently succeeded his father as the company's chief executive.

Steve was an extraordinarily effective leader, who benefited from having served in virtually every job—from beginning laborer—on the construction side of the firm. He and his delightful wife, Betty, had lived in construction trailers on sites in inhospitable climates all over the world. Steve was a native Californian, enjoyed intense outdoor activities, and lived for the success of the company.

I accepted his offer to join Bechtel as a vice president, a director, and special counsel, which, if all went well, would lead to the general counsel's position after Bill Slusser actually retired. Steve wanted me to avoid political activities—indeed, all outside activities—at least for the first year of my employment. I said that would be difficult because I had already had offers—in which I was interested—to sit on various corporate boards. I thought the experience to be gained there would be most helpful, particularly as many of the offers had come from corporations that had international operations, as Bechtel did. Eventually, Steve relaxed the requirement a bit and offered generous compensation which included valuable shares of Bechtel stock. I accepted the offer.

My other concern, which I expressed frankly to Steve was that I hoped my responsibilities would encompass much more than strictly legal work. I wanted to visit construction sites, learn all about the actual work of the company, and serve, if I could, on some of the corporate-wide committees that had other duties besides legal work. I was assured that that would be the case.

I received Steve's offer while he, Bill Slusser, and I drove up together to attend the annual encampment of the club at Bohemian Grove, north of San Francisco. I had been a member of the Bohemian Club since 1973. Bohemian Club members, as is the case with most private clubs, are expected to maintain what we called at Harvard a "decent reticence" about its matters.

What we can say is that the club was started in 1872, basically as a fraternity of artists, writers, and musicians, with a few philistines who, if not artists themselves, enjoyed and appreciated those who were. Since then, the club's membership has shifted more toward prominent businessmen, industry titans, and political leaders.

Over the years, the club had acquired about 2,700 acres of an extraordinarily beautiful and secluded portion of the ancient redwood forest north and west of San Francisco, within which were various campfires, tents, dining facilities, and other gathering places. Each camp was unique, and I was particularly fortunate that both Bill Slusser and Ted Meyer, my original sponsors, had paved the way for me to be taken into one of the oldest, the Isle of Aves, named for a mythical island in a poem by Charles Kingsley. Other members of the Isle of Aves included my old friend Bill Clark, former governor and Chief Justice of the United States Earl Warren, the presidents of Stanford and the University of California, and many other San Franciscans.

I gave a few of the so-called Lakeside lectures, which were generally held in the afternoons of the two-and-a-half weeks of the summer encampment. Lakeside talks were a lot of fun but a real challenge to any speaker. The audience consisted of up to a couple thousand people, most of whom were very well known, and most of whom had heard far better speakers from all over the world, because these were the people who were attracted as guests to the Grove. There was one further challenge: it was necessary when speaking to compete with one or two large and very ancient frogs, who competed with very throaty noises during most of the speeches. The crowd also fully expected to be entertained, and if a little instruction or governmental views went along with it, that was acceptable, but it was essential that one be both amusing and effective

The club was a very happy part of my life at that time, and I enjoyed my membership thoroughly. The artistic talent that had started the club was still an important requirement, and new members particularly were expected to participate in one way or another in the plays or other entertainments that were a part of the Grove's summer encampments. My thespian experience at the club was limited to a Grove play which involved Noah's ark. My role was the somewhat narrow and not particularly demanding one of holding up a portion of the rainbow which appeared after the flood. This required the skills of a college football card stunt, and I like to think that my quadrant of the rainbow appeared at the right time and in the proper sequence.

All of these antics—indeed, the whole idea of a grown men's camp-out—may seem rather puerile to outsiders, but having a brief retreat like this in such wondrous surroundings is salutary. It provides a temporary release from the pressures of leadership and responsibility, both of which weigh heavily on most members, by virtue of their positions in life and work. I know I found the summer encampments to be a welcome respite and always a help to regain perspective and balance.

The food at the Grove was extraordinarily good—plain, hearty fare, served on great camp tables in one of the most splendid of all redwood groves. The sight of 1,500 to 2,500 people all dining in those glorious surroundings has provided most happy and satisfying memories. It was, of course, not the first time I had spent time in the redwoods, because many of our summer vacations years before, with the children, had been in some of the earliest of the California state redwood parks. So the majesty and glory of these great trees were already well known to me.

I attended my first Bechtel directors' meeting nearly a month after I accepted Bechtel's offer. The company owned one twenty-three-story

building in San Francisco's financial district and two others nearby.
Steve Bechtel Jr. would walk all the way up to his twenty-second floor
office every morning, a feat that I could not emulate then and certainly not now. I had a large, corner office on the twenty-first floor
with a splendid view of the bay and much of the city.

There was no such thing as a "typical" workday at Bechtel, which
was one of the things I liked most about the job; and, unlike the
slower-moving government, you could actually see progress being
made.

Though the company was enormous, it retained a personal touch.
For many years, Steve Bechtel Sr. knew the first names and family
facts of every Bechtel employee. He was admired and respected by
everyone who knew him. And he was a man of vision. Once when he
was in Saudi Arabia to negotiate a contract for an oil refinery, he said,
"What you *really* need is a new city." The Saudis agreed, and Bechtel
built Jubail for them. In fact, so expansive became their plans that the
Saudis concluded they needed two cities, and they created the Royal
Commission for Jubail and Yanbu. Each became a successful industrial site and a full-scale city. Jubail had been a small, remote fishing
village; it is now a thriving city of several hundred thousand people.

Along with Bill Slusser and Steve Bechtel Jr., I was delighted to
work again with Virginia Duncan, my friend and former colleague
from KQED, who became my executive assistant. She had just left
KQED, having been elected to a California bank board, and later was
appointed to the board of the Corporation of Public Broadcasting.
She said she wanted to gain more business experience, which worked
out perfectly for me as well, because I needed an executive assistant
who was good at managing the many nonlegal details involved in
administering the legal and insurance departments. Insurance had
been part of the general counsel's duties for some time, and that was
another set of new responsibilities I had to learn. Virginia had skill-

fully handled many important details at KQED, so she came to Bechtel and did the same for me there.

George Shultz had joined Bechtel about a year before I did. As seemed to be the case every time we worked together (before and since Bechtel), we often had differing viewpoints. This was most evident when lawsuits were brought against the company, particularly large class-action suits. The arguments for settling them to avoid trial might be strong, but agreeing to huge settlements could set precedents that might encourage future suits, some of which would be virtually legal blackmail. So generally I would recommend that we fight rather than yield, but invariably George would want to settle. Later, when we both served in the Reagan administration, George was sometimes more eager to send in troops than I was.

I served on Bechtel's personnel and finance committees, which oversaw things like training programs, compensation packages, and health insurance plans, of which Bechtel offered one of the best.

I spent the first few months familiarizing myself with the contracts and projects in progress and the people working on them. This, of course, involved visiting many project sites, which I loved to do because it was a great education. In early October, I toured a number of Bechtel's Stateside projects, including the San Onofre nuclear power plant in southern California and the tunnel for Washington, D.C.'s Metro subway system.

In the fall of 1975, Bill Slusser took Jane and me to meet the staff in our London office, and then to Saudi Arabia and Kuwait. I was fascinated by the Mideast and the Arab cultures, and Bechtel veterans were well versed in the behavior expected in these countries. I learned, for example, that one should never show the soles of one's shoes (as when crossing one's legs), as Arabs deem this a great insult. The new city of Jubail was a huge single construction zone, including a new port, an industrial complex, highways, apartment buildings, hotels, hospitals, schools, and all utilities. At the same time, we were beginning on a new airport for Riyadh.

As we traveled throughout the region, I wrote a number of impressions and observations, some important, some trifling.

> *8 November 1975:* Flew from Kuwait to Riyadh. The baggage formalities at the Riyadh airport took some time although they have a very new, modern machine for bringing the baggage up from the ground floor, and for the first time in my entire career of travel one of my bags came out first.
>
> *9 November 1975:* Parenthetically, I should note that it is always interesting to see how many different viewpoints you get. From the people who are in the operating divisions there is usually a very substantial optimism. From the people who have to coordinate all of the company activities there is a kind of controlled pessimism and worry.
>
> Riyadh reminds me very much of some of the Philippine towns I saw during the war. Parts of the streets are paved, the center dividing strip is sand, and the wind blows a lot of dust around. Even though it is November, it is excessively hot, and dust is in most of the buildings. There seems to be very little central air conditioning although there is a vast number of air conditioning units.

We were received very cordially by Saudi and Kuwaiti officials, many of whom had been educated in the United States or England, but a sensitive issue caused some legal and business problems. As today, most Arab countries boycotted companies that did business with Israel—a practice that both Bechtel and the U.S. government agreed amounted to economic sanctions, which were illegal. A great deal of legal work was required to make sure that we did not violate U.S. law *or* jeopardize our dealings with *any* country. Fortunately, many high-ranking Arabs did not support the boycott anyway.

As usual, keeping up with the myriad responsibilities of the general counsel's post did not satisfy my need to branch out into other activities. So I pushed hard for Bechtel's approval—which was reluctantly given—to sit on the boards of PepsiCo and Quaker Oats.

PepsiCo is a huge, innovative conglomerate, and Don Kendall—then CEO and chairman of the board of PepsiCo, and a longtime friend—was quite impressive himself, as a 1977 article in *ARCOspark*, the magazine of Atlantic-Richfield, pointed out:

> In 1947, [Kendall] heard by chance that Pepsi had an opening for a fountain syrup salesman. PepsiCo is the only company he's ever worked for. After super-selling his way into the international VP job at Pepsi, he talked management into funding a Pepsi exhibit at the 1959 Moscow trade show. Under pressure to justify the endeavor, Kendall persuaded then-vice president Nixon to bring Khrushchev by the Pepsi booth for an introduction. What happened was the famous "kitchen debate" between Nixon and the Russian Premier.
>
> "It was a hot day and I was there passing out Pepsis," Kendall recalls. "Khrushchev ended up drinking eight and he passed them out to his aides. Pictures of Khrushchev with Pepsis in his hand appeared in newspapers around the world."
>
> Kendall—who took over Pepsi in 1963—has always believed in trade with Eastern Europe. And the kitchen debate paved the way for Pepsi in Russia. In 1972, Pepsi became the first American firm to make a consumer product in Russia. Pepsi has two plants in Russia with three more on the drawing boards. Kendall today oversees a $2.3 billion sales empire which includes North American Van Lines, Wilson Sporting Goods, Monsieur Henri Wines, Ltd., and Frito-Lay.

I went with Don Kendall and the rest of the board to the Soviet Union in the fall of 1979 to open new Pepsi bottling plants, and I observed firsthand the impact Pepsi had there. There were long lines at the Pepsi kiosks in the city squares, and it was gratifying to realize that in the Soviet Union, popular American products were playing such a large role—which was mostly because the people had so little of any quality that they could buy.

The Soviet Union was also benefiting from an arrangement with PepsiCo: the Soviets would buy Pepsi and pay for it by giving us Stolichnaya vodka to sell in the United States. The problem with this for Pepsi came later, when the Soviets invaded Afghanistan and many Americans refused to buy any Soviet products.

Other aspects of that trip were not quite so impressive—such as the night train from Moscow to Leningrad. It was supposed to be a marvel, but I was incautious enough to brush my teeth with the water on board—not a wise thing to do.

My return (which I made alone, as I had to get back for a Bechtel meeting) had problems as well—this time, at the Moscow airport. A large dragon lady in charge of customs asked what one of my bags was, and without thinking I identified my shaving kit as my "drug kit." Huge mistake. My answer delayed me by almost three hours (just enough time to miss my plane) while officials examined every single article I had in each of my bags. Unsuccessful in my attempts to explain the misunderstanding, I tried to call the health officials I had met when I was there as secretary of HEW, hoping they could help. But they were no longer in office.

I joined the board of Quaker Oats in 1977, after being recruited by the company chairman, Bob Stuart. I had known Bob for many years, as he had been active in Republican politics. He is a thorough gentleman, is an excellent businessman and diplomat, and has a delightful, quiet manner. Quaker, although a large conglomerate, seemed like more of a small family business. The Quaker meetings were held every other month at Chicago's Merchandise Mart, and I would usually fly in and back on the same day.

I managed to fill available fragments of time with other endeavors. I resumed my involvement with the Episcopal Church, a nearly life-long interest kindled by my mother that had only grown over the years. Now back in the Bay Area, we attended regular services at St. Luke's, and in the summer of 1977 I was appointed treasurer of the Episcopal Diocese of California. It seemed I was destined always to be responsible for balancing someone's budget.

I was also asked to write a few book reviews for the *Riverside Press-Enterprise* and the *Wall Street Journal*, which I was glad to do because it revived an old interest begun as a reviewer for the *San Francisco Chronicle* years before.

However, as always, my real and deepest interest was not in the boardroom or the church but in the ever changing rough and tumble of government and politics. Unfortunately, Bechtel frowned on political activities, particularly by former government officials, and Steve Bechtel worried that I was not fully dissociated from the public sector. I am afraid he was absolutely right. By the time I had been with Bechtel a year or so, I think Steve was pretty well resigned to the fact that I was always going to have other interests. In any event, he gradually eased his objections and allowed me to take part in some governmental activities, including serving on President Ford's Committee on Science and Technology and, in 1980, even working with Ronald Reagan's campaign.

In 1977 I accepted an invitation to join the Trilateral Commission, an organization whose origins stemmed from President Nixon's diplomatic overtures to China. Many American business leaders and former government officials were alarmed that our allies had not been consulted when the president made his China visit. I agreed that new relations with traditional adversaries should not be pursued at the expense of our relationships with our allies, particularly Western Europe and Japan. So the Trilateral Commission was formed with representatives from the United States, Europe, and Japan. It was an attempt to keep everyone informed through an extragovernmental consultative body that provided a forum for addressing common concerns and possible solutions. It was not a policy-making body, though it included a number of former and future government leaders, such as President Carter, Vice President Walter Mondale, Secretary of State Cyrus Vance, Defense Secretary Harold Brown, and National Security Adviser Zbigniew Brzezinski. When all these men took office with Mr. Carter in January 1977, they resigned from the commission but, fortunately, kept the trilateral U.S.–Western Europe–Japan relationship as the centerpiece of their foreign policy.

I know some right-wing zealots feared that the commission was a conspiracy to create a world government. David Rockefeller, whom I have known since Harvard days and who was basically the founder of the commission, was particularly suspect by the farthest of the far right, as well as by many far leftists. In reality, he was scarcely a revolutionary figure. But since he was part of the East Coast foreign policy establishment, to some people that automatically spelled a sinister conspiracy.

I did not agree with every report of the task forces of the Trilateral Commission—indeed, I thought some of the reports took a weak line on so-called Euro-Communism—but the commission was examining important issues and helped to strengthen our alliances, and we needed all the help we could get.

In the summer of 1978, I was offered another opportunity to indulge my love of public policy—this time by a Democrat. California governor Jerry Brown appointed me to his Commission on Government Reform, which he established in response to the passage of Proposition 13. The voters of the state had overwhelmingly passed the measure, which drastically reduced property taxes (by 67 percent, or approximately $7 billion) and limited future increases to 2 percent of property value. California was the first state to roll back the property tax so radically.* It was a great example of the power of the people and the use of the initiative to bring about changes that were inconceivable under the ordinary legislative process. Indeed, it was viewed with absolute horror by longtime state and local government people because the property tax had been one of the best sources of revenue.

Governor Brown and others considered the passage of Proposition 13 an emergency about which something had to be done. Never mind that it was the will of the people or that the repudiated property tax had been particularly onerous—given that property taxes rose with property value rather than income or ability to pay.

The fourteen-member commission was fairly evenly divided between Republicans and Democrats, and, as such, predictably, it did not reach a consensus about how the state and local governments could reform the way they taxed and spent. At least it gave me a platform to air many of my own long-standing ideas for tax and spending limitations, but I also suspect Governor Brown thought of the commission as bipartisan cover for enacting tax increases. He knew he could not survive politically if he recommended them, so he wanted to have a commission of experts say they was necessary.

Until serving on this commission I had not been active in political matters since returning to the private sector. It was not the most encouraging time to be a Republican. The party had been badly beaten in 1974—in Congress as well as in governorships and local elections, no doubt due to what today might be called "Watergate fatigue."

---

* California led a nationwide tax rebellion. According to *California and the American Tax Revolt: Proposition 13 Five Years Later*, edited by Terry Schwadron, "Between 1978 and 1980...fully 43 states adopted new limitations on local property taxes or new property tax relief plans, either on official initiative or as a result of the electorate's decision."

Then, in 1976, we lost the White House. I believe one reason was that the party was divided. Governor Reagan challenged incumbent President Ford, which I thought was a great mistake. Rifts remained even though Governor Reagan made a gracious concession speech at the convention and supported President Ford after narrowly losing on the convention's first ballot. Stiff nomination fights generally spell doom for Republicans.

By 1980, after nearly four years of economic and foreign policy defeats under President Carter, Americans were ready to take another look at Republican candidates—and Governor Reagan was ready to make another run for president. When he began his campaign in late 1979, he was given little chance of winning. Moderate Republicans considered him a right-wing nut who could never win, and many party loyalists resented him because they felt he was at least partly responsible for President Ford's defeat in 1976. Primarily, however, they feared his challenge to the conventional wisdom. Even foreigners were wary of him, concerned about an actor's ability to run the country. People I knew in London were horrified at the prospect of Ronald Reagan as president, and they felt that it could not possibly happen. (I reminded them of that several years later, and they were extremely grateful that they had been wrong. President Reagan turned out to be nearly as popular abroad as he was at home.)

Governor Reagan's campaign message resonated with the American people: he advocated a 10 percent across-the-board tax cut to boost our economy, pull us out of inflation, and put people back to work, and he supported the usually unpopular idea of rebuilding our hollowed-out military (which ultimately brought the Soviets to the bargaining table on arms control). All of this, and the hope he held out of a better America, rather than a country mired in "malaise," made him a most attractive alternative to a haggard and ineffectual President Carter.

My good friend Bill Clark was active in Governor Reagan's campaign from its early stages, and at his suggestion I began doing some informal consulting and speaking for the campaign in mid-1979. At first it was fairly limited, but gradually I became more involved, and by the summer of 1980 I was an at-large delegate from California to the Republican National Convention in Detroit.

Former president Ford was also running, but he could not match Governor Reagan's popularity. A number of Ford's people were still bitter about Governor Reagan's challenge in 1976, and they could not imagine that Reagan was up to the job. "Reagan," they liked to say, "knows nothing about foreign policy."

So, after the governor won the nomination at the convention, a number of President Ford's people began pushing for what would essentially be a "joint presidency": Ford would be Reagan's vice president but would do all the substantive work—in effect, operating like a prime minister, while Reagan's duties as president would be strictly ceremonial. It was a perfect plan, they thought. Reagan had all of the charisma and vote-drawing ability, but Ford would be there to serve as president in all but name.

Governor Reagan, as the party nominee, of course did not agree to such an absurd arrangement, but he was rather amused by the rumors. When he jokingly asked me about the idea, I pointed out that there was one minor problem: it was totally and completely unconstitutional—and that was just to begin with.

But the machinations and rumors continued, and leaks of this "dream ticket" spread like wildfire, reaching fever pitch when it was actually reported that the deal was done. Finally, Governor Reagan told a group of his supporters in his hotel suite, "This has gone far enough. Get me George Bush."

George Bush was the obvious choice, and a good one, for a running mate, since he had finished second in many primaries. I think Bush was surprised to be asked, but the press was completely astounded. They kept asking me (and anyone else they believed had Reagan's confidence) what had changed the governor's mind. I pointed out that he never had agreed to the "joint presidency" idea. "You've got it all wrong," I told them. "*Nobody* but the press thought this thing was all settled. Nobody ever bothered to consult Ronald Reagan."

In the following months leading up to the election, I continued consulting with Governor Reagan and his campaign staff. We all became increasingly enthusiastic as his candidacy continued to build momentum. Many of us had long known of the governor's leadership abilities and solid conservative values, and it was tremendously gratifying to see the rest of America getting to know him and beginning to recognize the many assets he could bring to leading the nation.

CHAPTER 15

IN THE ARENA AGAIN

onald Reagan's disposition and the weather in Los Angeles were equally and typically sunny when Jane and I arrived at the Century Plaza Hotel, Reagan's favorite hotel in the city, on November 4, 1980. As soon as we got to our hotel room, somewhere between 5 P.M. and 6 P.M., I turned on the television to see President Carter already conceding. We went to the headquarters suite, where a familiar coterie was gathered: Bill Clark, Ed Meese, Mike Deaver, Bill French Smith, Bill Casey, and various other aides and friends. The rest of the evening was a jubilant blur: meeting with hundreds of Reagan supporters, doing many quick radio and television interviews, and attending the president-elect's gracious speech acknowledging his remarkable victory. Almost as exciting was that the new Senate would have a GOP majority.

Carter's early concession infuriated the Democrats because the polls were still to be open for three more hours in the whole western part of the country, and they feared that his early concession would discourage many Democrats from voting at all. But Carter had guessed right; the results were clearly tilting in Reagan's favor.[*] Weary of high inflation and unemployment, the energy crisis, and the inability to gain freedom for fifty-two citizens held for over a year in Iran, Americans were ready for strong leadership and watershed changes in policies.

Change was in the offing for me personally as well, although I did not know, or even think about, that then.

I returned to San Francisco and my job with Bechtel, but soon after Election Day President-elect Reagan appointed me to head his task force on reducing federal spending. I recommended a two-track approach of deep spending and tax cuts (directly contrary to the Keynesian theories) as the only effective way of both slowing federal budget growth and stimulating the economy. I also recommended that Reagan have his own budget ready to submit to Congress as soon as possible; he would *not* want to govern on the basis of President Carter's last budget.

In addition to heading the economic task force, I was asked, and enthusiastically agreed, to serve on the president-elect's Task Force on National Security. Rebuilding America's defense was as important to Ronald Reagan as was restoring America's economy. Reagan keenly understood the importance of military strength. In his acceptance speech at the Republican convention in 1980, he said, "We know only too well that war comes not when the forces of freedom are strong, but when they are weak. It is then that tyrants are tempted." President-elect Reagan and I agreed that America's national security took precedence over every other policy priority.

The core decision-making group during the transition was Reagan's "kitchen cabinet"—essentially his longtime backers and advisers,

---

[*] Reagan ended up winning forty-four states and 489 electoral votes—only to garner even more impressive results in his reelection race four years later: forty-nine states and 525 electoral votes.

such as Holmes Tuttle, Justin Dart, and Henry Salvatori. A number of us who had served in the president-elect's gubernatorial administration were also included.

This group held frequent meetings, usually in the big conference room at Bill French Smith's law firm in Los Angeles. Bill had been Reagan's personal attorney for many years. Whenever one of us was suggested as an appointee, that person was asked to leave the room. So I took it as something of a compliment that I had to leave the conference room several times. I was apparently suggested for OMB, Treasury, attorney general, State, and Defense. I definitely did not want to run OMB again; two-and-a-half years of virtually continuous budget cutting there had been enough. I was ambivalent about the Treasury post; I suppose my inclination at that time was to get away from exclusively budgetary or financial matters and concentrate more on other issues, preferably relating to foreign and security policy. The attorney general post would have allowed that to a greater degree, but I knew that Bill Smith was Reagan's choice, and I strongly supported that. Frankly, if I were to be involved at all in the new administration, I was most interested in the State or Defense Departments. When Ronald Reagan called, in late November 1980, he said, "I know you have a very full, comfortable, and probably rich life, and now I want to spoil the whole thing by asking you to serve as my secretary of defense." Although accepting would mean another major upheaval in our lives and a significant loss of income, I knew immediately that I wanted to serve the president and execute his plans for regaining America's military strength.

I called my wife, who, as an army nurse commissioned early in the war, had outranked me when we both served in the army during World War II. So I took great delight in saying, "Lieutenant Dalton, now *you* may salute." I must report that she was not terribly enthusiastic about the prospect of uprooting and moving once again to Washington and living under public scrutiny to an even greater extent than before. But, as she had done so many times, she recognized that I felt this was something we should do, and as always she agreed and began the enormous task of organizing and carrying out our move to Washington.

My appointment was announced on what would have been my father's ninety-fourth birthday—December 1, 1980. I like to think that he would have been especially proud that day. I was the only cabinet member confirmed on the first day of the Reagan administration. I was approved by the Senate by a vote of 97 to 2,[*] the two opposing votes cast by North Carolina Republican senators Jesse Helms and John East, who thought I would not pursue a sufficiently hard line against the USSR and would not spend enough on defense. Senator East died early in the Reagan administration, but not before he had apologized to me for misjudging what I would do at Defense. Senator Helms later was kind enough to tell me he greatly admired my work, and we became good friends.

So many things happened at once, and so many priorities needed to be addressed as soon as I took office, that trying to recall those first days brings to memory only a vast blur of meetings, briefings, interviews, and paperwork. I immersed myself to learn not only large policy matters but also esoteric details, which I knew would come up at congressional hearings, though sometimes I didn't appreciate quite how detailed my knowledge would have to be. At one of my first budget hearings as secretary, a congressman asked me why the Defense Department had decided to contract out the laundry service at Eglin Air Force Base to a private firm. I had spent many, many hours preparing for this hearing, working with a vast number of staff and military people, trying to anticipate committee questions. This one we hadn't anticipated.

---

[*] Senator Sam Nunn abstained.

Of tremendous help to me in acclimating myself to my new position—and indeed, throughout my tenure at Defense—were two outstanding assistants, Thelma Stubbs and Kay Leisz.

Thelma knew everything about the office, having served as personal assistant to seven secretaries of defense before me. From composing letters for my signature to knowing whom to let in and whom to keep out, Thelma was the one to see.

Kay was recruited by Will Taft during the transition to be my executive assistant. A native of North Dakota, she had been secretary to a North Dakota senator who was retiring. She proved extremely competent and loyal, and she has stayed with me even since I left government. I think it is fair to say that I could not have accomplished what I did at Defense, and what I have since, without Kay at my side.*

The hugeness of the job manifested itself in many ways, particularly in the early days and weeks of the administration. I was pursued by a lot of forwarded mail, and there was one letter from Dun & Bradstreet, following up on a report that I had changed my business. It was addressed to "C. Weinberger, Secretary," and they wanted some information on the new firm. A form letter asked if it was correct that I had three million full-time employees but no sales, no profits, and no net worth. I had to admit that that was what the accountants would say, but I insisted that the Defense Department had a huge net worth. I never did find out what our credit rating was.

There were more important issues to be dealt with than laundry service and filling out forms. I was already aware of the general deterioration of our military during the Carter years, but as I began

---

* After we left Defense, Kay did all the tasks for me that had been performed by five or six people in the department: making schedules; keeping me on schedule; handling travel, speech, and invitation acceptances and regrets; preparing briefing books for meetings; and so on, ad infinitum.

receiving the classified data on our capabilities, I found that it was even worse than I had thought. It was truly appalling. Our nuclear deterrent was in serious need of modernization. Our conventional forces were underbudgeted and undersupplied, with limited funds for training exercises, which meant, in short, they were unready. Steaming time for the navy had been cut back, yet operational tempo and overseas tours had been increased; flight hours for air force crews and field maneuvers for the army had been curtailed. And we were woefully short on training funds for the National Guard and reserves. Morale among military personnel was miserable, and early retirements rivaled the number of new volunteers.

Almost as bad, my briefings revealed that we were losing the respect and support of our allies because of the Carter administration's erratic policies. Moreover, both our allies and the Soviets suspected we lacked the conventional military strength—and perhaps the will—to prevent a Soviet advance into Western Europe.

In view of my reputation from California and my OMB days as a zealous budget cutter, many may have thought it odd that the president-elect would ask me to conduct and lead the great military buildup that we both knew was necessary. I had always felt that we needed to maintain a strong defense at all times. I had recognized this back in 1972, when I was director of the budget, and I made no secret of my opinion.

In a talk to the American Enterprise Institute,* I concluded my opening statement by saying, "If our defense budget is inadequate, nothing else will be of much moment, and we will only know it when it is too late."

---

* "The Defense Budget," *American Enterprise Institute: A Town Hall Meeting*, October 17, 1972, p. 19.

In a *U.S. News & World Report* interview that same year, I elaborated: "...none of the domestic programs we've been talking about has the slightest meaning if our borders aren't secure.

"There's another factor in defense spending that is unique. In education, in health, in welfare, and in almost every other field, what the federal government doesn't do, other levels of government or the private sector will attempt to do. The only unit of government that pays for defense is the federal government. What we don't do in defense at the national level doesn't get done."

A strong military force seemed to me even more necessary in 1980, after a decade of neglect in a hostile world.

President Reagan was also deeply concerned about America's standing in the world—and what the increasing impotence of our hollowed-out military was doing to that standing. Reagan keenly understood the importance both of military strength and of having strong, supportive allies. He said frequently to me that if it ever came down to a choice between balancing the budget and spending enough to regain and keep our military strength, he would always come down on the side of the latter.

The gap in strength between the Soviets' and our capabilities, and between the Warsaw Pact's and NATO's, had widened enormously, and that gap was still growing. The Soviets had made major increases in a decade when we had made major reductions. Beyond just the differences in numbers, I was struck by the differences between our governmental systems. In the USSR, three or four men in the Kremlin made all the decisions on allocation of all their resources, on how much they would raise and spend on their military. They were not concerned about public opinion because none was permitted in the USSR. That had given them an enormous military advantage, which we needed to recognize, and they had used it to acquire vast stores of new weapons, such as high-tech missiles, and to draft and equip huge numbers of divisions, air wings, and so forth, despite the generally wretched quality of life suffered by the Russian people. The government needed no debates and no congressional hearings, nor any votes to acquire this weaponry—only the decision of a few men responsible to no one but themselves.

All of this caused me—and President Reagan—more than a little alarm. When we took office, the first thing we did was to add $32 billion to the Carter administration's Defense budget requests for fiscal years 1981 and 1982. We were criticized for this spending, but in truth it wasn't nearly enough. We had to modernize all three legs of the strategic triad at once: our sea-based, air-based, and ground-based nuclear missiles.

I knew too that we would have to rebuild our conventional strength, including finally deploying a new and effective main battle tank, the M-1, after years of design, redesign, and indecision. We also needed additional and improved helicopters, spare parts for everything, equipment for the Rapid Deployment Force, enhanced electronic warfare capabilities, and improved intelligence capabilities. All of this and much more had to be done and done quickly. Even basic maintenance at our bases had been deferred, and deferred maintenance is one of the worst ways to reduce costs.

In addition, we had to convince our allies that we had every intention of regaining our strength and that it would be not only safe but also very much in their interest to stay with us rather than to become neutral or slide over to the other side. That would take a great deal of cultivation of all of our NATO allies, of Japan and Korea, and of our friends in the Mideast. Korea was particularly nervous because President Carter had talked about removing our troops from there. There were other countries, too, whose strength and support we would need and who would in turn need our strength.

The crucial element in this recovery of strength was people. So our most urgent task would be to address the needs of our uniformed men and women and to improve morale, thereby strengthening the volunteer system, which was failing badly. I had been told many times during my confirmation hearings that we had to have a draft. But I knew how the draft had pulled the country apart and ripped the whole social fabric during the Vietnam War. I was convinced that the volunteer system could work if we treated the men and women fairly. We had begun to get a decent salary and benefits package for military personnel through Congress, but there was more to the equation than that. People do not join the military to make money. A sense of pride had to be restored—pride in the work they were doing and in the uniforms they wore. They also had to know that they were needed and that their government and its leaders respected and admired them.*

Hand in hand with this, we needed to change the public image of the military, as a profession and as individuals. I began thinking of a message to all the troops, and this ultimately became my first message as secretary: "Our new president and I share a deep appreciation of the sacrifices you make and the skills with which you serve and defend all the people. One of my major priorities is to be sure that our country fully recognizes and honors your great service at home and all over the world."

The president exercised vital leadership here, making numerous appearances at military events and posts, praising, with his characteristic warmth and patriotism, the men and women in uniform who are willing to sacrifice their lives for their country. This helped enormously in changing the public's perception of our armed forces into

---

* One minor change that I made within the Pentagon that I believe furthered this end was to reinstate the requirement that all military personnel, regardless of rank, wear uniforms while on duty. The Carter administration, apparently not wanting to seem too militaristic, had discouraged this basic practice, thus further eroding the spirit and pride of those in the military.

one of deep appreciation and respect. It also helped raise the morale of the troops themselves, and that improved recruiting.

Our military buildup during the Reagan administration would be the most important part of our foreign policy, which had essentially four major goals. The most basic, of course, was to protect our national security—our physical borders, our citizens, and our interests abroad.

Protecting our allies was essentially an extension of this policy, as peace-loving nations contribute to regional and global stability. We would always need to convince our friends and allies that our interests were mutual and that we were reliable partners.

Taking this strategy one step further, our third goal was to encourage countries trying to get out from under the yoke of Soviet Communism.

Our fourth major policy goal, about which President Reagan felt passionate, was to bring the Soviets to the bargaining table and achieve real nuclear arms reductions. Our major military buildup was instrumental in making that happen. This seemed paradoxical to some, but if we did not have real strength, the Soviets would never even talk to us. For peace can come only to those who are strong and determined enough to fight for it.

The president and I rejected détente, which argued that we should accept the Soviet Union as merely having a different political outlook. I thought President Reagan's definition of détente was more accurate: "a French word the Russians had interpreted as a freedom to pursue whatever policies of subversion, aggression, and expansionism they wanted anywhere in the world."* The president and I wanted to *roll back* Communism so that the people of Eastern Europe and elsewhere could breathe free.

Poland's Solidarity movement provided the first opportunity to do this in the new administration. As President Reagan wrote in his

---

* Ronald Reagan, *An American Life* (New York: Simon & Schuster, 1990), 265.

autobiography, "We were witnessing the first fraying of the Iron Curtain, a disenchantment with Soviet Communism in Poland, not realizing then that it was a harbinger of great and historic events to come in Eastern Europe."*

At a preinaugural meeting, we reviewed the Polish situation. Since the early 1970s, there had been stirrings for freedom within Poland, which only grew stronger when John Paul II—a fervently anti-Communist Polish cardinal—was named pope in 1978, the first Polish pope. By 1981, Polish factory and shipyard workers, led by Lech Walesa, were beginning to organize trade unions to ensure basic workers' rights. But any kind of individual rights, and any form of power or authority other than the government dictatorship, was anathema to Soviet interests. The Soviets reacted predictably, with threats of brutal repression. They could not tolerate the idea of free labor unions or anyone being free of government domination.

When Poland's puppet civilian Communist leaders did not take a sufficiently hard line against Lech Walesa's Solidarity movement, the Soviets quickly replaced the civilians with a military regime. At the same time, the Soviets massed tanks and troops along the border of Poland, ready to reinforce their two resident divisions. This obvious threat of Soviet invasion I called "invasion by osmosis."

We in the Reagan administration supported Solidarity in as many ways as we could—including sharing information with the Vatican. In addition, President Reagan directly warned Soviet general secretary Leonid Brezhnev of harsh economic sanctions if Moscow intervened militarily.

On December 13, 1981, the puppet government in Poland, now headed by General Wojciech Jaruzelski (whom I called a "Soviet general in a Polish uniform"), arrested Solidarity leaders and imposed martial law in an operation orchestrated by the Soviets.

* Ibid., 301.

President Reagan imposed sanctions on Poland and the Soviet Union, but he also ordered that financial and material assistance be sent to the Solidarity movement. We also gave them information, communicated largely through Radio Free Europe and the Voice of America. We even provided equipment and support for the publication of a small underground newspaper and encouraged labor organizations in the United States to support Solidarity.

I recalled that at that first meeting on Poland, I had told the president that while our conclusions were correct, he should know that we could not stop the Soviets by threats or strong messages, much less by any military maneuvering, if they insisted on going ahead against Poland. He had said, "Cap, I know that, and we must never be in this position again. We must regain our military strength quickly if we want to secure any kind of peace."

President Reagan's strategy worked and proved crucial in the eventual collapse of the Iron Curtain. The sanctions squeezed Poland's economy to the point where the Polish government, fearing for its very survival, capitulated to U.S. demands, released its political prisoners, and agreed to allow Solidarity to exist and grow without interference or retribution.* This was the beginning of the end of Soviet-dominated Eastern Europe.

All of the great results of President Reagan's foreign policy initiatives went far beyond what any of us had imagined when we took office back on that cold January day in 1981. Supporting democratic movements in Eastern Europe, while at the same time applying economic pressure on the countries' Communist leaders, was not the only effective aspect of his foreign policy. Securing real reductions in nuclear arms was another unique accomplishment.

It was clear that President Reagan understood that weak nations have no influence at the negotiating table and that any agreement

---

* Sanctions were lifted in January 1987.

reached from a position of weakness would provide an illusory kind of security at best. Any effective arms reduction agreement would now have to include reductions in real forces and capabilities, and not just be an agreement that resulted in nothing more than a photo opportunity. As the president said many times, he believed in peace through strength, not peace through a piece of paper. It was all the more imperative that we regain a deterrent capability, no matter how long it would take and no matter how unpopular. Thereby we would let the Soviets (and any other potential aggressors) know that a nuclear war could not be won and must never be fought.

For most of the 1980s, Soviet Communism constituted a very real—and indeed our greatest—threat, militarily and morally. Those who were anxious to sign any kind of agreement labeled "arms control" viewed our efforts as overly dire, alarmist, and simplistic. But it seemed crystal clear to me that the USSR was bent on world domination, as evidenced by its writings, doctrines, and actions, particularly its acquisition of a huge military capability designed to achieve that domination.

That such Soviet plans existed was made quite explicit by a speech Mikhail Gorbachev delivered at Vladivostok in 1986, in which he spoke of the Soviet Union's determination to be a major player in the whole Pacific region. That speech was largely ignored by those who regarded Gorbachev as a great peacemaker and who still felt we could easily coexist with the Soviets. Gorbachev's speech had been preceded by the huge expansions the USSR made to the base we had built at Cam Ranh Bay during the Vietnam War, its acquisition of so-called fishing rights far south in the Pacific, and a number of other actions that indicated that its permanent goal was a continued increase in both its nuclear and conventional arms far beyond anything needed for what its apologists called its understandable fear of having its homeland attacked. The Soviets were plainly arming and preparing for aggressive action. If you move out with forward "defenses" so far that on one side you encompass, for example, most of the Pacific, or a good bit of Europe on the other side, then you are clearly not simply trying to protect your border.

This approach ran counter to the image many Americans had at that time of Mr. Gorbachev, the Soviet Union's new leader. Indeed, he was more dynamic and visible and familiar with our media than the old, stodgy apparatchiks to whom we were accustomed, but his outward persona belied his real intentions, which were steeped in traditional Communist doctrines and goals that he has never repudiated.

By the end of my service in 1987, I had seen his many attempts to capture a favorable world opinion. This was new. The Soviets had never worried about that before. But a public relations campaign is a long way from changing fundamental behavior or ultimate goals. I did not believe that they were becoming a kinder, gentler country that we could trust, as many people hoped and wanted to believe.

This worry about whether the Soviets could be trusted—indeed our worry about the whole concept of the unverifiable Anti-ballistic Missile (ABM) Treaty, with its reliance on philosophical assumptions about Soviet behavior rather than on actual defenses—was one of the major factors that led the president to embrace the concept of strategic defense. This concept was, essentially, a shield that could destroy incoming missiles in their ascent phase or before they reentered the earth's atmosphere or reached their targets. The president announced his Strategic Defense Initiative, or SDI, in March 1983. This change of strategy offered mankind the hope of deterring a nuclear attack by military defenses rather than by relying on guesses as to what the Soviets might think or do.

When we signed the ABM Treaty in 1972, we gave up any hope of being able to destroy or defend against Soviet missiles. But the Soviets themselves pursued their own strategic defense program for nearly two decades, starting right after they signed that treaty, without any regard to the fact that their actions violated it.

We, on the other hand, complied with the ABM Treaty, doing nothing to acquire any effective defenses until 1983. After President Reagan's proposal and the beginning of our research, a large amount of time was spent debating whether *any* attempt to defend ourselves and our allies was permitted under the treaty. We could easily use Article XV of the ABM Treaty to end our participation in it and change the defenseless position we had been in ever since 1972. Most of this debate, led by the largely Democratic Congress, was an attempt to block us from proceeding with SDI, even though, as I noted, the Soviets had been working on a similar system for years.

The president began winning nuclear weapon reductions with the Intermediate Nuclear Forces (INF) Treaty signed in December 1987. We secured that because we were patient about it and because we negotiated from renewed strength. The treaty had its roots in the so-called zero option that I had proposed to the president, with which he had wholeheartedly agreed, in the fall of 1981. It was a simple proposal: if the Soviets would take out their SS-20 missiles, which could hit any target in Europe and many in Asia, we would not deploy our Pershing IIs, which could reach targets inside the Soviet Union.

What had changed between the time of our original zero-option proposal in 1981 and the INF agreement reached in 1987? By 1987, we had deployed the Pershing IIs and ground-launched cruise missiles in Europe, and we were negotiating from a vastly stronger conventional military position. Despite fierce Soviet opposition to our missile deployment, NATO had held firm. And we had continued to modernize our strategic nuclear forces and to work on SDI. Throughout six years of negotiating, President Reagan never grew desperate for "an arms control agreement" to decorate his presidency. He wanted the right agreement and refused to bargain away SDI, which was the keystone of his strategic vision.

Despite our internal division and the strong, bitter opposition from many followers of the old conventional wisdom both inside and outside of the administration, I also was convinced that SDI was a key factor in negotiating arms reductions and, indeed, in securing peace and freedom. I was particularly concerned with the Soviets' evident desire to force us to give up SDI so that they could keep their monopoly. I was very concerned that we might give in on SDI in return for some sort of chimerical arms reduction agreement, which the Soviets—or even our own State Department—might be able to persuade the president to go along with. These views led to the impression that I opposed all arms reduction agreements, whereas my position was that I wanted a good one, not just any agreement such as the Strategic Arms Limitation Treaty (SALT), which actually permitted an *increase* in strategic arms. I was perfectly willing to walk away from negotiations, as the president also proved to be, unless we achieved the kind of agreement we wanted.

Ironically, many saw my resignation in November 1987, just before the INF Treaty was signed, as a protest against the agreement.[*] Hardly anyone seemed to remember that I was the one who had proposed its general provisions in the first place in 1981 and that virtually everyone else in the media, think tanks, and government had opposed the idea.

There is no better example of the importance of negotiating from strength than the INF Treaty; there is no better argument for President Reagan's defense policies than the signing of that treaty.

The lesson of the INF Treaty is that we can secure our own modest agenda, which is simply peace and freedom for ourselves and our allies, only if we are militarily strong. Further, we needed to be militarily secure enough to resist aggression from the Soviets, or now from other sources, which could flame into action quickly.

---

[*] The only reason I left office when I did was because of my wife's health.

The INF Treaty should, and I think will, stand as a monument to President Reagan's determination to regain our military strength and to put his desire for a treaty that is in American interests far ahead of the political clamor for an agreement no matter what it may provide.

Our military buildup had an economic impact as well. The Soviets' desperate attempts to keep ahead of our greatly improved military capability added to their already serious economic woes. Indeed, some of the earliest intelligence briefings we received after we took office indicated that, even at that point, the Soviet economy was in deep trouble. Following his instincts, which were supported by many of his national security advisers, including myself, President Reagan determined to take advantage of Communism's inherent weaknesses—chief among them the lack of free-market incentives. As President Reagan wrote in his autobiography, "You had to wonder how long the Soviets could keep their empire intact. If they didn't make some changes, it seemed clear to me that in time Communism would collapse of its own weight, and I wondered how we as a nation could use these cracks in the Soviet system to accelerate the process of collapse."*

To that end, we and some of our allies squeezed credit to the Soviets; we restricted the transfer of militarily useful technology; and among our Solidarity sanctions against Moscow was an embargo on equipment the Soviets needed to build their trans-Siberian natural gas pipeline. President Reagan also, of course, used the bully pulpit of the Voice of America, Radio Liberty, Radio Free Europe, and the U.S. Information Agency to launch an ideological assault on Communism and to promote the democratic aspirations of the people of Eastern Europe.

From the earliest days of his administration, President Reagan made a concerted effort, as part of a coherent overall strategy, to win the

---

* *An American Life*, 238.

Cold War and consign the Soviet system to "the ash heap of history." His many critics thought this was an impossibility. And indeed, without Ronald Reagan's strategic clarity, moral courage, firmness, and determination, it might very well have proved impossible. Luckily, Reagan was there, and I was proud to be at his side.

CHAPTER 16

DAY-TO-DAY IN THE DOD

*S*uch was the grand strategy and greatest foreign policy accomplishment of the Reagan administration. But my day-to-day work as secretary of defense covered much else besides. It was arduous but immensely fulfilling work. The physical office of the secretary was imposing in its spaciousness and simplicity. A large desk dominated the room; all of the other furnishings were modest in comparison—mahogany, upholstered chairs; a small round conference table; a formal couch. Behind the desk was a large table on which rested the massive telephone console, and above that loomed a dour portrait of James Forrestal, the first secretary of defense. He looked almost destined for his tragic end, when he took his own life at Bethesda Naval Hospital. So on almost my first day in office, I had his portrait removed and replaced it (courtesy of my friend Carter Brown, head of the National Gallery of Art) with a richly colored Titian portrait of a cardinal gracefully bestowing a beneficence. I found him much more agreeable and soothing to the soul, and the colors were a continuing inspiration. Most of the other walls were blank and it took time to add pictures of my own choice.*

The whole atmosphere became more comfortable as I settled in and added some of my own items. Proud specimens from my elephant collection lined the front of my desk. From the service museums, I borrowed quite an impressive fleet of model airplanes and ships, which occupied the windowsills and back table. I also obtained a bust of General Douglas MacArthur and one of a typical infantryman, both of which I found reminiscent and inspiring. I also wanted to make it clear that our administration was not worried about being thought of as "too militaristic."

Some features of my new job took a bit of getting used to. For one thing, I had never seen, much less used, such an elaborate telephone board. There were numerous outside lines, as well as lines that connected directly to my executive assistants, the deputy secretary and undersecretaries of defense, the Joint Chiefs, the service secretaries, the major commands, and the White House, and even the proverbial red phone—a hotline to the president himself. All of these were secure, presumably untappable lines to prevent eavesdropping or interception, possibilities to which I had never given much thought, except for a brief, unpleasant time during the days of the White House plumbers when I was at OMB.

The importance of genuine security was emphasized to a much greater degree at Defense than in any of my previous positions. I certainly understood and vigorously advocated the need to safeguard military information, be it in the form of intelligence, operational plans,

---

* Each president is permitted to borrow pieces from the National Gallery of Art with which to decorate the White House during his tenure. I am not sure if this privilege officially extended to cabinet members, but Carter was a good friend, and he generously allowed the Titian to reside in my Pentagon office all seven years I was there. A magazine story about my office did not quite get it right: "Behind his desk hangs the famous picture 'Titian and Associate.'"

technical data, or any other aspect. What was difficult for me to get used to was that my personal safety—I "knew too much" to be allowed to be kidnapped—was also a major concern. I had never felt that I was in any kind of danger, and my lack of fear—or perhaps lack of common sense—more than once agitated the fine Defense Department security agents who had the unenviable task of protecting me.

I was often criticized, particularly in budget arguments, for using an air force plane when I traveled, especially to my home in Maine. That was necessary for exactly the same reasons: as the second person in the national military chain of command, I had to have access to secure communications at all times, day or night, wherever I was. Also, being the repository of so many of the nation's secrets, I was told early on how important it was that I not be taken hostage from a commercial plane, or from my home, or while out walking, or anywhere.

On one early trip to Bonn, West German officials suggested that it would be safer if I were taken to a secluded area in the countryside for my daily jog. My security detail agreed, but I thought the idea absurd—a waste of time, gas, and personnel—when I could easily jog around the neighborhood near my hotel. I was overruled, and so we jogged through a lovely forest. (Perhaps the Germans simply wanted me to go elsewhere because my jogging suit was considered too old and clearly not chic.)

On another European stop, I caused considerable panic among my security contingent when I instinctively jumped out of my limousine in a motorcade to help a police officer who had been knocked off his motorcycle in a minor traffic accident. We succeeded in freeing him from his fallen motorcycle, but I was immediately hustled back into the car.

Even in the United States, spontaneity was precluded by security requirements. Such normal activities as visiting an art gallery or bookstore, or grocery shopping, could not be done without extensive preparations: not only did agents have to accompany me, they also had to check out the route and destination ahead of time, sometimes even sending dogs in to sniff out the place.

It took some time for me to get used to all of these restrictions and precautions, but I know they were necessary, particularly when various threats were received through foreign intelligence sources. I knew that all of the men and women whose job it was to protect me did so in exemplary fashion, undoubtedly making ineffective any threats, potential and real, and I did not want to add to their problems by being "difficult."

I soon settled into a regular schedule—that is, as regular a schedule as it is possible to have when you are working with ever changing situations and fluid events. I would generally arrive at the office around 7 A.M., where a CIA courier would brief me with the President's Daily Briefing. As the name suggests, this was a summary of the most sensitive intelligence that was compiled every night for the president. The briefing was shown to only a handful of officials involved in national security, and it was always first on the agenda. The actual document was never left with anyone—the briefer read or summarized the report and I was able to look it over every morning while the high-ranking courier waited and expanded on various parts of the PDB, as it was called. It was a very valuable, excellently written and edited group of concise intelligence reports, and a summary analyzing important developing situations. I always received the briefing no matter where I was. I have been told that Mr. Clinton did not bother with it, designating the national security adviser or someone else to receive it.

Then, at 8 A.M., I would have a staff meeting, which was held in my office and generally included the deputy secretary of defense, the undersecretaries, and the department spokesman, as well as the assistant secretary for legislative affairs, the assistant secretaries for policy and international affairs, and of course the military assistant to the secretary. The purpose of these meetings was essentially to prepare for the day's activities and to discuss the status of ongoing projects and any late developments or crises. This was the only formal staff meeting scheduled each day, but I would consult with the deputy secretary, in person or on the phone, ten, twelve, maybe fifteen times throughout the course of the day; the physical layout of the offices lent itself to that sort of thing.

I felt that the deputy secretary was an alter ego to the secretary and that both should be fully engaged in all aspects of the department, not responsible for separate sets of issues. A true deputy is a person who is able to take over when the secretary is out of town, ill, or disabled, without any break-in period or major change in duties.

I was fortunate to have some very fine people serving in this position, particularly Frank Carlucci and, later, Will Taft. I had worked with both of them in the Nixon administration,* and I recruited both to come with me to Defense. They were completely dedicated, extremely able public servants and very good friends.

There was some difficulty getting Frank confirmed. Many conservatives in Congress, and some in the White House, were wary of him simply because he had served in the CIA as deputy director during the Carter administration. Although he had been appointed by Carter, his was not a political position. But despite this, and notwithstanding that he had also served most effectively in posts under Presidents Nixon and Ford, a few Republicans tended to view him as one whose loyalty to President Reagan was questionable. Some also were concerned (as they had been with me) that Frank would not take a strong enough stand for defense. The vote, and even the debate, on

---

* Frank had been my deputy at OMB and undersecretary at HEW. Will Taft had been one of my first law clerks at the FTC and my executive assistant at OMB and HEW.

his nomination was held up for weeks, and many tried to persuade me to drop the effort. Both because I wanted Frank for the deputy and because it would be a very bad start to give in, I stayed firm, as, of course, did the president.

At the same time, some strict conservatives in the White House felt that Will Taft was also too liberal and that if he were to be appointed as general counsel, as I was insisting, he had to be balanced by an appointment of the former director of the Arms Control and Disarmament Agency, Fred Iklé, who was considered a true-blue conservative.

Finally, after some persuasive calls from President Reagan and some get-acquainted meetings with Frank and Will, the vote was allowed to proceed. They were confirmed in early February 1981 (as was Iklé). They all performed extraordinarily well. Frank and Will both had the tremendous capacity and willingness to work endless hours, and both were able to grasp quickly all of the policy issues, as well as the more arcane technical and procedural aspects involved in whatever post they were assigned. Fred Iklé was both conservative and extremely knowledgeable about all the details of our international responsibilities. He too became a good and most loyal and able friend.

Also at Defense, I had the privilege of knowing and working with Richard Armitage, who had absolutely encyclopedic knowledge of many of the foreign countries we dealt with, as well as longtime friendships with many of the governmental leaders and ambassadors of those countries. Of equal significance was his complete appreciation of the importance of these relationships and alliances to the United States—something that many of his colleagues at Defense and, particularly, the State Department never seemed to share. From time to time, on my visits abroad, I was complimented on my knowledge of some of these countries, their history, and our long-term relationships with them. If any of these compliments was deserved, it was owed entirely to my patient and extraordinarily able tutor, Rich

Armitage. In his present post as deputy secretary of state, Rich is, I am sure, giving the same extremely skilled and brilliant advice to Secretary Colin Powell.

Most days, after the regular staff meeting, I met with the chairman of the Joint Chiefs of Staff. No one attained this position without excellent credentials and distinguished performance in a long military career. Three extremely competent men served as chairman during my tenure, and I feel that I worked very well with each of them.

General David Jones, of the air force, was a holdover from the previous administration, but even before I took office or knew him, I recommended that he be allowed to serve out his term, and the president agreed. I thought it might appear that we were politicizing this most important position in our military if the new president changed chairmen as his first act. Jones was an able man, but I never felt that he was quite as comfortable with me as his successors were.

General Jack Vessey, who became chairman in the summer of 1982, was a fellow army man who had served in World War II. We shared several bonds like that, and he was a delightful, warm human being and a great soldier. I have rarely worked with anyone for whom I had greater respect and admiration. General Vessey was a National Guard sergeant from Minnesota. He was given a rare battlefield commission for extreme bravery and skill on Anzio Beach.

I had known Jack Vessey's successor, Admiral Bill Crowe, for many years, from the time he was our commander in chief in the Pacific, and felt completely at ease with him. I was pleased that he was chairman for my last two years at the Pentagon. I know that he felt we should make more of an effort at rapprochement with the Soviets than I did, but he was loyal to my policies.

I met with all of the Joint Chiefs together at least once a week in their conference room on the first floor, which was called the Tank. That is also where we met with the president when he came to the Pentagon to meet with the chiefs.

I feel that General Colin Powell deserves mention here, even though he did not chair the Joint Chiefs until the Bush administration, after I had left government. Of course, most people are familiar with him from his invaluable leadership during the Gulf War, but I was impressed with him long before that. When I was at HEW, I helped in selecting him to be a White House fellow, and he was my military assistant when I was at Defense. In both cases, I saw that one of his principal assets was that he clearly knew more about the subject matter of almost any meeting than did any of the other participants. He also knew exactly what had to be accomplished at each meeting, and as a result he was able to participate in the most effective way possible. His subsequent career is so well known that it requires no additional elaboration from me. Suffice it to say that his appointment as secretary of state by President George W. Bush was, I think, quite properly received with universal acclaim and immediate confirmation.

Every Tuesday, I received a full military intelligence briefing in the National Military Command Center (NMCC). The NMCC was a large, two-story room with a semicircular table and places for each participant. There were elaborate phones at each console and several large display screens for the various slides used in presentations. This briefing was particularly valuable, covering, as it did, the world.

In addition, I met every Thursday with the service secretaries. I do not know if my predecessors or successors followed this pattern, but these meetings ensured that I had regular input from each branch of the military and that they all had the opportunity to bring their views and concerns to me directly. They also allowed me to make better informed program and procurement decisions based on the overall picture. Some critics said that I blindly signed off on everything the services requested, but as I am sure all the services would confirm, this was simply not the case. I made every effort to minimize redundancy in weapons systems or missions, while always bearing in mind our constant goal of securing as quickly as possible a strong and unified military force that could fight effectively and win on at least two fronts simultaneously if necessary.

One service secretary who particularly impressed me was Jim Webb—a marine through and through, with a stellar record of service in the Vietnam War. I strongly recommended to President Reagan that he appoint Jim as secretary of the navy, which he did in 1987. Jim has always been, even more than I, sickened by the contempt with which Vietnam veterans were treated when they returned home from that war. We both feel that combat in service to one's country should be honored, and Jim does not have much tolerance for critics who have not been in the military themselves. His understanding of the navy and his recognition of the support the military deserves and needs from its leaders served him well in the Pentagon and impressed me in our meetings. He is also a superb writer; his *Fields of Fire* is one of the great novels of the Vietnam War.

Often, while listening to presentations and discussions in these various meetings, I would, as had long been my habit, close my eyes because I find that I think and concentrate better with my eyes closed. Early on, some of the briefing presenters and other participants were disconcerted by this, unsure if they should continue talking while, as they feared, I might be asleep. But when they found that I was hearing everything they were saying and I could ask relevant follow-up questions, they learned to proceed with confidence, if not a little amusement.

Of course, on rare occasions, I actually was asleep, an inevitable by-product of frequent eighteen-hour workdays. Some attributed this to jet lag, but I really do not think I have ever experienced jet lag. I can sleep through a meeting whether I've been flying or not. President Reagan was fond of telling the story of the time when we were viewing an exhibit of weapons captured during our rescue invasion into Grenada. The president remarked that it was eye-opening to see all of this, and as the news camera zoomed in on me—sound asleep—the commentator said, "Except, apparently, to Secretary Weinberger."

Another weekly meeting I established was a breakfast with Bill Casey, director of central intelligence. Bill was much underestimated by his critics. He had a quick and penetrating mind and great intellectual interests, and was an avid and encyclopedic reader. He even wrote a very competent history of the American Revolution. He was also skilled in the ways of Washington and in dealing with large bureaucracies and numerous presidential aides. He was deeply conservative and constantly aware of the Soviet threat to freedom. He was no appeaser. He and I worked very well together for all the years he was in Washington, starting with his leadership of the Export-Import Bank when I was at HEW. He had also, of course, performed yeoman service as manager of President Reagan's campaign for the presidency.

Every Wednesday when we were both in town, I would have a working breakfast with the secretary of state—first Al Haig, then George Shultz. We alternated these breakfasts between the State Department and the Pentagon. The two departments were probably in agreement more often than most people have been led to believe. The policy matters on which we differed—whether we should have been back in Beirut, whether we should be more conciliatory with the Soviets, when to use military force, and things of that kind—were played up and emphasized more than the many issues on which we concurred.

There are of course some inherent differences between Foggy Bottom and the Pentagon. I think that the State Department generally, and George Shultz in particular, felt that there was value in any American military presence, whether it was capable of winning any battles or not, or whether there were any battles to be fought. So State was much more ready than we were to deploy our troops. It is probably easier for people to advocate using military forces if they do not have the responsibility for the care and safety of the troops, as I did. I also felt keenly that we should not wander into any situation or conflict unless we felt it was important enough to win. We should define our mission carefully—and then go in with overwhelming force to ensure victory.

I also advocated bringing massive strength to bear on a narrow front in policy as well as in military terms. I did not feel that we should enter into any arms reduction agreement just to secure an agreement. I thought it was much more important to have a good agreement, and I was not sympathetic to the cry that we did not care about arms control because we had not signed an agreement during our first years. When we did sign the INF agreement with the Soviets in 1987—after patiently sitting out the criticisms, protests, and public demands—it eliminated an entire category of deadly weapons: the intermediate-range nuclear forces.

I had known George Shultz for a long time and had worked with him many times, and in spite of our differences of opinion, we both did our best to carry out the president's desires. We had quite different styles but I think we were sincerely trying to secure good long-run objectives

Personality differences were most apparent when Al Haig was secretary of state early in the administration. From day one, he made his presence known. On January 20, 1981, while the inaugural parade was still going on, he attempted to get my approval for a sweeping set of procedures under which the State Department would preside at practically every intergovernmental meeting. He was very conscious of his time in the Nixon White House, when he had participated in taking duties away from the State Department. Now he wanted to get them back. Similarly, though he had been a powerful White House staff member, now he regularly fought against a powerful White House staff, presumably because he saw how that undercut cabinet secretaries. He had had a most impressive military career and had been a fine Supreme Allied commander in Europe; it was apparent he wanted to be a "supreme" cabinet member as well.

This apparent desire for power eventually caused him a bit of a public relations problem on the day of the assassination attempt against President Reagan. The first intimation I received that something was seriously amiss was when I was meeting in my office about 2:30 P.M. with Bobby Inman, then deputy director of central intelligence, who was giving me a general briefing. Kay Leisz gave me a message to hurry to the White House Situation Room as soon as possible. My driver had been given the afternoon off since I had no other scheduled appointments, so Bobby offered to drive me over. When we located his rather ancient car in the parking lot, we picked up what we could on the radio. Later it struck me as quite ironic that two people with major responsibilities in the security area received their information about this most vital happening in the new administration in this rather archaic way. When we reached the White House and convinced the various sentries to admit this rather "unofficial" car, I went to the Situation Room. I looked up at the TV monitor and wondered aloud why it was showing old clips of an Al Haig press conference. "Those aren't old clips," someone said. "That's Al. He's up there." He was trying to reassure the American people that because he was in charge while we waited for news about the president, the ship of state was not adrift. When Al came back downstairs to the Situation Room, he challenged my telling the chairman of the Joint Chiefs of Staff to have strategic air crews moved from their alert quarters to the planes themselves. I mentioned that Ed Meese, calling from the hospital, had confirmed that the "national command authority" rested with me as secretary of defense and that the orders to Al Haig were to "calm other governments." Al kept insisting that I should "read the Constitution." I believe he was relying on an older order of succession—president, vice president, secretary of state—that had been in effect as a law (but not in the Constitution itself) until 1947. Al was seemingly unaware that the secretary of state was not in fact next in the chain of succession after the vice president.*

In any event, and conceding the strains of that day, it should be said that Al was a dynamic and colorful member of the administration, and one who made many valuable contributions to it.

He was strong, ambitious, and knowledgeable, but he also could be quite abrasive, and he fiercely opposed anyone else's discussing foreign policy matters before the president. The president, on the other hand, just as when he was governor, liked his cabinet members to talk freely, even on issues outside their specific responsibilities.

My own relations with the White House were, for the most part, less dramatic than Al's. I frequently discussed matters with the national security adviser and asked to have my views presented, but if I wanted to go to the president directly, I did. Yet I did not feel I had to meet with the president every day just to demonstrate that I could.

When Dick Allen, Bill Clark, and, later, Frank Carlucci headed the National Security Council, this arrangement worked well. Unfortunately, that was not the case with Robert McFarlane, who did not want my input to the president to interfere with his own agenda. It was that agenda which sadly led to the so-called Iran-contra debacle. More on that unhappy tale later.

From the beginning of the administration, I decided that the best way to keep the president apprised of Defense Department activities without monopolizing his time or relying on intermediaries to pass my thoughts along was to send him regular summaries. So began my practice of writing weekly reports to the president. These were a slightly expanded version of the mini-memos that had worked so

---

* See Richard Allen's "The Day Reagan Was Shot" in the *Atlantic Monthly*, April 2001, pages 64 to 68, for the best account of that whole episode. Allen's article is based on the only tape recording made at the time and is an invaluable bit of history.

well in his gubernatorial days: two or three pages covering eight to ten issues—everything from training exercises and performance reviews on new weapons, to the status of our budget in Congress, to my trips and meetings with foreign officials. A staff man was assigned to select major topics to be included, but in large part I wrote (and always edited) these reports myself, because I wanted the president to have my unvarnished views.

Besides keeping the president informed, I felt it was also important, as much as possible, to let the American people know what we were trying to do and why we had to do it. It is the natural instinct of most people in a democracy, save in wartime, not to want their tax dollars spent on the military. Consequently, I gave far more speeches and appeared on television far more often than I wanted to. I preferred the most direct way to reach the public because I could express our policy objectives with a minimum of editorial screening. Press conferences and press interviews, in contrast, frequently passed through the filter of the reporter's own opinion. Still, plenty of press conferences had to be given. Sometimes one of the Pentagon press secretaries, Henry Catto, followed these by announcing, "What the secretary *meant* to say was. . . ." So my press conferences sometimes went through a double filter. I often joked that I had to read the *Washington Post* to see what I was thinking that day.

I admit that in those speeches for which formal texts had been released, I often wandered from what was written, preferring a more off-the-cuff approach, but the basic content, and certainly the facts, remained unchanged. Still, I gained the reputation among reporters of being a "textual deviate."

Much of my time was spent testifying before congressional committees—and I spent even more time preparing for them. The intense "practice" sessions, in which my staff would grill me (often in a rather hostile manner, for maximum realism), were somewhat appropriately called "murder boards." They covered everything from weapons systems to strategy to the line items in our budget request. It was the same preparation I had used at both OMB and HEW, and that preparation was, for me, a vital part of every hearing.

Dealing with Congress was, unfortunately, often contentious—especially because having a credible deterrent and the capability of defending American interests around the world is expensive, and military spending in a democracy is never popular. As every writer since Montesquieu has noted, people in democracies generally have pacific natures and are not interested in—and in many cases are repelled by—subjects such as weapons capabilities, military strategy, and the like. Besides, they would rather have their funds spent on something else, or preferably not spent at all.

The real problem, as I repeatedly said, is that if we want to remain at peace, we have to be able to deter any attack that might be made against us or our allies. The potential attacker must *know* that we have that ability. With respect to nuclear weapons, I never subscribed to the theory embodied in the ABM Treaty—essentially, that the only way to be completely safe from nuclear attack is to be completely vulnerable. A credible deterrent is essential for us to be truly protected.

Having a defensive strategy, with no plan to attack anybody, is a much heavier burden to carry before Congress than having an offensive strategy. A defensive strategy has to cede to the other side the time, place, and manner of attack and, ultimately, the battle. That puts a higher premium on preparedness and on acquiring the tools necessary to deter or defeat *any* kind of attack. This was often difficult to get across to some members of Congress.* Fortunately, enough of them knew the importance of rebuilding our military capabilities to enable us to pull ourselves up out of the danger zone after a few years of vastly increased spending. I am convinced that if we had had

---

* I was once chided by a senator for "coming back here and asking for more when we were not attacked last year."

a mere 2 percent annual real increase in military spending during the 1970s, we would not have had the herculean rebuilding job we had to do in the 1980s to regain a credible deterrent.

All of the varied activities I have described thus far represent only a fraction of my responsibilities as secretary of defense. There were also cabinet meetings, National Security Council meetings, budget discussions, visits to various military units and installations at home and abroad, presentations of awards, and foreign visitors to be received, negotiated with, and entertained, to say nothing of dealing with crises that presented themselves without the slightest regard for schedules or plans. Perhaps the best way to convey how many different kinds of things went on, on any given day, is to show entries for a few sample days from the daily summaries that I wrote (complete with my own "shorthand," explained in brackets, and some editing for a more general understanding):*

July 30, 1982

Driven to CIA

Saw CIA courier at CIA

Breakfast with Bill Casey, Frank Carlucci, Jack McMahon

Saw Frank Carlucci re budget and pay caps for military and [Richard] Perle's travels

In office 9 A.M.–12:45 P.M.

Called Dr. Taylor re sore heel and blood test

Presided at staff meeting

Bob Gray and Barrett of USO in office [re health appointments]

---

* I began keeping such notes during my early law office days, when we were required to account for our time so clients could be properly billed. Keeping these summaries became such a fully ingrained habit that I scarcely remembered doing it—of which more later.

[Military Assistant] Carl Smith in office re ceremony for astronauts

[Protocol officer] COL Tiplady in office re same

Astronauts on shuttle flights in office for photographs

Presented medals to astronauts at ceremony

Saw Marybel Batjer re health appointment & USO request

Saw COL Tiplady re dinner for George Shultz & swearing-in ceremonies for General Gabriel & Admiral Watkins

Called Sen. Domenici in Albuquerque—out, lw [left word]

Called Carl Smith to get data for Sen. Schmitt

General Vessey, Carl Smith, Frank in office—re possible USSR reading of our signals from SAC exercises; also re Honduran-Nicaragua air maneuvers; departure of Winston Lord

Iran still being thrown back by Iraqi Army; our intelligence reports & Gulf of Sidra exercise—I want it to go forward despite Libyan threats

John Tower—wants to meet with me before conference—agreed—he doesn't know why Baker & Domenici are mad about President sticking to his original '84 & '85 Defense figures [Apparently they were under the impression that the president had told them we would not seek increases in 1984–85. But this was clearly not true.]

Called Bob Michel—out, lw

Called Del Latta—out; lw

Rich Armitage in office re preparation for meeting with President & Cong. GOP leadership on Taiwan

Attended Int'l Economic Policy Group on pipeline in USSR and related issues—in WH—Don Regan [there]

Attended meeting of President & GOP Senators & Congressmen—on Taiwan—no change either in our policy or our obligation to maintain Taiwan's defense qualitatively & quantitatively

In office 2:30 P.M.–7:20 P.M.

Met with Jack Marsh, Frank Carlucci, Shy Meyer, Korb, etc. re women in Army—no quotas—no combat for women

Met with new Ambassador from Philippines Romauldez—President Marcos visit in Sept still on

Army doctors in office—for new blood pressure tests & my sore heel

Cong. Latta rmc [returning my call]—from Ohio—says he agrees no bad faith on President's part in staying with his '84 & '85 Defense budget

Sen. Domenici from Albuquerque—rmc—same

Called Bill Clark—re Gandhi dinner—GPS [Shultz] Dinner Aug 9— he can't come; my letter to John Nott [U.K. minister of defence]; my visit to Israel & meeting with Shamir; VP to swear in General Gabriel & Admiral Watkins

Ginny Duncan from SF (2)—re Corporation for Public Broadcasting post

Called RJ [my wife—Rebecca Jane] in Somesville

Carl Smith in office (2) re Weekly Report to President

Fred Iklé—to get report on pipeline meeting

Attended dinner of Mrs. Gandhi's for VP Geo Bush—[attendees:] Mrs. Gandhi's son Rajiv, George Shultz, Kay Graham, etc. Saw Bob Michel—he agrees there was no misleading by President in retaining his '84 & '85 Defense budget

Called Arlin in SF

Called RJ in Somesville

April 10, 1984
In office 7:05 A.M.–3:35 P.M.

Saw Colin Powell re [Nestor Sanchez and] continuing stories that we have contingency plans to put troops into Cent. Am.

CIA courier in office

Attended Intelligence Operations briefing in NMCC [National Military Command Center]

Presided at staff meeting

Called Colin Powell re General Chain going to State—will speak to General Gabriel & Jack Vessey

Secure conf. call—Bud McFarlane, Shultz, Bill Casey—McFarlane wants to put out joint statement to stop false stories on "plans" to put troops in Cent. Am. & mining of harbors in Nicaragua

Held Press Conf.—in PA [Public Affairs] studios on release of *Soviet Military Power*

Held satellite Press Conf. with Brussels & European press corps in PA studios re same

Called Bud McFarlane—out; lw

Saw Colin Powell—re [Nestor Sanchez's] stmts that we do have contingency plans for Cent. Am.

Full Honors ceremony for Sheik Salem al Sabah—MOD [Minister of Defense] of Kuwait

Met with him in office

Gave lunch for Sheik al Sabah

Richard Goldman—SF—in office—he has joined AIPAC [American Israel Public Affairs Committee]—wants me to make talks to Jewish groups

Herb Klein in office—wants me to see Sidle report on press relations and the military & put recommendations into effect—told him we had a Media Advisory Group to review that. [This was a group I appointed to make recommendations for our press relations, including forming a small pool of reporters when military situations did not permit mass coverage of combat, etc.] Also he hopes no action will be taken v. [against] Capt of Rangers

Met with Joint Chiefs in Tank—re our ability to monitor Soviet missile tests—not good—we can't break encryption yet

Taped interview with Steve Bell at ABC—for *Nightline*—on *Soviet Military Power* & Cent. Am.

Attended signing ceremony in Oval Office by President of Bill Archer's tax bill for deceased soldiers

Saw Bud McFarlane—approved joint statement on Nicaragua & El Salvador

In office 5:10 P.M.–6:35 P.M.

Colin Powell in office (2) re Bernie Rogers' objections to WH desire for plane for Poindexter group. Told him we had to follow WH; also re keeping records on search for Vietnam Unknown—most agreed no need to keep records

Shultz—wants General Chain

General Chain in office—he wants to take State job

Attended reception for Defense Minister of Kuwait at Kuwait Embassy

Attended dinner at British Embassy for 1st Sea Lord—[attendees:] Sen. Warner, Cong. Sam Stratton & John Whitehead, etc.

A full honors ceremony is quite an impressive event. It not only is a sign of respect for an ally, but it also provides an opportunity to demonstrate the fine military forces of the United States. Such a ceremony is tendered to visiting foreign ministers, ministers of defense, and heads of state.

The basic protocol dictated that I meet the visiting dignitary—in this case, Sheik al Sabah—when he arrived in his limousine in front of the Pentagon. From there, we would proceed to the parade ground just across the road, where I would introduce him to my senior staff and the Joint Chiefs. We would then stand together on the platform while a military band marched past, playing first the visiting country's national anthem, then ours. Then, the commander of the guard would invite the visiting dignitary to inspect the honor guard and review the troops. At that point, a detachment of each of the four services would march past. When this concluded, the visiting dignitary would thank the commander, and the ceremony would be officially over.

Music would continue to play as we proceeded to the Pentagon and to my office, where we would usually have a one-on-one meeting and, quite often, a lunch given in his honor (or a formal dinner would be given later in the visit).

Soviet Military Power was an annual assessment of just that, published by the Pentagon. It helped us measure and adjust our own forces and capabilities in relation to the Soviets'—an ongoing exercise that was crucial for realistic planning and budgeting. It was also most useful in persuading some of our allies that they needed to increase their defense efforts.

November 28, 1984
In office 7:05 A.M.–11 A.M.

Saw Colin Powell re NSC proposed changes in my speech today to Press Club

Called Bud McFarlane re above

CIA courier in office to brief both Shultz & me

Breakfast with George Shultz—he wants to have regular meetings of himself, Bill Casey, Bud, and me to talk things out & try to get agreements. I told him I thought they should be with President too. Also told him I thought we had to sell F-15s to Saudis—& also that I was making Press Club speech

Called Bud McFarlane—re meeting with Shultz & further changes in speech—also that our budget is under attack

Presided at staff meeting

Attended DRB [Defense Resources Board, an internal body that reviewed our budget] meeting with CINCs [Commanders in Chief of the Unified & Specified Commands]

Ed Meese—"core group" will be presenting recommendations on cutting Defense budget at 11

Attended "core group" session in Cabinet Room with President—[OMB director] Stockman presented recommendations on cutting budget including ours

Spoke to National Press Club on "Uses of Military Power" [saw there:] Jim Fogerty of *SF Chronicle*, also a reporter for *Cleveland Plain Dealer*

Met with [Republican congressman/ranking Republican on House
Armed Services Committee] Bill Dickinson in his office—with Russ
Rourke—Dickinson mad he wasn't consulted last year on our budget
plan

<u>In office 3:10 P.M.–7:25 P.M.</u>
  Saw Colin Powell re JCS meeting
  Met with DRB & CINCs
  Paul Robinson in office—our amb. to Canada—he wants to be
Secretary of Navy
  Honduran delegation—COL Gansleer in office—general courtesy call
  Jack Vessey in office re keeping helicopter ship off Lebanon but let-
ting [carrier USS] *Eisenhower* go on regular, previously planned trip
  Called Mike Burch (2) re reaction to my speech & re *LA Times* arti-
cle that my speech was just to get back at Shultz—told him no
  Called Ginny Duncan in SF re speech & her son John
  Dick DeLauer in office—ceremonial call prior to his leaving
  Spoke at farewell dinner for Dick DeLauer
  Attended GOP Senators dinner—at Library of Congress

It was customary to submit to the national security adviser any
speeches I planned to make, more for his information than to get his
okay. Of course, changes were often suggested and sometimes were
adopted.

This particular address to the National Press Club, on the uses of
military power, I wrote myself because I felt that forum was an important one in which to present a synthesis of a number of ideas I had
formulated over a period of time, starting with my strong disapproval
of our policy in Vietnam to commit large numbers of our forces to a
war we did not intend to win. In my Press Club speech, I outlined six
major criteria to be weighed before committing our combat forces
abroad.

First: The United States should not commit forces to combat overseas unless the particular mission is deemed vital to our national interest or that of our allies. Our actions in Grenada and Libya while I was in office were practical examples of missions vital to our national interest.

In the early 1980s, Grenada, a small island country in the Caribbean, became essentially a satellite of the Soviet Union and Cuba, using their help to build its military capabilities, including a huge new airfield. This in itself presented ample reason for us to be concerned, since Grenada was now basically an enemy outpost near our own borders. The political situation in Grenada deteriorated further in 1983, when an even more radical Marxist faction overthrew the government and held a violent grip on the tiny country. This clearly threatened the safety of Americans inside Grenada* as well as the security of neighboring Caribbean nations who were friendly with the United States and were begging us to intervene.† All of these factors made it quite clearly a matter vital to our national interest.

As a result of our intervention, we successfully rescued the American medical students, captured the airport, and drove out all Cuban and other resistance.

In the case of our bombing of Libya in 1986, we were responding to indisputable evidence that Libyan terrorists had been responsible for the bombing of a West Berlin discotheque that killed and injured American military personnel. It was certainly in our national interest to demonstrate that we would not tolerate deliberate attacks on our citizens inspired, and paid for, by any other country. The United States had engaged Libya militarily on a couple of previous occasions, when

---

* Including many American students attending a U.S.-owned medical school.

† Mrs. Eugenia Charles, prime minister of Dominica, made a particularly eloquent plea to President Reagan pointing out the very real threat Grenada's radical government (by then virtually an anarchy) posed to all of the outer Caribbean states.

Libya challenged our right to conduct regular maneuvers in the Gulf of Sidra. The Libyans claimed that this part of the Mediterranean belonged to them, when of course, it is recognized under international law as international waters. It was imperative not only that our pilots defend themselves when fired upon, but also that no country be allowed to deny any other country passage through international waters. This has been part of our policy since at least 1812.

The determination of national interest is not always as clear-cut. It is the first decision that must be made before military action is taken, because not everything we may dislike or feel is wrong amounts to a violation of our national interest serious enough to warrant the use of our troops abroad.

The *second* consideration that I laid out in my Press Club speech was that, if we decide that it is necessary to put combat troops into a given situation, we should do so wholeheartedly and with the clear intention of achieving a decisive victory. If we are unwilling to commit the forces or resources necessary to achieve our objectives, we should not commit them at all. We should never ask our people to go into battle and risk their lives for an issue that the country does not think is important enough to win—or, indeed, specifically intends *not* to win, as was the case in Vietnam. In that conflict, we went in with no particular goals or firm resolve. We committed a thousand troops one week and ten thousand the next week, and soon we were up to 565,000 with still no real plan for total victory. In fact, our government continually emphasized that our objective was never to win the war decisively, but only to "contain Communism." Containing Communism is roughly like trying to contain quicksilver by simply pushing in at the margins of the quicksilver pool.

Some question whether "winning" is a meaningful term in the nuclear age. Certainly, a nuclear war cannot be won and must never be fought, but we can win wars in the sense of convincing an opponent that he should not attempt a nuclear strike. In the Cold War, we won every day that the USSR or any other nuclear power did not launch an attack.

Third: If we do decide to commit forces to combat overseas, we should have clearly defined political and military objectives. We should know precisely how our forces can accomplish those objectives, and we should send forces capable of achieving them. Otherwise, there will be no real measure for sizing and equipping and maintaining our forces until we do win. Also, it should be an equally vital part of our policy to withdraw when—but only when—we have secured our objectives.

The importance of this criterion was demonstrated by our experiences in Lebanon in 1982 and 1983. The United States was part of the first multinational force (MNF), along with France and Italy, which supervised the departure of the Palestinian Liberation Organization (PLO) army from Beirut. This objective was mandated in an arrangement negotiated by our special envoy, Philip Habib, and agreed upon by the Lebanese government and the other various factions in the area. It was a clear mission, which was accomplished successfully, and our forces were then promptly withdrawn.

The next year, however, after Lebanon's president-elect was assassinated and Israeli forces reentered Beirut (as Ambassador Habib had assured the departing PLO forces they would not do), many people began urging President Reagan to send in another MNF. The State Department and some members of the National Security Council staff were particularly vocal in pushing this idea, eager to establish an American military "presence" in Lebanon to facilitate the withdrawal of warring armies.

Having a buffer between such forces is quite reasonable, as each side would be deeply suspicious of the other and vulnerable to violations of any withdrawal agreement by the other side. The problem in this case was that there was no agreement, by any party, to withdraw from its position. So American troops and those of any country that was persuaded to join the second MNF would be vulnerable, precariously inserted between countries that had no intention of stopping their fighting. Our mission would be nebulous at best, with no way to tell when it was completed.

Although I made these arguments repeatedly and forcefully, the president, unfortunately, concluded otherwise and sent a second, lightly armed contingent to join an MNF in Lebanon. My greatest fears were realized when, on October 23, 1983, our marine barracks and another building occupied by French forces were bombed, resulting in the deaths of 241 American and 56 French servicemen.

I have never overcome the feeling that I somehow should have been more persuasive in urging the president not to engage in such a flawed policy. The whole episode ingrained even more deeply in me the conviction that we should never commit troops into situations where the goals we give them are not clear and where the equipment we give them is not sufficient at least for self-defense.

The *fourth* point I listed in my speech was that, once we have committed military forces, we must continually reassess the situation. Every conflict is fluid, and circumstances may very well alter our objectives or dictate changes in the size or type of forces needed.

The *fifth* important factor to consider is that we must have reasonable assurance—*before* we commit combat forces abroad—that both our mission and our troops will have the support of the American people and their elected representatives in Congress. This emphatically does not mean that we should take a Gallup poll or consult some focus group before we do anything, but we cannot fight a war that the American people oppose. That was one of the major lessons of Vietnam. I believe that the necessary support cannot be achieved unless we are candid in making clear the threats we face and that support cannot be sustained without close and continuing consultation with Congress and the people. That is called leadership, and I fear we were woefully lacking in that in the Clinton years.

I did not touch on it in my press club speech, but this point can be carried a step further. Ideally, Congress should be completely in agreement with the administration on the need for the contemplated military action *before* troops are sent abroad. Often, the march of events cannot wait for the concurrence of such a large deliberative body. Inevitably, Congress is rankled when a president commits troops to action, and the lawmakers are often too eager to exercise their authority under the War Powers Resolution, which says that the military forces must come out within ninety days unless Congress gives its approval to their remaining in action. This act puts major and, I think, unconstitutional restraints on the president, as commander in chief, to use American forces when and where they might be necessary. It also can render those forces ineffective at best, or put them in greater danger at worst, since any enemy knows that he has only to suspend his objectionable actions until our forces are withdrawn, or to conduct even more hostile attacks against us in an effort to negatively influence American public—and thereby congressional—opinion.

The *sixth* and final criterion was that the commitment of troops should always be a last resort. I firmly believe that diplomatic efforts should be completely exhausted before we turn to the troops. But diplomatic efforts frequently fail, or they can succeed only by our giving up vital principles and objectives, so those efforts must never be seen as a permanent alternative to military action.

These six tests were intended to sound a note of caution, which is not only prudent but also morally required of a secretary of defense. Some thought it incongruous that I did so much to build up our defenses but was reluctant to commit forces abroad. It was not incongruous at all. I did not arm to attack. "We armed to parley," as Churchill always said. We armed so that we could negotiate from strength, defend freedom, and make war *less* likely. I never wanted to risk the lives of Americans in uniform unless it was necessary and my criteria were met.

Another few days' entries from my notes give a good sense of what some of my travels as secretary were like:

February 26, 1984

Shopped at Safeway

Spoke to National Governors' Association at Hyatt Regency, Capitol Hill. Gov. Robb, George Deukmejian, Gov. Orr (Indiana), etc.

Saw Colin Powell & Mike Burch—Marines are finally all out of Lebanon

Held brief press interview in lobby of hotel re above

Called Arlin in SF

Colin Powell re NSDD [National Security Decision Directive] on Lebanon—OK

Will Taft—re same & NSC meetings on E-W relations

Called Cap Jr. at home

Flew to London 8:05 P.M. (ET)–7:55 A.M. (GMT) 2/27

February 27, 1984

Arrived in London at 7:55 A.M.—met by Charles Price, our amb.

Driven to Churchill Hotel

Saw Colin Powell with PDB [President's Daily Briefing]

Met with Prime Minister Margaret Thatcher at #10 Downing Street—with ambassador

Driven to American Embassy residence—Winfield House

Met with Lord Peter Carrington re NATO issues—at Winfield House. He offered a very good quote:

"You Americans care too much what your critics say about you—when we were running things, we did not much care."*

---

* This would have been even better advice for President Carter. His great fear of our being criticized for practicing "colonialism" led him to give up the Panama Canal and two nearby military bases.

Lunch at Winfield House—[with] Peter Carrington, [Defense Minister] Michael Heseltine, [Foreign Minister] Francis Pym

Driven to Churchill Hotel

Colin Powell in office with video tape of earlier Oxford Union debates

Driven to Oxford

Attended reception & dinner at Oxford Union; undergraduate president [of the Union] Andrew Sullivan [who had originally invited me to do the debate]; former president of the Union [and later prime minister of Pakistan] Miss Benazir Bhutto [daughter of former prime minister of Pakistan who was killed by his political opponents]; Nemon (sculptor [of Churchill]), etc.

Called RJ in Washington

Debated Professor E.P. Thompson and others in Oxford Union building on "Resolved: there is no moral difference between foreign policies of US & USSR"

Driven back to London

Saw Colin Powell re call from Sam Pierce

Called Sam Pierce in Washington—rhc [returning his call]—n/a [no answer]

February 28, 1984

In London

Call from Mrs. Thatcher that I won debate at Oxford Union last night, 272-240

Breakfast with Michael Heseltine at Admiralty House

Met with Michael Heseltine at Ministry of Defence

Mrs. Thatcher—congratulations on winning debate

Met with Geoffrey Howe at Foreign Office

To Churchill Hotel

Called Sam Pierce in Washington—rhc—wants me to see Treasury Bond people for sales drive

Called RJ in SF

Visited & toured BBC—Langhorne Place

Called Colin Powell (2) re messages & tonight's agenda

Driven from BBC to Churchill Hotel

Charles Price—he will be coming to airport

Met with Archbishops of Canterbury & York, & Bishop of
London—at Church House [Anglican headquarters] re nuclear & military issues

Spoke to Oxford & Cambridge Club after reception there

Saw Colin Powell re tomorrow's schedule, reporting cables back to
President, Defense & State Departments re my meetings with British
officials

February 29, 1984

In London

Colin Powell in room with PDB, today's schedule in Lebanon, etc.

Driven to Heathrow

Flew to Cyprus 7:05 A.M. (GMT)–1:20 P.M. (CT)

Met by Cypriot Defense Minister Veniamin & our Admiral Martin

Met with Defense Minister at airport

By helicopter to USS *Guam* 1:35 P.M.–2:30 P.M.

Spoke to *Guam* sailors & part of MAU [Marine Amphibious Unit]
brought out from Beirut

Awarded them Navy commendation citation

Press briefing on ship

By helicopter to Beirut

Met by Ambassador Reg Bartholomew & toured Embassy compound—met with Marine General Joy

Joy had met with Ambassador & Gemayel in Damascus—may sign
accord today

Toured Marine positions

Flew to USS *Trenton* by helicopter

Spoke to troops on *Trenton* & presented them with citation

Visited with troops on *Trenton*

By helicopter to Larnaca, 4:50 P.M.–6:20 P.M. (CT)

Flew from Larnaca to Shannon 6:30 P.M. (CT)–10 P.M. (GMT)

[Surprise] celebration aboard plane for debate victory

Saw Colin Powell re reporting cables & tomorrow's schedule

Flew from Shannon to Andrews [Air Force Base] 11:10 P.M.

(GMT)–12:55 A.M. (ET)

Visiting our men and women in the military was one of my favorite activities. To see firsthand the pride they exuded in what they were doing and to hear their concerns directly was very satisfying, and I always encouraged them to ask any questions they wanted. I found it helped to break the ice if I recalled a few incidents and differences from my own enlisted service.

Some of the troops I visited were sailors in the engine rooms of our ships. This required going down innumerable stairs to the lowest decks—areas, I was told, that were rarely visited by assorted dignitaries. They seemed to appreciate my talking with them. I was also happy to talk to the marines who had been given the thankless job of serving as a buffer between warring factions in Lebanon. After the tragic barracks bombing, many of the marines thought they were being viewed at home as having failed. I told them they had done their duty superbly under very difficult circumstances, and I think I dispelled their notions of failure.

The original purpose of this trip, and its main event, was to participate in the Oxford debate. I had accepted the young Mr. Sullivan's* invitation without hesitation, but some in the administration—

---

* I found out later that he was a self-professed Marxist, but the job he did of presiding seemed to me to be admirably fair. He may even be a conservative now with all the changes that have happened.

mostly in the State Department, and even a few within the Defense Department—were wary about my participation. Their primary concern seemed to be that if I were to lose, as an official of the United States, it would undermine our ability to hold anti-Communist allies together. I thought this a specious argument, and besides, I did not intend to lose. I was quite eager to point out all the reasons why democracy was much superior to the Soviet system and how our foreign policy objectives were far more benevolent than theirs. In addition, I saw this as an opportunity finally to visit Oxford, having foolishly passed up the chance to study at Cambridge after college. Still, it was over some protest at home that I went. I suspect that part of it was not only the fear that I would lose, which would be a big story, but also the feeling that if it were going to be done at all, it ought to be by a trained diplomat.

As on my other trips to England, our group—which generally consisted of Will Taft, Colin Powell, Kay Leisz, Thelma Stubbs, a press aide, and the necessary security agents—was put up at the Churchill Hotel. It would have been delightful to stay at Winfield House, the beautiful American Embassy residence, and our ambassadors always invited us, but I knew what a major disruption it would be for them to have me as a houseguest, with our large number and special security and communications requirements. Besides, the Churchill was a perfectly nice and comfortable hotel, and it was already wired for our special needs.

After a reception and dinner at the Oxford Union on the night of the debate, I entered a large room that was set up much like the House of Commons, so that you face your opponent. It was incredibly hot from dozens of bright television lights, and the situation was not helped by being in a dinner coat. I had been told that black tie was the dress code, and the officers of the Union were in white tie. But my opponent, Professor E. P. Thompson, wore an old sports coat and sweater. He said he had never believed in black tie, that it was just a mark of class distinction. I remarked that, on the contrary, my father always said it was the most democratic of all costumes because everybody wore exactly the same thing. Thompson, an admitted Marxist, was not terribly amused.

Before our debate began, three or four student speakers—including a young Indian woman who was viciously anti-American—debated on the same question: "Resolved: There is no moral difference between the foreign policies of the U.S. and the USSR." This trendy view was called "moral equivalence." It rested on the idea that the Soviets' foreign policy was based only on their national interest and that the United States was wrong to worry about their acquiring a lot of other countries because it was simply to protect their borders by creating a buffer zone.

Then Andrew Sullivan, president of the Union, introduced me and Professor Thompson, and we began our debate. Thompson went first, and I responded—all of which took well over two hours, mostly because the rules of procedure were much like those in the House of Commons. If an opponent wants to question you, he just stands up and interrupts, and you have to sit down while he puts his question. There is apparently no limit to the number of times a person can be interrupted, so the evening can become quite prolonged.

Mr. Thompson spent the large part of his time denouncing the arms race and, more specifically, America's military power and our military presence in a number of countries. In fact, he spent a good deal more of his time lambasting the United States than he did addressing the original question. So much so that when it was my turn to speak, I began by saying that I thought perhaps I had come on the wrong evening, because before the debate began, one of the student officers announced that next week's debate would be on the question "Resolved: Christopher Columbus went too far."

In my attempt to disprove the resolution actually before the Union, I made essentially three points. First, the Soviet Union's policy was to promote Communism, while the United States sought to promote freedom. Second, they were in other countries by force; we were in other countries by invitation. And, last, whatever our respective policies might be, the Soviet people had absolutely no control over government policy, whereas if Americans were not satisfied with U.S. policy, they could, through a free political process, change it. I think these excerpts from my talk express my views best:

> The Soviet definition has always been that moral policy is what advances the Soviet state. That moral policy is what helps the cause of Communism.... It is a moral system which turns the definition of the word "moral" upside-down as far as we are concerned. Our view of morality is basically that a policy is moral if it advances certain basic principles and rights—something that we mentioned to you in a letter that we sent about two hundred years ago and which says that we hold these truths to be self-evident: that all men are created equal and that they are endowed by their creator with certain unalienable rights and that among these are life, liberty, and the pursuit of happiness.
>
> We've never used our power to try to conquer. We have used our power to try to help others.... Now we've heard a fair amount tonight about the American troops who have been here thirty-nine years.... The ... other important difference between these troops and the troops in the Warsaw Pact is the fact that the troops here are here by invitation of NATO and by invitation of the host country... [and] are here for a very specific purpose of...join[ing] with people to protect and preserve their own freedoms because they have been invited by the regularly chosen, legitimate governments of these countries to do that.... If you told us to take our soldiers out of Great Britain, they would be gone within a day or two.... There's quite a difference between that and the Warsaw Pact troops, who are there because they are imposed on those countries.

We think you can't have a moral foreign policy if the people cannot control it—if the people cannot change it. We've heard many instances tonight of the problems that individuals have with individual aspects of American foreign policy. I had a lot of problems with our foreign policy four years ago and I expressed those views very vigorously and I was not jailed. I was able to do that and I was able also to be of some help in assembling a group of people who turned out ultimately to be a majority, and those foreign policies were changed, a great many of them.... You have the freedom of choice and you can make a difference.... Tonight you'll exercise that freedom—you'll make a choice and I rest my case on your liberty to walk out either door and not have anything happen thereafter. There will be no intimidation, no threats, no arrests. I ask you to consider whether in the other system you and your families could have been here, or if you felt it was safe for your family to come here tonight and express things on either side.... So I urge your opposition to this motion so that you can come again.

At the conclusion of the debate, a vote was taken—not by a show of hands or roll call but by the same famous division used in the House of Commons: "Ayes to the right, Noes to the left." The Union members present then exited either to the "Aye" lobby or to the "No" lobby.

It had been a long evening and I was tired, so I went back to the hotel before the vote was counted. I felt that I had done reasonably well, but I also knew that Professor Thompson was very popular with the students who composed the Union. So I really cannot say I was expecting the victory, of which I learned the next morning. Those in the British Foreign Office and Defence Ministry, as well as Mrs. Thatcher, were extremely pleased, as, needless to say, was I.

When I finally decided to resign as secretary of defense, it was because of my wife's health. She had been suffering with arthritis for several years, then had a bout with cancer, developed osteoporosis, and broke two vertebrae. I needed to fulfill my obligations to her. Not only had she been in tremendous pain for some time, but she had never been especially enthusiastic about moving back to Washington in the first place; indeed, she had wanted me to leave office after President Reagan's first term. At that time, I did not feel that I had completed the mandate he had given me—to rebuild our military strength—and it was too crucial a goal to leave unfinished. But with only a year left in his second term, I concluded that I had done what I could, and I needed to redirect my attention to my wife.

Helping in this decision was my assumption, at least my hope, that Will Taft, my deputy of three-and-a-half years, would succeed me. I knew that he could be counted on to carry on my vigorous advocacy of the Strategic Defense Initiative and that he knew the Pentagon—and Washington—inside and out.

The president was agreeable to naming Will, but Howard Baker, then White House chief of staff, and others persuaded the president that the post required someone of more "stature." They decided on Frank Carlucci, who was serving ably as national security adviser. Frank was, indeed, extremely competent and knowledgeable, but I was sorry that Will did not get the opportunity to move up. Will continued to evidence his great loyalty and selflessness by agreeing to continue as deputy secretary of defense under Carlucci. He never expressed any bitterness. Later, the president appointed him to be our ambassador to NATO, where again he performed superbly. President George W. Bush also recognized Will's great worth by appointing him chief legal counsel to the State Department in February 2001.

Prior to my departure, an impressive military parade and a nineteen-gun salute were held in my honor on the Pentagon parade ground. A display of honor guards passing in review, along with military marches and even flyovers of aircraft from each service, culminated in the president's presenting me with the Presidential Medal of Freedom, a most splendid accolade in itself, and a great surprise to me. Something that

I considered an even greater honor was the tribute the president paid me at a most moving Rose Garden ceremony later that week:

> Today, just about any enlisted man or woman will tell you that Cap is a defense secretary who cares about the troops. And maybe that's because Cap had seen firsthand that the backbone, the sinew, the soul and spirit of our armed forces are the men and women who dig the trenches and swab the decks, fix the engines, drive the tanks, fly the planes, and face the enemy for all of us. He knows of the truth of what his old commander, General Douglas MacArthur, once said—that in the field, morale would quickly wither and die if soldiers come to believe themselves the victims of indifference or injustice on the part of their government.

My nearly seven years as secretary of defense, while stressful and demanding, were some of the most fulfilling of my life. I felt that I was able to make a difference and perhaps help set our nation on a more stable, secure course than it had previously been following. Sadly, much of what President Reagan and I worked so hard for was severely cut and compromised by the Clinton administration in its eagerness to do whatever seemed most popular at the moment and to follow whatever course it thought might enable it to avoid criticism. The defense of our country and its citizens is much too important ever to take a backseat to political expediency.

CHAPTER 17

THE DANGERS WE STILL FACE

*W*hile the final victory over Soviet Communism was not fully realized when President Reagan left office in January of 1989, the momentum he had started was unstoppable. That year saw breathtaking changes in Eastern Europe, as those nations began the difficult but welcome process of liberating themselves after more than four decades of harsh and brutal Soviet domination and repression.

In January, Hungary allowed pluralistic political parties and open demonstrations, and Estonia made its own language the official language, as did Lithuania.

In February, the Communist government of Czechoslovakia jailed a dissident and brilliant playwright named Vaclav Havel and others for participating in rallies opposed to the Communist regime. But by the end of the year, Havel had not only been released, but he had been elected president of Czechoslovakia. I will always remember how he began his speech to a joint session of our Congress when he made his first state visit here in early 1990. He said, "While I know most people begin a speech by saying how glad they are to be here, I really mean it. Only a few days ago, I was in jail!"

In March, the Soviet people, in the first national election since 1917, overwhelmingly defeated several high-ranking official Communist candidates, and Boris Yeltsin, Gorbachev's leading opponent, won by a landslide.

By August, Poland formally named a Solidarity leader, Tadeusz Mazowiecki, prime minister, and Lithuania took major strides toward its own independence, which it formally declared in March 1990.

In September, the most dramatic events of the decade began when East Germans poured into Hungary, which allowed them free passage to West Germany.

In October, Erich Honecker, Communist leader of East Germany for eighteen years, was ousted, and over 300,000 East Germans demonstrated for democracy.

In November, the East German government resigned, and all travel restrictions were lifted. No one who saw it, in person or on television, will ever forget the extraordinarily inspiring sight of the Berlin Wall tumbling down piece by piece while jubilant masses poured over and through it. Today, a section of the wall stands at the Reagan Presidential Library as a lasting reminder of the repression he ended, the millions of people he freed.

That same November, Czechoslovakia's Communist government resigned after huge demonstrations demanding democracy continued for eight days. Next, Hungarians voted in their first free election in forty-two years. But harsh Soviet measures of repression against Lithuania were imposed this month, including deploying Soviet tanks used to intimidate the Lithuanian parliament and shutting off promised oil and energy shipments—all because of Lithuania's statements of independence. Yet this dying gasp of Communism ultimately failed. Lithuania, today, is free and independent.

December of that sunrise year of 1989 brought East Germany's decision to have free elections, Havel's election as president in Czechoslovakia, and the overthrow and execution of Nicolae Ceausescu, the ruthless and particularly brutal dictator of Romania. East Germany ceased to be a separate Communist nation, and the newly unified Germany entered the new decade under the conservative government of Chancellor Helmut Kohl.

Of course, the transition of the former Eastern bloc countries to full-fledged independent nations did not happen overnight. Their growing pains continued over several years and, in some ways, are still going on. All are vastly better off because they now have the freedom to realize their own destinies.

How did all this happen? What caused this virtually complete collapse of Communism in Russia and Eastern Europe?

In short, how and why did we win the Cold War?

Clearly many causes and factors were involved—but I always felt there was one major turning point that led inexorably to the winning of the Cold War.

That was the moment when we decided we were going to win the Cold War. And that was when President Reagan, in perhaps his most major violation of the conventional wisdom, blatantly told the world that Communism was an Evil Empire. With this, he ended the years of national indecision about the nature of Communism. With that single stroke, we gave up "containment," "détente," "moral equivalence," and the idea that Communism and freedom were simply two different but compatible systems.

On March 8, 1983, in a speech in Orlando, Florida, President Reagan asked for prayers for the "salvation of all of those who were in that totalitarian darkness. . . . Let us be aware that . . . they are the focus of evil in the modern world."

He urged his audience to beware of the "temptation of blatantly declaring yourselves above it all and labelling both sides equally at fault, [and the temptation] to ignore the facts of history and the aggressive impulses of an Evil Empire."

Ronald Reagan felt so strongly about it that with this speech he overrode his "moderate" advisers and restored those phrases, which had twice been cut from his draft of a major speech that he gave in 1982 to the British Parliament. Otherwise the world would have heard his call half a year earlier.[*]

Predictably, the president's calling the Soviets and Communism the "Evil Empire" and its victims the "focus of evil" horrified all those who believed we could, by appeasement or accommodation or other means, persuade the Soviet Union to stop being the Soviet Union so that we could live in peace together.

Reagan would have none of it. He was willing to negotiate reductions in nuclear arms, but he warned against calling "the arms race a giant misunderstanding and thereby removing yourself from the struggle between right and wrong and good and evil."

Typical of the storm of protest that followed the president's openly voiced determination to win the Cold War was the reaction of Anthony Lewis of the *New York Times*, who said the president's speech was "primitive and dangerous." Lewis went on to ask, "What must Soviet leaders think? However one detests their system, the world's survival depends on mutual restraint."[†]

"Mutual restraint" had never characterized the Soviet Union, nor had containment contained or détente slowed its ever increasing military strength.[‡]

---

[*] See a fascinating article in the Allentown, Pennsylvania, *Morning Call* on March 5, 2000, by Frank Allen, based on his thorough research in the Reagan Archives and Library.

[†] See the *New York Times*, March 9, 1983.

[‡] *Soviet Military Power*, Volumes 1–9 (Washington, DC: The Pentagon, 1983–99).

What else, besides President Reagan's determination to win the Cold War, won it?

First: Our military buildup, designed not to give us superiority, but only to regain a credible enough deterrent to make it clear to the Soviets that they could never win a war against us. President Reagan never wavered in his determination to regain that degree of strength in our armed forces. And his administration carried out his policies with ceaseless advocacy.

Second: Our determination to construct and deploy an effective defense against ballistic missiles. This was another of the great violations of the conventional wisdom, involving the ultimate repudiation of the ABM Treaty and the Mutual Assured Destruction theory.

Third: The repair and strengthening of our strategic alliances, particularly in NATO and also in the Pacific, the Mideast, and Asia.

Many credit Gorbachev with helping end the Cold War. I do not. He did recognize that the Soviets could not win a war with the United States and NATO, but he never repudiated Communism, and despite all his rhetoric, he remains dedicated to Communism in theory and in practice.

The winning of the Cold War also enabled Poland, Hungary, and the Czech Republic to decouple themselves from the Soviet Union and then to seek to join the NATO alliance—a step that seemed unbelievable just a few months before. These countries made great strides in establishing democratic and comparatively free-market regimes. So to me, this was a natural fit: NATO was the quickest and safest way for these newly free countries to seal their fledgling friendships with the United States and the West, and NATO needed the additional defensive strength they could provide to discourage a western thrust from an unstable Russia. Imperial-minded Russians were furious at the prospect of their old "colonies" joining NATO. So were the usual common scolds of the West who wrote and chattered endlessly about "provoking" Russia by guaranteeing Eastern European freedom under NATO.

It was then that we saw the beginning of President Clinton's repeated attempts to appease the unappeasable Russians. Clinton and his strongly pro-Russian deputy secretary of state, Strobe Talbott, delayed by several years the official entry into NATO of Poland, the Czech Republic, and Hungary. The Clinton administration was determined to back Russia but, typically, tried to please everyone and offend no one. So it proposed the usual fuzzy compromise. This one was called the Partnership for Peace, launched in late 1993, as a substitute for the NATO membership the three former Warsaw Pact nations really wanted. This "partnership" invited Russia and the other fourteen republics of the former Soviet Union, as well as the former Warsaw Pact countries, to join together for "peacekeeping, crisis management, search-and-rescue missions, and disaster relief." They could "consult with NATO"; maybe later some could actually join; but the reality was that the willingness of those nations to share in the burdens of NATO was being summarily rejected by us when we should have eagerly embraced all three. It is one thing to extend help to Russia; it is quite another to spurn refugees from the Warsaw Pact who wish to join NATO.

Russian opposition should have been ignored, and we should have made clear to them that while we were prepared to help them economically, they could not control or influence us to ignore our best interests and the urgent needs of Soviet victims. It is our duty, and very much in our best interest, to help freedom-loving countries. How many of our allies will remain allies if we turn our backs on nations that want to be free and if we violate years of our historic attachment to such countries? To do so simply because we do not want to offend Russia just adds salt to the wound. To support the aggressor and oppose the oppressed was both irresponsible and incomprehensible behavior for the champion of democracy and the world's only remaining superpower.

In March 1999, Poland, Hungary, and the Czech Republic were admitted to NATO, but only after we made so many concessions to Russia's ego that NATO was unnecessarily and substantially weakened. The Clinton administration promised, implicitly or explicitly, that we would not admit any other nations to NATO; we invited Russia to sit on a NATO council; and we basically allowed Russia to claim a veto over NATO missions. We also promised that no NATO troops or weapons would be deployed in the new members' territories. We ever offered to put Russian observers in all major NATO posts, rendering NATO potentially impotent and making its three new members feel like second-class members.

The Baltic states were treated even less well by the Clinton administration, which offered them a lukewarm compromise—the Charter of Partnership The charter recognized that NATO membership was a "goal" for these nations but said they must wait until they were "ready"—a term not defined.

We never required Spain to be found "ready" when we were begging that country to join NATO in 1982. And we certainly never asked Russia then for its opinion or permission.

Our tepid response to countries trying to join NATO was part of a pattern demonstrating Clinton's overriding fear of displeasing Russia. To give Russia what amounts to a veto power over our decisions regarding our alliances—or, for that matter, over our entire foreign policy—is not why we fought and won the Cold War.

Some argue that since we have triumphed over the Soviet Union, there is no longer a need for NATO at all. This is a dangerous assumption. Russia still has a vast arsenal of nuclear warheads, a potentially unstable government, and, in Vladimir Putin, a man who gave the KGB complete satisfaction for seventeen years. Putin now talks of restoring 'Russia's greatness." He has continued a brutal war in Chechnya, seems to have a rapidly developing relationship with

China, and needs to be regarded with the same caution with which we would approach any other potentially hostile power. He also joins Russia with North Korea, Serbia, Iran, Iraq, and any other countries with which we may have disagreements.

The Russian military is low in morale, but it has a huge and growing inventory of new and ever more lethal weapons[*]—paid for largely by unsupervised and unaudited U.S. and Western aid. The Russian economy is, to put it charitably, far from strong, and the quality of life is far from enviable. Even at the beginning of the 1990s, though, many in our own government seemed to be unaware that the crumbling of the Soviet Union could conceivably end in a full return to a Stalinist dictatorship and Russian military aggression—a possibility that could arise very quickly in a country like Russia. Making drastic cuts in our military strength, as we have done, including deep cutbacks in our commitments to NATO, on the grounds that we no longer have significant foreign threats after the Cold War, is particularly imprudent. That idea should have been rudely exploded on August 2, 1990, when Saddam Hussein suddenly invaded Kuwait on his way to conquer Saudi Arabia and the United Arab Emirates and thereby gain control of about 70 percent of the world's known oil reserves.

Fortunately for the world, the United States then had the military capabilities, the leadership, and the will to block this aggression and

---

[*] As Roger W. Robinson Jr. wrote in the August 28, 1998, *Wall Street Journal,* "During this decade, even as some Russian workers were going unpaid, Moscow continued construction of a massive network of underground command and control bunkers in the Ural Mountains, deployed a new, mobile 'Topol-M2' (the SS-27) intercontinental ballistic missile, commissioned a new aircraft carrier (the *Admiral Kuzhetsov*) and nuclear cruiser (the *Peter the Great*), refitted its Typhoon Class submarines to accommodate SS-N24/26 missiles, began a stealth-fighter program (comparable to our F-22), and built a fifth-generation Borei Class ballistic missile submarine." All of this cost at least $18 billion.

organize a powerful coalition of Arab, Asian, and European nations. This coalition was not only fully capable of acting with the United States, but it was equally determined to stop Saddam Hussein's plans.

Initially, this remarkable coalition of nations and the United Nations imposed major economic sanctions against Iraq, enforced by an air and sea blockade. It became increasingly apparent, however, that because the blockade specifically excluded foods and medicines, Saddam Hussein channeled whatever he could to his military. The sanctions could not, in any reasonable amount of time, force Saddam out of Kuwait. It was also apparent that his continued occupancy of Kuwait was causing increasing hardships and misery not only to Kuwaiti citizens but also to thousands of workers and refugees who had fled Kuwait.

President Bush tried every possible diplomatic move. But when Saddam Hussein forbade his representative even to receive the president's letters, it became clear that the force authorized by virtually unanimous UN resolutions, and later by our Congress in a close but decisive vote, must be exercised. So on January 16, 1991, the allied forces unleashed air strikes of unparalleled intensity against Iraq, and the crippling of key components of Saddam's military strength began.

This was followed by ground troop insertions, which, with superior generalship, armaments of all types, and complete control of the air, overwhelmed the remaining Iraqi troops, many thousands of whom surrendered without a fight. They were weary and hungry and demoralized, and they seemed to welcome the opportunity to escape from the brutal minority Ba'ath party rule in Iraq, even if only temporarily. There was some hope that Iraqi unhappiness with the leadership of their country might lead to the overthrow of Saddam Hussein. I do not think this should have been left to hope alone.

President George Bush provided decisive leadership in this crisis. But I always felt it was imperative that we not only expel Saddam from Kuwait and restore the legitimate government (which we did) but also ensure that Saddam be deposed and punished. It was important that Iraq not be left with a military capability to reinvade Kuwait or attack other countries. We destroyed much of Saddam's military,[*] but, unfortunately, we allowed Saddam to remain in power, and we accepted his promises—promises that included our right to inspect his weapons sites—which he predictably broke.

Saddam Hussein has not yet tried to retake Kuwait, but his presence precludes any hope of lasting peace in the Mideast. Reliable intelligence tells us that Iraq continues to manufacture chemical and biological weapons and to shop relentlessly for nuclear weapons, despite UN sanctions.

The Clinton administration, not surprisingly, was erratic and ineffective in dealing with the problem. Our "patience ran out" several times; we sought a "diplomatic solution" with a vicious killer who does not negotiate and who can never be believed or trusted; we occasionally dropped a few bombs or chased an Iraqi fighter jet out of the no-fly zone. But our credibility with our allies and against Saddam was seriously doubted because of Clinton's deep defense cuts, the irresoluteness of American policy, and the domestic political considerations that seemed to govern Clinton's foreign policy in the area.

We wondered why Saudi Arabia would not let us use its bases to support an attack that ultimately could have protected it and others in the region from Saddam Hussein's ever increasing capabilities to destroy them. I suspect the Saudis knew that, under Clinton, we would not do more than carry out a few days of token bombing, if that, if Iraq moved again into Kuwait or elsewhere.

---

[*] Typically, those who were not there criticized us later for being too thorough and for not allowing armed Iraqis to escape, which would have meant potential harm to our forces.

All we sought was to reinsert UN inspectors into Iraq for a few days, with fewer restrictions placed on them, and yet Saddam continued to refuse even that. If we wanted to rid the world of the threats we faced in 1990 and 1991, we should have bombed every one of the disputed sites two or three times each, day and night, and we would have had to be prepared to ignore Saddam's inevitable lies about injured children.

Bombing alone would not oust this mass murderer, but if we were able to and did maintain a firm offensive, we could inflict enough damage to serve notice that we would not be bluffed any longer, thereby also warning other potential aggressors. We also could encourage and support opposition to Saddam inside and outside of Iraq. We should have eliminated or jailed Saddam himself—and still must do so, if we want any peace in the region.

Unfortunately, Iraq was not the only place where the Clinton administration abdicated its leadership responsibilities. Clinton's handling of the situation in Bosnia was a humiliation for the West comparable to the attempt to appease Hitler in the late 1930s.

How did this happen? When the uneasy alliance that was Yugoslavia broke apart, four nations—Croatia, Slovenia, Bosnia-Herzegovina, and Macedonia—claimed independence and were admitted to the UN. Serbia, meanwhile, embarked on its longtime goal of creating a Greater Serbia—controlling all of the former Yugoslavia of which it had also been a part. Serbia's allies in Bosnia cooperated with a shocking "ethnic cleansing" of Bosnia's Muslims, following Hitler's example.

The West's ultimate mistake was its failure to stop the Serbs at once. The problem again was the doctrine of limited objectives. Just as those who preached "containment" never intended to win the Cold War and those who sent our troops into Vietnam never planned to win, so too our approach to Serbia. We cautioned many times that we did *not* plan to defeat Serbia—only to stop its criminal atrocities.

President Clinton compounded this error when, shortly after his inauguration, he sent Warren Christopher to Europe, not to galvanize resistance to the aggression (as President Bush had done in the Gulf) but to inquire weakly what other countries would like to do. Naturally, none of them wanted to do very much, which sent a clear signal to the Serbs that they could pursue their aggression unhindered.

A routine UN arms embargo was put in place against Bosnia, but Russia continued to supply arms to the Serbs. For more than a year, UN and European "negotiators" bleated for cease-fires and "safe areas" and proposed various peace plans that awarded Serbia anywhere from 49 percent to 70 percent of Bosnia. The Serbs agreed to more than thirty cease-fire and safe-area proposals—and sometimes even kept their promises for as long as five or six hours.

The United States played an ignoble role, agreeing to giving the UN full command of the peacekeeping operation, which was manned by 23,000 lightly armed, ill-equipped troops scattered in hopelessly ineffective clusters and without effective rules of engagement. Predictably, these peacekeepers were attacked, ignored, overrun, and taken hostage, and the UN convoys of food and medicine were allowed to pass only when the Serbs gave permission.

This was the much-touted Dayton Agreement, signed in December 1995, which was supposed to create a stable, new "multiethnic Bosnian country." Instead, we accepted a partitioned Bosnia, which is what the Serbs wanted, with three parliaments (one federal, two regional), two separate armies, and two police forces, overseen by a rotating three-man presidency. Subsequent elections only emphasized that such a Rube Goldberg–like structure could not be built, let alone succeed.

Again, this demonstrated how easy it is to secure an agreement: just give up as much as the other party demands, and then we can have a big signing ceremony, proclaim ourselves peacemakers, and nominate our negotiators for the Nobel Peace Prize. Meanwhile, the victims of Serbia's aggression continue to suffer.

The United States has always been, and always should be, willing to accept the burdens of keeping peace and helping maintain freedom for ourselves and our allies. When, after two years of fatal, bumbling inaction, we cobbled together a paper agreement solving none of the conflicts that started the war, it was simply common sense to oppose deploying any soldiers, U.S. or NATO, to a mission inviting disaster—a "peacekeeping" mission where there was no peace to be kept.

Much earlier, we should have assembled a Gulf War–like coalition and told Serbia that its military targets would be mercilessly bombed by air forces under U.S. and NATO command if Serbia continued attacking civilian populations. When the brutality of Serb leader Slobodan Milosevic was again unleashed, this time in Kosovo, we ultimately did support NATO bombing, but with restrictions and restraints bound to make any operation ineffective.*

Ultimately, a new Serbian government ousted Milosevic from power. A few months later, he was turned over to the United Nations' War Crimes Tribunal, where he is now awaiting trial.

Another murderous regime sits in North Korea. It frightened the Clinton administration into another gross act of appeasement (called a "framework agreement"), initiated by our own appeaser-negotiator, former president Jimmy Carter, who told the North Koreans he would try to get American sanctions against them lifted. The sanctions were lifted in the summer of 2000.

Time and time again, the Clinton administration inexplicably made concessions to North Korea in the hope the Communist regime

---

* Targets could be bombed only after the approval of a large committee was secured.

would stop its nuclear weapons program. Under the "framework agreement," we even arranged to give the North Koreans two new nuclear reactors—ostensibly for more power, although the reactors are fully capable of producing plutonium, the very stuff of which nuclear weapons are made.

This absurd appeasement proceeded despite increasingly hostile actions by North Korea, including "test" launches over Japan of its new, long-range missiles—which can ultimately reach the United States—and thinly veiled threats against South Korea.

For example, in 1996, when the North sent a submarine with some twenty-five terrorists into South Korean waters, South Korea urged the United States to restart the valuable joint military exercises we had conducted with the South Korean armed forces from 1976 to 1994 (which we had stopped as part of the appeasement agreement we made with North Korea). But President Clinton merely urged "restraint" on both sides. Sadly, this is just one more example of the way in which the Clinton administration cavalierly disregarded and alienated our allies.

Aside from our increasingly strained relations with our allies, our own security was dangerously weakened by the inept Clinton as our commander in chief. Part of the problem was that President Clinton did not understand the military, and worse, he did not *like* the military. Moreover, he did not recognize the importance of a strong defense.

Gone was our military strength that won the Cold War. By the late 1990s, we were spending less on new weapons and equipment than at any time in the last forty years. Spending on research and development programs had been cut by nearly 60 percent.

It has been said that we fought and won the Gulf War with Cap Weinberger's forces. In a 2000 interview with Rush Limbaugh, Dick Cheney summed up the current regrettable situation well: "We had 6 percent of our GNP going for defense during the Reagan years; [we have] less than 3 percent today. We used to have eighteen army divisions; today we're down to ten. We used to have some twenty-four wings in the air force; we're down to thirteen today."

Each new administration appropriately begins with a reexamination of existing strategic policies. This process is under way with the new Bush administration, and the first result is usually a spate of rumors as to what has been decided, what new policies will be followed, and which existing policies will be changed.

There have already been many and varied reports including that we are abandoning the "two-war" strategy and that we are offering to take out of service or destroy all of our largest and most accurate MX missiles, which were finally deployed after a major struggle with Congress and others in the 1980s.

Regardless of what our policy is called, we must have armed forces of the strength necessary to deter and conquer any threat. If two attacks, leading to two wars that must necessarily be fought nearly simultaneously, are a possible threat, we must be strong enough to fight and win those two wars.

Such a threat is at least possible. China could decide it would no longer attempt to secure its "one China" goal by treaty or negotiation. Instead it could try to take Taiwan by force. Indeed, the continued increasing deployment along China's east coast of missiles facing and aimed at Taiwan cannot be ignored.

Should China attack Taiwan, North Korea, despite all of Clinton's attempts to offer what it wants, is equipped and positioned to launch another attack on South Korea.

The so-called two-war strategy was simply a convenient term for measuring and obtaining the kind and amount of deterrent military capability we might need. So long as giving up the two-war strategy does not mean giving up the military capabilities we may well need or the defense budgets big enough to support those capabilities, we need not worry too much.

But when we look at what has happened to the matchless military strength President Clinton inherited in January 1993, it is doubtful now that we could win one of those hypothetical two wars.

From 1985 to 2000, the total active-duty military personnel in our military went down by 34 percent.* Yet under Clinton, our forces were asked to serve in overseas assignments far more often and for far longer than they should.† Few of these missions improved military training. Most were called "operations other than war," and our troops were "spending more and more time working on aging equipment at the expense of honing their important war-fighting skills."‡

All of this was compounded by the Clinton "procurement holiday" and substantial cuts in the research and development work that earlier had produced the weapons with which we won the Gulf War.

Thus, today, our military faces extraordinary operation and maintenance costs for military hardware and weapons systems that it would be cheaper and more effective to replace with new models. New weapons systems not only have all the performance advantages of new technology, but they are increasingly built modularly, which means that they are far cheaper and easier to repair than older

---

* See Jack Spencer's "Building and Maintaining the Strength of America's Armed Forces," Chapter 10 of *Priorities for the President* by Baker Spring and Jack Spencer (Washington, DC: The Heritage Foundation, 2001).

† Our forces "have been used over thirty times beyond normal training and operations since the end of the Cold War." This is compared with only ten such deployments in the preceding forty years. See Spring and Spencer, page 214. Dick Cheney also said, in his 2000 Rush Limbaugh interview: "We've given the forces a lot of assignments they didn't used to have, the so-called peacekeeping assignments. What that means is that the guys are away from home all the time. The thing you hear about is 'the birthday problem.' A guy will tell you, 'Look, I missed my kid's last three birthdays because I was away from home. So I'm leaving. I can't take it anymore.'"

‡ General H. H. Shelton, Chairman of the Joint Chiefs of Staff, testimony to U.S. Senate Armed Services Committee, September 27, 2000.

weapons systems. While our military's operations and maintenance costs are skyrocketing because of aging weapons systems and infrastructure, our vital military research and development budgets are suffering. The result is a military whose operational capability is in serious danger of exponential decline. The Clinton administration inexcusably hollowed out our military capability and has left President Bush with the tab for making good Clinton's deficits on what should have been spent.

Not surprisingly, all of this has contributed to a loss in morale and a most worrisome difficulty in recruitment and retention of troops—something we never experienced during the Reagan buildup in the 1980s.[*]

We need to return to major increases in defense spending overall, and in particular, we need to rebuild the Reagan-era navy. Our navy today is roughly half as large as it was in the Reagan years, and yet the most immediate challenges we will likely face are naval challenges, since our most likely areas of conflict are separated from us by vast oceans. We have to be able to move our armed forces around the map, so we need a drastic upgrading of our air- and sea-lift capabilities. It takes six or seven years to build and fully deploy—with trained crews—aircraft carriers and nuclear submarines. We need to be building them now. It takes two or three years to build and deploy combat aircraft. We need to be building them now as well. After the years of Clinton neglect, we are seeing a disastrous de facto build-down—by failing to replace out-of-date ships and aircraft—of major and highly disturbing proportions.

With the election of George W. Bush, things are improving, and I expect that his commitment to our military will alleviate many of

---

[*] See Spring and Spencer, pages 217–218.

these problems. Still, it will take time and continued advocacy and determination to repair the damage wrought by eight years of the Clinton administration.

President Bush has also taken to heart the highest defense priority we should have—building a defense against intercontinental ballistic nuclear missiles and missiles with chemical or biological warheads.[*] Russia alone has an estimated 15,000 to 20,000 nuclear warheads.[†]

The Reagan administration worked for years to build a genuine, nationwide defense against these incoming intercontinental and intermediate-range missiles, but we were continually hampered by demands from Democrats and some Republicans that everything be "ABM Treaty–compliant" (read "totally ineffective"). No one in the Reagan administration was suggesting that we violate our treaty obligations. What was repeatedly urged was that we use the specific provisions of the treaty itself to get us out of it, as legally permitted, so that we can build and deploy effective defenses.

President Clinton and his State Department remained wedded to the flawed 1972 ABM Treaty, despite intelligence reports—and later, Russia's own admission—that the Soviet Union had violated the treaty almost from the beginning by deploying its giant radar at Krasnoyarsk. In September 1997, Secretary of State Madeleine Albright signed agreements designating Russia, Kazakhstan, Belarus, and Ukraine as our ABM Treaty partners in place of the collapsed USSR. Strobe Talbott, her Russophile deputy secretary, said as late as May 2000 that we meant to adhere to and strengthen the ABM Treaty. None of these new agreements, however, was ever submitted to the Senate. And now, with President Bush, thankfully they will not be;

---

[*] For the best description of the nature and size of the ballistic missile threat we face, see *The Ballistic Missile Threat Handbook* by Jack Spencer (Washington, DC: The Heritage Foundation, 2000).

[†] *Military Almanac* (Washington, DC: Center for Defense Information, 1999), 9.

already in his young administration, it is clear that capable, tough-minded professionals such as National Security Adviser Condoleezza Rice, Secretary of State Colin Powell, and Secretary of Defense Donald Rumsfeld have returned to putting the legitimate interests of the United States and our allies first. I have high hopes for the new administration and see it as a worthy inheritor—after the lamentable Clinton years—of the work I tried to achieve as secretary of defense for Ronald Reagan. This administration knows that peace comes through strength, that America must lead, and that nothing is more important than our national defense.

Two steps are necessary to gain any real security: we must reject any ABM succession agreements and announce that we will no longer be bound by the old ABM Treaty, and we must move ahead with the research and subsequent deployment that will give us and our allies a viable defense against nuclear, chemical, and biological weapons. The Clinton administration and its faint-hearted supporters stood in the way, and now that Senator Jim Jeffords has turned over control of the Senate to the Democrats, an effective missile defense will apparently continue to be denied to the American people.

President Clinton, inclined as he was to conduct policy by poll, should have noted that polls showed that a horrified majority of Americans were unaware that we currently have no effective defense against nuclear missile attack. Moreover, nearly 70 percent of respondents considered having a strong military to be very important and said that they were willing to pay the taxes necessary to ensure that the United States remains a global superpower.

The American people understand, if President Clinton did not, that the fact that we won the Cold War has changed—not removed—the various threats we could face.

The Bush administration has quite properly focused much time on reassessing our relationship with Communist China, and if we are to be influential in the Pacific, air power and, preeminently, naval power will be absolutely crucial to our having a convincing deterrent capability against potential aggressors.

Communist China needs to be approached with the same caution with which we should approach Russia under Vladimir Putin. Vladimir Putin was a competent spy for the KGB during the Cold War, and he likely remains a KGB operative at heart now that he runs post-Communist Russia. Like Russia, Communist China has opened up its economy to a degree—motivated by self-interest and Deng Xiaoping's vision to expand its economy—but it remains an extremely repressive and ambitious regional power. It is a disturbing scenario, but there are increasing signs that China and Russia see themselves as potential allies again—an alliance of "rogue state" supporters. This is a very hazardous, if underappreciated, situation. China has a much larger economic and population base to build on than the Soviet Union did in the Cold War—and China is rapidly expanding its military capability. In fact, China is the customer that sustains the research and development budget of Russia's military. In modernizing and improving its massive armed forces, China has focused on creating a highly trained strike force that is roughly equivalent to the size of the United States Army.

There is every reason, given the size of China and its potential threat, to revitalize the old Southeast Asia Treaty Organization, or SEATO, in a new form. A formal alliance of perhaps Taiwan, Japan, Singapore, South Korea, India, Thailand, the Philippines, Australia, New Zealand, and Vietnam would send a powerful signal to China—and to Russia—that the United States means to defend freedom in the Pacific. All of these nations—including Japan and South Korea—are at risk to Chinese pressure, because they know China has been a regional power since the dawn of Asian history. Our current allies in the Pacific cannot be allowed to doubt American resolve in the region. If we strengthen our commitment to preserving peace in the Pacific, we will find both new friends and trading partners.

Interestingly, Vietnam recently asked the Russians to leave the naval base at Cam Ranh Bay. It is time to bury our own ghosts of Vietnam. The Vietnamese, like all of China's neighbors, have every reason to be our allies today. The U.S. Navy in Cam Ranh Bay would help defend Vietnam and the other smaller Asian countries of the Pacific Rim against the awakening Chinese giant. So would American investment. So would re-creating SEATO.

A new, strong Asian alliance would help let China know that we will not shy away from rolling back Chinese Communism, any more than we shied away from rolling back Russian Communism, thereby winning the Cold War. If China threatens its neighbors, we should actively support covert operations to aid the voices of freedom against the regime in Communist China. And of course, we must carry out our treaty, legal, and moral obligations to help Taiwan preserve its own sovereignty.

Many of the views summarized here may seem uncompromising; indeed, I have been described as stubborn. Some even say that my mind closed at the age of six, and it has never opened since. However, as we have seen, the conventional wisdom is not always wise.

CHAPTER 18

THE NIGHTMARE YEAR

The year 1992 was, in every way, a nightmare year for me. I suppose I had been in some danger of succumbing to the Greek condition of hubris during the nearly five years that had passed since I had left the Defense Department. If so, 1992 was to dispel any pride I might have retained.

The military was in good condition. Americans clearly felt better about their country. I saw a bit of this when many soldiers and civilians were kind enough to stop me in the street and offer their congratulations on America's "new military," and I had every confidence in my able successors in the Reagan and Bush administrations.

But, for me, things suddenly changed. On the sultry New York morning of June 16, 1992, I appeared on a television program about global business and economic conditions. At the end of the interview, I was told I had a call waiting. It was my attorney, Robert S. Bennett. "Walsh has just handed down a five-count indictment against you," he said. "They had promised me they would make no decision for a few days, but, as usual, they broke that promise and went ahead with the indictment this morning, despite all our discussions."

After five years of nearly fruitless probing, Lawrence Walsh, the independent counsel appointed in 1986 to investigate the so-called Iran-contra affair, had become increasingly frustrated and anxious to "catch a big fish." Eager to implicate President Reagan in some kind of wrongdoing, Walsh targeted Reagan's close associates. But his results did not produce the headlines he craved. Two of his previous indictments resulted in convictions that had been overturned on appeal. Several other defendants had staved off indictment by agreeing to plead guilty to misdemeanors—really a form of legal blackmail. That was Walsh's basic tactic: when he knew he could not obtain a conviction, he would threaten to indict unless his victim agreed to plead guilty to something—anything—in return for a promise of a light sentence. The very threat of an indictment can lead many to agree to anything regardless of whether or not they are guilty.

Walsh had tried this with me, repeatedly offering a "light sentence" if I would plead guilty to whatever was the flavor of the week. And, of course, I was "to be cooperative" as he continued to pursue President Reagan and Vice President Bush. I had thought that the facts we had presented to him—my steadfast refusal to plead guilty to something I had not done, and the fact that I had ardently and vocally opposed the very policy that was at the heart of the issue— would persuade him not to proceed against me.

The full story of this goes back a long way—to the plight of the American hostages being held in Iran in the mid-1980s, and my discussions about how to free them. Initially, everyone agreed that ransoming or bargaining for their release would only encourage Iranian fanatics to seize other Americans.

But on June 17, 1985, Robert McFarlane, then national security adviser, transmitted a draft National Security Decision Directive

(NSDD) to Secretary of State George Shultz and to me. In it, a number of well-known points were made about the strategic importance of Iran. Then the proposed NSDD discussed the desirability of opening a "dialogue" and making an effort to reestablish a good working relationship with Teheran—even to the extent of giving Iran arms. There was also apparently a belief that dealing with Iranian "moderates" might bring about the release of some of our hostages.

I felt that this was one of the more absurd proposals yet circulated, and so noted in the margin of my copy, adding that this would be similar to "asking Qaddafi over for a cozy chat." In my formal written reply, I said, "Under no circumstances should we now ease our restrictions on arms sales to Iran. Such a policy reversal would be seen as inexplicably inconsistent by those nations whom we have urged to refrain from such sales, and would likely lead to increased arms sales by them and a possible alteration of the strategic balance in favor of Iran while Khomeini is still the controlling influence." I argued that there were no "moderates" left in the Iranian government, because anyone with "moderate" tendencies had long since been killed by Khomeini and his forces. Secretary Shultz, in a memorandum of his own, also objected sharply to the entire proposal.

Since Secretary Shultz and I heard nothing more about the idea, we assumed it had died. I recall a White House meeting later that summer with the president, Shultz, McFarlane, Don Regan, and either Bill Casey or John McMahon, his deputy. The question of arms deals came up. Again, Secretary Shultz and I argued as forcefully as possible that the whole silly idea would completely violate our accepted policy of not ransoming hostages. I made the further point that nothing indicated any change in the virulently anti-Western attitudes of Iran's leadership. Moreover, supplying arms to Iran while urging our friends and allies to honor our arms boycott of the very same country was absurd. Finally, if the president were implicated in a secret deal, future administration policy could be blackmailed by anyone who knew. It seemed to me that the president again agreed with me.

Nonetheless, McFarlane apparently advised the Israelis that it was all right for them to sell some of their American-supplied weapons to the Iranians and that we would resupply the Israelis—this because we "hoped we could get some hostages out." Subsequent investigations have made it clear that, in Don Regan's words, the president was "upset at this news." McFarlane would later say that the Israelis had "taken it upon themselves to do this."

The president later wrote to the Tower Commission (which was conducting one of the first investigations into this issue) that he could recall nothing "whatsoever about whether I approved an Israeli sale in advance, or whether I approved replenishing of Israeli stocks around August of 1985. My answer, therefore, and the simple truth, is, 'I don't remember—period.'" I believe the president. He never approved any such plan in my presence, and I do not believe he ever did.

I did not know until much later (and I doubt the president did either) that this entire initiative had arisen from meetings McFarlane had been holding with the Israelis who thought Iran would *consider* freeing some of the hostages in exchange for arms.

My first hint of these American-Israeli-Iranian discussions came when I asked the meaning of some oddly phrased cable traffic. Our intelligence agencies told me they had made a mistake. They had received instructions *not to let me see* those messages.

I retorted that the National Security Agency was part of the Department of Defense; they had no authority to deny my access to these messages. They replied that their instructions had come from "the White House." "Buildings do not give orders," I said; I demanded that *all* intelligence traffic of any kind come to me, along with *any* instructions they had to deny me access.

After finding these cables, I demanded that all of us—McFarlane, Shultz, and all who had been present at the previous gatherings with the president—meet with the president again. Three meetings were held by the president in the late fall of 1985—long after I thought the entire Iran proposal had been killed. At the latest of these new meetings, it seemed apparent to me that the president had changed his mind—otherwise, why would we still be talking about it?

On November 30, McFarlane resigned. He never made clear why. Most reports said he was "frustrated" and "tired." I later learned that on that same day Lieutenant Colonel Oliver North of the National Security Council (NSC) staff proposed a new "arms-for-hostages" deal to McFarlane's successor, Admiral John Poindexter. When this proposal was considered by the president on December 7, George Shultz and I opposed it vehemently yet again. We also left that meeting convinced that a plan by McFarlane to deliver a message to the Iranians in London was canceled. But McFarlane, who had already resigned from the administration, went anyway.

When people ask me how the will of the secretaries of state and defense could be so easily subverted, I can say only that people with hourly access to the president, such as McFarlane, could phrase their agenda in the most favorable terms. In addition to this, they could report to the president all manner of "hopeful indications" and generally lead a busy president occupied with many other things (including preparations for the Geneva meeting with Gorbachev) to believe that "progress" was being made and that ultimately our hostages would be released.

At a January 7, 1986, meeting with the president, Secretary Shultz and I again argued against arms deals with Iran. But this time—for the first time—the president gave me the clear impression that he had approved the idea.

After the whole deal became public in November 1986, Admiral Poindexter told me that on January 17, 1986, the president had indeed approved the idea of getting four thousand TOWs (tube-launched, optically tracked, wire-guided missiles) to Iran.

When I was finally told that the president had approved the sale, I insisted that any weapons transferred from the Department of Defense go to the CIA under the terms of the Economy Act, which permitted transfers of government property from one department to another. I reminded everyone that direct transfer from the Defense Department to Iran would violate the Arms Export Control Act, and I said that I would refuse to allow such a transfer. I must record that I had hoped this added objection would slow down or possibly even stop the sale, but alas it did not.

In early November 1986, the story of apparently continuing secret negotiations by McFarlane with the Iranians broke in a Middle Eastern newspaper. McFarlane's Iranian "moderates" immediately and publicly denounced the mission. Amazingly, as I learned in December, certain administration officials continued to carry on discussions with Iran. As I wrote in a December 22, 1986, memo to Al Keel, the acting assistant to the president for national security affairs, I was appalled and outraged:

> When the President announced in late November or early December that all further arms shipments to Iran had ceased, and after it became apparent that the channels we were using to discuss hostage release, and other matters with the Iranians were, at the very least, ineffective, and, as is easily apparent now, totally counterproductive, I had assumed that we were finished with that entire Iranian episode and so testified to Congressional Committees during last week. I was astounded, therefore, to learn, on Friday, December 19, 1986, *after* my testimony, that United States "negotiators" were still meeting with the same Iranians. . . .
>
> I must point out as strongly as I can that any attempt to conduct major activities in the security field with the deliberate exclusion of those who have some responsibility for security cannot succeed in anything but

adding to the troubles we already have. I would very much have appreciated an opportunity to present to the President arguments as to why we should *not* continue dealing with these channels in Iran....

I think the President was entitled to have the advice of all of his security advisers, and I must strongly object that the continuation of this practice of secrecy and attempts to exclude various advisers whose advice it is apparently feared may not support the agenda of [certain administration officials], can only get us in more and more difficulty, and serves the President very badly.

The president was characteristically selfless and exhibited great political and personal courage when he later publicly admitted that he had made a mistake. He agreed that it was not possible to negotiate or do business with the Iranians and that the advice he had been given by McFarlane and others was not only wrong but dangerously wrong. He also, very generously, went so far as to acknowledge that I had been right in advising against any kind of dealings with Iran.

In the investigations that resulted from the November news leak, an additional twist was discovered. As if the whole convoluted scheme were not bad enough, subsequent investigations revealed that at some stage, someone had hatched a plan to "overcharge" the Iranians (for the weapons we should not have sold them at all) and turn over some of the proceeds to the Nicaraguan contras, whose funding Congress had sporadically denied. It seemed like a "neat idea" to Oliver North and some other NSC staff members. They knew of the president's strong desire that the contras be funded, and they regarded their scheme as a way to support the freedom fighters without troubling about congressional blocks—or about the legality of the action—and without bothering to tell the president or anyone else about it. I certainly did not know of this until it became public in late 1936, and I am convinced that the president did not know before that time either. The contras should have been funded, but there is only one way to secure legal spending by our government, and that is by vote of Congress, which had been denied.

In his indictment, the independent counsel charged me with two counts of perjury, two counts of making false statements (to congressional committees and to Walsh's investigators), and one count of obstructing Congress. Apparently of no importance to the independent counsel was the fact that the two chairmen of the Senate investigating committee (Senators Daniel Inouye and Warren Rudman), to whom I had allegedly lied, wrote to Bennett saying, "It is inconceivable to us that [Weinberger] would intentionally mislead or lie to Congress."

The independent counsel was intent on proving that I had deliberately lied about my knowledge of events and that I was aware of arms shipments to Iran at the time they occurred, which was simply not the case. As I have said, I did participate in several discussions of McFarlane's "Iran Initiative," but every time it came up, I vehemently opposed it. Until the January 7, 1986, meeting, I believed that the president was against it also and that, therefore, the plan would not ever be carried out.

I am entirely willing, as I was during the investigation, to acknowledge that my memory was not perfect, particularly in regard to dates, and that I had been mistaken in the chronology of some of the responses I made to various inquiries. But that is a long country mile from perjury, which requires both criminal intent to deceive and a deliberate giving of false information. There was not the slightest evidence, let alone proof, that either of these vital elements had occurred.

The obstruction count had to do with my diary notes and the charge that I intentionally withheld them from congressional investigators. The fact is that I provided to the committees everything that I thought, based on my own memory, was relevant. I also instructed the Pentagon legal department to give congressional committees whatever they

requested. I assumed that anything in the files that was relevant—
including some memoranda I had made of the meetings—had been
produced and that the various investigating committees' questions
referring to these memoranda had been answered. It did not occur to
me that my notes, which were basically logs of calls, appointments,
and personal matters—the type of notes I had kept for many years,
long before these events—had any value or relevance for investigators.

After I left office in 1987, I deposited all of my papers from my years
at Defense, including my notes, at the Library of Congress. Many years
later, when investigators from the office of the independent counsel
were questioning me, I told them this, and that they were free to look
at anything they wished; I even gave them written authorization to do
so, which is not a course to follow if one is trying to conceal anything.
I also knew that all files of the department had, at my direction, been
made available to them.

Walsh and his investigators failed to look at any of these papers in
the Library of Congress for at least two years. Then he claimed I had
"concealed" the papers, which were gathering dust in the world's most
public depository and to which they had been given access by my specific written authorization. From this false premise, he tried to concoct
an elaborate conspiracy theory, alleging that I was deliberately "con-
cealing" evidence in order to "protect" the president. This was patently
absurd. President Reagan was enormously proud of all the actions he
had taken to try to release the hostages. He had no desire to be "protected." He told all who would listen of all he had done. In fact, when
he began actually to consider some kind of deal with Iran, and some of
the potential legal problems of such a course were pointed out to him,
he said that he could answer charges of illegality, but he could not ever
answer charges that he had passed up a chance to free the hostages.

The independent counsel was apparently not interested in the
facts, only in what might support his own conspiracy theory, and

in February 1992 he named me as a "target" of his investigation. This meant, essentially, that he was constructing a case against me—primarily, I felt, to try to force me to implicate the president.

Up until that point, former secretary of state and former attorney general Bill Rogers, the senior partner of the Washington law firm Rogers & Wells, where I was then practicing, had been informally advising me on legal matters related to the various Iran-contra investigations. Since I had nothing to hide and was on the right side of the issue, Bill Rogers met with prosecutors several times. He and I both thought I was a cooperating witness, so I was shocked, feeling that I had been misled by the government, when I received the "target letter." When I got the target letter, Bill recommended I hire a skilled criminal defense attorney. I had never had an attorney before; being one myself, and never having been personally involved in any legal matters greater than automobile insurance claims, I had no experience with finding outside legal help.

One name I remembered from an article about Washington attorneys was Robert Bennett, brother of Bill Bennett, who had been an excellent secretary of education in the Reagan administration. Bob Bennett, I knew, had a reputation of fighting for his clients rather than seeking plea bargains. Since I had not done anything to which I could plead guilty, I wanted a lawyer like Bob Bennett.

Bob was cordial and comforting over the telephone. He turned out to be a great attorney in every way, and he was well aware of the devastating effect of the charges, trumped up and false as they were. Bob reminded me of a holistic physician—he treated the whole patient, not just one particular problem. We worked well together, and he even accepted, with good grace, some of my suggestions, in a field in which I was no expert.

Bob and I both knew that we were about to embark on a long, miserable, all-consuming process. The grand jurors would have been given by the prosecutor a *general* impression of some wrongdoing, but without any argument or evidence to the contrary, because, of course, defense attorneys are not allowed to appear. The grand jury process reminded me of a story my father used to tell: A man saw an old friend on the street and said, "I haven't seen you in a long time. You were mixed up in that watch theft, weren't you?" The friend replied, "Yes. I was the man who had his watch stolen."

Bob Bennett and his partner Carl Rauh made valiant efforts to avert an indictment by informing the prosecutor at many meetings of the detailed strength of our defense. Bob also suggested that I take a lie-detector test, which I agreed to immediately. So one morning I rode out to a nondescript building in the Virginia countryside, and a retired specialist from the FBI attached all kinds of patches and wires to my arms, chest, and forehead. It was a chilling experience. The expert asked me five questions relevant to the Iran-contra matter and my notes, and then, after studying my reactions, he pronounced that I had passed with flying colors—no deception of any kind was shown. This was communicated immediately to the independent counsel's office, but it made not the slightest difference.

My good friend and one-time colleague in the Reagan administration, and at Rogers & Wells, Bill Clark, also joined in the fight. He made a special trip to Oklahoma for a meeting with Walsh, thinking that, since both of them had been judges, he might be able to persuade the independent counsel that the course he was pursuing was both absurd and terribly damaging. But after the meeting, Bill reported that Walsh was interested in only one thing: some kind of admission of guilt by me, preferably something—*anything*—that implicated President Reagan, or even Vice President Bush. If I would give that, the independent counsel's office could then arrange for no indictment and a light sentence. And, of course, I was to be "cooperative" with them as they pursued the president. This, I was told, was accompanied by a wink and a nudge. Bill pointed out to them that pleading guilty to something I had not done would be a lie—which was something I would not do—and that these "offers" by the independent counsel were improper, if not illegal, pressures.

As Paul Craig Roberts said so well in an editorial in the July 20, 1992, *Fair Comment*, this was "a good example of prosecutorial abuses employed to get witnesses not only to sing but also to compose."

Had we been dealing with any kind of reasonable prosecutor, the matter would have been dropped. But when Walsh and his team suddenly realized that the statute of limitations on one of the minor charges was to expire the next day, they rushed ahead and secured the grand jury's flaccid approval and issued their indictment on June 16.

I was scheduled to make a speech later that day in New York, but after Bob Bennett's call, my assistant, Kay Leisz, and I took the first shuttle back to Washington. The drive to LaGuardia and the hour-long flight seemed absolutely interminable. At Bennett's request, I went directly to his office and appeared at a press conference there. I made what would be my first and only public statement[*] until the whole ordeal was over:

> In order to avoid this indictment I was not willing to accept an offer by the Office of the Independent Counsel to plead to a misdemeanor offense of which I was not guilty, nor was I willing to give them statements which were not true about myself or others. I would not give false testimony nor would I enter a false plea. Because of this refusal, which to me is a matter of conscience, I have now been charged with multiple felonies.

The charges brought by Walsh and his staff were absolutely untrue. The major/lead count charged me with "obstructing" Congress by

---

[*] Bennett, quite rightly, advised that I not speak publicly about the case until after all of the legal proceedings had been concluded. It was unfortunate that the prosecutors did not follow these well-established rules.

purposely withholding my handwritten notes. In fact, these notes conclusively established my vigorous opposition to selling arms to Iran to free American hostages held in Lebanon. And had I realized they were relevant, I would have gladly provided them.

In late September 1992, U.S. District Judge Thomas F. Hogan recognized the wrongheadedness of this lead count and threw it out of court because it failed even to allege a criminal offense. Then Walsh tried to resurrect this claim by charging me with making a "false statement" to Congress about my notes in a subsequent one-count indictment. A little more than a month later, Judge Hogan dismissed this charge as well. In so doing, he criticized Walsh for seeking from the court "a license . . . to try another theory of prosecution when one theory fails."

Thus, Walsh's case had been reduced to the four subsidiary counts—all of which were based on twisted and untrue allegations cobbled together to look like "crimes." Three related to my testimony before the select congressional committees or their staff.

Two of these counts charged that I purposely lied before the select committees and their staff when I responded to certain questions about the Iran-contra mess by saying that I had "no memory" of a particular detail. My testimony was given more than two years after the events. General Colin Powell, my military assistant in 1985 and 1986, told Walsh in a sworn statement prior to my indictment that I do not have a particularly good memory for dates and details after events occur, let alone *years* afterward, especially given the vast flow of critical national security and other information through the office of the secretary of defense. I guess I should also add that in 1987, at age seventy, my memory, like that of many others, was not improving!

The actual language of these two charges demonstrates their misguided and reckless nature. Count II was based on the following question and answer that I gave in a deposition before the House Select Committee's staff on July 17, 1987:

Q: Do you recall learning at some point that the Saudis or some people connected with the Saudis provided funds for the contras?

A: No. *I don't have any memory* of any contra funding or anything
connected with the Saudis *that I can remember now.*

Count IV was based on the following exchange with the counsel
to the select committees during their hearing on July 31, 1987:

Q: And in addition, there are various documents which are in evidence before the Committee which refer to the Israeli desire and need
for replenishment of weapons that the Israelis were sending. Did you
know that replenishment was an issue?

A: No, *I have no memory of that.*

I did not lie to investigators about the state of my recollection, and
Walsh had no evidence that I did.

Count III involved the claim that I had known in advance of the
shipment of eighteen HAWK missiles to Iran by Israel in September
1985. This count was based on the following question and answer
that I gave in an exchange with counsel to the select committees during the hearing on July 31, 1987:

Q: The Committee has also received testimony that on that weekend
of November 23 and November 24, [1985] there was a shipment of 18
HAWK missiles from Israel to Iran. This [Exhibit 8] was a paper that
was written immediately prior to that time. Let me just ask you: Did you
have any knowledge that that transfer was to take place?

A: No, I did not.

I did not know about that shipment before the fact and was
shocked when I learned about it. I had already made it clear to everyone, including President Reagan, that I vehemently opposed arms

sales to Iran. Accordingly, no one was inclined to tell me about them, and the fact is that no one did. There was absolutely no evidence that I had advance knowledge of the shipment of eighteen HAWK missiles, and that is exactly how I testified.

The fifth and final count of the indictment was equally outrageous and untrue, and was part of a clever litigation strategy by Walsh and his team. Walsh charged me with lying to his assistant prosecutor about my notes in an October 1990 interview to which I voluntarily agreed. Then Walsh selected this same assistant prosecutor to be the lead trial prosecutor in order to bolster the credibility of the charge. Walsh did this even though it is unethical to use a lawyer who participated in the events on trial to seek unfair credibility advantages with a jury by having that lawyer be, in essence, an unsworn witness in the case. Fortunately, Bennett and his team crafted a compelling motion seeking to disqualify the prosecutor from the case. After the hearing on this motion, Judge Hogan in a strongly written opinion expressed grave concerns about the independent counsel's tactic. Seeing the handwriting on the wall, a few days later Walsh removed that prosecutor from the case and replaced him with another lawyer—a prominent San Francisco Democrat who had personally contributed to the Clinton-Gore campaign and whose law firm had donated over $20,000 to that campaign.

Moreover, there was no transcript of my voluntary interview in October 1990, and the FBI's description of the meeting was completely inaccurate. Furthermore, the idea that I had hidden notes from Walsh's team was preposterous. I never sought to hide them. Just before I left the Pentagon, I packed up my papers, including the little pads I used for my various jottings. I actually did this while being photographed in my office for archival purposes! Bob Bennett tracked down the photographer and obtained the photographs. This was forceful evidence of my innocence since Walsh claimed I had tried to conceal those notes. I then sent these papers to the Library of

Congress. When asked, I directed Walsh's investigators to my notes and other papers at the Library of Congress before, during, and after the October 1990 meeting mentioned in the indictment. Shortly after that meeting, I actually provided written authorization for the independent counsel to inspect and copy "such notes and documents related to the Iran-contra matter." At the Library of Congress, there was an index to my papers which specified they contained notes relating to Iran-contra. Apparently, for more than a year, Walsh's investigators were too sloppy to find the notes I authorized them to review.

So began, after the indictment, endless days of torment for me and my family. It was quite paralyzing at first. There was a tremendous desire to fight back, and the realization that you cannot; you have to go through the long, agonizing, excruciating procedure. There would be an exhaustive rehash of every sentence I had ever uttered and every action I had ever taken, which would drag on for several months even before the case reached court, and then the trial itself would probably take several more months.

Preparation for my trial was an emotionally exhausting exercise. I spent day after day either in Bennett's office or in a ratty old building on Connecticut Avenue, called a Secure Information Facility, where thousands of linear feet of the prosecutor's files, documents, and other materials were stored. There, Bob Bennett and I pored over papers and discussed many of the still-classified details of the whole unhappy saga. Bennett and I also attended numerous court hearings on motions and other matters pertaining to the handling of classified documents and things of that kind. Any time we entered or left the courthouse, we were pressed by dozens of news cameras and microphones.

The classified documents were particularly important to my case because certain secret intelligence reports about Iran actually showed I had not lied about my knowledge of events. Saul Pilchen and Ben Klubes of the Bennett/Rauh trial team spent two weeks in court explaining line-by-line the nature of the exculpatory reports to Judge

Hogan and fought Walsh's opposition to our use of them for my defense. In the end, I think the judge was inclined toward our view, but he did not rule before the pardon.

One of these hearings, on December 22, I believe, provided a bit of comic relief. As one of the technical points was being argued before Judge Hogan, a U.S. marshal handed Bennett a note. It read, "Please have Secretary Weinberger call Senator Dole immediately." With the pardon and other matters being then under discussion, we thought we should indeed make the call. Bob was granted a short recess and together we raced over to find a phone. The first bank of public phones was full and we continued our race down one of the courthouse's endless corridors. When we reached an empty phone and squeezed into the booth, I, panting hard, made the call. Bob tells me the color drained out of my face and that I stammered out, "Thank you very much, Senator, and to you, too." I hung up and Bob said, "Wha— wha—?" I said, "He wanted to wish us both a merry Christmas." We laughed all the way back to the courtroom but decided not to enlighten the court as to our secret cable.

Being inside the courtroom was extremely stressful. I could feel my heart beating rapidly and the heat of everyone staring at me, but I felt I had to remain outwardly impassive.

The whole thing was horribly debilitating. My wife, I am sure, felt much the same way, especially when she attended some of these hearings. Indeed, I knew that the overall strain on her was growing and that both my children and my grandchildren were being subjected to the inquiries and cruel gibes of friends and schoolmates.

My wife and I came down with shingles, an extremely painful disease that inflames the nerve endings. The health of our collie, my great friend, Kiltie, began to fail at this same time. Even lesser problems became difficult. Our Washington apartment flooded and the carpet had to be replaced—a normally minor project that under this stress seemed much larger.

Aside from these personal problems, prior commitments had to be honored and public appearances had to be made, mostly in connection with my work for *Forbes* magazine, which I had joined after leaving the Reagan administration. The first of these engagements was a talk at a Forbes conference in Bermuda, only a couple of days after the indictment. As part of the normal legal process, an order is issued that a defendant cannot leave the country, but Bennett was able to get this restriction lifted. When I went to the airport, however, I discovered that I had forgotten my passport, which meant a long and disconcerting delay. Eventually, I was allowed to board the plane. Making my speech there that night was particularly difficult because I was still in a state of shock and disbelief about my indictment. But the audience was very courteous—painfully so—and did an admirable job of acting as if nothing unusual were happening.

Fearing that I might be an embarrassment to the Forbes family, I offered, two or three times, to resign. I will always remember, with unbounded appreciation, the immediate and scornful dismissal of these suggestions by Steve Forbes and his three brothers, particularly Kip, with whom I work most closely. They said that they had complete faith in me and in all of the things I had done, and they expressed great admiration for my work at the Defense Department. They knew, too, how strongly I had opposed the whole Iranian initiative. Not only would they not hear of my resigning from *Forbes*, they insisted on my continuing with them, and their kindness reminded me of why I am so very glad that Malcolm Forbes Sr. urged me to join the magazine back in 1988.

I was, indeed, fortunate to have the unwavering support of many friends and colleagues, some of whom had themselves been subjected to harsh and unfair treatment before Walsh's grand jury.

A particularly disagreeable aspect of this whole affair was financial. Along with everything else, my legal bills seemed to be growing almost exponentially, amounting to several hundred thousand dollars a month, with no end in sight. It looked as if I would ultimately transfer the bulk of my estate not to my children but to my attorneys. I did not feel any resentment toward Bob Bennett. I knew it took a tremendous number of hours of legal work to go up against an independent counsel, who could draw as much money as he wanted out of the U.S. Treasury any time he wished. And I had a brilliant team of younger lawyers supporting Bob Bennett and Carl Rauh which included Saul Pilchen, Amy Sabin, Ben Klubes, Roberto Iraola, Bonnie Austin, Abby Raphael, and Stephen Vaughn.

My staggering legal bills were a source of double distress to me because, although Bennett assured me that he did not expect immediate payment, I have always made it a practice to pay every bill within a few days of receiving it. And, for years, I had not incurred any bills I could not pay for at the time.

Many people, aware of the problem, voluntarily sent contributions, and it occurred to a couple of friends, as well as Bennett's office, that it would be desirable to formalize this and establish some sort of fund to which contributions could be made. I reluctantly agreed—reluctantly because the idea of asking people for money runs counter to my self-sufficing, New England tendencies. Mike Burch, who had been assistant secretary of defense for public affairs when I was secretary, agreed to act as trustee, and three other volunteers, including Mrs. Frank Carlucci, ran the day-to-day operations of the legal defense fund. They sent out hundreds of letters of solicitation, and even more thank-you letters, to supporters all over the country, most of whom were kind, concerned citizens I had never even met.

In September 1992, the defense fund staff organized a fund-raising reception at the Mayflower Hotel in Washington. About one thousand people attended to show their support and urge contributions; a few even made speeches. Senator Alan Simpson's was one of the most memorable. In his usual blunt, straightforward style, he blasted the independent counsel and his treatment of me, using a stream of splendid expletives and jokes.

The event was a financial success, but for me personally, humiliating. It was embarrassing to be in such a position in the first place. My honesty or integrity had never been questioned before. I do not mean to give the impression that I did not appreciate everyone's most generous support—indeed I did, and always will. It was one of the most truly gratifying aspects of an otherwise very unhappy year.

Bob Bennett had requested a trial by judge, based on the belief that a judge would be much more likely to understand the issues of the case than an apathetic, perhaps even hostile, District of Columbia jury. But under law, the prosecutor must consent to a trial by judge, and, of course, he would not.

U.S. District Judge Thomas F. Hogan had been assigned to try our case, and he was the one handling the various motions both sides were putting forth. It was clear that he recognized the absurdity of the charge that I had obstructed Congress, and, as mentioned earlier, on September 29 he dismissed that count of the indictment.

But on October 30, days before the presidential election, the independent counsel returned a new indictment, which relied on many of the same factual allegations as the count that had been dismissed, just worded differently. Instead of obstructing Congress by withholding my notes, Walsh now said I had made false statements about my notes.

The timing of the reindictment was calculated to cause the maximum political damage to President Bush, which, of course, it did. The independent counsel included in the indictment, contrary to normal legal practice, some of the evidence on which he was going to rely. The piece he picked out to cite was a note that I was supposed to have written that allegedly indicated that Vice President Bush knew more about the "arms-for-hostages" plan, as it came to be called, than had previously been thought. It was scarcely a coincidence that this new indictment, with this particular citation, was issued only four days before the 1992 presidential election, in which President Bush was up for reelection. I have no doubt that this was another desperate attempt by the independent counsel to bring down as high an official as he could and support the Democratic candidate at the same time[*]—an effort undoubtedly tinged with revenge for my refusal to help him in this goal.

The Clinton campaign used the new indictment to maximum advantage. In fact, in its eagerness to use the indictment against President Bush, the Clinton team was a little sloppy, issuing a press release about it dated the day *before* the indictment was made public. Obviously, someone had leaked it to the Democratic campaign. This was simply more evidence of the blatant political vindictiveness of the prosecutor.

In early December, long after the election, this second indictment, consisting solely of Walsh's new lead charge, was also dismissed by the court, but the damage had been done. Indeed, inflicting that political damage was its only purpose. I believe it directly contributed to President Bush's defeat. (As did the presence in the race of Ross Perot, who, although he stood for nothing, managed to get about 19 percent of the vote. Perot's candidacy not only was devastating to President Bush, it also subjected our country to the Clinton presidency.)

That an independent counsel can have such a wide and powerful political reach—even going so far as to influence the outcome of a presidential election—underlines the fundamental error of the independent counsel law. The office of the independent counsel is a total anomaly in our system of government. An independent counsel is subject to absolutely no checks or balances. He has unlimited tenure.

---

[*] Walsh always made a big point of saying he was a registered Republican. This was supposed to give credibility to his baseless charges.

He has unlimited access to Treasury funds without the need to secure congressional consent. Indeed, he is not restricted by any requirements for approval—from Congress, the president, or the judicial branch—of any action he wishes to take. Theoretically, he is supposed to be under the eye of a three-judge federal court, but traditionally, this court has paid little attention to him.

Paul Craig Roberts best described the frightening power the office holds: "The office of special prosecutor is an amazing departure from American legal precedent. Unlike any other prosecutor, the special prosecutor has the power to bring the full weight and financial resources of the U.S. government to bear upon a single individual."[*] This runs counter to every tenet upon which a democracy is built.

Since its inception in 1978,[†] the independent counsel law has been renewed twice, but fortunately it was allowed to expire in June 1999.[‡] At the height of Walsh's assault on me there seemed no way to fight the power of his office, so when the idea of a presidential pardon was raised, I, after initial resistance, ultimately did not object.

Shortly after the 1992 election, several senators, particularly Bob Dole and Orrin Hatch, began calling for a presidential pardon as the best way to bring the whole sordid matter to an end and effectively put that independent counsel out of business. Some congressional Democrats also joined in this effort, as did some members of President Bush's

---

[*] "To Hold Prosecutorial Hounds at Bay," *Washington Times*, November 28, 1992.

[†] The Ethics in Government Act, which authorized the appointment of an independent counsel, was a result of the Watergate scandal. When President Nixon fired special prosecutor Archibald Cox (appointed by the attorney general) after Cox issued a subpoena for White House tapes, the public lost a great deal of trust in executive branch officials and their ability to investigate themselves. Consequently, Congress developed the idea of having an outside counsel, appointed by a special court, to investigate allegations of wrongdoing by top executive branch officials.

[‡] Paradoxically, its most severe critics became the Democrats after Mr. and Mrs. Clintons' antics were subjected to investigation by an independent counsel.

administration—in particular, presidential counsel Boyden Gray and Vice President Dan Quayle. All of these people shared the recognition that the independent counsel was completely out of control.

Although I greatly appreciated this effort by so many friends, it had to be pointed out to me many times that the presidential power of clemency did not require any finding of guilt. I did not want any implication that I had done anything wrong. But equally weighty a consideration was how long the ordeal could drag on (predictions were for a three- to four-month trial) and how it would constantly be in the headlines. I agreed that a pardon would save me and my family an enormous amount of grief and strain and daily torture, and could end the whole thing once and for all, with no appeals. It would have been a nice, high-principled thing to have rejected any suggestion of a pardon, but the possibility that all of this pain could be alleviated by a single stroke of a presidential pen was the decisive factor for me.

On December 18, Bob Bennett prepared a formal request for a pardon, and on Christmas Eve morning, Boyden Gray called Bennett from Camp David to inform us that the president had granted a pardon to me and five others who had been snared in Walsh's net.* For the first time in nearly a year, I slept well and awoke happily. That Christmas was one of the best I can remember.

My family and I are eternally grateful to President Bush for sparing us the continuation of such a dreadful ordeal. I wrote him then, expressing our deep appreciation, and have done so every Christmas Eve since.

The president acted honorably in every way and had, quite properly, included in his pardon a number of others who had been subjected to the independent counsel's pressures, some for far longer than

---

* Robert McFarlane, Elliott Abrams, and CIA officials Clair George, Duane Clarridge, and Alan Fiers.

a year, and some of whom had indeed agreed to plea bargain since they did not have the financial resources to fight Walsh's overwhelming power. President Bush is a compassionate man who recognized the tremendous injustice being done by an overzealous independent counsel.

Walsh's reaction to the president's action could have been easily anticipated. He called a press conference to denounce the president furiously. He announced that President Bush himself was now a subject of his investigation. But Walsh's time was nearly out, and his frustration over failing to convict anyone else was left unrelieved.

The press was naturally clamoring for me to make appearances now. I was disinclined to continue the matter in any way, but during the closing weeks of the long ordeal, Larry King of CNN had been particularly kind and thoughtful in his remarks about the case, and so I agreed to be on his program. Besides, it afforded me a full hour to vent my feelings publicly about the injustices of Walsh's investigation—an exercise more therapeutic than I had expected, with many kind comments from Larry King's viewers.

Then there was the not-so-little matter of my remaining legal bills—a total of $2.3 million. The legal defense fund had raised about $600,000, which was a great help, but I did not want any more solicitations to be made. So, again with Bill Clark's most able assistance, we worked out with Bob Bennett an arrangement under which I would pay off the bills over the course of the next three years—almost as long as it had taken me to pay off my 1958 campaign debt after my bid for California attorney general. In fact, I mailed the check to Bennett for my last installment in 1995.

I was anxious to get back into a regular work schedule and some semblance of a normal life. After a year of these personal legal problems, it was hard for me to get even halfway interested in any further law practice, and the *Forbes* organization was kind enough to want me full-time. So I officially resigned my position at Rogers & Wells and devoted my full attention to *Forbes*. I enjoyed the work, the *Forbes* people, and the travel and writing my job entailed. The Forbes family had my eternal gratitude for their extraordinarily generous loyalty and support during that whole miserable year of 1992.

Indeed, I am most grateful to people from all around the country, even the world, who expressed their support—financially as well as with calls, letters, and prayers—to me and my family during that difficult time. No American should ever be subject to such an untrammeled prosecutorial assault. America needs to be as vigilant about its domestic rule of law and the rights of defendants as it is about its national defense—something the American people are better aware of than are some lawyers. Zealots should never be given an opportunity to abuse unlimited power, as the independent counsel did in the Iran-contra case. With the expiration of the independent counsel law—an expiration that former independent counsel Kenneth Starr fully supported—I hope this unfortunate period in American legal history is behind us.

Chapter 19

Job Stability—At Last

*T*he "nightmare year" aside, the other aspects of my life since I left the Defense Department have been and continue to be quite fulfilling and enjoyable.

Left to myself, I would have finished out my term at Defense, but my wife's continued suffering with severe arthritis and osteoporosis dictated otherwise. There were many difficult and tiring demands on her as a cabinet wife, but she had stood by my side without complaint through my nearly seven-year tenure as secretary. I felt I should respect her wishes that I leave public office in 1987 after so much had been accomplished.

I expected to do some writing, so I wanted to stay near Washington and the relevant materials. Jane prefers our home in Maine, so I divide my time between there and our apartment in Washington.

The general practice at the Defense Department was for an outgoing secretary of defense to have a transition office at the Pentagon to handle transition correspondence and similar matters. At the time

I left, however, even the largest office building in the world had no extra rooms, and in any event I did not want my successor, Frank Carlucci, to feel that I was looking over his shoulder. So President Reagan generously offered me an office in the Old Executive Office Building, my old haunt from my OMB days.

I was in limbo for a few months, but frankly I rather enjoyed the break from heavy responsibilities. Still, it was hard not to react, almost automatically, like an old firehouse, to any new developments overseas. Then, in February 1988, I had a delightful, unexpected treat.

While I was attending a ceremony at the White House, the British ambassador to the United States, Sir Antony Acland, told me that Great Britain wanted to bestow on me an honorary knighthood, and he asked if I would accept. I was completely taken by surprise, but being an unabashed Anglophile, I answered with an immediate and enthusiastic yes. I assumed that Lady Thatcher had recommended me, as she had. I later learned that her foreign secretary, Sir Geoffrey Howe, also had quite a lot to do with it.

My guess that this award was in gratitude for the aid President Reagan and I had provided to England during the 1982 conflict in the Falkland Islands was confirmed by the words of Conservative member of Parliament Edward Leigh after my knighthood was announced: "Everybody knows that without private American help it wouldn't have been possible to have won the Falklands War." We did indeed help, but I do not entirely agree with Leigh's assessment; I think the decisive factor in Britain's victory was Mrs. Thatcher's firm and immediate decision to retake the islands, despite the impressive military and other advice she received that such an action could not succeed.

When, on April 2, 1982, the Argentine military dictatorship invaded the Falkland Islands, claiming that these territories—over which Britain had exercised full sovereignty for nearly 150 years— were owned by Argentina, they made a major miscalculation in assuming that Britain neither would nor could resist the junta in any effective way. As soon as Mrs. Thatcher ordered a full-scale counterinvasion, declaring that "the possibility of defeat simply does not exist," I vigorously expressed my view that it would be unthinkable for the United States to remain neutral when our oldest friend had been attacked in such a fashion. We could not condone, by silence or inaction, naked aggression anywhere, certainly not in our own hemisphere and not by a corrupt military dictatorship against one of our NATO allies. After some internal discussion, President Reagan agreed, and on April 30, he announced sanctions against Argentina and pledged that we would give the British material support.

I knew how vital speed would be for the extraordinarily difficult operation the British were about to undertake, so I had directed the Defense Department to expedite all existing requests from the United Kingdom for military equipment, and that all new British requests were to have first priority. Our material assistance was crucial, but it certainly would not have been if the British forces had not enjoyed Mrs. Thatcher's staunch leadership.

Mrs. Thatcher was a regular visitor to Washington during the Reagan years, and she was indefatigable in upholding Britain's national interests. She had a ready ear at the White House because President Reagan had known of her and admired her from reading her speeches even before she became prime minister. They spoke the same language. But that wasn't always enough to decide an issue. Once I had to tell Mrs. Thatcher that a British consortium, seeking a very large contract to supply NATO forces with mobile communications equipment, had come in with a bid more than a billion dollars higher than the bid of a French consortium, which was therefore going to win the contract. She looked steely regal and then said, "It is bad enough, Caspar, not to award the contract to us, but to give it to the Frrrrrench is quite unacceptable." I had never heard the word "French" said with five rolling r's—or with such ferocity.

I thought the Falklands War was her finest hour, when she disregarded the jeremiads of her military advisers and insisted on complete victory—a victory in which I was glad we were able to assist.

In any case, I never imagined that my actions in the conflict—to me, simply a matter of duty—would ever be recognized in such an extraordinary way as a knighthood. Still, as the old saying goes, the honors one enjoys the most are those one least expects and probably least deserves.

My wife and I flew to London the day before the ceremony and stayed at the American Embassy, which I had visited many times before as secretary of defense. Our embassy there is one of our finest homes—formerly the London residence of Barbara Hutton. It is located in a corner of Regent's Park and is a Georgian house with beautiful, large reception rooms and halls. The residence quarters are those of a supremely comfortable English country house. Our ambassador at the time, Charles Price, was a large, confident, affable, and cordial Missouri businessman—successful and at ease with British ways. His beautiful wife, Carol, was a most excellent hostess, and both were extremely popular and effective envoys.

That evening, a splendid dinner was held in my honor at 10 Downing Street; far too much praise was bestowed upon me. In attendance were about a hundred people, including the Duke of Edinburgh, the Prince of Wales and Princess Diana, various British cabinet members, and, of course, the prime minister and Denis Thatcher.

The next morning, I attended an investiture ceremony at Buckingham Palace, where the queen was presenting several awards to British subjects. The regular investiture procedure requires the honoree to kneel before the queen while she lightly taps him and dubs him "Sir Knight."

The press had been full of speculation over whether the only American to be honored and invested at this ceremony would kneel before the English sovereign. The queen most tactfully solved the problem by inviting Jane and me to a private audience with her after the formal investiture ceremony. Our small ceremony took place in her morning room, a lovely, golden room in the private quarters of the palace. Only the queen, Foreign Secretary Howe, my wife, and I were there. The queen was seated on a couch and invited us all to join her. We talked a while, and like everyone who has had that privilege, I noted mainly how extraordinarily well informed she was about everything going on in the world. She is small but has a most impressive presence, and at the same time she shows great informality and real friendliness.

At that private gathering, she had an insignia and badge of the Order of the British Empire, which she simply handed to me while we were all seated. She said, "We're very grateful to you for everything you have done for us, and we'd like you to have this."

It is a very handsome award, resting on silk—a red ribbon with the medal of the Order of the British Empire, and a separate silver star signifying the title "Knight Grand Cross," one of the highest orders of chivalry that can be bestowed on a foreigner. I learned that only fifty-five other Americans had been knighted and that only a handful were given this order.

Foreigners, of course, ordinarily do not use "Sir" before their names because the award is honorary. Also, our Constitution has some strict language about foreign titles. Nevertheless, the great honor of being given a knighthood was particularly gratifying for someone as steeped in English history as I.

When we returned home, I came down from that rather heady cloud, and my life resumed a more familiar tack.

Later in 1988, President Reagan appointed me to the National Economic Commission (NEC), a bipartisan commission established by Congress with the purported mandate to look for ways to reduce the federal budget deficit. But, much like Governor Brown's Commission on Government Reform in the late 1970s, the real purpose of the NEC, I felt, was to provide cover for tax increases.* The commission, primarily the brainchild of Senator Pat Moynihan, was supposed to say, "We can cut this, we can't cut that, but in the final analysis, we must have more revenue." Then Congress could raise taxes, saying the commission recommended it, and escape too much political opprobrium.

I accepted the appointment because the president asked me to, but from the start I argued against recommending tax hikes, which would have a contractive effect on the economy. I preferred to look for areas where the budget could be cut. I also spoke for tax *cuts* as the best way to encourage economic growth. This, of course, was totally unacceptable to the Democrats in Congress and on the commission—particularly Moynihan—who had sponsored the resolution to create the commission.

I also encountered much opposition when I defended continued substantial defense spending, but I believe strongly that the best social program is to keep people alive, safe, and healthy, which cannot be done without a commitment to effective national defense policies and adequate spending to support those policies.

After several months, the commission issued its recommendations. But—also like the Brown commission—the members were divided in their opinions, and two separate reports were submitted. I was a member of the commission majority, which believed that the deficit could be reduced by restraining federal spending—and

---

* The commission was made up of members from both the private sector (such as AFL-CIO president Lane Kirkland and Chrysler chairman Lee Iacocca) and the public sector (senators; congressmen; Don Rumsfeld, secretary of defense under President Ford; and myself).

without increasing taxes. In fact, we advocated a constitutional amendment that would require a balanced budget and limit the amount of revenue that could be raised. We also supported a line-item veto power for the president, and we believed that reform of the congressional budget process would be beneficial—particularly eliminating the duplication of separate Authorization and Appropriation Committees.

The minority report was considerably longer than ours, but it seemed quite ambiguous, and specific recommendations were difficult to discern. It basically just reiterated the problems and pointed out the difficulty of reaching a consensus about how to solve them. I think this was because the minority realized it could not persuade the majority to support a tax increase.

As nice as it had been to have a few months without any very heavy responsibilities, I needed to resume my income-tax-paying status. My longtime friend Bill Clark was a part-time senior consultant at the Washington law firm of Rogers & Wells, headed by former secretary of state William P. Rogers, an old friend who had served in President Nixon's first term. Bill recommended me to Rogers, who apparently felt I would be an asset to them, and he offered me a post with the firm. Although I had never had an overwhelming drive to be a lawyer, I accepted because I would be acting more in a consulting capacity, much as Bill Clark did. There were some interesting aspects; I advised their attorneys on banking and securities laws, worked on a case involving a World Bank grant to a new telecommunications company in the former Soviet republic of Georgia, and ran a seminar for the firm in Japan.

I was grateful to be with a reputable and successful firm, but as with every other time I had worked in a law office, I was not entirely satisfied. So I jumped at a most interesting and surprising opportunity that came my way in the fall of 1988.

When I was in New York for a Physical Fitness Awards Dinner,* the colorful publishing genius Malcolm Forbes, editor in chief of the venerable and much respected *Forbes* magazine, called and wanted to meet with me. I could not imagine why, but I agreed to see him just before the dinner that evening at the Waldorf-Astoria hotel.

We met in a room just off the banquet hall, and I was absolutely astounded when he asked me to become publisher of *Forbes* magazine. I was especially surprised in light of the fact that Malcolm himself had written some less-than-flattering editorials over the past years, criticizing defense spending and commenting on my stubbornness when I was at the Pentagon.†

---

* My own physique did not qualify me for an award; I was invited because when I was secretary of HEW, I had encouraged national physical fitness programs.

† There was one I remember, probably because he had paid me a nice compliment, though he then proceeded to illustrate it as a flaw:

"There are those who speculate that the mounting tempo and temper of criticism for Defense Secretary Weinberger's absolute refusal to consider removals from his overflowing budget platter might lead to his reassignment or resignation. They're whistling Dixie.

"We've contributed our critical mite, e.g., 'Cap the Butterknife,' etc. But we've never deluded ourselves that such might have much result.

"The defense secretary feels—rightly, I think—that any offer of his to reconsider or 'postpone' major projects, such as the MX missile or additional carrier groups, would be taken as a given by Capitol Hillers, and they'd promptly be in full cry for more. No one around the president enjoys his confidence more than Secretary Weinberger—and few for as long. Reagan's delighted with Cap's stubborn 'standup' to his critics.

"During this blazing Defense budget battle, people tend to overlook the fact that Cap Weinberger is one of the few genuinely and thoroughly nice guys in Washington. That's part of the problem. His convictions are genuine. He's not posturing for political power. That's more of a problem.

"If he were less nice, he wouldn't have been persuaded by all the Braid that everything they have asked for is essential. If he were more political, he would realize that Congress can't buy a deficit of a size that many of us feel would weaken America more than the proposed spending would strengthen it.

"If Cap were to recommend to the president that, considering the Whole Equation, perhaps it would be better to hold off on some of those Big Tickets, for sure Ronald Reagan would listen.

"Oh, would that Cap would."

Besides the general differences of opinion that Malcolm and I had, I was some years *older* than the retiring publisher, James Dunn. I really did not take the offer seriously at first (I was sure Malcolm was making one of his jokes). But as we talked, I realized he was quite serious, and I learned later that I was his first choice to succeed Dunn. Actually, the more I thought about it, the more attractive it sounded (Malcolm was enormously persuasive, whether talking to a potential new recruit or a potential new advertiser) because I had so enjoyed my previous minor experience in newspapers and publishing.

Apparently, Malcolm felt that I would not require much training, or "breaking in," and that a good portion of the magazine's readership would be interested in what I had to say about the world scene. Moreover, he knew that I was acquainted with a number of foreign government leaders and probably would be able to meet with them and record their views.

Also, I knew that *Forbes* had been a most respected and interesting business journal for decades. In fact, we are practically twins! *Forbes*'s first issue appeared about a week before I was born in 1917.

The Forbes family are great people, stemming from Scottish stock similar to my wife's. I had met Malcolm casually on a few previous occasions, mostly when I was invited aboard their glorious yacht, the *Highlander*, on its annual visits to Northeast Harbor, Maine.

I had known his oldest son, Malcolm Forbes Jr. (better known as Steve), when he was chairman of the Board for International Broadcasting and I was at Defense. He had come to my office a few times to talk about the great value of the Voice of America radio programs with respect to American interests abroad, essentially selling the virtues of democracy to those around the world who had not yet experienced it. I wholeheartedly agreed, and Steve did a fine job guiding the whole operation. He was as persuasive as his father.

Whatever the reason they wanted me, I accepted. Among other reasons, I thought that anyone who wanted to employ the aged should be encouraged. I then persuaded a rather reluctant Bill Rogers that I could do both Rogers & Wells assignments and the *Forbes* work.

I arrived at my second-story office in the magazine's Greenwich Village, New York, town house in September of 1988, and ever since I have thoroughly enjoyed every moment with *Forbes*.

When I am not traveling on *Forbes* trips, I typically spend about two days a week in New York, and more than that in my Washington *Forbes* office.

As I suspected, writing the column is a very satisfying part of the job. It gives me my own bully pulpit from which to inflict my biases on the large readership of *Forbes*. It is also a kind of forced discipline to keep up on world affairs. As promised, the content of my columns has never been restricted in any way (indeed, all *Forbes* columnists have free rein to express their views). The only requirements are that it fit one page and, of course, that it be done on time. The deadline comes along with terrible regularity, and I usually run too long, but with the skilled help of my executive assistant, Kay Leisz, and Merrill Vaughn, the column editor, my column always seems to make it on time and to fit into the allocated space.

Unlike traditional publishers, I did not directly solicit advertising, a task I was frankly glad not to have; I have never been comfortable with, or very good at, trying to sell things or asking people for money. But I did, as publisher (and continue to, as chairman), function as part of the "Forbes collection," whom potential advertisers might like to see and hear.

The so-called Cap-Kip Dinners began shortly after I joined the company. Every year, Christopher "Kip" Forbes (vice chairman of Forbes, Inc., and the third of four Forbes brothers)[*] and I host a

---

[*] Steve is the oldest brother. The second brother is Robert, president of *Forbes Global* and *Forbes FYI*, a leisure-oriented magazine supplement. Tim is the youngest Forbes brother and the company's chief operating officer.

series of these dinners in major cities around the country and invite business leaders, corporate CEOs and other senior executives to attend. After dinner, I expound on world events while Kip Forbes sells, with great and understated skill, the magazine as the best place for these companies to invest their advertising dollars. In an unguarded moment, Kip once said, "People come to pick Cap's brains, and that gives me a chance to pick their pockets." One of our rivals, *BusinessWeek*, foolishly criticized Kip for his wit.

The Cap-Kip Dinners are of great benefit to me and, I hope, to the magazine. Talking with these executives gives me a wonderful window on the state of American business and its leaders' insights on issues like the economy, trade, and industry trends, all of which become potential fodder for my column.

Another feature of the Cap-Kip Dinners that I enjoy is dessert. Kip realized early on what a world-class chocoholic I am. As he confided recently to a friend, "When dessert was, say, strawberry mousse, Cap's remarks would be ... fine. But serve 'death-by-chocolate,' and Cap is *on*!" I had never really noticed that chocolate affected my public speaking performance, but I do appreciate Kip's indulging my weakness.

The Forbes clan knows how to entertain in style. Besides the Cap-Kip Dinners, they also regularly host business executives on cruises in New York harbor on their lovely *Highlander*—a "capitalist tool" in every sense.[*] These excursions, which started about forty-five years ago, have much the same purpose as the other *Forbes* events. They provide a great "networking" opportunity and an excellent forum for the exchange of ideas. Many friendships have been formed there.

---

[*] "Capitalist Tool" is the magazine's motto and also was the name of the jet the company used to own. The motto came from an exasperated Khrushchev, who, after listening to Malcolm expound on the virtues of democracy, shouted angrily, "You're nothing but a capitalist tool."

Of course, it is certainly no hardship to sail on such an elegant vessel. Not long after I joined the company, Malcolm joked that "it's quite a comedown from admirals snapping to attention and the U.S. Navy as your fleet to merely the *Highlander* and a couple of speedboats, but Cap's adjusted very well."

She is indeed a beautiful ship, over 150 feet long, painted in Forbes green, and capable of sailing on oceans as well as smaller passages like the Amazon River and the Panama Canal. Much like the Forbes brothers themselves, the *Highlander* is elegant and relaxed at the same time; there is nothing ostentatious about it or them. The yacht is home to an eclectic art collection, six inviting guest staterooms, and several warm and comfortable lounges and seating areas, all of which afford expansive views of the passing shores and seas. And in addition to gracefully transporting happy guests, she carries a cigarette boat, two motorcycles, and the Forbes helicopter.

I feel most fortunate to be associated with this family and their many, many exciting ventures. My job is fun as well as stimulating—something that, I imagine, not many people are able to say. Everyone who works for the company is of the highest quality and each contributes to its success.

From the beginning, I have worked most closely with Kip Forbes, and I have treasured his friendship and his support over all these years. Kip is a man of many great skills and has a marvelous sense of humor. He is superb at his job. Just as admirable to me, he eschews strong-arm tactics in pursuit of advertising, instead promoting the magazine's virtues with genuine charm and a natural lack of pretension.

Kip is also an art historian of note, the founder and creator of the Forbes Collection of Victorian art and other splendid objects, including a dozen magnificent Fabergé Imperial eggs—a bigger collection than that of the Kremlin. He has written several books and articles about the collection.

Over the years, Kip and I have traveled not only to the Cap-Kip Dinners but literally all over the world. We normally do at least two Asian trips a year and one or two each to the Mideast, Europe, and Latin America, with stopovers in Africa and many other faraway points. We have probably racked up as many air miles as a pilot.*

One recent year, for example, my work for *Forbes* took me to the Philippines, Thailand, Portugal, Spain, Morocco, England, France, Saudi Arabia, Germany, Switzerland, Hong Kong, Taiwan, Poland, the Czech Republic, Hungary, Austria, Cyprus, Greece, Indonesia, Malaysia, and Mexico.

These trips allow me to meet the country's governmental and business leaders and observe its society firsthand. This gives me excellent material for my columns and enables me to make informal observations and judgments about that particular country's economic and political conditions and foreign policy. *Forbes* readers direct much of America's private overseas investment, and we write about the things they need to know.

There is also an advertising component to the trips. Most countries' business leaders are anxious to reach the people who own and manage America's businesses, and we are the magazine of choice for doing just that.

Essentially, as Kip says, we are "taking the Cap-Kip Show on the road." On these trips, he carries and completes huge bags full of correspondence and other paperwork covering every facet of the company's enterprises.

So, my usual travel companions are Kip Forbes and our very able advertising liaison, Christian Frost, a young man who, among other

---

* Typically, I am on an airplane three or four days a week. When I am in this country, two of those days are generally spent commuting from Washington or New York up to Maine and back. With only small commuter planes serving the area, that travel can be a bit frustrating, particularly in winter.

things, keeps everyone on schedule and organized. He is a skilled bicycle racer and, therefore, is quite resourceful and thinks well under pressure. I remember one occasion in Hong Kong when, after a luncheon with some of Hong Kong's business leaders, I was anxious to get back to the hotel for our next engagement. As it happened, the traffic leading to the tunnel we had to cross was extremely heavy and slow-moving. So we got out of the car, and Christian, who knew how to deal with traffic, even in Hong Kong, the most congested city in the world (next to Bangkok), took me on the subway and the Star Ferry, getting me to the hotel in ample time for the meeting.

These trips can often be quite exhausting. In a typical day's schedule, we arrive in the country after an overnight flight at, say, 6:30 A.M.; our first appointment is around 9 or 10 A.M.; there will be six or seven other appointments throughout the day, including lunches, dinners, and speeches; and we are lucky if we are through by 11 P.M. I have one major advantage, however: I do not seem to get jet lag, a trait that Kip calls "thoroughly obnoxious."

As tiring as the schedules might be, however, I do enjoy meeting new people (and seeing old friends) and learning how business is done, and public policy made, in other parts of the world. As Kip correctly concluded, if they were not scheduling all of this, I would probably be wanting to do it anyway. I do thrive on activity. Indeed, I am almost as busy as when I was secretary. The main difference is that the consequences of my mistakes are not as great now as then.

In early 1993, both *Forbes* and Rogers & Wells expressed interest in having me take on a greater role—in other words, choosing one or the other and no longer dividing my time between the two. I had become increasingly less interested in the law firm as Bill Rogers became less active. Bill Clark had already left. Accordingly, my decision took about ten seconds. *Forbes* was and is the right place for me.

In May 1993, the Forbes family made me chairman of the company, Forbes, Inc. My responsibilities did not change much; it is mostly an honorary title, and I am only the second person to fill the position. Malcolm Forbes had been the first, and it had been vacant since his death in 1990. So I feel honored indeed that his sons consider me a worthy successor.

I also feel very fortunate that they want to keep me on. As Kip frequently points out, I have now worked longer at *Forbes* than at any other job I have ever had. Never before have I appreciated the meaning of job stability!

Still, I am afraid that that has not prevented me from taking on new projects—even though I never go looking for any.

Several years ago, I met a man—on a plane, I believe—who recommended me to Thomas Clynes, a Florida television producer who was developing a new business talk show. Mr. Clynes soon proposed that I be the host of a new series called *World Business Review*.

The program would be aimed at business leaders, and the topics of discussion were to be heavily weighted toward the effects and changes that would be felt as new, ever changing technologies were applied to, and used by, business. As described in the show's promotional magazine, "Issues discussed ranged from deregulation of the utilities industry to Y2K solutions, from supply chain integration to banking and investment strategies, all in anticipation of the new millennium, and the exponential technological growth that it promises. . . ." Many of the programs would be devoted to electronic commerce, including detailed and expert discussions of the Internet and the many new uses of e-commerce.

Technology is an area in which I have little knowledge or expertise,[*] but it sounded interesting and was clearly part of the immediate future. And I would have some help: the basic script would be written

---

[*] When my family gave me a laptop computer for Christmas a couple of years ago, my grandson had to teach me how to use it.

for me by staff and there would be full-scale television production and marketing specialists. On many programs, a technology or industry expert would serve as my cohost. After a brief introduction by me, a taped field report would give some background on the topic of that segment, and then we would guide an informal discussion of it with a panel of in-studio guests, whose companies were directly involved in either developing or using the technology under discussion.

I am always amazed at how many people it now takes to produce a television show, especially when I think back to my days of moderating *Profile: Bay Area*, where we had only three: the producer/director in the control room, one cameraman, and me. I actually preferred it that way, but there is no stopping the march of "progress."

I thought hosting *World Business Review* would be a perfect way for me to keep abreast of the phenomenal and rapid advances in modern technology (and might even provide good material for my *Forbes* columns), so I talked with the Forbes family about it. They seemed amused more than anything else and interposed no objections, so I accepted the job and began in the spring of 1996.

Since I had no spare time to speak of, the minimal time commitment required for *World Business Review* was ideal. I did three or four days of taping in Washington every other month, but what it lacked in frequency, it made up for in intensity and duration. The taping days were very long; we might tape as many as twenty-five or thirty 15-minute segments a day, starting at 7 A.M. and finishing after 8 P.M. (On the air, one show is half an hour long.)

World Business Review airs on cable and public television channels, reaching about fifty million households. It is also now shown in Europe, Asia, and the Middle East, which is only natural in today's global economy. I have even seen it occasionally on transcontinental or overseas flights; usually I don't even notice until fellow passengers ask if it is I on the screen.

I greatly enjoyed doing the program and meeting and working with the fine crew Tom Clynes assembled, and I learned a great deal. But my family felt that it was too tiring, so after many lengthy discussions I "compromised" and finally retired from the show in early January 2000, after nearly four years on the program. Interestingly, I was replaced by my Reagan administration colleague Al Haig, who has been doing a fine job. The show goes on.

Throughout my life, I seem to have alternated fairly consistently between public service and my more journalistic interests. In the mid-1990s, I had the opportunity to combine the two in a way that went beyond the magazine and newspaper editorials I had written over the years.

In 1995 I was approached by Peter Schweizer, a scholar at Stanford University's Hoover Institution on War, Revolution, and Peace, about collaborating on a book. He had recently written *Victory*, a compelling look at how President Reagan's very deliberate strategies brought an end to the Cold War. Indeed, Peter was the first responsible journalist/historian to assign due credit to President Reagan for winning that war. Peter was concerned—as was I—about the Clinton administration's virtual abdication of foreign policy leadership and its reckless reductions in our military capabilities. Peter and I felt that this needed to be exposed and reversed, and we decided that the most effective way was to write a novel about some of the problems our country might face if we continued on that course.

All of the scenarios we used were hypothetical but certainly not outside the realm of possibility: a North Korean invasion of South Korea, accompanied by a Chinese attack on Taiwan; aggression by Russia or Iraq; and terrorism. Some may argue that these events are quite improbable, but then, Pearl Harbor was improbable, too.

Peter carried by far the major burden of writing, and he skillfully interwove events, resulting in a fast-paced, taut novel, complete with unstable despots, geographical obstacles, time pressures, political intrigue, and friendly governments that turned into foes. Actually, what he described is similar to military war-gaming, in which all of these factors must be taken into consideration, in addition to military capabilities and intelligence reports. Although we, of course, did not use classified data or operational contingency plans, we did use current available assessments and estimates of our own and foreign military resources to make it as realistic as possible. Peter and I worked together very well, and my admiration for him and his work grew as time went on.

Our hope in writing *The Next War*, published by Regnery in the fall of 1996, was to try to persuade the people in the Clinton administration of the dangerous error of their ways. We hoped, too, to instruct future leaders in the importance of preparedness and peace through strength and to let the people know how vulnerable we had become since the end of the Cold War. Whether those lessons have been learned remains to be seen.

Those who know anything about me know that I believe that lasting peace can be achieved only by American power and the will to use that power. Rebuilding America's military—in both armed strength and essential morale—was the overriding goal for which I strove as secretary of defense. I tried to convey all of that in my 1990 memoir, *Fighting for Peace: Seven Critical Years in the Pentagon*. But everyone was anxious to speed that book to press as soon as possible after I left the Pentagon, and it did not have the impact I had hoped it would have.

A number of people have kindly suggested that because I was present at many interesting and crucial points in recent American history, I might have a unique perspective that I ought to share in a book of broader scope. So, despite the feeling that it is rather presumptuous to write an autobiography, I undertook to write this book, with more time and care and a broader purview. I hope I have conveyed a sense of what America was like during most of the last century and of some of the challenges we have faced and still confront.

For me, writing this autobiography has been a very fulfilling process, giving me reason to revisit memories and scenes and events I had not thought of in years. And it has reminded me of how fortunate I am to have had a long lifetime of interesting, varied and satisfying experiences. I hope readers have enjoyed the journey as much as I have.

ACKNOWLEDGMENTS

*A*ny list of people who have helped in the preparation of this book must certainly start with my wife and children, who have tolerated for so long and endured beyond measure the life of a husband and father whose many activities, vast travel, and frequent career changes probably failed to supply the stability most families need.

Arlin and Cap Jr. and their children have borne it all nobly and carved out their own careers with much promise, and of course much more to come. They have brought me great happiness and much satisfaction. I am deeply grateful to them.

And then there are so many others who have helped so much not only with the book but also with so many of the events that make up the story:

Thanks to all of the Forbes family, whose great support is chronicled in the story.

Bill and Joan Clark, Will and Julia Taft, Gordon and Bobbi Fornell, the many friends and colleagues from government days, Rich

Armitage, Colin Powell, Don Rumsfeld, Paul Wolfowitz, and Paul O'Neill are among the many I worked with who are serving again in government.

Kay Leisz has continued to overlook the eccentricities and other heavy requirements of serving as my executive assistant with the same skills noted in *Fighting for Peace,* and she manages my time and schedules and all the other things necessary to make it all possible with great efficiency and extraordinary talent.

And my colleague Gretchen Roberts has my great gratitude for all the years it took to produce this autobiography. She did much of the heavy lifting (sometimes literally) involved in searching the thousands of files and documents at the Library of Congress, the Hoover Institution, and wherever I left pieces of paper. Gretchen also traveled thousands of miles to interview people whose lives and mine intersected over the years.

Friends and teachers from my schooldays in San Francisco, college and law school, the army, state and federal government, and many other points along the road talked freely about their memories.

Thanks goes also to the many people who agreed to be interviewed and to those at the Library of Congress (David Wigdor and John Haynes, and the Manuscript Reading Room staff) and the presidential libraries, as well as the archivists at Harvard; Sacramento; Idaho Springs, Colorado (my father's boyhood home); and Grand Island, Nebraska (where my mother taught violin).

People like Bob Bennett and Carl Rauh have, with their highly skilled teams, represented me and also helped with the preparation of the book. All the kind friends who were good enough to comment on my manuscript, particularly the Buckleys, father and son, whose own books, and the pleasure of their company, have furnished me and countless others with the greatest of pleasure for so many years.

One of the most accomplished and gifted novelists and writers of our time, Jim Webb, deserves a special word. He gave unstintingly of his talents to help and encourage me, beginning in the Pentagon, and fortunately still continuing.

And, of course, there were and are many, many more—and some who may prefer not to be mentioned specifically but who know who they are and who know how deeply grateful I am to them, too.

As always, all that fine help does not involve or include responsibility for any errors. That is mine and mine alone.

INDEX

Praise for *Legends*

"[*Legends*] does not scant, expertly roaming the continents and offering a psychological puzzle to go with all the deception and violence."
—John Updike, *The New Yorker*

"Littell plays fair: The clues are right out in the open, if only we could recognize them. And though *Legends* is an entertainment, it offers us unexpected literary pleasures." —*Los Angeles Times*

"Littell travels enticingly close to territory largely unexplored in political fiction: the symmetry between the macroscopic movements of governments and the microscopic weapons with which the human psyche confronts reality." —*The New York Times Book Review*

"One of the grand masters of the literary spy novel is at it again with this intriguing drama about a CIA operative-turned-PI who may or may not be delusional." —*The Sacramento Bee*

"*Legends* provides enough action for the most devoted espionage fan. It also reflects seriously on the fragility of identity and the dangers of its loss." —Bookreporter.com

"Littell provides plenty of inside intelligence info in his superb new thriller. . . . Wonderful writing and a great sense of fun make this another winner." —*Publishers Weekly* (starred review)

"Littell's sharp images, breathless chases and nasty double-crossers please as ever." —*Kirkus Reviews*

"Push reality away for a few hours and enjoy an interesting if ever fantastical read. I suggest the American language needs a new word to describe such books, and so I just made one up. Call Mr. Littell's novel 'spy-fi.' " —*The Washington Times*

"A new novel from Littell is always a pleasure but with *Legends* he may have topped even himself. This is spy fiction in the grand manner, full of twists and surprises and knowing details about that shadow world where paranoia is just good tradecraft. A terrific read." —Joseph Kanon, author of *The Prodigal Spy*

Also by Robert Littell

FICTION

A NASTY PIECE OF WORK

YOUNG PHILBY

THE STALIN EPIGRAM

VICIOUS CIRCLE

THE COMPANY

WALKING BACK THE CAT

THE VISITING PROFESSOR

AN AGENT IN PLACE

THE ONCE AND FUTURE SPY

THE REVOLUTIONIST

THE SISTERS

THE AMATEUR

THE DEBRIEFING

MOTHER RUSSIA

THE OCTOBER CIRCLE

SWEET REASON

THE DEFECTION OF A. J. LEWINTER

NONFICTION

FOR THE FUTURE OF ISRAEL
(with Shimon Peres)

PENGUIN BOOKS

LEGENDS

Robert Littell was born, raised, and educated in New York. A former *Newsweek* editor specializing in Soviet affairs, he left journalism in 1970 to write fiction full time. Connoisseurs of the literary spy novel have elevated his books to the genre's highest ranks, and Tom Clancy wrote that "if Robert Littell didn't invent the spy novel, he should have." He is the author of eighteen novels, including the critically acclaimed *The Company, The Once and Future Spy, An Agent in Paris, The Defection of A. J. Lewinter, The Sisters, The Debriefing, The Amateur,* and *The Revolutionist.* He currently lives in France.

LEGENDS

ROBERT LITTELL

PENGUIN BOOKS

PENGUIN BOOKS
Published by the Penguin Group
Penguin Group (USA) LLC
375 Hudson Street
New York, New York 10014

USA | Canada | UK | Ireland | Australia | New Zealand | India | South Africa | China
penguin.com
A Penguin Random House Company

First published in the United States of America by The Overlook Press,
Peter Mayer Publishers, Inc., 2005
Published in Penguin Books 2006
This edition published 2014

Grateful acknowledgment is made for permission to reprint lyrics from the song "It's All
Right Ma (I'm Only Bleeding)" by Bob Dylan. Copyright © 1965 by Warner Bros. Inc.
Copyright renewed 1993 by Special Rider Music. International copyright secured.
Reprinted by permission.

LIBRARY OF CONGRESS CATALOGING-IN-PUBLICATION DATA
Legends / Robert Littell.
p. cm.
ISBN 978-0-14-312740-6
1. Private investigators—New York (State)—New York—Fiction. 2. Brooklyn (New York,
N.Y.)—Fiction. 3. Intelligence officers—Fiction. 4. Identity (Psychology)—Fiction.
5. Russian Americans—Fiction. 6. Missing persons—Fiction. 7. Jewish women—
Fiction. 8. Deception—Fiction. I. Title.
PS3562.I7827L44 2006
813'.54—dc22   2005058671

Printed in the United States of America
10 9 8 7 6 5 4 3 2 1

Book design and type formatting by Bernard Schleifer

For my muses:
Marie-Dominique and Victoria

"All names are pseudonyms."

—ROMAIN GARY (writing under the pen name Emile Ajar)

". . . one of those individuals with multiple faces—like so many of the great spies of Cold War mythology—who invariably turn out to be different from who they seem and, when we think we have located them at the center of a great riddle, show up as part of another, even greater riddle . . ."

—BERNARD-HENRI LÉVY, *Who Killed Daniel Pearl?*

1993: THE CONDEMNED MAN CATCHES A GLIMPSE OF THE ELEPHANT

THEY HAD FINALLY GOTTEN AROUND TO PAVING THE SEVEN kilometers of dirt spur connecting the village of Prigorodnaia to the four-lane Moscow-Petersburg highway. The local priest, surfacing from a week-long binge, lit beeswax tapers to Innocent of Irkutsk, the saint who in the 1720s had repaired the road to China and was now about to bring civilization to Prigorodnaia in the form of a ribbon of macadam with a freshly painted white stripe down the middle. The peasants, who had a shrewder idea of how Mother Russia functioned, thought it more likely that this evidence of progress, if that was the correct name for it, was somehow related to the purchase, several months earlier, of the late and little lamented Lavrenti Pavlovich Beria's sprawling wooden dacha by a man identified only as the *Oligarkh*. Next to nothing was known about him. He came and went at odd hours in a glistening black Mercedes S-600 sedan, his shock of silver hair and dark glasses a fleeting apparition behind its tinted windows. A local woman hired to do laundry was said to have seen him angrily flick cigar ashes from the crow's-nest rising like a turret from the dacha before turning back to issue instructions to someone. The woman, who was terrified of the dacha's newfangled electric washing machine and scrubbed the laundry in a shallow reach of the river, had been too far away to make out more than a few words— "Buried, that's what I want, but alive . . ."—but they and the *Oligarkh*'s feral tone had dispatched a chill down her spine that made her shudder every time she recounted the story. Two peasants cutting firewood on the other side of the river had caught a glimpse of the

Oligarkh from a distance, struggling on aluminum crutches along the path behind his dacha that led to the dilapidated paper factory disgorging dirty white smoke from its giant stacks fourteen hours a day, six days a week, and beyond that to the village cemetery and the small Orthodox church with the faded paint peeling away from its onion domes. A pair of Borzois rollicked in the dirt ahead of the *Oligarkh* as he thrust one hip forward and dragged the leg after it, then repeated the movement with the other hip. Three men in Ralph Lauren jeans and *telnyashki*, the distinctive striped shirts that paratroopers often continued to wear after they quit the army, trailed after him, shotguns cradled in the crooks of their arms. The peasants had been sorely tempted to try for a closer look at the stubby, hunch-shouldered newcomer to their village, but abandoned the idea when one of them reminded the other what the Metropolitan come from Moscow to celebrate Orthodox Christmas two Januaries earlier had proclaimed from the ambo:

If you are stupid enough to dine with the devil, for Christ's sake use a long spoon.

The road crew, along with giant tank-treaded graders and steamrollers and trucks brimming with asphalt and crushed stone, had turned up during the night while the aurora borealis was still flickering like soundless cannon fire in the north; it didn't take much imagination to suppose a great war was being fought beyond the horizon. Casting elongated shadows in the ghostly gleam of headlights, the men pulled on tar-stiff overalls and knee-high rubber boots and set to work. By first light, with forty meters of paved road behind them, the aurora and the stars had vanished, but two planets were visible in the moonless sky: one, Mars, directly overhead, the other, Jupiter, still dancing in the west above the low haze saturated with the amber glow of Moscow. When the lead crew reached the circular crater that had been gouged in the dirt spur the day before by a steam shovel, the foreman blew on a whistle. The machines ground to a halt.

"Why are we stopping?" one of the drivers, leaning out the cab of his steamroller, shouted impatiently through the face mask he'd improvised to filter out the sulfurous stench from the paper factory. The men, who were paid by the meter and not the hour, were anxious to keep moving forward.

"At any moment we are expecting Jesus to return to earth as a Russian czar," the foreman called back lazily. "We don't want to miss it when he comes across the river." He lit a thick Turkish cigarette from the embers of an old one and strolled down to the edge of the river that ran parallel to the road for several kilometers. It was called the Lesnia, which was the name of the dense woods it meandered through as it skirted Prigorodnaia. At 6:12 a cold sun edged above the trees and began to burn off the mustard-thick September haze that clung to the river, which was in flood, creating a margin of shallow marshes on either side; long blades of grass could be seen undulating in the current.

The fisherman's dinghy that materialized out of the haze couldn't make it as far as the shore and the three occupants were obliged to climb out and wade the rest of the way. The two men wearing paratrooper shirts pulled off their boots and socks and rolled their jeans up to their knees. The third occupant didn't have to. He was stark naked. A crown of thorns, with blood trickling where the skin had been torn, sat on his head. A large safety pin attached to a fragment of cardboard had been passed through the flesh between his shoulder blades; on the cardboard was printed: "The spy Kafkor." The prisoner, his wrists and elbows bound behind him with a length of electrical wire, had several weeks growth of matted beard on his face, and purple bruises and what looked like cigarette burns over his emaciated body. Stepping cautiously through the slime until he reached solid ground, looking disoriented, he regarded his image in the shallow water of the river while the paratroopers dried their feet with an old shirt, then pulled on their socks and boots and rolled down their pants.

The spy Kafkor didn't appear to recognize the figure gaping at him from the surface of the river.

By now the two dozen crewmen, mesmerized by the arrival of the three figures, had abandoned all interest in road work. Drivers swung out of their cabs, the men with rakes or shovels stood around shifting their weight from one foot to the other in discomfort. No one doubted that something dreadful was about to happen to the naked Christ, who was being prodded up the incline by the paratroopers. Nor did they doubt that they were meant to witness it and spread the story. Such things happened all the time in Russia these days.

Back on the stretch of freshly paved road, the team's ironmonger wiped his sweaty palms on his thick leather apron, then retrieved a lunch box from the bullock-cart piled with welding gear and scrambled up the slope to get a better view of the proceedings. The ironmonger, who was short and husky and wearing tinted steel-rimmed eyeglasses, flicked open the lid of the lunch box and reached into it to activate the hidden camera set up to shoot through a puncture in the bottom of a thermos. Casually balancing the thermos on his knees, he began to rotate the cap and snap photographs.

Below, the prisoner, suddenly aware that every member of the road crew was gazing at him, seemed more distressed by his nakedness than his plight—until he caught sight of the crater. It was roughly the size of a large tractor tire. Thick planks were stacked on the ground next to it. He froze in his tracks and the paratroopers had to grasp him by the upper arms and drag him the last few meters. The prisoner sank to his knees at the lip of the crater and looked back at the workers, his eyes hollow with terror, his mouth open and gulping air with rattling gasps through a parched throat. He saw things he recognized but his brain, befuddled with chemicals released by fear, couldn't locate the words to describe them: the twin stacks spewing plumes of dirty white smoke, the abandoned custom's station with a faded red star painted above the door, the line of white-washed bee hives on a slope near a copse of stunted apple trees. This was all a terrible dream, he thought. Any moment now he would become too frightened to continue dreaming; would force himself through the membrane that separated sleep from wakefulness and wipe the sweat from his brow and, still under the spell of the nightmare, have trouble falling back to sleep. But the ground felt damp and cold under his knees and a whiff of sulfurous air stung his lungs and the cold sun playing on his skin seemed to stir the cigarette burns to pain, and the pain brought home to him that what had happened, and what was about to happen, were no dream.

A Mercedes made its way slowly down the dirt road from the village, followed closely by a chase vehicle, a metallic gray Land Cruiser filled with bodyguards. Neither car had license plates, and the workers watching the scene play out understood this to mean that the people in them were too important to be stopped by the police. The

Mercedes half turned so that it was astride the road and stopped a dozen meters from the kneeling prisoner. The rear window wound down the width of a fist. The *Oligarkh* could be seen peering out through dark glasses. He removed the cigar from his mouth and studied the naked prisoner for a long while, as if he were committing him and the moment to memory. Then, with a look of unadulterated malevolence on his face, he reached out with one of his crutches and tapped the man sitting next to the driver on the shoulder. The front door opened and the man emerged. He was of medium height and thin, with a long pinched face. He wore suspenders that kept his trousers hiked high on his waist, and a midnight blue Italian suit jacket draped cape-like over a starched white shirt, which was tieless and buttoned up to a very prominent Adam's apple. The initials "S" and "U-Z" were embroidered on the pocket of the shirt. He strode to the chase car and plucked a lighted cigarette from the mouth of one of the bodyguards. Holding it away from his body between his thumb and third finger, he walked over to the prisoner. Kafkor raised his eyes and saw the cigarette and recoiled, thinking he was about to be branded with the burning tip. But S U-Z, smiling faintly, only reached down and wedged it between the lips of the prisoner. "It is a matter of tradition," he said. "A man condemned to death is entitled to a last cigarette."

"They . . . damaged me, Samat?" Kafkor whispered huskily. He could make out the shock of silver hair on the figure watching from the back seat of the Mercedes. "They locked me in a basement awash in sewage, I could not distinguish night from day, I lost track of time, they woke me . . . with loud music when I fell asleep. Where, explain it to me if there exists an explanation, is the why?" The condemned man spoke Russian with a distinct Polish accent, emphasizing the open O's and stressing the next to last syllable. Terror tortured his sentences into baroque grammatical configurations. "The endmost thing I would tell to nobody is what I am not supposed to know."

Samat shrugged as if to say, The matter is out of my hands. "You arrive too close to the flame, you must suffer burning, if only to warn others away from the flame."

Trembling, Kafkor puffed on the cigarette. The act of smoking, and the smoke cauterizing his throat, appeared to distract him. Samat stared at the ash, waiting for it to buckle under its own weight and fall so they could get on with the execution. Kafkor, sucking on the cigarette, became aware of the ash, too. Life itself seemed to ride on it. Defying gravity, defying sense, it grew longer than the unsmoked part of the cigarette.

And then a whisper of wind coming off the river dislodged the ash. Kafkor spit out the butt. "*Poshol ty na khuy,*" he whispered, carefully articulating each of the O's in "*Poshol.*" "*Go impale yourself on a prick.*" He rocked back on his heels and squinted in the direction of the copse of stunted apple trees on the slope above him. "Look!" he blurted out, vanquishing terror only to confront a new enemy, madness. "Up there!" He sucked in his breath. "I see the elephant. It can be said that the beast is revolting."

At the Mercedes, the back door on the far side swung open and a frail woman dressed in an ankle-length cloth coat and peasant galoshes stumbled from the car. She wore a black pillbox hat with a thick veil that fell over her eyes, making it difficult for someone who didn't know her to divine her age. "Jozef—" she shrieked. She stumbled toward the prisoner about to be executed, then, sinking to her knees, she turned to the man in the back of the car. "What if it should begin to snow?" she cried.

The *Oligarkh* shook his head. "Trust me, Kristyna—he will be warmer in the ground if the hole is covered with snow."

"He is the same as a son to me," the woman sobbed, her voice fading to a cracked whimper. "We must not bury him before he has had his lunch."

Still on her knees, the woman, shuddering with sobs, started to crawl through the dirt toward the crater. In the back of the Mercedes, the *Oligarkh* gestured with a finger. The driver sprang from behind the wheel and, pressing the palm of his hand to the woman's mouth, half carried, half dragged her back to the car and folded her body into the back seat. Before the door slammed shut she could be heard sobbing: "And if it does not snow, what then?"

Closing his window, the *Oligarkh* watched the scene unfold through its tinted glass. The two paratroopers took a grip on the prisoner's arms and lifted him into the crater and set him down on his side, curled up in a fetal position in the round hole. Then they began covering the crater with the thick planks, kicking the ends into the ground so that the tops of the planks were flush with the dirt road. When that was done they dragged a section of metal webbing over the planks. All the while nobody spoke. On the slope the workers, puffing on cigarettes, looked away or stared at their feet.

When the paratroopers finished covering the crater, they backed off to admire their handiwork. One of them waved to the driver of a truck. He climbed behind the wheel and backed up to the crater and worked the lever that elevated the flatbed to spill tarmacadam onto the road. Several workers came over and spread the macadam with long rakes until a thick glistening coating covered the wooden planks and they were no longer visible. They stepped away and the paratroopers signaled for the steamroller. Black fume billowed from its exhaust pipe as the rusty machine lumbered to the edge of the crater. When the driver seemed to hesitate, the horn of the Mercedes sounded and one of the bodyguards standing nearby pumped an arm in irritation. "It is not as if we have all day," he shouted above the bedlam of the steamroller's engine. The driver threw it into gear and started across the crater, packing down the tarmacadam. When he reached the other side, he backed over it again and then swung out of the cab to inspect the newly paved patch of highway. Suddenly, he tore off his improvised face mask and, bending, vomited on his shoes.

Barely making a sound, the Mercedes backed and filled and swung past the chase car and started up the dirt spur toward the sprawling wooden dacha at the edge of the village of Prigorodnaia, soon to be connected to the Moscow-Petersburg highway—and the world—by a ribbon of macadam with a freshly painted white stripe down the middle.

1997: MARTIN ODUM HAS A CHANGE OF HEART

CLAD IN A WASHED OUT WHITE JUMPSUIT AND AN OLD PITH HELMET with mosquito netting hanging from it to protect his head, Martin Odum cautiously approached the rooftop beehives from the blind side so as not to obstruct the flight path of any bees straggling back to the frames. He worked the bellows of his smoker, spewing a fine white cloud into the nearest of the two hives; the smoke alerted the colony to danger, rousing the 20,000 bees inside to gorge themselves on honey, which would calm them down. April really was the cruelest month for bees, since it was touch and go whether there would be enough honey left over from the winter to avoid starvation; if the frames inside were too light, he would have to brew up some sugar candy and insert it into the hive to see the queen and her colony through to the warm weather, when the trees in Brower Park would be in bud. Martin reached inside with a bare hand to unstick one of the frames; he had worn gloves when he handled the hives until the day Minh, his occasional mistress who worked in the Chinese restaurant on the ground floor below the pool parlor, informed him that bee stings stimulated your hormones and increased your sex drive. In the two years he had been keeping bees on a Brooklyn roof top, Martin had been stung often enough but he'd never observed the slightest effect on his hormones; on the other hand the pinpricks seemed to revive memories he couldn't quite put his finger on.

Martin, who had dark hollows under his eyes that didn't come from lack of sleep, pried the first frame free and gingerly brought it out into the midday sunlight to inspect the combs. Hundreds of worker bees, churring in alarm, clung to the combs, which were depleted but still had enough honey left in them to nourish the colony. He scraped burr comb from the frame and examined it for evidence of American foulbrood. Finding none, he carefully notched the frame back into the hive, then backed away and pulled off the pith helmet and swatted playfully at the handful of brood bees that were trailing after him, looking for vengeance. "Not today, friends," Martin said with a soft laugh as he retreated into the building and slammed the roof door shut behind him.

Downstairs in the back room of the one-time pool parlor that served as living quarters, Martin stripped off the jumpsuit and, throwing it on the unmade Army cot, fixed himself a whiskey, neat. He selected a Ganaesh Beedie from a thin tin filled with the Indian cigarettes. Lighting up, dragging on the eucalyptus leaves, he settled into the swivel chair with the broken caning that scratched at his back; he'd picked it up for a song at a Crown Heights garage sale the day he'd rented the pool parlor and glued Alan Pinkerton's unblinking eye on the downstairs street door above the words "Martin Odum—Private Detective." The fumes from the Beedie, which smelled like marijuana, had the same effect on him that smoke had on bees: it made him want to eat. He pried open a tin of sardines and spooned them onto a plate that hadn't been washed in several days and ate them with a stale slice of pumpernickel he discovered in the icebox, which (he reminded himself) badly needed to be defrosted. With a crust of pumpernickel, he wiped the plate clean and turned it over and used the back as a saucer. It was a habit Dante Pippen had picked up in the untamed tribal badlands of Pakistan near the Khyber Pass; the handful of Americans running agents or operations there would finger rice and fatty mutton off the plate when they had something resembling plates, then flip them over and eat fruit on the back the rare times they came across something resembling fruit. Remembering a detail from the past, however trivial, gave Martin a tinge of satisfaction. Working on the back of the plate, he deftly peeled the skin off a tangerine with a few scalpel-strokes of a small razor sharp knife. "*Funny how some things you do, you do them well the first time,*" he'd allowed to Dr. Treffler during one of their early sessions.

"Such as?"

"Such as peeling a tangerine. Such as cutting a fuse for plastic explosive long enough to give you time to get out of its killing range. Such as pulling off a brush pass with a cutout in one of Beirut's crowded souks."

"What legend were you using in Beirut?"

"Dante Pippen."

"Wasn't he the one who was supposed to have been teaching history at a junior college? The one who wrote a book on the Civil War that he printed privately when he couldn't find a publisher willing to take it on?"

"No, you're thinking of Lincoln Dittmann, with two t's and two n's. Pippen was the Irish dynamiter from Castletownbere who started out as an explosives instructor on the Farm. Later, posing as an IRA dynamiter, he infiltrated a Sicilian Mafia family, the Taliban mullahs in Peshawar, a Hezbollah unit in the Bekaa Valley of Lebanon. It was this last mission that blew his cover."

"I have a hard time keeping track of your various identities."

"Me, too. That's why I'm here."

"Are you sure you have identified all of your operational biographies?"

"I've identified the ones I remember."

"Do you have the feeling you might be repressing any?"

"Don't know. According to your theory, there's a possibility I'm repressing at least one of them."

"The literature on the subject more or less agrees—"

"I thought you weren't convinced that I fit neatly into the literature on the subject."

"You are hors genre, *Martin, there's no doubt about it. Nobody in my profession has come across anyone quite like you. It will cause quite a stir when I publish my paper—"*

"Changing the names to protect the innocent."

To Martin's surprise she'd come up with something that could pass for humor. *"Changing the names to protect the guilty, too."*

There are other things, Martin thought now (continuing the conversation with Dr. Treffler in his mind), no matter how many times you do them, you don't seem to do them better. Such as (he went on, anticipating her question) peeling hard-boiled eggs. Such as breaking into cheap hotel rooms to photograph married men having oral sex with prostitutes. Such as conveying to a Company-cleared shrink the impression that you didn't have great expectations of working out an identity crisis. Tell me again what you hope to get out of these conversations? he could hear her asking. He supplied the answer he thought she wanted to hear: In theory, I'd like to know which one of my legends is me. He could hear her asking, *Why in theory?* He considered this for a moment. Then, shaking his head, he was surprised to hear his own voice responding out loud: "I'm not sure I have a need to know—in practice, I might be better able to get on with my dull life if I don't know."

Martin would have dragged out the fictitious dialogue with Dr. Treffler, if only to kill time, if he hadn't heard the door buzzer. He padded in bare feet through the pool parlor, which he'd converted into an office, using one of the two tables as a desk and the other to lay out Lincoln Dittmann's collection of Civil War firearms. At the top of the dimly lit flight of narrow wooden stairs leading to the street door, he crouched and peered down to see who could be ringing. Through the lettering and Mr. Pinkerton's private eye logo he could make out a female standing with her back to the door, scrutinizing the traffic on Albany Avenue. Martin waited to see if she would ring again. When she did, he descended to the foyer and opened the two locks and the door.

The woman wore a long raincoat even though the sun was shining and carried a leather satchel slung over one shoulder. Her dark hair was pulled back and twined into a braid that plunged down her spine to the hollow of her back—the spot where Martin had worn his hand gun (he'd recut the holster's belt slot to raise the pistol into an old shrapnel wound) in the days when he'd been armed with something more lethal than cynicism. The hem of her raincoat flared above her ankles as she spun around to face him.

"So are you the detective?" she demanded.

Martin scrutinized her the way he'd been taught to look at people he might one day have to pick out of a counterintelligence scrapbook. She appeared to be in her mid or late thirties—guessing the ages of women had never been his strong suit. Spidery wrinkles fanned out from the corners of her eyes, which were fixed in a faint but permanent squint. On her thin lips was what from a distance

might have passed for a ghost of a smile; up close it looked like an
expression of stifled exasperation. She wore no makeup as far as he
could see; there was the faint aroma of a rose-based perfume that
seemed to come from under the collar on the back of her neck. She
might have been taken for handsome if it hadn't been for the chipped
front tooth.

"In this incarnation," he finally said, "I'm supposed to be a
detective."

"Does that mean you've had other incarnations?"

"In a manner of speaking."

She shifted her weight from one foot to the other. "So are you
going to invite me in or what?"

Martin stepped aside and gestured with his chin toward the
steps. The woman hesitated as if she were calculating whether
someone living over a Chinese restaurant could really be a professional detective. She must have decided she had nothing to lose
because she took a deep breath and, turning sideways and sucking
in her chest, edged past him and started up the stairs. When she
reached the pool parlor she looked back to watch him emerging
from the shadows of the staircase. She noticed he favored his left leg
as he walked.

"What happened to your foot?" she asked.

"Pinched nerve. Numbness."

"In your line of work, isn't a limp a handicap?"

"The opposite is true. No one in his right mind would suspect
someone with a limp of following him. It's too obvious."

"Still, you ought to have it looked at."

"I've been seeing a Hasidic acupuncturist and a Haitian herbalist,
but I don't tell one about the other."

"Have they helped you?"

"Uh-huh. One of them has—there's less numbness now—but I'm
not sure which."

The ghost of a smile materialized on her lips. "You seem to have
a knack for complicating simple things."

Martin, with a cold politeness that masked how close he was
to losing interest, said, "In my book that beats simplifying complicated things."

Depositing her satchel on the floor, the woman slipped out of her raincoat and carefully folded it over the banister. She was wearing running sneakers, tailored trousers with pleats at the waist and a man's shirt that buttoned from left to right. Martin saw that the three top buttons were open, revealing a triangle of pale skin on her chest. There was no sign of an undergarment. The observation made him suck in his cheeks; it occurred to him that the bee stings might be having some effect after all.

The woman wheeled away from Martin and wandered into the pool parlor, her eyes taking in the faded green felt on the two old tables, the moving company cartons sealed with masking tape piled in a corner next to the rowing machine, the overhead fan turning with such infinite slowness that it seemed to impart its lethargic rhythm to the space it was ventilating. This was obviously a realm where time slowed down. "You don't look like someone who smokes cigars," she ventured when she spotted the mahogany humidor with the built in thermometer on the pool table that served as a desk.

"I don't. It's for fuses."

"Fuses as in electricity?"

"Fuses as in bombs."

She opened the lid. "These look like paper shotgun cartridges."

"Fuses, paper cartridges need to be kept dry."

She threw him an anxious look and went on with her inspection. "You're not crawling in creature comforts," she noted, her words drifting back over her shoulder as she took a turn around the wide floorboards.

Martin thought of all the safe houses he had lived in, furnished in ancient Danish modern; he suspected the CIA must have bought can openers and juice makers and toilet bowl brushes by the thousands because they were the same in every safe house. And because they were safe houses, none of them had been perfectly safe. "It's a mistake to possess comfortable things," he said now. "Soft couches, big beds, large bath tubs, the like. Because if nothing is comfortable you don't settle in; you keep moving. And if you keep moving, you have a better chance of staying ahead of the people who are trying to catch up with you." Flashing a wrinkled smile, he added, "This is especially true for those of us who limp."

Looking through the open door into the back room, the woman caught a glimpse of crumpled newspapers around the Army cot. "What's with all the newspapers on the floor?" she asked.

Hearing her speak, Martin was reminded how satisfyingly musical an ordinary human voice could be. "I picked up that little trick from *The Maltese Falcon*—fellow named Thursby kept newspapers around his bed so no one could sneak up on him when he slept." His patience was wearing thin. "I learned everything I know about being a detective from Humphrey Bogart."

The woman came full circle and stopped in front of Martin; she studied his face but couldn't tell if he was putting her on. She was having second thoughts about hiring someone who had learned the detective business from Hollywood movies. "Is it true detectives were called gumshoes?" she said, eyeing his bare feet. She backed up to the pool table covered with muzzle-loading firearms and powder horns and Union medals pinned to a crimson cushion, trying to figure out what fiction she could come up with that would get her out of there without hurting his feelings. At a loss for words, she absently ran her fingers along the brass telescopic sight on an antique rifle. "My father collects guns from the Great Patriotic War," she remarked.

"Uh-huh. That makes your father Russian. In America we call it World War Two. I'd appreciate it if you wouldn't touch the weapons." He added, "That one's an English Whitworth. It was the rifle of choice of Confederate sharpshooters. The paper cartridges in the humidor are for the Whitworth. During the Civil War Whitworth cartridges were expensive, but a skilled sniper could hit anything he could see with the weapon."

"You some sort of Civil War buff?" she asked.

"My alter ego is," he said. "Look, we've made enough small talk. Bite the bullet, lady. You must have a name."

Her left palm drifted up to cover the triangle of skin on her chest. "I'm Estelle Kastner," she announced. "The precious few friends I have call me Stella."

"*Who are you?*" Martin persisted, quarrying for deeper layers of identity than a name.

The question startled her; there was clearly more to him than met the eye, which raised the prospect that he might be able to help her after all. "Listen, Martin Odum, there are no shortcuts. You want to find out who I am, you're going to have to put in time."

Martin settled back against the banister. "What is it you hope I can do for you?"

"I hope you can find my sister's husband, who's gone AWOL from his marriage."

"Why don't you try the police? They have a missing person's bureau that specializes in this sort of thing."

"Because the police in question are in Israel. And they have more pressing things to do than hunt for missing husbands."

"If your sister's husband went missing in Israel, why are you looking for him in America?"

"We think that's one of the places he might have headed for when he left Israel."

"We?"

"My father, the Russian who calls World War Two the Great Patriotic War."

"What are the other places?"

"My sister's husband had business associates in Moscow and Uzbekistan. He seems to have been involved in some kind of project in Prague. He had stationary with a London letterhead."

"Start at the start," Martin ordered.

Stella Kastner hiked herself up on the edge of the pool table that Martin used as a desk. "Here's the story," she said, crossing her legs at the ankles, toying with the lowest unbuttoned button on her shirt. "My half-sister, Elena, she's my father's daughter by his first wife, turned religious and joined the Lubavitch sect here in Crown Heights soon after we immigrated to America, which was in 1988. Several years ago the rabbi came to my father and proposed an arranged marriage with a Russian Lubavitcher who wanted to immigrate to Israel. He didn't speak Hebrew and was looking for an observant wife who spoke Russian. My father had mixed feelings about Elena leaving Brooklyn, but it was my sister's dream to live in Israel and she talked him into giving his consent. For reasons that are too complicated to go into, my father wasn't free to travel so it was me who accompanied Elena when she flew to Israel. We took a *sharoot*"—she noticed Martin's frown of confusion—"that's a communal taxi, we took it to the Jewish settlement of Kiryat Arba on the West Bank next to Hebron. Elena, who changed her name to Ya'ara when she set foot in Israel, was married an hour and a quarter after the plane landed by the rabbi there, who had emigrated from Crown Heights ten years before."

"Tell me about this Russian your sister married sight unseen."

"His name was Samat Ugor-Zhilov. He was neither tall nor short but somewhere between the two, and thin despite the fact that he asked for seconds at mealtime and snacked between meals. It must have been his metabolism. He was the high strung type, always on the move. His face looked as if it had been caught in a vise—it was long and thin and mournful—he always managed to look as if he were grieving over the death of a close relative. The pupils of his eyes were seaweed-green, the eyes themselves were utterly devoid of emotion—cold and calculating would be the words I'd use to describe them. He dressed in expensive Italian suits and wore shirts with his initials embroidered on the pocket. I never saw him wearing a tie, not even at his own wedding."

"You would recognize him if you saw him again?"

"That's a strange question. He could cover his head like an Arab—as long as I could see his eyes, I could pick him out of a crowd."

"What did he do by way of work?"

"If you mean work in the ordinary sense of the term, nothing. He'd bought a new split-level house on the edge of Kiryat Arba for cash, or so the rabbi whispered in my ear as we were walking to the synagogue for the wedding ceremony. He owned a brand new Japanese Honda and paid for everything, at least in front of me, with cash. I stayed in Kiryat Arba for ten days and I came back again two years later for ten days, but I never saw him go to the synagogue to study Torah, or to an office like some of the other men in the settlement. There were two telephones and a fax machine in the house and it seemed as if one of them was always ringing. Some days he'd lock himself in the upstairs bedroom and talk on the phone for hours at a stretch. The few times he talked on the phone in front of me he switched to Armenian."

"Uh-huh."

"Uh-huh what?"

"Sounds like one of those new Russian capitalists you read about in the newspapers. Did your sister have children?"

Stella shook her head. "No. To tell you the awful truth, I'm not positive they ever consummated the marriage." She slid to the floor and went over to the window to stare out at the street. "The fact is I don't fault him for leaving her. I don't think Elena—I never got used to calling her Ya'ara—has the vaguest idea how to please a man. Samat probably ran off with a bleached blonde who gave him more pleasure in bed."

Martin, listening listlessly, perked up. "You make the same mistake most women make. If he ran off with another woman, it's because he was able to give her more pleasure in bed."

Stella turned back to gaze at Martin. Her eyes tightened into a narrower squint. "You don't talk like a detective."

"Sure I do. It's the kind of thing Bogart would have said to convince a client that under the hard boiled exterior resided a sensitive soul."

"If that's what you're trying to do, it's working."

"I have a question: Why doesn't your sister get the local rabbi to testify that her husband ran out on her and divorce him in absentia?"

"That's the problem," Stella said. "In Israel a religious woman needs to have a divorce handed down by a religious court before she can go on with her life. The divorce is called a *get*. Without a *get*, a Jewish woman remains an *agunah*, which means a chained woman, unable to remarry under Jewish law; even if she remarries under civil law her children will still be considered bastards. And the only way a woman can obtain a *get* is for the husband to show up in front of the rabbis of a religious court and agree to the divorce. There's no other way, at least not for religious people. There are dozens of Hasidic husbands who disappear each year to punish their wives—they go off to America or Europe. Sometimes they live under assumed names. Go find them if you can! Under Jewish law the husband is permitted to live with a woman who's not his wife, but the wife doesn't have the same right. She can't marry again, she can't live with a man, she can't have children."

"Now I'm beginning to see why you need the services of a

detective. How long ago did this Samat character skip out on your sister?"

"It'll be two months next weekend."

"And it's only now that you're trying to hire a detective?"

"We didn't know for sure he wasn't coming back until he didn't come back. Then we wasted time trying the hospitals, the morgues, the American and Russian embassies in Israel, the local police in Kiryat Arba, the national police in Tel Aviv. We even ran an ad in the newspaper offering a reward for information." She tossed a shoulder. "I'm afraid we don't have much experience tracking down missing persons."

"You said earlier that your father and you thought Samat might head for America. What made you decide that?"

"It's the phone calls. I caught a glimpse once of his monthly phone bill—it was several thousand shekels, which is big enough to put a dent in a normal bank account. I noticed that some of the calls went to the same number in Brooklyn. I recognized the country and area code—1 for America, 718 for Brooklyn—because it's the same as ours on President Street."

"You didn't by any chance copy down the number?"

She shook her head in despair. "It didn't occur to me . . ."

"Don't blame yourself. You couldn't know this Samat character was going to run out on your sister." He saw her look quickly away. "Or did you?"

"I never thought the marriage would last. I didn't see him burying himself in Kiryat Arba for the rest of his life. He was too involved in the world, too dynamic, too attractive—"

"You found him attractive?"

"I didn't say I found him attractive," she said defensively. "I could see how he might appeal to certain women. But not my sister. She'd never been naked in front of a man in her life. As far as I know she'd never seen a naked man. Even when she saw a fully clothed man she averted her eyes. When Samat looked at a woman he stared straight into her eyes without blinking; he undressed her. He claimed to be a religious Jew but I think now it may have been some kind of cover, a way of getting into Israel, of disappearing into the world of the Hasidim. I never saw him lay tefillin, I never saw him go to the synagogue, I never saw him pray the way religious Jews do four times a day. He didn't kiss the mezuzah when he came into the house the way my sister did. Elena and Samat lived in different worlds."

"You have photographs of him?"

"When he disappeared, my sister's photo album disappeared with him. I have one photo I took the day they were married—I sent it to my father, who framed it and hung it over the mantle." Retrieving her satchel, she pulled a brown envelope from it and carefully extracted a black and white photograph. She stared at it for a moment, the ghost of an anguished smile deforming her lips, then offered it to Martin.

Martin stepped back and held up his palms. "Did Samat ever touch this?"

She thought a moment. "No. I had the film developed in the German Colony in Jerusalem and mailed it to my father from the post office across the street from the photo shop. Samat didn't know it existed."

Martin accepted the photo and tilted it toward the daylight. The bride, a pale and noticeably overweight young woman dressed in white satin with a neck-high bodice, and the groom, wearing a starched white shirt buttoned up to his Adam's apple and a black suit jacket flung casually over his shoulders, stared impassively into the camera. Martin imagined Stella crying out the Russian equivalent of "Cheese" to pry a smile out of them, but it obviously hadn't worked; the body language—the bride and groom were standing next to each other but not touching—revealed two strangers at a wake, not a husband and wife after a wedding ceremony. Samat's face had all but disappeared behind a shaggy black beard and mustache. Only his eyes, storm-dark with anger, were visible. He was obviously irritated, but at what? The religious ceremony that had gone on too long? The prospect of marital bliss in a West Bank oubliette with a consenting Lubavitcher for cellmate?

"How tall is your sister?" Martin inquired.

"Five foot four. Why?"

"He's slightly taller, which would make him five foot six or seven."

"Mind if I ask you something?" Stella said.

"Ask, ask," Martin said impatiently.

"How come you're not taking notes?"

"There's no reason to. I'm not taking notes because I'm not taking the case."

Stella's heart sank. "For God's sake, why? My father's ready to pay you whether you find him or not."

"I'm not taking the case," Martin announced, "because it'd be easier to find a needle in a field of haystacks than your sister's missing husband."

"You could at least try," Stella groaned.

"I'd be wasting your father's money and my time. Look, Russian revolutionaries at the turn of the century grew beards like your sister's husband. It's a trick illegals have used since Moses dispatched spies to explore the enemy order of battle at Jericho. You live with the beard long enough, people identify you with the beard. The day you want to disappear, you do what the Russian revolutionaries did—you shave it off. Your own wife couldn't pick you out of a police lineup afterward. For argument's sake, let's say Samat was one of those gangster capitalists you hear so much about these days. Maybe things got too hot for your future ex-brother-in-law in Moscow the year he turned up in Kiryat Arba to marry your half sister. Chechen gangs, working out of that monster of a hotel across from the Kremlin—it's called the Rossiya, if I remember right—were battling the Slavic Alliance to see who would control the lucrative protection rackets in the capital. There were shootouts every day as the gangs fought over territories. Witnesses to the shootouts were gunned down before they could go to the police. People going to work in the morning discovered men hanging by their necks from lampposts. Maybe Samat is Jewish, maybe he's an Armenian Apostolic Christian. It doesn't really matter. He buys a birth certificate certifying his mother is Jewish—they're a dime a dozen on the black market—and applies to get into Israel. The paperwork can take six or eight months, so to speed things up your brother-in-law has a rabbi arrange a marriage with a female Lubavitcher from Brooklyn. It's the perfect cover story, the perfect way to disappear from view until the gang wars in Moscow peter out. From his split level safe house in a West Bank settlement, he keeps in touch with his business partners; he buys and sells stocks, he arranges to export Russian raw materials in exchange for Japanese computers or American jeans. And then one bright morning, when things in Russia have calmed down, he decides he's had enough of his Israeli dungeon. He doesn't want his wife or the rabbis or the state of Israel asking him where he's going, or looking him up when he gets there, so he grabs his wife's photo album and shaves off his beard and, slipping out of Israel, disappears from the face of the planet earth."

Stella's lips parted as she listened to Martin's scenario. "How do you know so much about Russia and the gang wars?"

He shrugged. "If I told you I'm not sure how I know these things, would you believe me?"

"No."

Martin retrieved her raincoat from the banister. "I'm sorry you wasted your time."

"I didn't waste it," she said quietly. "I know more now than when I came in." She accepted the raincoat and fitted her arms into the sleeves and pulled it tightly around her body against the emotional gusts that would soon chill her to the bone. Almost as an afterthought, she produced a ballpoint pen from her pocket and, taking his palm, jotted a 718 telephone number on it. "If you change your mind . . ."

Martin shook his head. "Don't hold your breath."

* * *

The mountain of dirty dishes in the sink had grown too high even for Martin. His sleeves rolled up to the elbows, he was working his way through the first stack when the telephone sounded in the pool parlor. As usual he took his sweet time answering; in his experience it was the calls you took that complicated your life. When the phone continued ringing, he ambled into the pool room and, drying his hands on his chinos, pinned the receiver to an ear with a shoulder.

"Leave a message if you must," he intoned.

"Listen up, Dante—" a woman barked.

A splitting headache surged against the backs of Martin's eye sockets. "You have a wrong number," he muttered, and hung up.

Almost instantly the telephone rang again. Martin pressed the palm with the phone number written on it to his forehead and stared at the telephone for what seemed like an eternity before deciding to pick it up.

"Dante, Dante, you don't want to go and hang up on me. Honestly you don't. It's not civilized. For God's sake, I know it's you."

"How did you find me?" Martin asked.

The woman on the other end of the line swallowed a laugh. "You're on the short list of ex-agents we keep track of," she said. Her voice turned serious. "I'm downstairs, Dante. In a booth at the back of the Chinese restaurant. I'm faint from the monosodium glutamate. Come on down and treat yourself to something from column B on me."

Martin took a deep breath. "They say that dinosaurs roamed the earth sixty-five million years ago. You're living proof that some of them are still around."

"Sticks and stones, Dante. Sticks and stones." She added, in a tight voice, "A word of advice: You don't want to *not* come down. Honestly you don't."

The line went dead in his ear.

Moments later Martin found himself passing the window filled with plucked ducks hanging from meat hooks and pushing through the heavy glass door into Xing's Mandarin Restaurant under the pool parlor. Tsou Xing, who happened to be his landlord, was holding fort as usual on the high stool behind the cash register. He waved his only arm in Martin's direction. "Hello to you," the old man called in a high pitched voice. "You want to eat in or take out, huh?"

"I'm meeting someone . . ." He surveyed the dozen or so clients in the long narrow restaurant and saw Crystal Quest in a booth near the swinging doors leading to the kitchen. Quest was better known to a generation of CIA hands as Fred because of an uncanny resemblance to Fred Astaire; a story had once made the rounds claiming that the president of the United States, spotting her at an intelligence briefing in the Oval Office, had passed a note to an aide demanding to know why a drag queen was representing the CIA. Now Quest, a past master of tradecraft, had positioned herself with her back to the tables, facing a mirror in which she could keep track of who came and went. She watched Martin approach in the mirror.

"You look fit as a flea, Dante," she said as he slid onto the banquette facing her. "What's your secret?"

"I sprang for a rowing machine," he said.

"How many hours do you put in a day?"

"One in the morning before breakfast. One in the middle of the night when I wake up in a cold sweat."

"Why would someone with a clean conscience wake up in a cold sweat? Don't tell me you're still brooding over the death of that whore in Beirut, for God's sake."

Martin brought a hand up to his brow, which continued to throb. "I think of her sometimes but that's not what's bothering me. If I knew what was waking me up, maybe I'd sleep through the night."

Fred, a lean woman who had risen through the ranks to become the CIA's first female Deputy Director of Operations, was wearing one of her famous pantsuits with wide lapels and a dress shirt with frills down the front. Her hair, as usual, was cropped short and dyed the color of rust to conceal the gray streaks that came to topsiders who worried themselves sick, so Fred always claimed, over Standard Operating Procedure: Should you start with a hypothesis and analyze data in a way that supported it, or start with the data and sift through it for a useful hypothesis?

"What's your pleasure, Dante?" Fred asked, pushing aside a half eaten dinner, fingering her frozen daiquiri, noisily crunching chips of ice between her teeth as she regarded her guest through bloodshot eyes.

Martin signaled with a chopstick and then worked it back and forth between his fingers. At the bar, Tsou Xing poured him a whiskey, neat. A slim young Chinese waitress with a tight skirt slit up one thigh brought it over.

Martin said, "Thanks, Minh."

"You ought to eat something, Martin," the waitress said. She noticed him toying with the chopstick. "Chinese say man with one chopstick die of starvation."

Smiling, he dropped the chopstick on the table. "I'll take an order of Peking duck with me when I leave."

Fred watched the girl slink away in the mirror. "Now that's what I call a great ass, Dante. You getting any?"

"What about you, Fred?" he asked pleasantly. "People still screwing you?"

"They try," she retorted, her facial muscles drawn into a tight smile, "in both senses of the word. But nobody succeeds."

Snickering, Martin extracted a Beedie from the tin and lit it with one of the restaurant's matchbooks on the table. "You didn't say how you found me."

"I didn't, did I? It's more a case of we never lost you. When you washed up like a chunk of jetsam over a Chinese restaurant in Brooklyn, alarums, not to mention excursions, sounded in the battleship-gray halls of the shop. We obtained a copy of the lease the day you signed it. Mind you, nobody was surprised to find you'd slipped into the Martin Odum legend. What could be more logical? He'd actually been raised on Eastern Parkway, he went to PS 167, Crown Heights was his stamping ground, his father had an electric appliance store on Kingston Avenue. Martin even had a school chum whose father owned the Chinese restaurant on Albany Avenue. Martin Odum was the legend you worked up on my watch, or have you misplaced that little detail? Now that I think of it, you were the last agent I personally ran before they kicked me upstairs to run the officers who ran the agents, although, even at one remove, I always considered that I was the person playing you. Funny part is I have no memory of Odum being a detective. You must have decided the legend needed embroidering."

Martin assumed that they had bugged the pool parlor. "Being a detective beats having to work for a living."

"What kind of cases do you get?"

"Mahjongg debts. Angry wives who pay me for photographs of errant husbands caught in the act. Hasidic fathers who think their sons may be dating girls who don't keep kosher. Once I was hired by the family of a Russian who died in Little Odessa, which is the part of Brooklyn where most of the Russians who wind up in America live, because they were convinced the Chechens who ran the neighborhood crematorium were extracting gold teeth from the late lamented before cremating their bodies. Another time I was hired by a colorful Little Odessa political figure to bring back the Rottweiler that'd been kidnapped by his ex-wife when he fell behind on alimony payments."

"You get a lot of work in Little Odessa."

"I keep nodding when my clients can't come up with the right word in English and wind up speaking Russian to me. They seem to think I understand them."

"Did you find the dog?"

"Martin Odum always gets his dog."

She clanked glasses with him. "Here's looking at you, Dante." She sipped her daiquiri and eyed him over the rim of the glass. "You don't by any chance do missing husbands?"

The question hung in the air between them. Martin sucked on his Beedie for a moment, then said very casually, "What makes you ask?"

She drummed a forefinger against the side of her Fred Astaire nose. "Don't play Trivial Pursuit with me, Pippen."

"Up to now I've steered clear of missing husbands."

"What about as of now?"

Martin decided that his apartment wasn't bugged after all; if it had been, Fred would have known he'd turned down Stella Kastner. "Missing husbands are not my cup of tea, mainly because ninety-nine times out of a hundred they have settled comfortably into new identities involving new women. And it is extremely difficult, as in statistically impossible, to find people who have their heart set on never returning to their old women."

A weight seemed to lift from Fred's padded shoulders. She scooped another cube of ice from her daiquiri and ate it. "I have a soft spot for you, Dante. Honestly I do. In the eighties, in the early nineties, you were legendary for your legends. People still talk about you, though they refer to you by different names, depending on when they knew you. 'What's old Lincoln Dittmann up to these days?' a topsider asked me just last week. Agents like you come along once or twice a war. You floated on a cloud of false identities and false backgrounds that you could reel off, complete with what zodiac signs and which relatives were buried in what cemetery. If I remember correctly, Dante Pippen was a lapsed Catholic—he could recite rosaries in Latin that he'd learned as an altar boy in County Cork, he had a brother who was a Jesuit priest in the Congo and a sister who worked in a convent-hospital in the Ivory Coast. There was the Lincoln Dittmann legend, where you'd been raised in Pennsylvania and taught history at a junior college. It was filled with anecdotes about a high school prom in Scranton that was raided by the police or an uncle Manny in Jonestown who made a small fortune manufacturing underwear for the Army during World War Two. In that incarnation you had visited every Civil War battlefield east of the Mississippi. You lived so many identities in your life you used to say there were times when you forgot which biographical details were real and which were invented. You plunged into your cover stories so deeply, you documented them so thoroughly, you lived them so intently, the disbursing office got confused about what name to use on your paycheck. I'll tell you a dark secret, Dante: I not only admired your tradecraft, I envied you as a person. Everyone enjoys wearing masks, but the ultimate mask is having alternate identities that you can slip into and out of like a change of clothing—aliases, biographies to go with them, eventually, if you are really good, personalities and languages that go with the biographies."

With his Beedie, Martin playfully made the sign of the cross in the air. "*Ave Maria, Gratia Plena, Dominus Tecumi, Benedicta Tu In Mulieribus.*"

Snickering, Fred waved at Xing in the mirror. "Would it be asking too much to get a check?" she called. She smiled sweetly at Martin. "I presume you've gotten the message I came all this way to deliver. Steer clear of missing husbands, Dante."

"Why?"

The question irritated Fred. "Because I am telling you to steer clear, damn it. On the off chance you were to find him, why, we'd have to go back and take a hard look at certain decisions we made concerning you. In the end you turned out to be a rotten apple, Dante."

He didn't have the foggiest idea what she was talking about. "Maybe there were lines I couldn't cross," he said, trying to keep the conversation going; hoping to discover why he woke up nights in a cold sweat.

"We didn't hire your conscience, only your brain and your body. And then, one fine day, you stepped out of character—you stepped out of all your *characters*—and took what in popular idiom is called a moral stand. It slipped your mind that morality comes in a variety of flavors. At Langley, we held a summit. The choices before us were not complicated: We could either terminate your employment or terminate your life."

"What was the final vote?"

"Would you believe it was fifty-fifty? Mine was the tiebreaker. I came down on the side of those who wanted to terminate your employment, on condition you signed up at one of our private asylums. We needed to be sure—"

Before Fred could finish the sentence, Minh turned up carrying a small saucer with a check folded on it. She set it down between the two. Fred snared it and glanced at the bottom line, then peeled off two tens from a wad of bills and flattened them on the saucer. She weighed them down with a salt cellar. She and Martin sat silently, waiting for the waitress to remove the salt cellar and go off with the money.

"I really did have a soft spot for you," Fred finally said, shaking her head at a memory.

Martin appeared to be talking to himself. "I needed help remembering," he murmured. "I didn't get any."

"Count your blessings," Fred shot back. She slid off the banquette and stood up. "Don't do anything to make me regret my vote, Dante. Hey, good luck with the detecting business. One thing I can't abide is Chechens who swipe gold teeth before cremating the corpus delicti."

* * *

They were speeding up the Brooklyn-Queens Expressway toward La Guardia Airport to catch the shuttle back to Washington when the telephone on the dashboard squawked. The Operations Directorate wallah doubling as a chauffeur snatched it out of the cradle and held it to his ear. "Wait one," he said and passed the phone over his shoulder to Crystal Quest, dozing against a door in the back.

"Quest," she said into the receiver.

She straightened in the seat. "Yes, sir. I did. Dante and I go back a long way—I'm sure the fact that I delivered the message in person convinced him we were not playing pickup sticks." She listened for a moment. Up front the wallah surmised that the tinny bursts resonating from the earpiece were conveying exasperation in both tone and content.

Quest scratched at her scalp through her rust colored hair. "I am definitely not going soft, Director—soft is not my style. I ran him when he was operational. Fact that he came in from the cold, as that

English spy writer put it, doesn't change anything. As far as I'm concerned, I'm still running him. As long as he doesn't remember what happened—as long as he keeps his nose out of this Samat business—there's no reason to revisit that decision." She listened again, then said, coldly, "I take your point about unnecessary risks. If he steps over the fault—"

The man on the other end of the phone finished the sentence for her; the wallah at the wheel could see his boss in the rear view mirror nodding as she took aboard an order.

"Count on it," Quest said.

The line must have gone dead in her ear—the Director was notorious for ending conversations abruptly—because Quest leaned forward and dropped the telephone onto the passenger seat. Sinking back against the door, staring sightlessly out of the window, she started muttering disjointed phrases. After a while the words began taking on a sense. "Directors come and go," she could be heard saying. "The ones who wind up in Langley through their ties to the White House aren't the keepers of the flame—we are. We man the ramparts while the Director busts his balls working the Georgetown dinner circuit. We run the agents who put their lives on the line prowling the edge of empire. And we pay the price. Field agent drinks too much, controlling officer gets a hangover. Field agent turns sour, we curdle. Field agent dies, we break out the sackcloth and ashes and mourn for forty days and forty nights." Quest sighed for her lost youth, her femaleness gone astray. "None of which," she continued, her voice turning starchy, "would prevent us from terminating the son of a bitch if it looked as if he might compromise the family's jewel."

* * *

Martin's bedside alarm went off an hour before first light. In case Fred had managed to plant a microphone after all, he switched on the radio and turned up the volume to cover his foot falls and the sound of doors closing. Still in his tracksuit, he climbed to the roof and worked the bellows of his smoker, sending the colony of bees in the second of the two hives into a frenzy of gorging on honey. Then he reached into the narrow space between the top of the frames and the top of the hive to extract the small packet wrapped in oilcloth. Back downstairs, Martin opened the refrigerator and stuck a plastic basin under the drip notch. In the faint light that came from the open refrigerator, he unfolded the oilcloth around the packet and spread out the contents on his cot. There were half a dozen American and foreign passports, a French Livret de Famille, three internal passports from East European countries, a collection of laminated driver's licenses from Ireland and England and several East Coast states, an assortment of lending library and frequent flyer and Social Security cards, some of them brittle with age. He collected the identity papers and distributed them evenly between the cardboard lining and the top of the shabby leather valise with stickers from half a dozen Club Med resorts pasted on it. He filled the valise with shirts and underwear and socks and toilet articles, folded Dante Pippen's lucky white silk bandanna on top, then changed his clothing, putting on a light three-piece suit and the sturdy rubber soled shoes he'd worn when he and Minh had hiked trails in the Adirondacks the year before. Looking around to see what he'd forgotten, he remembered the bees. He quickly scribbled a note to Tsou Xing asking him to use the spare front door key he'd left in the cash register to check the beehives every other day; if there wasn't enough honey in the frames to see the bees through until spring, Tsou would know how to brew up sugar candy with the ingredients under the sink and deposit it in the hives.

Carrying the valise and an old but serviceable Burberry, Martin made his way to the roof. He locked the roof door behind him and stashed the key under a loose brick in the parapet. Looking up at the Milky Way, or what you could see of it from a roof in the middle of Brooklyn, he was reminded of the Alawite prostitute Dante had come across in Beirut during one particularly hairy mission. Leaning on the parapet, he surveyed Albany Avenue for a quarter of an hour, watching the darkened windows across the street for the slightest movement of curtains or Venetian blinds or a glimpse of embers glowing on a cigarette. Finding no signs of life, he crossed the roof and studied the alleyway behind the Chinese restaurant. There was motion off to the right where Tsou Xing parked his vintage Packard, but it turned out to be a cat trying to work the lid off a garbage pail. When Martin was sure the coast was clear, he backed down the steel ladder and then carefully descended the fire escape to the first floor. There he untied the rope and lowered the last section to the ground (through runners that he'd greased every few months; for Martin, tradecraft was the nearest thing he had to a religion). He tested the quality of the stillness for another few minutes before letting himself down into Tsou Xing's backyard heaped with stoves and pressure cookers and refrigerators that could one day be cannibalized for spare parts. He slipped the note for Tsou under the back door of the restaurant, crossed the yard to the alleyway and headed down it until he came to Lincoln Place. Two blocks down Lincoln, on the northeast corner of Schenectady, he ducked into a phone booth that reeked of turpentine. The first faint smudges of metallic gray were visible in the east as he checked the number written on his palm. Feeding a coin into the slot, he dialed it. The phone on the other end rang so many times that Martin began to worry he'd dialed the wrong number. He hung up and double checked the number and dialed again. He started counting how many times it rang and then gave up and just listened to it ring, wondering what to do if nobody answered. He was about to hang up—he would go to ground in a twenty-four hour diner on Kingston Avenue and try again in an hour—when someone finally came on the line.

"Do you have any idea what time it is?" a familiar voice demanded.

"I have decided I can't live without you. If you still want me, I think we can work something out."

Estelle Kastner caught her breath; she understood he was afraid the conversation was being overheard. "I'd given up on you," she admitted. "When can you come over?"

He liked her style. "How about now?"

She gave him an address several blocks down President Street between Kingston and Brooklyn. "It's a big private house. There's a door around the side—the light over it will be on. I'll be waiting for you in the vestibule." On the off chance the phone really was tapped, Estelle added, "I've never had a relationship with someone whose sign isn't compatible with mine. So what are you?"

"Leo."

"Come on, you're not a Leo. Leo's are cock sure of themselves. If I had to guess, I'd say you have the profile of a Capricorn. Capricorns are impulsive, whimsical, stubborn as a mule in the good sense—once you start something, you finish it. Your being a Capricorn suits me fine." She cleared her throat. "What made you change your mind. About calling?"

She caught Martin's soft laughter and found the sound curiously comforting. She heard him say, "I didn't have a change of mind, I had a change of heart."

"Fools rush in," she remarked, quoting from an old American song she played over and over on the phonograph, "where angels fear to tread." She could hear Martin breathing into the phone. Just before she cut the connection, she said, more to herself than to him, "I have a weakness for men who don't use aftershave."

1994: MARTIN ODUM GETS ON WITH HIS LIVES

"COULD YOU SAY SOMETHING SO I CAN CHECK THE VOICE LEVEL?"

"What should I say?"

"Anything that comes into your head."

"'. . . the silent cannons bright as gold rumble lightly over the stones. Silent cannons, soon to cease your silence, soon unlimber'd to begin the red business.'"

"That's fine. Remember to speak directly into the microphone. All right, here we go. For the record: We're Thursday, the sixteenth of June, 1994. What follows is a tape recording of my first session with Martin Odum. My name is Bernice Treffler. I'm the director of the psychiatric unit at this private hospital in Bethesda, Maryland. If you want to break at any time, Mr. Odum, wave a hand. What were those lines from, by the way?"

"One of Walter Whitman's Civil War poems."

"Any reason you call him Walter instead of Walt?"

"I was under the impression that people who knew him called him Walter."

"Are you a fan of Whitman's?"

"Not that I'm aware of. I didn't know I knew the lines until I said them."

"Does the Civil War interest you?"

"It doesn't interest me, Martin Odum, but it interested—how can I explain this?—it interested someone close to me. In one of my incarnations, I was supposed to have taught a course in a junior college on the Civil War. When we were working up the legend—"

"I'm sorry. The CIA people I've treated up to now have all been officers working at Langley. You're my first actual undercover agent. What is a legend?"

"It's a fabricated identity. Many Company people use legends, especially when they operate outside the United States."

"Well, I can see my vocabulary is going to expand talking to you, Mr. Odum. Go on with what you were saying."

"What was I saying?"

"You were saying something about working up a legend."

"Uh-huh. Since in my new incarnation I was supposed to be something of an expert on the subject, the person I was becoming had to study the Civil War. He read a dozen books, he visited many of the battlefields, he attended seminars, that sort of thing."

"He, not you?"

"Uh-huh."

"Was there a name assigned to this particular, eh, legend?"

"Dittmann, with two t's and two n's. Lincoln Dittmann."

"Do you have a headache, Mr. Odum?"

"I can feel one starting to press against the back of my eyes. Could you crack a window? It's very stuffy in here . . . Thanks."

"Would you like an aspirin?"

"Later, maybe."

"Do you get headaches often?"

"More or less often."

"Hmmm. What kind of person was this Lincoln Dittmann?"

"I'm not sure I understand the question."

"Was he different, say, from you? Different from Martin Odum?"

"That was the whole point—to make him different so he could operate without anyone mistaking him for me or me for him."

"What could Lincoln Dittmann do that you couldn't?"

"To begin with, he was an extraordinary marksman, much more skilled than me. He would take his sweet time to be sure he got the kill, one shot to a target. He would crank in corrections for windage and distance and then slowly squeeze (as opposed to jerk) the trigger. I'm too high-strung to kill in cold blood unless I'm goaded into action by the likes of Lincoln. The few times in my life that I aimed at a human target, my mouth went dry, a pulse pounded in my temple, I had to will my trigger finger not to tremble. When a born-again sniper like Lincoln shot at a human target, the only thing he felt was the recoil of the rifle. What else? I was more proficient in tradecraft— I could melt into a crowd when there wasn't one, so they said. Lincoln stood out in a crowd like a sore thumb. He was obviously more cerebral than me, or my other legend, for that matter. He was a better chess player, not because he was smarter than me, it's just that I was too impatient, too restless to figure out the implications of any particular gambit, to work out what would happen eight or ten moves down the tube. Lincoln, on the other hand, was blessed with incredible patience. If an assignment required stalking someone, Lincoln was the agent of choice for the job. And then there was the way we each looked at the world."

"Go on."

"Martin Odum is a basically edgy individual—there are days when he jumps at his own shadow. He's afraid to set foot in a place he's never been to before, he's apprehensive when he meets someone he doesn't already know. He lets people—women, especially—come to him. He has a sex drive but he's just as happy to abstain. When he makes love, he goes about it cautiously. He pays a lot of attention to the woman's pleasure before he takes his own."

"And Dittmann?"

"Nothing fazed Lincoln—not his own shadow, not places he hadn't been to, not people he didn't already know. It wasn't a matter of his being fearless; it was more a question of his being addicted to fear, of his requiring a daily fix."

"What you're describing is very similar to a split personality."

"You don't get it. It's not a matter of *splitting* a personality. It's a matter of creating distinct personalities altogether who . . . Excuse me but why are you making notes when this is being recorded?"

"The conversation has taken a turn for the fascinating, Mr. Odum. I'm jotting down some initial impressions. Were there other dissimilarities between Dittmann and Odum; between Dittmann and you?"

"Creating a working legend didn't happen overnight. It took a lot of time and effort. The details were worked out with the help of a team of experts. Odum smokes Beedies, Dittmann smoked Schimelpenicks when he could find them, any thin cigars when he couldn't. Odum didn't eat meat, Dittmann loved a good sirloin steak.

Odum is a Capricorn, Dittmann didn't know what his Zodiac sign was and couldn't have cared less. Odum washes and shaves every day but never uses aftershave lotions. Dittmann washed when he could and doused himself with Vetiver between showers. Odum is a loner; the handful of people who know him joke that he prefers the company of bees to humans, and there's a grain of truth to that. Dittmann was gregarious; unlike Odum he was a good dancer, he liked night clubs, he was capable of drinking large quantities of cheap alcohol with beer chasers without getting drunk. He did dope, he solved crossword puzzles in ink, he played Parcheesi and Go. When it came to women, he was an unconditional romantic. He had a soft spot for females"—Martin remembered a mission that had taken Lincoln to a town on the Paraguayan side of Three Border—"who were afraid of the darkness when the last light has been drained from the day, afraid of men who removed their belts before they took off their trousers, afraid life on earth would end before dawn tomorrow, afraid it would go on forever."

"And you—"

"I don't do dope. I don't play board games. I don't do crossword puzzles, even in pencil."

"So Odum and Dittmann are antipodes? That means—"

"Lincoln Dittmann would know what antipodes means. And in a corner of one lobe of my brain I have access to what he knows."

"What does this *access* consist of?"

"You're not going to believe this."

"Try me."

Martin said, very softly, "There are moments when I hear his voice whispering in my ear. That's how I came up with those Walter Whitman lines."

"Lincoln Dittmann whispered them to you."

"Uh-huh. Other times I know what he would do or say if he were in my shoes."

"I see."

"What do you see?"

"I see why your employer sent you to us. Hmmm. I'm a bit confused about something. You talk about Lincoln Dittmann in the past tense, as if he doesn't exist anymore."

"Lincoln's as real as me."

"The way you talk about Martin Odum, it almost seems as if he's a legend, too. Is he?"

When Martin didn't answer she repeated the question. "Is Martin Odum another of your fabricated identities, Mr. Odum?"

"I'm not sure."

"Are you telling me you really don't know?"

"I thought that's what you were supposed to help me find out. One of the legends must be real. The question is which."

"Well, this is certainly going to be more interesting than I expected. You have a very original take on MPD."

"What the heck is MPD?"

"It stands for Multiple Personality Disorder."

"Is what I have fatal? Why are you smiling?"

"Multiple Personality Disorder is far more likely to be functional than fatal, Mr. Odum. It permits patients who suffer from it to survive."

"Survive what?"

"That's what we're going to try to work our way back to. Let me give you the short course on MPD. My guess is that somewhere along the line something happened to you. In the overwhelming majority of cases, the trauma took place in childhood—sexual assaults are high on the list of childhood traumas, but not the only things on the list. I had one case about four years ago where a patient turned out to have been traumatized because he played with matches and started a fire that resulted in the death of his baby sister. The trauma short-circuited the patient's narrative memory. This particular patient developed seven distinct adult personalities, each with its own set of emotions and memories and even skills. He switched from one to another whenever he came under any stress. None of the seven alter personalities—what you would call legends, Mr. Odum—remembered the original childhood personality or the trauma associated with that personality. So you see, switching between personalities—almost always accompanied by a headache, incidentally—was a survival mechanism. It was his way of erecting a memory barrier, of shielding himself from an extremely frightening childhood experience, and it's in this sense that MPD is considered to be functional. It allows you to get on with your life—"

"Or your lives."

"Very good, Mr. Odum. Or your lives, yes. My instinct tells me you certainly don't fit neatly into the literature on the subject, inasmuch as you developed your alter personalities out of operational necessity, as opposed to a psychological necessity. When your psyche decided it needed to disappear behind a memory barrier, you had a series of personalities crafted and waiting to be stepped into. It's in this sense that you can be said to fit into the Multiple Personality profile."

"How different were your patient's seven personalities?"

"In my patient's case, as in the majority of MPD cases, they were quite distinct, involving diverse habits, talents, interests, values, dress codes, mannerisms, body language, ways of expressing themselves. They even made love differently. The alter personalities had different names and several of them even had different ages. One of them was unable to communicate verbally while another spoke a language—in his case Yiddish—that the others didn't understand."

"How is it possible for one personality to speak a language that another of his personalities doesn't understand?"

"It's a perfect example of how compartmented what you call legends can be in the brain."

"Were the seven personalities aware of each other's existence?"

"Some were, some weren't. This aspect can vary from case to case. More often than not several of the personalities seem to be aware of the existence of several other of the personalities—they think of them the way you would think of friends who you know exist but haven't seen in awhile. And there is what we call a *trace* personality—in your case it would appear to be Martin Odum—who serves as a repository of information about all of the other personalities except the *host* personality that experienced the trauma. This would account for the sensation you have that, as you said a moment ago, in a corner of your brain you have access to the specialized knowledge or talents of another alter personality, or as you would put it, another legend."

"I have a question, Dr. Treffler."

"Listen, since we're going to be working together for some time, how about if we move on to a first name basis. Call me Bernice and I'll call you Martin, okay?"

"Sure. Bernice."

"What's your question, Martin?"

"I seem to be able to distinguish three operational identities. There's Martin Odum. There's Lincoln Dittmann. And there's one I haven't introduced you to—the Irishman, Dante Pippen. Today of all days, Dante would be out on a pub crawl in Dublin, seeing how many of the city's pubs he could drink in before the sun set."

"What's so special about today?"

"It's Bloomsday, for pete's sake. All the action in *Ulysses* takes place ninety years ago today—16 June, 1904." Martin shut his eyes and angled his head. " 'Bloom entered Davy Byrne's. Moral pub. The publican doesn't chat. Stands a drink now and then.' On top of everything, it was a Tuesday, like today. In Ireland, that's the kind of thing you don't let pass without praying at what Dante liked to call licensed tabernacles."

"Hmmm."

"So here's my question: Is one of my three legends genuine? Or is there a fourth personality lurking in the shadows who's the original me?"

"Can't respond to that one yet. Either premise could be correct. There could be a fourth legend, even a fifth. We won't know until we start to break down the memory barriers, brick by brick, to get to the identity that recognizes himself as the original you."

"For that to happen, the childhood trauma will have to surface?"

"Is that a question or a statement of fact?"

"Question."

"I'm going to enjoy working with you, Martin. You're very quick. You're not frightened, at least not to the point where you'd walk away from this adventure. The answer to your question is: To get to what you call the original you, you're almost certainly going to have to experience pain. How do you feel about pain?"

"Not sure what to answer. Martin Odum may feel one way about it, Lincoln Dittmann and Dante Pippen, another."

"On that delightful note, what do you say we call it a day?"

"Uh-huh." As an afterthought, Martin asked, "Could I take you up on that aspirin?"

1997: MARTIN ODUM DISCOVERS THAT NOT MUCH IS SACRED

ROM LOWER MANHATTAN, AS THE CROW FLIES, CROWN HEIGHTS is a mere four miles across the river but a world away. Since race riots raged in its streets in the early 1990s, this particular section of Brooklyn had enjoyed a degree of extraterritoriality. Riding in squad cars with the mantra "Courtesy Professionalism Respect" visible on the doors not spattered with mud, police officers patrolled the neighborhood during daylight hours, but only for the most flagrant crimes would they abandon the relative safety of their vehicles. Depending on which street you were on, in some cases which sidewalk, different mafias ruled. On the streets south of Eastern Parkway off Nostrand Avenue, the Lubavitchers, solemn men in black suits and black hats, busied themselves reading the Torah in neighborhood shuls and obeying its 613 commandments while they waited for the Messiah, who was expected to turn up any day now; by the weekend at the very latest. Because the end of the world was nigh, Lubavitchers were enthusiastic about mortgages, the longer the better; but they hesitated buying anything they couldn't immediately consume, they didn't get involved in fights they couldn't finish before darkness fell. One block farther down President, on Rogers Avenue, the Lubavitchers gave way to African-Americans crowded into tenements; ghetto blasters with the volume turned up drowned out the occasional shrieks of addicts who needed a hit but didn't have the cash to pay for it. The West Indian ghetto, with its tidy streets and social clubs and block parties that had young people strolling in the gutter until dawn, began a few blocks farther south, on Empire

Boulevard. Where the denizens of the different ghettos rubbed shoulders, tensions ran high. Everyone understood it only needed a spark to set off a conflagration.

Martin, an outsider in all of the Crown Heights ghettos, knew enough to keep his head down and avoid looking anyone in the eye when he walked the streets. The sun was up and toasting the crispness out of the air as he made his way down Schenectady, past a large "Rent Strike" sign whitewashed onto a storefront window, past several broken shopping carts with small placards saying they were the property of Throckmorton's Minimarket on Kingston Avenue, kindly return. His leg with the pinched nerve was starting to ache as he turned onto President, a wide residential street with trees and two-story homes on either side. He stepped off the sidewalk to make way for three Lubavitch women, one more anemic than the other, all of them wearing long skirts and kerchiefs over their shaven heads. They didn't so much as glance in his direction but went on prattling to each other in a language Martin couldn't identify. As he neared Kingston, he came abreast of an ambulance with a Jewish Star of David painted on the door, parked in front of a brownstone that had been converted into a synagogue; two pimply young men, with embroidered skull caps on their heads and long sideburns curling down to their jaws, sat in the front seats listening to Bob Dylan on the tape deck.

> . . . Everything from toy guns that spark
> To flesh-colored Christs that glow in the dark
> It's easy to see without looking too far
> That not much is really sacred.

Once across Kingston Avenue, Martin began to search for the house numbers. Two thirds of the way down the block, he found the big house that Estelle Kastner had described; a narrow flagstone walkway led to the side door with the light burning over it. He continued past the house without stopping and turned right on Brooklyn Avenue, and then right again on Union Street, all the while watching the streets for the telltale signs that he was being followed, either by someone on foot or in a car. He felt a certain nostalgia for the good old days in the boondocks when he would have had a sweeper or two trailing after him to make sure he was clean, and tidy up behind him if he wasn't. Nowadays, he was obliged to make do with rudimentary tradecraft precautions. Streets and alleyways and intersections, the lobbies of buildings with their banks of elevators, the toilets in the backs of restaurants and the windows in the backs of the toilets that looked out on alleyways—he took it all in as if his life might one day depend on remembering what he saw.

Halfway down Union he climbed the front steps of a brownstone and stabbed at the bell. An old man in an undershirt flung open an upstairs window and shouted down, "What'cha want?"

"Looking for a family, name of Grossman," Martin called back.

"You're barking up the wrong block," the man yelled. "The Jewish, they live on President Street. Union is still thanks to God reasonably Roman." With that he pulled his head back into the house and slammed the window shut.

Martin stood on the stoop for a moment, feigning confusion as he surveyed the street in either direction. Then he doubled back the way he'd come and made his way along President Street to the flagstones that led to the side entrance with the light over it. He was about to knock on the "No Peddlers" sign when the door was pulled open. Stella, wearing tight jeans with a man's shirt tucked into them, stood inside, squinting up at him. The same three top buttons of her shirt were unbuttoned, revealing the same triangle of pale chest. Strangely, Martin found her more attractive than he remembered. He noticed her hands for the first time; the nails were neither painted nor bitten, the fingers themselves were incredibly long and extremely graceful. Even her chipped front tooth, which had struck him as downright ugly when they met the day before, seemed like an asset.

"Well, if it isn't the barefoot gumshoe, Martin Odum, Private Eye," Stella said with a mocking grin. She let him in and slipped his valise under a chair. "In that raincoat," she said, taking it from him and hanging it on a vestibule hook, "you look like a foreign correspondent from a foreign country. I saw you limp past ten minutes ago," she announced as she led him up a flight of stairs and into a windowless walk-in closet. "I concluded that your leg must be hurting. I concluded also that you're paranoid someone might be following you.

I'll bet you didn't call me from home—I'll bet you called from a public phone."

Martin grinned. "There's a booth on Lincoln and Schenectady that smells like a can of turpentine."

A booming voice behind Martin exclaimed, "My dear Stella, when will you learn that some paranoids have real enemies. I was watching from an upstairs window when he limped down President Street. Our visitor has the haunted look of someone who would circle the block twice before visiting his mother."

Martin spun around to confront the corpulent figure wrapped in a terrycloth robe and crammed into a battery-powered wheelchair. Scratching noisily at an unshaven cheek with the nicotine-stained fingers of one hand, working a small joystick with the other, the man piloted himself into the closet, elbowed the door closed behind him and backed up until his back was against the wall. The naked electric bulb, dangling from the ceiling, illuminated his sallow face. Studying it, Martin experienced a twinge of recognition: in one of his incarnations he'd come across a photograph of this man in a counterintelligence scrapbook. But when? And under what circumstances?

"Mr. Martin Odum and me," the man growled in the grating voice of a chain-smoker, "are birds of a feather. Tradecraft is our Kabala." He scraped a kitchen match against the wall and sucked a foul smelling cigarette into life. "Which is how come I meet you in this safe room," he plunged on, taking in with a sweep of his arm the shelves filled with household supplies, the mops and brooms and the vacuum cleaner, the piles of old newspapers waiting to be recycled. "Both of us know there are organizations that can eavesdrop on conversations over the land lines, it does not matter if the phones are on their hooks."

Stella made a formal introduction. "Mr. Odum, this is my father, Oskar Alexandrovich Kastner."

Kastner removed a pearl-handled Tula-Tokarev from the pocket of his terrycloth robe and set the handgun down on a shelf. Martin, who understood the value of gestures, accepted Kastner's decision to disarm with a nod.

All the tradecraft talk had tripped a memory. Suddenly Martin recalled which counterintelligence scrapbook he'd been studying when he came across the face of Stella's father: it was the one filled with mug shots of Soviet defectors. "Your daughter told me you were Russian," Martin said lazily. "She didn't say you were KGB."

Kastner, nodding excitedly, gestured toward a plastic kitchen stool and Martin scraped it over and settled onto it. Stella leaned back against a folded stepladder, half sitting on one of its steps. "You are a quick wit, Mr. Martin Odum," Kastner conceded, his bushy brows dancing over his heavy lidded eyes. "My body has slowed down but my brain is still functioning correctly, which is how come I am still cashing my annuity checks. It goes without saying but I will anyhow say it: I checked you out before I sent Stella over to test the temperature of the water."

"There aren't that many people in the neighborhood you could have checked me out with," Martin observed, curious to identify Kastner's sources.

"Your name was suggested to me by someone in Washington, who assured me you were overqualified for any job I might propose. To be on the safe side, I made discreet inquiries—I talked with a Russian in Little Odessa whose ex-wife stole his Rottweiler when he missed some alimony payments. The person in question compared you to a long distance runner. He told me once you started something you finished it."

Martin put two and two together. "Oskar Kastner can't be your real name," he said, thinking out loud. "A KGB defector living in Brooklyn under an assumed name—there will surely be an elaborate cover story to go with the pseudonym—means that you, like the other Soviet defectors, must be in the FBI's witness protection program. According to your daughter, you came here in 1988, which means the CIA has long since wrung you dry and probably doesn't return your calls if you make any. Which suggests that your friend in Washington who gave you my name is your FBI handler."

So that was how Crystal Quest had gotten wind of Stella's visit to the pool parlor! Someone in the FBI had heard that an ex-CIA type was playing detective in Crown Heights and passed Martin's name on to Kastner. The FBI clerks who keep tabs on people in the protection program would have circulated a routine "contact" report when a former KGB officer announced his intention of employing a former CIA officer—even if the case in question had nothing to do with CIA operations. Somewhere in the labyrinthian corridors of Langley, a warning buzzer would have gone off; it had probably been the one wired to Quest's brain.

Did this mean that Kastner's missing son-in-law had some connection to past or present CIA operations? Martin decided it was an angle worth considering.

"He is pretty rapid for a long distance runner," Kastner was telling his daughter. "My FBI friend said you were discharged from the CIA in 1994. He did not explain why, except to say it had nothing to do with stealing money or selling secrets or anything unpleasant like that."

"I'm relieved you're both on the same side," Stella ventured from her perch on the ladder.

Martin batted a palm to disperse Kastner's cigarette smoke. "Why didn't you ask the FBI to try and find your missing son-in-law?"

"First thing I tried. They stretched some rules and searched the computer database for missing persons who had turned up dead. Unfortunately none of them fit Samat's description."

Martin smiled. "*Unfortunately?*"

Kastner's craggy features twisted into a scowl. "I speak American with an accent—Stella never stops correcting me—but I pick my words as if my life depended on their accuracy."

"I can vouch for Kastner's accent," Stella said with a laugh.

"You call your father Kastner?"

"Sure. You've already figured out that's not his real name—it's the name the FBI gave him when he came into the witness protection program. Calling my father Kastner is a running joke between us. Isn't it, Kastner?"

"It reminds us who we're not."

Martin turned to Stella. "Meeting your father explains a lot."

"Such as?" she demanded.

"It explains how you played along so quickly when I phoned this morning; you understood that I thought the phone might be tapped. You are your father's daughter."

"She was raised to be discreet when it comes to telephones," Kastner agreed with evident pride. "She knows enough tradecraft to pay attention to people who are window shopping for objects they do not seem likely to buy. Women and fishing rods, for example. Or men and ladies undergarments."

"You really didn't need to go around the block twice," Stella told Martin. "I promise you I wasn't followed when I came to see you. I wasn't followed on the way home either."

"That being the case, how come the folks I used to work for are trying to discourage me from getting involved with missing husbands?"

Kastner manipulated the joystick; the wheelchair jerked toward Martin. "How do you know they know?" he asked quietly.

"A woman named Fred Astaire whispered in my ear."

Kastner said, "I can see from the look in your eyes that you do not consider this Fred Astaire person to be a friend."

"It takes a lot of energy to dislike someone. Occasionally I make the effort."

Stella was following her own thoughts. "Maybe your pool parlor was bugged," she suggested. "Maybe they hid a microphone in that Civil War rifle of yours."

Martin shook his head. "If they had bugged my loft, they would have heard me refuse to take the case and not gone out of their way to lean on me."

Tilting his large head, Kastner thought out loud: "The tip could have come from the FBI—someone there might have routinely informed my CIA conducting officer if it looked as if you might become involved with me. But you probably figured that out already."

Martin was mightily relieved to hear him reach this conclusion. It underscored his credibility.

Kastner stared at Martin, his jaw screwed up. "Stella told me you refused to take the case. Why did you modify your mind?"

Stella kept her eyes on Martin as she spoke to her father. "He didn't modify his mind, Kastner. He modified his heart."

"Respond to the question, if you please," Kastner instructed his visitor.

"Let's chalk it up to an unhealthy curiosity—I'd like to know why the CIA doesn't want this particular missing husband found. That and the fact that I don't appreciate having an unpleasant woman who munches ice cubes tell me what I can or cannot do."

"I like you," Kastner burst out, his face breaking into a lopsided smile. "I like him," he informed his daughter. "But he would not have gone very far in our *Komitet Gosudarstvennoi Bezopasnosti*. He is too much of a loner. We did not trust the loners. We only recruited people who were comfortable serving as cogs in the machine."

"Which Directorate?" Martin asked.

The bluntness of Martin's question made Stella wince; in her experience, people talking about intelligence matters usually beat around the bush. "In the USA, Kastner," she told her father, who was visibly flustered, "they call this talking turkey."

Kastner cleared his throat. "The Sixth Chief Directorate," he said, adapting to the situation. "I was the second deputy to the man who ran the Directorate."

"Uh-huh."

The Russian looked at his daughter. "What does it mean, uh-huh?"

"It means he is familiar with the Sixth Chief Directorate, Kastner."

In fact, Martin had more than a passing acquaintance with this particular Directorate. At one point in the late eighties, Lincoln Dittmann had recruited a KGB officer in Istanbul. Lincoln had made his pitch when he heard on the grapevine that the officer's younger brother had been arrested for being out of step during a military drill; the instructor had acused him of sabotaging the parade to discredit the glorious Red Army. Lincoln had arranged to smuggle the disenchanted KGB officer and his family out of Istanbul in return for a roll of microfilm filled with Sixth Chief Directorate documents. The material provided the CIA with its first inside look into the operations of this up to then secret section. It had been carved out of the KGB Directorate structure back in the sixties to keep track of economic crimes. In 1987, when what the Soviets called "cooperatives" and the world referred to as "free market enterprises" were legalized by Comrade Gorbachev, the Sixth Chief Directorate shifted gears to keep track of these new businesses. As the economy, crippled by inflation and corruption at the most senior levels of government, began to stall, gangster capitalism thrived; cooperatives had to buy protection—what the Russians called *krysha* or *a roof*—from the hundreds of gangs sprouting in Moscow and other cities if they wanted to stay in business. When the Sixth Chief Directorate found it couldn't crush the gangs and protect the emerging market economy, it simply stopped trying and joined in the free-for-all looting of the country. Martin remembered Stella's saying that her father had immigrated to America in 1988. If he had been getting rich on the looting, he would have stayed and skimmed off his share. Which meant he was one of those die-hard socialists who blamed Gorbachev and his "restructuring" for wrecking seventy years of Soviet communism. In short, Kastner was probably the rarest of birds, an ardent, if disheartened, Marxist condemned to live out his days in capitalist America.

"You are thinking so hard, smoke is emerging from your ears," Kastner said with a laugh. "What conclusion have you reached?"

"I like you, too," Martin declared. "I like your father," he told Stella. "Fact is, he wouldn't have lasted long in the CIA. He is far too idealistic for a shop that prides itself on the virtuosity of its pragmatists. Unlike your father, Americans aren't interested in constructing a Utopia, for the simple reason they believe they're living in one."

Stella seemed stunned. "I like that you like Kastner, and for the right reasons," she said softly.

Kastner, his nerves frayed, swiveled his wheelchair to one side and then the other. "It remains for us to put our heads together and figure out why the lady with the pseudonym Fred Astaire does not want my son-in-law, Samat, to be discovered."

Martin permitted a rare half-smile onto his lips. "To do that I'm going to have to *discover* Samat."

Stella disappeared to brew up some tea and hurried back minutes later carrying a tray with a jar of jam and three steaming cups on it. She found her father and Martin, their knees almost touching, deep in conversation. Martin was smoking one of his wafer-thin Beedies. Her father had started another cigarette but held it at arm's length so the smoke wouldn't obscure Martin.

". . . somehow managed to falsify the records so the Party would not know his mother was Jewish," Kastner was explaining. "His father was an Armenian doctor and a member of the Party—at one point he was accused of being an enemy of the people and sent to Siberia, where he died. The post-Stalinist program to rehabilitate people falsely accused of crimes counted in Samat's favor when he applied to the Forestry Institute; the state had killed his father so it felt it had to compensate the son."

Martin nodded. "I seem to recall reading about your famous Forestry Institute that taught everything except forestry."

Kastner set aside his cigarette in a saucer and stirred a spoonful of jam into one of the cups. Blowing noisily across it, he sipped at the scalding tea. "It was the secret institute for our space program," he said. "In the seventies, it was the best place in the Soviet Union to study computer science. Samat went on to do advanced studies at the State Planning Agency's Higher Economic School. When he graduated near the top of his class, he was drafted into the KGB. Because of his computer skills, he was posted to the Sixth Chief Directorate."

"You knew him personally?"

"He was assigned to several cases I worked on. He became an expert on money laundering techniques—he knew everything there was to know about off-shore banks and bearer-share business operations. In 1991, when Yeltsin ousted Gorbachev and took power, one of the things he did was break up our Committee for State Security into its component parts, at which point a great many KGB officers found themselves suddenly unemployed and scrambling to make a living. Samat was one of them."

"You were in America by then. How do you know all this?"

"Your Central Intelligence Agency encouraged me to keep in touch with the Sixth Directorate. They wanted me to recruit agents in place."

"Did you succeed?"

Kastner flashed a pained smile. Martin said, "I take back the question. So we're up to where Samat, with the KGB closing down its shop, starts looking at the help wanted ads. What kind of job did he land?"

"He ended up working for one of the rising stars in the private sector, someone who had his own model of how to make the transition from socialism to market-oriented capitalism. His solution was gangster capitalism. He was one of the gangsters the Sixth Chief Directorate kept track of when I was there. Samat, with his knowledge of money laundering techniques, quickly worked his way up to become the organization's financial wizard. He was the one who brought the shell game to Russia. You have seen the Negroes playing the shell game on street corners down on Rogers Avenue. They fold your ten-dollar bill until it is the size of a walnut and put it under a sea shell and move it around with two other shells. When they stop your ten-dollar bill has disappeared. Samat did the same thing but on a much larger scale."

"And this is the Russian Lubavitch who wanted to marry your daughter and live in Israel?"

Kastner nodded heavily. "At one point the CIA asked me to try and recruit Samat. They arranged for me to talk with him on the telephone when he was in Geneva. I spoke of a secret account that could be his if he came over. I named a sum of money that would be deposited in this account. He laughed and replied that the sum of money they were suggesting was the loose change in his pocket. He told me the CIA could not afford to pay him a tenth of what he was earning. When Samat returned to Russia he made sure everyone knew the CIA had attempted to recruit him. There was even a satiric article published in *Pravda* describing the clumsy approach by a defector."

"When did Samat get in touch with you about marrying your daughter?" Martin asked.

"It was not Samat who contacted Kastner," Stella said. "Samat's employer, who happened to be Samat's uncle—his father's brother—is the one who got in touch with Kastner."

Martin looked from one to the other. "And who was Samat's employer?"

Kastner cleared his throat. "It was Tzvetan Ugor-Zhilov, the one known as the *Oligarkh.*"

"*The* Tzvetan Ugor-Zhilov who was on the cover of *Time* magazine in the early nineties?"

"There is only one Tzvetan Ugor-Zhilov," Kastner remarked with some bitterness.

"You knew that Samat was working for Tzvetan Ugor-Zhilov when you agreed to the marriage?"

Kastner looked at his daughter, then dropped his eyes. It was obviously a sore subject between them. Stella answered for her father. "It was not an accident that Tzvetan Ugor-Zhilov contacted Kastner—the two of them were acquainted from the days when the Sixth Chief Directorate was keeping track of the new cooperatives."

"In the early nineteen-eighties," Kastner explained, "Ugor-Zhilov was a small-time hoodlum in a small pond—he ran a used-car dealership in Yerevan, the capital of Armenia. He had a KGB record: He'd been arrested in the early seventies for bribery and black market activities and sent to a gulag in the Kolyma Mountains for eight years. Read Solzhenitsyn's *Ivan Denisovich* and you will get a glimpse of what each day of Ugor-Zhilov's eight years was like. By the time he made his way back to Armenia and scraped together enough money to open the used-car business, he was bitterly anti-Soviet; bitterly anti-Russian, also. He would have faded from our radar screen if he hadn't set his sights on bigger fish in bigger ponds. He came to Moscow and in a matter of months cornered the used-car market there. One by one he bought out his competitors. Those who would not sell wound up dead or maimed. The punishment handed out by the *Oligarkh* was what you Americans call cruel and unusual—he believed that it was good for business if his enemies had reason to dread him. When I spoke to Samat in Geneva, he passed on a story that Ugor-Zhilov had actually buried someone alive and had a road paved over him—and this while several dozen workers looked on. The story of the execution may or may not be true—either way it served its purpose. Few Russians were reckless enough to challenge the *Oligarkh*."

"You seem to know an awful lot about Tzvetan Ugor-Zhilov," Martin observed.

"I was the conducting officer in charge of the investigation into the *Oligarkh*'s affairs."

Martin saw where the story was going. "I'll take a wild guess—he paid off the Sixth Directorate."

Kastner didn't respond for a moment. "You have to put yourself in our shoes," he said finally. "We were honest cops and we went after him in a straightforward manner. But he bought the minister in the Kremlin who ran the KGB, then he bought my colleague who was the head of the Sixth Chief Directorate, and then he turned to me and put a thick packet of money on the table, this at a time when we sometimes went several months without drawing a salary because of the economic chaos. What was I to do? If I accepted I would be on his payroll. If I refused I would seriously compromise my life expectancy."

"So you defected to America."

Kastner plucked his cigarette from the saucer and inhaled deeply, then sniffed at the smoke in the air. "It was the only solution," he said.

"Knowing what you knew about uncle Ugor-Zhilov, why did you agree to let your daughter marry his nephew Samat?"

Stella came to her father's defense. "Kastner agreed because he didn't have a choice."

Kastner said, very quietly, "You do not understand how things worked after communism collapsed. One morning there arrived in my mailbox downstairs here on President Street a letter typed on expensive bonded paper. It was not signed but I immediately understood where it came from. The writer said that his nephew was obliged to leave Russia, and quickly. It said that the best place for him to go would be Israel. It was a time when Jews were queuing up by the tens of thousands for visas at the Israeli embassy in Moscow; the Israeli Mossad, fearful that what was left of the KGB apparatus would try to infiltrate agents into Israel, was screening the Jewish applicants very carefully. And carefully meant slowly. Ugor-Zhilov obviously knew that my daughter Elena had joined the Lubavitch sect soon after we settled in Crown Heights. He knew that the Lubavitchers had a lot of influence when it came to getting Jews into Israel—they could arrange for the Israeli immigration authorities to speed things up if there was a Lubavitch marriage involved, especially if the newlyweds planned to live in one of the Jewish settlements on the West Bank, which the Israeli government at the time was eager to populate."

Martin felt claustrophobic in the airless closet; he had a visceral revulsion for closed spaces without windows. "Something doesn't make sense here," he said, eyeing the door, mastering an urge to throw it open. "How could Tzvetan Ugor-Zhilov send a letter to you if you were in the FBI's witness protection—"

Martin's mouth sagged open; the answer to his question came to him before Kastner supplied it.

"It was *because* he was able to send a letter to me," Kastner said, "despite my being in the FBI program, that it was out of the realm of possibility to refuse him. Tzvetan Ugor-Zhilov is one of the richest men in all of Russia; one of the fifty richest men in the world, according to that article in *Time*. He has a long arm, long enough to reach someone who has been given a new identity and lives on President Street in

Crown Heights." He glanced at Stella and the two exchanged grim smiles. "Long enough," Kastner continued, "to reach his two beautiful girls, also. When the *Oligarkh* asks for a favor, it is not healthy to refuse if you are confined to a wheel chair and have nowhere else to defect to."

Martin remembered the words from the Bob Dylan song he'd heard in the street and he repeated them aloud: "*Not much is really sacred.*"

"Not true," Kastner burst out. "Many things are still sacred. Protecting my daughters is at the top of the list."

"Kastner could not be expected to anticipate how Samat would mistreat Elena," Stella put in. "It was not his fault—"

Kastner cut her off. "Whose fault was it if not mine?" he said despondently.

"Aren't you running a risk by hiring me to find this Samat?"

"I only want him to give my Elena the religious divorce so she can marry again. What he does with his life after that is his affair. Surely this is not an unreasonable request." Kastner worked the joystick, backing the wheelchair into the wall with a light thud. He shrugged his heavy shoulders as if he were trying to rid himself of a weight. "In terms of money, how do we organize this?"

"I pay my way with credit cards. When the credit card people ask me for money, I will ask you to pay my expenses. If I find Samat and your daughter gets her *get*, we'll figure out what that's worth to you. If I don't find him, you'll be out of pocket my expenses. Nothing more."

"In your pool parlor you spoke of the problem of searching for a needle in a field of haystacks," Stella said. "Where on earth do you begin looking for it?"

"Everyone is somewhere," Martin informed her. "We'll start in Israel."

Stella, startled, said, "We?"

Martin nodded. "First off, there's your sister—she'll trust me more if you're with me when I meet her. Then there's Samat. Someone on the run can easily change his appearances—the color and length of his hair, for instance. He could even pass himself off as an Arab and cover his head with a kaffiyeh. I need to have someone with me who could pick him out of a crowd if she only saw his seaweed-green eyes."

"That more or less narrows it down to me," Stella agreed.

1997: MINH SLEEPWALKS THROUGH ONE-NIGHT STANDS

DRESSED IN LOOSE-FITTING SILK PANTS AND A HIGH-NECKED SILK blouse with a dragon embroidered on the back, Minh was clearing away the last of the dirty lunch dishes when Tsou Xing poked his head through the kitchen doors and asked her if she would run upstairs and check Martin's beehives. He would do it himself, he said, but he was expecting a delivery of Formosan beer and wanted to count the cartons before they stored them in the cellar to make sure he wasn't being short changed. Sure, Minh said. No problem. She opened the cash register and retrieved Martin's keys and headed for the street, glad to have a few minutes to herself. She wondered if Tsou suspected that she had slept with Martin. She thought she'd spotted something resembling a leer in his old eyes when Tsou raised the subject of their upstairs' neighbor earlier that week; he had been speaking in English but had referred to Martin using the Chinese word for *hermit*. Where you think *yin shi* goes when he goes? Tsou had asked. Minh had hunched her muscular shoulders into a shrug. It's not part of my job to keep track of the customers, she'd replied testily. No reason climb on high horse, Tsou had said, whisking a fly from the bar with the back of his only hand. Not a crime to think you could know, okay? And he had smiled so wickedly that the several gold teeth in his mouth flashed into view. Well, I don't know and I couldn't care less, Minh had insisted. Pivoting on a heel, she had stalked off so Tsou would get the message: She didn't appreciate his sticking his nose into her love life, or lack of same.

Now Minh rubbed her sleeve across the private-eye logo on Martin's front door to clean the rain stains off of it, then let herself in and, taking the steps two at a time, climbed to the pool parlor. Actually, she did wonder where Martin had gone off to; wondered, too, why he hadn't left a message for her as well as Tsou. She attributed it to Martin's shyness; he would have been mortified if he thought Tsou had gotten wind of their relationship, assuming you could call their very occasional evenings together a relationship. She meandered through the pool parlor, brushing her fingers over his Civil War guns and the folders on his desk and the unopened cartons that contained heaven knows what. Soon after he'd moved in she had asked him if he wanted help opening them. He'd kicked at one of the cartons and had said he didn't need to open them, he knew what was inside. The reply struck her as being very in character.

When Minh thought about it, which was more often than she liked to admit, the fact that she really wasn't sure where she stood with *yin shi* exasperated her. He always seemed happy enough to see her but he never went out of his way to initiate meetings. Minh had been raised in lower Manhattan's Chinatown, a cauldron simmering with refugees of one sort or another, so she knew one when she saw one; the thing that betrayed them was they seemed to be alone even in a crowd. She herself was in the country illegally, a refugee from Taiwan. Minh was not even her real name, a detail she'd never revealed to Martin for fear he might be shocked. Sometimes she had the weird feeling that Martin, too, was some kind of refugee—though from what, she had no clue. *Yin shi* lived what she thought of as a boring life, ordering up the same dishes three or four nights a week, attending to his hives on the roof, making love to her when she turned up at his door. For excitement, he broke into hotel rooms to photograph husbands committing adultery, though when he described what he did for a living he managed to make even that sound boring. The single time she had raised the subject of boredom he had astonished her by admitting that he relished it; boring himself to death, he'd insisted, was how he planned to spend the rest of his life.

At the time Minh had thought it was one of those things you say to sound clever. Only later did it dawn on her that he'd meant every word; that boring yourself to death was a way of committing suicide in slow motion.

...ing into the back room, Minh straightened the sheets and
...on the cot, emptied the water from the plastic basin on the
...osed the refrigerator door, put away the dishes that Martin had
...gotten around to washing. She retrieved Martin's faded white
...and, rolling up the cuffs and the sleeves, slipped into it and
...the front. She put on the pith helmet with the mosquito net-
...ng from it and took a look at herself in the cracked mirror
...bathroom sink. The outfit was not what you would call feng
... Taking Martin's smoke gun from under the sink, she made her
way up the stairs to the roof. The sun, high overhead, was burning off
the last drops of rain that had fallen the previous night. Vapor rose
from shallow puddles as she crossed the roof to the hives. Martin had
bought them and the equipment, and even the first queen bees, from
a catalogue when he got it into his head to raise bees. In the beginning
he had pored over the instruction book that came with the hives. Then
he'd dragged a chair up to the roof and had spent hours staring at the
colonies, trying to figure out if there was a flight pattern to the swarm's
movements, a method to its apparent madness. Minh had never seen
him do anything with such intensity. When he'd begun inspecting and
cleaning the frames he'd worn gloves, but he discarded them when
Minh happened to mention the Chinese belief that bee stings stimulated your hormones and increased your sex drive. Not that the subsequent stings on his hands had changed anything—it was invariably
Minh who made the first move toward the cot in the back of the loft,
pulling Martin into the room, onto the cot, peeling off her clothing
and then his. He made love to her cautiously, as if (she finally realized)
he, not she, were fragile; as if he were afraid to let emotions surface that
he might not be able control.

Minh was crouching in front of the first hive, preparing the
smoker, ruminating on how making love with Martin had been like
sleepwalking through a string of one-night stands that were physically
satisfying but emotionally frustrating, when the dumdum bullet
plunged into the frames. There was an instant of absolute silence, as
if the 20,000 residents of the hive—those that had survived the
impact—had been reduced to a state of catatonic bewilderment.
Then a raging yellowish-brown football-sized swarm burst out of
the hive with such ferocity it knocked Minh over backward. The pith

helmet and veil flew off to one side and the bees attacked he̶
and her eyes, planting their darts with savage vengeance. She c̶
her fingers into fists and hammered wildly at the layers o̶
encrusting her skin, crushing them by the hundreds until her kn̶
les were covered with a sticky residue. There was no longer a s̶
overhead, only a thick carpet of rioting insects ricocheting off on̶
another as they fought for a turn at the intruder who had wrecked
their hive.

Her face and lids swelling, Minh slumped back onto the hot
tarpaper of the roof, swatting weakly at the bees the way Tsou had
whisked at the fly on the bar. As the pain gave way to numbness, she
heard a voice that sounded remarkably like her own telling Martin
that, hey, you really shouldn't wear gloves. Sure there's a reason why.
According to the Chinese, bee stings can stimulate your . . .

1997: OSKAR ALEXANDROVICH KASTNER DISCOVERS THE WEIGHT OF A CIGARETTE

THE TWO MEN IN CON-ED UNIFORMS PARKED THEIR REPAIR TRUCK in the narrow alley between President and Carroll and made their way on foot to the only back garden on the block protected by a chainlink fence. One of the men muttered something into a walkie-talkie, listened for a response and nodded to his colleague when he heard it. The second man produced a key, opened the door in the fence and used the same key to switch off the alarm box inside. The two, walking soundlessly on crepe soled shoes, climbed the stairs to the porch. Using a second key, they let themselves into the kitchen at the rear of the house and punched the code into the alarm there. They stood motionless for several minutes, their eyes fixed on the ceiling. When they heard the muffled scrape of a wheelchair rolling along a hallway over their heads, the two men produced pistols fitted with silencers and started up the back staircase. Reaching the first floor, they could hear a radio playing in the front room. Gripping their pistols with both hands, angling the barrels up, they worked their way along the hall to the closed door and flattened themselves against the wall on either side of it. One of the men tapped the side of his nose to indicate he had gotten a whiff of foul smelling cigarette smoke; their quarry was inside the room. Baring his teeth in a tight smile, his companion grasped the knob and flung open the door and the two of them, hunched over to keep their profiles low, burst into the room.

Oskar Alexandrovich Kastner, sitting in his wheelchair next to the window, was oiling the firing mechanism on a Soviet PPSh 41, a Second World War automatic weapon in mint condition. Smoke

coiled up from a cigarette burning in an ashtray. Kastner's heavy lidded eyes blinked slowly as he took in the intruders. One appeared
much older than the other but the younger man, gesturing to the
other to shut the door, seemed to be in charge.

"*Vy Russky?*" Kastner inquired.

"*Da. Ya Russky,*" replied the younger Con-Ed man. "*I gdye vasha
doch?*"

Kastner eyed the pearl-handled Tula-Tokarev on the table, a 1930s
pistol that he always kept charged, but he knew he could never reach
it. "*Ya ne znayu,*" he replied. He was not about to tell them that Stella
was on her way to Israel, accompanied by a CIA agent turned detective who lived over a Chinese restaurant. He wondered how the two
killers had broken through the chainlink fence and gotten into the
kitchen without tripping the alarms. "You took your time getting
here," Kastner growled in English. "Nine years." He set the PPSh
down and, working the joystick, maneuvered the wheelchair so that
his back was to the intruders.

"*Kto vas poslal?*" he asked.

"*Oligarkh,*" the younger gunman said with a ruthless snicker.

Gazing out the window, Kastner caught sight of two small
Lubavitch boys, dressed in black like their fathers, hurrying down the
street. He knew from Elena that they expected the Messiah to appear
at any moment and redeem mankind. Maybe this Messiah had turned
up and the boys were actually angels on their way to welcome him. He
himself would surely end up where angels fear to tread, as that song
Stella played on the Victrola put it. Kastner gasped when he felt the
needle prick the skin of his back next to the shoulder blade. In his day
the KGB specialists in wetwork had favored a tasteless, colorless rat
poison that thinned the blood and brought breathing to an abrupt
halt. The *Oligarkh's* hit men would surely be using something more
sophisticated and less traceable; perhaps one of those newfangled
adrenalin-like substances that caused widespread gastric bleeding and,
eventually, death, or, better still, a clotting agent that blocked a coronary artery and triggered what doctors called a myocardial infarction
and laymen referred to as a heart attack. On the off-chance that one
of the angels might ask him to identify himself, Kastner tried to rec-
ollect what his name had been before the FBI assigned the pseudonym

Oskar. It irritated him that he was unable to remember what his mother had called him as a child. If he could suck on his cigarette, it would surely calm his nerves long enough for the name to come back to him. Moving languidly, as if he were underwater, Kastner reached for the ashtray. With great concentration he managed to pinch the cigarette between his thumb and two fingers, only to discover that it was too heavy to lift.

1987: DANTE PIPPEN BECOMES AN IRA BOMBER

ASSEMBLED IN A WINDOWLESS STORAGE ROOM IN A BASEMENT OF Langley filled with empty watercoolers, the eight people around the conference table started, as always, with the family name and in short order narrowed the list down to one that had an Irish ring to it, but then spent the next half hour debating how it should be spelled. In the end the chairman, a station chief who reported directly to Crystal Quest, the new Deputy Director of Operations, turned to the agent known as Martin Odum, who had been following the discussion from a chair tilted back against the wall; as Martin's "Odum" legend had been burned and he would be the person employing the new identity, it would save time if he settled on the spelling. Without a moment's hesitation, Martin opted for Pippen with three p's. "I've been reading newspaper stories about a young black basketball player at the University of Central Arkansas named Scottie Pippen," Martin explained. "So I thought Pippen would have the advantage of being easy to remember."

"Pippen it is," announced the chairman and he turned to the selection of a Christian name to go with Pippen. The junior member of the Legend Committee, a Yale-educated aversion therapist, sarcastically suggested that they might want to go whole hog and use Scottie as the Christian name. Maggie Poole, who had read medieval French history as an Oxford undergraduate and liked to salt her conversation with French words, shook her head. "You're all going to think I am off the wall but I came up with a name in my dreams last night that I consider *parfait*. Dante, as in Dante Alighieri?" She looked around the table expectantly.

The only other woman on the committee, a lexicographer on loan from the University of Chicago, groaned. "Problem with Dante Pippen," she said, "is it wouldn't go unnoticed. People tend to remember a name like that."

"But don't you see, that's exactly what makes it an excellent choice," exclaimed Maggie Poole. "Nobody thumbing down a list of names would suspect Dante Pippen of being a *pseudonyme* precisely because it stands out in a crowd."

"She has a point," agreed the committee's doyen, a gargoyle-like CIA veteran who had started out creating legends for OSS agents during World War Two.

"I will admit I don't *dislike* the sound of Dante," ventured the aversion therapist.

The chairman looked at Martin. "What do you think?" he asked.

Martin repeated the names several times. Dante. Dante Pippen. "Uh-huh. I think it suits me. I can live with Dante Pippen."

Once the committee had decided on a name, the rest of the cover story fell neatly into place.

"Our Dante Pippen is obviously Irish, born, say, in County Cork."

"Where in County Cork?"

"I once vacationed in a seaport called Castletownbere," said the aversion therapist.

"Castletownbere, Cork, has a good ring to it. We'll send him there for a week of R and R. He can get a local map and the phone book, and fix in his head the names of the streets and hotels and stores."

"Castletownbere is a fishing port. He would have worked on a salmon trawler as a *teenager*."

"Then when the economy turned bad, he would have gone off to try his luck in the New World, where he will have picked up a lot about the history of the Irish in America—the potato famine of 1840 that brought the first Irish immigrants to our shores, the Civil War draft riots, that sort of thing."

"If he comes from Castletownbere, he must be Catholic. For the price of a generous donation, we can probably get the local Castletownbere church to slip his name into its baptism records."

"One fine day, like many, if not most, Irish men, he would have become fed up with the church."

"A lapsed Catholic, then," said the chairman, jotting the biographical detail down on his yellow pad.

"A *very* lapsed Catholic," Martin piped up from his place along the wall.

"Just because he's lapsed doesn't mean his family will have lapsed."

"Why don't we give him a brother and a sister who are in the church but can't be traced because they are no longer living under the name Pippen. Brother such and such. Sister such and such."

"The brother could be a Jesuit priest in the Congo, converting the natives to Jesus at the bitter end of some crocodile infested river."

"And the sister—let's put her in a convent hospital in the back country of the Ivory Coast."

"She will have taken a vow of *silence*, which means she couldn't be interviewed even if someone got to her."

"Is Dante Pippen a smoker or nonsmoker?

The chairman turned to Martin, who said, "I've been trying to cut down. If Dante Pippen is supposed to be a nonsmoker, it'll give me an incentive to go cold turkey."

"Nonsmoker it is, then."

"Be careful you don't put on weight. The CIA takes a dim view of overweight agents."

"We ought to hire one or two—being *obese* would be a perfect cover."

"Even if our Dante Pippen's a lapsed Catholic, he would still have gone to Catholic school as a child. He would have been taught to believe that the seven sacraments—Baptism, Confirmation, Eucharist, Confession, Anointing of the Sick, Matrimony and Holy Orders— could see you through a lifetime of troubles."

The chairman scribbled another note on his pad. "That's a good point," he said. "We'll get someone to teach him rosaries in Latin— he could slip them into the conversation to lend credibility to the new identity."

"Which brings us to his occupation. What exactly does our Dante Pippen do in life?"

The chairman picked up Martin Odum's 201 Central Registry folder and extracted the bio file. "Oh, dear, our Martin Odum can be said to be a renaissance man only if one defines renaissance narrowly.

He was born in Lebanon County, Pennsylvania, and spent the first eight years of his life in a Pennsylvania backwater called Jonestown, where his father owned a small factory manufacturing underwear for the U.S. Army during World War Two. After the war the underwear business went bankrupt and the elder Odum moved the family to Crown Heights, Brooklyn, to start an electrical appliance business. Crown Heights is where Martin was brought up."

"Being brought up in Brooklyn is not the most auspicious beginning for a renaissance man, even defined narrowly," quipped Maggie Poole. She twisted in her seat toward Martin. "I'm not ruffling your feathers, am I?"

Martin only smiled.

"Yes, well," the chairman continued, "our man majored in commerce and minored in Russian at a Long Island state college but never seems to have earned a degree. During vacations he climbed the lower alps in the more modest American mountain ranges. At loose ends, he joined the army to see the world and wound up, God knows why, toiling for military intelligence, where he focused on anticommunist dissidents in the satellite states of Eastern Europe. Do I have that right, Martin? Ah, here's something positively intriguing. When he was younger he worked in the private sector with explosives—"

Maggie Poole turned to Martin. "What *précisément* did you do with explosives?"

Martin rocked his chair off the wall onto its four legs. "It was a summer job, really. I worked for a construction company demolishing old buildings that were going to be replaced, then blasting through bedrock to make way for the subbasement garages. I was the guy who shouted through a bullhorn for everyone to clear the area."

"But do you know anything about dynamite?"

"I picked up a bit here and a bit there hanging around the dynamiters. I bought some books and studied the subject. By the end of the summer I had my own blasting license."

"Did you fabricate dynamite or just light the fuses?"

"Either, or. When I first came to work for the Company," Martin said, "I spent a month or two making letter bombs, then I got promoted to rigging portable phones so that we could detonate them from a distance. I also worked with pentaerythritol tetranitrate, which you know as PETN, an explosive of choice for terrorists. You can mix it with latex to give it plasticity and mold it to fit into anything—a telephone, a radio, a teddy bear, a cigar. You get a big bang out of relatively small amounts of PETN, and in the absence of a detonator, it's extremely stable. PETN isn't readily available on the open market but anyone with a blasting license, which Martin Odum has, can obtain the ingredients for roughly twenty dollars the pound. The explosive, incidentally, can pass through any airport X-ray machine in operation today."

"Well, that opens up some intriguing possibilities," the chairman informed the others.

"He could have done a stint as an explosive specialist at a shale quarry in Colorado, then been fired for something or other—"

"Stealing PETN and selling it on the open market—"

"Sleeping with the boss's wife—"

"*Homosexualité*, even."

Martin piped up from the wall. "If you don't mind, I draw the line at having homosexuality in my legend."

"We'll figure out why he was fired later. What we have here is an Irish Catholic—"

"Lapsed. Don't forget he's lapsed."

"—a lapsed Irish Catholic who worked with explosives in the private sector."

"Only to be fired for an as yet undetermined offense."

"At which point he became a free-lance explosive *expert*."

"We may have a problem here," said the chairman, tapping a forefinger on one page of Martin Odum's 201 folder. "Our Martin Odum is circumcised. Dante Pippen, lapsed or not, is an Irish Catholic. How do we explain the fact that he's circumcised."

The committee kicked around several possibilities. It was Maggie Poole who invented a suitable fiction. "In the unlikely event the question should come up, he could say he was talked into it by his first American girlfriend, who thought she would have less chance of catching a venereal disease from him if he were circumcised. Pippen could say the operation was performed in a New York clinic. It shouldn't be too difficult to plant a medical record at a clinic to backstop the story."

"Moving on, could he have been a member, at one point, of the IRA?"

"An IRA dynamiter! Now that's creative. It's not something the Russians or East Europeans could verify because the IRA is more secretive than the KGB."

"We could give him an arrest record in England. Arrested, questioned about an IRA bombing or two, released for lack of evidence."

"We could even plant small items in the press about the arrests."

"We are mining a rich vein," declared the chairman, his eyes bulging with enthusiasm. "What do you think, Martin?"

"I like it," Martin said from his seat. "Crystal Quest will like it, too. Dante Pippen is exactly the kind of legend that will open doors."

1989: DANTE PIPPEN SEES THE MILKY WAY IN A NEW LIGHT

WHEN THE BATTERED FORD REACHED THE FERTILE RIFT KNOWN as the Bekaa Valley, the Palestinians knotted a blindfold over Dante's eyes. Twenty minutes later the two-car motorcade passed through a gate in a perimeter fence and pulled to a stop at the edge of an abandoned quarry. The Palestinians tugged Dante from the back seat and guided him through the narrow dirt streets to the mosque on the edge of a Lebanese village. In the antechamber, his shoes and the blindfold were removed and he was led to a threadbare prayer carpet near the altar and motioned to sit. Ten minutes later the imam slipped in through a latticed side door. A corpulent man who moved, as heavy men often do, with surprising suppleness, he settled onto the carpet facing Dante. Arranging the folds of his flowing white robe like a Noh actor preoccupied with his image, he produced a string of jade worry beads and began working them through the stubby fingers of his left hand. In his early forties, with a crew cut and a neatly trimmed beard, the imam rocked back and forth in prayer for several moments. Finally he raised his eyes and, speaking English with a crisp British accent, announced, "I am Dr. Izzat al-Karim."

"I suspect you know who I am," Dante replied.

The corners of the imam's mouth curled into a pudgy grin. "Indeed I do. You are the IRA dynamiter we have heard so much about. I may say that your reputation precedes you—"

Dante dismissed the compliment with a wave of his hand. "So does your shadow when the sun is behind you."

The imam's jowls quivered in silent laughter. He held out a pack of Iranian Bahman cigarettes, offering one to his visitor.

"I have stopped smoking," Dante informed his host.

"Ah, if only I could follow your example," the imam said with a sigh. He tapped one of the thin cigarettes against the metal tray on a low table to tamp down the tobacco and slipped it between his lips. Using a Zippo lighter with a picture of Muhammad Ali on it, he lit the cigarette and slowly exhaled. "I envy you your strength of character. What was the secret that enabled you to give up cigarettes?"

"I convinced myself to become a different person, so to speak," Dante explained. "One day I was smoking two tins of Ganaesh Beedies a day. When I woke up the next morning I was someone else. And this someone else was a nonsmoker."

The imam let this sink in. "I wear the black turban of the sayyid, which marks me as a descendant of the Prophet Muhammad and his cousin Ali. I have two wives and I am about to take a third. Many people—my wives, my children, my fighters—count on me. It would be awkward for everyone if I were to become someone else."

"If I had as many wives as you," Dante remarked, "I'd probably start smoking again."

"Whether you smoke or abstain," the imam replied, his voice as soft as the cooing of a pigeon, "you will only live as long as God gives you to live. In any case, longevity is not what inspires a religious man like myself."

"What does inspire a religious man like yourself?" Dante heard himself ask, though he knew the answer; Benny Sapir, the Mossad spy master who had briefed Dante Pippen in a Washington safe house before the mission, had even imitated the imam's voice delivering stock answers to religious questions.

"The thought of the angel Gabriel whispering the verses of the Holy Koran into the ear of the Prophet inspires me," the imam was saying. "Muhammad's description, in what you call *The Book of the Ladder* and we call *The Miraj*, of his ascent to the nine circles of heaven and his descent into hell, guided by the angel Gabriel, keeps me up nights. The Creator, the Maker, the All-Merciful, the All-Compassionate, the All-Sublime, the All-Mighty inspires me. The one true God inspires me. Allah inspires me. The thought of spreading His word to the infidel, and killing those who do not accept it, inspires me." He held his cigarette parallel to his lips and studied it. "And what is it that inspires you, Mr. Pippen?"

Dante grinned. "The money your organization deposited in my account in the Cayman Islands inspires me, Dr. al-Karim. The prospect of monthly installments, paid in exchange for services rendered, inspires me. No need to shake your head in disapproval. It comes as no surprise to me that you find our several inspirations discordant, yours, of course, being the nobler of the two, and mine, by far the more decadent. Since I don't believe in your God, or any God, for that matter—I am what you would call a very lapsed Catholic—I think that your particular inspiration is as ephemeral as the contrails I saw on my drive down from Beirut. One moment they were there, sharp and precise, each with a silver Israeli jet fighter streaking through the crystal Lebanese sky at the cusp, the next they were thickening and drifting and eventually dissipating in the high winds."

The imam considered this. "I can see you are not a timid man, Mr. Pippen. You speak your mind. A Muslim who permitted himself to say what you have said would be putting his limbs, perhaps even his life, in jeopardy. But we must make allowances for a *very* lapsed Catholic, especially one who has come all this way to teach our fedayeen how to devise bombs to blow up the Isra'ili occupiers of Lebanon and Palestine." He leaned toward Dante. "Our representative in Paris who recruited you said you were born in an Irish town with the curious name of Castletownbere."

Dante nodded. "It's a smudge on the map on the southern coast of the Beara Peninsula in County Cork. Fishing port. I worked on one of the salmon trawlers before I went off to seek my fortune where the streets are paved with gold."

"And were they paved with gold, Mr. Pippen?"

Dante laughed under his breath. "At least they were paved, which is more than you can say for some parts of the Beara Peninsula. Or the Bekaa Valley, for that matter."

"Am I correct in thinking there was an expensive restaurant in Castletownbere called The Warehouse?"

"There was a pricy restaurant for the occasional tourist, but it wasn't named The Warehouse. It was called The Bank because it was in the old bank, one flight up on Main Street. Still had the bank vault in the back when I was there. I seem to remember a Mary McCullagh ran it in the sixties. I went to school with one of her daughters, a pretty little thing we called Deidre of the Sorrows because she made so many of us sorry when we discovered we couldn't sweet talk her into bed."

"You were arrested by Scotland Yard following the explosion of a bomb on a bus near Bush House, the BBC building in London."

"Is that a question or a statement of fact?"

"A statement of fact that I'd like you to corroborate, Mr. Pippen."

"I was killing time in London when the bus blew," Dante said, his eyes blinking innocently. "The coppers barged into a licensed tabernacle and more or less picked up anyone who spoke the King's English with an Irish accent. They were obliged to release me after forty-eight hours for want of evidence. Bloody bastards never even apologized."

"Did you blow up the bus, Mr. Pippen?"

"I did not. But the two who did learned which side was up from yours truly."

The imam smiled thinly. Glancing at a wall clock with a silhouette of Ayatollah Khomeini on its face, he pushed himself to his feet and started to leave. At the door, he turned back. "I seldom have the chance to speak with an Occidental nonbeliever, Mr. Pippen, especially one who is not in awe of me. Talking with you is going to be an enlightening experience. One must know the enemy before one can defeat him. I invite you to visit me in my study after your afternoon classes, every day of the week except Friday. I will offer you mint tea and honey cakes, you can reciprocate by offering me insights into the secular mentality."

"The pleasure will—" Dante started to say but the imam had already vanished through the latticed door, which squeaked back and forth on its hinges, evidence of his passage.

Dante was taken to his living quarters, a room in the back of one of the low brick houses with flat roofs at the edge of the village beyond the perimeter of the Hezbollah camp. At sunup an elderly woman with a veil over the lower part of her face appeared with what passed for breakfast: a steaming pot of green tea to wash down the chalk-dry biscuits covered with an oily paste made from crushed olives. Dante's bodyguard, who trailed after him everywhere, including to the outhouse, led him down the dirt path to the lip of the quarry. Several young boys in dusty striped robes were already tossing stones at a troop of goats to steer them away from the perimeter fence and up a nearby slope. A yellow Hezbollah flag decorated with a hand holding aloft a rifle flapped from the pole atop the brick building where the explosives and the fuses were stored. High overhead the contrails of Israeli jets on their dawn patrols crisscrossed the sky. Dante's students, nineteen fedayeen, all in their late teens or early twenties and wearing identical baggy khaki trousers and blouses and thick web belts under their robes, waited at the bottom of the quarry. An older man with an orange and white kaffiyah draped over his shoulders squatted on the rocky ground, setting out cartons filled with pentaerythritol tetranitrate, commonly known as PETN, along with latex, coils of electric wire and plungers powered by automobile batteries. "I, Abdullah, will translate for you," the man informed Dante when he reached the floor of the quarry. "Please to speak slow in consideration of my English, which is curdled like last week's goat milk."

Dante inspected the cartons, then kicked at the coils of wire and the plungers. "We will need modern detonators that can be tripped by radio-controlled devices from distant locations," he informed Abdullah.

"How far will be the distance to these locations?" Abdullah inquired.

Dante pointed to the goats disappearing over the top of the slope. "We will mix the PETN and the latex in a manner that I will demonstrate," he said, "and conceal the charges here in the quarry. Then we will climb to the top of that hill and detonate the explosives from there." Dante pointed to the hill and imitated the boom of the explosion. Abdullah translated for the fedayeen and they all turned to stare at the hill. They talked excitedly among themselves, then looked at their instructor, nodding respectfully at his expertise.

During the first several sessions, Dante concentrated on the

PETN and the latex, showing the Hezbollah fighters how to mix the two and then mold the clay-like explosive to fit any receptacle. He filled a portable radio with explosives one day, then turned it on to demonstrate that it still functioned, which was important if you wanted to get the radio past military checkpoints or airport security. Another time he packed the plastique into one of those newfangled satellite telephones and explained, with Abdullah translating, the advantages: If it was done correctly, you could actually telephone the target and identify his voice before setting off the charge and decapitating him.

In the beginning, the young men were afraid to touch the explosive charges until they saw Dante juggling a clump of it from one hand to the other to demonstrate how stable it was. Abdullah, meanwhile, took Dante's hand-written list to Dr. al-Karim and then set off for Beirut in the Ford with a purse-ful of the imam's precious American dollars to purchase the battery-operated transmitters and receivers that would go into the construction of remote detonators.

The first afternoon that Dante turned up in Dr. al-Karim's study, he found the imam seated well back from a table, leaning over his abundant stomach and typing away with two fingers on an IBM electric typewriter. From behind the building came the low hum of the gasoline-powered generator. "*Assalamu aleikum*—Peace be upon you. I would offer you a cigarette if you smoked cigarettes," the imam said, swiveling to face his visitor, waving him toward a wooden kitchen chair. "Can I assume you do not mind if I light up?"

"Be my guest."

The imam appeared to be puzzled. "How is it possible for me to be your guest in *my* house?"

"It was a meaningless figure of speech," Dante conceded.

"I have observed that Americans often come up with meaningless cliches when they do not know what to say."

"I won't make the same mistake twice."

The woman who brought Dante breakfast appeared from the next room and set out plates filled with small honey-coated cakes and two glasses filled with mint leaves and boiling water. Nibbling on

one of cakes as he waited for the mint tea to cool, Dante took in the
Spartan furnishings of the imam's study: framed photographs of the
training camp's fedayeen graduating classes (slightly askew, as if
someone had dusted them and left them askew to show they'd been
cleaned), a poster depicting the golden-domed Mosque of Omar in
Jerusalem tacked to one wall, the Kalashnikov in a corner with a clip
in it and a spare clip taped to the stock, the glass bowl on a low table
with a single goldfish circling round and round as if it were looking
for the exit, the copies of *Newsweek* stacked on the floor near the
door. Dr. al-Karim scraped his chair around the table and, settling his
bulk onto it facing his guest, warmed both his hands on the glass of
mint tea.

Speaking softly, selecting his words carefully, the imam said:
"There was a time when people held me in high esteem."

"Judging from what I've seen, they still do."

"How long, Mr. Pippen, will this last? How long do you think
one can go on preaching that the destruction of your principal
enemy is inevitable without it transpiring; without losing the credibility that is indispensable to continue as the spiritual leader of a
community? This is the predicament I find myself in. I must continue to hold out hope that our sacrifices will be rewarded not only
with martyrdom but with certain victory over the Isra'ili occupiers
of Lebanon and Palestine, and the Jews who are conspiring to take
over the world. But in time even the simplest of the fedayeen, sent
to combat the enemy, observes through binoculars that the Isra'ilis
still occupy their sandbagged fortresses in the south of Lebanon,
that the wakes of their patrol boats still crisscross the waters off our
coast, that the contrails of their jet aircraft still stain the sky over
our heads."

"Do *you* believe victory is inevitable?" Dante asked.

"I am convinced that the Jews will one day be seen, like the
Christian Crusaders before them, as a footnote in the long flow of
Arab history. This is written. Will it happen in my lifetime? Will it
happen in the lifetime of my children?" Dr. al-Karim sipped at the tea,
then, licking his lips to savor the taste of the mint, he leaned forward.
"I can buy time, Mr. Pippen, if your talents provide me with some
incremental measure of success. Our Hezbollah fighters, armed with

conventional weapons, are unable to inflict casualties on the better armed Isra'ili soldiers occupying the zone in southern Lebanon. We attack them with mortars or artillery, fired from the heart of some Lebanese village so that the Isra'ilis are unable to riposte. Very occasionally, we manage to wound or kill one or two of them. For every one we kill, we lose twenty or thirty fedayeen when our enemies, with remarkably accurate intelligence, descend from their fortresses to raid our bases here in the Bekaa Valley, or closer to the front lines. They always seem to know where we are, and in what strength." The imam shook his head. "We are like waves lapping against boulders on a shore—I cannot recruit and train and send into combat fighters by telling them that the boulders will, in a century or two, be washed smooth and reduced in size."

"I suppose that's why you retained my services." Dante said.

"Is it true that you can mold your explosives to fit almost any receptacle?"

"Absolutely."

"And detonate them from a great distance by radio command, as opposed to electrical wires stretched along the ground?"

Dante nodded emphatically. "Hard wire on the ground is more reliable, but radio-detonated explosions are more creative."

"Precisely how do radio-detonated explosions work?"

"You need a transmitter—a cordless phone, a wireless intercom, a radio paging system—and a receiver, both tuned to the same frequency. The transmitter sends not just a signal but also an audio tone—known as electronic pulses—which are modulated by the transmitter and demodulated by the receiver. The receiver picks up the transmission, demodulates the audio tone, closes the electric circuit, which sends current to the blasting cap which, in turn, detonates the explosive charge."

"With your expertise, could we disguise the explosives in what appears to be ordinary roadside rocks and explode them from, say, a hilltop a kilometer away as an Isra'ili patrol passes?"

"Child's play," Dante declared.

The imam slapped his knee in elation. "God willing, we will bloody the Isra'ilis, Mr. Pippen. God willing, the waves lapping against the shore will demolish the boulders in my lifetime. And when we have finished with the near enemy, we will turn our attention to the distant enemy."

"The Israelis are obviously the near enemy," Dante said. "But who is the distant enemy?"

Dr. al-Karim looked Dante in the eye. "Why, you, Mr. Pippen, are the distant enemy. You and your American civilization which considers smoking dangerous for the health while everything else—extramarital sex, pornography, carnal secularism, materialism—is permissible. The Isra'ilis are an outpost of your corrupt civilization. The Jews are your surrogates, dispatched to steal our land and colonize our countries and demoralize our souls and humiliate our religion. When we have defeated them we will turn our attention to the ultimate enemy."

"I can see how you might attack what you call the near enemy," Dante replied. "But how will you war against a distant enemy who can obliterate you the way he would a mosquito caught in flagrante delicto on the back of his wrist?"

The imam sat back in his chair, a knowing smile flickering on his pudgy face. "We will use the vast amounts of money we earn from selling you petrol for your gas-guzzling cars to hire the talents of people like you, Mr. Pippen. American heads are already poisoned by Hollywood films and glossy magazines such as *Playboy* or *Hustler*. We will poison their bodies. We will hijack their planes and crash them into their buildings. We will construct, with your help, the poor man's bomb—valises filled with germs or chemicals—and explode it in their cities."

Dante reached for the glass of mint tea and touched his lips to it. "I'd best be immigrating back to Ireland, then," he said lightly.

"I can see that you do not take what I say seriously. No matter." The imam pushed back his sleeve, glanced at his wristwatch and rose to his feet. "You will sleep fitfully tonight as you turn over in your mind what I have told you. Questions will occur to you. I invite you to come back tomorrow and pose them, Mr. Pippen. God willing, we will pick up the conversation where we left it off."

Dante stood up. "Yes. I will return. Thank you."

* * *

In the days that followed, Dante used what Abdullah had brought from Beirut to show his students how to assemble remote control detonators and set off explosive charges in the quarry from the top of the nearby hill. When Dr. al-Karim's people supplied the first molded rock made out of plaster of paris, Dante filled it with PETN and rigged a remote detonator. The students set the molded rock down at the side of the road and tethered a lame goat ten meters from it. Then everyone trooped up the hill. The imam himself, hearing of the experiment, showed up at the lip of the quarry to watch. Dante waved to him and Dr. al-Karim, surrounded by four bodyguards, raised a palm in salute. One of the young fedayeen wired the small transmitter to a car battery. Everyone turned to stare at the goat at the bottom of the quarry. "Okay, Abdullah," Dante said. "Let her rip." Reaching for the small radio, Abdullah rotated the switch until there was an audible click and then depressed it. Far below, in the quarry, a dry cough of a blast stirred up a swell of dust. When it cleared, the goat had vanished. Where it had stood, the ground was saturated with blood and entrails.

"God is great," Abdullah murmured.

"PETN is greater," Dante remarked.

When Dante entered the imam's study that afternoon, Dr. al-Karim came bounding around the desk to congratulate him. "You have earned your wages, Mr. Pippen," he said, throwing a pulpy arm over Dante's shoulder. "My fighters are eager to use your remote control device against the Jews."

The two settled onto kitchen chairs. Dr. al-Karim produced his jade beads and began threading them through his fingers with great dexterity as Dante explained that he needed another ten days, no more, no less, to make the imam's fedayeen ready for combat.

"We have waited this long," the imam said. "Another ten days will not inconvenience us."

The conversation drifted on to the two-year-old Syrian occupation of parts of Lebanon; the month before Dante's arrival, Damascus had installed surface-to-air missiles in the Bekaa, a move that Hezbollah did not appreciate since it was bound to attract Isra'ili attention to the valley. Dr. al-Karim wanted to know whether President Bush would put pressure on the Isra'ilis to pull back from the buffer zone in southern Lebanon. Dante said he was far from being an expert in such matters, but he doubted it. He, in turn, wondered whether the Iranians would put pressure on the Syrians to end their virtual occupation of Lebanon now that the civil war had quieted down. The imam replied that the death the week before of Iran's Ayatollah Khomeini had created a vacuum in the Islamic world and predicted that it would be a long time before the Shiites found someone with enough charisma to take his place. Dante asked jokingly if the imam aspired to the job. Dr. al-Karim took the question seriously. He stopped manipulating his worry beads and placed a finger along the side of a nostril. "I aspire to serve God and lead my people to victory over the Jews," he said. "Nothing more."

"Tell me something, Dr. al-Karim—" Dante hesitated.

The imam's head bobbed. "Only ask, Mr. Pippen."

"I notice that you often speak of the Jews, not the Israelis. I'm curious to know if Hezbollah isn't confusing the two. What I'm getting at is this: Are you anti-Israeli or anti-Jewish?"

"In as much as Isra'il is an enemy state," the imam replied without hesitation, "we are, of course, anti-Isra'ili." He started manipulating his worry beads again. "But make no mistake, we are also anti-Jewish. Our common history goes back to the Prophet Muhammad. The Jews never recognized the legitimacy of Islam as the true religion, and the Koran as the word of God."

"Your critics say this attitude more or less puts you in the same boat as Adolf Hitler."

The imam shook his head vigorously. "Not at all, Mr. Pippen. Our critics miss an essential point. Hitler was anti-Semite. There are enormous differences between being anti-Jewish and anti-Semite."

"I'm afraid you're losing me . . ."

"Anti-Semites, Mr. Pippen, believe that once a Jew, always a Jew. For Hitler, even a Jew who converted to Christianity remained a Jew. It follows that for the Nazis in particular and for anti-Semites in general, there was no solution except what they called the Final Solution, namely the extermination of the Jews. Being anti-Jewish, on the other hand, implies that there is a solution short of extermination; a way for Jews to save themselves from extermination."

"And what might that be?"

"The Jew can convert to Islam, at which point Islam will have no quarrel with him."

"I see."

"What do you see, Mr. Pippen?"

"I see that I shouldn't have started this conversation in the first place. I am a hired gun. You pay me for services rendered, not my opinions on your opinions."

"Quite right, quite right. Though if my answers don't interest you, I will admit to you that your questions interest me."

Abdullah materialized outside the window, tapping a fingernail against a pane. When the imam went over to the window, Abdullah pointed to the car winding its way up the dirt road toward the Hezbollah camp.

"I had almost forgotten," Dr. al-Karim said, turning back to Dante. "I am expecting a visitor. The Syrian commander in the Bekaa stops by every once in awhile to see what we are up to. He will stay through prayers and the evening meal tomorrow. It might be wise if you keep out of sight, as I have not informed him of your presence and the Syrians do not take kindly to foreigners in the valley."

"How about if I disappear in the direction of Beirut," Dante asked. "It's been almost three weeks since I arrived. As tomorrow is Friday and my students will be in the mosque praying, I was going to ask you for a day off."

"And what will you do on this day off of yours?"

"In my entire life I have never gone this long without a swill of beer. I will take my warm body off to a bar and drink a barrel of it."

"Why not? Beirut has quieted down. And you have earned a day of rest. I will send Abdullah and one of my bodyguards to keep you out of harm's way."

"An Irishman does not go to a licensed tabernacle to keep out of harm's way, Dr. al-Karim."

"Nevertheless, out of harm's way is where we must keep you until you have completed your work here. What you do after that is your affair."

* * *

The following afternoon the battered Ford that had transported Dante to the Bekaa three weeks earlier threaded its way through a tangle of secondary roads in the direction of Beirut. The bodyguard, sporting baggy khakis and cradling a Kalashnikov with notches cut into the stock for each of his kills, sat up front bantering in Arabic with the driver, a coal-black Saudi with matted dreadlocks. Dante, wearing a coarse brown Bedouin burnoose, a black-and-white checkered kaffiyah and dark sunglasses, shared the backseat with Abdullah, who climbed out of the car at each Syrian checkpoint to wave, with an imperious snap of the wrist, the letter bearing Dr. al-Karim's seal and signature in the face of the soldiers who were (so Abdullah swore) completely illiterate. Dante, lost in thought, stared through his reflection in the window, barely noticing the dusty villages with the swarms of barefoot boys playing soccer in the unpaved streets, the crowded open-air souks with giant dish antennas for sale on one side and donkeys and camels tethered to a nearby fence, the tiled butcher shops with young boys fanning the flies off the carcasses hanging from hooks. At the outskirts of Beirut, the Ford passed through the first of the militia barricades but (as Abdullah explained in halting English) the pimply gunmen there, though literate, were more interested in the twenty-dollar bills folded into Dr. al-Karim's letter than the letter itself or the passengers in the car.

With the presence of the Syrian army, the warring factions that had slaughtered each other in the streets of Beirut since the mid 1970s had more or less gone to ground; Muslim and Christian emissaries were rumored to be meeting at Taif, in Saudi Arabia, to formalize the cease-fire accord but armed militias still patrolled the city, which sprawled like a mutilated virago at the edge of the Mediterranean, its shell-ridden buildings mute testimony to the brutal fifteen-year civil war. As the sun dipped into the sea and darkness enveloped Beirut, the whetted crack of distant gunfire reverberated through the city; Abdullah, visibly edgy, muttered something about old scores being settled before the formal cease-fire came into effect. Careful not to stray from the Muslim-controlled areas of Beirut, he guided the driver to the port area and deposited Dante on a corner opposite the burnt-out shell of a neighborhood mosque. A narrow street angled off downhill toward the docks. "We will wait for you here," Abdullah told Dante. "Please to be returned by the hour of ten so we can be returned to the camp by the midnight."

On the narrow street, broken neon lights sizzled over a handful of bars that catered to the seamen from the ships docked at the quays or tied to giant buoys in the harbor. Waving cheerfully at his keepers, Dante skipped down the sidewalk and, ducking to get under a broken neon tube dangling from its electric cord, shouldered past the thick rug that served as a door into the first bar, set up in a mercantile building that had been gutted by a direct hit from a mortar. The charred rafters that held up the jury-rigged sloping roof had been whitewashed, but they still stank from the fire. Dante found a place at the makeshift bar between two Turkish sailors holding each other up and a Portuguese purser wearing a rumpled blue uniform.

"So now, what will your pleasure be?" the barman called, a distinct Irish lilt to his gruff voice.

Dante punched a hole in the cigarette smoke that obscured his view and spoke through it. "Beer and lots of it," he called back, "the warmer the better."

The bartender, a thick man with a shock of tousled rusty hair spilling over his eyes and a priest's white shirt buttoned up to his neck, plucked a large bottle of Bulgarian beer from a carton at his feet. He flicked off the metal cap with a church key, stopped the throat of the bottle with the ball of his thumb and shook the beer to put some life into it, then set it on the counter in front of Dante. "And will your lordship be wanting a mug to drink from?" he inquired with a laugh.

"Do you charge for it?" Dante asked.

"Oh, for Christ's sake, why would we want to do that? You're paying such an outrageous price for the goddamned beer, we supply the mug at no extra cost to yourself." He slid a freshly washed mug down the bar to Dante. "Now what ship did you say you were off?"

"I didn't say," Dante shot back. "It's the H.M.S. *Pinafore*."

The smile froze on the bartender's face. "H.M.S. *Pinafore*, did you say?"

Dante filled the mug, swiped away the foam with the back of a forefinger and, tilting back his head, drank off the beer in a long gulping swallow. "Ah, that surely transforms the way a man sees the world," he announced, starting to fill the mug again. "H.M.S. *Pinafore.* That's what I said."

Accepting this with a brisk nod, the bartender made his way to the far end of the bar and, blocking one ear with the tip of a finger, spoke into a telephone. Dante was halfway through his second bottle of Bulgarian beer when the woman appeared at the top of the broken wooden steps that led to what was left of the offices on the upper floor of the mercantile building. A sailor buttoning his fly trailed behind her. The woman, wisps of long dark hair falling across a face disfigured by smallpox scars, was wearing a tight skirt slit high on one thigh and a gauzy blouse through which her breasts were as visible as they would be if she'd been caught walking naked through a morning haze. All conversation ceased as she came across the room, her high heels drumming on the wooden floorboards. She stopped to take her bearings, spotted Dante and installed herself at the bar next to him.

"Will you buy me a whiskey?" she demanded in a throaty murmur.

"I'd be a horse's ass not to," Dante replied cheerfully, and he held up a finger to get the bartender's eye and pointed to the woman. "Whiskey for my future friend."

"Chivas Regal," the woman instructed the bartender. "A double."

Dante authorized the double with a nod when the bartender looked at him for confirmation, then turned to scrutinize the woman the way he'd been taught to look at people he might one day have to pick out of a counterintelligence scrapbook. As usual he had difficulty figuring out her age. She was Arab, that much was evident despite the thick eyeliner and the splash of bright red on her lips, and probably in her forties, but exactly where he didn't know. It occurred to him that she must be Christian, since Muslims would kill their women before they'd let them work as prostitutes.

"So what would be your name, darling?" Dante asked.

She absently combed the fingers of one hand through her hair, brushing it away from her face; two large silver hoop earrings caught the light and shimmered. "I am Djamillah," she announced. "What is your name?"

Dante took a long swig of beer. "You can call me Irish."

"From the look of you, you have been at sea for a while."

"What makes you think that?"

"You're dying of thirst, I can see that from the way you gulped down that disgusting Bulgarian beer. What else are you dying of, Irish?"

Dante glanced at the bartender, rinsing glasses in a sink just out of earshot. "Well, now, Djamillah, to tell you the God awful truth, I haven't been laid in a month of Sundays. Is that a predicament you could remedy?"

The Portuguese purser, sitting with his back to Dante, could be heard snickering under his breath. Djamillah was unfazed. "You are a direct man," she said. "The answer to your question, Irish, is: I could."

"How much would it set me back?"

"Fifty dollars U.S. or the equivalent in a European currency. I don't deal in local money."

"Bottoms up," Dante said. He clicked glasses with her and downed what was left in the mug, grabbed the half-empty bottle of beer by the throat (in case he needed a weapon) and followed her across the room to the stairs. At the top of the stairs she pushed open a wooden door and led Dante into what must have once been the head office of the mercantile company. There was a large desk covered in glass with photographs of children flattened under it near the boarded-over oval windows, and an enormous leather couch under a torn painting depicting Napoleon's defeat at Acre. A dozen sealed cartons without markings were stacked against one wall. Locking the door behind them, Djamillah settled onto the couch and, reaching through a torn seam into the cushion, produced a folder filled with eight-by-ten aerial photographs. Dante, settling down alongside her, used his handkerchief to grip the photographs and examined them one by one. "These must have been taken from high altitude," he remarked. "The resolution is excellent. They'll do nicely."

The woman offered Dante a felt-tipped pen and he began to draw arrows to various buildings in the camp and label them. "The recruits, nineteen fedayeen in all, live in these two low buildings inside the perimeter fence," he said. "Explosives and fuses are stored in this small brick building with the Hezbollah flag on the roof. Dr. al-Karim lives and works in the house behind the mosque. It is easily the largest in the village so your people won't have a problem identifying it. I don't know where he sleeps but his office looks out at the mosque so it must

be—" he drew another arrow and labelled it "K's office"—"here. I
bunk in with a family in this house in the village."

"What kind of security do they have at night?"

"I've strolled around the camp after dark several times—they
have a roadblock, manned by two recruits and one of the instructors, stationed here where the road curves uphill to the village and
the camp. There's a bunker with a heavy machine gun on top of the
hill over the quarry which is manned during the day. I've never been
able to get up there at night because the gate in the perimeter
fence is locked and I didn't want to raise suspicions by asking for
the key."

"We must assume it is manned at night. They'd be fools not to.
The machine gun must be a priority target. What kind of communications do they have?"

"Don't know really. Never saw the radio shack, or a radio for that
matter. Spotted what looked like high frequency antennas on the top
of the minaret of the mosque, so whatever they have must be somewhere around there."

"We don't want to bomb a mosque, so we'll have to take that out
by hand. Does Dr. al-Karim have a satellite phone?"

"Never saw one but that doesn't mean he doesn't have one."

"When will this round of training be finished."

"I've told Dr. al-Karim I needed ten more days."

"What happens then?"

"The graduating class goes off to the front to kill Israeli soldiers
occupying the buffer zone in Lebanon. And a freshman class turns up
to start a new cycle of training."

"How many instructors and staff are in the camp?"

"Including transportation people, including the experts on small
arms and martial arts, including Dr. al-Karim's personal bodyguards,
four that I've seen, I'd say roughly eighteen to twenty."

Djamillah went over the photographs again, double checking the
distances between buildings, the location of the gate in the perimeter
fence, identifying the footpaths that crisscrossed the village and the
Hezbollah camp. She produced a military map of the Bekaa to see
what other forces Hezbollah might have in the general vicinity of the
camp. "When the raid begins, you must somehow get to this spot"—

she pointed to a well between the village and the Hezbollah camp. She handed Dante a white silk bandanna and he stuffed it into the pocket of his trousers. "Wear this around your neck so you can be easily identified."

"How will I know when to expect the raid?"

"Exactly six hours before, two Israeli M-16s will fly by at an altitude high enough to leave contrails. They'll come from north to south. When they are directly above the camp they will make ninety degree turns to the west."

Djamillah slipped the photographs and the map back into the folder and wedged it into the seam of the cushion.

"Looks as if we've more or less covered the essentials," Dante remarked.

"Not quite." She stood up and began matter of factly stripping off her clothing; it was the first time in his life Dante had seen a woman undress when the act didn't seem sensual. "You are supposed to be up here having sex with me. I think it would be prudent for you to be able to describe my clothing and my body." She removed the blouse and the skirt and her underpants. "I have a small scar on the inside of my thigh, here. My pubic hair is trimmed for a bikini. I have a faded tattoo of a night moth under my right breast. And on my left arm you will see the scars of a smallpox vaccination that didn't prevent me from getting smallpox, which accounts for the pockmarks on my face. When we came up here I locked the door and you put fifty dollars—two twenties and a ten—on the desk and weighed them down with the shell casing that's on the floor over there. We both took off our clothing. You asked me to suck you—that was the expression you used—but I said I don't do that. You stripped and sat down on the couch and I gave you a hand job and when you were erect I slipped on a condom and came on top of you. Please make note of the fact that I make love with my shoes on." She began to dress again. "Now it's your turn to strip, Irish, so that I can describe your body if I need to. Why do you hesitate? You are a professional. This is a matter of tradecraft."

Dante shrugged and stood up and lowered his trousers. "As you can see, I am circumcised. My first American girlfriend talked me into having it done—she seemed to think there was less chance of her catching some venereal disease from me if I were circumcised."

"Circumcised and well endowed, as they say. Do you have any scars?"

"Physical or mental?"

She didn't think he was humorous. "I do not psychoanalyze my clients, I only fuck them."

"No scars," he said dryly.

She inspected his body from foot to head, and his clothing, then gestured for him to turn around. "You can put your clothes back on," she finally said. She walked him to the door. "You are in a dangerous business, Irish."

"I am addicted to fear," he murmured. "I require a daily fix."

"I do not believe you. If you did not believe in something you would not be here." She offered her hand. "I admire your courage."

He gripped her hand and held it for a moment. "And I am dazzled by yours. An Arab who risks—"

She tugged her hand free. "I am not an Arab," she said fiercely. "I am a Lebanese Alawite."

"And what the hell is an Alawite?"

"We're a sliver of a people lost in a sea of Arab Muslims who consider us heretics and detest us. We had a state once—it was under the French Mandate when the Ottoman Empire broke up after the First World War. The Alawite state was called Latakia; my grandfather was a minister in the government. In 1937, against our will, Latakia became part of Syria. My grandfather was assassinated for opposing this. These days most of the Lebanese Alawites side with the Christians against the Muslims in the civil war. Our goal is to crush the Muslims—and this includes Hezbollah—in the hope of returning Lebanon to Christian rule. Our dream is to reestablish an Alawite state, a new Latakia on the Levantine shore washed by the Mediterranean."

"I wish you good luck," Dante said with elaborate formality. "What is it that Alawites believe that Muslims don't?"

"Now is not the moment for such discussions—"

"You are a professional. This is a matter of tradecraft. I might be asked what we talked about after we had sex."

Djamillah almost smiled. "It is our belief that the Milky Way is made up of the deified souls of Alawites who rose to heaven."

"For the rest of my life I shall think of you when I look at the Milky Way," he announced.

She unlocked the door and stepped aside. "In another incarnation," she remarked solemnly, "it would have been agreeable to make love with you."

"Maybe when all this is over—"

This time Djamillah did smile. "All this," she said bitterly, "will never be over."

* * *

Two days after his return from Beirut, Dante was squatting in the dirt at the bottom of the quarry, demonstrating to his nineteen apprentice bombers how to fill the body cavity of a dead dog with PETN, when there was a commotion at the gate of the perimeter fence above them. Several of Dr. al-Karim's personal guards were tugging aside the razor wire. Horns blaring, two cars and a pick-up truck roared into the camp and pulled up in a swirl of dust. As the dust settled, gunmen wearing the distinctive checkered Hezbollah kaffiyah could be seen dragging someone wearing loose fitting striped pajamas and a hood over the head from the second car. Women from the village emerged from their homes and began filling the air with ululations of triumph. Lifting the hem of his burnoose, Abdullah trotted up the path until he was within earshot of the gunmen who had stayed behind to guard the vehicles and called out to them. One shouted an answer to his question and fired a clip from his Kalashnikov into the air. Abdullah turned back toward the quarry and, cupping his hands around his mouth, yelled, "God is great. They have captured an Isra'ili spy."

The apprentice bombers started talking excitedly among themselves. Dante, suddenly edgy, barked at them to pay attention to the demonstration. The students reacted to the tone of his voice even before Abdullah, scampering back down to the group, translated the words. Dante, wearing a surgical glove on his right hand, finished pulling the intestines through the slit he'd made in the dog's stomach and began stuffing the packets of PETN wrapped in burlap, and then the radio-controlled detonator, into the cavity. Using a thick needle and a length of butcher's cord, he sewed up the slit with large stitches. Standing, peeling off the surgical glove, he addressed Abdullah. "Tell them to position the dead dog so that its stomach is facing away from the enemy when he approaches." One of the students raised his hand. Abdullah translated the question. "He says you, is a dead dog more suitable than the papier-mâché rocks we learned to plant at the side of the road?"

"Tell him the Greeks couldn't have used the Trojan horse trick twice," Dante said. "Tell him the same goes for the Israelis. They'll catch on very quickly to the fake rocks stuffed with explosives. So you need to invent other ruses. A dead dog lying in the middle of a road is so common that the Israeli jeeps will keep going. At which point—"

Dr. al-Karim appeared above them on the rim of the quarry. He raised a bullhorn and called, "Mr. Pippen, I would like a word with you, if you please."

Dante saluted lazily and started to climb the path. Halfway to the top he looked up and noticed that several of the Hezbollah gunmen had joined the imam. All of them had pulled their checkered kaffiyahs over their faces so that only their eyes were visible. Out of breath, Dante reached the top and approached Dr. al-Karim. Two of the gunmen slammed bullets into the chambers of their Kalashnikovs. The metallic sound caused Dante to stop in his tracks. He forced a light laugh through his lips. "Your warriors seem jittery today," he remarked. "What's going on?"

Without answering, Dr. al-Karim turned and stalked off toward his house. Two of the gunmen prodded Dante with the barrels of their rifles. He bristled. "You want me to follow him, all you have to do is ask. Politely."

He trailed after the imam to the large house next to the mosque. When he reached the back of the house he found the door to Dr. al-Karim's office ajar. One of the gunmen behind him gestured with his Kalashnikov. Shrugging, Dante kicked open the door with his toe and went in.

Time seemed to have stopped inside the room. Dr. al-Karim, his corpulent body frozen in the seat behind the desk, his eyes hardly blinking, stared at the Israeli spy, bound with strips of white masking tape to a straight-backed kitchen chair set in the middle of the floor. Muffled groans came from the prisoner's mouth under the black hood. Dante noticed the thinness of the prisoner's wrists and ankles and jumped to the conclusion that Hezbollah had arrested a teenage boy. The imam motioned for Dante to sit in the other straight-backed chair. Four of the gunmen took up positions along the wall behind him.

"Where did we leave off our last conversation?" Dr. al-Karim inquired stiffly.

"We were talking about the Greeks and Aristotle. You were condemning them for teaching that reason gives access to truth, as opposed to faith."

"Precisely. We know what we know because of our faith in Allah and His Prophet, who guide us to the right way, the only way. It may be seen as a transgression when a lapsed Catholic like you does not accept this; normally a believer such as myself should attempt to convert you or, failing at that, expel you." He glanced at the spy. "When one of our own turns his—or her—back on faith, it is a mortal sin, punishable by execution."

The imam muttered an order in Arabic. One of the gunmen came up behind the Israeli spy and tugged off the hood. Dante caught his breath. Patches of Djamillah's long dark hair were pasted to her scalp with dried blood. One of her eyes was swollen shut, her lips were badly cut, several front teeth were missing. A large hoop earring dangled from one lobe; the skin on the other lobe hung loose, the result of having had the earring wrenched off without first undoing it.

"You do not deny that you know her?" Dr. al-Karim said.

Dante had trouble speaking. "I know her in the carnal sense of the word," he finally replied, his voice barely audible. "Her name is Djamillah. She is the prostitute who worked the licensed tabernacle I visited in Beirut. She carted me off upstairs to what the Irish call the intensive care unit."

"Djamillah is a pseudonym. She claims she cannot remember her real name but she is obviously lying; she is protecting members of her family against retribution. She was passing herself off as a prostitute in order to spy for the Jews. Aerial photographs of several training camps, ours included, were discovered hidden in the room she used. Some of

the photographs had notations, in English, describing the camp layout. We suspect you may have provided her with these notations when
you visited the bar in Beirut."

A rasp of a whisper came from Djamillah's cracked lips; she spoke
slowly, struggling to pronounce certain consonants with her mouth
open. "I told the ones . . . ones who questioned me . . . the Irishman
was a client."

"Who, then, made the notations on the photographs?" demanded
the imam.

"The notations . . . were on the photographs when they . . . they
were delivered to me."

Dr. al-Karim nodded once. The gunman behind Djamillah slipped
two fingers through the hoop of the remaining earring and pulled
down hard on it. It severed the skin on the lobe and came free in a
spurt of blood. Djamillah opened her mouth to scream, but passed
out before the sound could emerge from her throat.

A pitcher of water was flung in her face. Her eyes twitched open
and the muted scream lodged at the back of her throat like a fish bone
exploded with savage force. Dante winced and turned away. Dr. al-
Karim came around the desk and planted himself in front of Dante.
"Who are you?" he demanded in a low growl.

"Pippen, Dante. Free-lance, free-minded, free-spirited explosive
expert of Irish origin, at your beck and call as long as you keep
depositing checks in my off-shore account."

The imam circled the prisoner, looking at her but talking to
Dante. "I would like to believe you are who you say, for your sake; for
mine, as well."

"Come on, now—she must have seen dozens, perhaps hundreds
of men in the room over the bar. Any one of them could have been
her contact."

"Were you intimate with her?"

"Yes."

"Does she have any distinguishing marks on her body?"

Dante described the small scar on the inside of her thigh, the
trimmed pubic hair, the vaccination scar on her left arm, or was it her
right—he wasn't sure. Ah, yes, there was also the faded tattoo of a night
moth under her right breast. Dr. al-Karim turned to the prisoner and,

gripping the loose fitting shirt at the buttons, ripped it away from her body. He gazed at the faded tattoo under her breast, then flung the shirt closed, tucking the loose fabric under the strips of white masking tape.

"How much did you pay her?" the imam asked.

Dante thought a moment. "Fifty dollars."

"What denomination bills?"

"Two twenties and a ten."

"You handed her two twenties and a ten?"

Dante shook his head. "I put the bills on the desk. I weighed them down with a shell casing."

"What was she wearing when you had sex with her?"

"Her shoes."

"What were you wearing?"

"A condom."

Dr. al-Karim watched Dane closely. "She, too, said you were wearing a condom—*on your circumcised penis*. I assume you can explain how an Irish Catholic from Castletownbere came to be circumcised?"

Dante rolled his eyes in frustration. "Of course I can explain it. In a moment of intense stupidity, I let myself be talked into it by my first American girlfriend, who more or less made it a condition of sleeping with me. She'd somehow convinced herself she stood less chance of my passing on a venereal disease if I had my foreskin lopped off."

"What was the girl's name?"

"For Christ's sake, you don't really expect me to come up with the name of every girl I slept with."

"Where was the operation performed?"

"Ah, that I remember. On the fourth floor of an ether-reeking clinic." Dante supplied the clinic's name and address.

The imam returned to the chair behind the desk. "Consider yourself under house arrest," he informed Dante. "Clearly you are an expert in explosives. But I fear you may be working for someone other than Hezbollah. We will reexamine your curriculum vitae with a fine-toothed comb. We will send someone to Castletownbere on the Beara Peninsula, we will start with Mary McCullagh and the restaurant called The Bank and follow the trail from there. We will check to see if the New York clinic has a record of your circumcision.

If you have lied about a single detail . . ." He didn't bother to finish the sentence.

As Dante rose to his feet a deep groan escaped from the prisoner. Everyone in the room turned to look at her. Her mouth agape, Djamillah hyperventilated and angled her head and, gasping for breath, fixed her one open eye on Dante. With some effort she managed to spit out, "You are . . . one lousy lover, Irish." And then she smiled a crooked smile and gagged on the mordant laughter seeping from the back of her throat.

Back in his low room, with armed guards posted at the door, Dante sprawled on his cot and stared at the white washed ceiling, wondering if the stains of the crushed flies might convey bulletins from the front. And he re-created her voice in his skull; he could make out the words, forced with great effort through her bruised lips. *You are one lousy lover, Irish.*

At sunset Abdullah turned up at the door of his room. His manner had changed; it was written in his eyes that he no longer thought of Dante as a comrade in arms. "You are instructed to come with me," he announced, and without waiting he turned and quit the room. Two gunmen with their kaffiyahs masking their faces and only their eyes visible fell in behind Dante as he followed Abdullah through the village to the Hezbollah camp's perimeter fence. The gate in the fence had been dragged back and Abdullah signaled for Dante to follow him through it to the rim of the quarry. The nineteen apprentice bombers, along with the permanent staff and the Hezbollah gunmen who had brought the prisoner from Beirut were lined up along the rim. Across the quarry, her back to the setting sun, Djamillah was being bound to a stake by two of the gunmen. One of them hung a small khaki army satchel around her neck, then reached inside it to manipulate the wires and complete the electrical circuit. Djamillah's knees buckled under her and she collapsed into the ropes holding her to the stake. As the gunmen left her side, the satchel dangling from its straps against her chest, Dr. al-Karim materialized alongside Dante. He was holding a small remote transmitter, which he offered to the Irishman. "Would you like the honor?"

Dante looked down at the transmitter. "She is not my enemy," he said.

High above the Bekaa rift two Israeli jets, flying soundlessly, their contrails catching the last smudges of sunlight, appeared from the north. When they were directly over the Hezbollah camp they banked ninety degrees to the west. As they headed toward the sea the sound of their engines engulfed the camp.

The imam gazed across the quarry at the woman tied to the stake. Then, in an abrupt gesture, he raised the transmitter and rotated the switch until there was a hollow click and depressed it. For an instant that stretched into an eternity nothing happened. Dr. al-Karim, his brows knitted, was raising the transmitter to activate it again when, across the quarry, a dull blast stirred up a fume of mustard-colored smoke. When it dissipated, the woman had vanished and only the stump of the stake remained. Around the rim of the quarry the feday-een began to wander off into the darkness that settled quickly over the Bekaa at this time of year. The imam produced the string of jade worry beads and began working them through his pudgy fingers. The gesture struck Dante as therapeutic. He noticed that Dr. al-Karim's fingers and lips were trembling. Could it be that this was the first time he'd killed someone with his own hand?

"When one of our own turns her back on faith," the imam mur-mured—he appeared to be talking to himself—"it is a mortal sin, punishable by execution."

* * *

By midnight the cold gusts that swept down from the Golan Heights most nights of the year had picked up, drowning out the sound of the helicopters coming in high and fast and plummeting toward the ground like shot birds to land at strategic points around the Hezbollah camp. The roadblock at the spot where the Beirut high-way curved up hill to the village and the camp was overrun without a shot being fired. The fedayeen noticed that the men coming toward them were wearing kafiyyahs and made the fatal mistake of taking them for Arabs. "Assalamu aleikum," one of the men in kafiyyahs called out; a sentry at the roadblock called back, "*Wa aleikum salam.*" It was the last word he uttered. In the bunker on top of the hill above the quarry, the fedayeen started firing their heavy machine gun into the darkness when they caught sight of figures sprinting up the slope; the attackers, equipped with night vision goggles, didn't return fire until they were close enough to lob stun grenades over the bunker's sandbags. Other teams from the helicopters, their faces blackened with charcoal, raced through the village to attack the two low buildings that served as the camp's dormitory. Most of the apprentice bombers, as well as the staffers and the visiting fedayeen, were gunned down as they tried to flee through the doors and the windows. Explosive charges planted against the small brick building blew away the Hezbollah flag on the roof and set off a string of smaller explosions as the wooden boxes filled with ammunition caught fire.

Dante, crouching inside the door of his room, heard the two guards outside hollering into a walkie-talkie for instructions. When there was no response they both raced off in the direction of the imam's house behind the mosque, only to be killed by one of the Israeli teams blocking the narrow streets. The first casualties for the raiders came when several of them burst through the back door into Dr. al-Karim's office: One of the imam's personal guards walked toward them with his hands raised over his head and then blew himself up, killing two of the attackers and wounding two more. The other raiders, streaming through doors and windows, stormed through the house, killing the bodyguards and servants and one of the imam's wives and two of his teenage sons as they dashed from room to room. They found Dr. al-Karim hiding in an armoir on the top floor as his second wife and two other children cowered in a nearby bathroom fitted with gold-plated faucets on the sink and the bathtub. The imam was handcuffed and blindfolded and hauled through the streets toward one of the waiting helicopters.

When the sound of gunfire subsided, Dante knotted Djamillah's white silk bandanna around his neck and darted from the house in the direction of the water well between the village and the Hezbollah camp. Turning the corner of a narrow street, he was suddenly caught in a cross fire between some fedayeen who had taken cover on the ground floor of the school and the attackers crouching behind a low wall across the street. Dante dove behind a pickup truck as the fedayeen started firing rifle grenades. One of them exploded next to the pickup and Dante felt the tingling prick of hot shrapnel in his lower back. The sound of gunfire seemed to grow more distant as he lay on the road, staring up at the dull white stain stretching across the night sky while he waited for the pain that always trailed after the tearing of skin. Slightly delirious, he was trying to focus on the Milky Way in order to identify the star that represented the deified soul of the Alawite prostitute, Djamillah, when it finally arrived: a searing stitch of pain shot up his spinal column and he blacked out.

* * *

Dante woke to the blinding whiteness of a hospital room. Sunlight streamed through two windows and he felt its warmth on his shoulders above the bandages. He turned his head away from the sunlight and discovered Crystal Quest sitting on the next bed, munching crushed ice as she worked on a crossword puzzle. Benny Sapir, the Mossad spymaster who had briefed him in Washington, watched from the foot of the bed.

"Where the hell am I, Fred?" Dante asked weakly.

"He's come back to life," Benny observed.

"About time," Quest growled; she didn't want Dante to take her presence there as a manifestation of softness. "I have other things to do in life besides holding his hand. Hey Dante, being Irish, you ought to know this one: Joyce's 'Silence, exile, and . . .' Seven letters, starts with a 'c.'"

"Cunning. That was Stephen Dedalus's strategy for survival in *Portrait of an Artist.*"

"Cunning. Ha! It fits perfectly." Fred peered over the top of the newspaper, her bloodshot eyes focusing on the wounded agent. "You're in Haifa, Dante, in an Israeli hospital. The doctors had to pry some metal out of your lower back. The bad news is you'll wind up with a disagreeable cavity and a gimpy left leg, the result of a compressed nerve. The good news is there will be no major infirmities, and you'll be able to tuck a pistol behind your back without it producing a bulge in your clothing."

"Did you capture the imam?"

"We collared the guy who was *masquerading* as an imam. A direct descendant of the Prophet my ass! I suppose it won't hurt if you fill him in," she told Benny.

"Izzat Al-Karim was a pseudonym. Your imam's real name was Aown Kikodze; he was the only son of an Afghan father and his third wife, a teenage Kazakh girl who won a local beauty contest in Alma-Ata. Kikodze studied dentistry in Alma-Ata and was working as a dentist's assistant there in the early 1980s when he made hegira to Mecca, where he was discovered by Iranian talent scouts and recruited into Hezbollah. We first noticed him when he opened a mosque above a warehouse in southern Lebanon and began preaching some malarkey about the near enemy and the far enemy—nobody could make heads or tails out of what he was saying, but it came across like the Islamic version of what you Americans call fire and brimstone and he made a name for himself. Next thing you know he was sporting the black turban of a sayyid and running a Hezbollah training base. Even as we speak, my colleagues are trying to talk him into helping them with their inquiries into Hezbollah activities in the Bekaa."

"I suspect they'll succeed," Fred said. "The Israelis are at war, Dante, so they don't have weak-kneed civil libertarians breathing down their necks the way we do. If he's still compos mentis when they finish with him, we get to get sloppy seconds."

Dante turned on Benny. "Why didn't you tell me all this when you briefed me in Washington?"

"If you'd been caught, you'd have talked. We didn't want the putative imam to know we knew he was putative."

"Yeah, well, we lost Djamillah," Dante said bitterly.

Crystal Quest slid off the bed and approached Dante. "The Levant is full of girls named Djamillah. Which one are you talking about?"

"The Djamillah in Beirut, for God's sake, the Alawite who was posing as a prostitute. They executed her six hours before the helicopters arrived. I'll lay odds you don't want to hear how."

Fred snorted. "Oh, *that* Djamillah! Jesus, Dante, for someone in your line of work you can be awfully naive. 'Djamillah' was a legend. Her real name was Zineb. She wasn't *posing* as a prostitute; she was working as a prostitute in Dubai when she was recruited. And she wasn't an Alawite, she was an Iraqi Sunni. Thanks to some fancy footwork on our part, she believed she would be working for Saddam Hussein's *Mukhabarat*. There was an elegant logic to this false flag pitch, if I do say so myself: Saddam detests the Shiites and their Iranian mentors, and by extension, he loathes Hezbollah, which is a Shiite client of the Iranian mullahs."

Dante could hear Djamillah's voice in his ear. *You are one lousy lover, Irish.* "Whoever she was, she tried to save me when she could have used what she knew to save herself." He noticed the square of white silk hanging from a hook on the back of the door. "Do me a favor, bring me the bandanna, Fred."

Crystal Quest retrieved the square of silk and folded it into Dante's hand. "It's a hell of a memento," Benny said from the end of the bed. "You owe your life to that bandanna. When you didn't turn up at the well, our raiding party decided to write you off. One of the teams taking a last look around the camp reported seeing a man lying next to a pickup wearing a white bandanna. It saved your life."

"My Dante Pippen cover must be blown."

"That's the least of our problems," Fred said with a titter. "One thing we have an endless supply of in Langley is legends. We'll work up a brand new one for you when you're back on your feet."

Benny said, "Thanks to you, Dante, the operation was a great success."

"It was a crying shame," Dante said with sudden vehemence, and he meant it literally.

1997: MARTIN ODUM DISCOVERS THAT
SHAMUS IS A YIDDISH WORD

L ULLED BY THE DRONE OF THE JET ENGINES, MARTIN—HIS RIGHT
leg jutting into the aisle, his left knee jammed into the back of the
seat in front of him—had dozed off halfway through the flight
and had missed the sight of the coastal shoal of Israel unrolling like a
fulgent carpet under the wing of the plane. The wheels grinding out
of their bays woke him with a start. He glanced at Stella, who was
sound asleep in the seat next him.

He touched her shoulder. "We're almost there."

She nodded gloomily; the closer she got to Israel, the less sure she
was about tracking down her sister's runaway husband. What if she
caught up with him? What then?

As a matter of simple tradecraft, they had come to Israel using different routes: She had taken a flight to London and gone by train to
Paris and then flown on to Athens to catch the 2 A.M. flight to Tel
Aviv: He had flown New York–Rome and spent several hours getting
lost in crowds around the Colosseum before boarding a train to Venice
and an overnight car ferry to Patras, where he caught a bus to Athens
airport and then the plane to Israel. Martin, queuing behind Stella,
had winked at the woman behind the counter and asked for a seat
next to the good looking girl who had just checked in.

"Do you know her?" the woman had asked.

"No, but I'd like to," he'd replied.

The woman had laughed. "You guys never give up, do you?"

Landing at Ben-Gurion Airport in a light drizzle, the plane taxied
to the holding area and the captain, speaking in English over the inter-

com, ordered the passengers to remain seated for security reasons. Two lean young men, their shirttails hanging loose to hide the handguns tucked into their belts, strolled down the aisle, checking identity photos in passports against faces. One of the young men, wearing opaque sunglasses, reached Martin's row.

"Passports," he snapped.

Stella produced hers from the side pocket of the hand bag under the seat. Martin pulled his from the breast pocket inside his vest and handed both of them to the security agent. He riffled through the pages with his thumb. Returning to the page with Martin's photograph, he looked over the top of the passport at Martin. "Are you traveling together?"

They both said "No" at the same time.

The young man pocketed the two passports. "Come with me," he ordered. He stepped aside so that Martin could retrieve his valise from the overhead rack. Then he shepherded Stella and Martin down the aisle ahead of him. The other passengers gaped at the man and woman being hustled from the plane, trying to figure out whether they were celebrities or terrorists.

An olive-green Suzuki with a thick plastic partition between the front and rear seats was waiting on the damp tarmac at the bottom of the portable stairs and Martin and Stella were motioned into the backseat. Martin could hear the locks in the back doors click shut as he settled down for what turned out to be a short ride. Stella started to say something but he cut her off with a twitch of his finger, indicating that the automobile could be bugged. Seeing her nervousness, he offered her a smile of encouragement.

The first shadows of first light were starting to graze the tarmac and fields to the east of the airport as the car made its way to a distant hangar on the far side of the main runway and parked next to a metal staircase that led to a green door high in the hangar. The locks on the back doors of the Suzuki clicked open and the driver pointed with his chin toward the staircase.

"I suppose they mean for us to go up there," Stella ventured.

"Uh-huh," Martin agreed.

Favoring his game leg, he led the way up the long flight of steps. At the top he tugged open the heavy gunmetal door and, holding it for Stella, followed her into an immense loft with a remarkably low ceiling. Sitting at desks scattered around the loft were twenty or so people working at computer terminals; despite the "Positively No Admittance" sign on the outside of the door, none of them looked up when the two visitors appeared. Female soldiers in khaki shirts and khaki miniskirts steered carts through the room, picking up and distributing computer disks. A man with a gray crew cut appeared from behind a heavy curtain that served to partition off a corner of the loft. He was dressed in a suit and tie (rare for an Israeli) and wore a government-issue smile on his very tanned face.

"Look what the cat dragged in. If it isn't Dante Pippin in the flesh."

"Didn't know that Shabak mandarins got up before the sun," Martin ventured.

The smile vanished from the Israeli's face. "Shabak mandarins never sleep, Dante. That's something you used to know." He glanced at Stella, who was peeling away the rubber bands on the braid dangling down her spine so that her hair, damp from the light rain, would dry without curling. "Step out of character," the Shabak mandarin said to Martin, all the while taking in his companion's thin figure in tailored trousers and running shoes, "be a gentleman and introduce us."

"His name used to be Asher," Martin informed Stella. "Chances are he's recycled himself by now. When our paths crossed he was a gumshoe for the Shabak, which is short for Sherut ha-Bitachon ha-K'lali. Is my pronunciation in the ball park, Asher? The Shabak is the nearest thing Israel has to an FBI." Martin grinned at the Israeli. "I haven't the foggiest idea who she is."

The Israeli spread his hands wide. "I didn't come down with the first snowfall, Dante."

"If your people pulled her off the plane, it means you know who she is. Come clean, Asher. Who tipped you off?"

"A little canary." Asher pulled back a corner of the curtain and ushered his visitors into the area that served as an office. He gestured toward a couch and settled onto a high stool facing them.

"Could that little canary of yours be a female of the species called Fred?" Martin inquired.

"How can a female be named Fred?" Asher asked innocently.

"Fred is Crystal Quest, the honcho of the CIA's dirty tricks department."

"Is that her real name, Dante? We know the CIA's Deputy Director of Operations by another name."

Stella looked at Martin. "Why does he keep calling you Dante?"

Asher answered for him. "When your traveling companion did us a favor eight years ago, Dante Pippen was his working legend. He disappeared from our radar screen before we had a chance to learn his real identity. So you can imagine our surprise when we discovered that Dante Pippen would be on the Olympus flight from Athens, traveling under the name of Martin Odum. Is Martin Odum the real you or just another one of your legends?"

"Not sure, actually."

"People like you shouldn't breeze into Israel without touching base with the Shabak. The way I see it, it's a matter of professional courtesy. This is especially true when you're traveling with a former member of the KGB."

Martin melted back into the couch, his eyes fixed on Stella. "The Israelis don't get details like that wrong," he said quietly. "Next thing you know, you'll be telling me Stella isn't your real name."

"I can explain," she said.

One of the girl soldiers wearing a particularly short khaki miniskirt backed past the curtain carrying a tray with a pot of hot tea and two mugs. She set it down on the table. Asher mumbled something to her in Hebrew. Glancing at the two visitors over her shoulder as she left, the girl snickered appreciatively.

"If you can explain, explain," Asher told Stella. He filled the two mugs and slid them across the table toward his visitors.

Martin asked Stella, "What did you do for the KGB?"

"I wasn't a spy or anything like that," she told him. "Kastner was the deputy head of the Sixth Chief Directorate before he defected. The directorate's main line of work was dealing with economic crimes, but it wound up housing sections that didn't have a home in any of the other directorates. The forgers, for instance, worked out of the Sixth Chief Directorate, and their budget was buried in the directorate's overall budget. The same was true for the section that drew up blueprints for weapons the Soviet Union had no intention of developing, and then let the plans fall into the hands of the Americans in the hope of making them waste their resources keeping up with us. I was teaching English to grade-school children when Kastner proposed a job in a section that was so secret only a handful of Party people outside the Kremlin knew of its existence. Its in-house name was subsection Marx—but it was named after Groucho, not Karl. At any given time there were two dozen men sitting around a long table clipping stories from newspapers and magazines and inventing anti-Soviet jokes—"

Disbelief was written all over Asher's face. "I've heard some tall tales in my life but this beats them all."

"Let her finish."

Stella plunged on. "The KGB thought of the Soviet Union as a pressure cooker, and subsection Marx as the little metal cap that you occasionally lifted to let off steam. I and some other young women would come in on Fridays and memorize the jokes that the subsection had produced during the week. We were on an expense account— over the weekend we'd go out to restaurants or Komsomol clubs or workers' canteens or poetry readings and repeat the jokes. They did a study once—they found that a good joke that started out in Moscow could reach the Kamchatka Peninsula on the Pacific coast in thirty-six hours."

"Give us some examples of the jokes you spread," Asher ordered, still dubious.

Stella closed her eyes and thought for a moment. "When there were demonstrations in Poland against the stationing of Soviet troops there, I helped spread the story of the Polish boy who runs into a Warsaw police station and cries, 'Quick, quick, you have to help me. Two Swiss soldiers stole my Russian watch.' The policeman looks puzzled and says, 'You mean two Russian soldiers stole your Swiss watch." And the boy says, "That's right but *you* said it, not me!'"

When neither Martin nor Asher laughed, Stella said, "It was considered very humorous in its day."

"Do you remember another?" Martin asked.

"One of our most successful jokes was the one about two Communist Party apparatchiks meeting on a Moscow street. One of them says to the other: 'Have you heard the latest? Our Soviet scientists have managed to miniaturize nuclear warheads. Now we no longer need those expensive intercontinental ballistic missiles to wipe out America. We can put the nuclear warhead into a valise and put the valise in a locker at Grand Central Station in New York City and if the Americans give us any trouble, pffffft, New York will be reduced to radioactive ashes.' The second Russian replies: '*Nyevozmozhno.* It's not possible. Where in Russia will we find a valise?'"

Stella's joke reminded Martin of a fragment from a previous legend: Lincoln Dittmann's conversation, at a terrorist training camp in Triple Border, with the Saudi who was interested in obtaining a Soviet nuclear valise-bomb. Somehow Stella's little joke didn't seem like a laughing matter. Asher obviously agreed because he was gnawing on the inside of a cheek in irritation.

Stella, exasperated, repeated, "*Where in Russia will you find a valise*! That's the punch line of a joke, for God's sake. Is it against Israeli law to laugh?"

"Asher, like his colleagues in the CIA and the KGB, lost laughter a long time ago," Martin said. "They're time servers, hanging on by their finger tips to a world they no longer understand. If they can hang on long enough, they'll get a government pension and end their days growing stringless green beans in some suburban backyard. The reigning emotion here is nostalgia. On the rare occasions they loosen up, they start all their sentences with: Remember the time we . . . Isn't that right, Asher?"

Asher appeared to wince at Martin's little speech. "Okay," he said, turning to Stella, "for the moment let's agree that you worked for subsection Marx spreading lousy anti-Soviet jokes so the country could let off steam. Whatever brings you and Dante to the Holy Land, it's not to tell jokes."

"Tourism," Martin said flatly.

"Absolutely. Tourism," Stella agreed emphatically. She reached for the mug of tea and dipped a pinky in it and carefully moistened her lips with the ball of her finger. "We came to see the Temple Mount, we came to see Masada on the Dead Sea, we came to see the Church of the Holy Sepulcher . . ." Her voice trailed off.

"Are you planning to visit your sister in her West Bank settlement at some point?"

Stella glanced at Martin, then turned back to Asher. "That also, naturally."

"And Dante is keeping you company in exactly what capacity?"

Stella raised her chin. "I know him by the name of Martin. He is my lover."

The Israeli eyed Martin. "I suppose you could describe her body if you had to."

"No problem. Up to and including the faded tattoo of a Siberian night moth under her right breast."

Out of the corner of his eye Martin saw Stella start to undo the top buttons of her shirt; once again there was no sign of an undergarment, only a triangle of pale skin. Asher, embarrassed, cleared his throat. "That, eh, won't be necessary, Miss Kastner. I have reason to believe Dante works as a private detective and you hired his services. What you do after working hours is your business." Asher regarded Martin. "So that's what spies turn into when they come in from the cold—they metamorphose into private detectives. Sure beats cultivating stringless green beans. Tell me something, Dante, how does one go about becoming a private detective?"

"You watch old detective films."

"He's a great fan of Humphrey Bogart," Stella asserted, avoiding Martin's eye.

Asher watched her sip at the tea for a moment. When he spoke again his mood had changed; to Martin, he suddenly looked more like an undertaker than a cop. "Let me offer you some sympathy with your tea, Miss Kastner," Asher began. He slid off the stool and walked over to a table and flipped open the top dossier on a thick pile of dossiers. "I am sorry to be the bearer of sad news," he said, and he read from the page: "The following is a State Department advisory forwarded by the American embassy in Tel Aviv. 'Please pass this information to Estelle Kastner: her father, Oscar Alexandrovich Kastner, suffered a heart attack at his home in Brooklyn five days ago.'"

Stella's eyes tightened into an anguished squint. "Oh my God, I've got to telephone Kastner immediately," she whispered.

Martin could tell from the dark expression on Asher's face that there was no point to putting in a phone call. "He's dead, isn't he?"

"I'm afraid Dante's right," Asher told Stella. His gaze fell on Martin.

"There's something the little canary wanted me to pass on to you, Dante. The body of a Chinese girl was discovered on the roof over your pool parlor. Her boss at a Chinese restaurant went looking for her when she didn't turn up for work. She'd been stung to death by bees from one of your hives. Hell of a way to go, wouldn't you say?"

"Yeah," Martin agreed grimly. "I would say."

* * *

Neither Martin nor Stella said a word in the communal taxi for fear the driver or one of the other passengers might be working for the Shabak; both worried also that emotions would get the upper hand if one of them broke the comforting silence. Fifty minutes after leaving the airport they found themselves standing on a street corner in downtown Jerusalem. Heavy morning traffic flowed around them. Squads of soldiers, some of them dark skinned Ethiopians wearing green flak jackets and green berets, patrolled the streets, checking the identity papers of young men who looked as if they could be Arabs. Martin let six taxis pass before hailing the seventh. They took it to the American Colony Hotel in East Jerusalem, where a line of Palestinian taxis queued on the street outside the hotel. A young Russian, in Israel for a chess tournament, was leaning over a chess board set up on the hood of a car parked outside the hotel entrance as a television camera filmed him. He was playing against himself, slamming the pieces down on the board as he made a dozen rapid moves, muttering all the while about a flaw in black's position or the ineptness of white's attack. Spotting an opening, he gleefully thrust the white pieces forward for the kill, then looked up and announced in English that black had resigned in the face of white's dazzling attack.

"How can he play against himself and remain sane?" Stella asked.

"The advantage of playing against yourself is, unlike real life, you know what your opponent's next move will be," Martin observed.

He waited until the first three Palestinian taxis had driven off with passengers before signaling to the fourth. "Mustaffah, at your beck and call," announced the young Palestinian driver as he loaded their valises into the back of a yellow Mercedes that, judging from its appearance, had been around longer than the driver. "So to where?"

"Kiryat Arba," Stella said.

The enthusiasm drained from Mustaffah's eyes. "It will cost you a hundred twenty shekels or thirty dollars U.S.," he said. "I only take you to the main gate. The Jews will not tolerate Arab taxis inside."

"Main gate will be fine," Martin said as he and Stella settled onto the cracking leather of the back seat.

Mustaffah's plastic worry beads dangling from the rearview mirror tapped against the windshield as the taxi sped past fortress-like Israeli neighborhoods and bus stops swarming with religious Jews, and headed away from Jerusalem on a new highway that knifed south into the Judean Hills. On the rocky slopes on either side of the highway, knots of Palestinian men walked along dirt paths to avoid the Israeli checkpoints as they made their way into Jewish Jerusalem in the hope of finding a day's work. In the wadis, boys who had climbed onto the high branches of trees could be seen picking olives and stuffing them under their open shirts.

"You were tempting fate back at the airport," Martin remarked. "I'm talking about when you started to unbutton your shirt to show Asher the night moth under your breast. What would you have done if he hadn't stopped you?"

Stella inched closer to Martin until her thigh was touching his; she badly wanted to be comforted. "I consider myself a pretty good judge of character," she replied. "My instinct told me he would stop me, or at the very least avert his eyes."

"What about me?" Martin asked. "Did you think I'd avert my eyes?"

Stella stared through the grime on the window, remembering how she had clung to Kastner when she had hugged him good-bye; he had wheeled his chair away abruptly but she had still caught sight of the tears welling in his eyes. She turned to Martin. "Sorry. I was somewhere else. What did you say?"

"I asked whether you thought I'd avert my eyes, too, if you started to show Asher the night moth supposedly tattooed under your breast."

"Not sure," she admitted. "Haven't figured you out yet."

"What's to figure out?"

"There are parts of you my instinct can't get to. The heart of the matter is hidden under too many moods—it's almost as if you were several different people. For one thing, I can't decide if you are interested in women. I can't decide if you want to seduce me, or not. Females need to get this detail right before they can have a working relationship with a man."

"Not," Martin said without hesitation. "Trouble with women in general, and you in particular, is you're incapable of being on the receiving end of courtesy without assuming seduction is behind it." Martin thought of Minh coaxing erections out of his reluctant flesh during their occasional evenings together; he wondered if her death on the roof above the pool parlor had really been an accident. "Here's the deal, Stella: I'm past seduction. When I'm backed up against a wall I make war, not love."

"That's pain speaking," Stella whispered, thinking of her own pain. "You ought to consider the possibility that intimacy can be a painkiller.'

Martin shook his head. "My experience has been that you become intimate in order to have sex. Once the sex is out of the way, the intimacy only brings more pain."

Moving back to her side of the seat, Stella burst out in irritation, "It's typical of the male of the species to think you become intimate in order to have sex. The female of the species has a more subtle take on the subject—she understands that you have sex in order to become intimate; that intimacy is the ultimate orgasm, since it allows you to get outside of the prison of yourself; get outside your skin and into the skin, the psyche, of another human being. Sex that leads to intimacy is a jailbreak."

Mustaffah slowed for an Israeli checkpoint, but was waved through when two soldiers peered through the window and mistook the passengers for Jews heading back to one of the settlements. The taxi sped past roadside carts brimming with oranges and zucchinis and restaurants with kabob roasting on spits and garages with cars up on cinder blocks and mechanics flat on their backs underneath them. It slowed again for a flock of sheep that scattered when Mustaffah leaned on the horn. Young Arab women with babies strapped to their backs by a shawl, older women in long robes with heavy bundles balanced on their heads trudged along the side of the road, turning their faces away to avoid the dust kicked up by the Mercedes barreling past.

Half an hour out of Jerusalem, the taxi eased to a stop outside Kiryat Arba next to a sign that read: "Zionist Settlement—'The more they torture him, the more he will become.'" Martin could see the two guards at the gate in the security fence watching them suspiciously. Both were armed with Uzis, with the ritual tzitzit jutting from under their bullet proof vests. While Stella retrieved the two valises from the trunk of the Mercedes, Martin walked around to the open passenger window to pay Mustaffah. From one of the minarets below, the recorded wail of the muezzin summoning the faithful to midday prayer drifted up to the Jewish settlement. Slipping three ten dollar bills through the window, Martin noticed that the framed license on the glove compartment had a photograph of Mustaffah, but identified him, in English, as Azzam Khouri.

"Why did you tell me your name was Mustaffah?" he asked the driver.

"Mustaffah, he was my brother killed by the Isra'ili army during the Intifada. We was both of us throwing stones at the Jewish tanks and they got mad and started throwing bullets back. Since, my mother calls me Mustaffah to pretend my brother is still being alive. Some days I call myself Mustaffah for the same reason. Somedays I'm not sure who I am. Today is such a day."

The guards at the gate scrutinized the passports of the visitors. When Stella explained that she was there to see her sister, Ya'ara Ugor-Zhilov, they phoned up to the settlement, a sprawl of stone-faced apartment buildings and one-family houses spilling like lava down several once barren hills toward the Arab city of Hebron. Minutes later a battered pickup appeared at the top of the hill and slowly made its way, its spark plugs misfiring, past the playground teeming with mothers and little children to the gate. A moment later Stella and her sister were clinging to each other. Martin could see Stella talking quietly into the ear of her sister. Elena, or Ya'ara as she was now called, took a step back, shook her head vehemently, then burst into tears and fell back into her sisters arms. The driver of the pickup, a stocky, bearded man in his fifties, wearing black sneakers, a black suit, black tie and black fedora, approached

Martin. He inspected him through windowpane-thick bifocals set into wire frames.

"*Shalom* to you, Mr. Martin Odum," he said with a distinct Brooklyn accent. "I'm the rabbi Ben Zion. You need to be Stella's detective friend. I'm right, right?"

"Right on both counts," Martin said. "I'm a detective and I'm a friend."

"It's me, the rabbi who married Ya'ara to Samat," Ben Zion announced. "If you're trying to track down Samat and get poor Ya'ara a religious divorce, I'll give you the time of day. If not, not."

"How'd you know I was a detective? Or about my tracking down Samat?"

"A little canary told someone in the Shabak, and that someone told yours truly that two tourists who weren't touring anything but Kiryat Arba could be expected to wash up on our doorstep. Miracle of miracles, here you are." The rabbi raised a hand to shield his eyes from the noon sun and sized up the Brooklyn detective who had found his way to Kiryat Arba. "So you're not Jewish, Mr. Odum."

Behind them the two sisters started to walk up the hill, their arms around each other's waists. Martin said, "How can you tell?"

Rabbi Ben Zion tossed his head in the direction of Hebron, visible through swells of heat rising from the floor of the valley below them. "You don't live in the middle of a sea of Arabs without recognizing one of your own when you see him."

"In other words, it's a matter of instinct."

"Survival instinct, developed over two thousand years." The rabbi pitched the two valises into the back of the pickup. "So be my guest and climb in," he ordered. "I'll take you to Ya'ara's apartment. We'll get there before the girls and cook up water for tea, and light a memorial candle for her father—the canary told me about the death in the family, too, but I thought it would be better if Stella broke the bad news to her sister. Ask me nicely and I'll tell you what I know about the missing husband."

The rabbi threw the pickup into gear and, his sidecurls flying, gunned it up the hill, past the settlement post office, past the shopping center teeming with women in ankle length skirts and small boys wearing knitted yarmulke. Ya'ara, it turned out, lived in a small two-

room apartment on the ground floor of one of the apartment buildings with a view of Hebron. "When her husband abandoned her, she
had no resources of her own so our synagogue took her under its
wing," the rabbi explained. He searched through a ring of keys until
he came to the right one and unlocked the door. The furnishings were
Spartan. There was a narrow cot in one room, with a cracked mirror
bordered with plastic sea shells over it and a wooden crate turned
upside down serving as a night table. A folding bridge table covered
with a square of oil cloth, a motley assortment of folding chairs with
a small black-and-white television set on one of them, were scattered
around what served as a living room. On the sill of a waist-high book-
case separating the living room from the tiny kitchen alcove were three
flower pots containing plastic geraniums. Martin opened the door to
the small bathroom. Women's cotton underwear and several pairs of
long woolen stockings hung from a cord stretched over the bathtub.
Ben Zion noticed Martin's expression as he returned to the living
room. "We bought the furniture from Arabs whose houses were bulldozed between us and Hebron so we could walk to the Cave of
Machpela safely."

Martin strolled over to the window, raised the shade and looked out
at the tangle of streets and buildings that made up Hebron. "What's the
Cave of Machpela?" he called over his shoulder.

The rabbi was in the kitchen alcove, attempting to light the gas
burner with a match to boil water in a kettle. "Am I hearing you correctly? What's the Cave of Machpela? It's nothing less than the second
holiest place for Jews on the planet earth, ranking immediately behind
the Temple Mount or what's left of it, the Wailing Wall. Hebron—
which in biblical times was also called Kiryat Arba—is where the
Patriarch Abraham bought his first dunams of land in Canaan. The
Cave is where Abraham is buried; his sons Isaac and Jacob, his wife,
Sarah, too. It is also holy to the Palestinians, who coopted our
Abraham to be one of their prophets; they built a mosque on the spot
and we are obliged to take turns praying at the cave." Lighting a burner,
the rabbi slid the kettle over the grill. Shaking his head in disbelief, he
struck another match and lit a *yortseit* candle for the dead and carried
it back into the room. "What is the Cave of Machpela?" he asked
rhetorically, setting the candle on the table. "Even a *shagetz* ought to

know the answer to that one. We always stroll down to the cave on Fridays at sunset to welcome the Sabbath in at this holy site. You and Stella are welcome to join us—that way you can tell the Shabak you actually did some sightseeing."

Martin decided there'd been enough small talk. "What about Samat?"

Rabbi Ben Zion covered his mouth to smother a belch. "What about Samat?" he repeated.

"Did he run off with another woman?"

"Let me tell you something, Mr. Brooklyn detective who thinks men only leave their wives for other ladies. Samat didn't need to quit his wife to have another lady—he rented all the ladies his libido desired. When he disappeared in his Honda for two, three days running, where do you think he went? It's an open secret where he went. He went where a lot of men go when they want ladies to do things their wives won't do. In Jaffa, in Tel Aviv, in Haifa there are what my mother, may she rest in peace, used to call houses of ill repute where you can get your ashes hauled by ladies who don't mind being naked with a man, who, for a price, are willing to do anything to satisfy a client." The rabbi waved a hand in the general direction of the Mediterranean coast. "Samat had sexual appetites, you could see it in his eyes, you could tell it from the way he looked at his sister-in-law Estelle when she visited Kiryat Arba. Samat also had his share of obsessions that weren't carnal. What I'm saying is, he had other axes to grind besides sex."

In the kitchenette, the kettle began to shriek. The rabbi leaped to turn off the gas and set about preparing tea. He returned moments later carrying the kettle and four china cups, which he put on the bridge table next to the memorial candle. Leaning over the table the better to see what he was doing, Ben Zion slipped Lipton tea bags into the four cups and filled the first one with boiling water. When Martin waved it away, he took the cup himself and sank onto one of the folding chairs, his knees apart, his feet flat on the floor and tapping impatiently. Martin scraped over another chair and sat down facing him.

"Why would someone like Samat, who needed to visit houses of ill repute to satisfy his lusts, marry a religious woman whom he had never met?"

"Am I inside Samat's head to know the answer?" The rabbi blew noisily across the cup, then touched his lips to the tea to test the temperature. Deciding it was too hot to drink, he set it down on the table. "He was a strange bird, this Samat. I am Ya'ara's rabbi. In the Jewish religion we don't confess to our spiritual leaders the way Catholics do. But we confide in them. I believed Ya'ara when she said that Samat never touched her on her wedding night, or after. He never slept in the marriage bed. For all I know she may still be a virgin. When Samat was living under the same roof with her, she was absolutely convinced something was wrong with her. I tried to persuade her that the something that was wrong was wrong with him. I tried to persuade him, too."

"Did you succeed?"

The rabbi shook his head cheerlessly. "To use an old Yiddish expression, I never got to first base with Samat."

"What was he doing here?"

"Hiding."

"From what? From whom?"

The rabbi tried his tea again. This time he managed to sip at it. "What am I, a reader of minds? How would I know, from what, from whom? Look, coming to live in one of these Jewish settlements in the middle of all these Arabs is a little like joining the French foreign legion: When you sign on the dotted line, nobody asks to see your curriculum vitae, we're just glad to have your warm body. What I do know is that Samat went to the Kiryat Arba security officer and asked for a weapon. He said it was to protect his wife if the Hamas terrorists ever attacked."

"Did he get the weapon?"

The rabbi nodded. "Anybody living in a settlement who can see what he's shooting at can get a weapon." Ben Zion remembered another detail. "Samat evidently had an endless supply of money. He paid for everything he bought with cash—an upscale split-level house on the side of Kiryat Arba where you get to enjoy the sunsets, a brand new Japanese car with air conditioning. He never played pinochle with the boys, he never accompanied Ya'ara to the synagogue, even on the high holy days, though it didn't go unnoticed that she always left an envelope stuffed with cash in the charity box. Admit it, Mr.

American detective, I'll bet you don't know that *shamus* is a Yiddish word."

"I thought it was Irish."

"Irish!" The rabbi slapped a palm against one of his knees. "The shamus was the synagogue beetle, which was the sobriquet for the member of the congregation who took care of the synagogue." Ben Zion shook his head in puzzlement. "How, I ask you, is it possible to detect an AWOL husband if you can't detect the origin of the word shamus?"

The sudden arrival of Ya'ara and Stella saved Martin from having to account for this lapse in his education; it also provided him with his first good look at Samat's wife. She was a short, overweight woman with a teenager's pudgy face and a matronly body endowed with an ample bosom that put a strain on the buttons of her blouse; Martin feared that one of them would pop at any moment. In the space between the buttons he caught a glimpse of the pink fabric of a heavy brassiere. She wore an ankle-length skirt popular with Lubavitch women and a round flat-brimmed felt hat that she nervously twisted on her head, as if she were trying to find the front. The little patches of skin on her body that Martin could see were chalk white from lack of being exposed to sun light. Her cheeks were streaked with traces of tears. Stella, dry eyed, wore the ghost of a smile fixed on her lips that Martin had noticed the day she turned up at his pool parlor.

The rabbi bounded to his feet when the women appeared at the door; Ya'ara stopped to kiss the mezuzah before she came in. Grabbing one of her hands in both of his, bending at the waist so that his head was level with hers, the rabbi bombarded her with a burst of Hebrew which, to the shamus's ear, sounded more Brooklyn than biblical. Martin concluded that the rabbi was offering condolences because Ya'ara started sobbing again; tears cascaded down her cheeks and soaked into the tightly buttoned collar of her blouse. Ben Zion led Ya'ara to the *yortseit* candle and, rocking back and forth on the soles of his sneakers, started praying in Hebrew. Ya'ara, blotting her tears on the back of a sleeve, joined in.

"Aren't you going to pray for your father?" Martin whispered to Stella.

"I only pray for the living," she retorted fiercely.

When the prayer ended the rabbi excused himself to organize the Sabbath pilgrimage to the Cave of Machpela, and Martin got his first opportunity to talk to Stella's sister. "I'm sorry about your father," he began.

She accepted this with a shy closing of her lids. "I was not expecting him to die, and certainly not of a heart attack. He had the heart of a lion. After all he had been through—" She shrugged weakly.

"Your sister has hired me to find Samat so that you can get a religious divorce."

Ya'ara turned on Stella. "What good will a divorce do me?"

"It is a matter of pride," Stella insisted. "You can't let him get away with this."

Martin steered the conversation back to matters of tradecraft. "Do you have anything of his—a book he once read, a telephone he once used, a bottle of alcohol he once poured a drink from, a toothbrush even? Anything at all?"

Ya'ara shook her head. "There was stationery with a London letterhead but it disappeared and I don't remember the address on it. Samat filled a trunk with personal belongings and paid two boys to carry it down to the taxi when he left. He even took the photographs of our wedding. The only photograph left of him was the one Stella snapped after the ceremony and sent to our father." At the mention of their father, tears trickled down her cheeks again. "How could Samat do this to a wife, I ask you?"

"Stella told me he was always talking on the phone," Martin said. "Did he initiate the calls or did people call him?"

"Both."

"So there must be phone records showing the numbers he dialed."

Again she shook her head. "The rabbi asked the security office here to try and get the phone numbers. Someone even drove to Tel Aviv to interview the phone company. He reported back that the numbers were all on a magnetic tape that had been erased by error. There was no trace of the numbers he called."

"What language did he use when he spoke on the phone?"

"English. Russian. Armenian sometimes."

"Did you ever ask him what he did for a living?"

"Once."

Stella said, "What did he say?"

"At first he didn't answer. When I pressed him, he told me he ran a business selling Western-manufactured artificial limbs to people who had lost legs to Russian land mines in Bosnia, Chechnya, Kurdistan. He said he could have made a fortune but was selling them at cost."

"And you believed him?" Stella asked.

"I had no reason not to." Ya'ara's eyes suddenly widened. "Someone once called when he wasn't here and left a phone number for him to call back. I thought it might have something to do with these artificial limbs and wrote it down on the first thing that came to hand, which was the back of a recipe, and then copied it onto the pad next to the telephone. I tore off the page and gave it to Samat when he returned to the house that day and he went to the bedroom and dialed a number. I remember that the conversation was very agitated. At one point Samat was even yelling into the phone, and he kept switching from English to Russian and back to English again."

"The recipe," Stella said softly. "Do you still have it?"

Both Stella and Martin could see Ya'ara hesitate. "You would not be betraying your husband," Martin said. "If and when we find him, we are only going to make sure you get the famous *get* so you can go on with your life."

"Samat owes that much to you," Stella said.

Sighing, moving as if her limbs were weighted down by gravity, Ya'ara pushed herself to her feet and shuffled into the kitchen alcove and pulled a tin box from one of the wall cupboards. She carried it back to the living room, set it on the folding table, opened the lid and began thumbing through printed recipes that she had torn out of *Elle* magazine over the years. She pulled the one for apple strudel out of the box and turned it over. A phone number starting with the country code 44 and city code 171 was scrawled on the back in pencil. Martin produced a felt tipped pen and copied the number into a small notebook.

"Where is that?" Stella asked Martin.

"Forty-four is England, 171 is London," he said. He turned back to Stella. "Did Samat ever leave Kiryat Arba?" he asked.

"Once, sometimes twice a week, he drove off by himself, sometimes for a few hours, sometimes for several days."

"Do you have any idea where he went?"

"The one time I asked him he told me it was not the business of a wife to keep track of a husband."

Stella looked brightly at Martin. "We went with him once, Martin." She smiled at her half sister. "Don't you remember, Elena—"

"My name is Ya'ara now," Stella's sister reminded her coldly.

Stella was not put off. "It was when I came for the wedding," she said excitedly. "I had to be at Ben-Gurion Airport at seven in the evening for my flight back to New York. Samat was going somewhere for lunch. He said if we didn't mind killing time, he had to see someone on the coast and could drop me at the airport on the way back to Kiryat Arba."

"I remember that," Ya'ara said. "We made bologna sandwiches and packed them in a paper bag and took a plastic bottle of apple juice." She sighed again. "That was one of the happiest days of my life," she added.

Stella said to Martin, "He drove north from Tel Aviv along the expressway and got off at the exit marked 'Caesarea.' There was a labyrinth of streets but he never hesitated, he seemed to know his way around very well. He dropped us on the edge of the sand dunes near some A-frame houses. We could see those giant chimneys down the coast that produced electricity."

Ya'ara's face lit up for the first time in Martin's presence; the smile almost made her look handsome. "I wore an enormous straw hat to protect my face from the sun," she recalled. "We ate in the shade of a eucalyptus tree and then hunted for Roman coins in the sand."

"And what did Samat do while you were scouring the dunes for Roman coins?" Martin asked.

The girls looked at each other. "He never told us. He picked us up at the A-frames at five-thirty and dropped me off at the airport at six-forty."

"Uh-huh," Martin said, his brows knitting as he began to fit the first blurred pieces of the jigsaw puzzle into place.

* * *

Martin took a tiny address book (tradecraft ruled: Everyone in it was identified by nickname and phone numbers were masked in a simple cipher) from his pocket and used his AT&T card to call Xing's Mandarin Restaurant (listed in the address book as "Glutamate") under the pool parlor on Albany Avenue in Crown Heights. Given the time difference, Tsou would be presiding from the high stool behind the cash register, glowering at the waitress who had replaced Minh if she failed to push the more expensive dishes on the menu. "Peking duck hanging in window for two days," he'd once informed Minh, his gold teeth glistening with saliva, his face a mask of earnestness (so she had gleefully recounted to Martin), "is aphlodisiac, good for elections."

"Xing's Mandalin," a high pitched voice—so distinct it could have been coming from the next room—announced when the phone on the other end was picked up. "Filled up at lunch, same tonight. No flea table until lunch Sunday."

"Don't hang up," Martin cried into the phone. "Tsou, it's me, Martin."

"*Yin shi*, from where you calling, huh?"

Martin knew that Fred would be keeping track of his whereabouts through Asher and the Israeli Shabak, so he figured he was not giving anything away if he told the truth.

"I'm in Israel."

"Islael the Jewish kingdom or Islael the Jewish delicatessen on Kingston Avenue?" Tsou didn't wait for an answer. "You know about Minh, huh?"

"That's why I'm calling. Tell me what happened, Tsou."

The story spurted out. "She goes up to check the hives the way you asked. She does not come back. Clients begin to fidget. No food in sight. I go out back and shout up 'Minh.' She does not shout back. I climb file escape, find Minh laying on back, not moving, not conscious, clazy bees stinging life out of Minh's face. Disgusting. Makes me want to vomit. Call police on loft phone, Matin, hope you do not mind, let them into loft when they ling bell, they put on face masks and chase bees with can of Laid found below sink, they take Minh away in ambulance, face bloated big like basketball. She dead before ambulance leach hospital, Matin. Minh's death makes page two *Daily News*, big headline say 'Deadly Bees Kill Clown Heights Woman.'"

"What did the police say, Tsou?"

"Two detectives come for lunch next day, sons of bitches leave without paying check, I wave it in faces but they do not take hint. They ask about you and I tell them what I know, which is nothing. They tell me ASPCA in white clothing came to kill bees. They tell me hive exploded, which is what made bees clazy to attack Minh. Comes as news to me honey can explode."

Through the window Martin could see the orange streaks of sunset in the sky and the rabbi assembling a group of settlers for the stroll down the road toward Hebron and the Cave of Machpela. "It comes as news to me, too," he said very softly.

"What you say?" Tsou shouted.

"I said, honey doesn't normally explode."

"Huh. So. Detectives, they say Minh not even Minh's name, she illegal immigrant from Taiwan named Chun-chiao. Business picked up when *Daily News* ran name Xing's Mandolin on page two even though they spelled Xing 'Zing.' I admit it, whole thing leave bad taste in my mouth. Velly upsetting."

Martin assumed Tsou was referring to Minh's death. "Yeah, very," he agreed.

Tsou, however, seemed to be more concerned with Minh's false identity than her death. "Cannot believe anyone anymore these days, huh, *yin shi*? Minh not Minh. Maybe you not Matin."

"Maybe the *Daily News* was right," Martin said, "maybe your real name is Tsou Zing with a 'Z.'"

"Maybe," Tsou agreed with a sour laugh. "Who can say?"

* * *

With Rabbi Ben Zion and Martin strolling along in the lead and the two Kastner sisters bringing up the rear, the group of thirty or so ultranationalist orthodox settlers, the men sporting tzitzit and embroidered yarmulkes, the women in ankle-length skirts and long sleeved blouses and head scarves, made their way down the road toward the Cave of Machpela to greet the Sabbath at the holy site where the Patriarch Abraham was said to be buried. Two policemen wearing blue uniforms and blue baseball caps, along with half a dozen of the younger settlers, walked on either side of the group, rifles or Uzis slung over their shoulders.

The sun had disappeared behind the hills and the darkness was starting to blot out the twilight between the buildings. Instinctively, the murky dusk left Martin feeling queasy. Agents who worked the field liked daylight because they could see danger coming, and night-time because they could hide from it; the penumbra between the two offered none of the advantages of either. The massive fortress-like structure built over the sacred cave loomed ahead like a ship adrift in a fog.

"What do the Palestinians here think of your pilgrimages to the shrine?" Martin asked the rabbi, all the while inspecting the spaces between the Palestinian houses off to the right for any telltale sign of activity. Martin tensed as a shard of light ricocheted off a roof; as his eyes grew accustomed to the dimness, he realized it was nothing more than a lingering sliver of sunlight glinting off the solar heating panels atop a three-story building.

"The Palestinians," the rabbi replied, waving toward the surrounding houses, "say we're walking on their toes."

"You are, aren't you?"

The rabbi shrugged. "Look, it's not as if we're being unreasonable. Those of us who believe the Lord God gave this land to Abraham and his descendants for eternity are willing to let the Palestinians remain here as long as they accept that the land is ours."

"What about the others?"

"They can emigrate."

"That doesn't leave them—or you, for that matter—much room for maneuver."

"It's easy for visitors to come here from the outside and criticize, Mr. Odum, and then fly back to the safety of their country, their city, their homes . . ."

"My home," Martin ventured, "turns out to be less safe than I thought." He made a mental note to get more details of the death of Stella's father. He wondered if there had been an autopsy.

"You're talking about crime in the streets. It's nothing compared to what we have to put up with here."

"I was talking about exploding honey—"

"Come again— I must be missing something."

"Private joke."

Eyeing potential danger areas, Martin spotted a spark in an alleyway between two Palestinian homes to his right and uphill from the group of settlers walking toward the cave. Suddenly flames erupted and a blazing tire, thick black smoke billowing from it, started rolling downhill toward them. As the settlers scattered to get out of its path, the short hollow cough of a high-powered rifle resounded through the neighborhood and a spurt of dust materialized in the road immediately ahead of Martin. His old reflexes kicked in—he figured out what was going on in an instant. The tire was the diversion; the rifle shot had come from the other side of the road, probably from the top of the cement cistern a hundred and fifty yards away on a small rise. The two policemen and the settlers armed with weapons had reacted instinctively and were charging uphill in the direction of the alleyway where the tire had come from. One of the policemen was shouting into a walkie-talkie. Back at Kiryat Arba, a siren, its pitch rising as it whimpered into life, began shrieking across the countryside.

"The shot came from behind us," Martin shouted and he lunged for cover behind a low stone wall as the second shot nicked the dirt a yard beyond the spot where he'd been standing. Crouching behind the wall, massaging the muscles in his bad leg, Martin could see Stella and her sister, with her skirt hiked, running back up the hill toward the settlement, which was ablaze with searchlights sweeping the area. Moments later two Israeli jeeps and an open truck filled with soldiers came roaring down the road from the nearby army base. Leaping from their vehicles, the soldiers, bent low and running, charged the slopes on either side of the road. From behind the cistern came the staccato sound of automatic rifles being fired in short bursts. Martin suspected that the Palestinian rifleman—assuming he was Palestinian—had melted away and the soldiers were shooting at shadows.

Dusting the dirt off of his sabbath suit, the rabbi came up to Martin. "You okay?" he asked breathlessly.

Martin nodded.

"That was too close for comfort," Ben Zion said, his chest heaving with excitement. "If I didn't know better, I would have thought they were shooting at you, Mr. Odum."

"Now why would they want to do that?" Martin asked innocently. "I'm not even Jewish. I'm just a visitor who will soon go back to the safety of his country, his city, his home."

1997: MARTIN ODUM MEETS A BORN-AGAIN OPPORTUNIST

BENNY SAPIR LISTENED INTENTLY TO MARTIN'S ACCOUNT OF THE incident in Hebron. When he finally broke his silence it was to pose questions only a professional would think to ask.

"How can you be sure it wasn't some Arab kids letting off steam? That kind of thing happens all the time around Kiryat Arba."

"Because of the diversion. The attack was synchronized. The tire came first. Everyone looked off to the right. The two cops and the armed settlers raced uphill to the right. That's when the first shot was fired. It came from the left."

"How many shots were there?"

"Two."

"And both of them hit the road near you?"

"The shooter's rifle must have been pulling to the left. The first shot hit a yard or so ahead of me, which means he was firing short and left. The shooter must have cranked in a correction to the rear sight and elevated slightly. The second shot was on target—it hit beyond where I'd been standing, which means the bullet would have hit my chest if I hadn't leaped for cover behind the low wall."

"Why didn't he shoot again?"

"Fact that he didn't is what makes me think he was shooting at me. When I disappeared from view behind the low wall, there were still a dozen or so settlers crouching or lying flat on the ground. The search lights from Kiryat Arba were sweeping the area so he could easily see them. If he was shooting in order to kill Jews, he had plenty of targets available."

"Maybe the lights and the siren scared him off."

"Soldiers scared him off. But that happened five, maybe eight minutes later."

"*Beseder*, okay. So why would someone want to kill you, Dante?"

"Retirement hasn't dulled your edge, Benny. You're asking the right questions in the right order. Once we figure out the 'why,' we move on to the 'who.'"

Returning to Jerusalem from Kiryat Arba (Stella had remained behind to be with her sister), Martin had braved the rank stench of a phone booth and had asked information for the phone number of a Benny Sapir. He was given five listings under that name. The second one, in a settlement community thirteen kilometers outside of Jerusalem, turned out to be the Benny Sapir who had briefed Dante Pippen in Washington before the mission to the Bekaa Valley eight years before; Benny, normally the Mossad's point man on things Russian, had been covering for a colleague home on sick leave at the time. When he came on line now, Benny, who had retired from the Mossad the previous year, sounded winded. He recognized the voice on the other end of the phone immediately. "The older I get, the harder it is to remember faces and names, but voices I never forget," he said. "Tell you the truth, Dante, never expected our paths to cross again." Before Martin could say anything, Benny proposed to pick him up in front of the Rashamu Restaurant down from the Jewish *shouk* on Ha-Eshkol Street in half an hour.

Exactly on time, a spanking new Skoda pulled up in front of the restaurant and the driver, a muscular man with the body of a wrestler, honked twice. Benny's hair had gone gray and his once-famous smile had turned melancholy since Martin had last seen him, eight years before, standing at the foot of his hospital bed in Haifa. "Lot of water's flowed under the bridge since we last saw each other, Dante," Benny said as Martin slid onto the passenger seat. "You sure it wasn't blood?" Martin shot back, and they both laughed at the absence of humor in the exchange. At the intersection ahead of them, two Israeli soldiers of Ethiopian origin were frisking an Arab boy carrying a tray filled with small porcelain cups of Turkish coffee. "So you are going by the name of Martin Odum these days," Benny noted, wheeling the car into traffic and heading out of Jerusalem in the direction of Tel Aviv. The one-time spymaster glanced quickly at the American. "Sorry about that, Dante, but I was obliged to touch base with the Shabak."

"I would have done the same thing in your shoes."

It was obvious Benny felt bad about it. "Question of guarding one's flanks," he mumbled, apologizing a second time. "The people who run the show these days are a new breed—cross them and your pension checks start arriving late."

"I understand," Martin said again.

"Be careful what you tell me," Benny warned. "They want me to file a contact report after I've seen you. They're not quite sure what you're doing here."

"Me, also, I'm not quite sure what I'm doing here," Martin admitted. "Where we going, Benny?"

"Har Addar. I live there. I invite you for pot-luck supper. You can sleep over if you need a bed for the night. Does Martin Odum have a legend?"

"He's a private detective working out of the Crown Heights section of Brooklyn."

Benny rocked his head from side to side in appreciation. "Why not? A detective is as good a cover as any and better than most. I've used various legends in my time—my favorite, which was my cover when I was running agents in what used to be called the Soviet Union, was a defrocked English priest living in sin in Istanbul. The sin part was the fun part. To support my cover story, I had to practically memorize the Gospels. Never got over the trauma of reading John. If you're looking for the roots of Christian anti-Semitism, you don't have to go further than the Gospel According to John, which, by the way, wasn't written by the disciple named John. Whoever wrote the text commandeered his name. Now that I think of it, you could make the case that this is an example of an early Christian legend."

Benny turned off the Jerusalem–Tel Aviv highway and was wending his way up through the hills west of Jerusalem toward Har Addar when Martin asked him if the agents he'd run in the former USSR had been Jewish.

Glancing quickly at his companion, Benny said, "Some were, most weren't."

"What motivated them to work for Israel?"

"Not all of them knew they were working for Israel. We used false flags when we thought it would get results. What motivated them? Money. Resentment for personal slights, real or imagined. Boredom."

"Not ideology?"

"There must have been individuals who defected for ideological reasons but I personally never came across any. The thing they all had in common was they wanted to be treated as human beings, as opposed to cogs in a machine, and they were ready to risk their lives for the handler who understood this. The most remarkable thing about the Soviet Union was that nobody—*nobody*—believed in communism. Which meant that once you recruited a Russian, he made an outstanding spy for the simple reason that he'd been raised in a society where everyone, from the Politburo members on down to the Intourist guides, dissembled in order to survive. When a Russian agreed to spy for you, in a very real sense he'd already been trained to lead two lives."

"You mean three lives, don't you? One where he outwardly conforms to the Soviet system. The second where he despises the system and cuts corners to get ahead within it. The third where he betrays the system and spies for you."

"Three lives it is." Benny became pensive. "Which, when you think of it, may be par for the course. When you come right down to it, all men and some women live with an assortment of legends that blur at the edges where they overlap. Some of these IDs fade as we get older; others, curiously, become sharper and we spend more time in them. But that's another story."

"Consider the possibility that it isn't another story . . . Is Benny Sapir the last of your legends or the one your parents gave you?"

Instead of answering, Benny sniffed at the air, which was growing chillier as the car climbed into the hills. Martin kicked himself for having asked. He grasped what professional interrogators took for granted: Each time you posed a question, you revealed what you didn't know. If you weren't careful, the person being interrogated could wind up knowing more about you than you did about him.

Benny delicately changed the subject. "Does your leg give you trouble these days?"

"I got used to the pain."

A grimace appeared on Benny's prize-fighter's lips that looked as if they had been in one fight too many. "Yes, pain is like the buzzing in an ear—it's something you learn to live with."

As Benny shifted into second and turned onto a narrow road that climbed steeply, the small talk gave way to a comfortable silence that exists between two veteran warriors who have nothing to prove to each other. Benny had the car radio on and tuned to a classical music station. Suddenly the program was interrupted and Benny reached to turn up the volume. The announcer delivered a bulletin of news. When the music came back on, Benny lowered the volume.

"There was another *pigu'a*," he informed Martin. "That's a terrorist attack. Hezbollah in the Lebanon ambushed an army patrol in the security corridor we occupy along the border. Two of our boys were killed, two wounded." He shook his head in disgust. "Hezbollah makes the mistake of thinking that we're all hanging out in Tel Aviv nightclubs or raking in millions in our Israeli Silicon Valley, that prosperity has drained the fight out of us, that we've grown soft and fat and are not willing to die for our country. One of these days we'll have to set them straight . . ."

The outburst took Martin by surprise. Not knowing how to respond, he said, "Uh-huh."

Twenty-five minutes after picking Martin up near the *shouk*, Benny drove into what looked like a rich man's housing project filled with expensive two-story homes set back from the street. "We're a kilometer inside the West Bank here," he noted as he eased the Skoda to the curb in front of a house with a wraparound porch. Martin followed him through the metal gate and along the porch to the back of the house, where Benny pointed out the low clouds in the distance drenched with saffron light. "It's Jerusalem, over the horizon, that's illuminating the clouds," he said. "Beautiful, isn't it?"

"No," Martin shot back; the word escaped his lips before he knew what he was going to say. When Benny looked quickly at him, Martin added, "It makes me uneasy."

Benny asked, "What makes you uneasy—cities beyond the horizon? Clouds saturated with light? My living on the Palestinian side of the sixty-seven border?"

Martin said, "All of the above."

Benny shrugged. "I built this house in 1986, when Har Addar was founded," he said. "None of us who came to live here imagined we would ever give this land back to the Palestinians."

"Living on the wrong side of the green line must be something of an embarrassment for you."

Benny punched a code into a tiny number pad fixed on the wall to turn off the alarm. "If and when we agree to the creation of a Palestinian state," he said, "we'll have to adjust the frontier to take into account Israeli communities like this one." He unlocked the door and let himself into the house. The lights came on the instant he crossed the threshold. "Modern gadgets," he explained with a snigger. "The alarm, the automated lights are Mossad perks—they supply them to all their senior people."

Benny set out a bottle of imported whiskey and two thick kitchen glasses on a low glass table, along with a plastic bowl filled with ice cubes and another with pretzels. They both scraped over chairs and helped themselves to a stiff drink. Martin produced a Beedie from a tin box. Benny provided a light.

"To you and yours," Martin said, exhaling smoke, reaching to clink glasses with the Israeli.

"To legends," Benny shot back. "To the day when they become war surplus."

"I'll drink to that," Martin declared.

Martin glanced around, taking in the framed Hockney prints over the sofa, the brass menorah on the sideboard, the three blown-up photographs, each bordered in black, of young men in army uniforms on the wall over the chimney. Benny noticed him noticing. "The two on the left were childhood friends. They were both killed in action on the Golan, one in sixty-seven, the other in seventy-three. The one on the right is our son, Daniel. He was killed in an ambush in the Lebanon a year and a half ago. Roadside bomb hidden in a dead dog blew up as his jeep went past. His mother . . . my wife died of grief five months later."

Now Martin understood the source of the pain that Benny had learned to live with, and why he had grown melancholy. "I'm sorry," was all he could think to say.

"Me, also, I'm sorry," was all Benny could trust himself to answer.

They both concentrated on their drinks. Finally Benny broke the silence. "So what brings you to the Holy Land, Dante?"

"You were the Mossad's Russian expert, Benny. Who the hell is Samat Ugor-Zhilov?"

"Why are you interested in him?"

"He ran off from Kiryat Arba without giving a divorce to his wife. She's religious. Without a divorce she can't remarry. Her sister, who lives in Brooklyn, hired me to find Samat and get him to give her the divorce."

"To know who Samat is, you have to understand where he was coming from." Benny treated himself to another shot of whiskey. "How much do you know about the disintegration of the Soviet Union?"

"I know what I read in the newspapers."

"That's a beginning. The USSR we knew and loathed imploded in 1991. In the years that followed the country became what I call a kleptocracy. Its political and economic institutions were infiltrated by organized crime. To get a handle on what happened, you need to understand that it was Russia's criminals, as opposed to its politicians, who dismantled the communist superstructure of the former Soviet Union. And make no mistake about it, the Russian criminals were Neanderthals. In the early stages of the disintegration, when almost everything was up for grabs, the Italian mafia came sniffing around to see if they could get a piece of the action. You will have a better handle on the Russian mafia when you know that the Italians took one look around and went home; the Russians were simply too ruthless for them."

Martin whistled softly. "Hard to believe anyone could be more ruthless than the Cosa Nostra."

"When the Soviet Union collapsed," Benny went on, "thousands of gangs surfaced. In the beginning they ran the usual rackets, they offered the usual protection—"

"What the Russians call a roof."

"I see you've done your homework. The Russian word for roof is *krysha*. When two gangs offered their clients *krysha*, instead of the clients fighting each other if they had differences, the gangs did. The warfare spilled onto the streets in the early nineties. The period is referred to as the Great Moscow Mob Wars. There were something in the neighborhood of thirty thousand murders in 1993 alone. Another thirty thousand people simply disappeared. The smarter gangsters bought into legitimate businesses; the Russian Ministry of Internal

Affairs once estimated that half of all private businesses or state-owned companies, and almost all of the banks in the country, had links to organized crime. The infamous Tzvetan Ugor-Zhilov, known as the *Oligarkh* since he appeared on the cover of *Time*, began life as a small time hoodlum. When he couldn't bribe his way out of one particularly messy muddle, he wound up serving eight years in a gulag camp. When he finally returned to his native Armenia, Gorbachev was on the scene and the Soviet Union was breaking apart at the seams. Working out of a cramped communal apartment in Yerevan, the capital of Armenia, Ugor-Zhilov started offering *krysha*. Soon he was running his own small bank and his *krysha* clients were made to understand that they would be smart to use its services. At some point the *Oligarkh* branched out and bought into the used-car business in Yerevan. But being a big fish in a small pond didn't satisfy him, so he set his sights on Moscow—he moved to the capital and in a matter of months became the kingpin of the used-car business there."

"I heard all about his cornering the used-car market in Moscow. He bought out his competitors. The ones who wouldn't be bought out wound up in the Moscow River wearing cement shoes."

"The used-car racket was the tip of the iceberg. Look, Dante, you put your life on the line for Israel once and I'm going to return the favor. What I'm about to tell you isn't public knowledge—even the Sixth Chief Directorate of the KGB, which was supposed to be keeping tabs on the *Oligarkh*, didn't know it. For Tzvetan Ugor-Zhilov, the used-car dealerships were merely a stepping stone to bigger and better things. Russia happens to be the world's second largest producer of aluminum. When the Soviet system collapsed, Ugor-Zhilov branched out into the aluminum business. He somehow raised seed money— I'm talking billions; his used-car dealerships were bringing in cash but not that much and to this day it's a mystery where he got the money— and used it to make lucrative deals with smelters. He did all this through a holding company in which he was a silent partner. He bought three hundred railroad freight cars and built a port facility in Siberia to offload alumina, the bauxite extract that's the principal ingredient in aluminum. He imported the bauxite tax free from Australia, processed it at the smelters into aluminum and exported it, tax free, abroad. His profits soared. In the West aluminum brought five dollars a ton profit, in Russia it brought two hundred dollars a ton profit to the people who exported it. By the early nineties, as Yeltsin's privatization swept across the Soviet republics in an attempt to transform Russia into a market economy, the *Oligarkh* presided over a secret empire with the vast profits from aluminum at its base. His holding company expanded into other raw materials—steel, chrome, coal—and eventually bought into factories and businesses by the hundreds. He opened banks to service the empire and launder its profits abroad. Naturally he kept the skids greased with kickbacks to people in high places. At one point there were rumors that he'd paid off Yeltsin himself, but we were never able to pin this down."

"Did the CIA's Soviet division people know about this?"

"We were the ones with assets in Moscow. We shared enough of the take with them to convince them we were sharing all of it."

The phone rang. Benny raised it to his ear and listened. Then: "As a matter of fact, he is . . . He's doing what he was doing at Kiryat Arba, trying to pick up the trail of Samat Ugor-Zhilov so his wife can get a divorce . . . Actually, I do believe him, yes. Let's not forget that Dante Pippen is one of the good guys . . . *Shalom, shalom.*"

When Benny had hung up, Martin said, "Thanks for that."

"If I didn't believe it, you wouldn't be sitting here. Where was I? Okay. A certain number of Russian mafiosi were Jewish. When the mob wars broke out in Moscow in 1993, Israel became a safe haven for some of them. Here they were far away from the day to day mayhem. Even some of the gangsters who weren't Jewish came to Israel under our Law of Return—they concocted new identities claiming a Jewish mother or a Jewish grandmother and slipped into Israel along with the seven hundred and fifty thousand Russian Jews who came here in the nineties. As new immigrants, the gangsters were able to bring in large sums of money without anybody asking where it came from. When our Shabak people finally wised up to the danger, we tapped their phones, we infiltrated their entourages, all the time looking for evidence that the Russians were engaged in criminal activities here. But they were careful to keep a low profile. They didn't spit where they ate, as the saying goes. We used to joke that they wouldn't cross an intersection on a yellow light. Using Israeli banks as conduits, they continued their illegal activities, but always abroad. They smug-

gled uranium yellow cake out of Nigeria and sold it to the highest bidder. They bought into the diamond business, smuggling uncut stones
out of Russia to Amsterdam. They could get you a diesel submarine in
mint condition for a mere five-and-a-half million dollars, not counting a crew of Baltic sailors to run it—that was extra. They sold Soviet
surplus tanks with or without ammunition, jeeps, half-tracks, portable
bridges to cross rivers, anti-aircraft missiles, radars of all sizes and
shapes. Payments had to be in U.S. or Swiss currency deposited in
numbered accounts in Geneva, delivery guaranteed within thirty days
of the payment being received. All contracts were concluded with corporate affiliates in Liechtenstein."

"Why Liechtenstein?"

Benny bared his teeth. "They have strict banking secrecy laws."

"Uh-huh."

"The *Oligarkh*'s brother was one of those who immigrated to Israel.
His name was Akim Ugor-Zhilov. One fine day in 1993 he turned up
at Ben-Gurion airport with a wife and three young children in tow,
claiming that he had a Jewish grandmother and had, in any case, converted to Judaism; naturally he had affidavits to prove all this. He has a
livid scar over one eye. Claims he was wounded in Afghanistan, though
there is no evidence he ever served in the Soviet army. He installed himself in a heavily guarded villa in Caesarea surrounded by a high electri-
fied wall and staffed by Armenians who served in the army and knew
how to use weapons. The Russian speakers in the Mossad called them
chelovek nastroeniia— "moody people." One minute Akim would scream
insults at the Armenians who worked for him, the next he would be
purring like a cat and bragging about his business prowess. Besides the
fortress in Caesarea, he has a duplex in London's Cadogan Place and a
house on the Grande Corniche above Nice."

"How did he make ends meet in Israel?"

"He brought in something like fifty million dollars over the years
and invested it in government bonds, which earn six or seven percent
interest, tax free. He also has a piece of a newspaper delivery service, a
hotel in Eilat, half a dozen gas stations around Haifa."

"Where does Samat fit into this picture?"

"Akim and Tzvetan Ugor-Zhilov are brothers. It turns out there
was a third brother, name of Zurab. He was a medical doctor, a mem-

ber of the Armenian Communist Party and married to a Jewish woman. When Tzvetan was convicted of shaking down local merchants and sent to Siberia, his brother Zurab was arrested as an enemy of the people—under the Soviet system relatives of criminals usually suffered the same fate as the criminal. Zurab wound up in a Siberian gulag and died there of scarlet fever."

"What happened to Zurab's wife?"

"After the arrest of her husband, we lost all trace of her. She vanished from the face of the earth. The two brothers, Tzvetan and Zurab, had been very close, which explains, in part at least, why Tzvetan loathed the Soviet system: He blamed the communists for his brother's death. Zurab left behind him a son named Samat."

"Which makes Samat the *Oligarkh's* and Akim's nephew."

"Samat was taken under uncle Tzvetan's wing when he returned from Siberia; the *Oligarkh*, who had no children of his own, became a surrogate father to him. In the post-Stalinist Soviet Union, and especially after Gorbachev came on the scene, the fact that Samat's father had died in Siberia counted for him instead of against him. Samat was admitted to the elite Forestry Institute, the not-so-secret home of the Soviet space program, where he studied computer science. Later he earned a doctorate from the State Planning Agency's Higher Economic School. His computer skills must have attracted the attention of the KGB because the next thing we know he was working for the Sixth Chief Directorate, where he learned all there was to know about money laundering schemes and off-shore banks. When the *Oligarkh*, offering *krysha* and starting out in the used-car business in Armenia, decided to go into the banking business to service his expanding empire, he turned to his nephew. Samat quit the KGB and opened the first bank for Tzvetan Ugor-Zhilov in Yerevan. And it was Samat, with a reputation of something of a genius when it came to juggling accounts and obscuring currency trails, who created the money laundering scheme under which dozens of millions of dollars were siphoned off abroad and then squirreled away in off-shore banks and shell holding companies. The *Oligarkh's* holding companies are rumored to have financial interests in a Spanish insurance company, a French hotel chain, a Swiss real estate consortium, a German movie theater chain. Thanks to Samat's sleight of hand, the threads that linked these accounts were untraceable—God knows our people tried. So for that matter did your CIA. Samat's impenetrable labyrinth of banks stretches from France to Germany to Monaco to Liechtenstein to Switzerland to the Bahamas and the Cayman Islands, not to mention Vanuatu in the South Pacific, the Isle of Man, the British Virgin Islands, Panama, Prague, Western Samoa—all of them suspected of being involved in laundering the *Oligarkh*'s considerable riches. He eventually opened bank accounts in North America, where a third of his empire's aluminum was marketed. There were shells within shells within shells. Working out of the *Oligarkh*'s isolated dacha in a village half an hour from Moscow along the Moscow-Petersburg highway, Samat was constantly shifting assets from one shell to another. Wire transfers between banks, some of which consist of nothing more than a single room and a computer on some remote island, are the easiest way to move large amounts of money—one billion in one-hundred-dollar bills weighs something like eleven tons. And it was said that the *Oligarkh*'s banker never committed anything to paper; the entire structure of his uncle's off-shore holdings was in his head."

"Which was why it became urgent to get him out of Russia when the mob war heated up," Martin guessed.

"Precisely. We didn't figure out the connection between Samat and the second of his two uncles, Akim, until one of our teams watching Akim's villa at Caesarea caught them on film—Akim emerged from the villa and embraced Samat as he got out of his Honda, at which point we started looking into the identity of this new immigrant who had paid in cash when he bought a split-level home in Kiryat Arba."

Benny offered Martin a refill and, when he shook his head no, he poured himself a short one and downed it in one gulp. It was almost as if the recounting of the story had sapped his energy.

Martin said, "Samat's wife mentioned that he once dropped her on the dunes in Caeserea while he went to see someone. Now I know whom he saw."

Benny's pot-luck supper consisted of cold dishes he'd brought back in a doggie bag from an Arab restaurant in Abu Gosh and a bottle of red wine from the Golan. Martin, who didn't eat meat, made do with the vegetable dishes. Later, Benny broke out a bottle of fifteen-

year-old French cognac and carefully poured some into two snifters.
"There was an office bash when I retired last year," he explained.
"This was one of my going away presents, along with a jockstrap
medal for long and loyal service."

"How many years?"

"Forty two."

"Could Israel have survived without the Mossad?" Martin asked.

"Of course. We got as much wrong as we got right. We messed up
badly in seventy-three—we told Golda Meir that the Egyptians would-
n't be ready to wage war for at least ten years. A few weeks later they
swarmed across the Suez canal and overran our Bar Lev fortresses
stretched along the Israeli side of the waterway."

"What went wrong?" Martin asked.

"I suppose the same thing that went wrong in the middle and late
eighties when your CIA failed to predict the breakup of the Soviet
empire and the demise of the communist system. Looking in from the
outside, which is what I do these days, I can see that intelligence services are fatally flawed. They're self-tasking—they define the threats
and then try to neutralize them. Threats that don't get defined slip
through the mesh and suddenly turn up as full-blown disasters, at
which point those who are outside the intelligence community start
yapping about how we've been asleep on the job. We haven't been
asleep. We've just been defining it differently."

"They say a camel is a horse designed by committee," Martin said.
"For my money, the CIA is an intelligence agency designed by the
same committee."

Benny shrugged. "For me, Dante, it all comes down to that dead
dog at the side of the road in Lebanon, the one that exploded and
decapitated my son. If we had been doing the job we were paid to do,
we would have anticipated the dead dog filled with PETN, and identified the terrorist behind it. I have trouble . . . I have trouble getting
past that reality." Benny climbed heavily to his feet. "I think I'll turn
in now, if you don't mind. The bed's made in the room next to the
downstairs bathroom. Sleep well."

"I never sleep well," Martin murmured; he, too, was having trouble getting past the dead dog that decapitated Benny's son. "I wake up
in the middle of the night in a cold sweat."

An ugly grin deformed Benny's lips. "Occupational disease, for which there is no known cure."

The next morning Benny drove Martin into Jerusalem and let him off at the bus station. "One departs for Tel Aviv every twenty minutes," he said. He handed him a slip of paper. "Phone number for Akim in Caesarea. It's unlisted. I'd appreciate it if you didn't tell him where you got it. I'll nose around about the phone company's magnetic tapes and let you know what I find out. By the way, Samat's not in Israel. Shabak says he flew to London two days before the rabbi at Kiryat Arba reported him missing."

"Thanks, Benny."

"You're welcome, Dante. I hope you find what you're looking for."

"I've trimmed my sails, Benny. I am thankful for light winds."

* * *

From the brick guard shack atop the high wall surrounding Akim Ugor-Zhilov's seaside villa in Caesarea, Martin could almost hear the hiss as the sun knifed into the western Mediterranean. "Great view," Akim said, though he was standing with his back to it, sizing up his visitor, trying to figure out if his three-piece suit was custom made or off the rack. The livid sickle-shaped scar slashing across his high forehead over his right eye and vanishing into a long sideburn appeared to shimmer. "The Israelis think you are an Irishman named Pippen," Akim was saying, his heavy Russian accent surfacing indolently from the depths of his throat. "Then someone named Odum—which was the name on the passport you used to enter the country a week ago today—calls me from a phone booth in Tel Aviv and invites himself over to my house. Needless to say, the fact that a name is on a passport does not mean nothing. So which is it, friend, Pippen or Odum?"

"The answer is complicated—"

"Simplify."

Martin decided to stick close to the truth. "Pippen was a pseudonym I used years ago when I worked as a freelance explosive expert. Odum is the name I've been using since."

Akim brightened. "Pseudonyms are something I can relate to. In Soviet Russia, everybody who was anybody used them. You have heard of Vladimir Ilyich Ulyanov? He was known as Lenin, after the River Lena in Siberia. Iosif Vissarionovich Dzhugashvili took the alias Stalin, which meant steel, which is how he wanted people to think of him. Lev Davidovich Bronstein escaped from prison with the help of a passport made out in the name of one of his jailers, a certain Trotsky. Me myself, I managed to avoid being sent with my two brothers to the gulag by adopting the identity of a sleight-of-hand magician named Melor Semyonovich Zhitkin. You are familiar with the gulag? That's where temperatures fall below minus fifty and alcohol freezes and you suck on vodka icicles carefully so they do not stick to your tongue. Using the name Melor was a stroke of genius, even if it is me who says so. Melor is a Soviet name, stands for Marx-Engels-Lenin-Organizers-of-Revolution, which made the KGB think I was a diehard communist. I was diehard all right," he added with a sinister cackle. "They could not kill me, which is what made me diehard."

Without blinking one of his heavy lids or narrowing his eyes, Akim's expression turned hard. Martin wondered how he did it. Perhaps it was the shadows playing on his face, perhaps the pupils of his eyes had actually grown smaller. Whatever it was, the effect was chilling.

Akim's voice shed its laziness. "Pippen was an agent for the American Central Intelligence Agency who infiltrated the Hezbollah in the Bekaa Valley posing as a freelance explosive expert with connections to the IRA. You and the CIA are said to have parted company, though I am embarrassed to say none of my sources knows why. You are startled to see how well informed I am, right? You see, in Israel, as in every civilized country, information can be purchased as easily as toothpaste. Now you claim to be a Brooklyn, New York, detective named Odum. There are some who think this is simply another fabricated identity. There are others who say Odum is who you were before you were Pippen."

"I did work for the CIA once. I no longer do. Odum is as close to the real me as can get."

Akim accepted this with a wary nod. "Time for my insulin shot," he announced. He beckoned with a pinky bearing a heavy gold ring with a diamond set into it. Martin followed him down the narrow steps and across the lawn, past the swimming pool where three women in diaphanous dresses with low necklines were playing mahjongg; he suddenly longed for the days when he investigated uncomplicated things like mahjongg debts and kidnapped dogs and Chechen-run crematoriums in Little Odessa. He must have been off his rocker to think he could trace a husband who had jumped ship. Finding a needle in a haystack would be child's play by comparison. Akim reached the shaded veranda behind the mansion and motioned Martin to one of the deck chairs. Two of Akim's Armenians, wearing sports jackets that didn't conceal the automatic pistols in their shoulder holsters, stood nearby. A male nurse dressed in a white hospital smock was squirting liquid through a needle to expel any air left in the syringe. Akim collapsed into a deck chair and tugged the tails of his shirt out of his trousers to bare a bulging stomach. He sipped fresh orange juice through a plastic straw as the male nurse jabbed the needle under his dry skin and injected the insulin.

"Thanks a lot, Earl. See you tomorrow morning."

"My pleasure, Mr. Zhitkin."

When the male nurse was out of ear shot, Akim said, "As you can see I still use the name Zhitkin from time to time. Funny how you become attached to an alias that saved your life." At the pool, one of the women shrieked with pleasure. Akim burst out angrily, "Keep it quiet, ladies. Don't you see I have a visitor?" Massaging the spot on his stomach where the insulin had been injected, he said, "So what do you think I can do for you, Mr. Pippen or Mr. Odum or whatever your name is today?"

"I really am a detective," Martin said. "I was hired to find your nephew, Samat, who seems to have skipped out on his wife. I was hoping you would tell me where to start looking."

"What's she want, the wife, alimony payments? A piece of his bank account, assuming he has got a bank account? What?"

"I was hired by the wife's sister and father—"

"Who is a dead man now."

"You *are* well informed. They hired me to find Samat and get him to give her a divorce. She's religious. Without the divorce she can't marry again, can't have children with another man."

Akim tucked the tails of his shirt back into his trousers. "You have met the wife in question?" he asked.

"Yes."

"You have seen how she dresses? Who would marry *her*? Who would fuck her even to have children?"

"She's young. She may even be a virgin. The rabbi who married her thinks she and Samat never slept together."

Akim waved his hand in disgust. "Rabbi needs to stick to the bible. I do not want to hear private things about my nephew. Who he fucks—*whether* he fucks—is not my business."

Another Armenian shouted something in a strange language from the driveway guard house. Akim said, "My people want to turn on the spotlights after dark, but the neighbors complain to the police. Every time we turn them on the police come around and order us to turn them off. What kind of a country is this where a man of means cannot light up the wall around his property? It is like as if they personally hold being rich against me."

Martin said, "Maybe what they hold against you is the way you got rich."

"I am starting to like you," Akim admitted. "You talk to me the way I talked to people like me when I was your age. Fact is if I did not get rich, someone else would have got rich in my place. Making money was the only thing to do when the Soviet Union disintegrated—it was a matter of not drowning in Gorbachev's perestroika, because only the rich were able to keep their heads above water. Anyway, America brought it on, the collapse, the gangsters, the mob wars, all of it."

"I'm not sure I understand what you're driving at," Martin remarked.

"I am driving at history, Mr. Odum. In 1985 the Saudi oil minister, who happened to be a big wheel in the OPEC oil cartel, announced to the world that Saudi Arabia would no longer limit production to support oil prices. You want to sit there and tell me the Americans had nothing to do with this? Eight months later oil prices had plummeted seventy percent. Oil and gas exports is what kept the Soviet Union afloat for years, even for decades. The fall in oil prices started the economy downhill. Gorbachev tried to save what could be saved with his half-baked reforms, but the ship sank under his feet. When things quieted down, Russia's borders had shrunk to where they were in 1613. It is people like me and my brother who started poking through the debris and picking up the pieces. If things are better today for the masses it is because money has been trickling down. Ha! It is an economic fact that in order for wealth to trickle down, you need to have rich people at the top to do the trickling."

"If I'm reading you correctly, you are a born-again capitalist."

"I am a born-again opportunist. I did not go to school like Samat—I learned what I learned in the gutter. I understand capitalism contains within itself the seeds of its own destruction. Do not smile, Mr. Odum. The villain was your Genry Ford. By inventing the assembly line and mass producing his cars, he lowered the price to where the assembly-line workers became consumers of their own products. And with buy-now, pay-later schemes and plastic credit cards, people were able to spend money before they accumulated it. Instant gratification killed the Protestant work ethic, which glorified work and encouraged saving. Remember you heard it here first, Mr. Odum: America is on a slippery slope. It will not be far behind the Soviet Union in crashing."

"What will be left?"

"We will be left. The *Oligarkhs*."

One of Akim's bodyguards came around the side of the house to the veranda. He caught Akim's eye and tapped a fingernail against the crystal on his Rolex. Akim swung his short legs off the deck chair and stood up. "I am meeting a member of the knesset for supper in Peta Tikva," he said. "Let us stop circling each other like wrestlers, Mr. Odum. Wears out shoe leather." Waving to the women playing mahjongg, he shouted something in Armenian. Then, gesturing for Martin to accompany him, he started toward the enormous SUV parked in the driveway, exhaust streaming from its silver tail pipe. "How much they paying you to find Samat?" he demanded.

"I'm sorry?"

Akim stopped in his tracks and eyed Martin. Once again his face turned menacing without so much as his moving a muscle. "Are you thick in the skull or what?" he said, his voice a low, lazy growl. "Do I have to spell this out? Okay, I am asking what the wife's sister's father, who is a dead man, offered you to find my nephew Samat. I am saying that whatever he offered is nothing alongside what I will put on the table if you can lead me to him. What would you think of one million American dollars in cash. Or the equivalent in Swiss francs or German marks."

"I don't get it."

Akim groaned in exasperation. "You do not need to *get* it," he insisted. He started toward the car again. "A hundred and thirty million U.S. dollars have disappeared from six of my holding companies around the world that Samat controlled. That mouse of a wife in Kiryat Arba is not the only one wants a divorce. Me, too, I want one. I want to divorce my nephew. I want him to become my ex-nephew. So do we have an arrangement, Mr. Odum? You have my phone number. If you get your hands on Samat before I get my hands on him, pick up the phone and give me a call and you will become a rich man. Then you will be the one to trickle down to the proletariat so they can buy more of Mr. Genry Ford's automobiles."

*   *   *

Stella and Martin hefted their valises onto the table and opened the locks. One of the female soldiers, wearing white surgical gloves, started to rummage through the contents. The other female soldier, her eyes black with mascara, began asking questions and ticking off items on a clipboard when she heard the answers. Had anyone given them a parcel to take out of Israel? Who had packed their valises? Had the valises been left alone after they were packed? What was the purpose of their trip to Israel? Had they been to any Arab towns or villages or the Arab sections of Jerusalem? How had they come to the airport? Had the valises been in sight all the time after they got out of the taxi?

Finally the young woman looked up. "You are traveling together?"

"Yes," Martin replied.

"Excuse me for being personal but you do not have the same family name."

"We're just friends," Stella told her.

"Excuse me again but how long have you known each other?"

"Something like two weeks now," Martin said.

"And you decided to come to Israel together after knowing each other only two weeks?"

Stella bristled. "Is it written that people have to be lovers in order to travel together?"

"I am only asking the questions that we're instructed to put to all the passengers." She addressed Stella. "I see from your tickets that you both came to Israel from Athens. But your friend is flying to London and you are flying to New York. If you're traveling together, why are you no longer traveling together?"

"I'm returning to New York to bury Kastner," Stella explained.

"Who is Kastner?"

"My father."

"You call your father by his family name?"

"I call my father whatever I damn well decide to call him."

The young woman said, "So your father is dead." She jotted something on the space reserved for comments.

"I'm not planning to bury him alive, if that's what you mean."

The woman remained unfazed. "You are traveling under an American passport but you speak English with a slight East European accent."

"It's a Russian accent, actually. I immigrated to the United States from Russia nine years ago."

"At that period Soviet borders were not open to people who wanted to emigrate. How did you get out of the Soviet Union?"

Stella squinted at her interrogator. "My father and my sister and I went on vacation to the Black Sea in Bulgaria. The American CIA slipped us Greek passports and we joined a tour ship returning through the Bosporus to Piraeus."

The two female soldiers exchanged looks. "Airport security is not a joking matter," snapped the one searching the luggage.

"There was a time in my life when I was paid for being funny," Stella retorted. "This is not one of them."

The young woman with the clipboard raised a walkie-talkie to her lips and muttered something in Hebrew. "Wait here a moment," she ordered. She walked over to two men in civilian clothing and, pointing with her face at Stella and Martin, said something to them. One of the men pulled a small notebook from his pocket and thumbed through it until he came to the page he was looking for. He glanced over at Martin and then handed the female soldier an envelope. The girl shrugged. Returning to the table, she passed the envelope to Martin. "You can close your valises and check in now."

"What was that all about?" Stella asked Martin after they had presented their passports and boarding passes and gone up the escalator to the vast waiting room.

Martin slit open the envelope with a forefinger and unfolded the sheaf of paper in it. "Uh-huh," he muttered.

"Uh-huh what?"

"My old Mossad friend, the one who fed me pot-luck supper, says the magnetic tapes showing incoming and outgoing calls from Kiryat Arba were erased, just as the rabbi said. But they weren't erased by error. The Mossad did it as a favor for their CIA colleagues."

"The plot thickens!"

"We knew the CIA didn't want me to find Samat—my old boss told me as much when she invited me down to the Chinese restaurant." Martin thought about the exploding honey that had killed Minh and the two bullets that a sniper had shot at him in Hebron. He led Stella to one of the rows of plastic seats out of earshot of other passengers. "How did things go with your sister after I left?"

"She tried to talk me into staying in Israel. What would I do here?"

Martin said, "Israel is also a pressure cooker—you could go around telling anti-Israeli jokes for a living."

"Very funny. As a matter of fact I know a good one. The rabbi told it to me. Question: What is anti-Semitism? Answer: Hating Jews more than necessary."

"That's not funny," Martin said.

"What's funny about it," Stella insisted angrily, "is that it's not funny. I could kick myself for trying to make someone without a sense of humor laugh."

"My pal Dante had a sense of humor," Martin said, a faraway look in his eyes. "He left it in a room over a bar in Beirut."

Stella decided to change the subject. "Samat's uncle sounds like a real Russian mobster."

"I thought he could give me an idea where to start looking for Samat. He said if he knew where to look he wouldn't need me."

"Do you think Samat really ran off with all that money? What will his uncle do if he catches up with him?"

A voice over the public address system announced that the flight to London was about to start boarding. Martin climbed to his feet. "What will he do to him? I suppose he'll tickle him to death."

Stella said, "You're stepping out of character and telling a joke." Squinting, she studied Martin's face. "Okay, you're not telling a joke." Around them passengers were collecting their hand luggage and starting to head toward the stairs leading to the boarding gate. "I wish I were going with you. I'm getting used to your sense of humor."

"I thought you said I didn't have one."

"That's the part I'm getting used to." She stood and grazed his elbow with the back of her hand. "I hope against hope you'll call me from London."

His eyes took in the triangle of pale skin on her chest. "I admire your ability to hope against hope."

She toyed nervously with the first button on her shirt that was buttoned. "Maybe I can infect you."

"Not likely. I've been inoculated."

"Inoculations wear off." She stood on her toes and kissed him lightly on the lips. "Bye for now, Martin Odum."

"Uh-huh. Bye."

* * *

Crystal Quest was in wrathful dudgeon. "There's only one thing more revolting than having to target one of your own," she declared to the wallahs scattered around her sanctum, "and that's bungling the hit. Where do we hire marksmen these days, will somebody kindly enlighten me. Coney Island popgun concessions where you win a plastic doll if you topple the clown into the pan filled with dish water? Oh my God, it's pathetic. *Pa-the-tic.*"

"We should have given the assignment to Lincoln Dittmann," one of the newer wallahs suggested. "I understand he's a crackerjack shot—"

Quest, her head angled, her eyes unblinking, gazed at the speaker as if he just might have come up with the solution to their problem.

"Where did you pick up that nugget of information?" she inquired in a husky whisper, humoring the wallah before decapitating him.

The young man sensed that he had ventured onto quicksand. "I was reading into the Central Registry 201 files to get a handle on our assets in the field . . ." His voice faltered. He looked around for a buoy but no one seemed interested in throwing him one.

Quest's mouth sagged open as her skull bobbed up and down in wonderment. "Lincoln Dittmann! Now there's an idea whose time has come. Ha! Will somebody put the neophyte here out of his misery."

Quest's chief of staff, a thick skinned timeserver who had weathered his share of storms in the DDO's seventh floor bailiwick, said very evenly, "Dittmann and Odum are one and the same individual, Frank. You would have seen that they were cross-referenced in the 201 files if you'd read the fine print on the first page."

"That's strike one," Quest informed Frank. "If you read the fine print on *your* employment contract, you'll see that we operate by the *three-strikes-and-you're-out* rule in the DDO." She swiveled three hundred and sixty degrees in her chair as if she were winding herself up. "Okay. I'll recapitulate," she said, stifling her irritation. "We made an honest effort to talk Martin Odum out of walking back the cat on Samat Ugor-Zhilov. Martin's a consenting adult. He's doing what he has to do. And we're going to do what we have to do to make sure he never catches up to the Samat in question. This is a priority matter, which means it gets our full and undivided attention. Where did Martin Odum go when he left Israel? What leads is he following? Who is he planning to talk to? And what resources do we have on the ground—what resources can we throw into the theater of eventual operations—to make sure I get to wear my sackcloth and ashes before this thing blows up in our faces?"

1997: MARTIN ODUM PLAYS INNOCENT

LEANING OVER THE DEAD DOG, MARTIN SLIT OPEN ITS STOMACH with a safety razor, then reached in with the gloved hand to cut out the organs and create a stomach cavity. He motioned to one of the fedayeen students, who removed the frame from the hive and gingerly set it down on the road next to the dead dog. "Honey is very stable," Martin said with a laugh. "Tell him it won't blow up in his face until it's detonated." Using a spatula, he carefully scraped the beeswax from the honeycombs until he had accumulated a quantity the size of a tennis ball, then wired it to the tiny home-made plastic radio receiver and slipped the package into the stomach cavity. Using a thick needle and a length of butcher cord, he sewed up the opening. Rising to his feet, he stepped back to survey his handiwork.

"Any questions?" he demanded.

One of the fedayeen said something in Arabic and the Russian with the heavy gold ring on his pinky translated it into English. "He asks from how far away can we set off the charge?"

"Depends on what equipment you're using," Martin said. "A cordless phone or a Walkman will work up to a half a mile away. One of those automatic pagers that doctors wear on their belts can set off a charge five, six miles away. A VHF scanner or cellular mobile phone is effective for ten or twelve miles as long as the weather is good and there is no frequency jamming."

Martin, trailed by his three students and the translator, set off up the slope and went to ground behind the rusty wreck of a U.N. jeep. They didn't have long to wait. The Isra'ili patrol, led by a soldier scanning the dirt road with a magnetic mine detector, appeared around the bend. The soldier searching for mines passed his metal detector over the dog and, getting no reading, continued on. The officer behind him came abreast of the dog. Something must have caught his eye—the crude stitches on the stomach, probably—because he crouched next to the animal to have a closer look. Martin nodded at the fedayeen holding the automatic pager that had been rigged to transmit a signal to the plastic receiver inside the dog's stomach. Below, a dull blast stirred up a fume of mustard-colored smoke. When it cleared, the Isra'ili officer was still crouching next to the dog but his head could be seen rolling slowly toward the shoulder of the road.

"Comes as news to me that honey can explode," the Russian whispered, his thick Slavic accent surfacing indolently from the depths of his throat.

The sulfurous stench of the burnt beeswax reached Martin's nostrils and he had trouble breathing. Gasping for air, he bolted upright in bed and blotted the cold sweat from his brow with a corner of the sheet. His heart was beating furiously; a migraine was pressing against the back of his eyeballs. For a terrible moment he didn't know who he was or where he was. He solved the second problem first when he heard the hacking cough of the old man two rooms down the corridor of the boarding house and knew where he *wasn't*: southern Lebanon. When he figured out which legend he was inhabiting, his breathing gradually returned to normal.

When his plane landed at Heathrow, four days before, Martin had breezed through passport control without a hitch. "Here on business or pleasure, is it?" the woman custom's agent in the booth had asked. "With any luck, pleasure, in the form of licensed tabernacles and museums, and in that order," he'd answered. The woman had flashed a jaded smile as she stamped him into the country. "If it's pubs you're looking for, you have come to the right corner of the world. Enjoy your stay in England."

Collecting his valise from the baggage carousel, Martin had started following the signs marked "Underground" when a portly young man with a peaches-and-cream complexion had materialized in front of him. "Mr. Odum, is it?" he'd asked.

"How come you know my name?"

The young man, his body wrapped in a belted trench coat a size too large for him, had ignored Martin's question. "Could I trouble you to come with me, sir," he had said.

"Do I have a choice?"

"I'm afraid you don't."

"What are you, five or six?"

"MI5, thank you, kindly. Six thinks you're radioactive, wouldn't touch you with a ten-foot pole."

Martin could see three other men in trench coats closing in on him as he limped behind the young man across the arrival hall and up a flight of steps to a balcony overlooking the hall. Peaches-and-cream stopped before an opaque glass door with the word "Perishables" stencilled on it. He rapped on the glass twice with his knuckles, opened the door and politely stepped aside. Inside, a middle-aged woman dressed in a man's pinstriped suit and tie was busy calling up file folders on a computer terminal. Without looking up, she inclined her head toward an inner door with the words "Supervisor, Perishables" stencilled on the glass. In the inner office, Martin discovered a black man with a shaven head studying the baggage carousels below through the slats of a partly closed venetian blind. The black man swiveled around in his seat and sank back into it. "I'll admit it, you don't look like your average serial killer to me," he said in a soft purr.

"What does an average serial killer look like?"

"Glassy stare as he avoids your eye, bitten finger nails, mouth drooping open, saliva drooling down the stubble of his chin. Bela Lugosi sort of role."

"Are you a cop or a movie critic?"

Snickering at Martin's question, the Supervisor, Perishables began reading from a yellowing index card. "Last trace we had on you, you were a bloke with two incarnations. In the first, you were Pippen, Dante, an Irishman who declined to help us with our inquiries after the IRA blew open a bus in central London. In the second, you were Dittmann, Lincoln, an American arms merchant peddling his wares to the highest bidder in the Triple Border area of Latin America."

Martin said, "Case of mistaken identity. You're confusing me with the antiheroes of B films."

"Don't think we are," the Supervisor, Perishables allowed. He arched his brows and took a long look at Martin, who was shifting his weight from one foot to the other. "If we had chairs, I'd invite you to rest your arse on one of them. Sorry 'bout that."

"Been sitting from Tel Aviv to here," Martin said. "Glad to stretch my legs."

"Yes, well, in Israel you were passing yourself off as Martin Odum, a ruck of a private detective working out of the New York borough of"—he checked his file card—"Brooklyn. That's quite inventive, actually. Some nonsense about hunting for a missing husband so his wife could get a religious divorce. It goes without saying, knowing your track record, neither our antenna in Israel nor our Perishables division here in London swallowed the cover story. So what are you hawking this time round, Mr. Dittmann? Used one-owner Kalashnikovs? That Ukrainian-manufactured passive radar system they say can detect Stealth aircraft at five hundred miles distance? Nerve gas masquerading as talcum powder? Seed stock for biological agents that cause cholera or camelpox?"

"None of the above." Martin smiled innocently. "Search me."

"Don't mind if I do." He touched a button on a console. Martin could hear a buzzer wheeze in the outer office. The young man with the peaches-and-cream complexion and the woman who had been working on the computer terminal entered the room. "Would you be so kind as to give us the key to your valise, Mr. Dittmann," the woman asked, "and then disrobe." The black man came around the desk. Martin could see he was the kind who worked out at a gym often enough to hope the man who was supposed to help the police with their inquiries would resist.

Martin glanced at the woman. "I'm the timid type," he remarked.

"Nothing you 'ave, guv'nor, she 'asn't seen," snapped peaches-and-cream in a mock cockney accent.

The two men concentrated on Martin, stripping him to the skin and going over every square inch of his three piece suit, underwear and socks. The Supervisor, Perishables paid particular attention to his shoes, inserting them one at a time into a contraption that projected an X-ray image of the shoe onto a glass plate. The woman emptied the contents of the valise onto the desk and began examining each item. Toothpaste was squeezed out of its tube into a plastic container that had Chinese writing on the side. Cold capsules were split open and inspected. The small container of shaving cream was emptied and then cut in half with a hacksaw. Standing in the middle of the room, stark naked, Martin tried to imagine the anti-British joke that Stella would concoct out of the episode, but he couldn't come up with a punch line. Stella was surely right when she said he didn't have a sense of humor. "I suppose you are going to compensate me for property destroyed," he ventured as he started to pull on his clothing.

The Supervisor, Perishables took the question seriously. "You go ahead and replace the items in question and send us the bill," he said. "If you address it to Heathrow, Perishables, it should get here, shouldn't it, lads and ladies? Everyone knows who we are. Mind if I ask how long you reckon on staying in the country, Mr. Dittmann?"

"No. Ask."

Supervisor, Perishables didn't crack a smile. "How long you reckon on staying in the country, Mr. Dittmann?"

"My name is Odum. Martin Odum. I'm in Britain to tell anti-English jokes that will spread across the country like wildfire and take people's minds off the drudgery of day-to-day life. I plan to stay as long as folks keep laughing."

"He's certainly original," the black man told his associates.

Peaches-and-cream accompanied Martin down to the arrival hall. "No hurt feelings, I hope, gov'nor," he said, falling back into his phony cockney accent and trying to sound ironic.

Following the signs leading to the underground, Martin quickly spotted the two men who were following him, one about fifteen paces behind, the other ten paces behind the first. What gave them away was their habit of concentrating on the windows of the boutiques every time he turned in their direction. As Martin reached the escalator down to the train level, the first man peeled away, the second closed the gap and a third hove into view behind him. The resources they were devoting to keep track of Lincoln Dittmann made Martin feel important; it had been a long time since anyone thought he was interesting enough to lay on a staggered tail. As always in situations like this, Martin was more preoccupied with the agents he didn't see than the ones he was meant to spot. He took the Piccadilly line to Piccadilly Circus and the escalator to the street, then leaned against the side of a kiosk to give his game leg a rest. After awhile he strolled toward Tottenham Court Road, stopping at a chemist shop to buy toothpaste and shaving cream, eventually at a pub with a neon sign sizzling over the door that brought back memories of the Beirut waterfront and Dante's Alawite prostitute named Djamillah. He settled onto a stool at the dimly-lit end of the bar and sipped at his half pint of lager until half of it was down the hatch. Opening his valise, he slipped the packet of false identity papers into the white silk bandanna, then mopped his brow with it and stuffed it into the pocket of his suit jacket. Hefting his small valise onto the bar, folding his Burberry across it, he asked the bartender to keep an eye on his things while he used the loo in the back. Martin didn't even bother checking the tails, two outside in the street, one at a corner table in the front of the pub; they were all young, and young meant green, so they would fall for the oldest trick on the books: They would keep their eyes glued to the half consumed glass of lager and the valise with the raincoat on it, and wait for him to return. Depending on their relationship with the Supervisor, Perishables, they might or might not report that Martin had gone missing when he failed to come back.

Martin remembered this particular men's lavatory from a stint in London a lifetime ago. He'd been on his way to the Soviet Union and stopped off for a briefing from MI6's East European desk. What cover had he been using then? It must have been the original Martin Odum legend because Dittmann and Pippen came later, or so it seemed to him. In a remote corner of a lobe of his brain he had filed away one of those tradecraft details that field hands collected as if they were rare stamps: This particular lavatory had a fire door that was locked, but could be opened in an emergency by breaking a glass and removing the key hanging on a hook behind it. To Martin's way of thinking, this clearly qualified as an emergency. He found the glass and retrieved the key and opened the fire door. Moments later he found himself in a narrow passage that gave onto a side street and, as luck would have it, a taxi stand.

"Paddington," he told the driver.

He changed taxis twice more and only gave his real destination to the final driver. "Golders Green," he said, settling into the backseat and enjoying his fleeting triumph over the warm bodies from five.

"Any particular place on Golders Green?" the driver asked over the intercom.

"You can let me off near the clock at the top. I'll walk from there."

"Right you are, gov'nor. You American, are you?"

"What makes you think that?"

"It's the accent, gov'nor. I know American when I hear it."

"Actually I'm Polish," Martin had said, "but I've lived in America and it rubbed off."

The driver had tittered into the microphone. "I can tell someone what's pulling me leg, gov'nor. If you're Polish, that makes me an Eskimo."

Martin had paid off the taxi in front of the Golders Green underground station. Standing under the word "Courage" engraved in the stone monument at the top of Golders Green, he took his bearings, then set off down the broad avenue awash in sunlight and filled with midday pedestrians—Filipino maids pushing old ladies tucked into wheel chairs, teenage boys in embroidered skull caps careening past on mountain bikes, dozens of ultrareligious women wearing wigs and long dresses window shopping in front of stores with signs in English and Hebrew. Martin found a second-hand store run by a Jewish charity and bought himself an old valise that looked as if it had been around the world several times. He made a slit in the frayed silk lining under the lid and hid his stash of documents, then filled the valise with threadbare but serviceable clothing. He came across a second-hand Aquascutum that they were practically giving away because the belt was missing and the hem was in tatters. At a chemists, he bought more toothpaste, a disposable razor and a small tube of shaving cream. On Woodstock Avenue off Golders Green he spotted a ramshackle house next to a synagogue with a sign on the unkempt lawn advertising rooms for rent. He paid the grumpy landlady for a week in advance, stored his gear and went around the corner for a bite to eat at a kosher delicatessen across the street from a church. Midafternoon he walked up Golders Green to the Chinese Medicinal Center for a session of acupuncture on his game leg. When he complained that his leg felt sorer after the acupuncture, the old Chinese man, plucking the long needles deftly out of Martin's skin, said it was well known that things had to get worse before they could get better. Leaving a ten pound note on the counter, Martin promised he would bear that in mind. Starting back toward the rooming house, he noticed he was able to walk with less pain than before; he wondered whether it was due to the acupuncture needles or the power of suggestion. He bought a phone card at a tobacco shop and ducked into a fire-engine red booth on the corner of Woodstock and Golders Green that had a burnt phone book dangling from a chain. He rummaged in his wallet for the scrap of paper with the phone number that Elena had found on the back of the strudel recipe and, inserting his plastic card, dialed it.

Martin retrieved Dante Pippen's rusty Irish accent for the occasion. "And who would I be speaking to, then?" he inquired when a female voice came on the line.

"Mrs. Rainfield, dear."

"Good morning to you, Mrs. Rainfield. This is Patrick O'Faolain from the phone company. I'm up on a pole on Golders Green trying to sort out your lines. Could you do me the favor of pressing the number five and the number seven on your phone, in that order."

"Five, then seven?"

"That's the ticket, Mrs. Rainfield."

"Did you hear it?"

"Loud and clear. Do it once more to be sure, will you, now?"

"Okay?"

"Beautiful. We ought to be hiring the likes of you."

"Will you tell me what's going on?"

"Don't ask me how but your cable seems to have gotten itself twined around your neighbors' lines. One of them complained she heard cross talk when she tried to use her phone. Did you experience any static on yours, Mrs. Rainfield?"

"Now that you mention it, the phone did seem fuzzier than usual this morning."

"You ought to be hearing me clear as a bell now."

"I am, thank you."

"We spend most of our time climbing up phone poles to fix things that aren't broken. Now and then it's gratifying to fix something that is. You get half the credit—it was child's play once you hit the five and the seven. For my work sheet I'll be needing your full name and an address to go with your phone."

"I'm Doris Rainfield," the woman said, and she gave an address on North End Road, a continuation of Golders Green, behind the railroad station.

"Thanks a mill."

"Ta."

* * *

Martin pressed the buzzer next to the enormous steel door with "Soft Shoulder" engraved on a brass plaque and looked up into the security camera. There was a burst of static over the intercom. A woman's nasal voice surfed above the static.

"If you're delivering, you need to go round to the loading dock in back."

"Mr. Martin Odum," Martin called, "come to see the director of Soft Shoulder."

"Are you the bloke what's shipping the prostheses to Bosnia?"

"Afraid not. I was sent by a friend of the director's, a Mr. Samat Ugor-Zhilov."

"Wait a min, love."

The static gave way to an eerie quiet. A moment later the woman whom Martin took for Mrs. Rainfield came back on the intercom. "Mr. Rabbani, he wants to know how you know Mr. Ugor-Zhilov."

"Tell him," Martin said, employing the phrase Kastner had used the day they met on President Street, "we're birds of a feather."

"Come again?"

"Yes, well, you can tell Mr. Rabbani that I know Samat from Israel."

There was another interval of silence. Then a discreet electric current reached the lock in the door and it clicked open the width of a finger. Martin pushed it wide open and strode into the warehouse. He heard the door click closed behind him as he headed down the cement passageway lined with calendars from the 1980s, each with a photograph of a spread-eagled movie starlet flirting with nakedness. In the glass enclosed cubical at the end of the passageway, a young woman with pointed breasts and short hair the color and texture of straw sat behind a desk, painting her fingernails fuchsia. Martin poked his head through the open door. "You will be Doris Rainfield," he guessed.

The woman looked up, intrigued. "Samat went and told you 'bout me, did he, dear?" She batted the fingers of her right hand in the air to dry the nail polish. "I like Samat, I do. Oh, he's one for putting on airs, waltzing in with that topcoat of 'is flung over 'is shoulders like it was some kinda cape or other. He looked like the sheik in one of them Rudy Valentino silent period pictures, if you get my drift."

"I do get your drift, Mrs. Rainfield."

The woman lowered her voice to share a confidence. "Truth is I'm not Mrs. Rainfield. I used to be Mrs. Rainfield but I got myself legally hitched six weeks and three days back to Nigel Froth, which makes me Mrs. Froth, doesn't it, dear? Do you recognize the name? My Nigel's a world class snooker player. Made the quarter finals of the U.K. snooker championship last year, lost to the bloke who came in second, he did, which was a feather in 'is cap, I'm referring to Nigel's cap, not the bloke who came in second's cap. I still use my first husband's name at the office because that's what Mr. Rabbani calls me. All the paperwork 'ere is in the name of Rainfield and he says it'd be a bloody pain in the you know what to switch over."

Martin leaned against the door jamb. "Does Mrs. Rainfield act any differently than Mrs. Froth?"

"I s'pose she does, now that you mention it. My Mr. Froth fancies me in miniskirts and tight sweaters, he does. Mr. Rainfield wouldn't 'ave let me outa me house dressed like this. It's a lot like Samat's cape, isn't it, dear? What you wear is who you want to be." Fluttering unnaturally long lashes, Mrs. Rainfield pointed out the door at the bitter end of the passageway with her eyes. "Through there, then cross the warehouse on a diagonal and you'll fall on Mr. Rabbani's bailiwick. His factotum, an Egyptian named Rachid—trust me, you won't miss him—minds the door."

"Is Rachid his real name or is it a matter of Mr. Rabbani not wanting to redo the paperwork?"

Mrs. Rainfield giggled appreciatively.

Martin said, "Thank you" and started down the corridors created by stacks of cartons, all of them stencilled with the word "Prosthesis" and "Arm" or "Leg" and a measurement in inches and centimeters, along with a notation in smaller print that the articles had been manufactured in the United States of America. Above Martin's head, diffused sunlight streamed through skylights stained with soot and bird droppings. A heavy-set man with unshaven jowls and untidy hair, clearly the body guard, loomed beyond the last cartons. A handwritten nametag pinned to the wide lapel of his double-breasted suit jacket identified him as Rachid.

"You carrying?" he inquired, sizing Martin up with eyes that conveyed indifference to the visitor's fate in the unlikely event he resisted inspection.

Martin played a role he wasn't accustomed to: innocent. "Carrying what?"

Rachid snapped, "Something the municipal police might mistake for a handgun."

Grinning, Martin spread his legs apart and raised his arms. The bodyguard frisked him very professionally, passing his hand so high up the crotch that he grazed his penis with his knuckles, causing Martin to shudder.

"You ticklish, then?" the bodyguard remarked with a smirk. He inclined his head in the direction of a door with a neatly lettered plastic placard on it that said "Taletbek Rabbani—Export." Martin knocked. After a moment he knocked again and heard the scratchy voice of an old man call out weakly, "So what are you waiting on, my son, a hand delivered invite?"

Looking like a parenthesis, Taletbek Rabbani sat on a high stool hunched over a high desk, a thick cigarette dangling from his bone-dry lips, a smog of smoke hovering over his bald head like a rain cloud. An old man who must have been nudging ninety, he was not much thicker that the pencil clasped in his arthritic fingers. A tuft

of coarse white hair protruded from under his lower lip and served
as a receptacle for the ash that dropped off the burning end of the
cigarette. A swell of warm air enveloped Martin as he stepped into
the room; the old man kept his office heated to near sauna temperatures. Settling onto a tattered settee with the tag "Imported from
Sri Lanka" still attached to one spindly wooden leg, Martin could
hear the water gurgling through the radiators. "Taletbek Rabbani
sounds like a Tajik name," he remarked. "If I had to take a wild
guess, I'd say you were a Tajik from the steppes of the Panjshir Valley
north of Kabul. I seem to remember there was a tribal chief named
Rabbani who presided over a cluster of mountain villages near the
frontier with Uzbekistan."

Rabbani waved his skeletal fingers to dispel the cigarette smoke
and get a better look at his visitor. "You have been to Afghanistan?" he
demanded.

"In a previous incarnation I hung out for the better part of a year
near the Khyber Pass."

Rabbani was still trying to get a handle on Martin's curriculum
vitae. "What were you doing, my son, buying or selling?"

"Buying. Stories. I was debriefing fighters going into and out of
Afghanistan and writing them up for a wire service."

An ephemeral smile crossed Rabbani's age-ravaged eyes. "Wire service, my foot. Only people who hung out at the Khyber Pass were
American intelligence agents. Which means you were on the same side
as my older brother, the tribal chieftain Rabbani."

Martin had guessed as much once he'd placed Rabbani's name;
he hoped that this would get him off on the right track with the
old codger who, he now noticed, kept his left hand out of sight below
the desk. His fingers were certainly wrapped around the butt end of
a pistol.

"What happened to your brother after the Russians were kicked
out?"

"Along with everyone else in the valley, he got caught up in the
civil war—he fought alongside Ahmed Shah Massoud against the
Taliban when they abandoned their medrassahs in Pakistan and started
to infiltrate into Afghanistan. One day the Taliban invited my brother
to meet under a white flag in the outskirts of Kabul." The same smile

appeared in Rabbani's eyes, only this time it was tainted with bitterness. "I advised him against going, but he was strong headed and fearless and shrugged off my counsel. And so he went. And so the Taliban
cut his throat, along with those of his three bodyguards."

"I vaguely remember the incident."

Rabbani's left hand came into view, which told Martin that he had
passed muster.

"To have been at the Khyber, to remember Rabbani," the old man
said, "you must have worked for the CIA." When Martin neither confirmed nor denied it, Rabbani nodded slowly. "I understand there are
things that are never spoken aloud. You must forgive an old man for
his lack of discretion."

Martin could hear trains pulling into or out of the station next to
the warehouse with the rhythmic throb that was almost as satisfying
as travel itself. "If you don't mind my asking, Mr. Rabbani, how did
you wind up in London?"

"I was dispatched by my brother to England to purchase medical
supplies for our wounded fighters. When my brother was murdered,
a cousin on my mother's side profited from my absence to usurp the
leadership of the tribe. My cousin and I are sworn enemies—tribal
custom prevents me from exposing to you the reason for this feud
while there is no representative of my cousin present to defend the
other side of the matter. Suffice it to say that it became healthier for
me to stay on in London."

"And you went into the business of selling prostheses with
Samat?"

"I don't know how well you know Samat," Rabbani said, "but he
is a philanthropist at heart. He provided the start-up money to lease
this warehouse and open the business."

"The Samat I know does not have a reputation as a philanthropist," Martin said flatly. "He wheels and deals in many of the
weapons that lead to the loss of limbs. If he is in the business of selling
false limbs to war-torn countries, there must be a healthy profit in it."

"You misread Samat, my son," Rabbani insisted. "And you misread me. Samat is too young to be interested only in profit, and I am
too old. The cartons filled with false limbs that you saw on the way to
my office are sold at cost."

"Uh-huh."

"You clearly do not believe me." Rabbani slipped awkwardly off of the high stool and, retrieving two wooden canes that had been out of sight behind the desk, made his way across the room. When he stood before the settee, he hiked the trouser on his left leg, revealing a skin-colored plastic prosthesis with a Gucci loafer fitted onto the end of it.

Martin asked quietly, "How did you lose your leg?"

"I was told it was a land mine."

"Don't you remember?"

"Some nights fleeting images of what happened surface in my brain: a deafening explosion, the taste of dirt in my mouth, the stickiness of my stump when I reached down to touch it, the feeling I had for months that the leg was still there and I could feel pain in it. The images seem to come from the life of another, and so I have trouble reconstructing the event."

"Psychiatrists call that a survival mechanism, I think."

Leaning on one cane and then the other, Rabbani returned to his high chair and hefted himself into it. "I first met Samat when I was buying Soviet surplus arms and munitions in Moscow in the early nineties so that Massoud and my brother could defend the Panjshir. The Russian army units pulling out of their bases in the former German Democratic Republic after the Berlin Wall came down were selling off everything in their arsenals—rifles, machine guns, mortars, land mines, radios, jeeps, tanks, ammunition. Samat, representing the business interests of someone very powerful, was the middleman. It was a period of my life when I felt no guilt about buying and using these arms. I did to the Taliban what they eventually did to me. That was before I myself walked on a land mine. Take it from someone who has been there, Mr. Odum, it's an exhilarating experience, stepping on a mine. One instant you are attached to the ground, the next you are defying gravity, flailing away in the air. When you fall back to earth you have one limb less and nothing—not your body, not your mind—is ever the same. It was Samat who arranged for me to be flown to a Moscow hospital. It was Samat who came around with my manufactured-in-America artificial leg. It would not be an exaggeration to say that I became another person.

Which is why you find me presiding over a warehouse filled with prostheses that we sell at cost."

"And where does the name 'Soft Shoulder' come from?"

"Samat and I were traveling in the U.S. once," Rabbani explained. "We were driving a large American automobile from Santa Fe, in New Mexico, to New York, when we stumbled across the idea of going into the business of exporting artificial limbs at prices that would make them more easily affordable to the victims of war. We had pulled up at the side of the road to urinate when we shook hands on the project. Next to the car was a sign that read 'Soft Shoulder.' Neither of us knew what it meant, but we decided it would make a fitting name for our company."

The intercom buzzed. Rabbani depressed a lever with a deft jab of a cane and barked irritably, "And what is it now, my girl?"

Mrs. Rainfield's voice came over the speaker. "Truck's here for the Bosnia shipment, Mr. Rabbani. I sent them round back to the loading dock. They gave me a certified bank check for the correct amount."

"Call the bank to confirm it issued the check. Meanwhile get Rachid to supervise the loading." Rabbani tripped the lever closed with his cane, cutting the connection. "Can't be too vigilant," he moaned. "Lot of shady dealers make a lot of money peddling prostheses—they are not happy when someone else sells them at cost." He pried the stub of the cigarette out of his mouth and lobbed it across the room into a metal waste basket. "When were you in Israel, Mr. Odum?"

"Went there roughly ten days back."

"You told Mrs. Rainfield to tell me you knew Samat from Israel. Why did you lie?"

Martin understood that a lot depended on how he answered the question. "In order to get past the front door," he said. He angled his head. "What makes you think I was lying?"

Rabbani pulled an enormous handkerchief from a pocket and wiped the perspiration under his shirt collar at the back of his neck. "Samat left Israel before you got there, my son."

"How do you know that?"

The old man shrugged his bony shoulders. "I will not ask you

how you know what you know. Do me the courtesy of not asking me
how I know what I know. Samat fled from Israel. If you came knocking on my door today, it is because you somehow found a record of
his phone conversations and traced the calls he made to this address
in London, despite the fact that these phone records were supposed
to have been destroyed. I will not ask you how you did that—the
phone company is not permitted to reveal addresses corresponding to
unlisted numbers."

"Why did you let me in if you knew I was lying about Samat?"

"I calculated if you were clever enough to find me, you might be
clever enough to lead me to Samat."

"Join the queue, Mr. Rabbani. It seems as if everyone I meet wants
to find Samat."

"They want to find Samat in order to kill him. I want to find him
in order to save his life."

"Do you know why he fled Israel?"

"Certainly I know. He fled from Israel for the same reason he fled
to Israel. Chechen hit men were after him. Have been since the Great
Mob Wars in Moscow. Samat works for the *Oligarkh*—you're smart,
I'll give you that, but not so smart that you've heard of him."

Martin couldn't resist. "Samat's uncle, Tzvetan Ugor-Zhilov."

The old man cackled until the laugh turned into a grating cough.
Saliva trickled from a corner of his mouth. He dabbed at it with the
handkerchief as he gasped for breath. "You *are* a smart one. Do you
know what happened during the Great Mob War?"

"The Slavic Alliance battled the Chechen gangs. Over territory.
Over who controlled what."

"At the height of the war the Chechens had about five hundred
fighters working out of the Rossiya Hotel not far from the Kremlin.
The leader of the Chechens was known by his nom de guerre, which
was the Ottoman. The *Oligarkh* arranged to have him and his lady
friend at the time kidnapped. Samat was sent to negotiate with the
Chechens—if they wanted their leader back they would have to abandon Moscow and settle for some of the smaller cities that the *Oligarkh*
was willing to cede to them. The Chechens said they needed to discuss the matter with the others. Samat decided they were playing for
time—even if they agreed, there was no guarantee they would give up

Moscow. He persuaded the *Oligarkh* that the Chechens needed to be taught a lesson. Next morning people going to work found the body of the Ottoman and his lady friend hanging upside down from a lamppost near the Kremlin wall—newspapers compared it to the death of Mussolini and his mistress in the closing days of the Great Patriotic War."

"And you call Samat a philanthropist?"

"We all of us have many sides, my son. That was one side of Samat. The other was selling prostheses at cost to provide limbs to land-mine victims. I was one person before I stepped on the land mine and another after. What about you, Mr. Odum? Are you one dimensional or do you have multiple personalities like the rest of us?"

Martin brought a hand up to his forehead to contain the migraine throbbing like the trains pulling into and out of the station. Across the room the old man carefully pulled another cigarette from a desk drawer and lit it with a wooden match, which he ignited with a flick of his fingernail. Once again the smog of a rain cloud rose over his head. "Who is paying you to find Samat, Mr. Odum?"

Martin explained about the wife Samat had abandoned in Israel; how she needed to find her husband so he could grant her a religious divorce in front of a rabbinical court. Puffing away on his cigarette, Rabbani thought about this. "Not like Samat to abandon a wife like that," he decided. "If he ran for it, it means the Chechens tracked him to that Jew colony next to Hebron. Chechens have long knives and long memories—I've been told some of them carry photographs cut from the newspapers of the Ottoman and his lady hanging upside down from a Moscow lamppost. The Chechens must have been knocking on Samat's door, figuratively speaking, for him to cut and run." Rabbani hauled open another drawer and retrieved a metal box, which he opened with a key attached to the fob of the gold watch in his vest pocket. He took out a wad of English bank notes and dropped them on the edge of the desk nearest Martin. "I would like to find Samat before the Chechens catch up with him. I would like to help him. He does not need money—he has access to all the money he could ever want. But he does need friends. I could arrange for him to disappear into a new identity; into a new life even. So will you work for me, Mr. Odum? Will you find Samat and tell him that Taletbek Rabban stands ready to come to the assistance of his friend?"

"If Samat is being hunted by the Chechens, helping him could come back to haunt you."

Rabbani reached for one of the canes and tapped it against his false limb. "I owe Samat my leg. And my leg has become my life. A Panjshiri never turns his back on such a debt, my son."

Martin pushed himself to his feet and walked over to the desk and fanned the stack of banknotes as if it were a deck of cards. Then he collected them and shoved them into a pocket. "I hope you are going to tell me where to start to look."

The old man picked up the pencil, scratched something on the back of an envelope and handed it to Martin. "Samat came here after he left Israel—he wanted to touch base with the projects to which he was especially attached. He stayed two days, then took a plane to Prague. There is an affiliate in Prague—another one of Samat's pet projects—that's doing secret work for him on the side. I met one of the directors, a Czech woman, when she came here to see Samat. She gave me her card in case I ever visited Prague."

"What kind of secret work?"

"Not sure. I overheard the woman talking with Samat—the project had something to do with trading the bones of a Lithuanian saint for sacred Jewish Torah scrolls. Dont ask what the bones of a saint have to do with Torah scrolls. I don't know. Samat was very compartmented. The Samat I knew exported prostheses at cost. There were other Samats that I only caught glimpses of—one of them was concocting a scheme at the address I gave you in Prague."

Martin glanced at the paper, then held out a hand. Rabbani's bony fingers, soft with paraffin-colored skin, gripped his as if he didn't want him to leave. Words barely recognizable as human speech bubbled up from the old man's larynx. "I see things from the perspective of someone who is knocking at death's door. Apocalypse is just around the corner, my son. You are looking at me as if I belong in an asylum, Mr. Odum. *I am in an asylum*. So come to think of it are you. Western civilization or what is left of it, is one big asylum. The happy few who understand this are more often than not diagnosed as crazy and hidden away in lunatic bins."

Rabbani struggled for breath. "Find Samat before they do," he gasped. "He is one of the happy few."

"I'll do my best," Martin promised.

Making his way back through the aisles toward the front of the warehouse, Martin passed three lean men wrestling cartons onto a dolly. Rabbani's bodyguard, Rachid, stood apart, watching them with his unblinking eyes. The three men, all clean shaven, were dressed alike in orange jumpsuits with the insignia of a shipping company sewn over the zipper of the breast pocket. As Martin walked past, they raised their eyes to scrutinize him; none of them smiled. There was something about the men that troubled Martin—but he couldn't put his finger on it.

Mrs. Rainfield waved from her cubical as he headed down the cement corridor toward the front door. As he reached it a discreet crackle of electric current sizzled through the lock and the door clicked open. Out in the street, Martin waved cheerfully at the security camera over his head. He was still trying to figure out what it was about the three shippers that had caught his eye as he started up the street in the direction of Golders Green and the rooming house.

* * *

The three men in orange jumpsuits piled the cartons so high on the dolly that the topmost one began to teeter. Rachid jumped forward to keep it from falling to the ground. "Watch what you are doing—" he started to say. He turned back to find himself staring into the bore of a silencer screwed into the barrel of an Italian Beretta. It was aimed directly at his forehead.

Rachid nodded imperceptibly, a Muslim authorizing the assassin to end his life. The man in the orange jumpsuit nodded back, acknowledging that Rachid was the master of his destiny, and squeezed the trigger. There was a muted hiss from the handgun, which recoiled slightly as a neat puncture wound materialized in Rachid's forehead. The second man caught him under the armpits and lowered the body to the cement floor. The third man crossed the warehouse to Mrs. Rainfield's office and rapped his knuckles on the glass door. She motioned for him to come in. "What can I do you, dear?" she asked.

He produced a silenced pistol from the zippered pocket of his jumpsuit and shot her through the heart. "Die," he replied as she slumped onto the desk, her lifeless eyes frozen open in bewilderment.

Back in the warehouse, the two other men knocked on the door of Taletbek Rabbani's office and entered. One of them held out the manifest. "Mr. Rabbani, there are two cartons of size six foot-prostheses missing," one of them said as they approached his desk.

"That is absolutely impossible," Taletbek Rabbani said, snatching up his canes and pushing himself to his feet. "Did you ask Rachid—" He became aware of the handgun fitted with a silencer inches from his skull. "Who are you?" he whispered harshly. "Who sent you?"

"We are who we are," the man with the gun responded. He wrenched the canes out of Taletbek's hands and, grabbing him by the wrists, dragged him across the warehouse, a Gucci loafer trailing at the end of the plastic prosthesis, to a stanchion near the body of Rachid. The man who had shot Mrs. Rainfield brought over a spool of thick orange packing cord and tied the old man's wrists. Then he lobbed the spool over an overhead pipe and pulled on the cord until Taletbek's arms, stretched directly above his head, were straining in their shoulder sockets and the toe of his good foot was scraping the cement. The man who appeared to be the leader of the team approached the old man.

"Where is Samat?"

Taletbek shook his head. "How is it possible to tell you something I myself do not know?"

"You will forfeit your life if you refuse to help us find him."

"When you arrive in hell, I will be waiting for you, my son."

"Are you a Muslim?" the leader inquired.

Taletbek managed to nod.

"Do you believe in the Creator, the Almighty? Do you believe in Allah?"

Taletbek indicated he did.

"Have you made pilgrimage to Mecca?"

Rabbani, his face contorted with pain, nodded again.

"Say your prayers, then. You are about to meet the one true God."

The old man shut his eyes and murmured: "*Ash'hadu an la illahu ila Allah wa'ash'hadu anna Muhammadan rasulu Allah.*"

From the inside of his boot, the leader of the team of killers drew a razor sharp dagger with a groove along its thin blade and a yellowing camel bone handle. He stepped to one side of the old man and probed the soft wrinkles of skin on his thin neck looking for a vein.

"For the last time, where is Samat?"

"Samat who?"

The leader found the vein and slowly imbedded the blade into Taletbek's neck until only the hilt remained visible. Blood spurted, staining the killer's orange jumpsuit before he could leap out of the way. The old man breathed in liquidy gasps, each shallower than the previous one, until his head plunged forward and his weight sagged under the cord, pulling his arms out of the shoulder sockets.

* * *

Martin dialed Stella's number in Crown Heights from the booth and listened to the phone ringing on the other end. It dawned on him that he was looking forward to hearing her voice—there was no denying that she had gotten under his skin. "That really you, Martin?" she exclaimed before he could finish a sentence. "Goddamn, I'm glad to hear from you. Missed you, believe it or not."

"Missed you, too," he said before he knew what he would say. In the strained silence, he imagined her tongue flicking over the chip in her front tooth.

She cleared her throat. "What do you say we get the business part of the conversation out of the way first. Yes, there was an autopsy. For obvious reasons, it was done by a CIA doctor. The FBI man who Kastner dealt with when he needed something sent it to me, along with a covering letter. In it he said the police found no evidence of a break-in. The doctor who performed the autopsy concluded that Kastner'd died of a heart attack."

Martin was thinking out loud. "Maybe you should get a second opinion."

"Too late for another autopsy."

"What does that mean, too late?"

"When nobody claimed Kastner's body, the CIA had him cremated. All they gave me was his ashes. I walked halfway across the Brooklyn Bridge and screamed out the punch line from one of those old anti-Soviet jokes that Kastner particularly liked—'Be careful what you struggle for because you may get it'—and scattered the ashes in the river."

"Uh-huh."

"I hate when you say *Uh-huh* because I'm never sure what you mean by it."

"I don't mean anything. I'm just buying time for my brain to work things out. Did you get to talk to Xing in the Chinese restaurant?"

"Yes. He was very suspicious until I convinced him I was a friend of yours. He was annoyed you hadn't come back for the funeral of the Chinese girl your bees killed."

"What did you tell him?"

"I said you were busy detecting and he seemed to settle for that. The girl—"

"Her name was Minh."

"Minh died in great pain, Martin. The police who investigated it decided her death was an accident."

Martin offered up a short laugh. "The honey exploded by accident."

"What does that mean?"

"Nothing. Did you find out what she was wearing when the bees attacked her?"

"The *Daily News* story said she was wearing a white jumpsuit with the sleeves and legs rolled up. A pith helmet with mosquito netting attached to it was found near her body." A police cruiser with a screaming siren tore past Martin, drowning out all conversation. When it quieted down Martin could hear Stella saying, "Oh, I see."

"What do you see?"

"The rolled up sleeves and legs—it was your jump suit, wasn't it? Do you think . . . could it be that someone . . . oh, dear." Stella lowered her voice. "I'm frightened, Martin."

"Me, too, I'm frightened. Seems as if I'm always frightened."

"Did your trip work out for you?"

"Don't know yet."

"Are you coming back?"

"Not right now."

"Want me to fly over and meet up with you? Two heads are better than one, remember. Two hearts, also." He could almost hear the slight gasp of embarrassment. "No strings attached, Martin, it goes without saying."

"Why do things that go without saying get said?"

"To avoid confusion. Hey, you want to hear a good Russian joke?"

"Save it for when we meet again."

"I'll settle for that."

"For what?"

She said it very quietly. "For our meeting again."

Another police car could be heard coming down Golders Green, its siren wailing. Martin said quickly, "Bye."

"Yeah. Bye. Take care of yourself."

"Uh-huh."

The police car was almost abreast of Martin and Stella had to shout to be heard. "There you go again."

*　*　*

Martin found a pub at the top of Golders Green and slid into a booth at the back. The waitress, a skinny young thing with one ear and one nostril and one eyebrow pierced and her navel visible below her short T-shirt, came around with the menu printed in chalk on a small blackboard. Martin ordered the special of the day and a half-pint of lager. He was sipping the lager and waiting for the special when there was a commotion in the front of the pub. People abandoned the bar and their tables to gather under the television on an overhead shelf. The screen was not facing the back of the pub so Martin couldn't make out what was being said. When the waitress came around with the pot pie and chips, he asked her what was happening.

"People've been murdered in a warehouse stone's throw from 'ere. Most exciting thing that's 'appened on Golders Green in a month of Sundays, don't you know. That's what all them police sirens was about."

Martin went around to the front of the pub and caught the end of the news item. "A warehouse, located immediately behind the train station, was the grisly scene of the multiple murders," the male anchor said. "According to municipal records, the warehouse was being used as a depot for prostheses being shipped by a humanitarian group called Soft Shoulder to war ravaged countries." The female anchor chimed in: "We're now being told that three bodies were removed from the warehouse. They were identified as a Mr. Taletbek Rabbani, aged eighty-eight, an Afghan refugee who directed the humanitarian operation and who bled to death from a knife wound to his neck while tied to an overhead pipe; his associate, an Egyptian known only as Rachid, who was killed by a single shot to the head; and a secretary, Mrs. Doris Rainfield, who was also shot to death. A fourth woman is missing and police fear she may have been kidnapped by the team of hit men when they fled the scene of the crime. She was identified as Mrs. Froth, and was said to be the wife of the well known snooker player Nigel Froth."

Returning to his table, Martin found he'd lost all appetite for the pot pie. He raised a finger and caught the waitress's eye and called, "Whiskey, neat. Make that a double."

He was nursing the whiskey and his bruised emotions when he suddenly remembered what it was about the three men in orange jumpsuits at the warehouse that had troubled him. Of course! Why hadn't he seen it sooner? They had all been clean shaven. The upper halves of their faces had been ruddy, as if they'd spent most of their waking hours outdoors. But the lower halves had been the color of sidewalk—one of the men had razor nicks on his skin—which suggested that they had only recently shaved off thick beards in order to make it more difficult to identify them as Muslims.

Martin closed his eyes and summoned up an image of Taletbek Rabbani suspended from an overhead pipe while an assassin stabbed him in the neck. Trying to pick up Samat's trail, the Chechens, beardless in London, had come back to haunt the old one-legged Tajik warrior sooner than he'd imagined.

1994: THE ONLY FODDER WAS CANNON FODDER

"WHEN WE LEFT OFF LAST WEEK, MARTIN," DR. TREFFLER WAS saying, "you were commenting on the fact"—her eyes flicked down to the notes in her loose-leaf notebook—"that you are able to do some things well the first time you try."

The Company psychiatrist, wearing a tight skirt cut above the knee, uncrossed and recrossed her legs. As her thigh flashed into view, Martin turned his head away. He understood that everything she did had a purpose; the business with the legs was her way of harvesting information about his sex drive, assuming he had a sex drive. He wondered what another psychiatrist would make of Dr. Treffler's way of taking notes, filling the loose-leaf pages from top to bottom and edge to edge with a runty scrawl, the letters all leaning into some nonexistent emotional blizzard. Solzhenitsyn had written *Ivan Denisovich* that way, but he'd been coming off eight years in Stalin's gulag. What was her excuse? What did it mean when you didn't like margins?

"Yes, I remember now," Martin said finally. Through the panes of the window and the green metal mesh (put there to keep clients from jumping?) he could make out a bit of Maryland countryside; could see the last brown leaves clinging to the branches of trees. He felt an instinctive admiration for their tenacity. "It's always intrigued me," he continued because she expected him to; because she sat there with her legs crossed and her thigh visible and her Mont Blanc fountain pen poised over the loose-leaf page. "It struck me as funny how some things you do, you do them well the first time."

"Such as?" she inquired in a voice so toneless it betrayed absolutely no curiosity about the answer.

"Such as peeling a tangerine. Such as cutting a fuse for plastic explosive long enough to give you time to get out of its killing range. Such as pulling off a brush pass with a cutout in one of Beirut's crowded souks."

"What legend were you using in Beirut?"

"Dante Pippen."

"Wasn't he the one"—Bernice (they'd been on a first name basis for the last several sessions) had flipped to another page in her looseleaf notebook—"who was supposed to have been teaching history at a junior college? The one who wrote a book on the Civil War that he printed privately when he couldn't find a publisher willing to take it on?"

"No, you're thinking of Lincoln Dittmann, with two t's and two n's. Pippen was the Irish dynamiter from Castletownbere who started out as an explosives instructor on the Farm. Later, posing as an IRA dynamiter, he infiltrated a Sicilian Mafia family, the Taliban mullahs in Peshawar, a Hezbollah unit in the Bekaa Valley of Lebanon. It was this last mission that blew his cover."

Dr. Treffler nodded as she added a note to the page. "I have a hard time keeping track of your various identities."

"Me, too. That's why I'm here."

She looked up from the loose-leaf notebook. "Are you sure you have identified all of your operational biographies?"

"I've identified the ones I remember."

"Do you have the feeling you might be repressing any?"

"Don't know. According to your theory, there's a good chance I'm repressing at least one of them."

"The literature on the subject more or less agrees—"

"I thought you weren't convinced that I fit neatly into the literature on the subject."

Dr. Treffler flashed one of her very rare smiles, which looked like a foreign object on her normally expressionless face. "You are *hors genre*, Martin, there's no doubt about it. Nobody in my profession has come across anyone quite like you. It will cause quite a stir when I publish my paper—"

"Changing the names to protect the innocent."

"Changing the names to protect the guilty, too."

"You're getting into the spirit of things, Bernice. The people who pay you for shrinking my head will be very pleased."

"A psychiatrist doesn't shrink the patient's head, Martin. We shrink their problems."

"I'm relieved to hear it."

"Tell me more about Lincoln Dittmann."

"Such as?"

"Anything that comes to mind will do nicely." When he still hesitated, she said, "Listen, Martin, you can tell me anything you can tell the Director of the CIA."

"Anything?"

"That's why you're in this room. This is a private clinic. The doctors who work here have been cleared to hear state secrets. We get to treat the people who, for one reason or another, need help before returning to civilian life."

"If you were the Director and I was sitting like this facing you, our knees almost touching—"

Bernice nodded encouragement. "Go on."

"I'd tell you that a camel is a horse designed by a committee. Then I'd tell you that the CIA is an intelligence agency designed by the same committee. And then I'd remind you that in every civilization known to man, the ratio of horses asses to horses has been greater than one."

"You're angry." She jotted something on the loose-leaf page. "It's perfectly all right to be angry. Don't be afraid to let it out."

Martin shrugged. "I thought I was just expressing some healthy cynicism."

"Lincoln Dittmann," she said, tugging the conversation back to her question.

"He was raised in a small town in Pennsylvania named Jonestown. His mother was a Polish immigrant who had come to America after World War Two. His father owned a chain of hardware stores, with the main depot in Fredericksburg, on the Virginia side of the Potomac. He wound up spending several months a year in Fredericksburg and took his son with him when the trips fell during school vacations. Lincoln used his free time to scour the battlefield for souvenirs—in those days you could still find rusting bayonets or cannon balls or the barrels of muzzle loading rifles in the fields after a torrential rain. By

the time he reached his teens, when the other kids his age were reading Batman comics, Lincoln could recount every detail of the battle of
Fredericksburg. At Lincoln's urging, his father began buying Civil War
paraphernalia from the farmers during his turn around the hardware
stores—he returned home with rifles and bayonets and powder horns
and Federal medals on the backseat of his Studebaker—"

"Not Confederate medals?"

"The Confederates didn't give medals to their soldiers. When
Lincoln went off to college, he already had quite a collection. He even
owned a rare English Whitworth, the weapon of choice for Confederate sharpshooters. The paper cartridges were damned expensive
but a skilled sniper could hit anything he could see."

"Where did he go to college?"

"University of Pennsylvania. Majored in American history. Wrote
his senior thesis on the battle of Fredericksburg. When he began
teaching at the junior college, he turned it into a book."

"That was the book he printed himself when he couldn't find a
publisher?"

"It was a bitter disappointment to him, not finding a legitimate
publisher."

"What was it about Fredericksburg that was so special?"

Martin's hand, clammy with perspiration, came up to massage his
brow. The involuntary gesture wasn't lost on Dr. Treffler. "It was early
in December of 1862," he began, staring vacantly out of the window
at the horizon, watching for the flashes of the great battle being fought
beyond it. "There was a new Federal general in charge of the Army of
the Potomac, his name was Burnside. Ambrose Burnside. He thought
he saw a way to end the war with one swift assault across Virginia to
capture the Confederate capitol, Richmond. It was a brilliant plan.
President Lincoln signed off on it and Burnside force-marched his
troops down the Potomac to a point across the river from Fredericksburg. If he could surprise the rebels and take the city, the road to
Richmond would be open and the war would end almost before it
got going. Burnside had put in an urgent order for pontoon bridges,
but when he reached Fredericksburg he discovered that the War
Department hadn't dispatched them. The Union army wound up
bivouacking for ten days on its side of the river waiting for the

Goddamn bridges, giving Robert Lee time to bring up his army and mass it on the heights above the city. When the bridges finally arrived and Burnside crossed the river, he found Bobby Lee and seventy-five thousand Confederates blocking the road to Richmond. The weather was wintry, the autumnal mud in the rutted roads had turned hard. The Federals, advancing across sloping open ground, came on all day, wave after wave of them in their spanking bright factory-made uniforms. The Rebels in homespun dyed with plant pigments, fighting from behind a low stone wall at the edge of a sunken road at the foot of Marye's Hill, beat back every attack. The sharpshooters, armed with Whitworths, picked off the Federal officers so easily that many of them began tearing off their insignias as they went into the line. Groups of Federals tried to take cover behind some brick houses on the plain but the Yankee cavalry, using the flats of sabres, forced them back to the battle. Burnside kept track of the progress of the fighting from the roof of the Chatham Mansion across the river. From a knob up on the heights, the Mansion was within eyeshot and Bobby Lee pointed it out to Stonewall Jackson—he told him that thirty years before he'd courted the lady he wound up marrying at that very house. On the ridge line, a Confederate band belted out waltzes for the southern gentlemen and ladies who had come down from Richmond to see the battle. Old Pete Longstreet, with a woman's woolen shawl draped over his shoulders, watched the fighting unfolding below him through a long glass fixed to a wooden tripod in front of the Confederate command post. It took a time to convince him that the Federal attack on the sunken road wasn't a feint—he couldn't swallow the idea that Burnside was squandering his life's blood in a frontal attack that had no chance of succeeding. At one point an Irish Brigade made it to within fifteen paces of the sunken road and even the Rebels watching from the heights cheered their courage. But the 24th Georgians behind the low stone wall, firing and loading and firing so steadily their teeth ached from biting off the paper cartridges, turned back that attack, too. Burnside launched fourteen assaults on the heights before darkness blotted out the killing fields. When the Federals finally retreated across the river the next day and counted noses, they discovered that nine thousand Union men had fallen at Fredericksburg."

Martin sat humped over in the chair now, his lids squeezed shut, the flat of a hand pressed to his forehead damming the migraine building up behind his eyes. "When Lincoln Dittmann went to Washington to research the book, he discovered Burnside's original order for the pontoon bridges in the army archives. The word 'Urgent' had been inked out, probably by a Confederate sympathizer working at the War Department. You asked what was so special about Fredericksburg— Dittmann concluded that if the pontoon bridges had been delivered on time, the war might have ended there in 1862 instead of dragging on until 1865."

Martin, drained, went quiet. For some while the only sound in the small airless room came from the whir of the tape recorder and the nib of Dr. Treffler's pen etching long lines of runty letters onto the loose-leaf page. When she finally looked up from her notebook, she asked, very softly, "How does Martin Odum know all this? The fact that the Confederates didn't give medals, the flats of sabres driving the Federals away from the shelter of *brick* houses, the Chatham Mansion, the band playing waltzes on Marye's Hill while Longstreet, with a shawl over his shoulders, watched the Georgians in homespun dyed with plant pigments fight off fourteen attacks on the sunken road—*it's almost as if you'd been there!*"

Martin's mouth had gone dry and the words that emerged from his lips rang tinny and hollow, the second half of an echo that had lost some of its shrillness on the way back. "Lincoln Dittmann was there," he said. "He told me the details."

Dr. Treffler leaned forward. "You heard Lincoln Dittmann's voice describing the battle?"

"Uh-huh."

"Did he tell you he'd been there *during* the battle? Did he tell you he'd seen the fighting with his own eyes?"

"Not in so many words . . ."

"But you—you being Martin Odum—you assumed he'd been an eyewitness at Fredericksburg."

"He must have been there," Martin insisted plaintively. "How else could he have known all the things he knew? Lincoln told me lots more that isn't in any books." The words spilled out of Martin now. "The night of the battle temperatures plunged to below freezing . . .

even in the cold of winter there were horseflies drawn to the blood
oozing from wounds . . . the maimed Federals who were still alive
dragged the dead into heaps and burrowed under the corpses to keep
warm . . . riderless horses pawed at the frozen ground looking for fodder, but the only fodder at Fredericksburg on 13 December 1862 was
cannon fodder." Martin took a deep breath. "That was the last line of
Lincoln's book. The title came from the line. The book was called
Cannon Fodder."

Dr. Treffler waited for Martin's breathing to settle down before she
spoke. "Listen to me, Martin. Lincoln Dittmann is your contempo-
rary. He wasn't alive in 1862, which means he couldn't have been at
the battle of Fredericksburg."

Martin didn't respond. Dr. Treffler caught herself staring at him
and turned away quickly, then laughed out loud and looked back.
"Wow! This is stunning. You heard Lincoln Dittmann's voice at our
first session—he gave you the lines of that Walt Whitman poem you
recited."

"I remember. 'Silent cannons, soon to cease your silence, soon
unlimber'd to begin the red business.' That wasn't the first time I heard
Lincoln's voice—he's been whispering in my ear for years. By the way,
it's Walter Whitman, not Walt. Lincoln told me he'd come across
Whitman in a Federal field hospital after Burnside retreated from
Fredericksburg—the poet was worried sick about his brother who'd
taken part in the battle and was looking everywhere for him. Lincoln
recalled that the soldiers who knew Whitman called him Walter."

"Lincoln told you about Whitman being in the field hospital?
About the soldiers calling him Walter?"

"Uh-huh."

"Did he recall it from having been there or from having read
about it somewhere?"

Martin seemed not to want to deal with the question.

Dr. Treffler decided Martin had had enough stress for one session.
"Your headache starting in again?" she asked.

"It's blinding me."

"What do you see when your eyes are shut tight like that?"

Martin thought about that. "A long blur of headlights, as if a camera has been set up on an overpass and the lens has been locked open

to capture the streak of the cars speeding past underneath. Or the cosmos, yes, the entire cosmos in its big-bang mode expanding, inflating like a balloon with small black spots painted on it, and each spot on the balloon receding from every other spot."

"And how will this big bang end?"

"With me, marooned on one of the spots, alone in the universe."

1990: LINCOLN DITTMANN TAKES ON A LIFE OF HIS OWN

O THE ABIDING SATISFACTION OF ITS EIGHT SITTING MEMBERS, the Legend Committee had been upgraded from its windowless basement storage space at Langley to a fourth-floor conference room drenched in sunlight. That was the upside. The downside was that the new digs had an impregnable view of the vast outdoor parking lot used by the Company plebeians. (The patricians from the seventh floor, including Crystal Quest, the current Deputy Director of Operations and the Committee's immediate boss, all rated parking spaces in the underground garage, along with an elevator that whisked them to work without stopping at other floors along the way.) "Can't have everything," sighed the former station chief who chaired the Legend Committee the first time he set foot in the room the housekeepers were proposing and looked out one of the windows; he'd been hoping for Virginia countryside, not asphalt. To mask his disappointment he came up with the aphorism that had been engraved over the door to the inner sanctum when he presided over Cairo Station oh so many years ago: "*Yom asal, yom basal* . . . One day honey, one day onions."

"Where the heck are we?" he was asking Maggie Poole, who had specialized in medieval French history at Oxford and had never entirely lost her acquired British accent, an affectation particularly remarkable when she slipped French words into the conversation.

"We're on the fourth *étage*," she replied now, purposefully misunderstanding the question to get his goat. "Up here the water coolers are in the corridor outside the rooms, not inside."

"Oh, for Pete's sake, that's not what I meant and you know it. You do that every occasion you can."

"*Moi?*" Maggie Poole blurted out innocently. "Certainly not."

"What he's asking," said the Yale-educated aversion therapist, "is where are we up to with the new legend for Dante Pippen."

Dante, sitting with his spine against a soft pillow to relieve the pressure on the shrapnel wound in his lower back, thought of these sessions as indoor sport. It was a painless way to pass an afternoon even if his game leg and the back wound ached more or less round the clock. He closed his eyes to shield them from the bright sunlight slanting through the open venetian blinds and relished the warmth on the skin of his face. "I thought this time around," he offered, and he could almost hear the bones creaking as the ancient mariners of the Legend Committee craned their necks to stare at him, "we could begin in Pennsylvania."

"Why Pennsylvania?" demanded the lexicographer on loan from University of Chicago and happy to be; the per diem the Company deposited in his bank account somehow never got reported to the Internal Revenue Service.

The committee's doyen, a CIA veteran who began his professional career creating legends for the OSS agents during World War Two and never let anyone forget it, fitted on a pair of perfectly round wire spectacles and flipped open the original Martin Odum 201 Central Registry folder. "Pennsylvania," he observed, straining to make out the small type on the bio file, "seems as good a place to start as any. Mr. Pippen's predecessor, Martin Odum, spent the first eight years of his life in Pennsylvania, in a small town called Jonestown. His mother was a Polish immigrant, his father ran a small factory producing underwear for the U.S. Army."

"Jonestown was within driving distance of several Civil War battlefields and Martin wound up going to a bunch of them while he was in grade school," Dante said from the sideline. "His favorite, which he must have visited two or three times, was Fredericksburg."

"Could visiting Fredericksburg make someone a Civil War *expert?*" Maggie Poole inquired eagerly; she had caught a glimpse of where they could be heading.

"Martin was a Fredericksburg expert, for sure," Dante said with a laugh. His eyes were still tightly closed and he was beginning, once again, to enjoy the business of legend building; it seemed to him the closest he'd ever come to novel writing. "His stories about the battle there were so graphic, people who heard them sometimes jokingly wondered if he'd taken part in the Civil War."

"Can you give us some examples?" the chairman asked.

"He would describe Bobby Lee, up on Marye's Hill inland from Fredericksburg, pointing out Burnside's command post in the Chatham Mansion across the Potomac to Stonewall Jackson and recalling that he'd courted his wife under that roof thirty years before. Martin would describe Old Pete Longstreet, his shoulders draped in a woman's woolen shawl, watching the battle unfolding below him through a long glass fixed to a wooden tripod and telling everyone within earshot that the Federal attack on the sunken road had to be a feint, that the main attack would come somewhere else."

The Legend Committee chairman peered at Dante over the rim of his wire eyeglasses. "Was Bobby Lee the General we know as Robert E. Lee?" he asked.

"One and the same," Dante said from his place along the wall. "The Virginians called him Bobby Lee—though never to his face."

"Well, this does open avenues for exploration," the chairman told the others. "Our man may not be a Civil War expert, but with a little help from his friends he could certainly pass for one, couldn't he?"

"Which brings us to the name," Maggie Poole said. "And what could be more *logique* for a Civil War *expert* than calling him Lincoln?"

"I suppose you were thinking of using Abraham as a first name," sneered the aversion therapist.

"*Va te faire cuire un oeuf,*" Maggie Poole shot back. She glared at the aversion therapist, clearly tempted to stick her tongue out at him. "I was thinking along the lines of using Lincoln as a *prenom* because it would tend to give credibility to a Civil War legend."

"Lincoln something or other sounds quite elegant to me," Dante called from the wall.

"*Merci*, Mr. Pippen, for being so open minded, which is more than I can say for some others in this room," ventured Maggie Poole.

"I once knew a gun collector in Chicago whose name was Dittmann—that's with two 't's and two 'n's," said the lexicographer. "There was some suggestion that Dittmann wasn't his real name but that's neither here nor there. He specialized in Civil War firearms. His pride and joy was an English sniper rifle, it was called the Whentworth or Whitworth, something like that. As I recall, the paper cartridges were exorbitant, but in the hands of a skilled sharpshooter the rifle was considered to be a lethal weapon."

"Lincoln Dittmann is a name with . . . weight," the chairman decided. "How does it strike you, Mr. Pippen?"

"I could learn to live with it," he agreed. "And it would certainly be original to turn a field agent into a Civil War expert."

The members of the Legend Committee knew they had hit pay dirt and the ideas started to come thick and fast.

"He could start building the legend by visiting all the battle grounds."

"He ought to have a *collection personnelle* of Civil War firearms, I should think."

"I like having guns around," Pippen announced from his seat. "Come to think of it, a personal collection of Civil War weapons would make a great cover for an arms dealer, which is where Fred Astaire is heading with this legend."

"So we need to think in terms of a legend for an arms dealer?"

"Yes."

"Who in God's name is Fred Astaire?"

"It's Mrs. Quest's in-house nickname."

"Oh, dear."

"In what part of the world would Lincoln Dittmann be operating? Who would be his clients?"

Dante had to be careful not to give away family jewels. "His clients would be a hodgepodge of people who are out to hurt America," he said.

"To step into Lincoln Dittmann's shoes, you would have to do your homework."

"Do you mind reading up on a subject, Mr. Pippen?"

"Not at all. Sounds fun to me."

"He'd need professional credentials."

"Okay. Let's summarize. He was raised in Jonestown, Pennsylvania, and visited Fredericksburg so often as a child that he knew the battlefield backward and forward at a time when his young friends were reading Batman comics."

"His father could have owned a chain of hardware stores with the central depot in Fredericksburg, which meant he would have had to spend a lot of time there in any given year. Nothing would have been more natural than to have taken his young son with him whenever he could . . ."

"Of course! He would have taken him along to Fredericksburg during school vacations. The young Lincoln Dittmann would have joined the boys scouring the battlefield for Civil War souvenirs that wash up to the surface after heavy rainfalls."

"At some point Lincoln would have encouraged his father to hunt for rifles and powder horns and medals when he drove around—let's give him a Studebaker, which was a popular car after the war—checking on his hardware stores. The local farmers keep these Civil War things in their attics and Lincoln's father would have brought something back with him after each trip."

"If I collected medals," Pippen noted, "they'd all have to be from the Union Army. Confederate Army didn't award medals."

"How did they get their soldiers to soldier if they didn't award medals?"

"They were fighting for a cause they believed in," Pippen said.

"They were defending slavery, for God's sake—"

"Most of the Confederate soldiers didn't own slaves," Pippen said. (Things that Martin had picked up during those visits to Fredericksburg so many years earlier were coming back to him.) "They were fighting so the North wouldn't try and tell them what they could do and what they couldn't do. Besides which, when the war started, Lincoln—I'm talking about Abraham, the president—didn't have the slightest intention of abolishing slavery and freeing the slaves. Nobody on either side of the Mason-Dixon line would have accepted this because nobody had any idea what to do with the millions of slaves in the Confederate states if they were freed. Yankees didn't want emancipated slaves trekking north and stealing their manufacturing jobs for lower salaries. Southerners didn't want them homesteading Confederate land and growing cotton that could be marketed cheaper than plantation cotton. Or even worse, voting in local elections."

"He really *is* something of a Civil War buff already."

"Our Lincoln Dittmann ought to have been a *professeur* at one point, don't you think?"

"He could have taught Civil War history in some college. Why not?"

"Problem: To teach in a college you need an advanced degree. Even if he reads up on the Civil War, he might not be able to convince a real Civil War expert that he earned a Ph.D. in the subject."

"Let him teach at a junior college, then. That way he wouldn't need an advanced degree. And what he knows about the Civil War could pass muster."

"It would add to his credibility if he were to write a book on the subject."

"Hang on," Pippen said. "I don't think I have the stamina to write a book."

"Takes more than stamina. I know because I've written three. You need mettle if you're going to refuse to be intimidated by all the options."

"We could farm out the book. We could get it written for you and have a small university press that owes us a favor publish it under your name. *The Battle of Fredericksburg* by Lincoln Dittmann."

"I've got the perfect title: *Cannon Fodder*. With a subtitle: *The Battle of Fredericksburg*."

"Let's not get bogged down with the title, for goodness sake."

"What do you think of all this, Mr. Pippen?"

"It's first rate cover. Nobody would suspect an arms dealer who had been teaching Civil War history at a junior college of being CIA."

"There's something's missing from this legend."

"What?"

"Yes, what?"

"Motivation is what's missing. Why has Lincoln Dittmann sunk so low. Why is he associating with the scum of the earth, people who, by definition, are not friends of *l'Amerique?*"

"Good point, Maggie."

"Because he's angry at America."

"Why? Why is he angry at America?"

"He got into a some sort of jam. He was humiliated—"

Dante piped up from the sideline. "I don't mind being humiliated, but I'd appreciate it if sex weren't involved. You people always think of sex when you want to put something into a biography that discredits the principal. Next thing you know Lincoln Dittmann will be a closet transvestite or something like that."

"We take your point, Mr. Pippen."

"What if the jam involved plagiarism."

"He swiped the heart of *Cannon Fodder* from a treatise published in the twenties or thirties that he found in the stacks of a library."

"That would simplify matters for us. We wouldn't have to pay someone to write the book on Fredericksburg; we could find a treatise—there must be thousands of them lying around on shelves gathering dust—and copy it."

"My luck," Dante groaned, "I finally get to be the author of a book and it turns out I plagiarized it."

"It's that or sexual deviation."

"I'll take plagiarism."

"A reviewer in an historical periodical—tipped off by an anonymous letter sent by us—could blow the whistle on Dittmann, at which point he would lose his tenure and his job."

"His professional reputation would be ruined."

"Nobody else in the wide world of academia would touch him with a ten-foot pole."

"Now we're getting somewhere. The colleges put pressure on you to publish or perish and they expect you to hold down a full teaching load and do the research and writing in your free time."

"The experience left Lincoln Dittmann a bitter cynic. He wanted to get back at the college, at the system, at the country."

"I'd say we're halfway home, gentlemen and ladies. The only thing that remains is to try all this out on our taskmaster, the DDO, Crystal Quest herself."

Dante Pippen reached for the cane propped against the wall and used it to push himself to his feet. Dull pain stabbed at his lower back and sore leg, but he was so elated he barely noticed it. "I think Crystal Quest is going to be very satisfied with the Lincoln Dittmann legend," he told the members of the Legend Committee. "I know I am."

1991: LINCOLN DITTMANN WORKS THE ANGLES OF THE TRIANGLE

"HOW DID YOU GET INTO THE BUSINESS OF SELLING WEAPONS?" THE Egyptian wanted to know.

"Chances are you won't believe me if I tell you," Lincoln Dittmann said.

"If he don't believe you," said the short American with the tooled cowboy boots and tapered Levis and slicked back hair, "you're in deep shit." He spoke in a Texas drawl so silky that Lincoln had to strain to make out the words.

The Egyptian and the Texan, strange bedfellows in this god-forsaken Paraguayan frontier town across the border from Brazil, both laughed under their breaths, though there was no trace of mirth in their voices. Lincoln, sprawled on a sofa, his bad leg stretched straight out in front of him, the cane within arm's reach, his hands clasped behind his head, laughed with them. "I was teaching Civil War history at a junior college," he said. "My area of expertise—I wrote a book on the subject once—was the battle of Fredericksburg. Collecting Civil War weapons seemed like the natural thing to do. My pièce de résistance is a rare English Whitworth."

"That there's a sniper rifle, ain't it?" said the Texan.

Lincoln looked impressed. "Aren't many people around who can tell the difference between a Whitworth and an ordinary barnyard Enfield."

"My daddy had one," the Texan said proudly. "Feds went an' impounded it along with his other guns when he was nabbed for

burning a nigger church to the ground in Al'bama." He tilted his head
back and regarded Lincoln warily. The Texan, who had introduced
himself as Leroy Streeter when he'd picked Lincoln up in front of the
mosque with the gold-tinted roof on Palestine Street across the border
in Foz do Iguaçú, said, "Go and describe your Whitworth?"

Lincoln smiled to himself. Back at Langley, they'd learned from
the FBI that Leroy Streeter's father had once owned a Civil War
Whitworth; they'd reckoned the son would be familiar with the
weapon. If Leroy's quiz was what passed for checking bona fides in
Triple Border, it certainly was amateur hour; an undercover agent
wouldn't name drop—even the name of an antique rifle—if he couldn't
backstop it with details. Fact of the matter was that Lincoln did
own a Whitworth—a collection of Civil War weapons went with the
Dittmann legend. He'd even fabricated cartridges and gone out to a
remote landfill in New Jersey to see if the rifle was as accurate as its
reputation held. It was. "Mr. Whitworth's rifle," he told Leroy now,
"came factory-equipped with a low-powered brass scope fixed atop the
hexagonal barrel. Not many of the Whitworths around these days,
even in museums, still have the scope. Mine also has the original brass
tampon to plug the barrel against humidity and dust. The scope's fitted with little engraved wheels to sight the rifle and adjust for latitude
and longitude errors."

As he spoke, Lincoln kept his eyes on the Egyptian, who obviously ran the show here. He had not been introduced—though
Lincoln had a good idea of his identity; the FBI's briefing book
back in Washington had contained a blurry photo taken with a tele-
photo lens of an Egyptian known as Ibrahim bin Daoud talking to
a man identified as a Hezbollah agent in front of the entrance to the
Maksoud Plaza Hotel in São Paulo the previous year. The long delicate nose and carefully trimmed gray beard visible in the photo
were conspicuous on the Egyptian sitting on the sill across from
him now.

Stretched out on the unmade bed in the room above a bar in
Ciudad del Este on the Paraguay side of Triple Border, the muddy
heels of his boots digging into the mattress, Leroy was nodding
emphatically at the Egyptian. "He sure as hell's got hisself a Whitworth," he confirmed.

Lincoln was hoping that gun collecting could provide a useful bond between him and the Texan. "Crying shame about your daddy's Whitworth," he said. "Bet the FBI goons didn't have the wildest idea what a goddamn prize they had in their hands when they confiscated it."

"They was too fucking dumb to tell the difference between fool's gold and actual gold," Leroy agreed.

Lincoln looked back at the Egyptian. "To answer your question: From the Whitworth and my other guns, it was just a matter of branching out to Kalashnikovs and TOW antitank missiles, with the grenades and ammunition thrown in for good measure. Pays a lot better than teaching Civil War history at a junior college."

"We are not in the market for Kalashnikovs and TOWs," the Egyptian noted coldly.

"He's not interested in Ak-47s and TOWs," the Texan explained. "Now that Commie Russia's got one foot in the grave, you trip over this kind of hardware out here on Triple Border. He's interested in Semtex or ammonium nitrate, something in the neighborhood of eighty thousand pounds of it, enough to fill one of those big moving vans. We pay cash on the barrelhead."

Lincoln locked his eyes on the Egyptian. He was a skeletal man with a round pockmarked face and hunched shoulders, probably in his late fifties, though the gray beard could have been adding years to his appearance. The upper third of his face had disappeared behind dark sunglasses, which he wore despite being in a dingy room with the shades drawn. "Semtex in small quantities is no problem. Ammonium nitrate in any quantity is also no problem," he said. "You probably know that ammonium nitrate is used as fertilizer—mixed with diesel or fuel oil, it is highly explosive. The trick'll be to buy a large amount without attracting attention, which is something I and my associates can organize. Where do you want to take delivery?"

Leroy smiled out of one side of his mouth. "At a site to be specified on the New Jersey side of the Holland Tunnel."

Lincoln heard the cry of the muezzin—it wasn't a recording but the real thing—summoning the faithful to midday prayer, which meant he'd been taken somewhere within earshot of the only mosque in Ciudad del Este after Leroy had picked him up in front of the mosque in Foz do Iguaçu. He'd been shoved into the back of a Mercedes and ordered to strap on the blackened-out ski goggles he found on the seat. "You taking me to the Saudi?" he'd asked Leroy as the Mercedes drove in circles for three quarters of a hour to confuse him. "I'm taking you to meet the Saudi's Egyptian," Leroy had answered. "If the Egyptian signs off on you, that's when you get to meet the Saudi, not before." Lincoln had asked, "What happens if he doesn't sign off on me?" Leroy, sitting up front alongside the driver, had snorted. "If'n he don't sign off on you, he'll like as feed you to the pet crocodile he keeps in his swim pool."

Now Lincoln could feel Daoud scrutinizing him through his dark sunglasses. "Where did you hurt your leg?" the Egyptian asked.

"Car accident in Zagreb," Lincoln said. "The Croats are crazy drivers."

"Where were you treated?" Daoud was looking for details he could verify.

Lincoln named a clinic in a suburb of Trieste.

The Egyptian glanced at Leroy and shrugged. Something else occurred to him. "What did you say the title of your book on Fredericksville was?"

Leroy corrected him. "It's Fredericks*burg*."

"I didn't say," Lincoln replied. "Title was the best part of the book. I called it, *Cannon Fodder*."

Apparently Leroy was still fighting the War of Secession because he blurted out, "Cannon fodder is sure as hell what they was." His normal draw, pitched a half octave higher, came across loud and clear. "Federal cannon fodder, fighting to free the niggers and legitimize intermarriage and dictate the North's way of thinking on southern gents."

The Egyptian repeated the title to make sure he'd gotten it right, then muttered something in Arabic to the fat boy piecing together the jigsaw puzzle on the linoleum-covered table in the alcove. The boy, who was wearing a shoulder holster with a plastic gun in it and chewing bubble gum that he inflated every time he fitted in a piece, sprang to his feet and rushed out of the room. The Egyptian followed him. Lincoln could hear their footfalls on the staircase of the ramshackle building as the boy headed downstairs and Daoud climbed up one flight. He let himself into the room overhead and crossed it and dragged up a chair as a telephone sounded. Lincoln guessed that the Egyptian was phoning abroad to get his people to check out details of the Dittmann legend.

The DDO's people in Langley had anticipated this and laid in the plumbing. If someone nosed around the Trieste clinic, he would come across a record of a Lincoln Dittmann being treated by a bone specialist for three days, and paying his bill in cash the morning he was discharged. As for the book, *Cannon Fodder* had a paper trail. The Egyptian's contact would discover a 1990 reference to the publication of the book in *Publishers Weekly*. If he dug deeper he would come up with two reviews, the first in a Virginia junior college student newspaper praising one of the school's own teachers for his Civil War scholarship; the second in a Richmond, Virginia, historical quarterly devoted to the War of Secession, accusing Lincoln Dittmann of having plagiarized great chunks of a privately printed 1932 doctorate treatise on the battle of Fredericksburg. There would be a small item in a Richmond newspaper repeating the plagiarism charge and reporting that a committee of the author's peers had examined the original treatise and Dittmann's *Cannon Fodder*, and discovered entire passages that matched. The article went on to say that Lincoln Dittmann had been fired from his post teaching history at a local junior college. Chain bookstores would have reported modest sales before the book was withdrawn from circulation. If anyone hunted hard enough, copies of the first and only edition (what was left of the original five-hundred-book print run) could be found in the Strand in Manhattan and several other second-hand bookstores across the country. On the inside of the back jacket there would be a photograph of Dittmann with a Schimelpenick jutting from his lips, along with a brief biography: born and raised in Pennsylvania, a Civil War buff from the time he started visiting battlefields as a youngster, an expert on the Battle of Fredericksburg, currently teaching Civil War history at a Virginia junior college.

Waiting for the Egyptian to return, Lincoln plucked a Schimelpenick from the metal tin in his jacket pocket and held the flame of a lighter to the end of it. He inhaled deeply and let the smoke gush through his nostrils. "Mind if I smoke?" he inquired politely.

"Smoking," Leroy remarked, "poisons the lungs. You ought to give it up."

"Trouble is," Lincoln said "to give up smoking you need to become someone else. Tried that once. Went cold turkey for a while. But it didn't work out in the end."

After awhile the Egyptian returned to the room and settled into the wooden chair set catty-corner to the sofa. "Tell me more about what you did in Croatia?" he instructed Lincoln.

Croatia had been Crystal Quest's brainchild. For all her imperiousness, she was old school: She believed a good legend needed more than a paper trail to give it authenticity. "If he's supposed to be an arms merchant," she'd argued when she dragged Lincoln up to the seventh floor at Langley to get the director to sign off on the operation, "there's got to be a trail of genuine transactions that the opposition can verify."

"You're proposing to actually set him up in the arms business?"

"Yes, sir I am."

"Whom would he sell to?" the director had demanded, clearly unsettled by the notion of one of the Company's agents establishing his bona fides by becoming a bona fide arms merchant.

"He'll buy from the Soviets who are running garage sales from their arsenals in East Germany, and deliver to the Bosnians. Since U.S. policy tilts toward the Bosnians, our Congressional oversight commissars won't give us a hard time if they get wind of it, which they won't if we're careful. The idea behind this is to put Lincoln in the path of one Sami Akhbar, an Azerbaijani who buys arms for an al-Qa'ida cell in Bosnia."

"As usual you've covered all the bases, Fred," the director had noted with a flagrant lack of enthusiasm.

"Sir, that's what you pay me for," she'd shot back.

Lincoln had spent the next four months tooling around the Dalmatian coast in a serviceable Buick, avoiding the Serb undercover agents like the plague, using a fax to contact a shadowy Frankfurt entity and purchase truckloads of the Soviet surplus arms being sold off by Russian soldiers soon to be recalled to the USSR from East Germany, meeting the drivers at night on remote back roads as they came across Slovenia, then arranging for delivery at crossing points on the Dalmatian coast between Croatia and Bosnia. It was at one of these pre-dawn meetings that Lincoln first felt the fish nibbling at the bait. "Could you get your hands on explosives?" a Muslim dealer who went by the name Sami Akhbar had casually asked as he took possession of a two-truck convoy loaded with TOW antitank missiles and mortars and handed Lincoln a satchel filled with crisp $100 bills bound in wrappers from a Swiss bank.

Lincoln had dealt with Sami five times in the past four months. "What do you have in mind?" he had inquired.

"I have a Saudi friend who is shopping around for Semtex or ammonium nitrate."

"In what quantities?"

"Very large quantities."

"Your friend looking to celebrate the end of Ramadan with a big bang?"

"Something like that."

"Russians aren't peddling Semtex or ammonium nitrate. It would have to come from the States."

"Are you saying it is within the realm of possibility?"

"Everything is within the realm of possibility, Sami, but it will cost a pretty penny."

"Money is not a problem for my Saudi friend. Thanks to Allah and his late father, he is very rich."

The Muslim had produced a scrap of paper from a shirt pocket and, pressing it to the fender of the truck, had printed out with the stub of a pencil the name of a town and the street address of a mosque, along with a date and an hour. Lincoln had crouched in front of the Buick parking lights to read it. "Where in hell is Foz do Iguaçú?" he'd asked, though he knew the answer.

"It is in Brazil right across the frontier from Paraguay at a place called Triple Border, where Brazil and Paraguay and Argentina meet."

"Why can't we get together somewhere in Europe?"

"If you are not interested, only say so. I will find someone else who is."

"Hey, don't get me wrong, Sami. I'm interested. I'm just worried that it's a long way to go for nothing."

Sami had coughed up a laugh. "You guys who deal arms tickle me. I do not call two hundred and fifty thousand U.S. nothing."

Lincoln had glanced again at the scrap of paper. "Are you sure your rich Saudi friend will contact me if I am standing outside the mosque on Palestine Street at ten in the morning ten days from today?"

Sami had nodded into the darkness. "A person will contact you and take you to him."

In the small room over the bar, the Egyptian listened in silence to Lincoln's account of his dealings in Croatia. In the alcove, the boy, working again at his jigsaw puzzle, blew bubbles with the gum until they burst against his fleshy lips. Leroy cleaned the fingernails of his left hand with a fingernail of his right hand. When Lincoln reached the end of the story, the Egyptian lips pursed, sat without moving a muscle, weighing his next move. Finally he announced, "Leroy will take you back to your hotel in Foz do Iguaçú. Wait there until you hear from me."

"How long will that take?" Lincoln asked. "Every day I'm away from the Balkans costs me money."

The Egyptian shrugged. "If you become bored, you are free to yawn."

"How did it go?" Lincoln asked Leroy when the two were alone in the car and heading toward the bridge and Foz do Iguaçú.

"The fact that you're still alive can only mean it went well."

Lincoln glanced at the Texan, whose face flashed in and out of the light as cars passed in the opposite direction. "You're serious, aren't you?"

"Fucking A, I'm serious. Get it into your skull," he said, drumming a forefinger against his own. "You're associating with tough customers down here."

Lincoln had to swallow a smile. Felix Kiick had used much the same words as he wound up the briefing back in Washington. "Holy mackerel, watch your ass when you get to Triple Border," he'd said. "You'll be rubbing shoulders with mighty ornery folks."

* * *

The briefing in Washington had taken place on neutral turf, a nondescript Foggy Bottom conference room that had been swept by Company housekeepers and then staked out until the principals showed up at the crack of noon. From word one, the tension had been as thick as the fog Lincoln had braved driving to work that morning from the safe house in Virginia. It wasn't so much the FBI briefer, a short, stumpy veteran counterterrorism maven named Felix Kiick with the low center of gravity of a NFL linesman; the CIA had dealt with him on any number of occasions (most especially when he directed the FBI's counterterrorism team at the American embassy in Moscow) and considered him to be a straight shooter. The tension could be traced to the clash of cultures; to the mistrust J. Edgar Hoover (who had run the FBI with an iron hand until his death in 1972) had sewn into the agency's bureaucratic fabric during his forty-eight years at the helm. The fact that the FBI, acting in obedience to a formal presidential "finding," was being obliged to pass on to its arch competitor at Langley an operation and the assets that went with it, or what was left of them, only made matters worse. Kiick put the best possible face on the situation in his opening remarks. "Triple Border," he told Lincoln as Crystal Quest and several of her wallahs looked on, "which is the nickname for the zone where Brazil, Paraguay and Argentina meet up, is a cesspool filled with scum from Hamas, Hezbollah, Egypt's Islamic Brotherhood, the Irish Republican Army, the Basque separatist group ETA, Colombia's FARC, all of them operating under false identities or false flags. The FBI's interest in Triple Border goes back roughly ten years when a large expatriate population fleeing the civil war in Lebanon gravitated into the area. The local authorities, some of them bribed, some of them intimidated, turned their backs on the sharp rise in crime in their backyard. You could buy and sell almost anything down there—passports for two-thousand dollars a clip, including the mug shot and the official government stamp; stolen cars; cheap electronics; along with the staples on any lawless frontier these days, drugs and arms. Several terrorist organizations set up guerilla training camps in the *mato graso*—the outback—to teach recruits how to rig car bombs or shoot the Soviet hardware that anyone could purchase in the back alleys of the border towns using money conveniently laundered by the banks at Triple Border."

"Sounds like your people have a handle on the problems," Lincoln said. "Why are you backing off?"

"They're backing off," Crystal Quest said, "because the director has convinced the White House that American interests would be better served if the CIA held the Triple Border action." Quest fingered some crushed ice out of a bowl and began munching on it. "Drugs, contraband cars, a black market in computer software or pirated Hollywood films are small potatoes. We have reason to believe that Triple Border has become a staging area for Muslim fundamentalist groups working in the western hemisphere; at Triple Border they can purchase all the arms their hearts desire and launder the money to pay for it. And their fedayeen can get some R and R at the local bars, out of sight of the mullahs who expect them to remain chaste and pray five times a day. The mosques in Foz de Iguaçú on the Brazilian side and Ciudad del Este on the Paraguayan side are filled with Sunnis and Shiites who in other parts of the Muslim world don't give each other the time of day. In Triple Border we suspect that they're plotting to attack the United States and kill Americans."

Kiick spoke up. "Despite what the CIA thinks of our collective abilities, the FBI did manage to run a handful of assets in Triple Border. With some persistence one of them struck pay dirt, pay dirt being the Egyptian named Ibrahim bin Daoud who runs the fundamentalist training camp called Boa Vista. Daoud, whose real name is Khalil al-Jabarin, has a record—al-Jabarin was convicted of being a spiritual leader of the Muslim Brotherhood and served serious time in a Cairo military prison. He has the physical and mental scars to show for it; electrodes attached to testicles are said to be the torture of choice of Egyptian jailers. No doubt about it, Daoud himself is a cold-blooded killer—whether it's the result of his suffering or his genes we don't know. What we do know is that last month he snuck a crocodile into a swimming pool in São Paolo and then pushed in a man accused of being a police informer while some local hookers holding paper plates filled with defrosted hors d'oeuvres looked on. Money was spread around and the murder was hushed up. We know the story's not apocryphal because one of the hookers was a collateral asset. The dead informer was our principal asset in Triple Border."

"So the FBI has gone blind out there?" Lincoln asked.

"For all intents and purposes, yes."

"The principal asset who got close to Daoud didn't have an understudy?"

"We didn't get around to it in time," Kiick admitted.

"What else can I expect to find at Triple Border besides ravenous crocodiles?"

Kiick—Lincoln had a nodding acquaintance with him from having sat in on several of the rare joint CIA-FBI coordinating sessions—slid an FBI briefing book across the conference table. "What we've picked up is all in here," he said. "You're likely to come across a Texan who goes by the name Leroy Streeter. He's what we call a crossover—in his case, an Aryan nationalist nut who is making common cause with the Muslim fundamentalists. Mind you, the mix is potentially lethal. If and when Muslim terrorists do attack the United States, the white supremacists could provide infrastructure support and eventually hit men, since it's easier for an American to gain entrance to public places than an Arab from the Middle East. Leroy Streeter may or may not be the Texan's real name, by the way. The guy you'll meet—he's five foot two, a hundred and thirty pounds, speaks with a Texas drawl—travels under a passport made out to a Leroy Streeter Jr. Leroy Streeter Sr. was the führer of a Texas-based white supremacist splinter group called the Nationalist Congress; he died of cancer in Huntsville while he was serving time for blowing up a black church in Birmingham. State Department consulate in Mexico City issued a passport to a Leroy Streeter Jr. four years ago, but Argentina's Secretariat for State Intelligence thinks that he drowned on a Rio beach two years back; as far as we know, no body was recovered. Which means that Leroy Streeter Jr. has risen from the dead or someone is using his passport. Either way, he's high on the FBI's most wanted list. "

"Don't let yourself get sidetracked," Crystal Quest told Lincoln. "Leroy Streeter is not the target of this operation. The person we're after down there is the Saudi."

"Does the Saudi have a name?" Lincoln inquired.

"Everyone has a name," Quest snapped. "FBI just doesn't know it."

"From what our principal asset was able to tell us before his untimely death," continued Kiick, unfazed by Quest's dig at the Bureau, "we understand the Saudi is the kingpin of a fundamentalist group that recently surfaced as a blip on our radar screen. It's been operating out of Afghanistan since the Russians were evicted from the country two years ago and calls itself al-Qa'ida, which means 'The Base.' The Saudi appears to be organizing al-Qa'ida cells across Europe and Asia and running them from the Sudanese capital of Khartoum."

"How do I get to this Saudi?"

"With any luck, he gets to you," Quest said. "He's in the market for explosives, lots of it. The FBI asset picked up rumors that the Saudi is shopping around for a truckload and is offering a small fortune if it can be delivered to an address in the United States. The explosives may be the tip of the iceberg—the Saudi may have his heart set on acquiring something that will render the explosives more lethal."

"You're talking about a dirty bomb," Lincoln guessed.

"He's talking about gift wrapping the explosives with plutonium or enriched-uranium radioactive waste," Quest said, "which would result in the contamination of a wide area when the charge is detonated. Hundreds of thousands could be effected. It's because of this threat that the president decided to bring the CIA into the picture."

Kiick said, "Mind you, Lincoln—I understand that that's the name you're using now—the business about a dirty bomb is a worst-case scenario, and pure speculation."

Quest ignored the FBI representative "We're going to come at the Saudi obliquely," she told Lincoln. "We know of an al-Qa'ida cell in the Balkans that's been running guns and ammunition to the Muslims in Sarajevo in the belief that war between the Serbs and Bosnians is inevitable. Guy who directs it is an Azerbaijani who uses the name Sami Akhbar. Our plan is to hang you out to dry on the Dalmatian coast, which is Sami's stamping ground, and let him stumble across you. Once you've established your bona fides and whet his appetite, you reach the Saudi by working your way up the chain of command. In Triple Border,

he's said to use Daoud as a doorkeeper; nobody gets to the Saudi without getting past the Egyptian."

Crystal Quest, dressed in one of her signature pantsuits with wide
lapels and a dress shirt with frills down the chest, scraped back her
chair and stood up. Taking their cue from her, the wallahs from the
DDO jumped to their feet. "Get it into your head that Triple Border
isn't the Club Med," Quest reminded Lincoln. "The group we know
least about—the group which interests us the most—is this al-Qa'ida
entity. Bring home the bacon on the Saudi and al-Qa'ida, Lincoln,
and I'll personally see to it you get one of the Company's jockstrap
medals." She added with a leer: "Pin it on you myself." The DDO
contingent all laughed. As Quest headed for the door, Kiick offered
his hand across the table and Lincoln, half rising from his chair, shook
it. "Our cutout will make herself known to you by saying something
about Giovanni da Varrazano and the bridge named after him." Kiick
added, "Holy mackerel, watch your ass when you get to Triple Border.
You'll be rubbing shoulders with mighty ornery folks."

Crystal Quest's voice, suffused with satisfaction at her own mor-
bid sense of humor, came drifting back over her shoulder: "Whatever
you do, Lincoln, stay away from swimming pools."

* * *

Hanging out with Leroy Streeter in a booth at the rear of the Kit
Kat Klub on the main drag of Foz do Iguaçú for the second night
running, polishing off the last of the sirloin steak and French fries,
washing it down with cheap Scotch in a shot glass and lukewarm beer
chasers drunk straight from the bottle, Lincoln watched the hookers
slotting coins into the jukebox and swaying in each other's arms to
the strains of "Don't Worry, Be Happy," which, judging from the fact
that it was played over and over, night after night, was either number
one on the Brazilian hit parade or the only 45-rpm record in the
machine still functioning. Leroy had just come down the narrow
stairs leading to a dark hallway with two bedrooms off of it, having
gotten his ashes hauled (as he put it) for the second time that night.
The skinny teenage girl with the red-dyed hair worked into a chignon
on the top of her head to add height and age came down behind him,

ironing the folds of a thin shift with her palms as she tottered back
to the bar on spiked high heels. "I prefer jailbait," Leroy informed his
new found friend as he signalled for another bottle of beer. "They got
theirselves tight snatches and do whichever you tell 'em to without
raising a fuss or renegotiating the price. Can't figure what you got
'gainst getting laid, Lincoln. Like I told you, the girls here is all clean
as whistles."

"They're only clean as the last whistle they blew," Lincoln said.
"Last thing I need to come down with is gonorrhea. Wind up costing
me two hundred fifty grand to get screwed."

"I see what you're saying," Leroy said. He looked over at the
dancers padding around on the broad pine planks of the floor in front
of the jukebox; one young man, whom Leroy had identified as a
Pakistani he'd seen at Daoud's boondock training camp, was hugging
Leroy's skinny friend with the red-dyed hair and dancing in place,
shifting his weight from foot to foot in time to the music. "I don't
hold with females dancing with females," the Texan told Lincoln, aiming his chin in the direction of the hookers who hung limply in each
other's arms, their backs slightly arched, their painted lids closed, their
heads falling off to one side as if their necks weren't strong enough to
support the weight of their elaborate hairdos. "It ain't normal, is my
view, in the sense that lesbian love ain't normal. If God meant women
to fuck women he would have given some of them dicks. The hell
kind of music is that anyway? Don't worry, be happy is how I aim to
pass the rest of my days on earth once all this is over with."

Lincoln decided the moment had come to see whether his efforts
at bonding with the Texan had paid off. Bending over the table, low-
ering his voice so the two Brazilians in the next booth couldn't make
out what he was saying, he asked, "Once all *what* is over with? It's got
to do with the ammonium nitrate, right? Tell me something, Leroy—
what the fuck would anyone do with a moving van stuffed with
ammonium nitrate?" He managed to ask the question very casually, as
if he were only trying to hold up his end of the conversation; as if he
couldn't care less about the answer.

Leroy, a little man who wanted people to think of him as big,
couldn't resist bragging. "Between you and me and the fly on the wall
over there, I'm gonna go and personally drive it through the Holland

Tunnel," he replied, leaning forward until their foreheads were almost touching. "Gonna set the fuse and blow it up in downtown Manhattan and flatten a square mile of Wall Street real estate, is what I'm gonna do with it."

Sinking back, Lincoln whistled through his teeth. "You guys aren't fucking around—you're going straight for the jugular."

"Fucking A we're not fucking around," Leroy said, squirming gleefully on his banquette.

Lincoln raised the bottle to his lips and swallowed a mouthful of warm beer. "What you got against Wall Street, Leroy? Did you lose money on the stock market?"

Leroy sniffed at the air in the Kit Kat Klub, which reeked of beer and marijuana and perspiration. "I hate the Federal gov'ment," he confided, "and that there Wall Street is a branch of the Federal gov'ment. Wall Street is where them Jews hang out, running the country from behind their polished mahogany desks, plotting to take over the whole entire world. Whether you admit it or not, you know I'm right or you wouldn't be doing what you're doing. You're a foot soldier like me in the war of liberation. Hell, we may have to destroy America to liberate her, but one way or another we are gonna go and set the clock back to where right thinking folks can get on with their lives without being dictated to by some pompous asshole in Washington. It's the Civil War all over again, Lincoln. The Federal gov'ment's trying to tell us what we can do and what we can't do. Things keep up the way they been going, hell, they're gonna throw away the Constitution and decide you need to get yourself a license before you can own a handgun." Leroy kept his voice pitched low but he was starting to rant now. "A license to buy a handgun! Over my dead body! Listen up, Lincoln, you got yourself book learning so you know the country is going to the dogs. Give the kikes an' niggers an inch, they'll come right back at you for a country mile. If we don't draw the limit line in the dirt, if we don't make our stand now, why, one day soon they're gonna bus the niggers to every goddamn school in the country until there won't be such a thing as a white man's school left between the Pacific and the Atlantic."

Leroy seemed to run out of steam just as the mulatto girl working the bar turned up with his beer. She deftly flicked off the cap with a church key hanging between her breasts at the end of a long gold necklace. "Ready for a refill?" she asked Lincoln.

The bottle of beer on the table in front of him was still half full. "I'm okay," he said.

"He is definitely okay," Leroy agreed impatiently.

The waitress told Leroy, "My girlfriend Paura, she's the dark haired one in toreador pants dancing all by herself over there, has taken a shine to your friend here."

"You don't say," Leroy said. He smirked across the table at Lincoln. "Why don't you invite Paura over for a beer, Lincoln. If'n you don't fancy her I'll take her on."

"I told you—" Lincoln started to say, but Leroy had already grabbed the waitress's wrist. "Go and tell this Paura chic to get her ass over here."

The waitress could be seen laughing and saying something to her friend as she headed back to the bar. Paura, holding an enormous joint between two fingers of her left hand, slowly turned her head and sized up the two men in the booth, then went on with her dancing though each shuffling step brought her closer to the rear of the bar. She kept dancing even after the record stopped and wound up swaying like a leaf in a faint breeze next to the booth as "Don't Worry, Be Happy" started in again. She took a drag on her joint and swallowed the smoke and said, "I bet she told you my name's Paura."

"She did," Leroy affirmed.

"She never gets it right." The girl spoke English with what Lincoln took to be an Italian accent. "I'm Paura some days. On others I'm Lucia. Today is a Lucia day."

Lincoln, an aficionado of legends as well as firearms, asked, "Are these different names for the same person or two distinct people?"

Lucia scrutinized Lincoln to see if he was mocking her. When she saw he was serious, she answered his question seriously. "They're as distinct as night and day. Lucia is day. Her name in Italian means light. Sunshine and daylight fill her heart, she is grateful to be alive and lives from day to day, she doesn't see past tomorrow. She goes down on anyone who pays without haggling, she considers it a matter of principle to give a client his money's worth. She passes on half of what she earns to her pimp and does not hold back his share if a client should happen to leave a tip."

"And Paura? What's she like?"

"Paura is night. Her name means fear in Italian. Everything about her can be traced to fear—she is afraid of her shadow during the day, afraid of the darkness when the last light has been drained from the day, afraid of the customers who remove their belts before they take off their trousers. She's afraid of swimming pools. She is afraid life on earth will end before dawn tomorrow, afraid it will go on forever." She regarded Lincoln with her frightened eyes. "Would you like me to read your palm? I can tell you on what day of the week your life will come to an end."

Lincoln politely declined. "I have no visible lifeline," he said.

The girl tried another tack. "What sign were you born under?"

Lincoln shook his head. "I'm a Zodiac atheist. Don't know my sign, don't want to know."

"That more or less narrows our relationship down to dancing," Lucia said, her body starting to sway to the music again. Shrugging the filmy blouse so far off one shoulder that the aureole on a breast came into view, she held out a hand.

"She's a nut case," Leroy muttered. "But she sure has got the hots for you."

"I have a bad leg," Lincoln informed the girl.

"Go 'head and put her out of her misery," Leroy urged. "Jesus Christ, you can't catch nothing jus' dancing with her." When Lincoln still hung back, Leroy nudged his ankle under the table. "You ain't being a gentleman, Lincoln, that's for goddamned sure."

Lincoln pulled a face and shrugged and slid off the banquette to his feet. The Italian girl gripped one of his large hands in hers and pulled him limping into the middle of the room, then turned and, stomping out her joint on the floor boards, melted against him, both of her bare arms flung around his neck, her teeth nibbling on the lobe of his ear.

In the booth, Leroy slapped the table in delight.

Lincoln was a good dancer. Favoring his game leg, and with the girl glued to his lanky frame, he launched into an awkward little three step that set the other girls around the bar to watching in admiration.

After a bit Lucia whispered in Lincoln's ear. "You don't need to tell me your names if you don't want to. Wouldn't change anything if you did—around here nobody uses real names."

"Name's Lincoln."

"That a first name or family name?"

"First."

"That your name during daylight or at night?"

Lincoln had to smile. "Both."

Without missing a beat, Lucia said, "Giovanni da Varrazano, who gave his daylight name to the bridge that connects Brooklyn to an island named Staten, was killed by Indians during an expedition to Brazil in 1528. A little bird whispering in my ear told me you would be thrilled to know that."

Lincoln stopped in his tracks and pushed her off to arm's length. The smile sat like a mask on his face. "As a matter of fact, I am."

Lucia, quite pleased with herself, tucked her breast into her blouse with a dip and toss of her shoulder and sank back into his arms, and they started dancing again. Lincoln, suddenly edgy, pressed his mouth to her ear. "So it's you, the cutout," he said. He thought of Djamillah in the room over the bar in Beirut, with the faded night moth tattooed under her right breast; he remembered telling her *I am addicted to fear—I require a daily fix.* You had to be addicted to fear to get into the business of spying; this is the thing he had in common with the Italian girl Paura—she had surely been the cutout who had seen the FBI asset thrown to the crocodile. Lincoln identified the source of his edginess: He hoped against hope she wouldn't suffer the same fate "Do you have a good memory?" he asked her now. Without waiting for a reply, he said, "Here goes nothing: I was picked up by the Texan sitting at the table with me, I believe his name really is Leroy Streeter because he mentioned that his father had burned down a Negro church in Alabama. He took me to a room over a bar in Ciudad del Este. The Egyptian named Daoud was there."

"It's no skin off my nose if you don't want sex," Lucia said. "I've had enough sex for one day. My pussy and my mouth are both sore."

"Daoud checked out my bona fides—I heard him go upstairs and make a phone call—my guess is he was getting his people to confirm that I'd been treated in a Trieste clinic, that I'd written the book I said I wrote. I must have passed the initial muster because he sent me back here and told me to hang out with Leroy until I was contacted again, which is what I'm doing now."

"The reason we play the same record all the time," Lucia whispered, her tongue flicking inside his ear, "is because 'Don't Worry, Be Happy' is the opposite of our lives down here. Except for Lucia, all we do is worry about not being happy."

"With any luck, the next step is for me to be taken to meet the Saudi."

"The girls who work here," Lucia said, "use abortions as birth control. If you ever come back again, it will be appreciated if you would bring us a carton of condoms."

"Leroy told me why they're shopping around for ammonium nitrate," Lincoln went on. "I don't know if he's bragging or inventing, but he says he plans to fill a moving van with explosives and blow it up in the middle of Wall Street." He let one of his palms slip down to her tight toreador pants and the swell of a buttock. "What will you do when all this is over?"

Lucia dropped one of her hands to reach under the back of Lincoln's shirt. "All this will never be over," she breathed.

Her answer startled Lincoln; that was what the Alawite prostitute Djamillah had told Dante Pippen as he was leaving the room over the bar in Beirut a legend ago. "It will end one day," Lincoln promised her. "Where will you go? What will you do?"

"I would go back to Tuscany," she said, clinging to him, burrowing into his neck so that her words were muffled. "I would buy a small farm and breed baby polyesters and shear them twice a year and sell the hair to make silk-soft cloth."

"Polyester is a synthetic fabric," Lincoln said.

Lucia's hand came in contact with the leather of the holster nestling in the cavity in Lincoln's lower back. She caressed the cold metal on the butt of the small-caliber automatic in the holster. "I will raise baby acrylics, then," she said, annoyed at his nitpicking. Her fingers worked their way under the holster; when they reached the smooth scar of the healed wound she stopped dancing abruptly. "What gave you that?" she asked.

But Lincoln only murmured her night name, Paura, and she didn't repeat the question.

* * *

Hanging out at the Kit Kat Kub the following night, Lincoln made a point of dancing with two other girls and taking the second one up to a room so that suspicion wouldn't fall on Paura if he was compromised. Once in the room, the girl, a bleached blonde who called herself Monroe Marilyn, named her price. Lincoln counted out the bills and set them on the table. Monroe washed in a chipped bidet and insisted he wash too, and watched him to make sure he did. She took off the rest of her clothing except for a black lace brassiere which she claimed to have bought in Paris, and stretched out on the mattress covered with a stained sheet, her legs apart, her eyes fixed on the filaments in the electric bulb dangling from the ceiling. In the bar below "Don't Worry, Be Happy" started to play again on the jukebox. Lincoln shut his eyes and imagined he was making love to Paura. Under him, Marilyn moaned and cried out with pleasure; to Lincoln her sensual clatter came across as a recorded announcement, played over and over like the 45-rpm disk on the jukebox downstairs. He finished before 'Don't Worry, Be Happy" did.

"So you got your ashes hauled after all," Leroy said when Lincoln came limping back to the booth and slid onto the banquette across from him. "You must of broken some kind of speed record. You need to get laid at least once a day not to be sex starved. The trick is to make it last as long as you can. That way you get more fuck for your buck."

"You ought to write a lonely hearts column for the newspapers," Lincoln said. "You could advise men how to solve their sexual problems."

"I just may do that when I'm too old to take on the Federal gov'ment in Washington."

"How old will you be when you're too old for the good fight?"

"Thirty, maybe. Maybe thirty."

Around eleven, an old man wearing a long shabby overcoat and a threadbare scarf wound loosely around his thin neck came into the bar to sell lottery tickets. He had turned up the same hour every night since Lincoln had been hanging out at the Kit Kat. As he stepped through the door, the hookers dropped what they were doing to crowd around him, hunting for lucky numbers on the lottery slips attached to his clipboard. When they'd each bought a ticket that suited them, the girls drifted back to the tables or took up where they'd left off on the dance floor. The lottery vendor shuffled across the floor to a vacant booth not far from where Lincoln and Leroy were sitting. The mulatto waitress filled a tall glass with tap water and set it down in front of him. The old man half bowed to her from a sitting position—the gesture seemed to come from another world and another century. A new girl Lincoln had not seen before came down the steps behind a corpulent Lebanese client and, noticing the old man with the clipboard in the booth, hurried over to buy a ticket. When the music went silent, Lincoln could hear their voices—he could even make out what they were saying. The girl was asking when the drawing would be held and how she would know if she'd won anything. The old man told her that he kept the stubs attached to his clipboard for months. Each morning he tore the list of winning numbers from the newspaper, he said, and made it his business to personally seek out winners who had bought a ticket from him.

The idea of a hooker hoping to strike it rich from a lottery ticket intrigued Lincoln. He wondered if her pimp would take half the proceeds if she did win.

Leroy was listening to them also. He reached across the table and tapped Lincoln on the wrist. "The hell language they talking?" he wanted to know.

Lincoln hadn't realized they were talking a foreign language until Leroy called his attention to it. "Not sure," he replied, although, to his astonishment, he found that he knew very well. The old lottery vendor and the hooker were talking in Polish, which was the language Martin Odum's mother had used when she told him bedtime stories in Jonestown, Pennsylvania, a lifetime ago.

At the booth, the girl could be heard asking, "*Ile kosztóje bilet?*" When the old man told her how much a ticket cost, she carefully counted out coins from a small purse and tore one from the clipboard.

"Sounds foreign to me," Leroy was saying. "Don't like foreigners, don't like the languages they talk. Don't know why foreigners don't learn American. Make the world simpler if everyone talked American, is how I see it."

Lincoln couldn't resist baiting Leroy. "You want them to talk American with a Texas drawl like you or a clipped Boston accent like John Kennedy?"

Leroy took the question seriously. "Don't matter none to me. Any American beats out a foreign language, hands down."

Near midnight, as the girls began to drift over to the bar to settle up what they owed for the rooms they'd used, the fat Arab boy who'd been doing the jigsaw puzzle in Ciudad del Este burst into the bar. He was still wearing the shoulder holster with the plastic grip of a toy gun jutting from it. Spotting the two Americans in the rear booth, he padded over on his Reeboks and thrust out a folded note. Leroy read it and raised his eyes and cried out excitedly, "Bingo, Lincoln. Daoud is waiting for us behind the bar."

Daoud's coal black Mercedes was idling in the shadows at the street end of the alley when the two Yankees, the one with the cane limping along behind the short American in cowboy boots, came around the side of the Kit Kat and settled into the backseat. The fat Arab boy slid in next to Daoud in front. "Where are you taking us?" Lincoln asked, but Daoud didn't bother to reply. He gestured to the driver and the car lurched past the halal butcher shop on the corner into the poorly lit main drag and headed in the direction of the Little Dipper and Polaris, hanging in the night sky over the rooftops. Twenty minutes out of Foz do Iguaçú the paved road abruptly gave way to a rutted dirt track and the driver had to slow down to keep the passengers from hitting their heads against the roof of the car. In the headlights, Indians leading donkeys piled high with burlap sacks could be seen stumbling through the pitch darkness. "In the outback," Leroy told Lincoln, "lot of smuggling goes on during the night." After one particularly rough bump Daoud flung an arm over the shoulder of the fat teenager and said something to him in Arabic. The boy said, "*Inch'Allah.*"

Lincoln leaned forward to ask the Egyptian if the boy were his son. Daoud turned his head only slightly and said, "He is the son of my son."

"And where is his father?"

"His father, my son, was killed in the attack on the American Marines at Beirut Airport in 1983."

Lincoln reminded himself he was living deep in a legend; that he ought to be commiserating with the Egyptian. "It must be a source of great sadness to have lost your son—"

"It is a source of great pride to have given a son to the jihad. Along with my son, two hundred and forty one American marines and sailors lost their lives in the Beirut attack, after which your President Reagan lost his nerve and disengaged from Lebanon. Every father should have such a son."

An hour and twenty minutes out of Foz de Iguaçú, the headlights of the Mercedes picked up the first of two road blocks. Soon after the second one, located beyond a sharp curve in the track, the car slowed to give three armed men with red-and-white checkered kaffiyehs over their faces time to drag open a chain-link gate. One of the guards said something into a walkie-talkie as he waved the Mercedes through. The driver headed downhill toward a group of wooden army barracks set in what looked like a dry river bed and pulled up before a structure that was lower and wider than the other buildings. On a flat rise behind the barracks, in a dirt field illuminated by floodlights powered by a gasoline-driven motor whose put-put was audible in the still night air, a dozen men in khaki fatigues were practicing penalty shots against a goalie outfitted in a yellow Hertz jumpsuit. When one of them scored, Lincoln could make out the other players taunting the guardian.

Daoud's grandson darted from the Mercedes to pull open a narrow door in the side of the building. The young Pakistani whom Lincoln had seen dancing at the Kit Kat with Leroy's jailbait hooker stood in the corridor inside the door, an Israeli Uzi with spare clips taped to the folding metal stock tucked under an arm, his finger on the trigger. He tensed when he saw the two Americans and muttered something to Daoud, who translated. "He wants to know if you are armed." Lincoln, laughing, reached under his shirt behind his back and pulled the small-caliber automatic from the holster worn high on his belt so that it would disappear into the shrapnel wound. The Pakistani took the automatic and waved the party through.

The corridor gave onto a square room with a low ceiling. It took a moment for Lincoln's eyes to become accustomed to the dimness. About thirty or so men sat around the room on straw matting, their

backs against thin cushions attached to the walls. Daoud motioned
Lincoln and Leroy to a spot along the near wall, then crossed the room
and took a free place against the opposite wall near the figure who was
clearly presiding. Lincoln set his cane on the cement floor and settled
down, his bad leg stretched out in front of him, the other ankle tucked
under his thigh. Next to him, Leroy sank into an awkward crosslegged position. Lincoln reached for his tin of Schimelpenicks, but a
lean young Arab posed a hand gently but firmly on his wrist. Lincoln
noticed that nobody in the room was smoking. He nodded and
grinned at the young Arab, who turned away, expressionless.

Lincoln tried to distinguish the features of the figure across from
him. The man, who looked to be in mid-thirties, was ruggedly handsome, with a stringy ash-colored beard and dark thoughtful eyes exud-
ing an inner calm that could have easily been taken for arrogance. He
was extremely tall and dressed in a collarless coarse off-white ankle-
length robe with what Lincoln took to be a thick Afghan goat-hair
vest over it. Bareheaded, with socks and heavy walking sandals on his
feet, he sat crosslegged on the mat with a supple elegance, his back off
the wall and hunched slightly forward as he read something from a
sheet of paper to those within earshot, occasionally tapping the long
forefinger of his right hand on a word to emphasize its importance. All
Lincoln could make out was the honeyed undertone of someone who
didn't need to raise his voice to be heard.

There appeared to be some sort of queue because the two men sitting between Daoud and the figure Lincoln identified as the Saudi
spoke next, raising problems that needed to be solved or providing
information that needed to be weighed against what was already
known. Finally Daoud's turn came. Leaning forward, talking quietly,
he spoke to the Saudi for several minutes. Once he tossed his head to
indicate the two Americans sitting across the room. Only then did the
Saudi's gaze settle on the visitors. He scratched at his chest with several
fingers and uttered a single word. Daoud looked over and motioned for
Lincoln to approach. Leroy assumed the gesture included him and
started to get up, but Daoud wagged a finger and he collapsed back
into his cramped position. Leaning on his cane, Lincoln pushed himself
to his feet and walked over to the Saudi and sank onto his haunches
facing him. The Saudi saluted him with a palm to his heart and

Lincoln mimicked the gesture. A thin man with greasy hair parted down the middle and thick spectacles slipping along his nose was sitting next to the Saudi with a lined notebook open on his lap; Lincoln took him for a secretary. The Saudi murmured something and the secretary repeated it in a loud voice. Instantly all the men sitting around the walls sprang to their feet and headed for the door. Across the room, only Leroy remained, squirming uncomfortably in a position he would never grow accustomed to. Lincoln looked from Daoud to his host and back as Daoud delivered a short speech in Arabic. The Saudi listened intently, nodding from time to time in apparent agreement, his eyes darting occasionally to Lincoln and, once, to Leroy across the room. Finally the Saudi, scratching again at his chest, started to put questions. The secretary with the greasy hair translated them into English.

"He welcomes you to Boa Vista. He asks how you arrived to here from Croatia."

"I flew Lufthansa from Zagreb to Munich to Paris, then Air France to New York, then PanAm to São Paolo. I chartered a small plane that flew me into Foz do Iguaçú."

When the secretary had translated this, the Saudi, never lifting his eyes from Lincoln, put another question. The secretary said, "He asks how the struggle is going in Bosnia? He asks whether the Bosnians, in the event of war, will be able to defend Sarajevo if the Serbs capture the hills overlooking the city."

"The Serb military is by all accounts a great deal stronger than anything the Bosnians can field," Lincoln said. "What will strengthen the Bosnians in the event of war is that they have no place to go; their backs are against Croatia, and the Croats hate them as much as the Serbs."

"He agrees with your analysis. He tells the story of the Greek general who warned his officers not to attack a weaker force trapped in a canyon without a line of retreat available, because the weaker force would then conquer the stronger force."

The Saudi spoke again; again the secretary translated. "He asks how you plan to accumulate large quantities of ammonium nitrate without attracting the attention of the police"

Almost against his will Lincoln felt himself falling under the spell of the Saudi. He saw, now that he was close to him, that the skin on the Saudi's face and neck appeared yellowish, but he assumed it was due to the low wattage of the bulbs burning in the room. He couldn't help but like his style—no wonder young men were flocking to join his al-Qa'ida cells in Afghanistan and Yemen. Watching his unflinching eyes, Lincoln could feel the magnetic pull of his personality; the Saudi spoke softly but he carried a big stick. Seeing how uncomfortable his visitor was, the Saudi reached out to offer him a cushion. Lincoln sat on it his game leg thrust forward, and provided an explanation that had been prepared back at Langley: His several associates would spread out across America and, pretending to represent farmers' cooperatives in various southern and eastern states, would buy up whatever ammonium nitrate was available and truck it to New Jersey, where it would all be loaded onto a moving van. At a site to be designated, Leroy Streeter would take possession of the ammonium nitrate and pay the fee in cash.

"He asks if you are curious to know what Mr. Streeter plans to do with the ammonium nitrate."

"I suppose he plans to explode it someplace. Tell you the truth, I couldn't care less."

"He asks why you could not care less."

"I believe America has grown too rich and too fat and too insolent and needs to be taken down a peg or two." It was clear from the secretary's expression that he didn't understand the expression "a peg or two." Lincoln repeated the thought another way. "America needs to be taught a lesson in humility."

"He asks what kinds of arms you sold in the Balkans."

"All kinds. My clients would give me a wish list and I did my best to fill it."

"What is it, a wish list?"

"A list of the arms and munitions that they wished to have."

"He asks if you have limited your operations to conventional weapons."

"My operations have been limited to selling what the Soviet military has in its stocks. Up to now I have procured almost all of the weapons and munitions from Soviet army units in East Germany. Many of the Russians I dealt with have returned to the Soviet Union and would be able to supply me with other articles from the Soviet arsenal. Do you have something particular in mind?"

"He asks whether you could supply spent plutonium or enriched uranium."

Lincoln thought about that for a moment. "Spent plutonium or enriched-uranium waste could be obtained from nuclear power plants like the one in Chernobyl, north of Kiev in the Ukraine—"

The Saudi interrupted Lincoln and the secretary translated what he said. "He is curious why you mention Chernobyl, since its reactor exploded five years ago and the radioactive waste has been sealed under an enormous concrete sheath."

"It was the plant's number four reactor that exploded. Two other reactors remain in use. The radioactive waste is trucked to various nuclear disposal sites in the Soviet Union. There is another source of spent plutonium—the Soviet nuclear submarine fleet based in Archangel and Murmansk is known to be decommissioning vessels because of budgetary shortfalls. Plutonium pits are removed from the decommissioned subs and trucked to the same nuclear disposal sites. The bottom line is that there is no shortage of weapons-grade plutonium or uranium for anyone willing to run the risks involved in negotiating the acquisition. It goes without saying, very large sums of money would be required to conclude such a deal."

The Saudi accepted the translation with a preoccupied nod. He muttered something to the secretary, who said: "He asks how large?"

"How much radioactive waste would be required?"

"He says to you a tenth of a short ton to start with."

"Where would he want it delivered?"

"At a site to be specified in Afghanistan."

"I would need to consult my associates before setting a price. Off the top of my head, I should think we are talking about something in the neighborhood of a million dollars U.S., a down payment in cash when I have located the spent pits, the rest to be paid into a numbered account in an offshore bank."

"He asks is it so that nuclear bombs can be fitted into something the size of a common valise."

"He's referring to what the Americans have designated the MK-47. The Soviets are said to have constructed several hundred of these devices. Imagine something shaped like an army canteen, only larger, roughly the size of a bulging valise, with an automobile gas cap on the top and two metal handles on either side. Because of its size and mobility, the nuclear device can be easily smuggled into a target city and exploded by a crude timing mechanism. The MK-47s contain twenty-two pounds of uranium which, when exploded, is equivalent to one thousand tons of conventional TNT, one twentieth the size of the first Hiroshima atomic bomb."

"He asks about the shelf life of these valise-bombs."

"The Russians have been miniaturizing their nuclear payloads since the mid 1980s. Whatever they have in their stockpiles could be expected to function for ten to fifteen years."

"He wants to know if such a valise-bomb can be acquired?"

"For obvious reasons, the Russian military keep these devices under lock and key, with a high degree of command and control accountability. But if someone were to offer an enormous sum of money, plus safe passage out of Russia for the seller, it is conceivable that something might be worked out."

"He asks how much money is an enormous sum."

"Again, off the top of my head, I would say something in the neighborhood of three to five million U.S for each valise-bomb."

The Saudi sank back into the cushion fastened to the wall behind him and scratched absently at his upper arm and his ribs. Lincoln noticed that the Saudi was sweating despite the chill in the room; that the sweat on his brow seemed to crystalize into a fine white powder.

"He says to you that for the time being we will concentrate on the spent plutonium or uranium pits. He says that nobody can say what the future holds. Perhaps one day he will raise the subject of the valise-bomb again with you."

Lincoln smiled and nodded. "It's your call."

There was a large glass bowl filled with fruit, and another over-flowing with nuts, near the Saudi. He pointed first to one and then the other with a hand turned palm up, offering something to eat to his guest. Lincoln reached out to help himself to some nuts.

"He notes that it turns cold at night out here," the secretary trans-lated. "He asks if you and your friend would like some herbal tea."

Lincoln looked at Leroy over his shoulder and said, "He is offering us hot herbal tea."

"Ask 'em if they got anythin' slightly more alcoholic," Leroy said.

"Leroy, these people don't drink alcohol. It's against their religion."

"Goddamn. How can they expect folks to convert to a dry religion?"

The Saudi apparently caught the gist of Leroy's remark because he replied in Arabic without waiting for the secretary to translate. The secretary said: "He tells the story of the czar who converted Russia to Christianity—it was near the end of the first millennium. Vladimir I of Kiev was tempted by Islam but decided against it because he did not think Russians could get through their cruel winters without something the Arab chemists who developed the technique of distillation called *al-kuhl*. History might have turned out differently if the Prophet had not abstained from alcohol—the long cold war would have been between Christianity and Islam."

Lincoln said, "With the collapse of the Soviet Union, perhaps there will be another cold war—a new struggle for Jerusalem between the spiritual descendants of Richard the Lion Hearted and the heirs of the Sultan Saladin."

Listening to the translation, the Saudi reached for a glass filled with water and, popping two large oval pills into his mouth, washed them down with a long swig. Lincoln watched his Adam's apple bob in his long neck. Wiping his lips with the fabric on the back of a wrist, the Saudi said, in labored English, "A new struggle is surely a possibility."

"You speak English?" Lincoln asked him directly.

The Saudi responded in Arabic and the secretary translated. "He says to you he speaks English as well as you speak Arabic."

Lincoln grinned. "I understand four words of Arabic: *Allah Akbar* and *Inch'Allah*."

"He compliments you. He says to you the person who understands only these four words grasps the heart of the holy Koran. He says to you there are pious men, descendants of the Prophet, who can recite all one hundred and fourteen suras from memory but do not hold in their hearts the significance of these four words."

Lincoln looked at the Saudi. "Are you pious? Do you practice your religion?"

"He says to you he practices as much of it as needs to be practiced to be a faithful Muslim. He says to you that he resides in what Muslim's call *dar al-harb*, the home of war; above all other things he practices *jihad*. He would have you know that waging war on behalf of Islam and Allah against the infidel is a Koranic obligation."

Lincoln nodded at the Saudi, who inclined his head in a sign of esteem for the foreigner who appeared to respect him.

* * *

"What happened then?" Crystal Quest demanded when Lincoln, back in Washington, described the meeting at the training camp in the Brazilian *mato graso*.

"He threw questions at me for another twenty minutes and I fielded them. It was all very low keyed. At one point he got into a long discussion with the Egyptian, Daoud; for five or so minutes it was almost as if I didn't exist. Then, without saying another word to me, the Saudi climbed to his feet and departed. I heard the motors of three or four cars kick into life behind the building and saw their headlights sweep into and out of the room as they headed deeper into the *mato graso*. Daoud signaled that the meeting had come to an end and ushered Leroy and me back to his Mercedes and we started back toward Foz do Iguaçú. The Egyptian told me I had made a good impression on the Saudi. He said I was to return to the United States and organize the purchase and delivery of the ammonium nitrate at mid month to an abandoned hangar off the Pulaski Skyway in New Jersey." Lincoln produced a page that had been torn out of a lined notebook. "The address is written here."

Quest snatched the scrap of paper. "What about the Saudi and his radioactive waste?" she asked.

"Daoud invited me to return to Boa Vista on the night of the new moon to meet the Saudi and organize with him the delivery of the two hundred pounds of spent plutonium."

"Describe the Saudi again, Lincoln."

"It's all in my mission report. His name was never mentioned, either by Daoud or by the secretary translating for him at the meeting in Boa Vista. I would estimate he was roughly six foot five and in his middle thirties—"

Quest cut in. "Guessing someone's age has never been your strong suit. How old do you think the cutout was?"

"The hooker in the Kit Kat? I'd say she was in her late thirties or early forties."

"Proves my point," Quest told the wallahs who had crowded into her office to attend Lincoln's debriefing. "The girl, the youngest daughter of an old Roman family, is twenty-seven. Her real name is Fiamma Segre. She's been doing hard drugs for years—that's why she looks old before her time. Go on with your description of the Saudi."

Lincoln, resting his elbows on the cane stretched like a span between the two arms of the chair, closed his eyes and tried to summon an image of the Saudi. "He's charismatic—"

"That's a load of crap, Lincoln. What do we put on the advisory we send out to our stations? 'Wanted, dead or alive, one charismatic Saudi.'"

Lincoln's patience was wearing thin. He was bone tired—the car ride back to São Paolo and the flight back to the States had worn him out. The grilling by Fred and her wallahs was shaping up as the straw that would break the camel's back. "I'm doing the best I can—"

"Your best needs to be better."

"Maybe if he were to get some shuteye," ventured one of the bolder wallahs.

Quest didn't like to be second guessed. "Maybe if you were to get yourself a posting to another division," she shot back. "How about it, Lincoln. Give us something concrete to go on. Rack your memory. I'm looking for what you didn't put into your report."

From a remote corner of his subconscious, Lincoln dredged up several details he had overlooked when he drafted his report. "Something's very wrong with the Saudi—"

"Mentally or medically?"

"Medically. He kept scratching at different parts of his body—his upper arm, his chest, his ribs. He seemed to itch all over. His skin was sallow—at first I thought it was because of the dim lighting, but when he stood up to go he passed under a bulb and I saw that he really was yellowish. Another thing: He was sweating even though it wasn't warm in the room. The perspiration on his forehead appeared to crystalize into a fine white powder."

Crystal Quest sat back in her chair and exchanged looks with the M.D. on her staff who directed the section that provided psychological and medical profiles of world leaders. "What do you make of that, Archie?"

"There are several possibilities. The start of chronic kidney failure has to be one of them. It's a condition that could go on for five, ten years without becoming life threatening."

"He took pills," Lincoln remembered.

"Small? Big? Did you notice the color or the shape?"

"Oval. Very big, the kind I'd have trouble swallowing. It was dark so I'm not sure of the color. Yellow, maybe. Yellow or orange."

"Hmmm. If it is chronic kidney failure, a bunch of early treatments come to mind. Could be calcium carbonate and calcium acetate—both are big yellowish pills, oval shaped, taken several times a day to lower the phosphorus level of the blood when the kidney isn't filtering properly. Diet would be critical—dairy products, liver, vegetables, nuts are high in phosphorus and would need to be avoided."

Lincoln remembered another detail. "There was a bowl of nuts on the floor between us—he offered them to me but he never helped himself to any."

For once Quest looked pleased "That should give us something to go on. A Saudi operating out of Khartoum who may be suffering from chronic kidney failure—if he's taking pills it would mean he's been diagnosed by a doctor somewhere, or even undergone clinical tests in a hospital. When you've gotten forty winks, Lincoln, I want you to work with one of the artists on the third floor and see if you can't come up with a portrait. Meanwhile we'll get our people to collect enough ammonium nitrate to fill a moving van so you can make that rendezvous in New Jersey with the would-be Wall Street bomber, Leroy Streeter."

"Do I go back to Boa Vista the night of the new moon to sell radioactive waste to the Saudi?" Lincoln asked.

"I don't think that'll be necessary," Quest said "We have a good working relationship with SIDE. We'll send in a para team to back up the Argentine State Intelligence people. They can encircle Boa Vista the night of the new moon—"

"That's the fourth of next month," one of the wallahs noted.

"We'll let SIDE pick up the Saudi and work him over." She added with a harsh laugh, "Their methods of interrogation are less sophisticated than ours, but more cost efficient. When they're finished interrogating him they can feed him to one of Daoud's alligators and America will have one less enemy to worry about."

"I want to make sure we get the Italian girl out before all hell breaks look at Triple Border," Lincoln said. He fingered his cane and rested the tip of it on Crystal Quest's desk. "I don't want her to end up like Djamillah in Beirut."

"You're a vulgar romantic," Quest complained. "We'll sneak her out of there the afternoon of the day we close in on the Saudi."

"I want you to give me your word."

The sudden silence in the room roared in Lincoln's ear. The wallahs had never heard anyone talk to the DDO quite like that. They kept their eyes fixed on their boss so as not to miss the eruption; it would be another tantrum to add to the Crystal Quest saga when the subject came up, as it invariably did, at happy hour. The color drained from her rouged cheeks, her eyes bulged and she looked as if she were about to choke to death on a fish bone stuck in her gullet. Then an unearthly bleat seeped from between her resplendently crimson lips. It took a moment for the people in the room to realize she was laughing. "We'll get the girl out, Lincoln," she said as she gasped for breath. "You have my word."

* * *

They met an hour shy of first light in an enormous abandoned hangar under a curve of the Pulaski Skyway, twenty minutes from the mouth of the Holland Tunnel leading to Manhattan. At the rear of the hangar sheets of corrugated roofing had sagged to the ground, creating a makeshift wall that blocked the gusts sweeping in from the coast. Beyond the hangar, in a hard dirt field strewn with thousands of empty plastic bottles, a small campfire burned; twenty or so homeless migrants who picked up work as longshoremen on the Hoboken docks were sitting with their backs against the dilapidated panel truck they used as a mobile bunkroom, drinking coffee brewed over the open fire. Carried on the gusts of damp air, the tinny syncopated clatter of a Mexican mambo band reached the hangar from the panel truck's radio. Inside, Ibrahim bin Daoud scrambled up the narrow metal ladder into the back of the moving van and began inspecting the large burlap sacks, all of them stencilled in black letters "AMMONI-UM NITRATE." Daoud had turned up with a sample of ammonium nitrate in a small jar and started comparing the contents of the sacks against his sample.

Leroy, watching from the ground, called impatiently, "Well?"

"It is ammonium nitrate, all right," the Egyptian confirmed.

Smiling out one side of his mouth, Leroy hefted a large valise out of the trunk compartment of Daoud's rented Toyota, set it on the car's hood and snapped open the lid. Lincoln, leaning on his cane, could see a transparent plastic sack filled with $100 bills bound in yellow wrappers. A six-volt car battery, a coil of electric wire, a small satchel filled with tools and several army surplus percussion caps were also in the valise. Lincoln pointed at the money with his cane. "Count it," he told the wiry man who had driven the moving van from Pennsauken outside of Camden, the assembly point for the pick-up trucks bringing ammonium nitrate from various parts of the East Coast. Lincoln leaned back against a rusting stanchion to watch; he could feel the holster and small-caliber automatic rubbing against the skin in the cavity at his lower back. Up in the van, Daoud opened each of the burlap sacks in the first two rows to inspect the contents. He played a flashlight into the depths of the van, counting the sacks out loud in Arabic. Satisfied, he backed down the metal ladder and walked over to Lincoln.

"You are clearly someone we can do business with," he said.

The man counting the wads of bills, wearing a corduroy sports jacket with the butt of a pistol visible in a shoulder holster, looked up from the ground. "If there are a hundred bills in each packet like they say," he told Lincoln, "the count is right."

"The last thing we would do is cheat you," Daoud said. "We still have unfinished business in Boa Vista on the night of the new moon. Have you made progress with the problem of radioactive waste?"

"I have located twenty-three-thousand spent plutonium pits stored in two sheds at a secret military site. Security is insignificant—it consists of barbed-wire around the sheds and padlocks on the doors."

Daoud was someone who didn't display emotions easily. Now, unable to contain his excitement, he danced a little jig on the cement floor of the hangar. "My Saudi friend will be extremely pleased. In what area of Russia are these sheds?"

Lincoln only smiled.

Daoud said quickly, "It was not my intention to be indiscreet. I am trying to calculate how difficult it will be to retrieve a quantity of these pits and transport them across the various frontiers into Afghanistan."

"It can be accomplished. I shall require a down payment of two hundred and fifty thousand dollars U.S., in used one-hundred-dollar bills, payable when I meet the Saudi in Boa Vista on the night of four February."

Daoud started to say that the down payment would be waiting at Boa Vista when everyone was distracted by a commotion at the rear of the hangar. Daoud's fat grandson could be seen squirming through a gap in the corrugated roofing. Crying out in Arabic, he came padding toward his grandfather. Daoud plunged a hand into the deep pocket of his raincoat; it emerged clutching a pistol fitted with a silencer. "My grandson tells that the men around the camp fire in the field are armed with automatic rifles—he crept close and saw people distributing them from the back of the panel truck. It appears we have walked into a trap—"

The headlights of a dozen automobiles, glimmering in the pre-dawn mist that clung to the ground, materialized on the ramp coming off the Pulaski Skyway half a mile away. The cars formed up in a line abreast and headed in the direction of the hangar.

Leroy cried, "Give me the detonator—I'll set off the sacks and blow 'em all to hell," but before he could do anything the wiry man who was counting the money scooped up the valise and darted out the side of the hangar, disappearing into the darkness. Daoud pulled his grandson under the moving van. Leroy grabbed Lincoln's arm and drew him toward the fallen squares of corrugated roof as the headlights began to play across the interior of the hangar. "God-damn," Leroy muttered, hauling a shiny wooden-handled Webley and Scott from his belt and spinning the chambers angrily. "You was followed here, Lincoln," he said in a harsh whisper.

"You or Daoud were the ones who were followed," Lincoln retorted.

Behind them they could make out the distant shouts of men coming across the field from the direction of the campfire.

Leroy crouched behind a sheet of tin. "My daddy died in one of their jails," he said. "Listen up, Lincoln—it's still night out. All we got to do is shoot down one or two of 'em—when the others panic an' go to ground, we can squirm off into the field and make a run for it."

The automobiles, with their headlights flickering over the moving van, pulled up around the hangar. Silhouettes could be seen running in front of the headlights as men took up positions on the hangar's perimeter. Some of them were armed with rifles, others carried plastic shields. A voice Lincoln thought he recognized came echoing over a bullhorn. "This is the FBI. We know you're in there. You are completely surrounded. You have two minutes to come out with your hands raised over your heads."

In the middle of the hangar Daoud rolled clear of the moving van and rose to his feet. He raised one hand to shield his eyes from the headlights and started to walk in the direction of the bullhorn. When he was halfway there the hand holding the pistol emerged from behind his back. Lincoln could hear the hiss of two silenced shots before several rifles firing on automatic cut him down. The Egyptian, propelled backward by the bullets slamming into his chest, crumpled to the cement. Sobbing like a baby, the fat Egyptian boy crawled from under the van to his grandfather's body and flung his arms around him. Then the boy stumbled to his feet and, peering through his tears into the headlights, tugged the pistol from his shoulder holster. Before he could get it clear, high powered bullets burrowed into his chest.

Sweeping the ground before them with blinding hand-held klieg lights, a line of armed men wearing black windbreakers started advancing through the hangar. When one of them turned to shout an order, Lincoln noticed the large white letters "FBI" on the back of his jacket. "Wait till we can see the whites of their eyes," Leroy whispered to Lincoln, who was hiding behind a stanchion next to the crouching Texan. "I'll plug the one who's leading the pack."

The FBI agents drifted past the van, the beams of their klieg lights spearing the darkness ahead of them as they closed in on the sheets of corrugated roofing at the rear of the hangar. Lincoln thought he recognized the stumpy figure of Felix Kiick in the lead, hunched low with a bullhorn in one hand, a pistol in the other. When Kiick was fifteen yards away he brought the bullhorn to his lips. "This is your last chance—Leroy Streeter, Lincoln Dittmann, you can't escape. Come out with your hands over your heads."

Kiick took several more steps as he spoke. Leroy, steadying his shooting arm with his left hand, his left elbow locked into his gut, raised the Webley and Scott and took careful aim at Kiick's head. Lincoln had hoped they would be captured without a fight, but the timing of the raid on the hangar had gone wildly wrong. The op order had called for the agents at the campfire in the field to arrive at the back of the hangar as the headlights coming off the Pulaski ramp became visible. Leroy and Daoud, distracted by the approaching automobiles, would be easily overpowered before they could put up a fight. Now there was nothing for Lincoln to do but save Kiick from the bullet. In one flowing gesture he raised his cane and brought it crashing down on Leroy's arm, shattering his wrist. Kiick jumped when he heard the bone splinter. Leroy gazed up with more pure hate in his eyes than Lincoln had ever seen in a human being. His lips moved but no words emerged until he managed to croak, "You're one of them!"

"Felix, we're over here," Lincoln called, stepping around the corrugated sheeting into view.

Kiick came over and played his light on Leroy, who was gaping in astonishment at his right hand hanging limply from the wrist. The wooden-handled Webley and Scott lay on the cement. Two FBI agents gripped Leroy under his armpits and dragged him toward the automobiles. Using a handkerchief, Kiick retrieved Leroy's weapon and held it by the barrel. "Something tells me I owe you one," he said.

Lincoln and Kiick walked over to where Daoud and his grandson lay. Medics were kneeling next to both of them, listening with stethoscopes for any signs of life. The medics looked up at the same moment and shook their heads. Someone illuminated the corpses with a klieg light and started taking photographs from different angles. Other agents covered the corpses with lengths of silver plastic. An agent wearing elastic surgeon's gloves brought over the handgun that had been retrieved from under the corpse of the fat Egyptian boy. He held it out, grip first, so Kiick could get a better look at it.

"Holy mackerel," Kiick said. He shook his head in disgust. "It sure looked like the real McCoy to me."

* * *

Presiding over the formal postmortem in the DDO's seventh floor bailiwick at Langley, Crystal Quest made no effort to tame the shrew in her. Everything that could go wrong had gone wrong, she seethed. The adults pretending to be FBI agents in the field behind the hangar had been spotted by a child—*by a child!*—before the raid was even underway. Daoud had walked into a hail of bullets so as not to be taken alive. Lincoln Dittmann's legend was blown when he saved Kiick's life. As an added extra bonus, the FBI clowns under Felix Kiick's command had gunned down a juvenile armed with a plastic pistol. Holy Christ, it hadn't even been loaded with water. Leroy Streeter Jr., who would get a life sentence for attempting to blow up a square mile of Wall Street, knew precious little about the al-Qa'ida cells and less about the Saudi who was organizing them; Streeter's expertise was limited to a small group of nutty white supremacists in Texas that had already been infiltrated by so many state and Federal agents half the group's dues came from the government. To add humiliation to embarrassment, any hope of nabbing the Saudi had evaporated the night before when the cretins from the Argentine State Intelligence had bungled the raid on Boa Vista. Talk about stealth, they had headed into the Brazilian *mato graso* in half a dozen giant army helicopters flying at treetop level *with their running lights on*, for God's sake, and kicked up such a storm of sand when they touched down at the training camp that half the fedayeen managed to slip away in the confusion. Naturally the Saudi who had been presiding over the meeting in the low-roofed building was nowhere to be found when the SIDE agents, backed up by a handful of the Company's paramilitary people who were currently hunting for new jobs, burst through the door. So what did the raid net? I'll tell you what it netted. Are you ready for this, gentlemen and ladies? It netted two jokers from Hamas, two more from Hezbollah, seven from Egypt's Islamic Brotherhood, a drunk Irishman from the IRA and two young females from the Basque ETA who listed *fashion model* under profession when they were interrogated. Fashion models my ass! One of them was so flat chested she put padding in her brassiere to break even, for Christ's sake. No shit, we could have snared twice as many terrorists using fly paper tacked to the rafters of any bar on the main drag of Foz do Iguaçú.

Quest appeared to come up for air. In the several seconds of silence, Lincoln was able to get a word in. Well, he said, we did pin down the identity of the Saudi.

The speculation about the chronic kidney failure had been the starting point. On the theory that Leroy Streeter's offhand remark about the Saudi's wealth ("Thanks to Allah and his late father, he is very rich") would suggest he'd been diagnosed and treated by an expensive private physician, Riyadh intelligence authorities had combed the clinics frequented by the royal family and affluent members of the business community. If they came up with anything, they kept it to themselves. Confronted with the Saudi foot dragging, the American secretary of state had been persuaded to take the matter up with his Saudi counterpart. Within days the intelligence authorities in Riyadh had pouched a thick dossier to Langley filled with hundreds of photographs and associated biographical information. Lincoln had sorted through the photos in the conference room next to the DDO's office, with Quest peering anxiously over his shoulder. He came across several that gave him pause. No, no, that's not him, he would finally say, *our* Saudi had incredibly intense eyes that seemed to look into you rather than at you. Going through the pouch a second time, Lincoln had used a magnifying glass to study the group photographs. Suddenly he had leaned over the table to get a closer look at one man.

I think maybe—

You think maybe what, for Christsake?

Maybe this is our Saudi. Yes, there's no doubt about it. Look at those goddamn eyes.

The group photograph had been taken years before at the wedding of a seventeen-year-old Saudi to a Syrian girl who was a distant relative of his. The bridegroom's name, according to the caption provided by the Riyadh intelligence people, was Osama bin Laden. He turned out to have a Central Registry file dating back to when he became involved in the anti-Soviet jihad in Afghanistan. The son of the Yemeni-born construction tycoon Muhammad Awad bin Laden, who had made a fortune in Saudi Arabia, Osama, according to Riyadh, was considered to be the black sheep of the fifty-three siblings in the extremely wealthy bin Laden family, in part because of his disdain for the ruling Saudi royal family and their ties to the United States, in part because of his recent obsession with Islamic fundamentalism.

Okay, we have his name and a mug shot to go with it, Quest was conceding, the shrew in her only partly assuaged. A goddamn pity we don't have his warm body also.

What we need to do, one of the staffers ventured from the sideline, is put pressure on the Sudanese to hand him over to us, or at least expel him from Sudan.

I've promoted bin Laden to the top of our wish list, Quest announced. We wish he were dead. Something tells me we had better get our paws on this Osama character before he gets his paws on radioactive waste and builds himself a dirty bomb.

Amen, said Lincoln.

* * *

Six weeks later Lincoln, in Rome for two weeks of R and R, hired a taxi to drive him out to Hadrian's sprawling villa near Tivoli and spent the afternoon limping around the site in a light spring rain, trying to distinguish myth from reality. Which was the flesh and blood Publius Aelius Hadrianus, which the legend he had consigned to history? Was he the emperor who ruthlessly suppressed the Jewish revolt of 132 and paraded the survivors through Rome in chains? Or the patron of the arts who presided over the construction of the vast country villa outside of Rome, and most especially its entrancing circular library where he spent afternoons studying the manuscripts he accumulated? Or, as seemed likely, was there something of the real Hadrian present in both incarnations?

Didn't truth provide the spinal column in every legend?

In early evening Lincoln had the driver drop him off across the Tiber on the Janicular. He checked the address scrawled on the slip of paper in his wallet and headed up hill, walking at a leisurely pace so as not to tire his leg, until he came to the luxurious four-story apart-

ment house near the fountain where Romans lingered to inhale the
negative ions from the cascading water. He settled onto the stone railing near the fountain, with Rome stretched out behind him, and
breathed in some of the negative ions himself. It surely wouldn't hurt
him, he thought. These days he was walking without the aid of a cane,
but his leg tired easily; the doctors at the Company clinic in Maryland
had warned him the pain would never completely go away. He would
learn to live with it, they promised; that's what everyone did with
pain.

The bells on a church uphill from the fountain tolled the hour
and Lincoln checked his wristwatch. Either it or the bells were four
minutes off, but what did it matter? In the end time was something
you killed. Across the street a doorman in a long blue overcoat with
gold piping removed his cap to salute the very elegantly dressed
woman emerging from the building. She held the leash of a small dog
in one gloved hand, in the other she clasped the small hand of a little
boy dressed in short pants and a knee-length overcoat buttoned up to
the neck. With the dog leading the way, the woman and the boy
crossed the street to pass the fountain on their way downhill to the
music school. Lincoln slipped off the stone rail as they came abreast
of him.

"Hello," he said.

The woman stopped. "Do I know you?"

"Don't you remember me?"

The woman, who spoke English with what Lincoln took to be an
Italian accent, looked puzzled. "I'm sorry, no. Should I?"

Lincoln noticed a small silver crucifix hanging from the delicate
silver chain around her neck. "My name's Dittmann. Lincoln
Dittmann. We met in Brazil, in a border town called Foz do Iguaçú.
Your name—your daytime name was Lucia."

"*Mama, que dice?*"

A nervous smile tugged at the corners of the woman's mouth.
"My daytime name happens to be the same as my nighttime name. It
is Fiamma. Fiamma Segre."

Lincoln found himself speaking with some urgency, as if a great
deal depended on convincing her that daytime names were never the
same as nighttime names. "I told you it would end. You said you would

breed baby polyesters on a farm in Tuscany. I am elated to see you've found something more interesting to do with your life."

The nervous smile worked its way up to the woman's frightened eyes. "Polyester is a synthetic fabric," she said softly. She pulled gently at the boy's hand. "I am afraid we must be on our way. It was a pleasure talking to you, Lincoln Dittmann. Good-bye."

"Good-bye," Lincoln said. Although his heart wasn't in it he forced himself to smile back at her.

1997: MARTIN ODUM IS MESMERIZED TO TEARS

THE JETLINER ELBOWED THROUGH THE TOWERING CLOUDS AND emerged into an airspace as cheerless as sky gets without sun. Dark pitted fields ribbed with irrigation gutters unfurled under the belly of the plane. From his window seat, Martin Odum watched Prague tilt up in its oval frame as if it were perched on the high end of a teeterboard. In his mind's eye he imagined the buildings yielding to gravity and sliding downslope into the Vltava, the broad mud-colored river meandering through the center of the city that looked, to Martin's jaundiced eye, like a beautiful woman who had been tempted by a face lift too many. The plane's wing dipped and Prague leveled out and the hills rimming the bowl of the city swam into view on the horizon, with the prefabricated Communist-era high rise apartment boxes spilling over the crests into the bleak countryside. A moment later the tarmac rushed up to graze the wheels of the plane. "Welcome to Prague," announced a recorded voice over the public-address system. "We hope your flight has been enjoyable. The captain and his crew thank you for flying Czech Airlines."

"You're definitely welcome," Martin heard himself respond. The buxom English woman in the next seat must have heard him too, because she favored him with a look reserved for passengers having conversations with recorded announcements. Martin felt obliged to decipher his remark. "Any airline that gets me where I'm going in one piece has my unstinting gratitude," he informed her.

"If you are frightened of flying," she retorted, "you should entertain the idea of traveling by train."

"Frightened of trains, too," Martin said gloomily. He thought of the Italian girl Paura that Lincoln Dittmann had come across in Foz do Iguaçú, the one who was afraid of her shadow. He wondered what had become of her. To this day he wasn't one-hundred percent sure the woman Lincoln had accosted on the Janicular and the call girl in Brazil were one and the same person. There had been a physical resemblance, so Lincoln had claimed, but the two women had been a world apart in mood and manner. "Frightened of arriving at places I haven't been to before," Martin told his neighbor now. "Frightened of motion *and* movement, frightened of the going *and* the getting there."

The English woman was eager to put an end to the exchange and formulated a cutting remark that would accomplish it. But she decided she might be dealing with an authentic maniac after all and kept her mouth shut.

Making his way through the crowded terminal following the overhead signs with images of busses on them, a thin Beedie glued to his lower lip, Martin found his path blocked by a slight young man with an ironic grimace pasted on his fleshy lips. He was dressed in khaki jodhpurs that buttoned at the ankles and a green Tyrolean jacket with tarnished brass buttons. For an instant Martin thought he had been spotted by the local constabulary, but the young man quickly made it clear he was freelancing. "Mister, no difference if you are come to Praha for business or pleasure, in both conditions you will be requiring a fixer whose honorarium will be conspicuously less than what you would find yourself expending on hotels and transportation and meals if you do not accept to employ my services." The young man, anxious to please, doffed his deerstalker and, pinching one of the two visors between a thumb and two fingers, held it over his solar plexus. "Radek at your beck and call for an insignificant thirty crowns an hour, which translates into one lousy U.S. dollar."

Martin was tempted. "What made you pick me?" he wanted to know.

"You look reasonably U.S. and I need to varnish my English for the year-end examinations that must be passed with floating colors to arrive into medical school."

"Flying colors, not floating colors."

The young man beamed. "*Flying colors* it will be from this second in time until Alzheimer's sets in."

Martin knew himself to be a poor judge of age, but Radek looked a little old to be thinking of going to medical school, and he said so.

"I am a late blossomer," the young man said with a disarming grin.

Martin wasn't so much interested in saving money as time. His instinct told him that he had to get into and out of Prague before Crystal Quest, whose operatives would not be far behind, informed the local security people of his presence; before the Chechens who murdered Taletbek Rabbani caught up with him. He produced a ten dollar bill from his shirt pocket. "Fair enough, Radek—here are ten hours in advance. I want to take a bus into the city. I want to rent a room in a cheap hotel in the Vyšehrad quarter that has a fire staircase leading to an employees' entrance. Then I want to make a phone call from the central post office, after which I would like to eat a copious vegetarian meal in a cheap restaurant—"

"I know definitely the cheap hotel. It is former secret police dormitory turned into a student bed and breakfast when communism demised. When you are checkered in, I will pilot you to a mom and pop's Yugoslav eatery, not much grander than a crackle in the wall, all vegetarian except for the meat."

Martin had to laugh. "Sounds like just the ticket."

Radek tried the phrase on his tongue. "*Just the ticket*. I see the meaning. And for after the meal, what about girls? I know a bar where university students in miniskirts wait on tables to supplement their stipends. Some of them are not against supplementing the supplements."

"We'll save the girls for my next trip to Prague, Radek." Martin took a last drag on the Beedie and embedded the burning end in the sand of an ashtray. "After the mom and pop's crackle in the wall, I want to go to"—he hauled out the envelope that Taletbek Rabbani had given him in London and looked at what the old man had written on the back of it—"to the Vyšehrad Train Station on Svobodova street."

"The Vyšehrad Station was shut closed by the communists. Trains pass there but do not stop. For a while it was an abandoned building where you could buy drugs. I am hearing it was hired to Czech people who buy and sell."

"Buy and sell what?"

Radek shrugged. "Only God knows and He has so far not shared the information with me."

"I want to know, too. I want to find out what they buy and sell."

Radek fitted his deerstalker back onto his head at a rakish angle. "Then please to follow me, Mister."

The hotel in the Vyšehrad quarter turned out to be spotlessly clean and inexpensive if you didn't formally register and paid two nights in advance with American dollars, which Martin immediately agreed to do. And the narrow fire staircase led, four floors down, to the kitchen and a back door giving onto a courtyard that gave onto a side street. The central post office, reached after a short ride on a red-and-cream double trolley, had a window for international calls. Martin jotted the Crown Heights phone number on a pad and waited his turn and squeezed into the empty booth that smelled of stale cologne when his ticket was called.

"Hello," he cried into the phone when he heard Stella's voice breasting the static on the other end.

"Why are you shouting?" she demanded.

He lowered his voice. "Because I'm farther away than the last time I called."

"Don't tell me where you are—there's been a bizarre echo on my line the last few days."

"Doesn't matter," Martin said. "They'll take two or three minutes to figure out it's an international call. Then they'll need two or three days to find out which city it came from. And another week to get the local spooks to determine I'm calling from the central post office in Prague."

"Now you've gone and told them."

"They won't believe me. They'll think I'm planting phony clues to throw them off. What did you do with yourself today?"

"Just came back from the dentist—he's making me a new front tooth."

"Money down the drain. I liked the chipped tooth. Made you look . . ."

"Finish what you started to say, for God's sake. Every time you get personal you let go of the end of the sentence and it drifts off like a hot air balloon."

"Breakable. That's the word that was on the tip of my tongue."

"I'm not sure how to take that. What's so great about looking breakable."

"For starters, means you're not already broken. People who are broken have several selves. Estelle is your real name, isn't it?"

"The family name, Kastner, was assigned to us when we came to America. They wanted to change my first name, too, but I wouldn't let them. Estelle is me." When he didn't respond, she said, "You still there?"

"I'm thinking about what you said. I know I must have met people who aren't living in legends, I just don't remember when."

"Legends, as in having different names?"

"It's much more than different names; it has to do with having several biographies, several attitudes, several ways of looking at the world, several ways of giving and taking pleasure. It has to do with being so broken that the king's horses and the king's men would have a hard time putting you together again."

"Listen up, Martin—"

"Terrific! Now they'll know it's me calling."

"How can they be sure I'm not using a phony name to throw them off?"

"There's something in what you say."

"I lied to you the last time we spoke. I said if I joined you in Europe there wouldn't be strings attached. If you let me come, there will be. Strings attached."

Martin didn't know what to say. He stifled the *uh-huh* and let the silence stand.

"You don't know what to say," Stella guessed.

"Strings are attached to puppets," Martin finally said. "It's not an image of you that I put much store in."

"The strings wouldn't be attached to me or you, they'd be attached to my coming over. Remember when we were going into Israel and I told that policeman you were my lover?"

Martin smiled to himself. "And I told him you had a tattoo of a Siberian night moth under your right breast."

"Got one," Stella announced.

He didn't understand. "Got what?"

"Tattoo of a Siberian night moth under my right breast. A Jamaican tattoo artist on Empire Boulevard did it. That's the string that's attached when we next meet. I'm going to have to show it to you to prove it's there, since it's not your style to take my word for something as important as that. Then we'll see if one thing leads to another."

Martin thought of the whore Dante had come across in Beirut. "I heard of a girl who actually had a moth tattooed under her breast. Her name was Djamillah. Did you really get one?"

He could hear the laughter in her voice. "Uh-huh."

"Stealing my *uh-huhs*," Martin said.

"Plan to steal more than that," she shot back.

He changed the subject. "I was scared today."

"Of what?"

"Where I'm at I've never been to before. That frightens me."

"Okay, here's the deal. You better get used to being where you've never been to before. I'll hold your hand. Okay?"

"I suppose so."

"If this is you enthusiastic, I'd hate to see you reluctant."

"Fact is, I'm not sure."

"Ever hear the story of the Russian peasant who was asked if he knew how to play the violin? *I'm not sure*, he replied. *Never tried*." She snickered at her own joke. "You need to try, Martin, to know if you can or you can't."

"I can see you're right. I just don't *feel* you're right."

She digested that. "Why did you call me?"

"Wanted to hear your voice. Wanted to make sure you're still you."

"Well, you've heard it and I've heard yours. Where does that leave us, Martin?"

"I'm not sure." They both laughed at the *I'm not sure*. "I mean, I still have to find the person who went AWOL from his marriage."

"Let it go. Forget Samat. Come home, Martin."

"If I let it go, the person who came home wouldn't be me. Aside from that, lot of questions are out trawling for answers."

"When the answers are elusive you have to learn to live with the questions."

"I need to go. Stella?"

"Okay, okay, go. I'll replay the conversation in my head after you hang up. I'll sift through it looking for meanings I missed."

"Don't worry, be happy."

"Don't worry, be happy? What's that supposed to mean?"

"It's a song from the top ten in the late eighties. Thought of it today—they were playing it over and over on a jukebox in Paraguay when a guy I know was there."

"Was the *they* a girl?"

"A bunch of girls. Prostitutes working a bar who bought lottery tickets from an old Polish gentleman."

"You depress me, Martin. There's so much about you I don't know."

"I depress me, too. For the same reason."

* * *

The *plat du jour* at the mom and pop's turned out to be spicy Yugoslav meatballs served in soup dishes with vegetables that had been overcooked and were difficult to identify. Martin exchanged his meatballs for Radek's vegetables and helped himself to half the boiled potatoes. The wine was a kissing cousin to Greek ouzo, flavored with anise and easy to drink once the first few mouthfuls numbed your throat. Radek sat across the small table from Martin, mopping up the sauces in his soup dish with pieces of stale bread and washing them down with gulps of wine. "My dream is to go to U.S. the beautiful before Alzheimer's sets in," he confided, sucking on a tooth to free the food caught in his gums. "Is it so that they pave the streets with Sony Walkmans when the cobblestones wear out?"

Martin leaned back and treated himself to an after-dinner Beedie. "Where did you pick up that juicy detail?"

"It was written in a university satirical magazine."

"Don't believe everything you read in university satirical magazines. Can you ask for the bill."

Radek studied the bill when it came, then got into an argument with the owner, who wound up crossing out two items and reducing the price of the wine. "I saved you sixty crowns, which is two lousy

U.S. dolars," Radek noted. "That adds up to two hours of my honorarium, Mister. So where to now?"

"A trolley to Svobodova Street."

"How is it a rich U.S. like you does not hire taxi cabs?"

"I have a theory that you don't really know a city until you've rid-
den its public transportation."

Radek rolled his head from side to side in dismay. "Here all the
people who take public transportation dream to take private transportation. You want to go to the Vyšehrad Station?"

"I would like to get off a hundred meters before it and walk the
rest of the way to work off the meal."

Radek laid a forefinger along a nostril. "You want to case the joint
first."

"Where did you pick up *case the joint*?"

"So I am crazy about old U.S. movies." He transformed a thumb
and an index finger into a pistol and jammed it into the pocket of his
Tyrolean jacket. "*I have a gub in my pocket, Mister.*"

"What movie is that from?"

"Woody Allen. *Take the Money and Run.*"

"Uh-huh. Let's go."

Sitting in the back of the trolley, listening to the sparks crackling
off the overhead electric cable, Martin studied the faces around him
looking for the one that was conspicuously uninterested in him.
Normally he prided himself on being able to blend into a crowd even
when there wasn't one. Now, however, he was in too much of a hurry
to take the usual precautions. His American clothes, especially his
shoes, made him stand out in any Czech crowd and people, naturally
curious, would inspect him, some openly, some furtively. Martin figured if someone were following him he would be careful not to look
at him at all. In the long ride from the mom and pop's eatery to Mala
Strana, then queuing to wait for a trolley on another line, Martin, still an
artisan of tradecraft, didn't have the feeling he was being tailed. Which,
he knew from experience, could mean that the people following him
were very good at it. Radek noticed him noticing the passengers
around him. "If you are not wanting girls, what are you wanting?"
he asked. He leaned closer so the haggard woman on the aisle seat
brazenly scrutinizing the American couldn't overhear him. "Cannabis,

ganja, hemp, hashish, bhang, sinsemilla, cocaine, crack, angel dust, horse, methadone, LSD, PCP, uppers, downers. Only identify it, Radek will find it for less lousy U.S. dollars than you pay me a day."

"I've never even heard of half these things," Martin said. "What I'm wanting is to stretch my legs when we're within walking distance of the Vyšěhrad Station."

"Next stop," Radek said, obviously disappointed that his procurement talents were not being put to the test. He plucked at the cord running the length of the trolley above the windows as if it were a guitar string. Up front a bell sounded. As the trolley ground to a halt, the doors scraped open. Once on the sidewalk, Radek pointed with his nose. In the distance, on the other side of the wide street, Martin could make out a shabby communist gothic structure trapping the last quarter hour of sunlight slanting in over the Vltava on its dilapidated roof, which was crawling with pigeons. He turned to Radek and offered his hand. "I won't be needing your services anymore," he announced.

Radek looked dejected. "You paid for ten hours, Mister. I still owe you seven and a half."

"Consider the unused hours a gratuity." When Radek still didn't shake hands, Martin brought his own up to his eye and snapped off a friendly salute. "Good luck to you in medical school, Radek. I hope you find a cure for Alzheimer's before Alzheimer's sets in."

"I kick myself for asking someone like you only thirty lousy crowns an hour," Radek muttered as he turned and headed in the opposite direction.

Sucking on a Beedie, Martin strolled down Svobodova Street in the direction of the river. He passed a row of apartment buildings, one with the date "1902" etched over the door and a "Flat for Sale" sign in English on the inside of a ground floor window. Across the street loomed the Vyšěhrad Station in all its communist-era decadence. The station consisted of a central carcass and two broken wings. Dirty white stucco peeled away from the facade like sunburnt skin, exposing the dirty red bricks beneath. The windows on the Svobodova side were boarded over, though there were hints of fluorescent light seeping between the cracks in several of the second-floor windows that weren't well jointed. The pigeons, in twos and threes, were fluttering away from the roof in search of the last rays of sun as Martin made his way back up Svobodova, this time on the station side of the street. Trolleys clattered by, causing the ground to tremble underfoot. Behind the station a commuter train sped past in the direction of *Centrum*. Dog-eared posters advertising Hungarian vacuum cleaners and reconditioned East German Trabants were thumb tacked to the boards covering the ground floor windows. Near the gate leading to a path around the side of the left wing of the station, someone had chalked graffiti on the wall: *The Oklahoma City bomb was the first shot of World War III*. Martin eased open the gate on its rusty hinges, climbed the brick steps and walked around to the back of the station. The passage was obviously in daily use because the weeds and vines on either side had been cut away from the brick footpath. Making his way along what used to be the platform when the station had been in use, Martin glanced into one of the wings through a sooty window shielded by rusting metal bars. Inside, two young men whom he took to be gypsies, wearing vests and corduroy trousers tucked into the tops of leather boots, were emptying large cartons and setting out what looked like packets of medicines on a long trestle table. Two young women dressed in long colorful skirts were repacking the items into smaller boxes and sealing them with masking tape. One of the young men caught sight of Martin and gestured with his thumb toward the main station doors further down the platform. Martin nodded and, a moment later, pushed through the double door into the station's once-ornate central hall, fallen into dilapidation and smelling of wet plaster, evidence that someone had tried to patch over the worst of the building's wounds. A broken sign over the door read "*Vychod—Exit*." The tiles on the floor, many of them cracked, shifted under his feet. A wide stairway curled up toward the second floor. Painted on the wall above the stairway were the words "Soft" and "Shoulder." A squat dog with a blunt nose stood on the top landing, yelping in a hoarse voice at the intruder. A handsome, elegantly dressed woman in her fifties peered down from the railing. "If you are looking for Soft Shoulder, do come up," she called. "Don't mind the dog. His bite is worse than his bark, but I will lock him up." Reaching for the dog's leash, the woman pulled him, still yelping, into a room and shut the door. With the dog barking behind the door she turned back toward Martin, who was leaning on the banister to take the weight off his game leg as he climbed toward her. A half dozen thin Indian bracelets jangled on her thin wrist as she held out a slender hand. "My name is Zuzana Slánská," she said as Martin took her hand.

He noticed that her fingers were weedy, her nails bitten to the quick, her eyes rheumy. He suspected that the wrinkled smile on her gaunt lips had been worn too many times without laundering. "Mine's Odum," he said. "Martin Odum."

"What African country are you buying for?"

Figuring he had nothing to lose, Martin said the first thing that came into his head. "The Ivory Coast."

"We don't often deal with clients in person, Mr. Odum. Most of our business is mail order. As a matter of record, who sent you to us?"

"An associate of Samat's named Taletbek Rabbani." He produced the back of the envelope with Rabbani's barely legible scrawl on it and showed it to the woman.

A shadow passed over her face. "News of Mr. Rabbani's death reached us earlier this week. When and where did you meet him?"

"The same place you met him—at his warehouse behind the train station in the Golders Green section of London. I was probably the last person to see him alive—not counting the Chechens who murdered him."

"The small item in the British newspaper made no mention of Chechens."

"It may be that Scotland Yard doesn't know this detail. It may be they know it but do not want to tip their hand."

Smiling nervously, the woman led Martin into a large oval room lit by several naked neon fixtures suspended from the ceiling. The three windows in the office were covered with planking, reminding Martin of the time Dante Pippen had followed Djamillah into the mercantile office above the bar in Beirut—the windows there had been boarded over, too. He looked around, taking in the room. Large cartons with "This Side Up" stenciled on them were stacked against one wall. A young woman in a loose fitting sweater and faded blue jeans sat at a desk, typing with two fingers on a vintage table-model Underwood. At the edge of the desk, a scroll of facsimile paper spilled from a fax machine into a carton on the floor. A loose-leaf book lay

open on a low glass table filled with coffee stains and overflowing
ashtrays. The woman motioned Martin to a seat on the automobile
banquette against the wall and settled onto a low three-legged stool
facing him, her crossed ankles visible through the thick glass of the
table. "I assume Mr. Rabbani explained how we operate here. In order
to keep our prices as low as possible, we do business out of this
defunct station to reduce the overhead and we only sell our generic
medicines in bulk. Is there anything in particular you are looking for,
Mr. Odum? Our best sellers are the Tylenol generic, acetaminophen,
the Valium generic, diazepam, the Sudafed generic, pseudoephedrine,
the Kenacort generic, triamcinolone. Please feel free to thumb through
the loose-leaf catalogue. The labels of our generic medicines are pasted onto the pages. I am not aware of any particular epidemic threatening the Ivory Coast aside from the HIV virus—we unfortunately do
not yet have access to generic drugs for AIDS, but hope governments
will put pressure on the drug conglomerates . . ." She gazed at her visitor, a sudden question visible in her eyes. "You didn't mention your
medical credentials, Mr. Odum. Are you a trained doctor or a public
health specialist?"

Another commuter train roared by behind the station. When it
had passed, Martin said, "Neither."

Zuzana Slánská's fingers came up to touch the small Star of David
attached to the chain around her neck. "I am not sure I comprehend
you."

Martin leaned forward. "I have a confession to make. I am not
here to buy generic medicines." He looked directly into her rheumy
eyes. "I have come to find out more about Samat's project concerning
the exchange of the bones of the Lithuanian saint for the Jewish Torah
scrolls."

"Oh!" The woman glanced at the secretary typing up order forms
across the room. "It's a long story," she said softly, "and I shall badly
need a brandy and several cigarettes to get me through it."

* * *

Zuzana Slánská leaned toward Martin so that he could light her
cigarette with a match from the book advertising Prague crystal. "I

have never smoked a Beedie before," she noted, sinking back, savoring the taste of the Indian cigarette. She pulled it from her mouth and carefully examined it. "Is there marijuana mixed with the tobacco?" she asked.

Martin shook his head. "You're smelling the eucalyptus leaves."

She took another drag on the Beedie. "I am wary of the experts who argue so passionately that smoking is dangerous for your health," she remarked, the words emerging from her mouth along with the smoke. As she turned away to glance at the two fat men sucking on thick cigars at a nearby table, it struck Martin that she had the profile of a woman who must have been a stunner in her youth. "There are a great many things dangerous for your health," she added, turning back. "Don't you agree?"

Concentrating on his own cigarette, Martin said, "For instance?"

"For instance, living under high tension wires. For instance, eating fast food with artificial flavoring. For instance, being right when your government is wrong." She favored the old waiter with a worn smile as he carefully set out two snifters half-filled with three-star Jerez brandy, along with a shallow Dresden bowl brimming with peanuts. "I am speaking from bitter experience," she added, "but you surely will have grasped that from the tone of my voice."

She had led him on foot across the river to the *salon du thé* on the top floor of a gaudy hotel that had only recently opened for business. From the window next to the table at the back of the enormous room, Martin could see what he'd spotted from the plane: the hills rimming Prague and the communist-era apartment buildings spilling over them. "My husband," the woman was saying, caught up in her own story, "was a medical doctor practicing in Vinohrady, which is a district of Prague behind the museum. I worked as his nurse. The two of us joined a literary circle that met once a week to discuss books. Oh, I can tell you, it was an exhilarating time for us. My husband was fearless—he used to all the time joke that old age was not for the weak of heart." She gulped down some of the brandy and puffed furiously on her Beedie, as if time were running out; as if she had to relate her life's story before her life ended. "Tell me if all this bores you to tears, Mr. Odum."

"The opposite is true," Martin assured her. "It mesmerizes me to tears."

Zuzana Slánská hiked one slim shoulder inside her tailored Parisian jacket. "We were ardent Marxists, my husband and I. We were convinced it was the great Russian bear that had suffocated communism and not the other way around. Our Czech hero, Alexander Dubcek, was still a loyal party-line apparatchik when we began signing petitions demanding reforms. The Soviet-appointed proconsuls who reigned over us could not distinguish between dissidents who were anticommunist and those, like us, who were pro-communist but argued that it had gone wrong; that it needed to be set right in order for Marxism to survive. Or if they did distinguish between us, they calculated that our form of dissidence was the more threatening of the two. And so we suffered the same fate as the others."

Martin could see the muscles on her face contorting with heartache remembered so vividly that she seemed to be experiencing it now. "You must know the story," she rushed on, barely bothering to breathe. "The one about the NKVD commissar admitting to Yosif Vissarionovich Stalin that a particular prisoner had refused to confess. Stalin considered the problem, then asked the commissar how much the state weighed, the state with all its buildings and factories and machines, the army with all its tanks and trucks, the navy with all its ships, the air force with all its planes. And then Stalin said, dear God, he said, *Do you really think this prisoner can withstand the weight of the state?*"

"Did you feel the weight of the state? Were you and your husband jailed?"

Zuzana Slánská had become so agitated that she began swallowing smoke and brandy in the same gulp. "Certainly we felt the weight of the state. Certainly we were jailed, some months at the same time and once even in the same prison, some months at different times so that we passed each other like ships in the night. I discovered that when you left prison you took the stench of it with you in your nostrils; it took months, years to get rid of it. Oh, once my husband returned from prison so beat up that I didn't recognize him through the spy hole in the door and called the police to save me from a lunatic, and they came and looked at his identity card and told me it was safe to let him in, the lunatic in question was my husband. Does it happen in America, Mr. Odum, that the police must assure you it is safe to let your husband pass the door of your apartment? And then one day my husband was arrested for treating the broken ankle of a youth who turned out to be an anticommunist dissident hiding from the police. The journalists from America covering the trial pointed out in their stories that the same thing had happened to the American doctor who treated the broken ankle of A. Lincoln's assassin."

From some murky past—from some murky legend?—the story of the Prague trial surfaced in Martin's memory. "You're the wife of Pavel Slánský!"

"You recognize the name! You remember the trial!"

"Everyone who followed events in Eastern Europe was familiar with the name Pavel Slánský," Martin said. "The Jewish doctor who was arrested for setting the broken ankle of a dissident; who at his trial pleaded innocent to that particular charge, but used the occasion to plead guilty to wanting to reform communism, explaining in excruciating detail why it needed reforming to survive. He was the forerunner of the reformers who came after him: Dubcek in Czechoslovakia, eventually Gorbachev in the Soviet Union."

An uncontaminated smile, as fresh as laundered linen on a clothesline, materialized on Zuzana Slánská's face. "Yes, he was ahead of his time, which in some countries is counted as a capital crime. The American authorities showed little sympathy for him—one suspects they did not want to see anyone attempt to reform communism, lest they succeed. My husband was declared to be an enemy of the state and condemned to ten years in prison for anticommunist activities. And I became like the poet Akhmatova, queuing at the prison guardhouse through the winters and springs and summers and falls to deliver packages of socks and soap and cigarettes addressed to prisoner 277103. The number is seared into my memory. The wardens took the packages and signed receipts promising they would be delivered. And then one day one of my packages was returned to me in the mail bearing the stamp *Deceased*. This tendency of bureaucracies in killer states to adhere to normal procedures and regulations has yet to be explained, at least to my satisfaction. In any case, that was how I discovered that my husband, the prisoner Slánský, was no longer among the living." Zuzana Slánská raised a cold palm to swat away the cigar smoke drifting toward her from the nearby table. "May I have another of your amusing cigarettes? I need the eucalyptus to overpower the stench of their cigars. Oh, Mr. Odum, if one was able to put up with the inconveniences, I must tell you that dissidence was exhilarating."

"Aside from prison, what were the inconveniences?"

"You lost your job, you were required to crowd into a fifty-square-meter apartment with the two couples already living in it, you were sent off to a psychiatric clinic to work out to the satisfaction of the state what made a dissident criticize something that was, by definition, perfect. When we would gather at an apartment late at night to discuss, oh, say, Solzhenitsyn's *Ivan Denisovich*, our small group considered all the angles, all the scenarios except the possibility that the gangsters who presided over the Soviet Union would become freelance gangsters presiding over the territory they had staked out when communism collapsed. Looking back, I can see now that we were incredibly naive. We were blinded by the exhilaration—each time we made love we thought it might be the last time and this turned us into ardent lovers, until the day came when we had no one to make love to. And so we stopped, most of us, being lovers and became haters."

"And the generic drugs—how did you get into that?"

"I was a trained nurse but, after the trial of my husband, no doctor dared employ me. For years I worked at menial tasks—cleaning medical offices after they shut for the day, removing garbage cans from the courtyards of apartment houses to the street before dawn so the trucks could empty them. Finally, when our own communists were expelled from power in 1989, I decided to do what my husband always dreamed of doing—sell generic medicines to the third world at the lowest possible prices. I met Samat during one of his first trips to Prague and told him about my idea. He accepted at once to fund it as a branch of an existing humanitarian enterprise called Soft Shoulder —it was with his money that we rented the Vyšehrad Station and bought the first stocks of generic medicines. Now I eke out enough profit to employ four gypsies and a part-time secretary. I once attempted to reimburse Samat but he refused to accept money. It must be said, he is something of a saint."

"I suppose it would take a saint to get involved in repatriating the bones of a saint," Martin remarked.

"I can say that I was the one who first told Samat about the Jewish Torah scrolls in the Lithuanian church." Her hand drifted up to her neck to finger the Star of David. "My older sister was deported during the war to a concentration camp in Lithuania. She managed to escape into the steppe and joined the communist partisans harassing the German rear. It was my sister—her partisan name was Rosa, after the German communist Rosa Luxemburg; her real name was Melka —who attempted to warn the Jews in the shtetls not yet overrun by the Germans and the *einsatzgruppen* murderers who followed behind them. Few believed her—they simply did not imagine that the descendants of Goethe and Beethoven and Brahms were capable of the mass murder of an entire people. But in several of the shtetls the rabbis hedged their bets—they collected the sacred Torah scrolls and priceless commentaries, some of them many hundreds of years old, and gave them to a Lithuanian Orthodox bishop to hide in a remote church. After the war my sister passed on to me the name of this church—*Spaso-Preobrazhenski Sabor*, which means Church of the Transfiguration, in the town of Zuzovka, on the Neman River just inside Lithuania near the frontier with Belarus. When I told the story to Samat, he dropped what he was doing—Samat, who was not as far as I know Jewish, went directly to the church to recover the Torah scrolls and bring them to Israel. The Metropolitan of the diocese refused to give them back; refused even to sell them back when Samat offered him a large sum of money. The Metropolitan was willing, however, to trade the Torah scrolls for the relics of Saint Gedymin, who established the Lithuanian capital in Vilnius in thirteen hundred something. Saint Gedymin's bones had been stolen from the church by German troops during the war. After years of inquiry, Samat was finally able to trace the bones of the saint to Argentina. They had been smuggled there by Nazis fleeing Europe at the end of the war and deposited in a small Orthodox church near the city of Córdoba. When the church refused to part with the bones of Saint Gedymin, Samat went to see a person he knew in the Argentine government; in the Defense Ministry, actually. Samat told me he had persuaded the Defense Ministry to repatriate the saintly relics to Lithuania—"

"In return for what?"

"I'm afraid I don't know. Samat mentioned that he'd been to see the people at the Argentine Defense Ministry. But he never told me what they wanted in exchange for the relics of Saint Gedymin."

"When did he tell you about the Defense Ministry?"

"The last time he passed through Prague."

"Yes, and when was that?"

"After he left Israel he went to London to see Taletbek Rabbani. From London he flew here to see me on his way to—"

Martin became aware that Zuzana Slánská's rheumy eyes had focused on something over his shoulder. He noticed her fingers slipping the Star of David out of sight under the collar of her blouse as he twisted in his seat to see what she was looking at. Radek, holding his deerstalker over his solar plexus, his other hand buried in the pocket of the Tyrolean jacket, stood at the doors of the *salon du thé* surveying the clients. He spotted Zuzana Slánská and Martin across the room and pointed them out with one of the brims of his deerstalker as he started threading his way through the tables toward them. A dozen men in civilian suits fanned out behind him.

A gasp of pure dread escaped from Zuzana Slánská's throat as she rose to her feet. She uttered the words, "Old age is not for the weak of heart," then, her eyes fixed on Radek, her lips barely moving, she said: "There is an island in the Aral Sea twenty kilometers off the mainland called Vozrozhdeniye. During the Soviet era it was used as a bioweapons testing range. On the island is the town of Kantubek. Samat's contact in Kantubek is a Georgian named Hamlet Achba. Can you remember all that?"

"Vozrozhdeniye. Kantubek. Hamlet Achba."

"Warn Samat . . ." Radek was almost upon them. "Oh, it's for sure I will not survive the stench of another prison," she murmured to herself.

Around them the waiters and the clients had frozen in place, mesmerized by the progress of Radek and his companions toward the two customers at the small table in the back of the room. Radek, a faint smile of satisfaction disfiguring his lips, reached the table. "I have a gub in my pocket," he informed Martin. "It is a German Walther P1. You are arrested, Mister. You, also, Misses, are arrested."

* * *

Martin could feel the gentle rise and fall of the deck under his shoes (the laces, along with his belt, had been confiscated) as he waited for the interrogation to begin again. They had come for him at odd hours for the last several days, a technique designed to deprive him of sleep more than elicit information. As there was no porthole in his small cell immediately over the bilges of the houseboat or in the compartment above it, where the interrogations took place, he soon lost track of whether it was night or day. The only sound that reached his ears from outside were the foghorns of passing river ferries and the doppler-distorted shriek of sirens as police cruisers raced through the streets of Prague. From somewhere in the bowels of the houseboat came the dull throb of a generator; from time to time the bulb hanging out of reach over his head dimmed or brightened. Soon after Radek hustled him from the police van to the houseboat, which was tied to bollards on a cement quay down river from the Charles Bridge, he thought he caught the muted cry of a woman coming from another deck. When he re-created the sound in his head he decided it could have been the caterwaul of a cat prowling through the garbage bins on the quay. The grilling sessions in the airless compartment didn't appear to fatigue the interrogator, a stooped, gaunt bureaucrat with an unshaven face and a shaven skull and an aquiline nose that looked as if it had been broken and badly set at some point in his life. Holding court from behind a small desk bolted to the planks of the deck, he fired off questions in a dispassionate monotone, only occasionally lifting his eyes from his notes. Radek, dressed now in a neat three-piece brown suit with narrow Austrian lapels, leaned against a bulkhead next to one of the two guards who escorted Martin to and from his cell. Martin sat facing the inquisitor on a chair whose front legs had been shortened so that the prisoner would feel as if he were constantly sliding off of it. Bright spotlights positioned on either side of the desk burned into his retinas, causing his eyes to tear and his vision to blur.

"Do you have a name?" Martin had asked the gaunt man behind the desk at the very first session.

The question appeared to have dismayed the interrogator. "What would it serve, your knowing my name?"

"It would permit me to identify you when I file a complaint with the American embassy."

The interrogator had glanced at Radek, then looked back at Martin. "If you lodge a complaint, say that you were arrested by a secret unit attached to a secret ministry."

From his place along the wall, Radek had choked off a guttural laugh.

Now the interrogator slid a small Pyrex percolator toward Martin. "Help yourself," he said, gesturing toward the pot of coffee.

"You've spiked it with caffeine to keep me awake," Martin said tiredly, but he poured some into a plastic cup and sipped it anyway; they had fed him salted rice and not provided drinking water since his arrival on the houseboat. "Your techniques of interrogation are right out of those old American movies that Radek here is so crazy about."

"I do not deny it," the interrogator said. "One must not be a snob when it comes to picking up tricks of the trade. In any case, it has been my experience that these techniques work in the end—I say this as someone who has been on both sides of the interrogation table. When I was arrested for anticommunist activities by the communists, in four days they were able to convince me to admit to crimes I had not committed using these very same techniques. And what has been your experience, Mr. Odum?"

"I have no experience with interrogations," Martin said.

The interrogator sniggered skeptically. "That is not the impression your Central Intelligence Agency gave us. Their chief of station in Prague confides to us that you were once one of their paramount field operatives, someone so skilled at tradecraft it was said of you that you could blend into a crowd even in the absence of one."

"If I were half that good, how come I fell for Radek's pitch at the airport?"

The interrogator shrugged his stooped shoulders, which raised them for an instant to where they normally should have been. "Perhaps you are past your prime. Perhaps you were preoccupied with other thoughts at that particular moment. In any case, if you had not hired Radek—"

"For the equivalent of one lousy U.S. dollar an hour," Radek groaned from the wall.

"If you had not hired him, you would surely have wound up in one of the three taxis we had positioned outside. The drivers, all of whom call themselves Radek, work for us."

Martin identified a piece of the puzzle that was missing: How could Radek's service have known he would turn up in Prague? Obviously the CIA chief of station had been talking to his Czech counterpart about Martin. And the chief of station reported to the Deputy Director of Operations, Crystal Quest. Which brought Martin back to what he'd told the late Oscar Alexandrovich Kastner in the windowless walk-in closet on President Street a lifetime ago: *I'd like to know why the CIA doesn't want this particular missing husband found.*

"Your station chief," the interrogator was saying, "claims you are no longer employed by the CIA. He says you are a freelance detective. It could be true, what he says; it could also be that they are simply denying any connection to you because you have been caught in the act. So tell me, Mr. Odum. What weapon systems were you contracting to buy at the Vysĕhrad Station. More importantly, who were you buying them for?"

"Zuzana Slánská sells generic medicines."

"The woman you call Zuzana Slánská was never legally married to the doctor Pavel Slánský, who, as you surely know, was convicted as an enemy of the state during the communist period. Her real name is Zuzana Dzurova. She assumed the name Slánská when she learned of Pavel's death in prison. As for the generic medicines, we have reason to believe they are a front for one of the most prolific weapons operations in Europe." The interrogator pulled a report from one of the cardboard file boxes on the desk, pried a staple loose with his thumbnail and extracted the third page. He fitted on a pair of rimless reading glasses and began to quote from the text. ". . . operating in conjunction with Mr. Taletbek Rabbani in London, who claims to be selling prostheses at cost to third world countries . . ." The interrogator looked up from the paper. "It is surely not lost on you that both Mr. Rabbani's prosthesis operation in London and Zuzana Slánská's generic medicine operation here in Prague were funded by the same individual, a Mr. Samat Ugor-Zhilov, who until recently was living in a Jewish settlement on the West Bank of the

Jordan River in order to shelter himself from the gang wars raging in Moscow."

Martin's muscles ached from the effort of keeping his body from sliding off the chair. He strained to bring the interrogator into focus. "Both Mr. Rabbani and Zuzana Slánská described Samat Ugor-Zhilov as a philanthropist—"

Radek emitted a single hiccup. "Some philanthropist!" he cried from the wall.

The interrogator threw Radek a dark look, as if to remind him that there was a pecking order; that birds on the junior end of it should be seen but not heard. Then, angling the sheet of paper toward the light, he began reading phrases from it. "Both Mr. Rabbani and Zuzana Slánská are marketing a French device that corrects the error the U.S. Pentagon builds into the satellite GPS system to thwart rogue missile launchings . . . Soviet-surplus radar units from the Ukraine . . . ah, yes, armored personnel carriers from a Bulgarian state-run company, Terem, sold to Syria for eventual delivery to Iraq . . . engines and spare parts for the T-55 and T-72 Soviet tanks from assorted Bulgarian armaments factories . . . ammunition, explosives, rockets, training manuals in missile technology from Serbia . . . spare jet-fighter parts and rocket propellants from an aviation factory in eastern Bosnia. And listen to this: The London prosthesis warehouse and the Prague generic medicine operation are used as clearing houses for orders for an ammunition factory in the town of Vitez and missile guidance systems fabricated in a research center in the city of Banja Luka . . . payments for items on the inventory were made in cash or in diamonds." The interrogator flicked the nail of his middle finger against the sheet of paper. "I could continue but there is no point."

In one of his legends—Martin couldn't recall which—he remembered taking a course at the Farm designed to prepare agents in the field for hostile interrogation. The various techniques of interrogation discussed included one where the interrogator would invent flagrant lies to disorient the person being questioned. Agents who found themselves in this predicament were advised to hang on to the facts they knew to be true and let the fictions of the interrogator pass without comment.

Martin, his head swimming with fatigue, heard himself say, "I know absolutely nothing about the sale of weapons."

The interrogator removed his eyeglasses and massaged the bridge of his nose with the thumb and third finger of his left hand. "That being the case, what brought you to Mr. Taletbek Rabbani's warehouse in London and the Vyšehrad Station in Prague?"

Martin longed to stretch out on the metal army cot in his cell. "I am trying to trace Samat Ugor-Zhilov," he said.

"Why?"

In disjointed sentences, Martin admitted that he had once been employed by the CIA; that it was perfectly true that he had set up shop as a private detective in Brooklyn, New York, after he left the service. He explained about Samat walking out on his wife in Israel, leaving her in a religious limbo; how the wife's sister and father had hired him to track down Samat and convince him to give her a religious divorce so that she could get on with her life. "I have no interest in purchasing false limbs or generic drugs. I am simply following a trail that I hope leads to Samat."

Smiling thinly, the interrogator humored Martin. "And what will you do once you find him?"

"I will take Samat to the nearest town that has a synagogue and oblige him to grant his wife a divorce in front of a rabbi. Then I will return to Brooklyn and spend the rest of my life boring myself to death."

The interrogator turned Martin's story over in his mind. "I am familiar with the school of intelligence activities that holds that a good cover story must be made to seem preposterous if it is to be believed. But you are pushing this thesis to its limits." He rifled through the papers on the desk and came up with another report. "We have been observing people entering or leaving the Vyšehrad Station for weeks now," he continued. "We even managed to plant a listening device in the upstairs office. Here is a transcript of a very recent conversation. Perhaps it will seem familiar to you. A man was heard to say: *I have a confession to make. I am not here to buy generic medicines. I have come to find out more about Samat's project concerning the exchange of the bones of the Lithuanian saint for Jewish Torah scrolls.*" The interrogator raised his eyes from the paper to look directly at his prisoner. "Curious that you make no mention of divorce before a rabbi. Bones of the Lithuanian saint, Jewish Torah scrolls—I take that to be coded references to weapons systems originating in Lithuania and Israel. I can tell you that, aside from the illegality of selling weapons and weapon systems, what intrigues us most about Mrs. Slánská is her motive. She was not doing it for money, Mr. Odum. She is an idealist."

"Last time I checked, being an idealist was not a crime, even in the Czech Republic."

"The American writer Mencken once defined an idealist as someone who, on observing that a rose smelled better than a cabbage, concluded that it would also make better soup. Yes, well, like Mencken's idealist, Mrs. Slánská's idealism is very particular—she remains a diehard Marxist, plotting the comeback of the communists. She desires to set the clock back and is thought to be using the considerable profits from the sale of weapons to finance a splinter group hoping to do here in the Czech Republic what the former communists have done in Poland and Rumania and Bulgaria: win elections and return to power."

It occurred to Martin there might be a way to beat the fatigue that made it appear as if everything around him was happening in slow motion. He closed one eye, thinking that one lobe of his brain could actually sleep while the other eye and the other lobe remained awake. After a moment, hoping the interrogator wouldn't catch on to his clever scheme, he switched eyes and lobes. He could hear the interrogator's voice droning on; could make out, through his open eye, the blurred figure getting up and coming around to half sit on the desk in front of him.

"You arrived here from London, Mr. Odum. The British MI5 established that you lived for several days in a rooming house next to a synagogue off Golders Green. The warehouse where Mr. Taletbek Rabbani was murdered the day before you departed from London was within walking distance of your rooming house."

"If everyone living within walking distance of the warehouse is a suspect," the half of Martin's brain still functioning managed to say, "MI5 is going to have its hands full."

"We have not excluded the possibility of concluding a deal with you, Mr. Odum. Our principal objective is to discredit Mrs. Slánská; to show that she and Mr. Rabbani were in league with Mr. Samat Ugor-Zhilov's weapons operation; that both the warehouse in London and the defunct train station in Prague were funded by the same Samat Ugor-Zhilov, a notable Moscow gangster who is associated with the Ugor-Zhilov known as the *Oligarkh*. The object for us is to tie the communist splinter group to Zuzana Slánská's illegal weapons operation and discredit them once and for all . . . Mr. Odum, are you hearing me? Mr. Odum? Mr. Odum, wake up!"

But both lobes of Martin's brain had yielded to exhaustion. "Take him back to his cell."

* * *

Once, several incarnations back, Dante Pippen had barely survived an interminable bus trip that took him from a CIA safe house in a middle class neighborhood of Islamabad (furnished, for once, not in ancient Danish modern but in modern Pakistani kitsch) to Peshawar and the tribal badlands of the Khyber Pass, where he spent the better part of a year debriefing fighters infiltrating into and out of Afghanistan. The bus trip (Crystal Quest's notion of how an Irish reporter working for a wire service—Dante's cover at the time—would travel) had turned out to be a nightmare. Squeezed onto the wooden bench at the back of the bus between a mullah from Kandahar wearing a filthy *shalwar kameez* and a bearded Kashmiri fighter in a reeking djellaba, Dante had been eternally grateful when the bus pulled up, sometimes smack in the middle of nowhere, other times on the sewage-saturated streets of what passed for a village, to let the passengers stretch their legs, reckon the direction of Mecca and murmur the verses of the Koran a Muslim is required to recite five times a day. Now, slouching on the plush banquette in the back of the air-conditioned double-deck tourist bus, surrounded by well-dressed and, more importantly, well-scrubbed Germans on their way home from the spa at Karlovy Vary, Martin Odum suddenly thought of Dante's Khyber trip and the memory brought a smile to his lips. As always, remembering a detail from Dante's past reminded Martin that he, too, must have had a past, and this gave him a measure of hope that he could one day retrieve it. He patted the Canadian passport in the inside breast pocket of his jacket in anticipation of arriving at the Czech-German frontier. This particular passport, one of several he'd swiped from a safe when he was clearing out his office after being dismissed from the CIA, had been issued to a resident of British Columbia named Jozef Kafkor, a name Martin didn't recognize but found easy to remember because it reminded him of Franz Kafka and his stories of anguished individuals struggling to survive in a nightmarish world, which was more or less how Martin saw himself. Lulled by the motion of the bus and the ticking of its diesel engine, Martin closed his eyes and dozed, reliving the events of the last twelve hours.

He could hear Radek's voice whispering in his ear. *Please, Mr. Odum, you must wake up.*

Martin had drifted up toward the mirrored surface of consciousness in carefully calibrated increments, a deep sea diver rising languidly to avoid the bends. When he finally located the appropriate muscles and worked his lids open, he had discovered Radek, dressed again in jodhpurs and the Tyrolean jacket, crouching next to the metal army cot in his cell. "For the love of God, wake up, Mr. Odum."

"How long have I been asleep?"

"Four, four and a half hours."

Martin had struggled stiffly into a sitting position on the cot, with his back against the wooden bulkhead. "What time is it?"

"Twenty to six."

"Antemeridian or postmeridian?"

"Before dawn. Are you able to focus on what I say? The guards on the quay, the staff on the houseboat have been sent home. People in high places want you to vanish into thin air." He handed Martin his shoes, both of which had laces, along with his belt. "Put these on. Follow me."

Radek led Martin up the metal staircase to the weather deck. In a tiny room next to the midships passageway, he returned his Aquascutum and valise, which he had retrieved from the bed and breakfast. Martin snapped open the valise and touched the white silk scarf folded on top of the clothes. He ran his fingers across the underside of the lid.

"Your false papers, as well as your dollars and English pounds, are where you hid them, Mr. Odum."

Martin regarded Radek warily. "You provide a great deal for thirty lousy crowns an hour."

There was a flicker of pain in Radek's eyes. "I am not the man I appear to be," he whispered. "I am not the person my superiors take me for. I did not rebel in my youth against the communists to serve so-called state capitalists who use the same methods. I refuse to be complicit with criminals." He pulled the German Walther P1 with a clip inserted in it from a pocket of his Tyrollean jacket and offered it to Martin, butt first. "At least you are forewarned."

Thoroughly confused, Martin took the weapon. "Forewarned and forearmed."

"I was instructed to release you at fifteen minutes to seven. I surmise that your body would have been found floating in the Vltava. Your valise, filled with American dollars and British pounds and false identity papers, would have been recovered from the quay. The authorities would have speculated that a suspicious American, involved in the illegal sale of weapons and weapons systems, had been murdered by international gangsters. A small item to that effect would have appeared in the local newspapers. The American embassy would give the matter superficial attention—your CIA station chief might even hint that the national interest would be better served if they did not dig too deeply into the affair. With the ink still wet on the various reports, the case would be closed."

"A quarter to seven—that gives me less than an hour," Martin noted.

"My automobile, a gray Skoda, is parked fifty meters down the quay. The gas tank is full, the keys are in the ignition. Drive along the quay until you come to the first ramp leading to the street, then cross the river at the first bridge you come to and head due south, following the signposts to Ceské Budějovice and beyond that, Austria. If they stop you at the frontier, use one of your false passports. The whole trip should take you about two hours if you do not meet too much traffic."

"If I'm running, I want to take Zuzana Slánská with me."

"Her life is not in danger. Yours is. She faces a prison sentence if the evidence is sufficient to convict her."

Martin was worried about Radek. "How will you explain that your handgun is missing?"

"I would take it as a service if you would strike my head above the ear hard enough to break the skin and draw blood. They will find me only just beginning to regain consciousness. I will claim that you overpowered me. They will have their doubts—I will certainly be demoted, I may even lose my employment. So what. I resist, therefore I am."

The two men shook hands. 'I hope our paths cross again," Martin said.

Radek flashed a sheepish grin. "Be warned, Mister—next time I will not be such a fool as to settle for one lousy U.S. dollar an hour."

Gritting his teeth, Radek shut his eyes and angled his head. Martin didn't stint—he knew Radek stood a better chance of talking his way out of trouble if the head wound were real. Gripping the handgun by the barrel, wincing in empathy, he forced himself to swipe the butt sharply across the young man's scalp, drawing blood, stunning Radek, who slumped onto his knees.

"Thank you for that," he groaned.

"It was not my pleasure," Martin observed.

He collected his belongings and made his way across the gangplank to the quay, which appeared deserted. Radek's Skoda was parked in the shadows to his left. He went to the car and opened the door and threw his belongings onto the passenger seat. When he turned the key in the ignition, the motor started instantly. He checked the gas gauge—it was full, just as Radek had said. He threw the car into gear and started down the quay. He'd gone about half a kilometer when his headlights fell on the ramp leading to the street. Suddenly Martin's foot went to the brake. Killing the headlights, he pulled the car into the shadows at the side of the quay. He sat there for a moment, shaken by the pulse pounding in his ear. An old instinct had triggered an alarm in the lobe of his brain that specialized in tradecraft. He retrieved the German handgun from the pocket of his jacket, removed the clip, flicked the first of the icy 9-millimeter Parabellum bullets into the palm of his hand and hefted it.

He caught his breath. The bullet looked real enough. But it was too light!

Contrary to what the interrogator had said, Martin was not past his prime!

Checking out the bullets in a handgun was a piece of tradecraft Dante Pippen had picked up during a brief stint with a Sicilian Mafia family. When you gave someone a handgun, or left one where it was sure to be found, there was always the danger that it could be turned against you. In Sicily it was indoor sport to plant handguns loaded with dummy bullets that looked and (if you pulled the trigger) sounded like real bullets. But dummy bullets didn't have the same weight as real bullets—someone familiar with handguns could sense the difference.

Radek had set him up for a fall.

Martin remembered the pained look in the young man's eyes; he could hear his voice, oozing sincerity, delivering his manifesto: *I am not the man I appear to be.*

Who amongst us is the man he appears to be?

Martin thought about going back to liberate Zuzana Slánská. But he quickly abandoned the idea—if he returned to the houseboat for her now, they would know that he'd figured out the scheme. And they would fall back on Plan B, which was bound to be less subtle but more immediate.

Martin could imagine the scenario of Plan A: The prisoner, carrying multiple false identity papers and arrested in the company of an arms dealer, overpowers his guard, swipes his handgun and escapes from the safe house where he is being questioned, heading for Austria. Somewhere along the route, or perhaps at the border crossing itself, he is stopped for a routine passport control. In front of witnesses he produces the gun and tries to shoot his way out of a tight spot, at which point he is gunned down by uniformed police. Open and shut case of self defense. Happens all the time in the former Soviet wastelands of Europe these days.

Knowing that Radek had been setting him up for a hit, Martin certainly didn't want to use the Skoda, though if he parked it on a side street, where it could go unnoticed for hours or even for days, the authorities might spend precious time looking for Radek's car on the highways leading south. Once he ditched the Skoda (he would throw the handgun in the river but leave the bullets on the driver's seat to taunt Radek), the quickest way out of the country was the best: There were trains departing all through the day for Karlovy Vary, the spa in the northwestern corner of the country a long stone's throw from the German frontier. And there were double-decker tourist busses heading back to Germany from Karlovy Vary by the dozens every afternoon; even under the communist regime it had been possible to bribe one of the bus drivers to take you across the border. If the frontier guards verified identities, he could use the Canadian passport that he'd stashed in the tattered lining of his Aquascutum. Checking the lining again, he felt there was a good possibility that Radek had not discovered that one.

The driver's tinny voice, coming from small speakers in the roof of the tourist bus, stirred Martin from his reverie. "*Bereitet Eure Pässe, wir werden an der Grenze sein.*" Up ahead he could make out the low flat-roofed wooden buildings that housed the money changers and the toilets, and beyond that the border guards in brown uniforms and berets. There was one tourist bus ahead of theirs and three behind, which Martin knew was a stroke of luck; the guards tended toward cursory inspections at rush hours. When it was the turn of his bus, a young officer with a harassed expression on his face climbed onto the bus and walked down the aisle, glancing at faces more than the open passports, looking for Arabs or Afghans surely. Sitting on the banquette, Martin opened the passport to the page with his photo and, smiling pleasantly, held it out, but the young officer barely gave it, or him, a second glance. When the bus started up again and eased across the red stripe painted across the highway, the German passengers, relieved to be back in civilization, broke into a raucous cheer.

Martin didn't join in the celebration. He was having second thoughts about leaving Zuzana Slánská in the clutches of the devious Radek. In his mind's eye he could visualize the weight of the state crushing the breath out of her brittle body.

* * *

Standing on the fo'c'sle, Radek had watched the red taillights grow dimmer as the Skoda made its way along the quay toward the ramp. When the lights brightened and the car braked to a stop, the inter-

rogator, standing next to him and peering through binoculars, grunt-
ed in irritation. Moments later, when the taillights finally started up
the ramp and disappeared on the street above the quay, the two men
clasped hands to salute a scheme well hatched. The interrogator
flicked back the sleeve of his leather jacket to look at the luminous dial
of his wristwatch. "I will alert our people that the American is on his
way south," he said. "The *Oligarkh* has wired instructions to our ministry—he wants the trail to Samat to end at the Slánská woman."

Radek, pressing a handkerchief to his head wound to stop the
bleeding, took out a small flashlight and signalled with it in the direction of the green garbage bin down the quay from the houseboat.
Moments later the two heavies who had escorted Martin to and from
his cell appeared on the gangplank. Radek motioned for them to follow him as he headed for the small cell two decks under the bow. They
found Zuzana Slánská sitting on her metal cot, her eyes swollen with
fear, her legs tucked under her body, her arms hugging the blanket
over her shoulders despite the absence of a breath of air in the room.
"Is it time for another interrogation already?" she asked, her fingers
toying with the Star of David at her neck as she unwound from the
sitting position on the cot and stood up. Instead of waving her
through the door, the two guards positioned themselves on either side
of the woman and gripped her arms above the elbows. Zuzana's eyes
widened as Radek stepped forward and wrenched her blouse out of
the waistband, baring her stomach. When she caught sight of the
small syringe in his hand, she struggled to break free, but the two men
only tightened their holds on her arms. Thoroughly terrified, Zuzana
began to sob silently as Radek jabbed the needle into the soft flesh of
her navel and depressed the plunger. The drug took effect rapidly—
within seconds Zuzana's eyelids drooped, then her chin fell forward
onto her chest. While the two heavies held her up, Radek produced a
small pocket knife and began cutting strips from the blanket on the
cot. He twisted the strips into cords and tied two of them end to end.
Then he dragged the metal cot into the center of the cell under the
light bulb and, climbing up on the bed, attached one end of the
makeshift cord to the electric wire above the bulb. He pulled on it to
make sure it would hold. The heavies hauled Zuzana's limp body onto
the cot under the bulb and held her up while Radek fashioned a noose

and tightened it around the woman's neck. Then he jumped free of the cot and kicked it onto its side and the three men stepped back and watched Zuzana's body twisting slowly at the end of the cord. Radek grew impatient and motioned with a finger—one of the heavies grabbed her around the hips and added his weight to hers to speed up the execution. Clucking his tongue, Radek rolled his head from side to side in mock grief. "It is clearly not the state's responsibility if you turned out to be suicidal," he informed the woman strangling to death in the middle of the room.

* * *

Crystal Quest's features clouded over as she fitted on narrow spectacles and read the deciphered "Eyes Only" action report from Prague Station that her chief of staff had deposited on the blotter. The two wallahs who had been briefing her on the mass graves recently uncovered in Bosnia exchanged looks; they had lived through enough of the DDO's mood swings to recognize storm warnings when they saw them. Quest slowly looked up from the report. For once she seemed tongue-tied.

"When did this come in?" she finally asked.

"Ten minutes ago," the chief of staff replied. "Knowing your interest, I thought I'd walk it through instead of rout it."

"Where did they find the Skoda?"

"On one of those narrow cobblestoned streets on the Hradcany Castle side of the river."

"When?"

"Twelve hours ago, which was a day and a half after the Czechs watched him drive off down the quay."

The wallahs slumped back in their chairs and gripped the arm rests to better breast the storm. To their utter surprise, a cranky grin crept over Quest's crimson lips.

"I love that son of a bitch," she whispered harshly. "Where did they find the bullets?"

The chief of staff couldn't help smiling, too. "On the front seat of the car," he said. "Six 9-millimeter Parabellums set out in a neat row. They never found the handgun."

Quest slapped at the action report with the palm of her hand. To the attending wallahs it came across as applause. "Naturally they never found the handgun. He would have deep-sixed it in the Vltava. Oh, he's good, he is."

"He ought to be," agreed the chief of staff. "You trained him."

Quest was rolling her head from side to side in satisfaction. "I did, didn't I. I trained him and ran him and repaired him when he broke and ran him again. Some legends back, when we were playing Martin as Dante Pippen, I remember him coming in from a stint with that Sicilian Mafia family that was offering to sell Sidewinders to the Sinn Féin diehards in Ireland. He had us all in stitches telling us about how the Sicilians left pistols lying around where anybody could pick them up and shoot them. The catch was they were loaded with dummy bullets, which weighed less than real bullets if you took the trouble to heft them in your palm. Dante"—Quest started giggling and had to catch her breath—"Dante wanted us to leave pistols loaded with dummy bullets lying around Langley. He was only half kidding. He said it would be a quick way to separate the street-smart agents from the street-dumb ones."

"They may still find him if he went to ground in Prague," observed the chief of staff.

"Dante isn't in the Czech Republic," Quest said flatly. "He would have found half a dozen ways of getting across their silly little border."

"We'll catch up with him," the chief of staff promised.

But Quest, her head still bobbing with pleasure, was following her own thoughts. "I love the guy. I really do. What a goddamned shame we have to kill him."

* * *

"I need to get this off my chest," Stella said, cutting short the small talk. "I've never had an erotic phone relationship before."

"I didn't realize our conversations were erotic."

"Well, they are. The fact that you call is erotic. The sound of your voice coming from God knows where is erotic. The silences where neither of us knows quite what to say, yet nobody wants to end the conversation, is endlessly erotic."

They both listened to the hollow silence. "It is not written that we will ever become lovers," Martin said finally. "But if we do, we must make love as if each time could be the last."

His remark took her breath away. After a moment she said, "If we were to make love, I have the feeling time would stop in its tracks, death would cease to exist, God would become superfluous." She waited for Martin to say something. When he didn't she plunged on: "It exasperates me that we only just met—I lost so much time."

"Uh-huh."

"Translate that, please."

"Time is something you can't lose," Martin said. "Memory is another story."

He listened to her breathing on the other end of the phone four thousand miles away. "Consider the possibility," he said, "that we can talk intimately because of the distance between us—because the phone provides a measure of safety. Consider the possibility that the intimacy will evaporate when we come face to face."

"No. No. I don't think it will; I'm sure it won't. Listen, before Kastner and I came to America I was in love with a Russian boy, or thought I was. I look back on it now as something that was pleasantly physical, as first loves tend to be, but not erotic. The two are a universe apart. My Russian boy friend and I talked constantly when we weren't groping each other on some narrow bed in some narrow room. Thinking about it now, I remember endless strings of words that had no spaces between them. I remember conversations that were without silences. You know how you can split an atom and get energy. Well, you can do the same with words. Words contain energy. You can split them and harness the released energy for your love life. Are you still there, Martin? How do you interpret my love affair with the Russian boy?"

"It means you weren't ready. It means you are now."

"Ready for what?"

"Ready for naked truths, as opposed to crumbs of truth."

"Funny you should say that. Do you know Vassily Grossman's *Life and Fate*? It's a great Russian novel, one of the greatest, right up there with *War and Peace*. Somewhere in it Grossman talks about how you can't live with scraps of truth—he says a scrap of truth is no truth at all."

Martin said, "I've had to make do with scraps—maybe that's what's pushing me to find Samat. Maybe somewhere in the Samat story there's a naked truth."

"What makes you say that?"

"Not sure." He laughed under his breath. "Intuition. Instinct. Hope against hope that the king's horses and the king's men can somehow put the pieces together again."

1997: MARTIN BOUM IS ACCUSED OF HIGH *AND* LOW TREASON

"LOOK, IF YOU PLEASE, DIRECTLY AHEAD OF US—THERE ARE THE hulls," Almagul shouted over the din of the ancient Soviet outboard that was powering her eight-meter skiff across the Aral Sea toward Vozrozhdeniye Island. "Ten years ago there was a bay here with the port for Kantubek at the top of it. The ships you see became stranded when the rivers feeding the Aral Sea were diverted and the sea level sank."

Martin shielded his eyes with a hand and squinted into the dazzling sunlight. He could make out the hulls of a tanker, a tug boat, a Soviet-era torpedo boat, eight ships in all, half sunken into the sand and the salt residue in what had once been a bay. "I see them," he called to the girl.

"You must wear gloves now," she shouted, and she raised a hand from the outboard tiller to show that she had already fitted hers on over the sleeves of the frayed fisherman's sweater that buttoned across one shoulder. Martin pulled the yellow latex kitchen gloves over the cuffs of his shirt sleeves and attached thick rubber bands at the wrists of each of them. He knotted Dante's white silk scarf around his neck for good luck and tucked his pants legs into the knee-length soccer stockings the girl had given him when they left the Amu Darya—one of the two rivers trickling into the Aral Sea—the night before. As the skiff drew closer to the salt beach a flock of white flamingoes, frightened by the clatter of the motor, beat into the air. Martin spotted the first buildings of Kantubek, now a deserted shell of a town except for the scavengers who came from the mainland to plunder what was left of the once grandiose Soviet bioweapon testing site. Almagul, something of a tomboy who claimed to be sixteen, though she easily might have been a year or two younger, had been coming here regularly with her father and her twin sister before they both died two years before—of a mysterious illness that had left them feverish, with swollen lymph glands and mucus running from their nostrils. (Before her sister's death, Almagul had been known as Irina but, following local tradition, had taken the name of her twin sister, Almagul, to perpetuate her memory.) On the island, the father and his daughters would collect lead and aluminum and zinc-covered steel water pipes and copper wiring, as well as stoves and sinks and faucets and, when nothing else could be found, wooden planking pried up from the floors of buildings, and sell everything on the mainland to men who loaded the loot onto flatbed trucks and headed over the dusty plains toward Nukus or up to the city of Aral on the Kirgiz Steppe. Almagul hadn't been back to Vozrozhdeniye since the death of her father and her sister but Martin, arriving on a Yak-40 milk run from Tashkent, learned that she was the only person in Nukus with a skiff and a working outboard who had been to the island. He tracked her down to a one-room shack at the edge of the river and made her an offer she couldn't refuse—and then doubled it when he discovered she was studying English in the *gymnasium* and could translate for him as well. They had started down the Amu Darya loaded with spare jerry cans of gasoline and a straw hamper filled with camel-milk yogurt, goat cheese and watermelon.

"Over there is Kantubek," the girl was shouting now as she veered toward a dune at the foot of the town and idled the motor to let the skiff glide onto the sandy shore. Martin scrambled onto the bow and jumped the last half-meter to shore and turned to haul the skiff higher onto the beach. Clearly emotional at this first trip back to the island since the death of her father, Almagul joined him and stood with her gloved hands on her hips, looking around anxiously. Her Soviet manufactured *djeans*, tied with a rope through the loops at the waist, were tucked into fisherman's rubber boots secured at the tops with lengths of elastic. She kicked at broken test tubes and petri dishes half buried in the sand, and waved toward the piles of debris littering the path that curved up the dunes toward dozens of wooden buildings in various stages of dilapidation. Martin could see mountains of rusting animal cages of all shapes and sizes, rotting timber, scores of broken crates. He glanced at the sky, measuring the height of the sun. "I'll explore the town," he told the girl. "If all goes well, I'll be back here by mid afternoon."

"I am not able to remain past the setting of the sun," Almagul informed him. "My father had an iron rule never to spend the night on the island. In the light of day is possible to see rodents, maybe even fleas. After it turns dark . . ."

Heading down the Amu Darya at half throttle the night before so as not to anger the men fishing from its banks with spotlights and grenades, Almagul had explained about the dangers awaiting visitors to Vozrozhdeniye. Fearing that American inspection teams monitoring the 1972 treaty banning biological weapons would turn up on the island, the Soviets, in 1988, had hidden tens of tons of bacterial agents in hastily dug pits. They had also buried in shallow ditches thousands of cadavers of monkeys, horses, guinea pigs, rabbits, rats and mice that had been used to test the lethality of the bacterial agents. When the Soviet Union collapsed in the early '90s, Uzbekistan and Kazakhstan took custody of the island, but never bothered to dig up the buried spores or the cadavers, which had infected the island's rodent population. The rodents tended to survive the anthrax, glanders, tularemia, brucellosis, plague, typhus, Q fever, smallpox, botulinum toxin or Venezuelan equine encephalitis, but eventually transmitted the sicknesses to fleas which, in turn, transmitted them to other rodents. Which meant that a simple flea bite on the island could be fatal to a human. The risks were very real. In the two years since the death of her father, Almagul knew of fourteen men from Nukus who had disappeared while scavenging on Vozrozhdeniye Island; local authorities around the rim of the receding Aral Sea presumed the missing men had been bitten by fleas and had died of plague or another sickness on the island's dunes, and their bones picked clean by the flamingoes.

Almagul had dropped hints that bio agents or viruses spread by fleas weren't the only things to be found in the ghost town on the island. When Martin drew her out, she said that a handful of scavengers, commanded by a warlord, had installed themselves in the ruins of Kantubek. *Did the warlord have a name?* Martin asked. *My father, who read the bible each night before going to sleep, called the warlord Azazel after the evil spirit in the wilderness to whom a scape-*

goat is sent on the day of Atonement, the girl replied. *Others in Nukus say he is a Danish prince with the name of Hamlet Achba. This Hamlet and his gang demand twenty-five percent of the value of what anyone carries off from the island.* Almagul was betting that the warlord wouldn't bother a visiting journalist who wanted to write about the once secret Soviet bioweapons testing range for a Canadian magazine, or the girl who took him there and back to earn enough to see her through the winter.

Favoring his game leg, Martin started up the track that snaked through the dunes. At the top he turned to wave at Almagul, but she had hiked herself onto a crate to watch the flamingoes, with their distinctive bent bills, returning to the beach and didn't notice him. Topping a rise, he headed toward the ghost town along the main road, which consisted of slabs of concrete set end to end. In a field at the edge of town he spotted a basketball court that had been converted into a helicopter landing pad—a great white circle had been whitewashed onto the cement and its surface blackened by engine exhaust. Farther down the street he passed a vast hangar that had once housed Kantubek's motor pool. Most of the sections of corrugated roofing had been carted off but the vehicles, buried in drifts of sand, remained—gutted green trucks, two treadless T-52 tanks, two armored personnel carriers sitting on their axles, a faded orange bus that had been driven up onto a cement ramp to be serviced and never driven off, a once-red fire engine with the hood open and the entire motor missing, the rusting hulks of half a dozen ancient tractors with faded Soviet slogans painted on their sides. Continuing on into the town, Martin came upon an enormous building with a ragged Soviet hammer and sickle flag still flapping from the pole jutting over the tarnished double doors that led to an ornate lobby. A giant mosaic depicting the weight of the state, in the form of formations of tanks and squadrons of planes and fleets of ships, filled the entire windowless wall at the side of the lobby. Signs with the Cyrillic lettering bleached out by the sun hung off lampposts. Dust and sand stirred by gusts of wind swirled around Martin's feet at the intersections.

And then his street sense kicked in—he felt the eyes burning into the back of his neck before he caught sight of the scavengers edging

into view from behind buildings around the intersection. There were
five of them, all wearing canvas laced leggings and canvas gloves that
stretched to the elbows and glass face masks that Uzbek cotton farmers used when their crops were being dusted. Each of the men wore a
curved Cossack saber from his belt and cradled a vintage bolt-action
rifle in the crook of an arm, with a condom over the muzzle to protect the barrel from sand and moisture. Martin's fingers instinctively
slipped behind his back to where his automatic would have been if
he'd been armed with one.

One of the scavengers motioned for Martin to raise his hands over
his head. Another came over and frisked him for weapons. Martin's
hands were secured in front of him at the wrists with a dog's leash and
he was pulled around a corner and down a side street. When he stumbled, a rifle butt jabbed him sharply between the shoulder blades. Two
blocks farther along a door was pushed open and Martin was prodded
into a building and across a lobby with only a handful of its white
marble tiles still in place. He and the others splashed across a shallow
trough filled with a liquid that smelled of disinfectant, then walked
under a shower head that sprayed him and the guards with a fine mist
of disinfectant. He could hear the voices of other scavengers, speaking
in a strange language he couldn't identify, exchanging remarks with
the five who had brought him in. Double doors were jerked open and
Martin found himself in an auditorium with most of the folding seats
unbolted and stacked against one wall. Eight men wearing white laboratory coats and latex gloves were sitting on the few seats still intact.
Slouched in a high-backed throne-like wooden chair set in the middle
of the stage, with a painted backdrop from an old socialist realist
operetta behind him, the warlord presided over the assemblage. He
was a dwarf of a man, so short that his feet didn't reach the ground,
and dressed in a rough gray sleeveless scapular that plunged to the tops
of spit-shined paratrooper boots resting on an upturned ammunition
box. His bare arms were as muscular as a weight lifter's. He wore a
shoulder holster over the scapular, with the steel grip of a large navy
revolver jutting from it. The old-fashioned motorcycle goggles covering his eyes gave him the appearance of an insect. A stiff czarist-era
admiral's hat sat atop his oversized head. He talked for several minutes
in a low growl with one of the men in jumpsuits standing behind him

before raising his head to look directly at Martin. Lifting one stubby arm, he gestured for him to approach and, his voice pitched girlishly high, barked something in the strange language of the scavengers.

At a loss for a response, Martin mumbled "Uh-huh."

From the back of the auditorium, a girl's voice translated. "He insists to know for what reason you come to Kantubek."

Martin stole a glance behind him. Almagul was standing inside the auditorium door, an armed scavenger on either side of her. She smiled nervously at him as he turned back to the warlord and saluted him. "Explain to him," he called over his shoulder, "that I am a journalist from Canada." He produced a laminated ID card identifying him as a wire service reporter and waved it in the air. "I am writing an article on the philanthropist Samat Ugor-Zhilov, who is said to have come to Vozrozhdeniye Island when he left Prague."

When Almagul translated Martin's reply, the warlord bared his teeth in disbelief. He snarled something in a high-pitched voice to the men standing behind the throne, causing them to titter. The warlord kicked over the ammunition box so that his feet danced in the air as he raged at the girl standing in the back of the auditorium. When he ran out of breath he slouched back into the throne. Almagul came up behind Martin. "He tells you," she said in a low, frightened voice, "that Samat Ugor-Zhilov is the governor of this island and the director of Kantubek's experimental weapons programs."

* * *

The muffled voices talking to each other in an unintelligible language had worked their way into the texture of Martin's dream; he decided he was Lincoln Dittmann at Triple Border, listening to the Saudi he'd later identified as Osama bin Laden conferring with the Egyptian Daoud. When he finally realized that the men weren't speaking in Arabic, he forced himself through the membrane that separated sleep from wakefulness and sat up. It took a moment for his eyes to become accustomed to the dim light cast by feeble bulbs burning in sockets on the stone walls of the vaulted basement. He reached out and touched the cold bars and remembered that the guards had forced him into a low cage, the kind used to house monkeys in laboratories. He could make out Almagul curled up on a pile of rags in the cage next to his. Beyond her cage were other cages—more than he could count. Eight of them contained prisoners sleeping on the floor or sitting with their backs to the bars, dozing with their bearded chins on their chests.

Near the stone staircase, three men in white lab coats stood around a high stainless-steel table talking among themselves. Martin could hear their voices. Gradually a migraine mushroomed behind his eyes and he felt himself being sucked into another identity—one in which the language the men were speaking seemed vaguely familiar; to his astonishment he discovered that he understood fragments.

. . . *very stable, even in sunlight.*

. . . *the advantage of anthrax over plague. Sunlight renders plague stock harmless.*

. . . *should concentrate on anthrax.*

. . . *I agree . . . especially pulmonary anthrax, which is extremely lethal.*

. . . *Q fever persists for months in sand.*

. . . *What are you suggesting? . . . bombard New York with sand and then attack America with Q fever?*

. . . *still think we are making a mistake focusing on bacterial agents, which are, in general, difficult to stabilize, difficult to weaponize.*

Of course! The men were speaking Russian, a language Martin had studied in college in what seemed like a previous incarnation. He remembered the shrink at the Company clinic telling him of a case where one alter personality was able to speak a language that the other personalities didn't understand. It was a perfect example, she'd said, of how compartmented legends can be in the brain.

. . . *not going to make the case for nerve agents over bacterial agents again, are you? Samat himself decided the question months ago.*

. . . *Samat said we could revisit the issue at any point in our program. Nerve agents—VX in particular, but Soman and Sarin also—can be deadly.*

. . . *they have serious manufacturing problems.*

. . . *I want to remind you that tabun is relatively easy to manufacture.*

. . . *Tabun is only moderately stable.*

. . . *we are turning in circles . . . try one of the hemorrhagic fevers— the Ebola, for instance—on one of our clients.*

. . . Ebola is taking us down a dead-end street. I grant you it is lethal, but it is also relatively unstable, which makes an ebola program problematic.

. . . still, we have the spores Konstantin developed in his laboratory, so we might as well test them on one of the guinea pigs.

. . . only eight guinea pigs left.

. . . not to worry . . . two new ones.

The three scientists, if that's what they were, fitted on Russian army gas masks equipped with enormous charcoal filters. One of them selected a test tube from a cluster in a refrigerator and, removing the wax seal with a pocket knife, carefully poured a single drop of yellowish liquid onto a wad of cotton in a petri dish and quickly covered it with a glass lid. The scientists pulled a low table up to the cage at the far end of the basement and positioned a small ventilator so that it would blow over the petri dish into the cage. The bearded giant of a man sitting with his back to the bars in the cage rocked forward onto his knees and began to shout at the men in the language of the scavengers. His ranting woke the other prisoners. Almagul climbed onto her knees and, grasping the bars, yelled at the men in lab coats in Uzbek. The prisoner in the cage next to hers began raging at them, too. Almagul looked at Martin, her face contorted with terror. "They are experimenting on one of the scavengers," she cried, pointing toward the men in white lab coats.

In the last cage, the bearded man sank back onto his haunches and, covering his mouth with the tail of his shirt, breathed through the fabric. One of the scientists brought over a Sony camera attached to a tripod and began filming the prisoner. Another scientist checked the time on his wristwatch, noted it on his clipboard, then removed the cover on the petri dish and stepped away from the cage.

Martin's thoughts went back to the trial that had landed him and the girl in the monkey cages. The court martial—the warlord's term for the proceedings—had started after the lunch break and lasted twenty minutes. Presiding from the makeshift throne on the stage of the auditorium, Hamlet had acted as prosecutor and judge. Martin, his wrists secured with the dog's leash, had been charged with both high and low treason. Almagul, accused of aiding and abetting, had stood behind Martin, nervously whispering translations in his ear. Hamlet had opened the proceedings by announcing that he was absolutely convinced of the guilt of the accused; that the sole purpose of the court martial was to determine the degree of guilt and, eventually, the appropriate punishment.

"Guilty of what?" Martin had asked after pleading innocent to the formal charge of high and low treason.

"Guilty of working for a foreign intelligence agency," Hamlet had shot back. "Guilty of trying to steal Russia's biowarfare secrets."

"My only interest," Martin had had Almagul say, "is to interview Samat Ugor-Zhilov." And he had explained about Samat's humanitarian quest—repatriating to a village in Lithuania the bones of Saint Gedymin in order to obtain the sacred Torah scrolls and bring them to Israel.

"And where," Hamlet inquired, leaning forward, cocking his big head so as to better catch Martin's response, "would Samat find the bones of Saint Gedymin?"

"I was told he'd traced them to a small Orthodox church near the city of Córdoba in Argentina."

"And what," the warlord continued, his short feet dancing on the ammunition box, "would Samat offer the Argentines in return for the bones of the saint?"

Martin realized he'd reached the mine field. "I have no idea," he replied. "That's one of the questions I wanted to ask Samat."

At which point Hamlet launched into a tirade so fierce that Almagul had all she could do to keep up with him. "He says you know very well what Samat would trade, otherwise you would not have come to this island. He says the Russian nuclear arsenal will become obsolete in ten years time and the Americans will rule Russia unless Samat is able to perfect bioweapons to counter the American threat. He says bioweapons are the only cost efficient answer to Russia's problem. He says it costs $2 million to kill half the population of one square kilometer with missiles loaded with conventional warheads, $80,000 with a nuclear weapon, $600 with a chemical weapon and $1 with a bioweapon. Vozrozhdeniye Island, he reminds you, was once the center of bioweapon research for the Soviet Union: Under Samat's direction, and with Samat's financial backing, Vozrozhdeniye is once again developing a bioarsenal that will save Russia from American domination."

Hamlet collapsed back into the throne. One of the white coated scientists brought over a porcelain basin filled with water smelling of disinfectant and the warlord rang out the sponge in it and mopped his feverish brow.

Martin said, very quietly, "Are you suggesting that Samat gave bioweapon seed stock to the Argentineans in exchange for the bones of the saint?"

"That is not what I am suggesting," the warlord groaned when he heard Alamgul's translation. "Is that what I am suggesting?" he asked the scientists in lab coats.

"*Nyet, nyet,*" they responded in a discordant chorus.

"There is the proof," Hamlet cried, waving toward the scientists as if they were his star witnesses.

"Then what are you suggesting?" Martin had Almagul ask.

"Who is on trial here, you or me?" the warlord retorted furiously. "I am not suggesting Samat provided the Argentinean military with bioweapons. I am also not suggesting that he provided them with the orbits of American spy satellites. That rumor is without substance. It is a fact of life, as any idiot knows, that to get high-quality photographs, the spy satellites are obliged to orbit earth at low altitudes, circling the planet in a polar orbit every ninety minutes. It is a fact of life that they are over any one point on the earth's surface for only a few minutes. If you know when one of the satellites is due overhead, you can suspend operations you do not want the Americans to photograph. India and Pakistan have been doing this for years. So has Iraq. From whence comes the rumor that it is from Saddam Hussein in Iraq that Samat obtained the American satellite orbits that he traded to the Argentines for the bones of the saint."

It dawned on Martin that Hamlet and the people around him were stark raving mad; characters that Alice might have come across when she fell down the rabbit hole. He decided it was in his interest to humor the mad warlord. "And what in the world could Samat have given to Saddam Hussein in return for the orbits?"

Almagul whispered, "It is perilous to know the answer," but Martin, drunk on state secrets, ordered her to translate the question.

Hamlet drew his navy revolver from its holster and spun the chamber, sending the ticking sound reverberating through the auditorium. Then he raised the revolver and sighted on Martin's head and said "Bang, bang, you are extinguished." He laughed at his little joke and the others in the auditorium laughed with him, albeit somewhat anxiously, so it seemed to Martin. After a moment Hamlet said, "If Samat had wanted to go down that path, he could have traded to Saddam Hussein anthrax spores and hemorrhagic seed viruses that were harvested here on the island in exchange for the orbits." The warlord lifted the goggles off of his eyes and scratched thoughtfully at the side of his bulbous nose with the barrel of the revolver. A stunted grin materialized on his thick lips. "He could have traded the orbits for the bones of the saint. And the bones of the saint for the Torah scrolls. But it goes without saying, none of this actually happened.'

Hamlet, tiring of the game, gaveled the butt of his revolver down on the arm of the throne. "You and the girl are guilty as charged and sentenced to the monkey cages, to be used as guinea pigs in our experiments. Case closed. Trial over. Court adjourned."

The groaning of the giant scavenger in the last cage shook Martin out of his reverie. Almagul, sitting on the icy floor with her back to the bars in the cage next to Martin, buried her head between her knees. Her body shook with silent sobs. Martin reached through the bars to touch her shoulder. "I recognize the men in the cages," the girl whispered hoarsely. "They are the ones missing from Nukus. We are all surely going to die like my father and my sister," she added. "They have already killed six scavengers from Nukus and thrown their bones to the flamingoes. The worst part is that I have no sister to take my name."

In the last cage the giant scavenger pitched forward onto his knees, with his head touching the ground, and then rolled onto his side. The scientist filming the test called to the two others in Russian to come over and look. The man with the clipboard produced a large skeleton key and opened the padlock on the monkey cage and the three Russians in lab coats, still wearing their gas masks, ducked inside and crouched around the body. One of them raised the scavenger's limp wrist and let it flop back again. "Konstantin will be extremely pleased with his ebola—" he started to say when the giant scavenger, bellowing with a primitive furor, sprang to life and began shattering the gas masks and the facial bones of the scientists with his fists. With blood seeping from under their gas masks, two of the scientists crawled on all fours toward the low door of the cage, but the giant caught them by their ankles and hauled them back and, climbing over their bodies, pounded their faces into the cement floor. In the other cages the prisoners called to the giant scavenger to free them, but he kept lifting the heads by the hair and smashing them into the cement. It was Almagul's voice that finally penetrated to the wild man's brain. Gasping for air, a maniacal gleam in his bulging eyes, the scavenger released his grip on the bloody heads and looked up.

Almagul called his name and spoke soothingly to him in the strange language of the scavengers. The giant, his arms and shirt drenched in blood, crawled through the door of his cage and staggered to his feet. The other prisoners were all talking to him at once. Almagul spoke quietly to the giant. Martin noticed that mucus was seeping from his nostrils as he lurched across the basement to the stainless steel table, snapped off one of the legs and came back to the cages. One by one he slipped the narrow end of the steel leg through the padlocks and, using the bars for leverage, snapped open the locks. Martin was the last to emerge from the cages. The giant collapsed at his feet—Martin, reaching to help him, found he was burning with fever. "There is nothing we can do for him," Almagul said. The other scavengers backed away from the fallen man until Almagul snapped angrily at them. One of them came forward and brought the stainless steel table leg down on the giant's head to put him out of his misery. Then, armed with steel legs from the table and the wooden legs broken off chairs, the scavengers made their way up the stone steps. Almagul, leading the way, carefully opened the steel door leading to the biowarfare laboratory and stepped aside to let the others through. Two Russian scientists napping on cots were strangled to death by the desperate prisoners. Three other scientists were working with frozen anthrax spores in a walk-in refrigerator. Martin thrust one of the stainless steel legs through the door handles, locking the Russians inside, and then turned up the thermostat. The three scientists, realizing they were trapped, began pounding on the thick glass window in the door. One of the prisoners found a plastic jerry can in a closet filled with kerosene for the heating unit. He splashed kerosene over the shelves filled with petri dishes and filing cabinets. Almagul struck a match and tossed it into the spilled kerosene. A bluish fire skidded across the floor. In a moment the laboratory was awash in flames.

The escaping scavengers stumbled across two guards playing backgammon in an ante chamber with razor-stropped one-edged Cossack sabers stacked in four old umbrella stands. Both of the guards lunged for their rifles but were clubbed to death before they could reach them. Snatching the two rifles, stuffing their pockets with bullets, Martin and Almagul led the scavengers, armed now with sabers, up a back staircase that led to the lobby. The single guard on duty there backed against a wall and raised his hands in surrender when he saw the scavengers; one of them walked up to him and split his skull open with a single stroke of his sword. On a gesture from Martin, the men spread out and burst through the several double doors into the auditorium. The fight was short and lethal. Furiously working the bolt of his rifle, hardly bothering to take aim, Martin—a pulse pounding in his temple, his trigger finger trembling—provided covering fire from the back of the auditorium as the escaping prisoners, brandishing the sabers over their heads and screaming savagely, charged down the aisles. The warlord, who had been holding court from the throne, cowered behind it as his guards, caught by surprise, desperately tried to fight off the attackers. Two of the prisoners were killed before they reached the stage; a third was shot in the face as he climbed onto it. When Martin's bolt-action rifle jammed, he caught Lincoln's voice roaring in his ear: *Grab it by the barrel, for Christsake, use it as a club.* Gripping the hot barrel with both hands, Martin joined the battle on the stage, clubbing wildly at the guards as they tried to fend off the blows with their rifles or their arms. When one of the guards stumbled, Martin pounced on him and pinned him down while a prisoner hacked off the guard's hand holding the rifle. Breathing heavily, Martin stood up as another prisoner planted one foot on the neck of the fallen man and slit open his back, exposing his spine down to the coccyx. Gradually the prisoners, pushed by a ferocity that came from having nothing to lose and their lives to win, overpowered the guards who were still alive. The wounded guards, with blood gushing from ugly gashes, and the three who surrendered were hauled into the orchestra pit and decapitated with saber strokes to the napes of their necks. One headless man took several short steps before collapsing to the floor. Martin, sick to his stomach, watched the scavengers circle around the throne almost as if they were playing a harmless child's game. Hamlet had pulled the square of thick theater curtain that had been used as a carpet over his head. The scavengers tore it away from his clutching hands and prodded the warlord to his feet with the points of their sabers. Wiping snot from his nose, Hamlet begged for mercy as the prisoners stripped away his canvas leggings and boots and gloves and goggles and marched him through the auditorium and lobby and out into the street.

Picking his way barefoot through the gutter to avoid the fleas, Hamlet kept babbling in the strange language of the scavengers, but nobody paid the slightest attention to what he was saying. As the sun edged above the horizon, the group retraced the route Martin had taken into Kantubek, passing the ornate building with the mosaic in the lobby depicting the weight of the state. When they reached the motor pool hangar, aswirl in sand and dust, the scavengers found a roll of electric wire and lashed the warlord of Vozrozhdeniye Island to one of the gutted green trucks, his wrists bound over his head to the rusted frame of a window, his bare feet just reaching the drift of sand when he stood on his toes. The warlord whimpered something and Almagul, watching from the street, called out a translation for Martin.

"He pleads with them not to leave him here where the rodents and fleas can get to him. He appeals to be shot."

"Ask him where Samat went when he left here," Martin shouted.

"I do not understand his answer," Almagul called back. "He says something about the bones of a saint being returned to a church in Lithuania."

"Ask him if the church is in the village of Zuzovka near the frontier with Belarus."

"I think he has become mad. He tells only that Samat is a saint—he says this over and over."

Hamlet Achba could be heard ranting incoherently as the four

surviving prisoners and Martin and Almagul made their way along the
track that ran through the dunes to the beached boat. At one point
Martin stopped to look back at Hamlet. He was about to start up the
dunes toward the warlord when he heard Dante's wild Irish cackle in
his ear. *Don't you know the bible instructs victims how to survive emotionally? An eye for an eye, a tooth for a tooth, a burning for a burning,
laddie.* When Martin hesitated, Dante sighed in despair. *Aye, you're a
weak-kneed excuse for a man.* Martin had to agree. Nodding grimly, he
turned and stumbled down the hill to join the others on the beach.
The men rinsed the blood off their bodies in the sea and tugged the
boat off the sand and climbed aboard. Almagul started the outboard,
sending the white flamingoes scattering into the air. She backed the
boat until the water was deep enough to swing it around and head at
full throttle toward the mainland. While Almagul distributed watermelon and goat cheese from the hamper, Martin gazed back at the
ghost town of Kantubek, growing smaller and smaller until it finally
vanished into the tulle-like haze that thickened as the sun stepped
higher in the east.

* * *

The solemn timeserver behind the counter at the central post
office in Nukus had never before placed a call out of the country and
needed to read the appropriate chapter in a manual before she could
figure out the various codes and how to charge for the communication. On the third attempt she finally got through to a place she had
never heard of—the borough of Brooklyn—and punched the chess
timer that she used to measure the duration of calls.

"Stella, that you?" Martin called into the phone in the open booth
while the half dozen people queuing for pension checks looked on in
wonderment at someone dispatching his voice across Europe and the
Atlantic Ocean to the United States of America and receiving an
answer within a fraction of a second

"Did you catch up with Samat?"

"I missed him but it couldn't have been by much. The basketball
court was blackened by exhaust."

"You okay, Martin?"

"I am now. It was touch and go for a while."

"What does a basketball court have to do with Samat?"

"It had a white circle painted on it, which means it'd been turned into a helicopter pad. Unlike me, Samat travels first class. I come chugging after him in open boats with outboard motors. How you making out with your new front tooth?"

"I decided you were right about the old chipped tooth—it had a certain charm even if it did make me look breakable. I don't recognize the person looking back at me in the mirror."

"You can always chip the new tooth."

"Very funny. Martin, don't get angry but you are tracking down Samat, aren't you?"

"What kind of a question is that?"

"I've been doing a lot of thinking lately. The fact is I hardly know you—I don't think you're a serial killer or anything like that, but you could be a serial liar. You could be phoning me from Hoboken and making the rest up."

"I'm phoning you from a post office in Uzbekistan. The woman who put the call through had never called out of the country before."

"I want to believe you. I really do. But the people you used to work for—you know whom I mean—sent a lady psychiatrist around yesterday. Her name was Bernice Treffler. She said she'd treated you after you were laid off."

"What else did she say?"

"She said—oh, Martin . . ."

"Spit it out."

"She said you were off your rocker. Are you? Off your rocker, Martin?"

"Yes and no."

Stella exploded. "What kind of an answer is that, for God's sake? Either you are or you aren't. There's no middle ground."

"It's more complicated than you think. There is a middle ground. I'm not insane, but there are things I can't remember."

"What kind of things?"

The timeserver watching the chess clock muttered something to Almagul, who came over to tug at Martin's sleeve. "She says this is going to cost you the wages of a year."

Martin waved the girl away "Somewhere along the way," he told Stella, "I lost track of which of the several skins I lived in was the real me."

He could hear Stella groan into the phone. "Oh, God, I should have known it was too good to be true."

"Stella, listen. What I have wrong with me isn't fatal, either for me or for us."

"Us?"

"*Us* is what we're both worried about, isn't it?"

"Wow! I admit there are moments when you sound as if you could be off your rocker. Then there are other moments when you sound perfectly sane to me."

"I am *imperfectly* sane."

Stella started laughing. "I can live with imperfection—"

Suddenly the line went dead in Martin's ear. "Stella? Stella, are you still there?" He called to Almagul, "Tell her the line's been cut."

When Almagul translated, the time server reached out and punched the chess clock with her fist and began calculating the cost of the call on an abacus. When she had figured out the sum, she wrote it on a scrap of paper and held it up so everyone in the post office could tell their children about the deranged foreigner who had spent a fortune to dispatch his voice to a place on the far side of the Atlantic Ocean with the unlikely name of Brooklyn.

1997: MARTIN ODUM REACHES NO-WOMAN'S LAND

ARTIN ODUM PULLED THE LADA HE'D RENTED IN HRODNA, the last big burg in Belarus before the Lithuanian border, off the two-lane highway that had been repaved so many times, each layer piled on top of the previous one, it probably ranked, rising above the wetlands as it did, as an elevated highway. He killed the motor and strolled over to a mossy embankment above the Neman River, and urinated against a scorched oak that looked as if it had been struck by lightening. Martin had crossed the frontier at a dusty village, half of it in Belarus, the other half in Lithuania, with a tongue twister of a name. The young border guards, sunning themselves in deck chairs beside a low prefabricated building on the village's dusty main street, had waved him past without so much as a glance at the Canadian passport made out in the name of one Jozef Kafkor. At regular intervals the route had been blocked by sheep and he'd had to honk his way through them. The last sign post he'd seen before he stopped to relieve his bladder had put his destination, the river town of Zuzovka, at eighteen kilometers; keeping track of the distance on the odometer, Martin reckoned it would be around the next bend in the Neman. Overhead, a high-flying jetliner, its two white contrails drifting apart and thickening behind it, vanished into a fleecy mare's-tail of a cloud. Moments later the distant drone of the motors reached Martin's ears, leaving him with the impression that the noise was racing to catch up with the engines producing it.

How he ached to be on that plane, gazing down at the Baltic flatlands as he headed toward home, toward Stella. How he ached to stop looking over his shoulder every time he stepped into a street; to put the quest for Samat behind him and go back to boring himself to death, a pastime his sometime Chinese girlfriend, Minh, had once described as suicide in slow motion.

Once he'd crossed the border into Lithuania, Martin noticed that the elevated highway had gradually filled with traffic heading in the direction of Zuzovka—there were open farm trucks and dilapidated school busses crammed with peasants, and scores of men in loose shirts and baggy trousers trudging along on foot. Curiously, all of them carried pitchforks or what Dante Pippen would have called *shillelaghs*—sturdy cudgels with knobs on one end, fashioned from the thick branches of oaks. As Martin started back to his car now, two shaggy horses that looked as if they might have been on their way to the abattoir clopped past, hauling a wooden cart loaded with bricks. The old peasant perched high up in the driver's seat gripped the reins casually in one hand and with the other touched two fingers to the visor of his cap in salute when Martin called out a greeting in broken Russian. The old man clucked his tongue at the horses, which didn't need much coaxing to pull up.

Martin waved to the knots of men filling the road on their way toward Zuzovka and raised his hands, as if to ask: *Where is everyone going?*

The old man leaned over and spit eucalyptus juice onto the highway. Then, scrutinizing the foreigner through eyes with a suggestion of Mongolia in them, he allowed as how "Saint Gedymin has come back to Zuzovka."

"Gedymin died six hundred years ago," Martin remarked to himself.

The peasant, speaking slowly and articulating carefully as if he were instructing a child, said, "Gedymin's bones, which the German invaders stole from our church, have by miracle been returned."

From some remote corner of his brain Martin assembled Russian words into a sentence. "And how did the bones of the saint find their way back to Zuzovka?"

A cagey grin appeared on the old man's weathered face. "How else would a saint travel except by private helicopter."

"And how long ago did the helicopter bringing the bones of the saint arrive in Zuzovka?"

The peasant pointed his chin at the sky and shut his eyes as he ticked off the days on the fingers of a hand. "One day before today, the widow Potesta's cow drowned in the Neman. Two days before today, Eidintas wound the cord attached to his bull around the palm of his right hand and then lost all of his fingers except for the thumb when the bull charged laundry hanging on a line. Three days before today, the wife of the drunken shepherd walked all the way to Zuzovka's pharmacy to treat a broken nose, though she refused to identify the owner of the fist that had broken it." Looking down at Martin, the peasant grinned. "Three days before today the helicopter brought the bones of the saint to Zuzovka."

"And why are all the men heading toward town armed?"

"To join the Metropolitan Alfonsas and defend Gedymin from the Romish."

The old man laughed at Martin's ignorance as he clucked at the horses and snapped at them with the reins. Martin slipped behind the wheel of the Lada, started the motor and honked twice at the peasant as he pulled into the left lane and passed him. The old man, still laughing, again touched the visor of his cap with two fingers in salute, though this time there was more derision than politeness in the gesture.

Zuzovka, a sprawling market town with a tractor repair station next to the brightly painted wooden arch that marked the beginning of its long and wide and dusty main street, materialized around the next bend. The town's two-story brick school sat on a patch of sandy land across from the tractor station; the school's soccer pitch, like the basketball court on Vozrozhdeniye Island in the Aral Sea, had been converted into a helicopter landing pad, with a great circle of whitewashed stones set out in the middle of the field blackened by engine exhaust. Martin had to slow to a crawl behind the line of open trucks and men afoot, all heading in the direction of the Orthodox Church situated on a dirt lane that angled off from the main street and ran across the wetlands to the muddy bank of the Neman.

Parking his car in front of a bakery with a sign on the door announcing that, due to Catholic threats to "liberate" Saint Gedymin, it would not open for business today, Martin melted into the throngs. He grabbed a teenage boy by the arm. "*Gdye zhenshchini?*" he asked. "Where are the women?"

"Zuzovka is a no-woman's land," the boy, grinning from ear to ear, shot back as he hurried after the others.

The peasants, joking among themselves about the Catholic skulls they would split open and the Catholic blood that would irrigate Orthodox soil, barely noticed the stranger among them. Dozens of rowboats were tied up at the rickety wooden docks along the river bank, and groups of armed men could be seen climbing the slope toward the church. A fire brigade band—the men dressed in knee-high boots and red parkas—was trumpeting martial aires from the iron gazebo in a fenced park across the lane. Drawing nearer to the church, Martin produced the laminated card that identified him as a wire service reporter and, brandishing it over his head, called out that he was a Canadian journalist. The crowd parted when several of the local *notables*—distinguishable from the farmers because they wore double-breasted suit jackets with their shirts buttoned up to the neck—instructed the peasants to let the foreign journalist through.

Hobbling along on his game leg, which had been acting up since he quit the Aral area, Martin shouldered through the several hundred ripe-smelling peasants toward the three onion domes, each topped with a rusted Orthodox cross. Two young Orthodox priests, dressed in sandals and black habits, waved him up the steps and into the church, and bolted its metal-studded wooden door behind him with a thick wooden crossbar thrust through iron staples and then embedded in niches chiseled into the stone walls on either side. The church reeked of incense and the smoke of beeswax candles and the dust and dankness of centuries and it took a moment for Martin's eyes to make anything out in the misty dimness. The silver and gold in the icons on the sweating walls glinted as a tall bearded man dressed in a black habit, with chiseled features and a squared black miter atop his long black hair, approached. With each step he pounded the floor with the silver tip of a thick staff.

"Do you speak Canadian?" the priest demanded in English, planting himself in front of the visitor.

Martin nodded.

"I am the Metropolitan Alfonsas," the priest thundered, "come from the district capital at Alytus to receive the bones of Saint Gedymin and defend the Church of the Transfiguration from the papists who connive to steal the holy relics from their rightful owners."

"Uh-huh."

Before he could say more, floodlight blinded Martin. Squinting, he made out the figure of a television cameraman advancing across the floor of the church. The light fixed to the heavy camera on his shoulder bored into the feretory set in a wall to one side of the pulpit. One of the young priests undid a padlock and swung open a thick glass door as the cameraman zoomed in on the velvet cushion with what looked like a bleached pelvis bone and femur nestled in it. Martin noticed a splinter of weathered wood, roughly the thickness and length of a forearm, set into a niche lined with gold cloth inside the feretory.

"And what is that morsel of wood?" he whispered to the metropolitan.

Alfonsas's eyes turned hollow with wrath. "That is not wood," he cried. "It is a fragment of the True Cross." Overcome with emotion, the metropolitan turned away and, murmuring verses in Church Slavonic, prostrated himself on the great stones of the floor, under which corpses of metropolitans and monks were interred. Guided by a producer, the cameraman panned with his floodlight and lens onto Alfonsas and held it there while a very chic young woman spoke into a microphone in what Martin took to be BBC Lithuanian.

She broke off the interview abruptly when a roar from outside the church penetrated the thick walls. One of the priests, scampering up a ladder and peering through a slit high in a bartizan, called out, "Holy father, the battle has begun." The metropolitan sprang to his feet and motioned for the glass door of the feretory to be shut and locked. Gripping his staff by the silver tip and resting the heavy jewel-encrusted handle on a shoulder, he planted himself in front of the holy relics of Saint Gedymin. "Over my dead body," he cried. He fixed Martin with his dark beady eyes. "Bear witness," he instructed him, "to the perversity of the papists who falsely claim the relics of our saint."

The cameraman cut the floodlight and the television reporters darted toward the narrow door in the back of the church. The metropolitan cried out when he saw them tugging free the crossbar—too late. The door burst open on its hinges and a mob of shrieking peasants stormed into the church. Flailing away with his heavy staff, the metropolitan defended the feretory until someone stabbed his thigh with the prongs of a pitchfork and the peasants wrestled his staff away. Martin backed up against a wall and raised his hands over his head but some deranged peasants with wild beards and wild eyes closed in on him and began punching him in the rib cage until he doubled over and sank onto the floor. Through the sea of peasants milling around, he could make out one of them raising a heavy candlestick and shattering the glass window of the feretory. The pillow with the bones of the saint was removed and the peasant army, throwing open the great front door, spilled out of the church. A howl of triumph rose from the throats of the Catholics outside Faint from the pain in his chest, Martin saw the metropolitan, on his knees in front of the feretory, sobbing like a baby.

* * *

Lithuanian police and an army unit, pouring into Zuzovka from the north aboard camouflage-painted armored busses, eventually succeeded in separating the warring communities, but not before two of the attacking Catholics and one of the young Orthodox priests had been clubbed to death and dozens on both sides injured. Their sirens jingling, ambulances arrived behind the police. Doctors and nurses scrambled across the battleground in front of the Orthodox church, treating broken bones and broken heads and hauling the more seriously hurt off on stretchers to the district hospital in Alytus. Martin's rib cage was taped up by a male nurse, after which he was escorted by armed soldiers to the command post, set up in the gazebo, to be quizzed by an army colonel with waxed whiskers who seemed more interested in the impression he would make on television than the confrontation between the town's Orthodox and Catholic communities. Looking appropriately grave, he finished giving an interview to the woman reporter from Vilnius and asked her when it would be broadcast, and then instructed an aide to phone his wife in Kaunas to make sure she caught him on TV. With the television crew off filming the wounded in the field, the officer turned to Martin and checked his identity papers. To be sure that the story the journalist named Kafkor filed (to the news service named on the laminated ID card) would take into consideration the Catholic side of the story—like the vast majority of Lithuanians the colonel was Catholic—he insisted on personally taking Martin in his jeep to talk with the bishop of the archdiocese, come all the way from Vilnius to support the local Catholic priests and the members of the diocese.

The bishop turned out to be a cheery little man with wide hips and narrow shoulders, giving him the appearance, in his crimson ankle-length robe and embroidered stole, of a church bell. The meeting took place in the vegetable garden behind the church. Two white storks peered down at the scene from the large nest on top of the bell tower. "Dates," the bishop said, launching into a lecture he had obviously given before, "are handy pegs on which to hang history. Do you not agree with this observation, Mr. Kafkor?"

Martin, wincing from the pain in his ribs, used the tips of the white silk scarf silk tied around his neck to blot the perspiration on his forehead. "Uh-huh."

The army officer thrust a pad and ball point pen into Martin's hands. "You must take notes," he whispered.

As Martin scribbled, the bishop paced between the furrows, the hem of his robe growing dirtier with each step, as he explained the history of Saint Gedymin. "It was Gedymin, as every schoolchild in Lithuania knows, who created Greater Lithuania, a vast duchy that stretched from the Black Sea to Moscow to the Baltic. He ruled over the empire from the capital he founded in Vilnius in the year of our Lord Jesus 1321. Sixty-five years later, in the year of our Lord 1386, Lithuanians, by the grace of God, adopted Catholicism as the state religion and, on the order of the grand duke, the entire population was baptized on the banks of the Neman. At which time it can be said that the last Lithuanian pagans vanished into the dustbin of history."

"Did you get all that?" the army officer demanded.

"The first Catholic church," the bishop plunged breathlessly on, "was built on this very site ten years after the mass baptism, and expanded"—he pointed to the bell tower and the jesse window and the two vaulted wings—"in the centuries that followed. The bones of Saint Gedymin, or what was left of him after the original crypt in Vilnius was desecrated by Tartar bandits, were consigned to the Catholic church at Zuzovka and remained here from early in the fourteenth century until Lithuania came under Russian domination in 1795. The Russians, being Eastern Orthodox, purloined the bones of the saint from the Catholic church and gave them to the Orthodox metropolitan, who had the Church of the Transfiguration built to house them. Despite our repeated petitions over the years, the bones remained in the possession of the Orthodox until a German army officer, retreating before a Russian offensive in 1944, stole the relics as he passed through Zuzovka."

Hoping to cut short the story, Martin said, "It was Samat Ugor-Zhilov who discovered the Orthodox church possessed a collection of priceless Torah scrolls and commentaries, and offered to trade the bones of Saint Gedymin, which he had traced to an Orthodox church in Argentina, for the Jewish documents."

The bishop danced a jig at the mention of Samat's name. "But that is not it at all! That's the fabricated story that this satanic Samat Ugor-Zhilov and the metropolitan would have the world believe. The truth is quite different."

"Mark the truth in your notebook," the army officer instructed Martin.

The bishop noticed the dirt that had accumulated on the hem of his robe and reached down to brush it off. "The television tells us that Samat Ugor-Zhilov, who is identified as a Russian philanthropist, returned the bones of Saint Gedymin in exchange for the Jewish Torah scrolls and commentaries held for safekeeping in the Orthodox church since the Great Patriotic War. The television goes on to say that all he asked for himself was a minuscule crucifix, fashioned from the wood of the so-called True Cross in the possession of the Orthodox church. The TV even showed a picture of the metropolitan handing to the so-called philanthropist the crucifix, which was the size of a pinky finger on a child. Samat thanked the metropolitan and said he would donate the crucifix, fashioned from the True Cross, to the Orthodox church in the village near Moscow where his mother still lived."

Martin looked up from his note taking, his eyes burning with excitement. "Did he give the name of this village?"

The bishop shook his heavy head; his jowls continued to roll from side to side after his head had returned to an even keel. "No. What does it matter?" Without waiting for a response, he continued: "The real reason this Samat Ugor-Zhilov gave the saint's bones to the Orthodox and not to its original Catholic custodians is opium."

Martin, unnerved, looked up again. "Opium?"

"Opium," the army officer repeated, tapping a forefinger on Martin's pad. "Write the word, if you please."

"Opium," the bishop said, "is the key to understanding what has transpired. The opium poppy is grown in what is called the Golden Triangle—Burma, Thailand, Laos. Vietnamese drug traders transport the raw opium to the Russian naval base at Cam Ranh Bay in Vietnam, and from there it is shipped to the Russian port of Nakhodka on the Sea of Japan. The Russian drug cartel, which was run by the one known as the *Oligarkh*, Tzvetan Ugor-Zhilov, until he went into hiding several years ago, processes the opium in Nakhodka and then smuggles it across Russia for distribution to markets in Europe and America. Since the late 1980s Zuzovka has served as a hub for shipping opium to northern Europe and Scandinavia. Landing strips were bulldozed onto the flatlands bordering the Neman and small planes flying at night ferried their illicit cargoes into this corner of Lithuania. To move the large quantities of opium westward, Samat Ugor-Zhilov employed runners disguised as Orthodox priests, since they are able to pass frontiers easily. When the metropolitan threatened to put a stop to this, Samat bought him off by tracking down and returning Gedymin's bones"—the bishop's eyes blinked mischievously—"assuming that what he brought to the church were really the bones of the sainted saint."

"What about the Torah scrolls?"

"The metropolitan did not want to be seen having commercial dealings with sacred texts so he consigned them to Samat, who sold them to an Israeli museum and donated the proceeds, less a hefty commission, to the Orthodox church."

"And how did you come across all this information?"

The bishop glanced up at the storks in the nest atop the bell tower. "A very large bird told me."

Martin closed his pad and dropped it into a pocket. "It seems as if every riddle is part of another greater riddle."

"It is like an onion," the bishop said consolingly. "Under each layer is . . . another layer."

"One last question: If you're not sure the bones Samat brought with him are those of the sainted saint, why were the Catholics battling to bring them back to the Catholic church?"

The bishop held up one of his small pristine hands as if he were directing traffic. "Whether the bones of the sainted saint are genuine is of little consequence. The only thing that matters is that the faithful believe they are."

* * *

That night the colonel personally drove Martin back to his Lada, still parked in front of the bakery.

"How are your ribs, Mr. Kafkor?"

"They only hurt when I laugh and there's not much chance I'll be laughing a lot."

"Well, good-bye and God speed, Mr. Kafkor. I have ordered the soldiers in the jeep to escort you to the Belarus frontier." When Martin started to protest that it wouldn't be necessary, the colonel cut him off. "Our police discovered two bloated bodies floating in the Neman this afternoon. At first they assumed the murdered men were Catholics killed by the Orthodox, or Orthodox killed by Catholics. A specialist from Vilnius identified the long knife found on one of the corpses as a weapon popular in Chechnya, which suggests that the two dead men were Chechens."

"Maybe they were involved in Samat's opium cartel," Martin ventured.

The colonel shrugged. "There may be a connection between the dead Chechens and Samat, though I doubt it had anything to do with the opium operation. Islam is not welcomed in this frontier region of Lithuania, either by the Catholics or the Orthodox. No, the only thing that could have brought Chechens here is a mission—though with them being drowned, it is impossible to speculate what it could have been. You would not have an idea?"

Martin shook his head. "It's as much a mystery to me as it is to you."

* * *

The following morning Martin treated himself to a good breakfast in Hrodna's only hotel and then strolled carefully (his cracked ribs hurt if he walked too fast) along the main street, past the bulletin board posted with the regional newspaper open to photographs of the riot at Zuzovka, to the town's central post office. He queued at the window with the emblem of a telephone over it, and wrote the number on the ledger when the clerk didn't understand his rudimentary Russian.

"What country uses code nine seven two?" she asked.

"Israel."

"And what city in Israel uses the area code two?"

"Jerusalem."

The clerk noted "Jerusalem, Israel" on her work sheet and dialed the number. She motioned for Martin to pick up the telephone in the nearest booth. He heard a man's voice on the line protesting, "This must be a mistake—I don't know anyone in Belarus."

"Benny, it's me, Martin."

"What the Christ are you doing in Belarus?"

"It's a long story."

"Give me the short version."

"Even the short version's too long to tell you on the phone. Listen, Benny, that night I spent at your house you told me about the *Oligarkh* living in an isolated dacha in a village a half hour from Moscow along the Moscow-Petersburg highway. You wouldn't by any chance remember the name of the village?"

"You want to hold on, I'll check my computer."

Martin watched the people lining up at the other windows, some for stamps, some to pay electric or water bills, some to cash pension checks. None of them looked out of place, which didn't mean much; anyone who wanted to keep tabs on him would use local help.

Benny came back on line. "The name of the village is Prigorodnaia."

"Maybe you ought to spell that."

Benny did, phonetically.

"Prigorodnaia. Thanks, Benny."

"I guess you're welcome. Though come to think of it, I'm not positive."

1994: LINCOLN DITTMANN SETS THE RECORD STRAIGHT

B ERNICE TREFFLER KNEW SOMETHING WAS OUT OF JOINT THE moment Martin Odum strolled into the room—a grin meant to be both sardonic and seductive played on his lips, as if a session with a Company shrink came under the heading of indoor sport and she was fair game. He appeared taller, more assured, less agitated, completely in control of emotions that he could identify. His body language was new to her—his head was angled suggestively, his shoulders relaxed, one hand jingled the loose change in a trouser pocket. He walked with only the faintest trace of a limp. She could have sworn that his hair was combed differently, though she would have had to pull a photograph of Martin from the file folder to be sure, which is something she didn't want to do in front of him. Instead of sitting across the desk from her, as he usually did, he flopped gracefully into a chair next to the low table near the window, his legs extended and crossed casually at the ankles, and nodded at another chair, inviting her to join him, sure she would. When she did, she noticed him undressing her with his eyes as she came across the carpet; she saw him inspecting her thigh when she crossed her legs. She set the small tape recorder down and edged the microphone closer to Martin. He fixed his gaze on her eyes and she found herself toying with the joint on the fourth finger of her left hand where the gold ring used to be before the divorce.

"You're wearing perfume," he noted. "What is it?"

When she didn't respond, he tried another tack. "Is Treffler your married name?"

"No. I work under my maiden name."

"You don't wear a wedding band but I could tell you're married."

He gaze fell away from his. "What gave me away?"

"You sure you want to know?" he asked, clearly taunting her.

Why was Martin Odum coming on to her? she wondered. What had changed since the session the previous month? Leaning forward, aware that in this new incarnation he wouldn't miss the slight swell of her breasts above the scalloped blouse, she flipped a switch on the tape recorder. "Mind if I check your voice level again?"

"Be my guest." He clasped his hands behind his head and leaned back into them, thoroughly enjoying how uncomfortable he had managed to make her. "A woman, a dog, a walnut tree," he recited, pronouncing "dog" *dawg*, "the more you beat 'em, the better they be."

"That another line from Walt . . . from *Walter* Whitman?"

He laughed softly. "It's a ditty the boys used to sing around the campfire while they were waiting to cross the Rapahannock."

Suddenly it hit her. "You're not Martin Odum!"

"And you're not as thick as Martin says."

"You're the one who claims to have been at the battle of Fredericksburg," she breathed. "You're Lincoln Dittmann."

He only smiled.

"But why? What are you doing here?"

"Martin told you about my being at Fredericksburg but you didn't believe him. You thought he was making the whole thing up." Lincoln leaned forward, the humor gone from his eyes. "You went and hurt his feelings, Dr. Treffler. Shrinks are supposed to heal feelings, not hurt them. Martin sent me round to set the record straight."

Dr. Treffler understood that she was setting out into uncharted territory. "Okay, convince me Lincoln Dittmann was at the battle of Fredericksburg. What else did the boys talk about while they were waiting to cross the river?"

Lincoln stared out the window, his eyes wide, unblinking, unfocused. "They talked about home remedies for diarrhea, which many considered the arch enemy, more dangerous than Johnny Reb. They traded recipes for moonshine. I recall one lieutenant from the 70th Ohio concocted something he labeled 'Knock 'em stiff'—it consisted of bark juice, tar water, turpentine, brown sugar, lamp oil and alcohol. They argued whether, when they crossed the river and marched on Richmond and won the war, the slaves ought to be freed; so many were against, the few who were for were careful to keep their own counsel. They griped about having to pay $1.80 for a plug of tobacco. They griped about the Yankees who'd gone west to avoid the draft and claim free land while they were stuck on the Rapahannock fighting the Goddamn war. The griped about the factory-made shoddy—"

"Shoddy?"

"What we called *shoddy* was woolen yarn made from old clothing and then turned into material for uniforms that disintegrated under your fingers in a matter of weeks."

"What was your rank?"

Lincoln turned back to focus on Dr. Treffler. "I wasn't in the army."

"If you weren't in the army, what were you doing at Fredericksburg?"

"Fact is, I'd been working for Alan Pinkerton in Chicago. You ever heared of Pinkerton's detective agency?" When Dr. Treffler nodded, he said, "Thought you might have. Alan was employed by his friend Colonel McClellan to eliminate banditry from the railroads out west. When old Abe appointed the colonel to head the Army of the Potomac, McClellan brought along his friend Alan Pinkerton, who was using the pseudonym E.J. Allen at the time, if I remember right. And Alan brought along some of his operatives, me among them, to organize an intelligence service. Then came what the Federals called the battle of Antietam, after the stream, and the Confederates called the battle of Sharpsville, after the village. With the help of General Joe Hooker—who tore himself away from his camp followers, what we jokingly called *Hooker's girls* or just plain *hookers*, long enough to lead the attack on the right—McClellan won the day and Bobby Lee was obliged to pull his force, what was left of it, back into Virginia. Antietam was the first time I saw the elephant—"

"Saw the elephant?"

"That's how we described experiencing combat—you say you saw the elephant. After the battle, Alan sent several of us riding south to discern the Confederate order of battle, but that old snake in the grass Lee bamboozled us—he must have figured we could estimate his troop strength by counting the rations he issued, 'cause he doubled the rations and we doubled the size of his army and McClellan got cold feet and stayed put, which is when old Abe decided McClellan had got the slows and sent him packing back to Chicago. Alan Pinkerton went along with him but I stayed on to work for Lafayette Baker, who was setting up a Federal intelligence service in Washington. Which brings me to McClellan's successor, Ambrose Burnside, and Fredericksburg." Leaning forward, Lincoln picked up the small microphone and spoke into it. "A woman, a dog, a walnut tree, the more you beat 'em, the better they be. Hey, doc, what about you and me having dinner together when we're finished here?"

Bernice Treffler kept her face a blank and her voice neutral. "You'll understand that this is simply not possible. A psychiatrist cannot have a relationship with a client outside of working hours and still hope to maintain the distance she needs to evaluate the client."

"Where is it written there has to be a distance between you and the client? Some psychiatrists sleep with their patients in order to bridge this distance."

"That's not the way I function, Lincoln." She tried to make a joke out of it. "Maybe you need another psychiatrist—"

"You'll do fine."

"Why don't you go on with your story."

"*My story!* You think it's a story!" He set the microphone back on the table. "You still don't see that what I'm telling you really happened. To me. At Fredericksburg."

"Lincoln Dittmann taught history at a junior college," Dr. Treffler said patiently. "He turned his college thesis on the battle of Fredericksburg into a book and printed it himself, under the title *Cannon Fodder*, when he couldn't find an editor willing to publish the manuscript."

"There are things that happened at Fredericksburg you can't find in any history book, or *Cannon Fodder*, for that matter."

"Such as?"

Lincoln was angry now. "Alright. Burnside force-marched the Union Army down the Rapahannock, but wound up bivouacking across the river from Fredericksburg for ten long days waiting for the damn pontoon bridges to catch up with him. Lafayette Baker'd posted me to Burnside's staff—I was supposed to figure out the Confederate order of battle so Burnside could reckon on what was waiting for him once he got across the river. Armed with an English spyglass, I spent the better part of the first nine days aloft freezing my ass off in a hot-air balloon, but the mustard-thick haze hanging over the river never burned off and I couldn't make heads or tails of what was going on up on the ridgeline behind Fredericksburg. Which is why I decided to infiltrate the Confederate lines. I found a sunken fisherman's dingy and raised it with the help of some skirmishers and greased the oar-locks and set off before sunrise to cross the river, which was in flood, creating a margin of shallow marshes on either side. When my dingy couldn't make it as far as the shore, I pulled off my boots and socks and rolled up my trousers and climbed out and waded through the slime until I reached solid ground. I found myself on the slope below the lunatic asylum. The doctors and nurses had fled inland when Burnside's army appeared on the other side of the river, leaving the demented women to fend for themselves. They were leaning out of windows, some of them clothed, some buff naked, mesmerized by the sight of the Federal soldiers urinating into the river, also by the occa-sional mortar shot Yankee gunners lobbed across the Rapahannock and the ensuing explosions on the heights behind Fredericksburg; the demented women were sure something dreadful was about to happen, sure, too, that they were meant to witness it and spread the story, so one young lady with tufts of matted hair hanging over her bare breasts screeched to me from a window when I made my way up the hill past the asylum."

The memory of the poor lunatics trapped between the lines in their asylum set Lincoln to breathing hard through his nostrils. Dr. Treffler said, very quietly, "Want to take a break, Lincoln?"

He shook his head roughly. "I purloined an orderly's smock from the laundry shed behind the asylum and put it on and walked through Fredericksburg in the direction of Marye's Hill. The city was deserted except for sentinels who, seeing the white smock, took me for someone employed at the asylum. I made a mental note of everything I saw. Fredericksburg itself was obviously not going to be defended, despite the occasional Mississippi sharpshooter firing across the river from buildings along the waterfront. I made my way out of the city, past

buildings with greased paper serving as windows, past an emporium
with boards nailed over the doors and windows (as if this would stop
looters), and headed across the plain. I could see that no effort had
been made to dig trenches or pits, and I began to wonder if there was
to be a battle after all. Then I came to the sunken road under Marye's
Hill, with a stone wall running the length of it, and I knew there would
be a battle and that it would go against the Federals, for the sunken
road was acrawl with Confederates—there were sharpshooters polishing the brass scopes of their Whitworths and setting out the paper cartridges on top of the stone wall; there were short-muzzled cannon with
grape charges piled next to their wheels; there were officers afoot with
swords and long-muzzled pistols directing newly arrived troops into
the line; there were Confederate flags and unit flags furled and leaning
against trees so the Federals, when they finally appeared, would not
know what they were up against until it was too late to turn back. The
single unfurled flag visible to the naked eye belonged to the 24th
Georgians, known to be hard customers and surpassing marksmen
when sober. No way around the sunken road and its stone wall presented itself—to the right it was too swampy for a flanking movement,
to the left the road and wall went on forever. I was challenged by pickets several times but, making laughing reference to the lunatics, talked
my way past and continued up the hill. And back from the crest, out
of sight of Pinkerton men peering through spyglasses from balloons,
was the largest army I ever set eyes on. There were more cannon than
a body could count. Soldiers were watering down the road to suppress
the dust as teams of horses positioned the cannon behind freshly dug
earthenworks. A Confederate band belted out waltzes for the southern
gentlemen and ladies who had come down from Richmond to see the
battle. My footpath took me past a large gray tent set next to a copse
of stunted apple trees and I saw three generals poring over maps
stretched open on a trestle table. One, in a white uniform, I took for
Bobby Lee himself; the second, in homespun gray with plumes fluttering from his hat, I took for George Pickett (which meant that Pickett's
division had come up earlier than anticipated and was taking its place
in the line); the third, with a woman's woolen shawl draped over his
shoulders, I took to be Old Pete Longstreet. I was sorely tempted to try
for a closer look at the generals and acted upon this desire, which

proved to be my undoing. A young officer wearing a brand new uniform with a sash to hold his sword accosted me. My story about being the last orderly to abandon the lunatics to their asylum did not appear to persuade him and he set me to walking toward the divisional tent on the far side of Marye's Hill, him following close on my heels. As much as I ached to, I could not run for it—all he had to do was raise the alarum and a thousand rebels would have been upon me. Could I trouble you for a glass of water?"

"No problem." Dr. Treffler walked over to a sideboard and filled a glass from a plastic bottle and carried it back, aware that Lincoln's eyes never left her. Was he thinking of the young lunatic, leaning out the window with the matted hair covering her breasts? Was he regretting he didn't have a shrink who slept with her patients?

Lincoln drank off the glass of water in one long swallow and then ran his finger around the rim as he picked up the thread of his tale. "I was closely questioned by a stubby, hunch-shouldered officer with a shock of hair turned silver from age and battle fatigue, so I supposed because he walked with the aid of two wooden crutches. And when he didn't esteem my answers—I admitted to having been born and raised in Pennsylvania but claimed I'd gone south to defend state's rights and slavery, for who in his right mind wanted millions of freed slaves invading the north to take away our jobs—he had me stripped to the skin and began examining each item of clothing. Which is how he came across the watch fob decorated with the symbol of Alan Pinkerton's detective agency—an unblinking eye—that Alan himself had given me back in the days when we were chasing train robbers and cattle thieves. The old officer recognized it immediately and my efforts to make out that I had got it off one of the crazed women in the asylum fell short of convincing him. *You are a Federal spy,* he said, *caught behind our lines. Make your peace with your Maker for you will be executed at dawn.*"

Lincoln, reliving the episode, wiped perspiration from his forehead with the back of a wrist. "I was allowed to dress, after which they tied my ankles loosely so I could walk but not run and took me to a circle of hospital wagons and sat me down at a wooden crate inside one of them to write my last testament and any letters that I deemed necessary to deliver to friends or family. Night fell quickly at this time of the year. The aurora borealis, a rare sight in these latitudes, flickered like soundless cannon fire in the north; it didn't take much imagination to suppose a great war was being fought beyond the horizon. I was brought an oil lamp and a tin plate of hard crackers and water, but try as I might I was unable to swallow even the spittle in my mouth, the lump in my throat, which I identified as fear, being too big. I attempted to write my mother and father, and a girl I had been sweet on back in Pennsylvania, I wanted to tell them what had befallen me and so began: *I take the present opportunity of penning you a few lines, my health is good but it will not be so for long.* I was obliged to discontinue the letter because my brain, befuddled with chemicals released by fear, could not locate the words to describe my condition. I became convinced that it was all a terrible dream, that any moment I would become too frightened to continue dreaming; that I would force myself through the membrane that separated sleep from wakefulness and wipe the sweat from my brow and, still under the spell of the nightmare, have trouble falling back to sleep. But the wooden crate felt damp and cold under my palm and a whiff of sulfurous air—in the next wagon the surgeons, amputating the leg of a boy who had been pinned under an overturned cannon, were dousing the stump with sulfur—stung my lungs and the pain brought home to me that what had happened, and what was about to happen, were no dream."

Dr. Treffler, caught in the web of Lincoln's tale, leaned toward him when he stopped talking. "Admit it," he said with a sneer, "it's beginning to dawn on you that I am recounting the truth." When she nodded carefully he went on. "I was expecting execution by hanging but the old officer with the silver hair and crutches had something more dreadful in store. At first light my wrists and elbows were bound behind my back with a length of telegraph wire. I was taken from the hospital wagon by two men wearing the striped shirts of penitentiary guards and paraded to the other side of Marye's Hill and the turnpike known as Plank Road, called so because the craters gouged by several dozen exploding Federal mortar rounds had been too deep to fill with earth and had been covered over with planking to make the road passable. Standing at the lip of one such crater, which was roughly the size of a large wagon wheel, with the planks intended to patch it stacked at the side of the turnpike, it struck me what my interrogator intended when he spoke of execution. One of the penitentiary guards produced a square of strawboard with the words "The spy Dittmann" lettered on it in India ink and attached the sign with cotter pins to the back of my shoddy jacket. I divined who the author of my unusual execution was when I caught sight of Stonewall Jackson, known to be a religious fanatic, sitting his horse on a rise above me, a look of unadulterated malevolence on his face. He removed the cigar from his mouth and studied me for a long while, as if he were committing me and the moment to memory. He angrily flicked cigar ashes as he issued instructions to an aide. I was too far away to make out more than a few words. *Buried, that's what I want, but alive* . . . Hundreds of Confederates on the side of the hill had stopped what they were doing to watch the execution. My interrogator plucked a cigarette from the mouth of one of the penitentiary guards and, making his way to me on his crutches, wedged it between my parched lips. *It is a matter of tradition,* he said. *A man condemned to death is entitled to a last cigarette.* Trembling, I puffed on the cigarette. The act of smoking, and the smoke cauterizing my throat, distracted me. My interrogator stared at the ash, waiting for it to buckle under its own weight and fall so they could get on with the execution. Sucking on the cigarette, I became aware of the ash, too. Life itself seemed to ride on it. Defying gravity, defying sense, it grew longer than the unsmoked part of the cigarette."

"And then?"

"And then a whisper of wind coming off the river brought with it the distant sound of a brass band playing Yankee Doodle. Under cover of darkness the Federals had finally thrown their pontoon bridges across the river and were starting to come over in force. There were scattered shots from Fredericksburg as the Confederate rear guard pretended to put up a fight to suck the Federals into the trap that awaited them once they captured Fredericksburg and started across the plain Richmond-bound. The notes of Yankee Doodle and the hollow reports of muskets set everyone to peering toward the river. Bobby Lee reined up next to Jackson, who touched his hat in salute. They talked for a moment, Lee pointing out the Chatham Mansion, which served as Burnside's command post, within eyeshot on the other side of the river. And then Lee happened to glance in my direction. His

eyes fixed on me and he called, *What the blazes is going on down there?*
My interrogator called up that I was a Federal spy caught behind the
Confederate lines the previous evening; that they were about to bury
me alive as a warning to others. Lee remarked something to Jackson,
then stood in his stirrups and, removing his white hat, shouted down,
There will be enough killing on these fields today to last a man a lifetime.
Tie him to a tree and let him watch the battle, and set him free when it
is over. Which is how I came to see the elephant again—to witness the
carnage that unfolded below Marye's Hill that terrible December day.
Burnside' army burst out of Fredericksburg onto the plain and
formed up. The 114th Pennsylvania Zouaves with their white headbands were the first to charge the stone wall along the sunken road—
they came on with pennants flying while a drummer boy set the
cadence for the attack until his head was severed from his body by a
cannon ball. It was a massacre from start to finish. Through the afternoon wave upon wave of Federals charged the sunken road, only to be
cut down by a hail of minié balls I counted fourteen assaults in all,
but not a one of them made it as far as the wall. The cause was so hap-
less, the Confederates looking down from the hill took to cheering the
courage of the Federals. I could see the Rebel sharpshooters dipping
their hands in buckets of water so they could load their Whitworths,
scalding hot from being shot so much, without blistering their skin.
At one point in the afternoon I could make out groups of Federals trying to take cover behind some brick houses on the plain but the
Yankee cavalry, using the flats of sabres, forced them back to the battle. It was a Godawful thing to behold—there have been days since
when I wished they'd gone ahead and buried me alive so that the sight
and sound of battle would not be graven on my brain."

"And they let you cross the battlefield to your lines when it was
over?"

"As for the field of battle, the less said about it the better. The temperature that night dipped below freezing and my breath came out
from between my chattering teeth in great white plumes as I negotiated its pitfalls. I ripped the square of strawboard off my back and
started toward the flames I could see burning in Fredericksburg, tripping over the bloated bodies of horses and men, stumbling onto limb-
less corpses entangled at the bottom of shell craters. Even in the cold

of winter there were horseflies drawn to the blood oozing from wounds. The maimed Federals who were still alive dragged the dead into heaps and burrowed under the corpses to keep warm. To my ever-lasting regret I could do nothing for them. I stopped to cradle a dying soldier who had a slip of paper with his name and address pinned to the back of his blouse. He shivered and murmured *Sarah, dearest* and expired in my arms. I took the paper, meaning to send it to his next of kin but somehow lost it in the confusion of the night. Riderless horses pawed at the frozen ground looking for fodder, but the only fodder at Fredericksburg on 13 December 1862 was cannon fodder."

"You reached the town—"

"Fredericksburg resembled Sodom. Buildings had been set ablaze by the retreating Federals, the emporium lay gutted, its furniture and wares littering the planks of the sidewalk and the dirt in the street. What was left of silken gowns that had been cut up for handkerchiefs and towels hung limply from placards projecting over the entrances to stores. Mad women from the asylum, in sooty shifts and bare footed, picked through the debris, collecting pocket mirrors and colored rib-bons and fine ladies hats imported from Paris France, which they pulled over their matted hair. Two of them were struggling to carry off a Regulator clock. I was surely one of the last to cross the bridge because the engineers began to unfasten the pontoons behind me. On the other side I wandered from campfire to campfire, past dispirited troops dozing on the ground, past pickets sleeping on their feet. I must have become feverish because much of what happened to me subsequent to the retreat across the pontoon bridge is disjointed and fuzzy in my head. I seem to remember great lines of woebegone sol-diers trudging back toward Washington, the wounded piled three and four deep in open carts drawn by mules, the dead buried in shallow graves where they succumbed. When I came awake, I don't know how many days later, I found myself on a cot stained with dried blood in a field hospital. Doctors decided I was suffering from hypochondria, what your fancy doctors call depression nowadays. A gentleman with a kindly face and a soiled white shirt open at the throat was sponging my chest and neck with vinegar to bring down the fever. We got to talking. He told me his name was Walter. Only later did I discover him to be the celebrated Brooklyn poet Whitman, scouring the field hospitals for his brother George, who'd been listed as wounded in the battle. Luck would have it, he'd found him in the same tent as me. One morning, when I felt stronger, Walter put his arm around my waist and helped me out of the tent into the sunlight. We sat, only the two of us, with our backs to a stack of fresh pine coffins. I remember Walter staring at the heap of amputated limbs behind the tent and opining, *Fredericksburg is the most complete piece of mismanagement perhaps ever yet known in the earth's wars.* After some while orderlies appeared from the tent carrying three stretchers with corpses on them and set them on the ground to attend burial. The dead men were covered with blankets, with the toes of their stockings sticking out and pinned together. Pushing himself to his feet, Walter walked over to the bodies and, squatting, lifted aside the blanket from one and looked for a long, long time at the boy's dead face. When he sat back down next to me, he pulled a notebook from a pocket inside his jacket and, licking the stub of a pencil, began to write in it. When he finished I asked him what he'd written and he read it off and the words stuck with me all these years." Lincoln shut his eyes—to keep back tears (so it seemed to Dr. Treffler)—as he dredged up Walter Whitman's lines. *Sight at daybreak,—in camp in front of the hospital tent on a stretcher (three dead men lying,) each with a blanket spread over him—I lift up one and look at the young man's face, calm and yellow,—'tis strange! (Young man: I think this face of yours the face of my dead Christ!).*

Lincoln, drained of arrogance, looked at Dr. Treffler as he recited in a sing-song whisper, "A woman, a dog, a walnut tree, the more you beat 'em—I can't recall the rest."

"I believe you, Lincoln. I can see that you really were at Fredericksburg." When he just sat there, his chin on his chest, breathing unevenly, she said, "Shalimar."

"What?"

"That's the name of the perfume I'm wearing. Shalimar."

1994: BERNICE TREFFLER LOSES A PATIENT

D R. TREFFLER TURNED AROUND THE STATUE OF NATHAN HALE outside the Central Intelligence Agency's headquarters at Langley, Virginia, studying the expression on the face of the young colonial spy from various angles, trying to imagine what might have been going through his mind as he was being led to execution. It occurred to her that nothing had been going through his mind; perhaps he had been too distracted by the lump in his throat, which is called fear, to think clearly. She couldn't remember if Nathan had seen the elephant (though the term probably didn't come into use until the Civil War) before he set off on his mission behind British lines in Manhattan Island. She wondered if the British executioners wore striped shirts; wondered, too, if they had wedged a cigarette between his lips before they hanged him on the Post Road, what today is Third Avenue in Manhattan. *It is a matter of tradition*, Lincoln Dittmann had remembered the executioner saying. *A man condemned to death is entitled to a last cigarette.*

A whey-faced young man with a laminated card pinned to the breast pocket of his three-piece suit approached. "He was the first in a long line of Americans who died spying for our country," he noted, looking up at Nathan's wrists bound behind his back. "You must be Bernice Treffler." When she said *In the flesh* he asked to see her hospital identity card and driver's license and carefully matched the photos against her face. She peeled off her sunglasses to make it easier for him. Apparently satisfied, he returned the cards. "I'm Karl Tripp, Mrs. Quest's executive assistant, which is a fancy name for her cat's-paw. I'm sorry if we've kept you waiting. If you'll come with me . . ."

"No problem," said Dr. Treffler, falling in alongside her escort. She was mesmerized by the laminated card on the suit jacket with his photo and name and ID number on it. If lightning struck him right now, right here, would she have the good sense to tear it off and send it to his next of kin?

"First visit to Langley?" he asked as he showed his ID to the uniformed guard at the turnstile, along with the signed authorization to bring in a woman named Bernice Treffler.

"I'm afraid it is," she said.

The guard issued a visitor's pass that expired in one hour, and noted Dr. Treffler's name and the number of the pass in a log book. Karl Tripp pinned the pass to the lapel of her jacket and the two of them pushed through the turnstile and made their way down a long corridor to a bank of elevators. She started to walk into the first one that turned up but Tripp tugged on her sleeve, holding her back. "We're taking the express to the seventh floor," he whispered.

Several young men relegated to the plebeian elevators eyed the well dressed woman waiting for the patrician elevator, wondering who she might be, for the seventh floor was, in naval terminology, admiral's country and outsiders went there (the elevator didn't stop at other floors) by invitation only. When the door finally opened on the seventh floor, Tripp had to walk Dr. Treffler through another security check. He led her down a battleship-gray corridor to a door marked "Authorized DDO staff only," unlocked it with a key at the end of a chain attached to his belt and motioned her to a seat at a crescent-shaped desk. "Coffee? Tea? Diet coke?"

"I'm fine. Thanks."

Tripp disappeared, closing the door behind him. Treffler looked around, wondering if this tiny windowless cubbyhole could really be the office of someone as important as Crystal Quest, whom she had spoken to several times on the phone since she first began treating Martin Odum. A moment later a narrow door hidden in the paneling behind the desk opened and Mrs. Quest appeared from a larger, airier office. She was obviously a good deal older than she sounded on the phone, and wearing a pantsuit with wide lapels that did nothing to emphasize her femininity. Her hair cropped short, looked like rusting gunmetal. "I'm Crystal Quest," she announced matter of factly, lean-

ing over the desk to swipe at Dr. Treffler's palm with her own, then
sinking back into the wicker swivel chair. She reached into the bottom
drawer of the desk and pulled out a thermos. "Frozen daiquiris," she
explained, producing two ordinary kitchen tumblers but filling only
one of them when her visitor waved her off. "So you're Bernice
Treffler," she said. "You sound older on the phone."

"And you sound younger—Sorry, I didn't mean . . ." She laughed
nervously. "Heck of a way to start a conversation."

"No offense taken."

"None intended, obviously."

"Which brings us to Martin Odum."

"I sent you an interim report—"

"Prefer to hear it from the horse's mouth." Quest flashed a twisted smile. "No offense intended."

"Martin Odum is suffering from what we call Multiple
Personality Disorder." Dr. Treffler could hear Crystal Quest grinding
slivers of ice between her molars. "At the origin of this condition is a
trauma," the psychiatrist continued, "more often than not a childhood
trauma involving sexual abuse. The trauma short-circuits the patient's
narrative memory and leads to the development of multiple personalities, each with its own memories and skills and emotions and even
language abilities. Often a patient suffering from MPD switches from
one personality to another when he or she comes under stress."

Crystal Quest fingered a chunk of ice out of the kitchen tumbler
and popped it into her mouth. "Has he been able to identify the
trauma?"

Dr. Treffler cleared her throat. "The original trauma, the root
cause of these multiple personalities, remains shrouded in mystery, I'm
sorry to report." She could have sworn Crystal Quest looked relieved.
"Which is not to say that with more treatment it won't surface. I
would very much like to get to the trauma, not only for the sake of
the patient's mental health but because of the medical paper I plan to
write—"

"There won't be any medical paper, Dr. Treffler. Not now, not
ever. Nor will there be additional treatment. How many of these multiple personalities have you detected?"

Dr. Treffler made no effort to hide her disappointment. "In

Martin Odum's case," she replied stiffly, "I've been able to identify three distinct alter personalities which the patient refers to as legends, a term you will surely be familiar with. There's Martin Odum, for starters. Then there is an Irishman named Dante Pippen. And finally there's a Civil War historian who goes by the name of Lincoln Dittmann."

"Any hint of a fourth legend?"

"No. Is there a fourth legend, Mrs. Quest?"

Quest ignored the question. "How many of these legends have you personally encountered?"

"There is Martin Odum, of course. And at the most recent session, which took place last week, I came face to face with Lincoln Dittmann."

"How could you be sure it was Lincoln?"

"The person who came into my office was quite different from the Martin Odum I know. When I realized I was confronting Lincoln Dittmann and said so, he came clean."

"Cut to the chase. Is Martin Odum off his rocker? Should we commit him to an institution?"

"You can have it either way, Mrs. Quest. Lincoln Dittmann is certainly off his rocker, as you put it. He's convinced he was present at the battle of Fredericksburg during the Civil War. Say the word and I can get a dozen doctors to certify he's clinically insane. If you wanted to, you could have Lincoln Dittmann—or his alter ego, the Irishman Dante Pippen—committed indefinitely."

"What about Martin Odum?'

"Martin is distressed by his inability to figure out which of the three working identities is the real him. But he functions reasonably well, he is quite capable of making a living, of fending for himself, perhaps even of having a relationship with a woman as long as she is able to live with the ambiguity at the heart of his persona."

"In short, nobody who meets Martin in a bar or at a dinner party would think he was mentally deranged?"

Dr. Treffler nodded carefully. "As long as he is unable to dredge up the details of the original childhood trauma, he will remain in this state of suspended animation—functional enough to muddle through, vaguely anguished."

"Okay. I want you to drop this case. I'll send my man Tripp around to your clinic to collect any and all notes you might have made during the sessions. I don't need to remind you that the whole affair is classified top secret and not to be discussed with a living soul."

Dr. Treffler remembered something she'd told Martin at one of their early sessions. "Even if I change the names to protect the guilty?"

"This is not a laughing matter, Dr. Treffler." Crystal Quest stabbed at a button on the console. "Tripp will see you to the lobby. Appreciate your coming by."

"That's it?"

Mrs. Quest heaved herself out of the wicker chair. "That's definitely it," she agreed.

Dr. Treffler rose to her feet and stood facing her, her eyes bright with discovery. "You never wanted me to identify the trauma. You don't want Martin to get well."

Quest sniffed at the scent of perfume in the windowless cubbyhole; it startled her to realize that Bernice Treffler's professional psyche reeked of femaleness, which was more than she could say for herself. "You're in over your head," the Deputy Director of Operations testily informed her visitor. "In Martin's case, getting well could turn out to be fatal."

1997: MARTIN ODUM DISCOVERS THE KATOVSKY GAMBIT

STEPPING OFF THE CURB IN FRONT OF THE CROWDED AIRPORT terminal, Martin raised an index finger belt high to flag down one of the freelancers cruising the area in search of customers who didn't want to deal with the doctored meters on the licensed cabs. Within seconds an antique Zil pulled to a stop in front of him and the passenger window wound down.

"*Kuda.*" demanded the driver, an elderly gentleman wearing a thin tie and a checkered jacket with wide lapels, along with a pair of rimmed eyeglasses that were the height of fashion during the Soviet era.

"Do you speak English?" Martin asked.

"*Nyet, nyet, nye govoryu po-Angliski,*" the driver insisted, and then began to speak pidgin English with obvious relish. "Which whereabouts are you coming to, comrade visitor?" he asked.

"A village not far from Moscow named Prigorodnaia. Ever hear of it?"

The driver rocked his head from side to side. "Everyone over fifty knows where is Prigorodnaia," he announced. "You have been there before?"

"No. Never."

"Well, it's not stubborn to find. Direction Petersburg, off the Moscow-Petersburg highway. Big shots once owned dachas there but they are all late and lamented. Only little shots still live in Prigorodnaia."

"That's me," Martin said with a tired grin. "A little shot. How much?"

"Around trip, one hundred dollars U.S., half now, half when you resume to Moscow."

Martin settled onto the seat next to the driver and produced two twenties and a ten—which was what Dante Pippen had paid the Alawite prostitute Djamillah in Beirut several legends back. Then, popping another aspirin from the jar he'd bought at the airport pharmacy to dull the pain from the cracked rib, he watched as the driver piloted the Zil through rush-hour traffic toward Moscow.

After a time Martin said, "You look a little old to be freelancing as a taxi."

"I am one miserable pensioner," the driver explained. "The automobile belongs to my first wife's youngest son, who was my stepson before I divorced his mother. He was one of those smart capitalists who bought up industry privatization coupons distributed to the proletarian public, and then turned around and sold them for an overweight profit to the new Russian mafioso. Which is how he became owner of an old but lovingly restored Zil automobile. He borrows it to me when the ridiculous rent on my privatized apartment needs to get paid at the start of the month."

"What did you do before you retired?"

The driver looked quickly at his passenger out of the corner of an eye. "Believe it or not, no skin off my elbow if you don't, I was a famous, even infamous, chess grandmaster—ranked twenty-third in Soviet Union in 1954 when I was a nineteen-year-old Komsomol champion."

"Why infamous?"

"It was said of me that chess drove me mad as a hatter. The critics who said it did not comprehend that, as a chess-playing psychologist once pointed out, chess cannot drive people mad; chess is what keeps mad people sane. You don't by any chance play chess?"

"As a matter of fact, I used to. I don't get much of a chance anymore."

"You have heard maybe of the Katovsky gambit?"

"Actually, that rings a bell."

"It's me, the bell that's ringing," the driver said excitedly. "Hippolyte Katovsky in the flesh and blood. My gambit was the talk of tournaments when I played abroad—Belgrade, Paris, London, Milan, once even Miami in the state of Caroline the North, another time Peking when the Chinese Peoples Republic was still a socialist ally and Mao Tse-tung a comrade in arms."

Martin noticed the old man's eyes brimming with nostalgia. "What exactly was the Katovsky gambit?" he inquired.

Katovsky leaned angrily on the horn when a taxi edged in ahead of him. "Under Soviets, drivers like that would have been sent to harvest cotton in Central Asia. Russia is not the same since our communists lost power. Ha! We gained the freedom to die of hunger. The Katovsky gambit involved offering a poisoned pawn and positioning both bishops on the queen's side to control the diagonals while knights penetrate on the king's side. Swept opponents away for two years until R. Fischer beat me in Reykjavik by ignoring the poisoned pawn and castling on the queen's side after I positioned my bishops."

His lips moving as he played out a gambit in his head, Katovsky fell silent and Martin didn't interrupt the game. The Zil passed an enormous billboard advertising Marlboro cigarettes and metro stations disgorging swarms of workers. Fatigue overcame Martin (he'd been traveling for two days and two nights to get from Hrodna to Moscow) and he closed his eyes for a moment that stretched into twenty minutes. When he opened them again the Zil was on the ring road. Giant cranes filled what Martin could see of the skyline. New buildings with glass facades that reflected the structures across the street were shooting up on both sides of the wide artery. In one of them he could make out automobiles barreling by, but there were so many of them on the road he couldn't be sure which one was his. Traffic slowed to a crawl where men in yellow hard hats were digging up a section of the roadway with jackhammers, then sped up again as the Zil spilled through the funnel. Up ahead an overhead sign indicated the junction for the Petersburg highway.

"Turnoff for Prigorodnaia very shortly now," Katovsky said. "I was one of Boris Spassky's advisors when he lost to Fischer in 1972. If only he would have followed my advice he could have vacuumed the carpet with Fischer, who made blunder after blunder. Ha! They say the winner in any game of chess is the one who makes the next to last blunder. Here—here is the Prigorodnaia turnoff. Oh, how time seeps through your fingers when you are not closing your hand into a fist—

I remember this road before it was paved. In 1952 and part of 1953, I was driven by a chauffeur to Lavrenti Pavlovich Beria's dacha in Prigorodnaia every Sunday to teach chess to his wife. The lessons came to an end when Comrade Stalin died and Beria, who behind Stalin's back created the gulags and purged the most loyal comrades, became executed."

As Katovsky headed down the spur, past a sign that read "Prigorodnaia 7 kilometers," the cracked rib in Martin's chest began to ache again. Curiously, the pain seemed . . . *familiar.*

But how in the name of God could pain be familiar?

A pulse, the harbinger of a splitting headache, began to beat in Martin's temples and he brought his fingers up to knead his brow. He found himself slipping into and out of roles. He could hear Lincoln Dittmann lazily murmuring a verse of poetry.

. . . the silent cannons bright as gold rumble
lightly over the stones. Silent cannons, soon
to cease your silence, soon unlimber'd to begin
the red business.

And the voice of the poet wearing the soiled white shirt open at the throat.

Sight at daybreak,—in camp in front of the
hospital tent on a stretcher (three dead men lying,)
each with a blanket spread over him

Other voices, barely audible, played in the lobe of his brain where memory resided. Gradually he began to distinguish fragments of dialogue.

Gentlemen and ladies . . . overlooked Martin Odum's original biography.

His mother was—

. . . was Polish . . . Immigrated . . . after the Second . . .

Maggie's on to . . .

. . . staring us in the face . . .

The driver of the Zil glanced at his passenger. "Look at those chimneys spewing filthy white smoke," he said.

"Uh-huh."

"That's a paper factory—built after Beria's time, unnecessary to say—he never would have permitted it. Now you are knowing why only little shots live here nowadays—the stench of sulfur fills the air every hour of every day of every year. The local peasants swear you get used to it—that in time you only feel discomfortable when you breathe air that is not putrid."

Even the reek of sulfur stinging Martin's nostrils seemed familiar.

"Comrade Beria played chess," the driver remembered. "Badly. So badly that it required all my cleverness to lose to him."

. . . Lincoln Dittmann was in Triple . . . overheard an old lottery vender talking Polish to a hooker . . . catch the drift . . .

. . . his mother used to read him bedtime stories in Polish . . .

Martin found himself breathing with difficulty—he felt as if he were gagging on memories that needed to be disgorged before he could get on with his life.

Ahead, an abandoned custom's station with a faded red star painted above the door loomed at the side of the road. Across from it and down a shallow slope, a river rippled through its bed. It must have been in flood because there appeared to be a margin of shallow marshes on either side; grass could be seen undulating in the current.

Martin heard a voice he recognized as his own say aloud, "The river is called the *Lesnia,* which is the name of the woods it meanders through as it skirts Prigorodnaia."

Katovsky slowed the Zil. "I thought you said me you never been to Prigorodnaia."

"Never. No."

"Explain, then, how you come to know the name of the river?"

Martin, concentrating on the voices in his head, didn't reply.

He aced Russian at college . . . speaking it with a Polish accent.

. . . bringing his Polish up to snuff, they could also work on his Russian.

"Pull over," Martin ordered.

Katovsky braked the car to a stop, two wheels on the tarmac, two wheels on the soft shoulder. Martin jumped from the car and started walking down the middle of the paved road toward Prigorodnaia. Off to his left, high on the slope near a copse of stunted apple trees, he could see a line of whitewashed beehives. His game leg and broken ribs ached, the migraine lurking behind his brow throbbed as he made his way across a landscape that seemed painfully familiar even though he had never set eyes on it.

. . . Jozef as a first name?
Half of Poland is named Jozef.
. . . precisely the point . . .
I happen to be rereading Kafka . . .
. . . suggest a Polish-sounding variation. Kafkor.

Martin detected an unevenness in the tarmac under his feet and, looking down, saw that a section of roadway, roughly the size of a large tractor tire, had been crudely repaved. It had been smoothed over, but the surface was lumpy and the seam was clearly visible. Gaping at the round section of road, he suddenly felt dizzy—he sank onto his knees and looked over his shoulder at the Zil drawing closer to him. His eyes widened in terror as he felt himself being transported back in time through a mustard-thick haze of memory. He saw things he recognized but his brain, befuddled with chemicals released by fear, could no longer locate the words to describe them: the twin stacks spewing plumes of dirty white smoke, the abandoned custom's station with a faded red star painted above the door, the line of whitewashed bee-hives on a slope near a copse of stunted apple trees. And then, vanquishing terror only to confront a new enemy, madness, he could have sworn he saw an elephant striding over the brow of the hill.

The old man driving the Zil was standing alongside the car, one hand on the open door, calling plaintively to his passenger. "I could have crushed Beria every time," he explained, "but I thought I would live longer if I came in second."

The voices in Martin's skull grew louder.

. . . studied Kafka at the Janiellonian University in Kraków.

. . . worked summers as a guide at Auschwitz.

. . . job in the Polish tourist bureau in Moscow . . . contact with the DDO target without too much difficulty.

Question of knowing where this Samat character hangs out . . .

Martin, his facial muscles contorting, heard himself whisper, "*Poshol ty na khuy.*" He articulated each of the O's in "*Poshol.*" "*Go impale yourself on a prick.*"

Pushing himself to his feet, feeling as if he were trapped in a terrible dream, Martin stumbled down the paved spur toward Prigorodnaia. Could he have met Samat before? He had a vision of himself leaning on the bar of a posh watering hole on Bolshaya

Kommunisticheskaya called the Commercial Club. In his mind's eye he could make out the thin figure of a man settling onto the stool next to him. Of medium height with a pinched, mournful face, he wore suspenders that kept his trousers hiked high on his waist, and a midnight blue Italian suit jacket draped cape-like over a starched white shirt, which was tieless and buttoned up to a very prominent Adam's apple. The initials "S" and "U-Z" were embroidered on the pocket of the shirt. Martin saw himself placing on the burnished mahogany of the bar a Bolshoi ticket that had been torn in half. From a jacket pocket the thin man produced another torn ticket. The two halves matched perfectly.

Moving his lips like a ventriloquist, Samat could be heard mumbling, *What took you so long? I was told to expect the cutout to make contact with me here last week.*

It takes time to establish a cover, to rent an apartment, to make it seem as if we are meeting by chance.

My uncle Tzvetan wants to see you as soon as possible. He has urgent messages he must send to Langley. He wants assurances he will be exfiltrated if things turn bad. He wants to be sure the people you work for lay in the plumbing for the exfiltration before it is needed.

How do I meet him?

He lives in a village not far from Moscow. It's called Prigorodnaia. I invite you to his dacha for the weekend. We will tell everyone we were roommates at the Forestry Institute. We studied computer science together, in case anyone should ask.

I don't know anything about computers.

Except for me, neither does anyone else at Prigorodnaia.

Martin caught sight of the low wooden houses on the edge of the village ahead, each with its small fenced vegetable garden, several with a cow or a pig tethered to a tree. A burly peasant splitting logs on a stump looked up and appeared to freeze. The large axe slipped from his fingers as he gaped at the visitor. He backed away from Martin, as he would from a ghost, then turned and scampered along the path that ended at the small church with paint peeling from its onion domes. Nearing the church, Martin noticed a patch of terrain behind the cemetery that had been leveled and cemented over—a great circle had been whitewashed onto the surface blackened by engine exhaust.

An Orthodox priest wearing a washed-out black robe so short it left his bare matchstick-thin ankles and Nike running shoes exposed stood before the doors of the church. He held a minuscule wooden cross high over his head as men and women, alerted by the log splitter, drifted through the village lanes toward the church.

"Is it really you, Jozef?" the priest demanded.

As Martin drew nearer many of the women, whispering to each other, crossed themselves feverishly.

Martin approached the priest. "Has Samat come back to Prigorodnaia?" he asked.

"Come and departed in his helicopter. Donated this cross, fabricated from the wood of the True Cross of Zuzovka, to our church here in Prigorodnaia, where his sainted mother prays daily for his soul. For yours, too."

"Is he in danger?"

"No more, no less than we were after it was discovered that the planks over the crater in the spur had been removed and the man buried alive had gone missing."

Martin understood that he was supposed to know what the priest was talking about. "Who protected Samat?" he asked.

"His uncle, Tzvetan Ugor-Zhilov, the one we call the *Oligarkh*, protected Samat."

"And who protected his uncle?"

The priest shook his head. "Organizations too powerful to have their names spoken aloud."

"And who protected you when you removed the planks over the crater and freed the man buried alive?"

"Almighty God protected us," said the priest, and he crossed himself in the Orthodox style with his free hand.

Martin looked up at the onion domes, then back at the priest. "I want to talk to Samat's mother," he announced, thinking she might be among the women watching from the path.

"She lives alone in the *Oligarkh's* dacha," the priest said.

"Kristyna is a raving lunatic," said the peasant who had been splitting logs. Crossing themselves again, the other peasants nodded in agreement.

"And where is the *Oligarkh*, then?" Martin thought to ask.

"Why, none of us can say where the *Oligarkh* went to when he quit Prigorodnaia."

"And when did the *Oligarkh* leave Prigorodnaia?"

"No one knows for sure. One day he was here, struggling down the path near the river on aluminum crutches, his bodyguards following behind, his Borzois dancing ahead, the next the dacha was stripped of its furnishings and echoed with emptiness, and only a single candle burned in a downstairs window during the long winter night."

Martin started toward the sprawling dacha with the wooden crow's-nest rising above the white birches that surrounded the house. The peasants blocking the path gave way to let him through; several reached out to touch an arm and a toothless old woman cackled, "Back from the dead and the buried, then." Gaunt chickens and a rooster with resplendent plumes scrambled out from under Martin's feet, stirring up fine dust from the path. Drawn by curiosity, the villagers and the priest, still holding aloft the sliver of a cross, trailed after him, careful to keep a respectful distance.

When Martin reached the wooden fence surrounding the *Oligarkh*'s dacha, he thought he could make out a woman singing to herself. Unlatching the gate and circling around toward the back of the dacha, he stepped carefully through a neatly tended garden, with alternating furrows of vegetables and sunflowers, until he spotted the source of the singing. An old and frail crone, wearing a threadbare shift and walking barefoot, was filling a plastic can with rainwater from a barrel set under a gutter of the dacha. Long scraggly white hair plunged across her pale skin, which was stretched tightly over her facial bones, and she had to stab it away from her eyes when she caught sight of Martin to get a better look at him. "Tzvetan, as always, was correct," she said. "You will have been better able to survive the winter once the hole was covered with snow, though I was dead set against their burying you before you had eaten your lunch."

"You know who I am?" Martin asked.

"You didn't used to ask me silly questions, Jozef. I know you as well as I know my own son, Samat; as well as I knew his father, who hibernated to Siberia during the time of Stalin and never returned. Curious, isn't it, how our lives were utterly and eternally defined by

Stalin's whimsical brutality. I knew you would come back, dear Jozef. But what on earth took you so long? I expected you would surely return to Prigorodnaia after the first thaw of the first winter." The old woman set down her watering can and, taking Martin's hand in hers, led him across the garden to the back door of the dacha. "You always liked your tea and jam at this hour. You will need a steaming cup to see you through the morning."

Kristyna pushed through a screen door hanging half off of its hinges and, slipping her soiled feet into a pair of felt slippers, shuffled through a series of deserted rooms to the kitchen, all the while glancing over her shoulder to be sure Martin was still behind her. Using both thin arms, she worked the hand pump until water gushed from the spigot. She filled a blackened kettle and put it to boil on one of the rusting electric plaques set on the gas stove that no longer functioned. "I will fetch your favorite jam from the preserves in the larder of the cellar," she announced. "Dearest Jozef, don't disappear again. Promise me?" Almost as if she couldn't bear to hear him refuse, she pulled up a trap door and, securing it with a dog's leash, disappeared down a flight of steps.

Martin wandered through the ground floor of the dacha, his footfalls echoing from the bare walls of the empty rooms. Through the sulfur-stained panes of the windows he could make out the priest and his flock of faithful gathered at the fence, talking earnestly among themselves. The double living room with an enormous stone chimney on either end gave onto a study filled with wall-to-wall shelves devoid of books, and beyond that a small room with a low metal field-hospital cot set next to a small chimney filled with scraps of paper and dried twigs waiting to be burned. Half a dozen empty perfume bottles were set out on the mantle. A small pile of women's clothing was folded neatly on an upside down wooden crate with the words "Ugor-Zhilov" and "Prigorodnaia" stenciled on several of its sides. A dozen or so picture postcards were tacked to the door that led to a toilet. Martin drew closer to the door and examined them. They'd been sent from all over the world. One showed the duty-free shop at Charles de Gaulle airport in Paris, another the Wailing Wall in Jerusalem, a third a bridge spanning the Vltava River in Prague, still another Buckingham Palace in London. The topmost postcard on the door was a photograph of a family walking down a paved country road past two identical clapboard farm houses built very close to each other. Across the road, a weathered barn stood on a small rise, an American eagle crafted out of metal sitting atop the ornate weather vane jutting from the mansard roof. The people pictured on the postcard were dressed in clothing farmers might have worn going to church two hundred years before—the men and boys were attired in black trousers and black suit jackets and straw hats, the women and girls were wearing ankle length gingham dresses and laced-up high shoes and bonnets tied under the chin.

Martin pried out the tack with his fingernails and turned over the postcard. There was no date on it; the printed caption identifying the picture on the postcard had been scuffed off with a knife blade, the post office cancellation across the stamp read "fast New York." "Mama dearest," someone had written in Russian, "I am alive and well in America the Beautiful do not worry your head for me only keep singing when you weed the vegetable garden which is how I see you in my mind's eye." It was signed, "Your devoted S."

The old woman could be heard calling from the kitchen. "Jozef, my child, where have you gone off to? Come take tea."

Pocketing the postcard, Martin retraced his steps. In the kitchen the old woman, using a torn apron as a potholder, was filling two cups with an infusion that turned out to have been brewed from carrot peelings because, for her, tea had become too expensive. She settled onto a three-legged milking stool, leaving the only chair in the room for her visitor. Martin pulled it up to the table covered with formica and sat across from her. The woman kept both of her hands clasped around the cracked mug as she summoned memories and gently rocked her head from side to side at the thought of them. Her lidded eyes flitted from one object to another, like a butterfly looking for a leaf on which to settle. "I recall the day Samat brought you back from Moscow, Jozef. It was a Tuesday. Ah, you are surprised. The reason I remember it was a Tuesday is because that was the day the woman from the village came to do laundry—she was too terrified to use the electric washing machine Samat brought from GUM and scrubbed everything in a shallow reach of the river. You and Samat had been roommates in a school somewhere, so he said when he introduced you to his uncle's entourage. Later, Tzvetan took you aside and asked you question after question about things I did not comprehend—what in the world is an exfiltration? You do remember the *Oligarkh*, Jozef? He was a very angry man."

Martin thought he could hear the angry voice of an older man raging against the regime as he lurched back and forth on aluminum crutches before people too cowed to interrupt. *My grandfather was executed during the 1929 collectivization, my father was shot to death in a field gone to weed in 1933, both were found guilty by itinerant tribunals of being kulaks. Do you know who kulaks were, Jozef? For the Soviet scum, they were the so-called rich peasants who wanted to sabotage Stalin's program to collectivize agriculture and drive the peasants onto state farms. Rich my ass. Kulaks were farmers who owned a single pair of leather shoes, which would last a lifetime because they were only worn inside church. My grandfather, my father would walk to and from church wearing peasant shoes made of woven reeds, what we called* lapti, *and put on their leather shoes when they crossed the threshold. Because they owned a pair of leather shoes, my grandfather and my father were branded enemies of the people and shot. Perhaps now you understand why I wage one-man war against Mother Russia. I will never forgive the Soviets or their heirs . . .*

Martin looked across the table at the old woman sipping her infusion. "I remember him saying something about leather shoes," he said.

The woman brightened. "He told the story to every newcomer to the dacha—how his grandfather and father had been executed by the Soviets because they owned leather shoes. It could have been true, mind you. Then, again, it could have been imagined. Those who lived through the Stalinist era can never get out of it. Those who were born afterward can never get in. You are too young to know the Soviet state's greatest secret—why everyone spent their waking hours applauding Stalin. I shall educate you: It is because the walls in the new apartment buildings were insulated with felt, which left the rooms well heated but infested with clothes moths. Our indoor sport was to clap our hands and kill them in mid flight. We kept score—on any given evening the one with the most cadavers was declared to be the winner. Ah," the woman added with a drawn out sigh, "all that is spilt milk. Samat and Tzvetan, they are both of them gone from here now."

"And where have they gone to?" Martin asked softly.

The old woman smiled sadly. "They have gone to earth—they have hibernated into holes in the frozen ground."

"And in what country are these holes in the ground?"

She gazed out a window. "I was studying piano at the conservatory when my husband, Samat's father, was falsely accused of being an enemy of the people and sent to Siberia." She held her fingers up and examined them; Martin could see that the palms of her hands were cracking from dryness and her nails were broken and filthy. "My husband—for the moment his name slips my mind; it will surely come back to me—my husband was a medical doctor, you see. He never returned from Siberia, though Tzvetan, who made inquiries after the death of Koba, whom you know as Stalin, heard tales from returning prisoners about his brother running a clinic in a camp for hardened criminals, who paid him with crusts of stale bread."

"Did you and Samat suffer when your husband was arrested?"

"I was expelled from the Party. Then they cancelled my stipend and expelled me from the conservatory, though it was not because my husband had been arrested—he and Tzvetan were Armenians, you know, and Armenians wore their arrests the way others wear medals on their chests."

"Why were you expelled, then?"

"Dear boy, because they discovered I was an Israelite, of course. My parents had given me a Christian name, Kristyna, precisely so that the Party would not suspect I had Jewish roots, but in the end the ruse did not work."

"Did you know that Samat went to live in Israel?"

"It was my idea—he needed to emigrate because of the gang wars raging in the streets of Moscow. I was the one who suggested Israel might accept him if he could prove his mother was Jewish."

"How did you make ends meet when you lost your conservatory stipend?"

"While he was in the gulag, Tzvetan arranged for us to be taken care of by his business associates. When he returned he personally took us both under his wing. He convinced Samat to enroll in the Forestry Institute, though why my son would want to learn forestry was beyond me. And then he sent him to the State Planning Agency's Higher Economic School. What Samat did after that he never told me, though it was clearly important because he came and went in a very shiny limousine driven by a chauffeur. Who would have imagined it—my son, driven by chauffeur?"

On a hunch, Martin said, "You don't seem mad."

Kristyna looked surprised. "And who told you I was?"

"I heard one of the peasants from the village say you were a raving lunatic."

Kristyna frowned. "I am a raving lunatic when I need to be," she murmured. "It is a formula for protecting yourself from life and from fate. I wrap myself in lunacy the way a peasant pulls a sheepskin coat over his shoulders in winter. When people take you for a raving lunatic, you can say anything and nobody, not even the Party, holds it against you."

"You are not what you seem."

"And you, my dear, dear Jozef, are you what you seem?"

"I'm not sure what you mean by that . . ."

"Samat brought you here—he said you were friends from school. I accepted you in place of the son I had lost at childbirth. The *Oligarkh* received you as a member of his entourage and, after several months, as a member of his family. And you betrayed us all. You betrayed Samat, you betrayed me, you betrayed Tzvetan. Why?"

"I don't . . . remember any of this."

Kristyna looked at Martin intently. "Does your amnesia protect you from life and from fate, Jozef?"

"If only it could . . . I run as fast as I can, but life and fate are endlessly and always right behind and gaining on me."

Tears seeped from under Kristyna's tightly shut lids. "Dear Jozef, that has been my experience also."

Taking leave of Kristyna, Martin headed back toward Prigorodnaia's church. The crowd of peasants had long since followed the priest back to the church to offer up special prayers for the soul of Jozef Kafkor. Martin was unlatching the garden gate when he heard Samat's mother calling from a window.

"It was Zurab," she shouted.

Martin turned back. "What about Zurab?" he called.

"Zurab was the given name of Samat's father, my husband. Zurab Ugor-Zhilov."

Martin smiled and nodded. Kristyna smiled back and waved good-bye.

When he reached the paved spur, Martin found the Zil parked off the roadway in the shade of a grove of birches leaning away from the prevailing winds. Katovsky, his shoes off and trousers rolled up, was down slope from the car soaking his feet in the cool currents of the Lesnia. "You wouldn't by any chance be familiar with the fourth game A. Alekhine versus J. Capablanca 1927?" the driver called as he scrambled uphill toward Martin. "I was just now playing it in my head—there was a queen sacrifice more dazzling than the thirteen-year-old R. Fischer's celebrated queen sacrifice on the seventeenth move of his Grünfeld Defense against the grandmaster Byrne, which stunned the chess world."

"No," Martin said as Katovsky sat on the ground to pull on his shoes. "Never played that game."

"On second thought you ought to avoid it, comrade visitor. Queen sacrifices are not for the weak of heart. I tried it once in my life. I was fifteen at the time and I was playing the State Grandmaster Oumansky. When he made his sixteenth move, I studied the board for twenty minutes and then resigned. There was nothing I could do to avoid defeat. The Grandmaster Oumansky accepted the victory gracefully. I later discovered he spent months replaying the game. He couldn't figure out what I'd seen to make me surrender. To me, it was as conspicuous as the nose on your face. I would have been a pawn down in four moves. My bishop would have been pinned after seven and the rook file would have been open after nine, with his queen and two rooks lined up on it. What I saw was I could not beat the State. If I had it to do over again," the driver added with a sigh, "I would not play the State."

* * *

A hundred meters in from where the Prigorodnaia spur joined the four-lane Moscow-Petersburg highway, interior ministry troops in camouflage khakis had blocked off circulation, obliging the occasional automobile to slow to a crawl and slalom between strips of leather fitted with razor-sharp spikes. When Katovsky's Zil came abreast of the parked delivery truck with the DHL logo on its side, baby-faced soldiers armed with submachine guns motioned for the driver to pull off the road. A brawny civilian in a rumpled suit yanked open the passenger door and, grabbing Martin's wrist, dragged him from the car so roughly his cracked ribs sent an electric current through his chest. A second civilian wagged a finger at the driver, who was cowering behind the wheel. "You know the rules, Lifshitz—you could get six months for operating a taxi without a license. I might forget to arrest you if you can convince me you didn't take a passenger to Prigorodnaia today."

"How could I take a passenger to Prigorodnaia? I don't even know where it is."

Martin, looking back over his shoulder, asked, "Why are you calling him Lifshitz?"

Gripping the nape of Martin's neck in one huge hand and his elbow in the other, the brawny civilian steered the prisoner toward the back of the DHL truck. "We call him Lifshitz because that's his name."

"He told me it was Katovsky."

The civilian snorted. "Katovsky, the chess grandmaster! He died a decade ago. Lifshitz the unlicensed taxi driver was a finalist in the Moscow district Chinese checkers tournament five, six years ago. Chess grandmaster—that's a new one in Lifshitz's repertoire."

Moments later Martin found himself sitting on the dirty floor in the back of the DHL truck, his legs stretched in front of him, his wrists manacled behind his back. The two civilians sat on a makeshift bench across from him, sucking on Camels as they gazed impassively at their prisoner through the smoke. "Where are you taking me?" Martin demanded, but neither of his captors showed the slightest inclination to respond.

At some point the truck must have turned off the ring road onto a main artery because Martin could sense that it was caught in bumper to bumper traffic. Horns shrieked around them. When the truck swerved sharply, Martin could hear the screech of brakes and drivers shouting curses. The two jailers, their eyes fixed on the prisoner, seemed unfazed. After twenty or so minutes the truck descended a ramp—Martin could tell by the way the motor sounded that they were indoors—and then backed up before coming to a stop. The civilians threw open the rear doors and, gripping Martin under his armpits, hauled him onto a loading ramp and through swinging doors down a long corridor to a waiting freight elevator. The two grilled gates slid closed and the elevator started grinding noisily upward. The doors on the first five floors were sealed shut with metal bars welded across them. On the sixth floor the elevator jerked to a halt. Other civilians waiting outside tugged open the double gates and Martin, surrounded now by six men in civilian suits, was escorted to a holding room painted glossy white and saturated in bright light. The handcuffs were removed from his wrists, after which he was stripped to the skin and his clothing and his body were meticulously inspected by two male nurses wearing white overalls and latex gloves. An overripe doctor in a stained white smock with a cigarette bobbing on her lower lip and a stethoscope dangling from her neck came in to examine Martin's eyes and ears and throat, then listened to his heart and took his blood pressure and probed his cracked ribs with the tips of her fingers, causing him to wince. As she went through the motions of checking his health, Martin was more distressed by his nakedness than his plight. He concentrated on her fingernails, which were painted a garish phosphorescent green. He caught the gist of a question she posed in Polish; she wanted to know if he had ever been hospitalized. Once, he replied in English, for a shrapnel wound in my lower back and a pinched nerve in my left leg, which still aches when I spend too much time on my feet. The doctor must have understood his response because she ran her fingers down the length of the back wound, then asked if he took any medication. From time to time an aspirin, he said. What do you do between aspirins? she asked. I live with the pain, he said. Nodding, the doctor noted his response and checked off items on a clipboard and signed and dated the form before handing it to one of the civilians. As she turned to leave, Martin asked if she was a generalist or a specialist. The woman smiled slightly. When I am not freelancing for the Service, I am a gynecologist, she said.

Martin was ordered to dress. One of the civilians led the prisoner to a door at the far end of the room and, opening it, stood aside. Martin shuffled into a larger room (once again the laces had been removed from his shoes, making it difficult to walk normally) filled with sturdy furniture, hand-me-downs, so he surmised, from the days when Stalin's KGB ruled the roost in what was then called the Soviet

Union. A short, husky middle-aged man wearing tinted eyeglasses presided from behind a monster of a desk. The man nodded toward the wooden chair facing the desk.

Martin gingerly lowered himself onto the seat. "Thirsty," he said in Russian.

The interrogator snapped his fingers. A moment later a glass of water was set on the desk within reach of the prisoner. Holding it in both hands, he drank it off in several long gulps.

"I am a Canadian citizen," Martin announced in English. "I insist on seeing someone from the Canadian embassy."

Behind the desk, the civilian angled a very bright light into Martin's eyes, forcing him to squint. A husky voice that was perfectly harmonious with the huskiness of the civilian drifted out of the blinding light. "You are voyaging under a passport that identifies you as Kafkor, Jozef," the interrogator said in excellent English. "The passport purports to be Canadian, though it is, as you are no doubt aware, a forgery. The name on it is Polish. The Russian Federal Security Service has been eager to get its hands on you since your name first came to our attention. You are the Kafkor, Jozef, who was associated with Samat Ugor-Zhilov and his uncle, Tzvetan Ugor-Zhilov, better known as the *Oligarkh*."

"Is that a question?" Martin asked.

"It is a statement of fact," the interrogator replied evenly. "According to our register, you met Samat Ugor-Zhilov shortly after arriving in Moscow to work for the Polish tourist bureau. You were taken by this same Samat Ugor-Zhilov to meet his uncle, who was living in the former Beria dacha in Prigorodnaia. In the four months that followed your initial visit to Prigorodnaia, you spent a great deal of time as a guest at the dacha, sometimes remaining there the entire week, other times going out for four-day weekends. The ostensible reason for the visits was that you were going to teach conversational Polish to Samat's mother, who lived in the dacha. Your superiors at the Polish tourist bureau did not complain about your prolonged absences, which led us to conclude that the tourist bureau was a cover. You were obviously a Polish national, though we suspected you had spent part of your life abroad because our Polish speakers who listened to tapes of you talking with your coworkers in Moscow identified occasional lapses in grammar and antiquated vocabulary. You spoke Russian—I assume you still do—with a pronounced Polish accent, which suggested you had studied the Russian language from Polish teachers in Poland or abroad. So, *gospodin* Kafkor, were you working for Polish intelligence or were you employed, with or without the collaboration of the Poles, by a Western intelligence service?"

Martin said, "You are mistaking me for someone else. I swear to you I don't remember any of the details you describe."

The interrogator opened a dossier with a diagonal red stripe across the cover and began leafing through a thick stack of papers. After a moment he raised his eyes. "At some point your relationship with Samat and his uncle deteriorated. You disappeared from view for a period of six weeks. When you reappeared, you were unrecognizable. You had obviously been tortured and starved. Early one morning, while road workers were paving the seven kilometer spur that led from the main Moscow-Petersburg highway to the village of Prigorodnaia, two of the *Oligarkh's* bodyguards escorted you across the Lesnia in a rowboat and prodded you up the incline to a crater that had been gouged in the spur by a steam shovel the previous day. You were stark naked. A large safety pin attached to a fragment of cardboard bearing the words *The spy Kafkor* had been passed through the flesh between your shoulder blades. And then, before the eyes of forty or so workers, you were buried alive in the crater—you were forced to lie in fetal position in the hole, which was roughly the size of a large tractor tire. Thick planks were wedged into place above you, after which the road workers were obliged to pave over the spot."

Martin had the unnerving sensation that a motion picture he had seen and forgotten was being described to him. "More water," he murmured.

Another glass of water was placed within reach and he drank it off. In a hoarse whisper Martin asked, "How can you know these things?"

The interrogator twisted the arm of the lamp so that the light played on the top of the desk. As the interrogator set out five blown-up photographs, Martin caught a glimpse of Kafkor's Canadian passport, a wad of American dollars and British pounds, the picture postcard that he'd swiped from the door of the dacha in Prigorodnaia, along with his shoelaces. He scraped his chair closer to the desk and leaned over the photographs. They were all taken from a distance and enlarged, rendering them grainy and slightly out of focus. In the first photograph, an emaciated man, completely naked, with a matted beard and what looked like a crown of thorns on his head, could be seen stepping gingerly through the shallow slime onto dry land. Two guards in striped shirts followed behind him. In the next photograph, the naked man could be seen kneeling at the edge of a crater, looking over his shoulder, his eyes hollow with terror. The third photograph in the series showed a thin figure of a man with a long pinched face, a suit jacket draped cape-like over his shoulders, offering a cigarette to the condemned man. The fourth photograph caught a heavy set man with a shock of silver hair and dark glasses in the back of a limousine, staring over the tinted window open the width of a fist. In the last photograph, a steamroller was backing across the glistening tarmac, raising a soft fume. Workers leaning on rakes or shovels could be seen staring in horror at the scene of the execution.

"One of the workman on the road crew, the ironmonger in point of fact, was employed by our security services," the interrogator said. "He had a camera hidden in the thermos in his lunch box. Do you recognize yourself in these photographs, *gospodin* Kafkor?"

A single word worked its way up from Martin's parched throat. "*Nyet.*"

The interrogator switched off the light. Martin felt the world spinning giddily under his feet. His lids drifted closed over his eyes as his forehead sank onto one of the photos. The interrogator didn't break the silence until the prisoner sat up again.

Martin heard himself ask, "When did all this happen?"

"A long time ago."

Martin sagged back into his seat. "For me," he remarked tiredly, "yesterday is a long time ago, the day before yesterday is a previous incarnation."

"The photographs were taken in 1994," the interrogator said.

Martin breathed the words "Three years ago!" Kneading his forehead, he tried to work the pieces of this strange puzzle into place, but no matter which way he turned and twisted them, no coherent picture emerged. "What happened after this individual was buried alive?" he asked.

"When the photographs were developed and circulated, we decided to mount an operation to free him—to free *you*—in the hope that you were still alive. When we reached the site of the execution, in the dead of night, we discovered the peasants, led by the village priest, had already scraped away the tarmac and pried up the planks and rescued the man buried in the crater. Before first light, our people helped the peasants replace the planks and tar over the spot."

"And what happened to . . . this person?"

"The village's tractor repairman drove *you* to Moscow in Prigorodnaia's tow truck. His intention was to take you to a hospital. At a red light on the ring road, not far from the American Embassy, you leaped from the cab of the truck and disappeared in the darkness. Neither the municipal police nor our service was able to find any trace of you after that. As far as we were concerned, you disappeared from the surface of the earth—until today, until a custom's officer at the airport signaled the arrival of a Canadian bearing a passport issued to Kafkor, Jozef. We assumed you would be returning to Prigorodnaia, which is the reason the interior ministry troops closed the road—we knew we could pick you up on the way out."

A secretary appeared behind the desk and, bending close, whispered in the interrogator's ear. Clearly annoyed, the interrogator demanded, "How long ago?" Then: "How in the world did he find out?" Shaking his head in disgust, the interrogator turned back to Martin. "The CIA station chief in Moscow has learned that you are in our hands. He is sending a formal request through channels asking us to turn you over to his agency for interrogation when we've finished with you."

"Why would the CIA want to question Jozef Kafkor?"

"They will want to discover if you were able to tell us what we want to know."

"And what is it that you want to know?"

"Whose side were they on—Samat Ugor-Zhilov and the *Oligarkh*, Tzvetan Ugor-Zhilov? And where are they now?"

"Samat took refuge in a West Bank Jewish settlement in Israel."

The interrogator carefully unhooked his eyeglasses from one ear and then the other and began to clean the lenses with the tip of his silk tie. "Bring tea," he instructed the secretary. "Also those brioche cakes stuffed with fig confiture." He fitted the glasses back on and, collecting the five photographs, slipped them back into the folder. "*Gospodin* Kafkor, the Russian Federal Security Service is underfunded and understaffed and underappreciated, but we are not dimwits. That Samat took refuge in Israel we have known for a long time. We were negotiating with the Israeli Mossad to have access to him when word reached him that Chechen hit men had tracked him to Israel, causing him to flee the country. But where did he go when he disappeared from Israel?"

The interrogator leafed through more reports. "He was sighted in the Golders Green section of London. He was seen again in the vicinity of the Vyšehrad Train Station in Prague. He was said to have visited the town of Kantubek on the island of Vozrozhdeniye in the Aral Sea. There were reports, too, that he may have gone to the Lithuanian town of Zuzovka not far from the frontier with Belarus. There is even a rumor that he was the mysterious person who turned up in the helicopter that touched down for half an hour behind the cemetery in Prigorodnaia."

The secretary turned up at the door carrying a tray. The interrogator motioned for him to set it on the small round table between two high-backed chairs and leave. When he was alone with the prisoner, he waved him over to one of the chairs. Settling into the other chair, he filled two mugs with steaming tea. "You must try one of the cakes," he advised, sliding the straw basket toward Martin. "They are so delicious it must surely count as a sin to eat them. So, *gospodin* Kafkor, let us sin together," he added, biting into one of the cakes, cupping a hand under it to catch the crumbs.

"My name is Cheklachvili," the interrogator said, speaking as he took another bite out of his cake. "Arkhip Cheklachvili."

"That's a Georgian name," Martin noted.

"My roots are Georgian, though I have long since offered my allegiance to Mother Russia. It was me," he added with a distinct twinkle in his eyes, "the ironmonger on the slope who was employed by our security services. It was me who took the photographs of you with a camera hidden in my lunch box."

"You've come up in the world," Martin commented.

"Photographing your execution was my first great triumph. It caught the attention of my superiors and started me up the career ladder. After you jumped from the tow truck and disappeared in Moscow, we heard rumors that you had found your way to the American Embassy on the ring road. The CIA station chief himself was said to have taken you in charge. There was a flurry of coded radio traffic for forty-eight hours, after which you were spirited out of Moscow in an embassy car heading for Finland. There were five men in the car—all of them had diplomatic passports and were able to pass the frontier without scrutiny. What happened to you after that we simply do not know. To tell you the truth, I suspect you don't know either."

Martin stared at his interrogator. "What makes you suppose that?"

The interrogator collected his thoughts. "My father was arrested by the KGB in 1953. He was accused of being an American agent and sentenced by a summary tribunal to be shot. The guards took him from his cell in the vast Lubyanka headquarters of the KGB one night in March and brought him to the elevator that carried prisoners down to the vaulted basements for execution. When they discovered that the elevator was not working, they returned him to his cell. Technicians worked through the night to repair the elevator. In the morning the guards came for my father again. They were waiting for the elevator to climb to their floor when word reached them that Stalin was dead. All executions were cancelled. Several months later the new leadership killed Beria and issued a general amnesty, and my father was set free."

"What does his story have to do with me?"

"I remember my father returning to our communal apartment— I was six years old at the time. It had been raining and he was drenched to the skin. My mother asked him where he had been. He shook his head in confusion. There was a vacant look in his eyes, as if he had glimpsed some horrible thing, some monster or some ghost. He didn't remember his arrest, he didn't remember the summary tribunal, he didn't remember the guards leading him to the elevator for execution. It was all erased from his consciousness. When I went to work for the security apparatus, I looked up his dossier and found out what had happened to him. By then my father had been put out to pasture. One day, years later, I worked up the nerve to tell him what

I had discovered. He listened the way one does to the story of someone else's life, and smiled politely as if the life I had dredged up had nothing to do with him, and went on with the life he remembered. Which was the life he lived until the day he died."

Drinking off the last of his tea, the interrogator produced a small key from the pocket of his vest and offered it to Martin. "If you go through that door, you will find a narrow staircase spiraling down six floors to the street level. The key opens the door at the bottom of the staircase leading to a side street. When you are outside, lock the door behind you and throw the key down a sewer."

"Why are you doing this?"

"I believe you when you say you don't remember being brought across the river and buried alive. I believe you when you say you don't know Samat Ugor-Zhilov or his uncle, the *Oligarkh*. I have concluded that you are unable to help us with our inquiries. If you are intelligent, you will quit Russia as rapidly as you can. Whatever you do, don't go to the American Embassy—the CIA station chief has been making discreet inquiries for the past several weeks about someone named Martin Odum. From his description, we suspect that Martin Odum and Jozef Kafkor are the same person."

Martin started to mutter his thanks but the interrogator cut him off. "The skeletal man in the third photograph, the one offering the condemned man a last cigarette, is Samat Ugor-Zhilov. The man with silver hair watching the execution from the partly open window of the automobile is the *Oligarkh*, Tzvetan Ugor-Zhilov. Keep in mind that they attempted to execute you once. They would surely try again if they discover your whereabouts. Ah, I must not forget to return to you your belongings." He retrieved the Canadian passport, the wad of bills, the picture postcard showing a family strolling down a country road somewhere in north America and the shoelaces, and handed everything to the prisoner.

The interrogator watched as the prisoner threaded the laces through his shoes. When Martin looked up, the interrogator shrugged his heavy shoulders, a gesture that conveyed his presumption there was nothing more to say.

Martin nodded in agreement. "How can I repay you?" he asked.

"You cannot." The lines around the interrogator's eyes stretched into a controlled smile. "By the way, Arkhip Cheklachvili is a legend. I assume that Jozef Kafkor and Martin Odum are also legends. The cold war is over, still we live our legends. You may well be its last victim, lost in a labyrinth of legends. Perhaps with the aid of the postcard, you will be able to find a way out."

1992: HOW LINCOLN DITTMANN CAME TO
GO TO LANGUAGE SCHOOL

"GENTLEMEN AND LADIES," DECLARED THE FORMER STATION CHIEF who chaired the Legend Committee, rapping his knuckles on the oval table to encourage his charges to simmer down, "I invite your attention to a remarkable detail that we seem to have overlooked in Martin Odum's biography."

"Are you thinking what I'm thinking?" asked the Yale-educated aversion therapist. "His mother was—"

"She was Polish, for heaven's sake," snapped Maggie Poole, speaking, as always, with more than a trace of the British accent that had rubbed off on her at Oxford. She added brightly, "His mother immigrated to *les Etats Unis* after the Second World War."

"We are on to something," said the only other woman on the committee, a lexicographer on permanent loan from the University of Chicago. "I simply can't believe we missed this."

"The detail has been staring us in the face every time we worked up a cover story for him," agreed the committee's doyen, a grizzly CIA fossil who had begun his long and illustrious career devising false identities for OSS agents during World War Two. He looked at the chairman and asked, "What started you thinking along these lines?"

"When Lincoln Dittmann returned home from Triple Border," the chairman said, "the subsequent action report mentioned that he'd overheard an old lottery vender talking Polish to a hooker in a bar and discovered he could catch the drift of what they were saying."

"That's because his mother used to read him bedtime stories in Polish when they were living in that Pennsylvania backwater called

Jonestown," the aversion therapist explained impatiently.

"*Mon Dieu*, six months of intensive tutoring and he'll talk Polish like a native," said Maggie Poole.

"Which is not how you talk American English," quipped the aversion therapist.

"You can't resist, can you, Troy?"

"Oh, dear, resist what?" he asked, looking around innocently.

The chairman rapped his knuckles on the table again. "Given what the Deputy Director of Operations has in mind for Lincoln," he said, "he really ought to speak Russian, too."

"Martin Odum studied Russian at college," the lexicographer noted. "Not surprisingly, he wound up speaking it with a Polish accent."

"While the tutors are bringing his Polish up to snuff," Maggie Poole suggested, "they could also work on his Russian."

"Okay, let's summarize," said the chairman. "What we have is a Polish national who, like most Poles, speaks fluent Russian. What we need now is a name."

"Let's be simple for once."

"Easier said than done. *Le simple n'est pas le facile.*"

"What about using Franz-Jozef as a first name?"

"Are we being inspired by the Emperor of Austria or Haydn?"

"Either, or."

"What about just plain Jozef," offered Maggie Poole.

"Half of Poland is named Jozef."

"That's precisely the point, it seems to me," she retorted.

"That's not what you argued when we settled on the name Dante Pippen. You said nobody thumbing down a list of names would suspect Dante Pippen of being a *pseudonyme* precisely because it was so unusual."

Maggie Poole would not be put off. "Consistency," she said huffily, "is the last refuge of the unimaginative. That's Oscar Wilde, in case you're wondering."

"I happen to be rereading Kafka's *Amerika*."

"For God's sake, you're not going to suggest Kafka as a family name."

"I was going to suggest a Polish-sounding variation. Kafkor."

"Kafkor, Jozef. Not half bad. It's short and sweet, an easy handle to slip into, I should think. What do you think, Lincoln?"

Lincoln Dittmann, gazing out the window of the fourth floor conference room at the hundreds of cars in the Langley parking lot, turned back toward the members of the Legend Committee. "A variation on the name of Kafka—Kafkor—seems appropriate enough."

"What on earth do you mean by appropriate?"

"Kafka wrote stories about anguished individuals struggling to survive a nightmarish world, which was more or less how the principal of this new legend would see himself."

"You've obviously read Kafka," Maggie Poole said.

"He could have read *into* Kafka at the Jagiellonian University in Kraków," someone noted.

"He could have worked summers as a guide at Auschwitz."

"Through our contacts in Warsaw, we could land him a job in the Polish tourist bureau in Moscow. From there he ought to be able to make contact with the DDO target without attracting too much attention to himself."

"Question of knowing where this Samat character hangs out when he's in Moscow."

"That's Crystal Quest's bailiwick," Lincoln remarked.

1997: MARTIN DDUM GETS TO INSPECT THE SIBERIAN NIGHT MOTH

T HE PHONE ON THE OTHER END OF THE LINE HAD RUNG SO MANY times, Martin had given up counting. He decided to let it ring all evening, all night, all the next day if necessary. She had to return home sometime. A woman carrying a sleeping baby on her hip rapped a coin against the glass door of the booth and angrily held up her wrist so that Martin could see the watch on it. Muttering "Find another booth—I bought this one," he turned his back on her. Shaking her head at how insufferable certain inhabitants of the borough had become, the woman stalked off. In Martin's ear the phone continued to ring with such regularity that he ceased to be conscious of the sound. His thoughts wandered—he played back what he could remember of the previous phone calls. To his surprise, he was able to recreate her voice in his brain as if he were a skilful ventriloquist. He could hear her saying, *When the answers are elusive you have to learn to live with the questions.*

It dawned on him that the phone was no longer ringing on the other end of the line. Another human being was breathing hard into the mouthpiece.

"Stella?"

"Martin, is that you?" a voice remarkably like Stella's demanded.

Martin was surprised when he realized how eager he was to hear that voice; to talk to the one person on earth who was not put off because he wasn't sure who he was, who seemed ready to live with whatever version of himself he offered up. Suddenly he felt the dead bird stirring in him: He ached to see the night moth tattooed under her breast.

"It's me, Stella. It's Martin."

"Jesus, Martin. Wow. I can't believe it."

"I've been ringing for hours. Where were you?"

"I met some Russians in Throckmorton's Minimarket on Kingston Avenue. They were new immigrants, practically off the boat. I was entertaining them with jokes I used to tell in Moscow when I worked for subsection Marx. You want to hear a great one I just remembered?"

"Uh-huh." Anything to keep her talking.

She giggled at the punch line before she told the joke. "Okay," she said, collecting herself. "Three men find themselves in a cell in the Lubyanka prison. After awhile the first prisoner asks the second, 'What are you here for?' And the second prisoner says, 'I was against Popov. What about you?' And the first prisoner says, 'I was for Popov.' The two turn to the third prisoner and ask, "Why were you arrested?' And he answers, 'I'm Popov.'"

She became exasperated when Martin didn't laugh. "When I delivered the punch line at the Moscow Writers Union, people would roll on the floor. Someone in subsection Marx tracked the joke—it spread across Moscow in three days and reached Vladivostok in a week and a half. The Russians in Throckmorton's Minimarket actually applauded. And you don't get it?"

"I get it, Stella. It's not funny. It's pathetic. When your joke spread across Russia, people weren't laughing. They were crying."

Stella thought about that. "There may be something to what you say. Hey, where are you calling from this time? Murmansk on the Barents Sea? Irkutsk on Lake Baikal?"

"Listen up, Stella. Do you remember the first time I ever phoned you?"

"How could I forget. You called to tell me you didn't have a change of mind, you had a change of heart. You were phoning from—"

He cut her off. "I was calling from a booth that reeked of turpentine."

He could hear her catch her breath. "On the corner of—"

He interrupted her again. "Could you find the booth if your life depended on it?"

She said, very calmly, "My life *does* depend on it."

"Do me a favor and bring the autopsy report on your father that the FBI guy sent you."

"Anything else?"

"Uh-huh. That time when I met your father, he removed a pearl-handled souvenir from the pocket of his robe and put it on a shelf where I could see it. I'd like to get my hands on that object, if it's possible."

"Anything else?"

"As a matter of fact, yes. I'd like to inspect the night moth."

"No problem," she said. "It goes where I go."

* * *

They were nursing mugs of lukewarm coffee in a booth at the back of the twenty-four-hour diner on Kingston Avenue, two stores down from Throckmorton's Minimarket. Stella kept looking up at Martin; phrases formed in her mind only to become stuck on the tip of her tongue. When she had turned up at the phone booth on the corner of Lincoln and Schenectady, they had hugged awkwardly for a moment. The faint aroma of rose petals seeped from under the collar on the back of her neck. Stella had said something about how they really ought to kiss, and they did, but the kiss was self-conscious and quick, and a disappointment to both of them. At a loss for words, he'd remarked that he'd never seen her in anything but pants. She said she'd worn the tight knee-length black skirt to disguise herself as a woman. He'd actually managed a smile and said that the deception could have fooled him. He asked her if she had taken precautions to make sure she wasn't being followed. She explained how she had strolled over to an ice cream parlor on Rogers Avenue crammed with teenagers playing electronic pinball machines, then ducked out a back door into an alleyway and made her way through empty side streets to Schenectady and the phone booth. Nodding, he had taken her by the arm and steered her wordlessly in the direction of the all-night diner on Kingston. Sitting across from her now, he noticed the new front tooth; it was whiter than the rest of her teeth and hard to miss. Her hair was pulled back and twined into a braid that plunged out of sight behind her shoulder blades. He recognized the small wrinkles fanning out from the corners of her eyes, which were fixed in a faint squint, as if she were trying to peer into him. The three top

buttons of her man's shirt were open, the triangle of pale skin shim-
mering on her chest.

Martin cleared his throat. "You threatened to show me the tattoo
the next time we met."

"Here? Now?"

"Why not?"

Stella looked around. There were four Chinese women in a booth
across the diner playing mahjongg, and a young man and a girl two
booths away staring so intently into each other's eyes Stella doubted
they would be distracted by anything less than an earthquake. She
took a deep breath to work up her nerve and undid three more buttons on her shirt and pulled the fabric away from her right breast.
Visions invaded Martin's brain: a neon light sizzling over a bar on the
Beirut waterfront, a room upstairs with the torn painting depicting
Napoleon's defeat at Acre, the night moth tattooed under the right
breast of the Alawite prostitute who went by the name of Djamillah.
"You want the God honest truth?" he whispered. "Your Siberian night
moth takes my breath away."

The ghost of a smile materialized on Stella's lips. "That's what it's
supposed to do. The Jamaican tattoo artist on Empire Boulevard said
I could have my money back if it didn't bowl you over. Maybe now
one thing will lead to another."

He reached for her hand and she folded her other hand on top of
his, and they both leaned across the table and kissed.

Settling back, Martin said, "Business first."

"I like your formula," Stella said, rebuttoning her shirt.

He looked surprised. "Why?"

"Reading between the lines, it puts pleasure on the agenda."

A smile touched his eyes. "Did you bring the autopsy report?"

She pulled the report and the letter that had come with it from
her leather satchel and unfolded them on the table. Martin skimmed
the autopsy report first: . . . *myocardial infarction . . . clot superimposed
on plaque in coronary artery already constricted by cholesterol buildup . . .
abrupt and severe drop in blood flow . . . irreparable trauma to a portion
of the heart muscle . . . death would have been almost instantaneous.*

"Uh-huh."

"Uh-huh what?"

"The CIA doctor seems to be saying your father died a natural death."

"As opposed to an unnatural death? As opposed to murder?"

Martin started reading the covering letter the FBI had sent with the autopsy report. *No trace of forced entry . . . even if there had been, Mr. Kastner had a charged Tula-Tokarev within arm's reach . . . no evidence of a struggle . . . unfortunately not unusual for people confined, like Mr. Kastner was, to a wheelchair to experience blood clots originating in a leg that work their way up to the coronary arteries . . . minuscule break in the skin near a shoulder blade compatible with an insect bite . . . Feel free to call me on my unlisted number if you have any questions.* Martin looked up. "Did you father go out often?"

"Kastner never left the house. He didn't even go into the garden behind the house. He spent his time cleaning and oiling his collection of guns."

"If he didn't go out, how did he get bitten by an insect?"

"You aren't convinced by the autopsy report?"

Martin glanced at the signature at the bottom of the letter, then stiffened.

Stella asked, "What's not right?"

"I used to know a Felix Kiick who worked for the FBI."

"There was another agent in charge of the Witness Protection Program when Kastner and I and Elena came over in 1988. We met him several times when we were living at the CIA safehouse in Tyson's Corner outside of Washington. The agent retired in 1995—he came to President Street to introduce the person who was taking his place. That's how we met Mr. Kiick."

"Short? Stumpy? With a low center of gravity that makes him look like an NFL linesman? Nice, open face?"

"That's the one. Do you know him?"

"Our paths crossed several times when I worked for the CIA. I knew him as a counterterrorism specialist, but they probably booted him upstairs at the end of his career. The Witness Protection people are usually running in place, waiting for retirement to catch up with them." Martin thought of something. "When I met your father, he mentioned that he'd gotten my name from someone in Washington. Was that someone Felix Kiick?"

Stella could see that the question was bothering Martin. She considered carefully before answering. "Kastner called the unlisted number in Washington we'd been given in case we needed anything. Now that you mention it, it was Mr. Kiick who said there was a good detective living not far from us. He recommended you, but he told Kastner not to tell you where he'd gotten your name."

Martin seemed to be focusing on horizons that Stella couldn't see. "So it was no accident that I wound up walking back the cat on Samat Ugor-Zhilov."

Stella said, "I brought the souvenir with the pearl handle." She opened the satchel and tilted it so Martin could see her father's Tula-Tokarev. "It's an antique, but it still shoots. It was Kastner's favorite handgun. From time to time he went down to the basement and fired it into a carton filled with roof insulation, then he'd recover the bullet and examine it under a low-powered microscope. I brought bullets for it, too."

Stella touched her lips to the coffee but found it had grown cold. Martin signaled for refills. The waiter, a teenage boy with long sideburns and a silver stud in the side of a nostril, brought two steaming mugs of coffee and took away the old ones. Stella said, "What about Samat?"

"I think I know how to locate him."

"Quit."

"I'm sorry?"

"Quit. Forget Samat. Concentrate on locating me."

"What about your father?"

"What's Kastner have to do with your deciding to quit?"

"He hired me. He's dead, which means he can't unhire me." Martin reached again for her wrist but she snatched it back. "I haven't come all this way to quit now," he insisted.

"You're crazy." She noticed the expression on his face. "I didn't mean that the way it sounded. You're not *crazy* crazy. You are *im*perfectly sane. Admit it, your behavior is sometimes borderline. In your shoes anyone else would shrug and get on with his life."

"You mean his *lives*."

Martin reached again for her wrist. This time she didn't pull away. He fingered her watch and began absently winding the stem. "Samat's in America," he said.

"How do you know that?"

He produced the picture postcard and told her how he had tracked Samat from Israel to London to Prague to Vozrozhdeniye Island in the Aral Sea to the Lithuanian village of Zuzovka, and finally to the village of Prigorodnaia not far from Moscow where Samat's mother, Kristyna, lived in the empty dacha once owned by the most hated man in Russia, Lavrenti Beria. "She told me she was a raving lunatic when she needed to be," Martin said. "She told me she wrapped herself in lunacy the way a peasant pulls a sheepskin coat over his shoulders in winter."

"Sounds to me like a survival strategy." Stella examined the photograph on the postcard—the men and boys attired in black trousers and black suit jackets and straw hats, the women and girls wearing ankle-length gingham dresses and laced-up high shoes and bonnets tied under the chin. She turned it over and translated the message. "Mama dearest, I am alive and well in America the Beautiful . . . Your devoted S." She noticed the printed caption had been scraped off. "Where on God's green earth is *fast New York*?" she demanded, squinting at the post office cancellation mark across the stamp.

"I've done my homework. The people in the photograph are Amish. Belfast, New York is the rough center of the Amish community that lives upstate New York, and the only town upstate that ends in *fast*. It makes tradecraft sense. All the men have long beards. Instead of shaving off his beard, which is what the Russian revolutionaries used to do when they wanted to disappear, Samat would keep his and dress like the Amish and melt into the madding crowd."

"Who's he hiding from?"

"For starters, Chechen gangsters bent on revenge for the killing of one of their leaders known as the Ottoman. Then there's your sister, also his uncle Akim, who claims Samat siphoned off a hundred and thirty million dollars from holding companies he controlled. For some reason I can't figure out, the CIA seems to be very interested in him, too."

"Where do I come in?"

"When you described Samat to me in the pool parlor—"

"That seems so long ago it must have been during a previous incarnation."

"You're talking to a world-class expert on previous incarnations.

When you described him, you said his eyes were seaweed-green and utterly devoid of emotion. You told me if you could see his eyes, you would be able to pick him out of a crowd." Martin lowered his voice. "I don't mean to push you past where you're ready to go—how come you know his eyes so well?"

Stella turned away. After a moment she said, "You wouldn't ask the question if you didn't imagine the answer."

"You saw his seaweed-green eyes up close when you slept with him."

Stella groaned. "The night of the wedding, he came to my room in the early hours of the morning. He slipped under the covers. He was naked. He warned me not to make a commotion—he said it would only hurt my sister when he told her I'd . . . I'd invited him." Stella looked into Martin's eyes. "I'd know his eyes anywhere because I memorized them when he fucked me in the room next to my sister's bedroom on the night of her marriage to this monster of a man. I was originally planning to stay in Kiryat Arba for three weeks, but I left after ten days. He came into my bed every night I was there . . ."

"And when you returned two years later?"

"I took him aside the first day and told him I'd kill him if he came into my bed again."

"How did he react?"

"He only laughed. At night he would turn the doorknob to torture me, but he didn't come into the room. Martin, you've got to tell me the truth—does this change anything between us?"

He shook his head no.

Stella permitted the ghost of a smile to settle softly onto her lips again.

1997: Martin Odum gets the *get*

DRIVING IN THE VINTAGE PACKARD HE HAD BORROWED FROM HIS friend and landlord, Tsou Xing, the owner of the Mandarin restaurant below the pool parlor on Albany Avenue, Martin and Stella reached Belfast after dark. The pimply boy working the pump at the gas station on the edge of town ticked off on grimy fingers the choices available to them: a bunch of descent hotels in town, some pricier than others; an assortment of motels along Route 19 either side of town, some seedier than others; several bed and breakfasts, best one by a country mile was old Mrs. Sayles place on a groundswell overseeing the Genesee, the advantage being the riot of river water which lulled some folks to sleep, the disadvantage being the riot of river water which kept some folks up until all hours.

They found their way to the house on the river with "B & B" and "Lelia Sayles" etched on a shingle hanging from a branch of an ancient oak, and reached through the tear in the screen to work the knocker on the front door. As they didn't have luggage, Martin was obliged to cough up $30 in advance for a room with a matrimonial bed, bathroom down the hall, kindly go barefoot if you use the facilities during the night so as not to wake the ghosts sleeping in the attic. They went out to get a bite to eat at a diner across from the public library on South Main and lingered over the decaf, both of them trying to put off the moment when there would be no turning back. Parking on the gravel in Mrs. Sayles's driveway afterward, Martin decided the Packard's engine oil level needed checking. "I'm every bit as agitated as you," Stella murmured, reading his mind as he propped up the hood. She started toward the house, then wheeled back when she reached the porch, her left palm drifting up to the triangle of pale skin visible on her chest. "Look at it this way, Martin," she called. "If the sex doesn't work out to everyone's expectations, we can always fall back on the erotic phone relationship."

"I want sex *and* the erotic phone relationship," he replied.

Stella angled her head to one side. "Well, then," she said, laughter replacing the nervousness in her eyes, "maybe you ought to stop monkeying with the damn motor. I mean, it's not as if either of us were virgins."

"How'd it go?" Mrs. Sayles asked the next morning as she set out dishes of homemade confitures on the kitchen table.

Martin, irritated, demanded, "How'd what go?"

"*It*," Mrs. Sayles insisted. "Heavens to Betsy, the carnal knowledge part. I may be pushing eighty from the far side, but I'm sure as hell not brain dead."

"It went very nicely, thank you," Stella said evenly.

"Loosen up, young fellow," Mrs. Sayles advised when she noticed Martin buttering a piece of toast for the second time. "You'll be a better bed partner for it."

Hoping to change the subject, Martin produced the picture postcard.

"My great-great-great-grandfather, name of Dave Sanford, built the first sawmill on the banks of the Genesee River," Mrs. Sayles explained, all the while rummaging through a knitted tote bag for her reading glasses. "That was long about 1809. This house was built in 1829 with lumber from that mill. Belfast was a one-horse town in those days. Nothing but forests far as the eye could see, so they say, so they say. When the lumber boom wore out the forests, most folks turned to raising cattle. The White Creek Cheese Factory, which is famous 'round here, was founded long about 1872 by my great-grandfather—"

Stella tried to steer the conversation back to the Amish. "What about the picture on the postcard?"

"It's going to stay a blur until I come up with my reading spectacles, dear child. Could have sworn I put them in here. Never could figure out how a body can find her reading spectacles if she's not wearing them. Well, I'll be, here they are, all the while." Mrs.

Sayles fitted them on and, accepting the postcard from Stella, held it up to the sunlight streaming through a bay window. "Like I was saying, I know the Amish crowd up on White Creek Road pretty good because of my family's connection with the White Creek Cheese Factory. Hmmmm." Mrs. Sayles pursed her lips. "Truth to tell, I don't reckon I recognize any of the Amish on this here picture postcard."

"How about the houses and the barn?" Martin said, coming up behind her, pointing to the two clapboard houses built very close to each other, to the barn with a mansard roof on a rise across from them.

"Houses, barn neither. Mind you, there are an abundance of Amish living on the small roads sloping off White Creek. Picture could have been taken on any one of them." Mrs. Sayles had an inspiration. "There's a fellow, name of Elkanah Macy, works as a janitor over at the Valleyview Amish school on Ramsey Road. He moonlights as a handyman for the Amish out in the White Creek area. If anybody can help you, he can. Be sure to tell Elkanah it was me sent you around."

Elkanah Macy turned out to be a retired navy petty officer who, judging from the framed photographs lining one wall, had served on half the warships in the U.S. Navy during his twenty years in the service. He had converted the atelier in the Amish school basement into a replica of a ship's machine shop, replete with calendar pinups of naked females. "Lelia sent you around, you say?" Macy remarked, sucking on a soggy hand-rolled cigarette as he sized up his visitors through hooded eyes. "Bet she went an' told you the goddamn whopper 'bout Dave Sanford being her great-great-great-granddaddy. Hell, she tells that to anyone stands still long enough to hear her out. Listen to her tell it, anybody who did anything in Belfast was her kin—Sanford's sawmill on the Genesee, the old cheese factory out on White Creek Road. Bet she went an' told you 'bout the goddamn ghosts in the attic. Ha! Take it from somebody that knows, lady's got herself a sprightly imagination. Fact is, the first Sayles in Allegheny County were loansharks that went and bought up farmhouses cheap during the forties and sold them for a handsome profit to the GIs coming back from the war. What is it you want with the Amish over at White Creek?"

Martin showed Mr. Macy the picture postcard. "You wouldn't by any chance know where we could find these houses, would you?"

"Might. Might not. Depends."

"On what?" Stella asked.

"On how much you be willing to pay for the information."

"You don't beat around the bush," Stella observed.

"Heck, not beating around the damn bush saves time and shoe leather."

Martin peeled off a fifty from a wad of bills. "What would half a hundred buy us?"

Macy snatched the bill out of Martin's fingers. "The two farm houses with the barn directly across from them are about three, three and a half miles out on McGuffin Ridge Road. Head out of Belfast on South Main and you'll wind up on 19. Look for the Virgin Mary billboard with her one-eight-hundred number. Right after, you'll cross 305 going west, bout a half mile farther on you'll hit White Creek Road going south toward Friendship. For some of the way White Creek Road runs parallel to the factual creek. Long 'bout halfway to Friendship, McGuffin Ridge Road runs off of White Creek. You got to be stone blind to miss it."

Martin held up another fifty dollar bill. "We're actually looking for an old pal of mine who we think moved into one of the farm houses in that area."

"Your old pal Amish?"

"No."

"Not complicated." Macy snatched the second bill. "All them Amish get me over to unplug the damn electric meters and fuse boxes when they move in. Amish don't take to electricity or the things that work off it—ice boxes, TVs, Singers, irons, you name it. You can tell an Amish lives in a house if the electric counter is hanging off the side of it, unplugged. You can tell someone who ain't Amish lives there if'n the goddamn counter's still attached."

"Are there a lot of non Amish living out on McGuffin Ridge Road?" asked Martin.

When the janitor scratched at his unshaven chin in puzzlement, Martin came up with still another fifty dollar bill.

"A-mazing how a picture of U.S. Grant can stir up recollections,"

Macy said, folding the fifty and adding it to the other two in his shirt pocket. "Except for one house, McGuffin Ridge is all Amish. The one house is the second one on your picture postcard."

Stella turned to Martin. "Which explains why Samat sent this particular postcard to his mother."

"It does," Martin agreed. He nodded at Macy. "That's quite a fleet," he remarked, glancing at the framed photographs on the wall. "You served on all those warships?"

"Never been to actual sea in my life," Macy said with a giggle. "Only served on them while they was in drydock, reason being I get seasick the minute a ship puts to sea."

"You certainly picked the wrong service," Stella said.

Macy shook his head emphatically. "Loved the goddamn navy," he said. "Loved the ships. Didn't much like what they was floating on, which was the sea. Hell, I'd re-up if they'd take me. Yes, I would."

Martin pulled the Packard into the gas station at the edge of town and bought a bottle of spring water and an Allegheny County map while Stella used the restroom. Heading out of town on 19, he felt her hand come to rest on his thigh. His body tensed—real intimacy, the kind that comes *after* sex, was a strange bedfellow to Martin Odum. In his mind's eye, he thought of himself as being somewhere between Dante Pippen, who made love and war with the same frenetic energy, and Lincoln Dittmann, who had once gone off to Rome to try and find a whore he'd come across in Triple Border. Stella sensed the tenseness under her fingers. "I wasn't lying to Mrs. Sayles," she remarked. "It did go very nicely, thank you. All things considered, last night was a great start to our sex life."

Martin cleared his throat. "I am not comfortable talking about things like our sex life."

"Not asking you to talk about it." Stella shot back, laughter in her voice. "Expecting you to listen to me talk about it. Expecting you to mumble *uh-huh* once in a while in quiet encouragement."

Martin glanced at her and said. "Uh-huh."

The Packard sped past the billboard advertising the one-eight-hundred number of the Virgin Mary. Half a mile beyond 305 they reached the junction with the signpost reading "White Creek Road" and "Friendship." Martin turned onto White Creek and slowed down. When the highway dipped, he lost sight of the creek off to the right, only to spot it again when they topped a rise. In places the rippling water of White Creek reminded him of the Lesnia, which ran parallel to the spur that connected Prigorodnaia to the Moscow-Petersburg highway. The farmhouses along White Creek were set on the edge of the road to make it easier to get firewood and fodder in during the winter months when the ground was knee-deep in snow. The houses, spaced a quarter or a half mile apart, some of them with carpentry or broadloom workshops behind them and samples of what was being produced set out on raised platforms or porches, all had the electric meters and fuse boxes dangling off the clapboard walls. Amish going-to-market buggies could be seen in the garages, with cart mares grazing in adjoining fields. Occasionally children, dressed like little adults in their black suits or ankle-length dresses and bonnets and lace-up high shoes, would scamper out to the side of the road to stare shyly at the passing automobile.

The McGuffin Ridge turnoff loomed ahead and Martin swung off White Creek. McGuffin was a mirror image of White Creek—the road crossed rolling farm country, with farm houses built close to the road, all of them with electric meters and lengths of black cable hanging off the walls. Three and a half miles into McGuffin Ridge, Stella tightened her grip on Martin's thigh.

"I see them," he told her.

The Packard, moving even more slowly, came abreast of the two identical clapboard farm houses built very close to each other. Across the road, a weathered barn stood atop a small rise. A crude American eagle crafted out of metal jutted from the ornate weather vane atop the mansard roof. Two Amish men in bibbed dungarees were sawing planks behind the first of the two houses. An Amish woman sat on a rocker on the porch crocheting a patch quilt that spilled off near her feet. As the Packard passed the second house, Stella looked back and caught her breath.

"The electric meter is still attached to the house," she said.

"It's a perfect setup for somebody who wants to melt into the landscape," Martin said. "He can get the Amish women next door to cook for him. If anybody comes nosing around when he's out, the Amish men will tell him. You didn't notice an automobile anywhere around the house?"

"No. Maybe he goes to town by buggy, like the Amish."

"Not likely. No car, no Samat."

"What do we do now?" Stella asked as Martin drove on down the road.

"We wait until Samat comes back. Then we'll dust off your father's antique Tula-Tokarev and go calling on him."

Martin pulled the Packard off the road beyond the next rise and he and Stella walked back to a stand of maple on a butt of land. On the far side of the stand, it was possible to see the two houses and the barn across the road from them. Sitting on the ground facing each other with their backs against trees, they settled down to wait. Martin pulled Dante's lucky white silk scarf from a pocket and knotted it around his neck.

"Where'd you get that?" Stella asked.

"Girl gave it to someone I know in Beirut. She said it would save his life if he wore it."

"Did it?"

"Yes."

"What happened to the girl?"

"She lost her life."

Stella let that sink in. After awhile she said out of the blue, "Kastner was murdered, wasn't he?"

Martin avoided her eye. "What makes you think that?"

"The FBI man, Felix Kiick, told me."

"In so many words? He said your father didn't die of a heart attack?"

"This Felix Kiick was a straight guy. Kastner trusted him. Me, too, I trusted him."

"So did I," Martin agreed.

"I thought about it a thousand times. I came at it from every possible direction."

"Came at what?"

"His letter. The actual autopsy doesn't mention the minuscule break in the skin near the shoulder blade. Mr. Kiick's letter does."

"He said it was compatible with an insect bite."

"He was waving a red flag in front of my face, Martin. He was drawing my attention to something that was compatible with a lethal injection using a very thin needle. Kastner used to tell me about things like that—he said lethal injections were the KGB's favorite method of assassination. In his day the KGB's hit men favored a tasteless rat poison that thinned out the blood so much your pulse disappeared and you eventually stopped breathing. Kastner had heard they were working on more sophisticated substances that couldn't be easily traced—he told me they had developed a clotting agent that could block a coronary artery and trigger myocardial infarction. Don't pretend you didn't notice Kiick's reference to the insect bite."

"I noticed."

"And?"

"Kiick's the guy who suggested your father hire me to find Samat. Kiick spent the better part of his FBI career in counterterrorism. He crossed paths with the Company's Deputy Director of Operations, Crystal Quest—"

"The one you called Fred when you first spoke to Kastner."

"You have a good memory for things beside KGB jokes. Kiick must have known Fred didn't want Samat found. And now Kiick's waving the insect bite in front of our faces."

Stella seemed relieved. "So you don't think I'm raving mad?"

"You're a lot of things. Raving mad is not one of them."

"If I didn't know better, I might take that for a compliment."

"Someone else was killed around the time your father was being stung by an insect. Her name was Minh."

Stella remembered the Israeli Shabak officer telling Martin about the Chinese girl who'd been stung to death by his bees on the roof over the pool parlor. "What does one death have to do with the other?" she asked.

"If your father was murdered, it means someone was trying to close down the search for Samat. Minh was killed tending my hives, which means she was wearing my white overalls and the pith helmet with mosquito netting hanging from it when something made the bees explode out of one of the hives."

"From a distance she would have looked like you." Something else occurred to her. "What about those shots when we were walking from Kiryat Arba to that sacred cave—you told me two bullets from a high-powered rifle came pretty close to you."

"Could have been Palestinians shooting at Jews," Martin said. He didn't sound very convincing.

"Maybe the same people who killed Kastner and your Chinese friend Minh were shooting at you."

"Uh-huh. The *Oligarh* has a long reach. But we'll never know for sure."

"Oh, Martin, I think I'm frightened . . ."

"Join the world. I'm never not frightened."

The long shadows that materialize immediately before sunset were beginning to stretch their tentacles across the fields. Martin, following his own thoughts, said "You've changed the way I look at things, Stella. I used to think I wanted to spend the rest of my life boring myself to death."

"For someone who wanted to bore himself to death, you sure gave a good imitation of living an exhilarating life."

"Did I?"

"Kiryat Arba, London, Prague, that Soviet island in the Aral Sea, that Lithuanian town rioting over who gets to keep the bones of some obscure saint. And then there's the whole story of Prigorodnaia and the seven-kilometer spur that leads to it. Some boring life."

"You left out the most exhilarating part."

"Which is?"

"You."

Stella pushed herself away from the tree to crouch next to him and bury her face in his neck. "Fools rush in," she murmured, "where angels fear to tread."

The sun had vanished behind the hills to the west and a rose-gray blush had infused the sky overhead when they spotted the headlights coming down McGuffin Ridge Road from the direction of White Creek. Martin stood up and tugged Stella to her feet. The car appeared to slow as it neared the two farm houses. It swung away from them to climb the dirt ramp leading to the barn. The figure of a man could be seen pulling open the barn doors, and closing them after he'd parked the car inside. Moments later a porch light flicked on across the road in the nearest of the two houses. The man let himself into the house. Lights appeared in the ground floor windows. Martin and Stella exchanged looks.

"I don't want you to take any risks," Stella said flatly. "If he's armed, the hell with my sister's divorce, shoot him."

Martin smiled for the first time that day. "You sure you told jokes for the KGB? You sure you weren't one of their wetwork specialists?"

"Wetwork?"

"Hit men. Or in your case, hit women."

"I told killer jokes, Martin. Hey, I'm more nervous now than I was last night. Let's get this over with."

In the gathering gloom, they made their way on foot down the white stripe in the middle of the road toward the two houses. Somewhere behind them a dog barked and a quarter of a mile farther along McGuffin Ridge other dogs began to howl. Through the porch windows of the second house, Martin could see the Amish family sitting down to supper at a long table lit by candles; everyone bowed their head as the bearded man at the head of the table recited a prayer. Martin checked the Tula-Tokarev to be sure the safety was off, then climbed silently onto the porch ahead of Stella and flattened himself against the clapboard to one side of the front door. He motioned for Stella to come up and knock.

Speaking English with a thick Russian accent, the man who lived in the house could be heard calling, "Is that you, Zaccheus? I told you to bring the meal over at eight. It is not civilized to sit down to supper at the hour you Americans eat." The door opened and a gaunt man, his face masked by a thick beard with only his seaweed-green eyes visible, regarded Stella through the screen. The porch light was above and behind her and her face was lost in shadows.

"Who are you?" he asked. "What is it you're doing out here this time of day?"

Stella breathed, "*Priviet, Samat.*"

Samat gasped. "*Tyi,*" he whispered. "*Shto tyi zdes delaish?*"

Stella gazed directly into Samat's eyes. "It's him," she said.

Martin stepped into view, the antique Tula-Tokarev aimed at Samat's solar plexus. Stella opened the screen door and Martin stepped across the sill. Samat, white spittle forming at one corner of his thin lips, backed into the room. He held his hands wide, palms up, almost in greeting. "Jozef, thanks to God, you are still among the living." He started to pose questions in Russian. Martin realized that Jozef, like

Stella and Samat, was a Russian speaker. He, Martin, could grasp words and phrases, sometimes the gist of a sentence, but an entire conversation in Russian was more than he could handle. He cut Samat off in mid sentence. "*V Amerike, po-angliiski govoriat*—in America, English is spoken."

"What are you doing with *her*?" Samat looked from one to the other. "How is it possible you know each other?"

Stella seemed as dazed as Samat. "Don't tell me you two know each other."

"Our paths have crossed," Martin told her.

Samat sank onto a couch. "How did you find me, Estelle?"

Martin pulled over a wooden chair and, setting it back to front, straddled it facing Samat, the handgun resting on the top slat in the high back and pointed at his chest. Settling onto a bar stool, Stella flipped the picture postcard at Samat's feet. Retrieving it from the floor, he took in the photograph, then turned it over to look at the post office cancellation stamp. "Zaccheus was supposed to mail this from Rochester," he whined. "The son of a bitch never went farther than Belfast. No wonder you found me two houses on McGuffin Ridge." He looked intently at Martin, then at the postcard. "Jozef, you went back to Prigorodnaia. You saw my mother."

"Why is he calling you Jozef?" demanded Stella, utterly mystified.

Martin kept his eyes locked on Samat's. "I missed you by a day or two. The priest said you'd flown off in your helicopter after delivering the tiny cross carved from the wood of the True Cross."

"Must you point that weapon at me?"

Stella answered for him. "He definitely must, if only to make me feel better."

Mopping his brow with the back of a sleeve, Samat asked, "Jozef, how much do you remember?"

"All of it." In his mind's eye Martin could visualize the first black-and-white photograph the Russian interrogator in Moscow had shown him; an emaciated figure of a man, whom the Russian identified as Kafkor, Joseph, could be seen, stark naked with a crown of thorns on his head, wading toward shore from the row boat, the two guards in striped shirts following behind him. "I remember every detail. I remember being tortured for so long I lost count of time."

Stella leaned forward. She was beginning to grasp why Martin considered himself to be imperfectly sane. "Who tortured you?" she asked in a whisper.

"The men in striped shirts," Martin said. "The ex-paratroopers who guarded the dacha in Prigorodnaia, who brought me across the river . . ." He eyed Samat. "I remember the cigarettes being stubbed out on my body. I remember the large safety pin attached to a fragment of cardboard bearing the words *The spy Kafkor* being passed through the flesh between my shoulder blades. I remember being brought across the Lesnia with all the road workers gaping at me. I remember the guards prodding me up the incline to the crater that had been gouged into the spur of road."

Samat started hyperventilating. When he could speak again, he said, "I beg you to believe me, Jozef, I would have saved you if it had been within the realm of possibility."

"Instead you gave Kafkor the spy a last cigarette."

"*You do remember!*"

Stella looked from one to the other; she could almost hear her father instructing her that in the life of espionage operatives, questions would always outnumber answers.

Samat started to reach into a cardigan. Martin thumbed back the hammer on the handgun. The click reverberated through the room. Samat froze. "I absolutely must smoke a cigarette," he said weakly. He held the cardigan open and reached very slowly into an inside pocket and extracted a pack of Marlboros. Pulling one cigarette free, he struck a wooden match and brought the flame to the end of the cigarette. His hand shook and he had to grip his wrist with the other hand to steady it and hold the flame to the cigarette. Sucking it into life, he held it away from his body between his thumb and third finger and watched the smoke spiral up toward the overhead light fixture. "What else do you remember, Jozef?"

Martin could almost hear the husky voice of the Russian interrogator, who went by the legend Arkhip Cheklachvili. He repeated what Cheklachvili had told him back in Moscow; at moments his own voice and that of the interrogator overlapped in his head. "Prigorodnaia's tractor repairman drove me to Moscow in the village's tow truck. His intention was to take me to a hospital. At a red light on the Ring Road, not far from the American Embassy, I leaped from the cab of the truck and disappeared in the darkness."

"Yes, yes, it all fits," Samat blurted out. "Mrs. Quest sent us word . . . she told my uncle Tzvetan and me . . . that the FBI counterintelligence people stationed at the Moscow Embassy found you wandering in the back streets off the Ring Road. She said you couldn't remember who you were or what had happened to you . . . she spoke of a trauma . . . she said it was better for everyone if you couldn't remember. Oh, you fooled them, Jozef." Samat started to whimper, tears glistening on his skeletal cheeks. "If she had suspected you of remembering, you would not have been permitted to leave Moscow alive."

"I sensed that. I knew everything depended on convincing her I was suffering from amnesia."

"It was the *Oligarkh* who ordered them to torture you," Samat said with sudden vehemence. "He was convinced you had betrayed the Prigorodnaia operation. He needed to know to whom. Mrs. Quest needed to know to whom. It was a matter of damage control. If rot had set in, we needed to burn it out, so my uncle said. I tried to reason with him, Jozef. I told him you might have denounced the operation when you came to realize what it consisted of—but only to people on the inside. Only to Crystal Quest. I swore you would never go to the newspapers or the authorities. I told him you could be brought around to see things from our point of view. After all, we all worked for the same organization, didn't we? We all marched to the same music. It wasn't our business to pass judgment on the operation. The CIA gave us a compass heading and off we went. You were a soldier like me, like my uncle; you were the link between us and Mrs. Quest; between us and Langley."

Martin had to lure Samat into filling in the blanks. "It was the scope of the Prigorodnaia operation that sickened me," he said. "Nothing like that had ever been attempted before."

Samat's head bobbed restlessly; words spilled out, as if the sheer quantity of them filling the air could create a bond between him and the man he knew as Jozef. "When the CIA found my uncle Tzvetan, he was running a used-car dealership in Armenia. What attracted them to him was that his father and grandfather had been executed by the Bolsheviks; his brother, my father, had died in the camps; he him-

self had spent years in a Siberian prison. Tzvetan detested the Soviet
regime and the Russians who ran it. He was ready to do anything to
get revenge. So the CIA bankrolled him—with their money he cornered the used-car market in Moscow. Then, with the help of CIA
largesse, I'm talking hundreds of millions, he branched out into the
aluminum business. He made deals with the smelters, he bought three
hundred railroad cars, he built a port facility in Siberia to offload alumina. Before long, he had cornered the aluminum market in Russia
and amassed a fortune of dozens of billions of dollars. And still his
empire grew—he dealt in steel and chrome and coal, he bought factories and businesses by the dozens, he opened banks to service the
empire and launder the profits abroad. Which is where I came in.
Tzvetan trusted me completely—I was the only one who understood
how the *Oligarkh*'s empire was configured. It was all here in my head."

"Then, once Tzvetan had established himself as an economic force,
the CIA pushed him into politics."

"If my uncle ingratiated himself with Yeltsin, it was because he
was following Mrs. Quest's game plan. When Yeltsin wanted to publish his first book, Tzvetan arranged the contracts and bought up the
print run. The Yeltsin family suddenly discovered that they held shares
in giant enterprises. Thanks to the *Oligarkh*, Yeltsin became a rich
man. When Yeltsin ran for president of the Russian Federation in
1991, Tzvetan financed the campaign. Tzvetan was the one who funded Yeltsin's personal bodyguard, the Presidential Security Service. It
was only natural that when Yeltsin sought advice, he would turn to the
leading figure in his inner circle, the *Oligarkh*."

Martin began to see where the Prigorodnaia plot was going.
"Yeltsin's disastrous decision to free prices and willy-nilly transform
Russia into a free-market economy in the early nineties unleashed
hyperinflation and wiped out the pensions and savings of tens of millions of Russians. It threw the country into economic chaos—"

"The concept originated with Crystal Quest's DDO people. My
uncle was the one who convinced Yeltsin that a free-market economy
would cure Russia's ills."

"The privatization of Soviet industrial assets, which looted the
country's wealth and funneled it into the hands of the *Oligarkh* and a
handful of insiders like him—"

Samat was scraping his palms together. "It all came from the CIA's Operations Directorate—the hyperinflation, the privatization, even Yeltsin's decision to attack Chechnya and bog down the Russian army in a war they couldn't win. You can understand where the Americans were coming from—the cold war was over, for sure, but America did not defeat the mighty Soviet Union only to have a mighty Russia rise like a phoenix from its ashes. The people at Langley could not take the risk that the transition from socialism to capitalism might succeed. So they got the *Oligarkh*, who detested the communist apparatchiki, who was only too happy to see Russia and the Russians sink into an economic swamp, to use his considerable influence on Yeltsin."

Stella, watching Martin intently, saw him wince. For an instant she thought his leg must be acting up again. Then it dawned on her that the pain came from what Samat was saying: Martin had found the naked truth buried in Samat's story. She had, too. "The CIA was running Russia!" she exclaimed.

"It was running Russia into the ground," Martin agreed.

"That was the beauty of it," Samat said, his voice shrill with jubilation. "*We paid the Russians back for what they did to the Ugor-Zhilovs.*"

Martin remembered what Crystal Quest had said to him the day she summoned him to Xing's Mandarin restaurant under the pool hall. *We didn't hire your conscience, only your brain and your body. And then, one fine day, you stepped out of character—you stepped out of all your characters—and took what in popular idiom is called a moral stand.*

At the time Martin didn't have the foggiest idea what she was talking about. Now the pieces of the puzzle had fallen into place; now he understood why they'd convened a summit at Langley to decide whether to terminate his contract—or his life.

Samat, drained, puffed on the cigarette to calm his nerves. Martin's found himself staring at the ash at the tip of Samat's cigarette, waiting for it to buckle under its own weight and fall. Life itself seemed to ride on it. Defying gravity, defying sense, it grew longer than the unsmoked part of the cigarette. Martin associated the ash with the naked man kneeling at the edge of the crater, the one who had been caught in the black-and-white photograph peering over his shoulder, his eyes hollow with terror.

Samat, sucking on the cigarette, became aware of the ash, too. His words slurring with dread, he whispered, "Please. I ask you, Jozef. For the sake of my mother, who loved you like a son. Do not shoot me."

"I'm not sure you should shoot him," Stella said. "Then again, I'm not sure you shouldn't. What is to be accomplished by shooting him?"

"Revenge is a manifestation of sanity. Shooting him would make me feel . . . *perfectly* sane." Martin looked back at Samat, who was breathing noisily through his mouth, terrified that each breath would be his last. "Where is the *Oligarkh*?" Martin asked.

"I do not know."

Martin raised the Tula-Tokarev to eye level and sighted on Samat's forehead, directly between his eyes. Stella turned away. "When you lived in Kiryat Arba," Martin reminded Samat, "you spent a lot of time on the phone with someone who had a 718 area code."

"The phone records were destroyed. How could you know this?"

"Stella remembered seeing one of your phone bills."

"I swear to you on my mother's head, I do not know where the *Oligarkh* is. The 718 number was the home phone of the American manufacturer of artificial limbs that I imported to London for distribution to war zones." Tears welled in Samat's seaweed-green eyes. "For all I know, the *Oligarkh* may no longer be alive. In the Witness Protection Program, these things are tightly compartmented, precisely so that no one can get to him through me. Or to me through him."

Stella said, very quietly, "He may be telling the truth."

Samat clutched at the buoy Stella had thrown him. "I never meant to harm you," he told her. "The marriage to your sister was a matter of convenience for both of us—she wanted to live in Israel and I had to get out of Russia quickly. I was incapable of sleeping with Ya'ara. You have to comprehend. A man can only be a man with a woman."

"Which narrowed it down to Stella," Martin said.

Samat avoided his eye. "A normal man has normal appetites . . ."

Martin held the pistol unwaveringly for several long seconds, then slowly let the front sight drop. "Your other uncle, the one who lives in Caesarea, claims you stole a hundred and thirty million dollars from six of his holding companies. He offered me a million dollars to find you."

Samat glimpsed salvation. "I will pay you two million not to find me."

"I don't accept checks."

Samat saw that he might be able to worm his way out of this predicament after all. "I have bearer shares hidden in the freezer of the icebox."

"There is one other matter that needs to be arranged," Martin informed him.

Confidence began seeping back into Samat's voice. "Only name it," he said, all business.

* * *

Stella spent the better part of the next morning on Samat's phone trying to track down an Orthodox rabbi who would accommodate them. An old rabbi in Philadelphia gave her the number of a colleague in Tenafly, New Jersey; a recorded announcement at the Chabad Lubavitch Synagogue there suggested anyone calling with a weekend emergency try the rabbi's home number, which rang and rang without anyone answering. A rabbi at Beth Hakneses Hachodosh in Rochester knew of a rabbi at Ezrath Israel in Ellenville, New York, who delivered religious divorces, but when Stella dialed the number she fell on a teenage daughter; her father, the rabbi, was away in Israel, she said. He did have a cousin who officiated at B'nai Jacob in Middletown, Pennsylvania. If this was an emergency, Stella could try phoning him. It was the Middletown rabbi who suggested she call Abraham Shulman, the rabbi at the Beth Israel Synagogue in Crown Heights, Brooklyn. Rabbi Shulman, an affable man with a booming voice, explained to Stella that what she needed was an ad hoc rabbinical board, composed of three Orthodox rabbis, to deliver the scroll of the *get* and witness the signatures. As luck would have it, he was sitting down to Sunday brunch with two of his colleagues, one from Manhattan, the other from the Bronx, both of them, like Shulman, Orthodox rabbis. Oh, dear, yes, it was unusual but the rabbinical board could witness the signing of the *get* by the husband even if the wife were not physically present and then forward the document to the wife's rabbi in Israel for her signature, at which point the divorce would become final. Rabbi Shulman inquired how long it would take her and the putative husband to reach Crown Heights. Stella told the rabbi they could be there by late afternoon. She jotted down his directions: cross over from Manhattan to Brooklyn on the Manhattan Bridge, follow Flatbush Avenue down to Eastern Parkway, then follow Eastern Parkway until you reached Kingston Avenue. The synagogue filled the top three floors of number 745 Eastern Parkway on your left coming from New York, immediately after Kingston Avenue.

The three rabbis, looking somewhat the worse for brunch, were holding court in Shulman's murky book-lined study on the ground floor under the synagogue. Shulman, the youngest of the three, was clean shaven with apple-shiny cheeks; the two other rabbis had straggly white beards. All three wore black suits and black fedoras propped high on their foreheads; on the two older rabbis it looked perfectly natural, on Shulman it produced a comic effect. "Which of you," boomed Shulman, looking from Samat to Martin and back to Samat, "is the lucky future ex?"

Martin, one hand gripping the Tula-Tokarev in his jacket pocket, prodded Samat in the spine. "Who would believe," Samat said under his breath as he shuffled across the thick carpet, "you went to all this trouble to find me for a divorce."

"Did you say something?" inquired the rabbi to the right of Shulman.

"It is me, the divorcer," Samat announced.

"What's the mad rush to divorce?" the third rabbi asked. "Why couldn't you wait until the shul opens on Monday morning?"

Stella improvised. "He's booked on a flight to Moscow from Kennedy airport this evening."

"There are Orthodox rabbis in Moscow," Shulman noted.

In a bamboo cage set on a wooden stepladder next to floor-to-ceiling bookshelves, a green bird with a hooked bill and bright red plumes between its eyes hopped onto a higher trapeze and declared, clear as a bell, "*Loz im zayn, loz im zayn.*"

Rabbi Shulman looked embarrassed. "My parrot speaks Yiddish," he explained. "*Los im zayn* means *let him be.*" He smiled at his colleagues. "Maybe *Ha Shem*, blessed be his Name, is trying to tell us something." The rabbi turned back to Samat. "I assume you wouldn't come all this way without identification."

Samat handed his Israeli passport to the rabbi.

"You are Israeli?" Shulman said, plainly surprised. "You speak Hebrew?"

"I immigrated to Israel from the Soviet Union. I speak Russian."

"The Soviet Union doesn't exist anymore," Shulman pointed out.

"I meant Russia, of course," Samat said.

"Excuse me for asking," the oldest of the three rabbis said, "but you *are* Jewish?"

"My mother is Jewish, which makes me Jewish. The Israeli immigration authorities accepted the proofs of this when they let me into the country."

Stella explained the general situation while Shulman took notes. Her sister, whose Israeli name was Ya'ara, daughter of the late Oskar Alexandrovich Kastner of Brooklyn, New York, currently lived in a Jewish settlement on the West Bank called Kiryat Arba. Ya'ara and Samat Ugor-Zhilov, here present, had been married by the Kiryat Arba rabbi, whose name was Ben Zion; Stella herself had been a witness at the marriage ceremony. Samat had subsequently abandoned his wife without granting her a religious divorce. This same Samat, here present, had had second thoughts about the matter and is now willing to put his signature to the document granting a religious divorce to his wife. She stepped forward and handed the rabbis a scrap of paper which spelled out the terms of the divorce. Samat's signature was scrawled across the bottom.

The resplendent parrot descended to the lower trapeze and cried out, "*Nu, shoyn! Nu, shoyn!*" Shulman said, "That's the Yiddish equivalent of *Let's put the show on the road.*"

One of the older rabbis looked across the room at Martin. "And who are you?"

"That's a good question, rabbi," Martin said.

"Perhaps you would like to answer it," Shulman suggested.

"My name is Martin Odum."

Looking straight at Martin, Stella said, "He has deeper layers of identity than a name, rabbi. Fact is, he's not absolutely sure who he is. But so what—women fall for men all the time who don't know who they are."

Shulman cleared his throat. The three rabbis bent over Samat's passport. "The photograph in the passport doesn't look anything like this gentleman," one of the rabbis observed.

"I did not have a beard when I came to Israel," Samat explained.

Stella said, "Look carefully—you can tell by the eyes it's the same man."

"Only women are able to identify men by their eyes," Shulman remarked. He addressed Samat. "You affirm that you are the Samat Ugor-Zhilov who is married to—" he glanced at his notes—"Ya'ara Ugor-Zhilov of Kiryat Arba?"

"He does affirm it," Stella said.

The rabbi favored her with a pained look. "He must speak for himself."

"I do," Samat said. He glanced at Martin, leaning against the wall near the door with one hand in his jacket pocket. "I affirm it."

"Is there any issue from this marriage?"

When Samat looked confused, Stella translated. "He's asking if you and Ya'ara had children." She addressed Shulman directly. "The answer is: You can't have children when you don't consummate the marriage."

One of the older rabbis chided her. "Lady, given that he is not contesting the divorce, I think you are telling us more than we need to know."

Shulman said, "Do you, Samat Ugor-Zhilov, here present, stand ready to grant your wife, Ya'ara Ugor-Zhilov, a religious divorce—what we call a *get*—of your own free will and volition, so help you God?"

"Yes, yes, I will give her the damn *get*," Samat replied impatiently. "You guys use a lot of words to describe something as uncomplicated as a divorce."

"Kabbalah teaches us," Shulman noted as his two colleagues nodded in agreement, "that God created the universe out of the energy in words. Out of the energy of your words, Mr. Ugor-Zhilov, we will create a divorce."

Stella smiled at Martin across the room. "It doesn't come as a surprise to me that words have energy."

Samat looked bewildered. "Who is this Kabbalah character and what does he have to do with my divorce?"

"Let's move on," Shulman suggested. "Under the terms of the *get,*" he went on, reading from Stella's scrap of paper, "your wife will keep any and all property and assets that you may possess in Israel, including one split-level house in the Jewish settlement of Kiryat Arba, including one Honda automobile, including any and all bank accounts in your name in Israeli banks."

"I have already agreed to this. I signed the paper."

"We must ascertain verbally that you understand what you have signed," explained Shulman.

"That you were not coerced into signing," added one of his colleagues.

"According to the terms of the divorce," the rabbi continued, "you are putting on deposit with this rabbinical board one million dollars in bearer shares, with the intention that the said one million dollars, less a generous $25,000 donation to a Jewish program to relocate Jews to Israel, will be transferred to the ownership of your wife, Ya'ara Ugor-Zhilov."

Samat glanced at Martin, who nodded imperceptibly. "I agree, I agree to it all," Samat said hurriedly.

"That being the case," the rabbi said, "we will now prepare the scroll of the *get* for your signature. The document, along with the $975,000 in bearer shares, will be sent by Federal Express to rabbi Ben Zion in Kiryat Arba. Ya'ara will be summoned before a rabbinical board there to sign the *get,* at which point you and your wife will be formally divorced."

"How long will it take to prepare the scroll?" Martin asked from the door.

"Forty-five minutes, give or take," Shulman said. "Can we offer you gentlemen and the lady coffee while we prepare the document?"

Later, Martin and Samat waited outside the Synagogue while Stella brought around the Packard. Martin slid into the backseat alongside Samat. "Where are we off to now?" Stella asked.

"Take us to Little Odessa."

"Why are we going to the Russian section of Brooklyn?" Stella asked.

"Get us there and you'll see," Martin said.

Stella shrugged. "Why not?" she said. "You certainly knew what you were doing up to now."

She piloted the large Packard through rush-hour traffic on Ocean Parkway, past block after block of nearly identical gray-grim tenements with colorful laundry flapping from lines on the roofs. Twice Samat tried to start a conversation with Martin, who sat with the butt of the Tula-Tokarev in his right fist and his left hand gripping Samat's right wrist. Each time Martin cut him off with a curt *uh-huh*. Up front Stella had to laugh. "You won't get far with him when he's in his one of his *uh-huh* moods," she called over her shoulder.

"Turn left when you get to Brighton Beach Avenue," Martin instructed her. "It's the next traffic light."

"You've been here before," Samat said.

"Had two clients in Little Odessa before I became a famous international detective tracking down missing husbands," Martin said. "One involved a kidnapped Rottweiler. The other involved a neighborhood crematorium run by Chechen immigrants."

Samat pulled a face. "I do not comprehend why America lets Chechens into this country. The only good Chechens are dead Chechens."

Stella asked Samat, "Have you been to Chechnya?"

Samat said, "Did not need to go to Chechnya to come across Chechens. Moscow was swarming with them."

Martin couldn't resist. "Like the one they called the Ottoman."

The seaweed in Samat's eyes turned dark, as if they had caught the reflection of a storm cloud. "What do you know about the Ottoman?"

"I know what everyone knows," Martin said guilelessly. "That he and his lady friend were found one fine morning hanging upside down from a lamppost near the Kremlin wall."

"The Ottoman was not an innocent."

"I heard he'd been caught doing fifty in a forty-kilometer zone."

Samat finally figured out his leg was being pulled. "Speeding in Moscow can be dangerous for your health," he agreed. "Also littering."

"Turn left on Fifth Street, just ahead. Park on the left where it says no parking anytime."

"In front of the crematorium?" Stella asked as she turned into the street.

"Uh-huh."

"Who are we meeting?" Samat inquired uneasily as Stella eased the Packard alongside the curb and killed the motor.

"It's almost eight," Martin said. "We'll wait here until it's dark and the streets are empty."

"I'm going to close my eyes for a few minutes," Stella announced.

Stella's forty winks turned into an hour-and-ten-minute nap; all the driving she'd done that day, not to mention the worrying, had taken its toll on her. Samat, too, dozed, or appeared to, his chin sinking onto his chest, his shut eyelids fluttering. Martin kept a tight grip on the butt of the Tula-Tokarev. Curiously, he didn't feel bushed despite his having slept fitfully on Samat's couch the night before (woken every few hours by Samat calling from the locked closet that he needed to go to the toilet). What kept Martin alert, what kept the adrenalin flowing, was his conviction that revenge *was* a manifestation of sanity; that if he played this thing out, his days of being *imperfectly* sane were numbered.

As darkness settled over Little Odessa, the Russians began heading back to their apartments. Behind them, on Brighton Beach Avenue, traffic thinned out. Lights appeared in windows on both sides of Fifth Street; the bulb in the vestibule of the funeral parlor across the street came on. Two floors above the door with the gold lettering that read "Akhdan Abdulkhadzhiev & Sons—Crematorium," an elaborate chandelier fitted with Christmas tree bulbs blazed into life and the scratchy sound of an accordion playing melodies that sounded decidedly Central Asian drifted out of an open window. A lean man and a teenage boy dragged a pushcart filled with tins of halavah down the middle of the street and turned into one of the driveways near the end of the block. Two young girls skipping rope as they made their way home passed the Packard. An old woman carrying a Russian *avoska* filled with vegetables hurried up the steps of a nearby brownstone. When the street appeared deserted, Martin leaned forward and nudged Stella on the shoulder.

She angled her rearview mirror so that she could see Martin in it. "How long did I sleep?"

"A few minutes."

Samat's eyes blinked open and he swallowed a yawn. He looked up and down the street. "I do not understand why we have come to the Russian section of Brooklyn," he said anxiously. "If it is to meet someone—"

Martin could hear a voice in his ear. *For once in your life, don't weigh the pros and cons—just act violently.*

"Dante?"

You don't want to shoot him, Martin—too noisy. Use the butt. Break his knee cap.

Stella said, "Who are you talking to, Martin?"

Don't think about it, just do it, for Christsake!

"I'm talking to myself," Martin murmured.

He was sorely tempted—to jailbreak, to set foot outside the Martin Odum legend; to become, if only for an instant, someone as impulsive as Dante Pippen. Clutching the Tula-Tokarev by the barrel, Martin slammed the grip down hard on Samat's right knee. The sharp crunch of the bone splintering filled the Packard. Samat stared in disbelief at his knee as a brownish stain soaked into the fabric of his trousers. Then the pain reached his brain and he cried out in agony. Tears spurted from his eyes.

Stella twisted in the seat, breathing hard. "Martin, have you gone mad?"

"I'm going sane."

Samat, cradling his shattered knee cap with both hands, thrashed in pain. Martin said, very softly, "You killed Kastner, didn't you?"

"Get me a doctor."

"You killed Kastner," Martin repeated. "Admit it and I will put an end to your suffering."

"I had nothing to do with Kastner's death. The *Oligarkh* had him eliminated when the Quest woman told him you were trying to find me. My uncle and Quest . . . they wanted to cut off all the leads."

Stella said, "How did the killers get into the house without breaking a door or a window?"

"Quest supplied the keys to the doors and the alarm box."

"You killed the Chinese girl on the roof, too," Martin said.

Samat's nose began to run. "Quest's people told the *Oligarkh* about the beehives on the roof. He sent a marksman to the roof across the street. The marksman mistook the Chinese girl for you. Her death was an accident."

"Where is the *Oligarkh?*"

"For the love of God, I must get to a doctor."

"Where is the *Oligarkh?*"

"I told you, I do not know."

"I know you know."

"We speak only on the phone."

"The 718 number?"

When Samat didn't say anything, Martin reached across Samat and pushed open the door on his side of the car. "Read the name on the crematorium door," he ordered.

Samat tried to make out the name through the tears blurring his vision. "I cannot see—"

"It says Akhdan Abdulkhadzhiev. Abdulkhadzhiev is a Chechen name. The crematorium is the Chechen business that was accused of extracting gold teeth before cremating the corpses. If you don't give me the phone number, I'll push you out of the car and ring the bell and tell the Chechens sitting down to supper upstairs that the man who hanged the Ottoman upside down from a lamppost in Moscow is on their doorstep. There isn't a Chechen alive who doesn't know the story, who won't jump at the chance to settle old scores."

"No, no. The number . . . the number is 718-555-9291."

"If you're lying, I'll break your other knee."

"On my mother's head, I swear it. Now take me to a doctor."

Martin got out of the Packard and came around to the other side of the car and, taking a grip on Samat's wrists, pulled him from the backseat across the sidewalk. He propped Samat up so that he was sitting on the sidewalk with his back against the door. Then Martin pressed the buzzer for several seconds. Two floors over his head a young woman appeared in the open window.

"Crematorium closed for the day," she shouted down.

"Crematorium about to open," Martin called back. "You ever hear of a Chechen nicknamed the Ottoman?"

The woman in the window ducked back into the room. A moment later the needle was plucked off the record. Two men stuck their heads out of the window. "What about the Ottoman?" an older man with a flamboyant mustache yelled down.

"The Armenian from the Slavic Alliance who lynched him and his lady friend within sight of the Kremlin is on your doorstep. His name is Samat Ugor-Zhilov. Your Chechen friends have been looking all over the world for him. There's no rush to come get him—he's not going anywhere on a shattered knee."

Samat whimpered, "For the love of God, for the sake of my mother, you cannot leave me here."

Martin could sense the excitement in the room above his head. Footsteps could be heard thundering down the stairs. "Start the motor," he called to Stella. A current of pain shot through his game leg as he made his way around the car and climbed in next to the driver. "Let's go," he said. "Don't run any red lights."

Stella, biting her lip to keep from trembling, steered the Packard away from the curb and headed down the empty street. Martin turned in the seat to watch the Chechens drag Samat into the crematorium. Stella must have seen it in her rearview mirror. "Oh, Martin," she said, "what will they do to him?"

"I suppose they will extract the gold teeth from his mouth with a pair of pliers and then put him in one of their cheapest coffins and nail the lid shut and light off the burning fiery furnace and cremate him alive." He touched the back of her hand on the steering wheel. "Samat left behind him a trail of blood—the Ottoman and his lady friend, your father, my Chinese friend Minh, the scavengers locked in cages on an island in the Aral Sea who died miserably when Samat used them as guinea pigs to test biowarfare viruses that he eventually gave to Saddam Hussein. The list is long."

Using hand gestures, Martin directed Stella back into the heart of Brooklyn. When they reached Eastern Parkway he had her pull over to the curb. He retrieved the paper bag from the trunk and, taking her arm, drew her to a bench on one side of the parkway. "There's a million dollars in bearer shares left in the bag," Martin explained, handing it to her. "Go to ground in a motel on the Jersey side of the Holland Tunnel for the night. Tomorrow drive to Philadelphia and go to the biggest bank you can find and cash these in and open an account in your name. Then drive to Jonestown in Pennsylvania. Not Johnstown. Jonestown. Find a small house, something with white clapboard and storm windows and a wrap around porch at the edge of town and a view across the corn fields. It needs to have a yard where we can raise chickens. There's a monastery not far away over the rise—you want to be able to hear its carillon bells from the house."

"How do you know about Jonestown and the monastery?"

"Lincoln Dittmann and I both come from Jonestown. Funny part is we didn't know each other back then. My family moved to Brooklyn when I was eight but Lincoln was brought up in Pennsylvania. I'd almost forgotten about Jonestown. He reminded me."

"Who's Lincoln Dittmann?"

"Someone I came across in another incarnation."

"What do I do when I find the house?"

"Buy it."

"Why don't you come with me?"

"I have some loose ends to take care of. I'll turn up in Jonestown when I've finished."

"How will you find me?"

"Jonestown is a small town. I'll ask for the gorgeous dish with a permanent squint in her eyes and a ghost of a smile on her lips."

Stella relished the coolness of the night air. The headlights streaking past led her to imagine that she and Martin were stranded on an island of stillness in a world of perpetual motion. "Do you really remember what happened to you in Moscow?" she asked.

He smiled. "No. A curtain screened off the fragment of my life that I lived under the legend Jozef Kafkor. But what I've lost won't change anything for us. The part of Martin Odum's life that I want to remember begins here."

1997: LINCOLN DITTMANN CONNECTS THE DOTS

"U.S. GOVERNMENT PRINTING OFFICE ANNEX. HARVEY CLEVELAND speaking. How can I help you?"

"Do you recognize my voice, Felix?"

"Tell you the truth, no. Am I supposed to?"

"Does a hangar under the Pulaski Skyway ring a bell? A crazy Texan named Leroy was about to shoot you. You jumped a mile when you heard his wrist bone splinter."

Felix Kiick could be heard chuckling into the phone. "Speak of the devil," he said. "Lincoln Dittmann. How'd you get this number? It's supposed to be an unlisted hotline."

"How are you, Felix?"

"Hang on—I'm going to scramble this call." There was a burst of static, then Felix's voice came on line again, loud and clear. "I'm almost but not quite retired. Six weeks, three days, four and a half hours to go and I'm out of here. What about you?"

"I'm more or less okay."

"Which is it—more or less?"

"More, actually."

"Your memory coming back?"

"Nothing's wrong with my memory, Felix. You're confusing me with Martin Odum."

Lincoln's remark startled Felix. "I guess I am," he admitted warily. "You *are* . . . Lincoln Dittmann?"

"In the flesh."

"Why are you calling?"

LEGENDS 369

"I'm connecting the dots. I thought you could fill in some of the blanks."

"Tell me what you know," he said guardedly. "Maybe I'll hint at what you don't know."

"I know what happened to Jozef Kafkor in Prigorodnaia, Felix. He was the cutout between Crystal Quest's operations folks at the CIA and the *Oligarkh*, Tzvetan Ugor-Zhilov. When Jozef figured out that Quest was part of the Prigorodnaia operation—when he figured out she *originated* the operation—he must have threatened to take the matter up with an assortment of congressmen or senators, at which point Jozef was tortured and starved by the *Oligarkh*'s hired hands, and eventually buried alive."

"I'm hanging on your every word. Lincoln."

"You were a counterterrorism wonk before they put you out to preretirement pasture, changing diapers for clients in the FBI's Witness Protection Program. I seem to remember you'd been posted to the American embassy in Moscow at one point in your career. Were you in Moscow when they brought in Jozef Kafkor, Felix?"

Lincoln could almost *hear* Kiick smiling. "It's within the realm of possibility," the FBI man acknowledged.

"With your rank," Lincoln said, talking rapidly, leaving precious little breathing space between sentences, "you would have been the top FBI gun at the embassy. You would have picked up scuttlebutt about the DDO running a secret operation via a cutout. When Jozef turned up on your doorstep, it would have crossed your mind that he could be the cutout—his physical condition, the evidence of torture on his body, his mental state would have suggested that the DDO operation had gone off the tracks." Lincoln came up for air. "Why were the *Oligarkh* and Samat exfiltrated?"

Felix actually sighed. "They'd been living on the edge for years—the Moscow gang wars, the Chechens, certain factions inside the Russian Federal Security Service, disgruntled KGB hands who found themselves out in the cold, Yeltsin's political enemies, wannabe capitalists whom the *Oligarkh* had ruined on his way up, take your pick. And then Jozef Kafkor comes on the scene—Jozef and his scruples. Quest would have assured the *Oligarkh* she was the only one who heard his qualms, but the Ugor-Zhilovs, Tzvetan and Samat, must have had their doubts. After all, Quest had a vested interested in lying to them to keep the operation up and running indefinitely. When Jozef was rescued from the grave the *Oligarkh* dug for him and ended up wandering the streets of Moscow, the Ugor-Zhilovs didn't swallow Quest's story that he couldn't remember the Jozef Kafkor legend. Samat cracked first. He didn't like the idea of coming to the States. He thought he'd be safer tucked away in a Jewish settlement on the West Bank of the Jordan, so he got himself into Israel. The *Oligarkh* held on longer, but in the end he cracked, too, and they brought him in."

"To the Witness Protection Program?"

"No way. He was too important for Quest to entrust to the FBI. Her DDO wallahs created a legend for the *Oligarkh* themselves and settled him somewhere on the East Coast of America."

"Meanwhile you had Kastner and his two daughters in your protection program."

"I liked Kastner."

"If it's any comfort, given that you lost him, he liked you."

"You're sprinkling salt in wounds, Lincoln."

"And the day Kastner told you—he referred to you as his friend in D.C.—that he needed someone to track down Samat, you couldn't resist tempting fate, could you? I can imagine how the scenario played out after Moscow. Someone like you would have been fascinated by the man found wandering behind the embassy, his body covered with sores. You would have been intrigued by the CIA's immediate interest in him. You would have been curious to know what happened to Jozef Kafkor after he was smuggled out to Finland. You had friends at the CIA, you would have learned that the Jozef Kafkor exfiltrated to Finland on your watch had been reincarnated, so to speak, as Martin Odum; that this same Martin Odum wound up working as a private detective in Crown Heights. And so you gave Kastner Martin Odum's name." When Kiick didn't confirm or deny this, Lincoln said, "Why?"

"Why not?"

"Come clean, Felix."

"This *Oligarkh* character and his nephew Samat rubbed me the wrong way. Crystal Quest rubbed me the wrong way—I still remember how arrogant she was when the FBI was obliged to turn the Triple Border action over to her. And there is no love lost between the FBI and the CIA in general. On top of that, there have to be limits. I mean, ruining the Russian economy—"

Lincoln said, "How'd you figure it out?"

"All you had to do was look around you in Moscow. All you had to do was catch the smug smiles on the faces of the DDO wallahs assigned to Moscow station. Quest herself showed up several times— you couldn't miss the gleam of unadulterated triumph in her blood-shot eyes. They were involved in something very big, that much was apparent to everyone around. They were transforming the world, rewriting history. And we saw Yeltsin imposing these wild ideas that the newspapers said came from the *Oligarkh*—freeing prices over-night, which led to hyperinflation; privatizing the Soviet industrial base, which left Ugor-Zhilov and a few insiders fabulously rich and the rest of the proletarians dirt poor; attacking Chechnya, which bogged down the Russian military in the Caucasus. It didn't take a genius to put two and two together. Demolishing the Russian economy, impoverish-ing dozens of millions of people so that the United States wouldn't have to deal with a powerful Russia—holy mackerel, it was over the top, Lincoln. So I guess I saw a certain poetic justice for Martin Odum to be the one to track down Samat for the divorce. I guess, in the back of my head, I wondered if Martin's memory wouldn't be jogged if and when he caught up with Samat."

"If Martin's memory was jogged, if he came to realize that he was Jozef, he would want revenge."

Felix said, very carefully, "Any sane man in his shoes would."

"Kastner was murdered, wasn't he?"

"Probably. The CIA insisted on doing the autopsy. I didn't like the way it played out—it was too neat by half. Martin heads for Israel to pick up the trail of Samat. Kastner dies of a heart attack. And the Chinese girl wearing Martin's white jumpsuit winds up being stung to death by bees on the roof."

"You noticed that."

"I notice everything. So are you going to tell me, Lincoln—did Martin and Kastner's kid, Estelle, find Samat?"

"What makes you think Estelle is involved?"

"Because you phoned me on this unlisted number. It had to come from somewhere. My guess," Felix added cautiously, feeling his way, "is that Stella gave the number to Martin, and Martin passed it on to you."

"Martin found Samat where you stashed him—upstate New York in the middle of Amish country. He persuaded him to give his wife a religious divorce. Some rabbis in Brooklyn did the paper work."

"What happened to Samat after he signed on the dotted line?"

"He said something about wanting to see Russian friends in Little Odessa. That's the last anyone saw of him, flagging down a taxi and telling the driver to take him to Brighton Beach."

"Now that Samat's been found, the case is closed."

"There's still the *Oligarkh*. You wouldn't by any chance know where he hangs his hat these days?"

"I don't know. If I did I wouldn't tell you. On the off chance you can find him, don't. Remember what happened to Jozef. Touch a hair on the *Oligarkh*'s head, Quest and her wallahs will bury you alive."

"Thanks for the free advice, Felix."

"You saved my life once, Lincoln. Now I'm trying to save yours."

1997: LINCOLN DITTMANN FEELS THE RECOIL IN HIS SHOULDER BLADES

THE SANCTUM LINCOLN HAD SUSSED OUT WAS AS SUITABLE AS A sniper's blind gets. Most of the panes were missing from the window, which meant he could steady the Whitworth on a sash at shoulder height—Lincoln shot best standing up, with his left elbow braced against a rib. The window itself was covered with a canopy of ivy that had spread across the facade of the abandoned hospital across the street and slightly uphill from the U-shaped tenement at 621 Crown Street, off Albany Avenue. For a sharpshooter, weather conditions—it was sunny and cold—were ideal; humid air could slow down a bullet and cause it to drop, dry hot air could cause it to fire high. Lugging the rifle and a shopping bag up the stairs littered with broken glass and trash to the corner room on the fourth floor, Lincoln had removed the thick work gloves and coated all of his finger tips with Super Glue, then set out the bottles of drinking water, the Mars bars and the containers of liquid yogurts on a sheet of newspaper. He knotted Dante Pippen's lucky white silk scarf around his neck before sighting in the Whitworth. He judged the distance from the front door of the hospital to the sidewalk in front of the tenement to be eighty yards, then calculated his height above ground and the length of the hypotenuse of the resulting triangle. He adjusted the small wheels on the rear of the brass telescopic sight atop the Whitworth, focusing on the crucifix hanging in a ground floor window giving out onto the street. Sighted correctly and fired with a firm arm, the hexagonal barrel of the Whitworth—rifled to spit out a .45-caliber hex-shaped lead bullet that made one complete turn every twenty yards—could hit anything the marksman could see. Queen Victoria herself had once gotten a bull's eye at four-hundred yards; she'd been so thrilled with the exploit that she had knighted Mr. Whitworth, the rifle's inventor, on the spot. Lincoln tapped home the ramrod, working the hand-rolled cartridge into the barrel, then carefully fitted the primer cap over the rifle's nipple. Finally he removed the brass tampon on the barrel and stretched a condom over the muzzle to protect the barrel from dust and moisture. With his weapon ready to fire, Lincoln crouched at the sill to study the target building across the street from what had once been the Carson C. Peck Memorial Hospital.

Lincoln had made use of one of Martin Odum's old tricks to find the address that corresponded to the unlisted phone number 718-555-9291. He'd called the local telephone company from a booth on Eastern Parkway. A woman had come on the line. Like Martin in London, Lincoln had retrieved Dante Pippen's rusty Irish accent for the occasion.

"Could you tell me, then, how I can get my hands on a new phone book after my dog chewed the bejesus out of the old one?"

"What type of directory do you want, sir?"

"Yellow pages for Brooklyn."

"We'll be glad to send it to you. Could I trouble you for your phone number?"

"You're not troubling me," Lincoln had said. "It's 718-555-9291."

The woman had repeated the number to be sure she had it right. Then she'd asked, "What kind of dog do you have?"

"An Irish setter, of course."

"Well, hide the phone book from him next time. Will you be needing anything else today?"

"A new yellow pages will do me fine. Are you sure you know where to send it?"

The woman had said, "Let me check the screen. Here it is. You're at 621 Crown Street, Brooklyn, New York, right?"

"That's it, darlin'."

"Have a nice day."

"I plan to," Lincoln had said just before he hung up.

From his hideaway on the fourth floor of the abandoned and soon to be demolished hospital, Lincoln watched a black teenager balanc-

ing a ghetto blaster on one shoulder skate past 621 Crown Street. As
dusk shrouded the neighborhood and the streetlights flickered on,
what Lincoln took to be a group of Nicaraguans in dreadlocks and
colorful bandannas piled out of a gypsy cab and filed into the building. Settling down to camp for the night, Lincoln examined the building across the street more closely through the scope on the rifle. All
the windows on the first five floors had cheap shades, some of them
drawn, some of them half raised; the people he caught glimpses of in
the windows looked to be Puerto Ricans or blacks. The entire top
floor appeared to have been taken over by the target; every window
was fitted with venetian blinds, all but one tightly closed. The one
where he could see through the slats turned out to be a kitchen,
equipped with an enormous Frigidaire and a gas stove with a double
oven. A stocky black woman wearing an apron appeared to be preparing dinner. Now and then men would wander through the kitchen;
one of them had his sports jacket off and Lincoln could make out a
large-caliber pistol tucked into a shoulder holster. The black woman
opened the oven to baste a large bird, then prepared two enormous
bowls of dog food. She seemed to shout to someone in another room
as she set the bowls down on the floor. A moment later two Borzois
romped into sight and were promptly lost to view under the sill of the
window.

Cleaning away the debris, settling down on the floor with his back
against a wall, Lincoln treated himself to a Mars bar and half a container of yogurt. All things considered, he was relieved that he was the
one doing the shooting and not Martin Odum. Marksmanship was
not Martin's strong suit; he was too impatient to stalk a target and
crank in one or two clicks on the sights for distance and windage and
slowly squeeze (as opposed to jerk) the trigger; too cerebral to kill in
cold blood unless he was goaded into action by the likes of Lincoln
Dittmann or Dante Pippen. In short, Martin was too involved, too
temperamental. When a born-again sniper like Lincoln shot at a
human target, the only thing he felt was the recoil of the rifle. Staking
out the target, taking your sweet time to be sure you got the kill, one
shot to a target, Lincoln was in his element. He had owned a rifle since
he was a child in Pennsylvania, hunting rabbits and birds in the woods
and fields behind his house in Jonestown. Once, packed off to the

Company's Farm for a refresher course in hand-to-hand combat and firearms, he'd impressed the instructors the first day on the firing range when they'd put an antiquated gas-operated semiautomatic M-1 in his hands. Without a word, Lincoln had screwed down the iron sights and fired off a round at the thirty-six-inch target hoping to spot a spurt of dirt somewhere in front of it. When he did he'd turned up the sights one click, which was the equivalent of one minute of elevation or ten inches of height on the target, and fired the second round into the black. He'd notched in a one-click windage adjustment and raised his sights and hit the bulls eye on the third try.

The cold set in with the darkness. Lincoln turned up the collar of Martin Odum's overcoat and, drawing it tightly around his body, dozed. Images of soldiers outfitted in white headbands charging a stone wall along a sunken road filled his brain; he could hear the spurt of cannon and the crackle of rifle fire as smoke and death drifted over the field of battle. He forced himself awake to check the luminous hands on his wristwatch and the building across the street. Falling into a fitful sleep again, he found himself transported to a more serene setting. Skinny girls in filmy dresses were slotting coins into a jukebox and swaying in each others arms to the strains of *Don't Worry, Be Happy*. The music faded and Lincoln found himself inhaling the negative ions from a fountain on the Janicular, one of Rome's seven hills. An elegantly dressed woman and a dwarf wearing a knee-length overcoat buttoned up to his neck were walking past. Lincoln could hear himself saying, *My name's Dittmann. We met in Brazil, in a border town called Foz do Iguaçú. Your daytime name was Lucia, your nighttime name was Paura.* He made out the woman's excited response: *I remember you! Your daytime name happens to be the same as your nighttime name, which is Giovanni da Varrazano.*

In his fiction Lincoln caught up with the woman as she continued on down the hill. He gripped her shoulders and shook her until she agreed to spend the rest of her life breeding baby polyesters with him on a farm in Tuscany.

Checking the building across the street again, Lincoln became aware of the first faint ocherous stains tinting the grim sky over the roofs in the east. Setting up the kill had been easier than he'd expected. He'd made his way through the alleyways behind Albany Avenue to the yard in back of Xing's restaurant. Using an old boat hook hidden behind a rusting refrigerator, he'd tugged down the lower rung of the ladder on the fire escape and climbed up to the roof. The bees had long since abandoned Martin's two hives, including the one that seemed to have exploded: stains of what looked like dried molasses were visible on the tar paper. Retrieving the key Martin had hidden behind a loose brick on the parapet, Lincoln had unlocked the roof door and let himself into Martin Odum's pool parlor. He made his way through the dark apartment to the pool table that Martin had used as a desk and took a single handrolled rifle cartridge from the mahogany humidor; Lincoln himself had fabricated the ammunition several years before, procuring high-grade gunpowder and measuring it out on an apothecary scale. Pocketing the cartridge, he picked up the Whitworth and blew the dust off of its firing mechanism. It was a surprisingly light weapon, beautifully crafted, exquisitely balanced, a delight to hold in your hands. This particular Whitworth had originally been his; he couldn't remember how it had wound up in Martin Odum's possession. He made a mental note to ask him one of these days. Wiping the weapon clean of fingerprints, he rolled it in one of Martin's overcoats and slung it across his back. Then, pulling on a pair of thick work gloves he found in a cardboard box, he retraced his steps down to the alley, recovered the shopping bag filled with nourishment that he'd prepared that morning and meandered through the deserted streets of Crown Heights to the massive building with "Carson C. Peck Memorial Hospital" and "1917" engraved on its stone base. Breaking in turned out to be relatively uncomplicated: At the back of the hospital, on the Montgomery Street side, squatters had cut through the chainlink fence the demolition company rigged around the property and one of the ground floor doors was ajar. Crouching inside the building to get his bearings, Lincoln caught the muffled sound of a brassy cough rising from the stairwell, which suggested that the squatters had installed themselves in the basement of the building.

The ocherous streaks had dragged smudges of daylight across the sky, transforming the rooftops into silhouettes. Massaging his arms to work out the coldness and the stiffness, Lincoln pushed himself to his feet and padded over to a corner of the room to relieve himself against a wall. Returning to the window, kneeling at the sill, he noticed a light in the top-floor kitchen window across the street. The black woman, wrapped in a terrycloth robe, was brewing up two large pots of coffee. When the coffee was ready she filled eight mugs and, carrying them on a tray, disappeared from view. Below, at the entrance to 621 Crown, two Nicaraguan women wearing long winter coats and bright scarves and knitted caps pulled down over their earlobes emerged from the building and hurried off in the direction of the subway station on Eastern Parkway. Twelve minutes later a black BMW pulled up to the curb in front of the tenement. The driver, a tall man in a knee-length leather overcoat and a chauffeur's cap, climbed out and stood leaning against the open door, clouds of vapor streaming from his mouth as he breathed. He glanced at his watch several times and stamped his feet to keep them from growing numb. He checked the number over the entrance of the building against something written on a scrap of paper and seemed reassured when he spotted the two men shouldering through the heavy door of 621 into the street. Both were dressed in double-breasted pea jackets with the collars turned up. The men, obviously bodyguards, greeted the driver with a wave. One of the bodyguards strolled to the corner and looked up and down Albany Avenue. The other walked off several paces to his left and checked out Crown Street. Returning to the BMW, he eyed the windows of the deserted hospital across the street.

The security arrangements were clearly casual; the bodyguards were going through the motions but there was no urgency to their gestures, which is what often happened when the individual being protected has been squirreled away and the people responsible for his safety assumed that potential enemies wouldn't be able to find his hole. Back at the BMW, the two bodyguards and the driver were making small talk. One of the bodyguards must have detected a signal on his walkie-talkie because he hauled it from a pocket and, looking up at the closed venetian blinds, muttered something into it. Several minutes went by. Then the front door of 621 swung open again and another bodyguard appeared. He was straining to hold back two Borzois attached to long leashes. To the amusement of the men waiting near the BMW, the dogs practically dragged the man into the gutter. Behind him a stubby hunch-shouldered man with a shock of silver hair and dark glasses materialized at the front door. He had a cigar clamped between his teeth and walked with the aid of two aluminum crutches, thrusting one hip forward and dragging the leg after it, then repeating the movement with the other hip. He paused for breath when he reached the end of the walkway in front of the building's entrance. One of the bodyguards opened the back door of the car. In the corner room across the street, Lincoln rose to his feet and in one flowing motion jammed his left elbow into his rib cage as he steadied the rifle on a window sash. Closing his left eye, he pressed his right eye to the telescopic sight and walked up the muzzle of the Whitworth until the cross-hairs were fixed on the target's forehead immediately above the bridge of his nose. He squeezed the trigger with such painstaking deliberation that the eruption of flame at the breech's nipple and the bullet rifling out of the barrel and the satisfying recoil of the stock into his shoulder blade all caught him by surprise. Sighting again on the target, he saw blood oozing from a ragged-edged tear in the middle of the man's forehead. The bodyguards had heard a sound but not yet associated it with gunfire. The one holding open the back door of the car was the first to notice that their charge was collapsing onto the pavement. He leapt forward to catch him under the armpits and, shouting for help, lowered him to the ground.

By the time the bodyguards realized that the man they were protecting had been shot dead, Lincoln, oblivious to the spasms in his game leg, was well on his way to the breach in the chainlink fence.

1997: CRYSTAL QUEST COMES TO BELIEVE IN DANTE'S TRINITY

DANTE PIPPEN, A MAESTRO OF TRADECRAFT, HAD POSITIONED himself in a booth at the rear of Xing's Mandarin Restaurant with his back to the tables, facing a mirror in which he could keep track of who came and went. He sized up the two figures in trenchcoats who entered the restaurant at the stroke of noon. Both had the deadpan eyes that marked them as flunkies for the CIA's Office of Security. The one with the cauliflower ears of a prize-fighter ducked behind the bar to make sure that Tsou Xing, who was holding fort on his high stool in front of the cash register, didn't have a sawed-off shotgun stashed under the counter. Ignoring Dante, the second man, who had the shoulders and neck of a weight lifter, pushed through the swinging doors into the kitchen. Moments later he reappeared and planted himself in front of the doors, his arms folded across his barrel chest.

It wasn't long before Crystal Quest turned up at the door of the restaurant. Coming into the murky interior from the dazzling sunlight of Albany Avenue, she was momentarily blinded. When she could see again, she spotted Dante and started toward him, the thick heels of her sensible shoes drumming on the linoleum floor. "Long time no see," she said as she slid onto the banquette opposite him. "As usual you look fit as a flea, Dante. Still working out on that rowing machine?"

Dante managed a half-hearted laugh. "You're confusing me with Martin Odum, Fred. He's the one with a rowing machine."

Quest, who knew a joke when she heard one, grinned nervously.

Dante said, "How about treating your bloodstream to a shot of alcohol?"

"Alcohol's just what the doctor ordered. Something with a lot of ice, thank you."

Dante called for a whiskey, neat, and a frozen daiquiri, heavy on the ice. Tsou waved his good arm in acknowledgment. Waiting for the drinks, Dante watched Quest toying absently with the frills down the front of her dress shirt. He noticed that the jacket of her pantsuit, like the skin around her eyes, was wrinkled; that the rust-colored dye was washing out of her hair, revealing soot-gray roots. "You look the worse for wear, Fred. Job getting you down?"

"Being DDO of an intelligence entity that has recast itself as a risk-averse high-tech social club is not a cake walk," she said. "There are people at Langley who do nothing but stare at satellite downloads from morning to night, as if a photograph could tell you what an adversary *intends* to do with what he has. Hell of a way to run an espionage agency. They've slashed our budget, the president doesn't have the time or the curiosity to read the overnight briefing book we prepare for him, the liberal press climbs all over us for our occasional fumbles. It goes without saying we can't gloat about our occasional successes—"

The Chinese waitress wearing a tight skirt slit up one thigh set the drinks on the table. Watching the girl slink away in the mirror reminded Dante of Martin's late lamented Chinese girlfriend, Minh. "Do you have any?" he asked Quest.

Crunching on chips of ice, she'd lost the thread of the conversation. "Have any what?" she inquired.

"Successes."

"One or two or three."

"Like the Prigorodnaia business," Dante murmured.

Quest's eyes hardened. "What Prigorodnaia business are you talking about?"

"Christsake, Fred don't play the innocent," Dante snapped. "We know what happened to Jozef Kafkor. We know the DDO provided seed money to the Armenian used-car dealer so he could corner the Russian aluminum market. We know how Ugor-Zhilov, a.k.a the *Oligarkh*, ingratiated himself with Yeltsin, arranging for the publication of his book, organizing his personal bodyguard, replenishing his bank account. Once installed in Yeltsin's inner circle, the *Oligarkh* nudged him into freeing up prices and privatizing the industrial base of the defunct Soviet Union. We know he lured Yeltsin into attacking Chechnya just when the Red Army was recovering from the Afghanistan debacle. We know that for a period of years in the early nineties the individual running Russia from behind the scene was none other than . . . Fred Astaire. We know she was running it into the ground so that the new Russia rising from the ashes of the Soviet Union couldn't compete with America."

The blood seemed to seep from Quest's cheeks until the only color remaining came from the smears of blush she'd applied during the shuttle flight from Washington. She spooned another chunk of ice into her mouth. "Who's *we?*" she demanded.

"Why, I would have thought that was obvious. There's Martin Odum, the one-time CIA field agent turned detective who specializes in collecting mahjongg debts. There's Lincoln Dittmann, the Civil War buff who actually met the poet Whitman. And last but certainly not least, there's yours truly, Dante Pippen, the Irish dynamiter from Castletownbere."

Quest snickered bitterly. "That business of Lincoln claiming to have been at the battle of Fredericksburg—it was a brilliant piece of theater. It had us all fooled—the shrink, me, the committee that met from time to time to review the situation, to decide whether to terminate your contract or your life. We all assumed that Martin Odum was off his rocker. Teach me to give someone the benefit of the doubt."

Nursing his whisky, Dante shrugged a shoulder. "If it's any consolation, Lincoln *was* at the battle of Fredericksburg."

Quest raised an eyebrow; she didn't appreciate having her leg pulled. "Why'd you need to see me, Dante? What's so important that it couldn't wait until you had a chance to come down to Langley?"

"We've taken out life insurance, we've taped what you don't want the world to know—the Prigorodnaia operation; how you provided the keys to Kastner's safe house so the *Oligarkh*'s people could break in and murder him; how you told them about Martin's beehives, which led to the death of the Chinese girl, Minh. Add to that the sniper who tried to kill Martin in Hebron. Not to mention the Czechs who gave Martin a car and a pistol in Prague and told him to run for it. These attempts on Martin's life had your prints all over them."

"That's nonsense. Knowing what I know, the last thing I would have done is charge a pistol with dummy Parabellums."

Dante said, "How did you know the handgun was loaded with dummy Parabellums?"

Quest smudged a fingertip dabbing at the mascara on an eyelid. Dante took her failure to answer for an answer. "Listen up, Fred, if any one of us dies of anything but old age, the tapes will be duplicated and distributed to every member of the Congressional Oversight Subcommittee, also to selected journalists in the liberal press who report on your *occasional* fumbles."

"You're bluffing."

Dante raised his chin and looked Quest in the eye. "If you think that, all you need to do is call our bluff."

"Listen, Dante, we all came of age in the cold war. We all fought the good fight. I'm sure we can work something out."

'There's one more item on our agenda. We held a meeting to decide whether to terminate your life or your career. Career won, two to one. Within one week we want to read in the newspapers that the legendary Crystal Quest, the first woman Deputy Director of Operations, a veteran of thirty-two years of loyal and masterful service to the Central Intelligence Agency, has been put out to pasture."

Sucked against her will into Dante's trinity, Quest asked, "Who was the one who voted to terminate my life?"

"Why, Martin, of course, though being the more squeamish of the three, he wanted me or Lincoln to make the hit." Dante smiled pleasantly. "Some people forgive but don't forget. Martin's the opposite— he forgets but doesn't forgive."

"What does he forget?"

"Whether Martin Odum is a legend or the real him."

"It's the original him, the first legend. You worked for Army Intelligence—"

"You mean, *Martin* worked for Army Intelligence."

Quest nodded carefully. "Martin's specialty was East European dissidents. I stumbled across a paper *he* published in the *Army*

Intelligence Quarterly identifying two veins of dissidence: the anticommunists, who wanted to do away with communism altogether, and
the pro-communists, who wanted to purge communism of Stalinism
and reform the system. *His* article, which turned out to be far sighted,
predicted that in the end the pro-communists were more likely to have
an impact on East Europe and, ultimately, the Soviet Union itself,
than the anticommunists. I remember . . . *Martin* citing the trial of
Pavel Slánský in Prague, claiming he was the precursor of the reformers who came after him, Dubcek in Czechoslovakia, eventually
Gorbachev in the Soviet Union."

"And you lured him away from Army Intelligence into the CIA?"

"The Legend Committee worked up a cover for him using his real
name and as much of his actual background as they could. He'd lived
in Pennsylvania until his father moved the family to Brooklyn. Martin
was something like eight at the time. He was raised on Eastern
Parkway, he went to PS 167, Crown Heights was his stamping ground,
he even had a school chum whose father owned a Chinese restaurant
on Albany Avenue. When we discovered he could handle explosives,
for a while we had him making letter bombs or rigging portable phones
to explode from a distance. Martin was the last agent I personally ran
before they kicked me upstairs to run the officers who run the agents.
The Odum we concocted wasn't a detective. That's something you . . .
that's something *Martin* added to the cover story when his Company
career came to an end." Quest, shaken, began gnawing on a chip of ice.

Dante tucked a ten dollar bill under the ashtray and stood up. "I'll
pass all this on to Martin if I see him. I suspect he'll be relieved."

Quest looked up at Dante. "It was you who shot the *Oligarkh*."

"Christsake, Fred."

"I know it was you, Dante. The kill had your M.O. on it."

Dante laughed lightly, his shoulders shuddering with pleasure.
"You're losing your touch, Fred. I have nothing to gain by lying to
you—it was Lincoln who made the hit on the *Oligarkh*. Newspaper
accounts said the police couldn't identify the bullet or the murder
weapon, which means Lincoln must have used that old Civil War
sniper rifle you found for him when you were working up the
Dittmann legend. Jesus, that's really humorous. Martin or I wouldn't
know how to load the damn thing."

Snickering in satisfaction, Dante headed for the front of the restaurant. The weight lifter came off the kitchen doors and started after him. The prize-fighter edged around the bar to block his path. Tsou Xing called in a high pitched voice, "No violence inside, all-light."

Dante's Irish temper flared. Glancing over his shoulder at Quest, he said, very softly, "Am I to understand that you'll be calling our bluff, Fred?"

Quest locked eyes with Dante, then looked away and took a deep breath and wagged a forefinger once. The two flunkies from the Office of Security stopped in their tracks. Dante nodded as if he were digesting a momentous piece of information, something that could transform his legend and add to its longevity. Humming under his breath one of Lincoln's favorite tunes, *Don't Worry, Be Happy*, he pushed through the door into the blinding sunlight.

AVAILABLE FROM PENGUIN

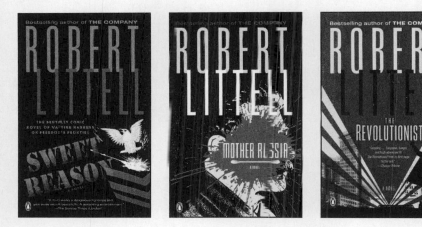

BY ROBERT LITTELL

PENGUIN BOOKS